Horse Owner's

VETERINARY

Handbook

Horse Owner's
VETERINARY
Handbook

Second Edition

James M. Giffin, M.D.
and
Tom Gore, D.V.M.

Howell Book House
New York

Copyright © 1989 by Howell Book House, 1998 by James M. Giffin, M.D. and Tom Gore, D.V.M.

Howell Book House
Published by Wiley Publishing, Inc., Hoboken, New Jersey
Published simultaneously in Canada

For general information about our other products and services, please contact our Customer Care Department within the United States at (800) 762-2974, outside the United States at (317) 572-3993 or fax (317) 572-4002.

Wiley also publishes its books in a variety of electronic formats. Some content that appears in print may not be available in electronic books. For more information about Wiley products, visit our web site at www.wiley.com.

Library of Congress Cataloging-in-Publication Data

Giffin, James M.
   Horse owner's veterinary handbook / James M. Giffin and Tom Gore.
—2nd ed.
        p.   cm.
   Includes index.
   ISBN 0-87605-606-0
   1. Horses—Diseases—Handbooks, manuals, etc.   2. Horses—Handbooks, manuals, etc.   I. Gore, Tom.   II. Title.
SF951.645 1997
616.1'0896—dc21   97-26490
                                                   CIP

Manufactured in the United States of America

15 14 13

Contents

Chapter 5—**EYES**—121

Chapter 9—RESPIRATORY SYSTEM—201

Chapter 10—CIRCULATORY SYSTEM—225

Chapter 15—**PREGNANCY AND FOALING**—397

Chapter 16—**PEDIATRICS**—427

Chapter 17—FEEDING AND NUTRITION—455

INTRODUCTION

Charles Chenevix Trench in A *History of Horsemanship* quotes an eighteenth-century Frenchman in part as follows:

> **God found it good to bestow on man a supreme mark of his favor, and so he created the horse. The horse was swifter than everything on the face of the earth; he could outrun the deer, leap higher than the goat, endure longer than the wolf. Man, encompassed by the elements which conspired to destroy him, would have been a slave, had not the horse made him king.**

The horse no longer is the source of man's power and dominance. And yet, the popularity of the horse has never been greater. In a world where the buggy has been replaced by the fax machine, cellular telephone, and modern sports car, there are more horses living today than ever before. In part this is because of the genuine pleasure people derive from owning and working the horse, and in part because of the horse industry, which has become increasingly active in promoting equestrian activities.

The past two decades have witnessed an explosion in technology and scientific research in equine medicine. The application of these discoveries has had far-reaching effects on the health and longevity of horses.

In this new, fully updated, and expanded edition, we have incorporated the latest information on veterinary horse care and disease prevention. Two new chapters, *Pediatrics* and *Geriatrics*, have been added in recognition of the importance of these specialty areas of interest. The well-cared-for horse at all stages of life, when given annual vaccinations, scheduled deworming, and good dental and foot care, suffers fewer illnesses and infirmities, costs less money to maintain, and will repay the small expenses many times over in the pride and pleasure of ownership.

The *Horse Owner's Veterinary Handbook* has a unique *Index of Signs and Symptoms* that you can use to determine the possible cause of your horse's ailment. With this information you will be in a better position to assess the potential seriousness of a symptom and can decide if treatment is urgently needed. Some health problems can be treated at home. Others require professional guidance. Knowing when to call your veterinarian can be of utmost importance.

A *veterinary handbook is not intended to be a substitute for professional care.* Book advice can never be as helpful or as safe as actual medical assistance. No text can replace the interview and physical examination, during which the veterinarian elicits the sort of information which leads to a speedy and accurate diagnosis. But the knowledge provided in this book will enable you to work in better understanding and more effective cooperation with your veterinarian.

The *Horse Owner's Veterinary Handbook* is the third in a series that includes the revised *Dog Owner's Home Veterinary Handbook* and the recently revised *Cat Owner's Home Veterinary Handbook* (both also published by Howell Book House). The experience gained in keeping these works up to date has helped us in planning and executing this revision.

The combined efforts of many people have made this book possible. We are especially indebted to Susan Stamilio (SKS Designs) for the many anatomical drawings throughout this book. All drawings, unless otherwise credited, were produced by SKS Designs.

A special note of thanks is due to Kjersten Darling, D.V.M., of KD Stables (Montrose, Colorado); to Billy Scales and Shelby Mighell of B & S Quarter Horses (Ridgway, Colorado); to Dick and Willa Sell of Real Impressive Paints (Montrose, Colorado); and to the many other gracious people who contributed advice and allowed us to photograph their horses.

Recognition would not be complete without mentioning the numerous researchers, clinicians, and educators whose works serve as a source of information for this edition. Among them are: *Current Therapy in Equine Medicine 3*, 1992 (W.B. Saunders Company); *Equine Clinical Nutrition: Feeding and Care* by Lon D. Lewis, D.V.M., Ph.D., 1995 (Williams & Wilkins); *Nutrient Requirements of Horses*, 5th ed.,1989 (National Research Council); *Guide to Lameness* by Ted S. Stashak, D.V.M., 1995 (Williams & Wilkins); *The Horse* by Calvin Kobluk, D.V.M., Trevor Ames, D.V.M., and Raymond Goer, D.V.Sc., 1995 (W.B. Saunders Company); *Student's Guide to Equine Clinics* by Chris Pasquini, D.V.M. and Susan Pasquini, 1993 (Sudz Publishing); and *The Stallion* by James P. McCall, Ph.D., 1995 (Howell Book House).

We would like to express appreciation to the publishers of *Adams' Lameness in Horses*, Edition IV, 1987 (Lea & Febinger) and *Equine Medicine and Surgery*, 1982 (American Veterinary Publications) for giving permission to use photographs and illustrations.

To Howell Book House and Sean Frawley, who gave us this opportunity, and to Madelyn Larsen for a great job of editing, we are indeed grateful.

Horse Owner's
VETERINARY
Handbook

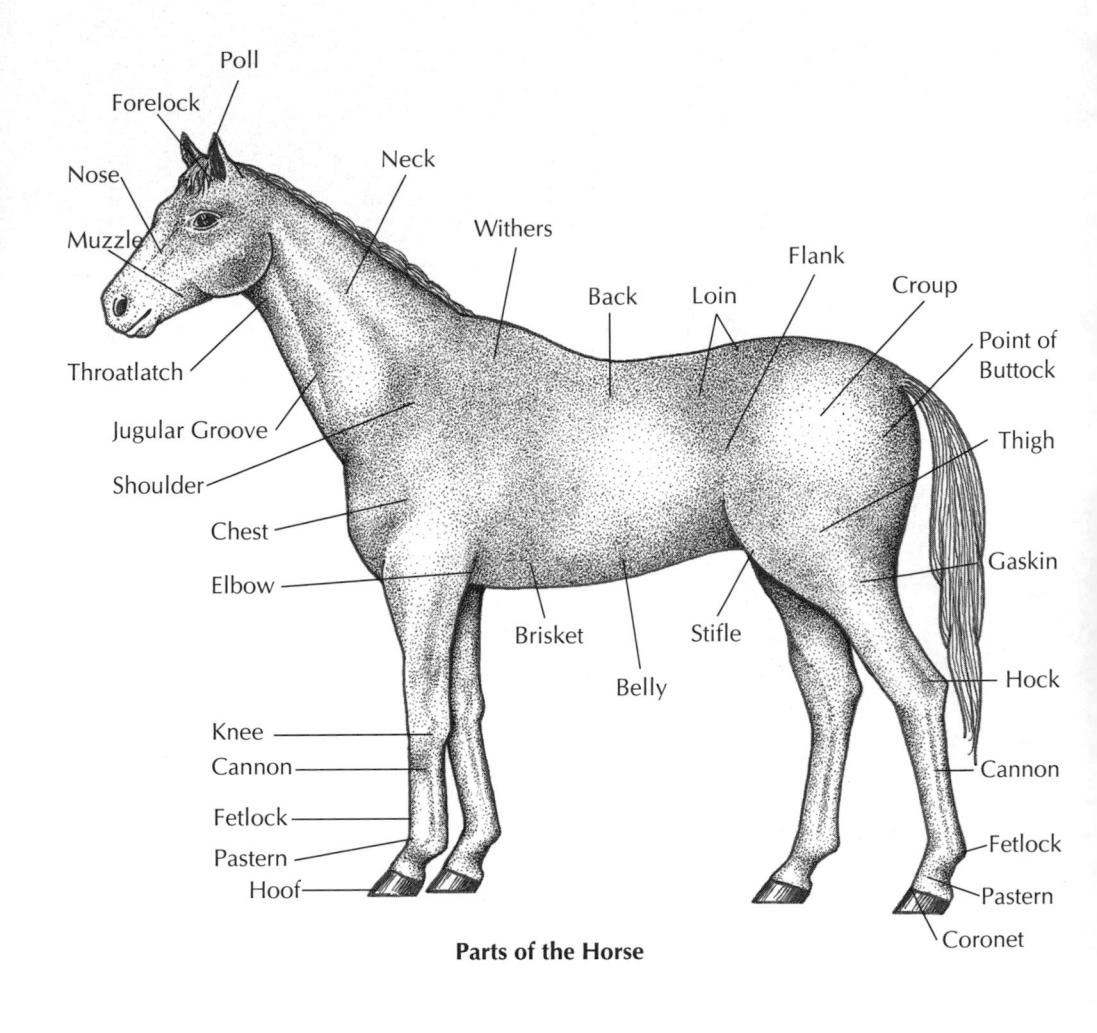

Parts of the Horse

EMERGENCIES

Abdominal Pain

Sudden severe pain in the abdomen in the horse is referred to as colic. A horse with colic appears anxious and upset, and may kick at the abdomen, roll on its back, kick its feet in the air, break out in a sweat, and strain as if to pass urine or stool.

Colic is a symptom rather than a specific disease. There are a great many diseases associated with signs of colic. Accordingly, veterinary examination is necessary to determine the nature and seriousness of the problem.

For more information, see DIGESTIVE SYSTEM: COLIC.

Cardiovascular Collapse

Too much stress on the heart can lead to sudden circulatory collapse. In racehorses, the stress is that of maximum physical exertion over a relatively short period of time. In hard-working performance and endurance horses, the stress is submaximal but occurs over an extended period of time. The initial signs are those of the exhausted horse syndrome. If the exercise is continued, collapse will occur.

SUDDEN COLLAPSE

During maximal physical exercise, the cardiac output of a racehorse increases to 7 times normal while the heart rate increases to 200 beats per minute. Blood flow through skeletal muscles may be 20 times that of the resting state.

Under such circumstances the equine heart muscle labors under a sustained deficiency of oxygen, a condition known as hypoxia. A switch to anaerobic

1

metabolism may sustain the heart for some time, but with continued exertion a point is eventually reached at which the heart can no longer supply enough oxygen to the muscles. At this point the heart may decompensate and the horse will collapse.

Cardiac arrhythmias are thought to be the immediate cause of sudden cardiovascular decompensation (see ARRHYTHMIAS). Contrary to popular belief, horses with arrhythmias usually do not drop dead under the rider. The first indication is an abrupt drop in running speed. This alerts the rider and allows him to pull up and dismount.

The ability of a horse to tolerate cardiovascular stress is directly related to athletic fitness. Fitness depends on how well the horse has been trained and conditioned. To achieve a high level of conditioning, a horse must be free of health problems, including anemia, valvular disease, myocarditis, intestinal parasites, bronchitis, and heaves—which compromise the efficiency of the heart and lungs.

To prevent sudden cardiovascular collapse in the competition horse, it is important to:

- Screen all horses for cardiac and respiratory diseases.
- Correct any medical problems that may exist.
- Institute a program of graduated exercise, aimed at obtaining maximum athletic fitness.
- Monitor and recognize the immediate signs of exhaustion, and rapidly correct dehydration and electrolyte deficits.

EXHAUSTED HORSE SYNDROME

This syndrome affects performance and endurance horses undergoing submaximal exertion over an extended length of time. After a short period of hard work, the glucose stored by muscles is depleted. When this happens, energy is generated by switching from glucose utilization (*aerobic* metabolism) to the utilization of fats (*anaerobic* metabolism). Anaerobic metabolism produces lactic acid and waste products which accumulate and cause fatigue of heart and skeletal muscles.

The basal metabolic rate increases 10 to 20 times in sustained exercise. This generates a tremendous amount of heat that must be dissipated to maintain normal body temperature. Sweating is the chief means of dissipating body heat in the horse. As much as 25 to 50 liters (6 to 12 gallons) of sweat can be lost during an endurance ride in hot, humid weather. Sweat contains substantial amounts of calcium, potassium, bicarbonate, sodium, chloride, and magnesium.

When fluid and electrolyte losses are severe, horses may lose the ability to sweat—even in the presence of a high rectal temperature (see HEAT STROKE).

Recognition of Impending Exhaustion. During endurance races, problems are recognized at veterinary checkpoints or mandatory rest stops. An exhausted horse shows an elevated rectal temperature along with a fast heart rate, flared nostrils, and a rapid breathing rate. If the horse is severely overheated, the breathing rate can actually be greater than the heart rate. There is a prolongation of the capillary refill time to greater than 3 seconds.

After 15 minutes, the heart rate should drop to less than 70 beats per minute and the breathing rate to less than 40. If this does not occur, the horse should be rested until it does occur.

While resting, the exhausted horse may exhibit muscle cramps, tremors, stiffness, and be unwilling or unable to move. This condition, called endurance-related myopathy, is not the same as the tying-up syndrome, although most of the signs are similar (see EXERTIONAL MYOPATHY).

A badly exhausted horse is apathetic, depressed, weak, unwilling to drink water, and appears febrile and dehydrated. Sweating may take place at a reduced rate or be absent altogether. Such horses should be removed from the race to prevent sudden heart failure or metabolic collapse.

Thumps. This condition, technically called synchronous diaphragmatic flutter (SDF), occurs in some exhausted horses. Thumps is caused by a low serum calcium in association with other electrolyte deficiencies. It is characterized by spasmodic contraction of one or both flanks, forceful enough to be felt or heard by the rider. The thumps themselves are caused by rapid contractions of the diaphragm in unison with the heartbeat. The diaphragmatic nerves that pass over the heart apparently respond to its electrical field. Thumps should be looked upon as a warning sign and an indication for further veterinary evaluation.

Post-Exhaustion Syndrome. Some severely exhausted horses do not recover after rest. These horses remain depressed, with persistently elevated heart and breathing rates. Liver and kidney failure can occur. This may lead to the death of the horse. Reports have shown that horses with the post-exhaustion syndrome have received Butazolidin or some other nonsteroidal anti-inflammatory drug early on. These drugs should be withheld until the horse is adequately rehydrated.

Treatment of the Exhausted Horse: Stop all exercise. Move the horse to a cooler environment. As soon as possible, begin to replace fluids and electrolytes. If the horse is unable to drink, replacement solutions should be given, either intravenously or orally by stomach tube. Large volumes (usually several gallons) of electrolyte-containing solution are required. A suitable oral electrolyte solution can be prepared by adding one tablespoon of common salt and one tablespoon of Lite salt to a gallon of water. Lite is half sodium chloride and half potassium chloride. It is readily available at grocery stores. This solution is high in chloride, the electrolyte lost in greatest amounts in sweat. It does not contain calcium. A number of commercial oral rehydrating solutions (containing sodium, potassium, chloride, calcium, bicarbonate, and glucose) are commercially available through your veterinarian or a horse supply store. Continue administering the electrolyte solution until the horse recovers sufficiently to drink water on its own.

Lower elevated body temperature as described in the section on HEAT STROKE. Thumps will disappear spontaneously with rehydration. A replacement solution containing calcium will expedite this process.

Prevention: A horse on a long, physically depleting ride needs an average of one gallon of water per hour. Statistics indicate that horses who drink frequently during an endurance race are much less likely to drop out of the race than those who do not. Accordingly, allow and encourage your horse to drink often, and let him drink as much as he wants. However, after the race the horse should be cooled for about one hour before being permitted to drink.

Sodium, chloride, potassium, bicarbonate, calcium, and magnesium are lost in the sweat and urine in proportion to the severity of stress, temperature, humidity, and individual sweating characteristics of the horse. To compensate for these losses, it may be advisable to give controlled amounts (perhaps several quarts) of electrolyte-enriched water during the race, even though it may not be needed by all horses. It will not harm the horse as long as fresh water is available and the horse is allowed to drink as much as he wants during rest stops. However, keep in mind that water is far more essential than electrolytes. Do not give electrolyte water as a substitute for fresh water.

It is best not to feed a competition horse before a race, even though some people like to feed hay to an endurance horse at rest stops. Feeding diverts energy to digestion. This energy can be better utilized in supplying cardiovascular and musculoskeletal needs.

Dehydration

Dehydration is loss of body fluids. It is not recognized until a 5 percent or greater loss of body weight occurs. A loss of 12 to 15 percent of body weight in water is life-threatening.

Signs of dehydration are weakness, depression, dry mucous membranes (mouth, tongue), sunken eyeballs, prolongation of the capillary refill time beyond 3 seconds, and a heart rate over 60 beats per minute. Circulatory collapse and shock are terminal events.

The degree of dehydration can be estimated by testing for skin elasticity. When the skin of the lower chest above the elbow is picked up into a fold, it should spring back into place. In moderate to severe dehydration, the skin stays up in a ridge or returns to its original position very slowly.

Severe dehydration is most often caused by profuse diarrhea, prolonged physical exertion in hot weather, acute gastric dilatation, intestinal obstruction, and peritonitis. The dehydration is often complicated by sepsis, electrolyte deficits, and acid-base imbalances.

Dehydration also can occur with fever, heat stroke, choke (esophageal blockage), and loss of consciousness (preventing the horse from drinking).

Treatment: Mild dehydration (for example, due to water deprivation for 24 hours) can be corrected by allowing the horse to drink small quantities at frequent intervals. Electrolyte-enriched water, as discussed in the section on EXHAUSTED HORSE SYNDROME, is indicated when water loss is accompanied by electrolyte loss.

Moderate to severe dehydration must be treated by a veterinarian. Corrective replacement solutions containing water and electrolytes can be given by stomach tube, assuming the horse does not have an intestinal problem such as diarrhea or bowel obstruction. The maximum rate of administration by nasogastric tube should not exceed 6 quarts of fluid every 2 hours.

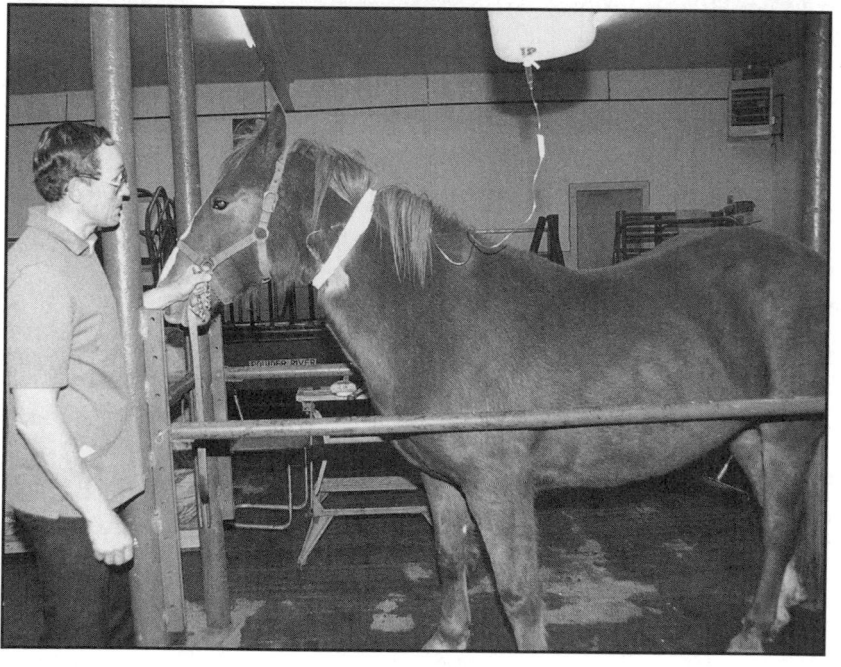

Large volumes of intravenous fluids are needed to correct moderate to severe dehydration.

Intravenous solutions are commonly given through the jugular veins, although other sites are available should circumstances require. Because the intravenous route allows for the most rapid replacement of fluid, it is the route most preferred for severe dehydration and for ongoing losses.

Exertional Myopathy
(Azoturia and the Tying-up Syndrome)

Azoturia and the tying-up syndrome represent degrees of the condition called exertional myopathy. Azoturia is the more severe form.

Both tend to occur in heavily exercised horses who continue to consume a high-carbohydrate diet even though the exercise is temporarily discontinued. As the activity is resumed, the horse finds it difficult and painful to move. The term "Monday morning disease" was first used to describe this condition, since it was noted that horses rested and fed a working ration over the weekend often became stiff and sore when returned to activity on Monday.

Azoturia and the tying-up syndrome are caused by an accumulation in the muscle of a carbohydrate storage compound called glycogen. Glycogen storage occurs to a much greater extent in horses than in other animals, and even more so in horses with exertional myopathy. With exercise, muscle glycogen is rapidly broken down to release blood sugar. This produces lactic acid in amounts well beyond that which can be removed by metabolism. Lactic acid damages skeletal muscle and causes it to release muscle enzymes and myoglobin. Myoglobin is excreted in the urine and blocks the nephrons, causing acute kidney failure.

Azoturia. Signs begin 15 to 60 minutes after the beginning of exercise. The horse becomes anxious, sweats profusely, and exhibits a rapid pulse. This is followed almost immediately by a stiffening of all major muscles, accompanied by staggering and wobbliness in the rear. Collapse is possible.

A horse with severe azoturia passes reddish-brown to black urine containing myoglobin pigment. With a mild attack, pigment will be found only on chemical analysis. The presence of myoglobinuria makes the diagnosis of azoturia and rules out endurance-related myopathy, colic, tetanus, and laminitis.

Tying-up. This milder syndrome occurs in race and performance horses during the cooling-out period after vigorous exercise. Signs include stiffness, muscle tremors, anxiety, and sometimes sweating. The muscles of the loin and hindquarters in particular are tense, hard, and painful. If myoglobinuria is present on urinalysis, the condition should be called azoturia.

Treatment: On first suspicion of exertional myopathy, stop all activity and enforce absolute rest. Any degree of activity, even returning to the stall, makes the condition much worse. Speak to the horse calmly to relieve anxiety. Cover the horse with a blanket and obtain veterinary assistance.

Signs of exertional myopathy may resemble those of colic. It is important to distinguish between these two conditions, since exercising or even walking a horse with acute exertional myopathy could be fatal.

Tranquilizers and pain relievers such as Acepromazine and Demerol help to relieve anxiety and may aid in the removal of lactic acid by improving circulation to the muscles. Oral anti-inflammatory drugs, particularly Naproxen, are especially effective in relieving stiffness. They should be continued for several days. If corticosteroids are given, they should be administered only during the first few hours. They should not be used thereafter, as steroids have been implicated in causing attacks and can contribute to the development of laminitis.

Severely affected horses are given large volumes of intravenous fluid along with an oral electrolyte solution by stomach tube to promote urine flow and protect the kidneys from myoglobin damage. Thiamin and pentathenic acid (both present in B complex vitamins) facilitate the elimination of lactic acid.

The outlook for recovery is good if the horse remains standing and its pulse returns to normal within 24 hours. It is also good if the horse goes down but is able to maintain a sternal position. If the horse remains on its side and the pulse does not return to normal within 24 hours, the prognosis is guarded. Death can occur from acute kidney failure or the complications of prolonged recumbency.

Prevention: A horse that has recovered from exertional myopathy is susceptible to recurrent attacks. In part, these attacks can be prevented by withholding grain during periods of inactivity, maintaining a regular exercise program with at least some exercise each day, and starting all exercise activities slowly and increasing them gradually.

Vitamin E and selenium may prevent recurrent attacks in some horses. Commercial preparations are available. They can be given once a month by injection, or can be added in low doses to the horse's feed. The anticonvulsant drug Dilantin has been reported to prevent some recurrences.

Electric Shock and Burns

ELECTRIC SHOCKS

Horses who chew on electric insulation can receive a shock sufficient to cause electrocution. Improperly grounded electric hot walkers are another cause of fatal shock. A horse can be electrocuted by coming into contact with a pool of water electrified by a downed wire.

Horses are occasionally killed by lightning. A horse does not have to be struck in order to be killed. A tall tree with deep roots and spreading branches can serve as a conduit for a bolt of lightning, conducting electricity through the ground to any animal standing in the immediate vicinity of the tree during a thunderstorm. The same thing can happen when lightning hits ponds and fences, or barns and stables not protected by lightning rods.

Electric walkers should be grounded to prevent accidental shock.

Most lightning strikes are fatal. The singed hair and skin of the dead horse gives evidence of the cause of death.

A horse who survives a major shock will often be knocked unconscious. Upon recovering, the horse may demonstrate signs of brain injury, including dizziness, altered vision, excitability, or paralysis.

Many electrocutions can be prevented. Faulty stable wiring should be replaced. Electric wire accessible to horses and rodents should be encased in metal housing. Lightning rods should be attached to all stables and barns. Electric walkers should be grounded. Fence wire connected to wooden posts is not well grounded and will conduct electricity. To ground the fence, replace a wooden post with a metal post every 50 yards. Keep horses out of wet pastures and away from small ponds during thunderstorms.

BURNS

Burns are caused by fire, electric shocks, skin friction, frostbite, and caustic chemicals.

Frostbite usually affects the ears and can lead to loss of skin and cartilage, leaving a cropped appearance.

Saddle sores, galls, rope burns, and friction injuries are discussed in the Skin chapter.

Acids, alkalis, iodine-containing solutions, and petroleum products are the most common causes of chemical burns.

Steam, hot water scalds, and flame burns cause damage to the skin and underlying tissue in proportion to the length and intensity of exposure. With a surface burn you will see skin redness, occasional blistering, perhaps slight swelling; and the burn is painful. With deep burns the skin appears white and the hair comes out easily when pulled. Paradoxically, deep burns are not necessarily painful since the nerve endings may have been destroyed.

When more than 20 percent of the body surface is involved in a deep burn, the outlook is poor. Fluid losses are excessive and shock will occur promptly.

Treatment: Apply cold water compresses or ice packs to local burns for 30 minutes to relieve pain. Replace as compresses become warm. Clip away hair and wash gently with a mild soap such as Ivory. Do not break blisters, as they provide a natural barrier to infection. Apply a topical antibiotic ointment such as Furacin, Silvadene Cream, or Triple Antibiotic Ointment. Aloe vera cream possesses medicinal properties and is particularly soothing on mild burns. Do not, however, apply oil, grease, or iodine-containing surgical cleansing solutions as they are irritating and will increase the depth of the burn and thus the potential for infection.

Burns can be treated open or closed, depending on the location of the injury. Where practical, protect the wound with an outer gauze dressing and change it daily (see WOUNDS).

Treat chemical, acid, and alkali burns by flushing copiously with large amounts of lukewarm water. To be effective, this must be done shortly after the injury.

Handling and Restraint

A horse who is frightened, injured, or in pain is a potential danger to itself as well as to its handlers. Do not handle or attempt to treat an agitated horse without professional assistance. In most cases, the horse will need to be given an intravenous sedative or tranquilized before treatment can be undertaken.

Most horses should be restrained for routine procedures such as shoeing, applying insecticides, floating the teeth, deworming, and giving injections. When restrained, a well-socialized horse recognizes that he is going to be handled and submits readily to the customary treatment.

The method of restraint will depend upon the horse's innate disposition and spirit, prior training, the duration of treatment, and whether the procedure is likely to cause pain. In general, it is best to begin with the least severe restraint that will allow examination.

Some specific methods for handling and restraint are discussed below.

Secure the horse with a halter and lead before beginning any sort of examination or treatment.

HEAD RESTRAINT

Even when a procedure is relatively minor and painless, it is still important to have an assistant restrain the horse's head. The assistant should hold the lead and be prepared to divert the horse's attention. The assistant should stand on the same side as the examiner in order to keep the horse from wheeling into (or kicking) the examiner. This should be the left side whenever possible, as horses are used to being handled on the left.

A simple and effective method of restraining the head is to have the assistant hold the muzzle with the left hand and the nape of the neck with the right. To prevent the horse from ducking, the left thumb is inserted beneath the nose band of the halter. This method is useful for procedures such as floating the teeth.

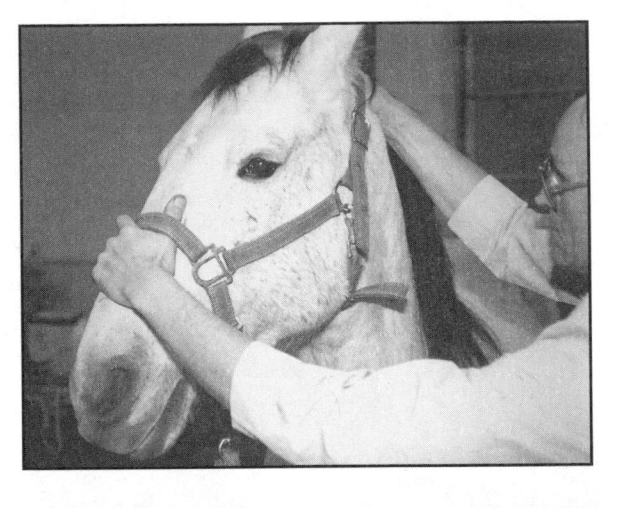

A simple way for an assistant to restrain the head for a short procedure such as giving an injection.

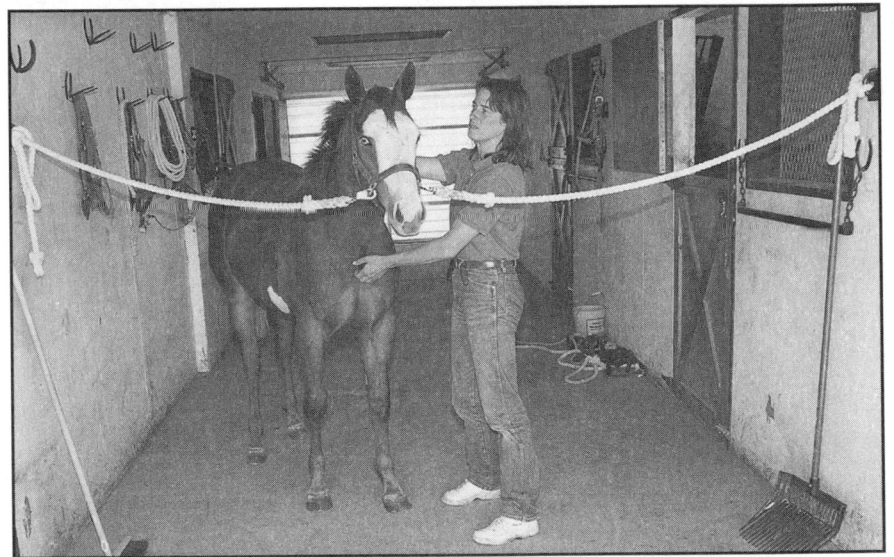

When working alone, it is safer to cross-tie the horse than tie him to a fence or post.

When an assistant is not available, you can restrain the horse's head by cross-tying the horse between two walls or posts. The tie ropes should be anchored firmly at about the level of the shoulders and snapped onto the halter. Tie the anchored ends with a slip knot for quick release.

HALTER AND LEAD

The first step in dealing with a frightened or stubborn horse is to gain mastery with the halter and lead. Approach the horse from the front while talking in a soothing and familiar manner. Never approach a horse from the rear or out of its line of vision.

If the horse is agitated, take as much time as necessary to gain its confidence. It is best to proceed from the left, as horses are used to being handled from that side. Rub the horse on the shoulder or neck for a few moments to establish physical contact and gentle the horse down; then slip the halter over the nose and tighten the buckle.

A chain across the gums is an effective restraint and keeps the horse from backing or rearing.

The chain can be placed through the mouth, as shown here, or over the nose.

Always lead from the left side, holding the shank about 18 inches from the halter. Hold the lead firmly but do not wrap it around your hand or thumb.

When administering treatment, don't tie the lead shank to a fence or post. Many horses so restrained for treatment will sit back forcefully on their haunches, invariably breaking the fence or a piece of tack. If the horse realizes he can escape by force, it will be extremely difficult to tie that horse up in the future. If forced to work alone, cross-tie the horse as described above.

In the situation in which a stubborn or fractious horse refuses to be led on a halter, you can rectify the situation by using a war bridle. A war bridle can be made by passing one end of a rope around the poll, across the gums of the upper teeth, and then out through a noose at the other end. With a halter in place, you can accomplish this restraint more easily by clipping the shank chain to one halter ring, passing it over the gums, and then sliding it out through the other halter ring (see illustration on preceding page). As a less aggressive restraint, the chain can be passed over the nose or through the mouth. With any of the above methods, a quick pull will cause pain and prevent the horse from jerking back or rearing.

The least aggressive restraint is to pass the lead shank under the horse's chin. This restraint will suffice for most handling situations. However, if the horse rears, do not jerk on the chain as it could cause him to fall over backward.

A chain shank or war bridle should be removed whenever a horse is tied. If the horse becomes upset and pulls back, the bridle or shank will constrict around its head or muzzle and cause serious injury.

Another method that can be used for a horse who refuses to advance on the lead (for example, through a door) is to blindfold the horse and then either lead or back him through the door.

A horse that refuses the lead can often be led when blindfolded.

TWITCHES

Twitches are among the oldest and most widely used methods of restraint. A twitch is thought to stimulate the release of endorphins in a manner similar to acupuncture, and to produce sedation comparable in degree to chemical tranquilization.

Some horses should not be twitched. Because of past abuse, they may greatly resent the twitch and even fight it. These horses should be restrained in some other manner.

The skin twitch is applied by grasping a fold of skin just in front of the horse's shoulder. It may provide adequate distraction for the performance of short procedures.

The ear twitch is applied by grasping and squeezing the ear with the heel of the hand pressed against the horse's scalp. Slight pressure is exerted downward. The major disadvantage of the ear twitch is that it can make the horse head-shy. Therefore the ear twitch should be used cautiously and only by experienced horsemen.

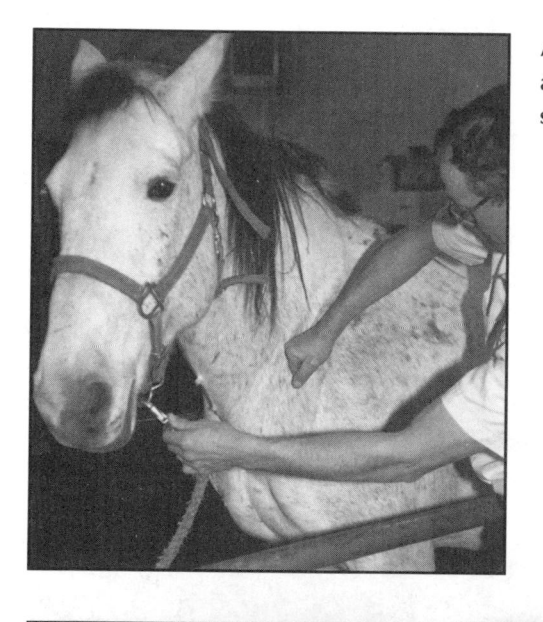

Apply the skin twitch by grasping a fold of skin in front of the shoulder.

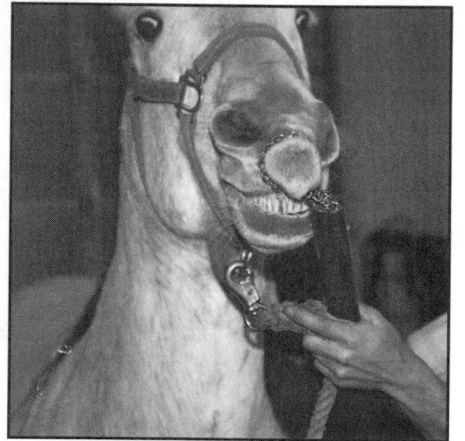

The nose twitch. Grasp the upper lip to steady the head. Slip the loop over the nose with the lips folded under.

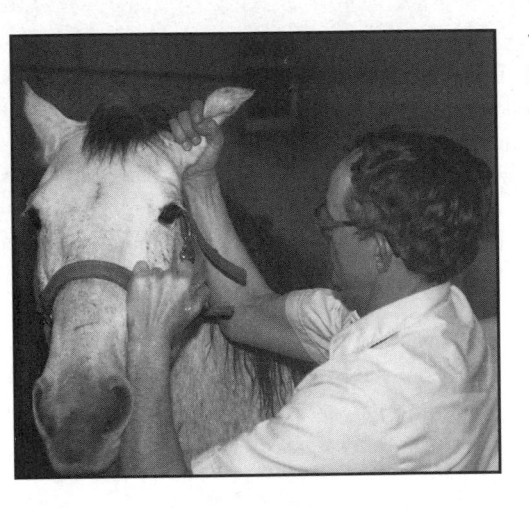

The ear twitch can make the horse head-shy. It should be used only by experienced handlers.

A lip twitch attached to the halter is useful when an assistant is unavailable.

The nose twitch and the lip twitch are used most often. However, they tend to lose their effectiveness when the skin becomes numb. To delay numbness, the twitch can be applied loosely and tightened as necessary. To apply a nose twitch, first grasp the upper lip between thumb and fingers to steady the head. Slip the loop over the horse's nose with the lip folded under so that the lining of the mouth is not exposed. Tighten the loop by twisting the handle.

The humane twitch is a lip twitch attached to the halter so that it can't come off during the procedure. It is especially useful when the handler is unfamiliar with horse restraints or is obliged to work alone.

HANDLING THE FEET

To pick up the front foot, stand to the side in case the horse strikes out. Slide your hand down the horse's leg while squeezing on either side of the flexor tendon above the fetlock. It may be necessary to push the horse onto the opposite leg while picking up the foot and flexing the joint.

When preparing to pick up a back foot, approach from the side. A horse who resents being approached from behind sometimes (but not always) gives evidence by moving away and taking weight off the leg in preparation for kicking. Even if the horse appears docile, do not approach from the rear.

To pick up the foot, slide your hand along the inside of the leg behind the cannon bone and draw the leg forward. The leg is lifted and supported on the examiner's thigh. Note that the stifle joint is extended and the hock and toe are held in a flexed position. This helps to restrict voluntary movement of the leg.

When releasing the feet, the above procedures are reversed.

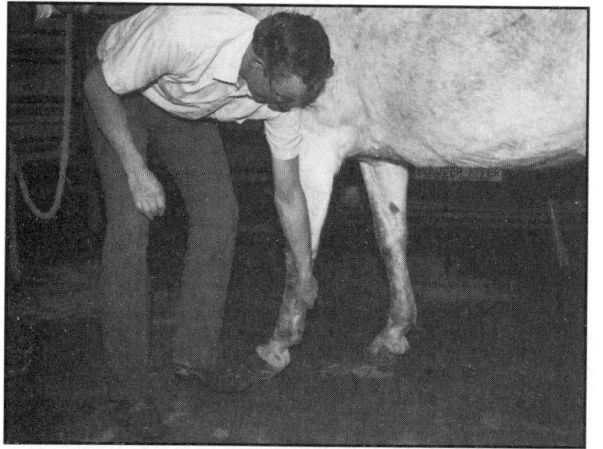

Picking up the front foot, with the handler standing well to the side.

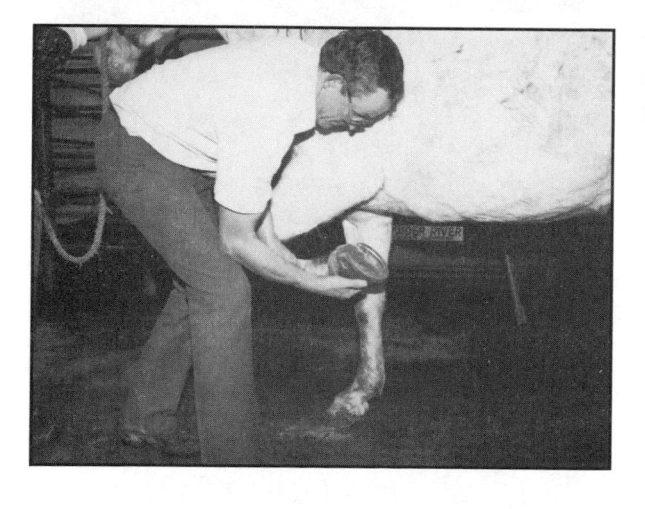

The knee is flexed to examine the sole and frog.

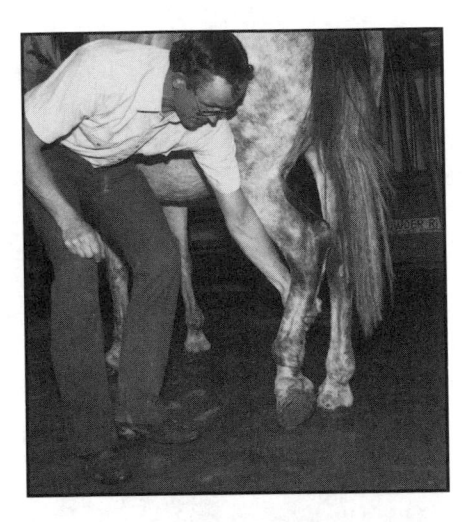

Picking up the back foot. Approach from the side. Slide the hand inside the cannon bone and draw the leg forward.

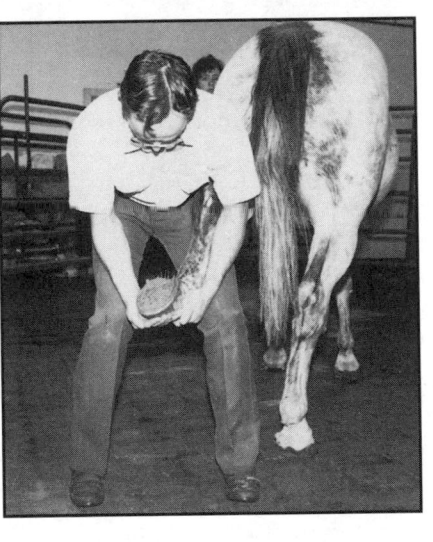

The leg is supported on the thigh with the stifle joint extended. This makes it difficult for the horse to pull free.

PREVENTING THE HORSE FROM KICKING

If a horse is inclined to kick while undergoing treatment, lifting a front leg will prevent him from doing so, as a horse cannot kick with one foot off the ground. The leg can be restrained by tying it up with a rope or strap. The rope or strap should be equipped with a quick-release mechanism in case the horse loses its balance. Tying up a back leg involves the use of a sideline.

Hobbling the hocks prevents kicking and allows the horse to bear weight on all four legs. This is important for long procedures or when a mare has to support the weight of a mounting stallion.

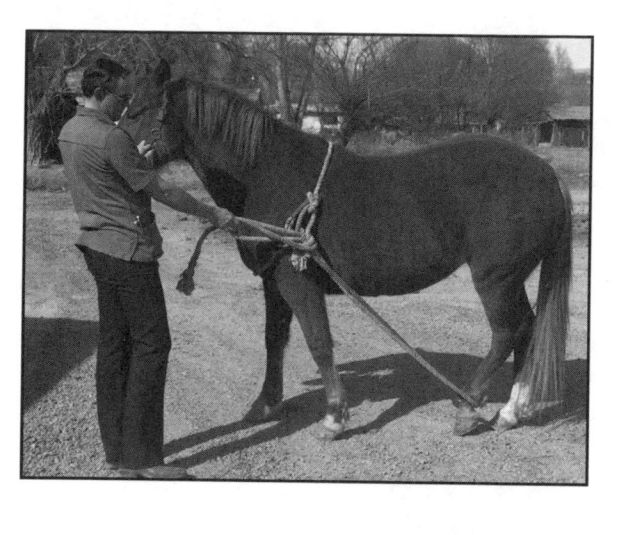

Tying up a back leg involves the use of a sideline.

STOCKS

For rectal and vaginal examinations, it is most convenient to restrain the horse in stocks or a palpation chute. In addition, stocks are particularly suitable for dental extractions and surgery on the standing horse. A partition at the back of the stock protects the examiner from being kicked. Once in stocks, the horse should be backed up against the partition to prevent him from kicking over the top.

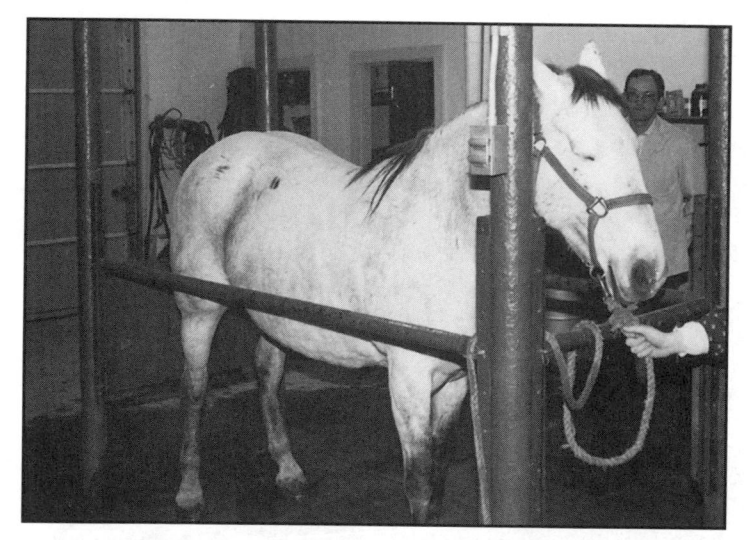

A stock with a kicking partition at the back is a safe restraint for rectal and vaginal examinations.

TAIL RESTRAINTS

A tail restraint is a good method for controlling weanlings that are not halter-broken. The restraint is employed by grasping the tail and pulling it over the back in a wheel while encircling the base of the neck with your other arm. This provides effective immobilization for short procedures such as passing a stomach tube or giving an injection. Forced tail flexion should be used with caution in older horses as coccygeal fractures and nerve injuries have occured.

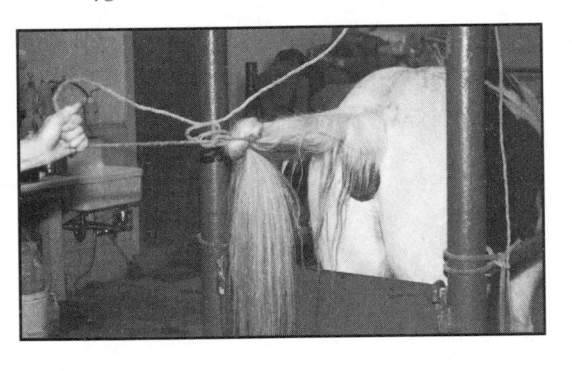

A tail restraint.

Tying a rope to the tail and pulling it straight back is a useful restraint for rectal and vaginal examinations. The rope should be held by an assistant and not tied to a stationary object.

RESTRAINING THE FOAL

Young foals that are not halter-broken but are wearing a halter should not be restrained by grasping the halter. These young horses often react by rearing back and falling. This can lead to a brain concussion or spine fracture.

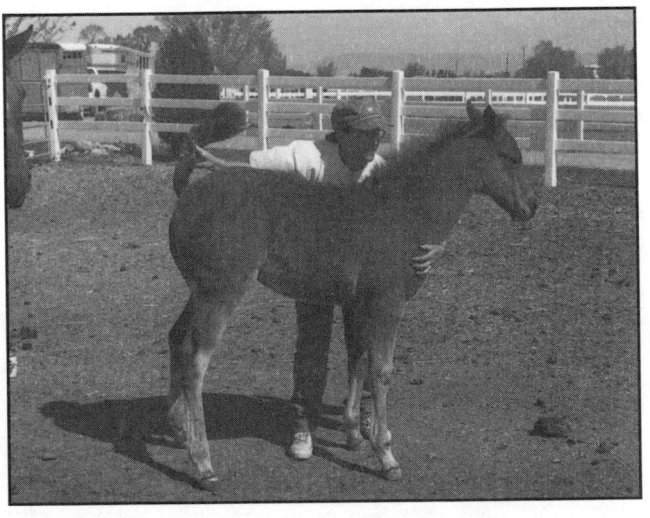

The correct method for restraining a foal.

Nursing foals become excessively agitated and difficult to control if separated from their dams. If the foal cannot be approached easily in the paddock or field, mother and foal should be led into a small enclosure such as a smooth-walled stall. The foal is then cornered and can be easily held with one arm encircling its chest and the other behind the rear legs above the hocks. The tail can be held over the back as described in the section above.

CHEMICAL RESTRAINT

Intravenous sedation is indicated for horses who resist physical restraint, and for those in whom a painful procedure is anticipated. Intravenous sedation is given by injection into the jugular vein.

Depending upon the circumstances, your veterinarian may select a drug or drug combination from the following classes:

Phenothiazines (such as acepromazine) are tranquilizers that act on the central nervous system to produce calming and deep drowsiness. Uncommonly, they produce extreme anxiety, muscle twitching, dropping of the penis, sweating, and convulsions.

Narcotics (such as morphine, Demerol, and butorphenol) are painkillers. When used in pain-free horses, they may produce excitation, apprehension, and increased muscular activity. Constipation and urinary retention can occur. Untoward effects can be reversed by giving an antidote.

Xylazine (Rompun) combines both tranquilization and pain control. It has a good margin of safety and can be used in combination with other drugs for better sedation and anesthesia. It is often the drug of choice for procedures requiring intravenous sedation.

Keep in mind that the effects of tranquilizers and sedatives are variable. A horse may still kick or strike even though thought to be fully tranquilized. Exercise the same precautions as you would around a nonsedated horse.

For more information on tranquilizers and sedatives, see ANESTHETICS AND TRANQUILIZERS.

Heat Stroke

Heat stroke is an emergency which requires immediate recognition and treatment.

Horses dissipate body heat primarily through sweating. When the humidity is high and air temperature is close to body temperature, cooling by sweating is not an efficient process. The horse then attempts to dissipate heat through rapid air exchange, or panting.

Common situations which predispose to overheating in horses are:

- Being transported in hot, poorly ventilated trailers.
- Being subjected to sustained exercise in warm, humid weather.

A horse trailer, if parked in the sun and improperly ventilated, is a
hazard for heat stroke.

- Being excessively dehydrated as a consequence of water deprivation,
  extreme exertion, or fever.
- Suffering from anhydrosis (the inability to sweat in response to exercise or
  heat production).

Heat stroke begins with symptoms like those described earlier for EXHAUSTED
HORSE SYNDROME. If these symptoms go unchecked, the thermoregulatory mechanism malfunctions; this allows body temperature to rise up to as high as 115 degrees F, well above levels of heat exhaustion. The horse loses its ability to sweat,
and becomes disoriented and unsteady on its feet. The situation is now critical,
and the horse may collapse and die at any moment.

Treatment: Rapid cooling must begin at once. While awaiting the veterinarian, move the horse to shade and spray it repeatedly with cold water. Apply ice
packs or alcohol sponges to the neck, flanks, and lower extremities. Fans are a very
effective means of cooling, although not always available. Cold water enemas,
administered by the veterinarian, produce rapid cooling.

Dehydration is always a factor and should be corrected with large volumes of
intravenous fluids containing electrolytes.

Heat stroke can be prevented by limiting exposure to predisposing situations
and by insuring that hard-working and endurance horses drink frequently during
prolonged exercise.

Insect Stings, Spiders, Scorpions, Lizards

The stings of bees, wasps, yellow jackets and ants all cause painful swelling at
the site of the sting. If an animal is stung many times, it could go into shock as the
result of absorbed toxins. Rarely, a hypersensitivity reaction (anaphylactic shock)
can occur if the horse was exposed in the past (see ANAPHYLACTIC SHOCK).

The stings of black widows, Missouri brown spiders, and tarantulas also are toxic to animals. The sign is sharp pain at the sting site. Later the horse can develop chills, fever, and labored breathing. An antivenin of equine origin is available for the treatment of the black widow bite. The antibiotic Dapsone is recommended for the treatment of brown spider bites.

The stings of centipedes and scorpions cause local reaction and at times severe illness. These bites heal slowly. Poisonous scorpions are found only in southern Arizona (two species).

Two species of poisonous lizard are found in the United States, both in southwestern states (the Gila monster and the Mexican bearded lizard).

Treatment of stings and bites:

1. Identify the insect.

2. Remove an embedded stinger with tweezers, or scrape it with a credit card (only bees leave their stingers behind).

3. Make a paste of baking soda and apply it directly to the sting.

4. Ice packs relieve swelling and pain.

5. Calamine lotion and Cortaid relieve itching.

6. If a lizard has a firm hold on the horse, pry open its jaws with pliers.

Poisoning

A poison is any substance harmful to the body. Animal baits are palatable poisons. Horses will readily consume them if given the opportunity. This also makes them an obvious choice for intentional poisoning.

Pastures contain a variety of plants, often unrecognized but potentially toxic. Poisonous substances can also be found in roughages and improperly stored grain and hay. Accidental ingestion of these compounds is the most common cause of poisoning in the horse.

The great variety of potentially poisonous plants and forages makes identification difficult, but most farm extension agents and veterinarians will be familiar with the common toxic plants and forages prevalent in your area.

Ingestion of plant and forage toxins causes a complete spectrum of toxic symptoms. They include mouth irritation, drooling and tongue paralysis, diarrhea, rapid heart rate, rapid labored breathing, cyanosis, depressed sensorium, abnormal gait, staggering and loss of balance, limb paralysis, muscle tremors and convulsions, collapse, coma, and death. Some plants can cause sudden death without premonitory signs. For more information on specific poisonings, see FORAGE TOXICITIES in Feeding and Nutrition.

Drugs and medications, when given in an overdose or by the wrong route, may cause the death of the animal. Occasionally a horse will suffer anaphylactic shock when given a drug by injection. This happens if the horse has a profound allergy to the drug (see ANAPHYLACTIC SHOCK).

TREATMENT OF POISONING

On suspicion of poisoning, contact your veterinarian at once. Locate the source of the poison and remove it to prevent further contact.

If the horse is down and having difficulty breathing, clear the airway (see SHOCK).

Signs of acute poisoning appear shortly after ingestion. Residual poison may be present in the horse's stomach. A gastric tube should be passed into the stomach and the contents suctioned and removed. The stomach is then washed out with large volumes of water to remove as much residual poison as possible.

After gastric lavage, an activated charcoal slurry is introduced through the stomach tube. The charcoal absorbs chemicals remaining in the stomach and small intestine. To prepare the slurry for an adult horse, mix 1 pound of activated charcoal with 2 quarts of water; for a foal, add $^1/_2$ pound of charcoal to 1 quart of water.

The next step is to prevent further absorption by eliminating the poison from the digestive tract. This is accomplished by giving a laxative immediately after the charcoal slurry. The two laxatives recommended for this purpose are magnesium sulfate (Epsom salt) and sodium sulfate (Glauber's salt). Sodium sulfate is preferred when used with activated charcoal, but either laxative is acceptable. Both are dissolved in water and given at a rate of 1 pound of laxative per gallon for a mature horse; or $^1/_3$ pound of laxative per $^1/_3$ gallon for a foal. The laxative can be repeated in 8 to 12 hours.

Mineral oil is a mild laxative and intestinal protectorant. It is preferred for some poisonings. The recommended dose is 3 to 4 quarts for a mature horse and 1 pint for a foal. Mineral oil must be given by stomach tube.

Large volumes of intravenous fluids are given in most acute poisonings to support the circulation, treat shock, and protect the kidneys. A large urine output may assist in eliminating the poison. Corticosteroids are often given for their antiinflammatory effects. A horse in coma may benefit from tracheal intubation and artificial ventilation during the phase of respiratory depression.

Convulsions caused by poisons are associated with prolonged periods of oxygen deficit and the potential for brain damage. Continuous or recurrent seizures should be controlled with intravenous Valium, phenobarbital, pentobarbital, or Robaxin.

Seizures caused by strychnine and other central nervous system poisons may be mistaken for epilepsy. This would be a mistake, as immediate veterinary attention is needed in cases of poisoning. In contrast to a poison seizure, epileptic seizures are brief, seldom last more than a minute, and are followed by a quiet period in which the horse appears dazed but is otherwise normal. Seizures caused by poisoning are often continuous or recur within minutes. Between episodes the horse is agitated and sweating, and may exhibit tremors, incoordination, weakness, colic, and diarrhea.

Specific antidotes are available for some poisons but cannot be administered unless the poison is known or suspected by the history of exposure. Most products containing chemicals are labeled for identification. If the label is not informative on the composition and toxicity of the product, call the National Animal Poison Control Center at (800) 548-2423 or (900) 680-0000. The hotline is open 24 hours a day. You can also call the emergency room at your local hospital and ask for information from the Poison Control Center.

If the horse has a poisonous substance on the skin or coat, wash the area thoroughly with soap and large volumes of water, or give the horse a complete bath in lukewarm water. Even if the substance is not irritating to the skin, it should be removed. Gasoline and oil stains can be removed by soaking the area with mineral or vegetable oil. Work the oil into the coat. Then wash the coat with a mild detergent such as Ivory soap.

POISON BAITS

Animal baits containing strychnine, sodium fluoroacetate, arsenic, phosphorus, zinc phosphide, metaldehyde, and other poisons are used in rural areas for control of gophers as well as coyotes and other predators. In stables and barns they are used to eliminate rodents. These poisons are now being used less frequently because of livestock losses, concerns about persistence in the environment, and the potential to poison pets and children.

A variety of toxic signs occur with poison baits. They include hyperexcitability, tremors, incoordination, weakness, seizures, coma, respiratory depression, and circulatory collapse. These poisons are extremely toxic and may produce death in a matter of minutes.

Strychnine. It is available commercially as coated pellets dyed purple, red, or green. Signs occur less than 2 hours after ingestion of the poison. The first signs are agitation, excitability, and apprehension. They are followed by intensely painful convulsions with rigid extension of all limbs. The horse arches its neck and is unable to breathe. Any slight stimulation, such as touching the horse or making a loud noise, will trigger a seizure.

Treat for poisoning as described above. Intravenous pentobarbital or phenobarbital is given during the first 48 hours to control seizures. Administer oxygen. Maintain a quiet environment and avoid unnecessary handling.

Sodium Fluoroacetate (Compound 1080). This highly potent rat and gopher poison is often mixed with cereal, bran, and other rat feeds. Signs of poisoning are agitation, profuse sweating, trembling, straining to urinate or defecate, a staggering gait, and terminal convulsions. Because of its rapid action, sudden death without observed signs may be the only indication of poisoning. Treat for poisoning as described above. An antidote (glyceryl monoacetin) is available through chemical supply stores. Intravenous calcium chloride or calcium gluconate may be needed to correct a low serum calcium.

Arsenic. This heavy metal is often combined with metaldehyde in slug and snail baits, and may appear in ant poisons, weed killers, and insecticides. Arsenic has a very rapid action and a major potential for unintentional poisoning. Fortunately, its use has been greatly curtailed. Death can occur before symptoms are observed. In less acute cases, the signs are severe colic, weakness, trembling, staggering, salivation, diarrhea, and paralysis.

Treat for poisoning as described above. A specific antidote (dimercaprol, also called British anti-Lewisite or BAL) is available. It should be given as soon as the diagnosis is suspected.

Metaldehyde. This poison (often combined with arsenic) is used commonly in rat, snail, and slug baits. It looks and tastes like dog food. The contents of the horse's stomach may have an odor of formaldehyde. Signs of toxicity are excitation, drooling and slobbering, uncoordinated gait, muscle tremors, and weakness which progresses to recumbency in a matter of hours. Death is by respiratory failure. Treat for poisoning as described above. Intravenous Valium or pentobarbital is given to control tremors. There is no antidote.

Phosphorus. This chemical is present in rat and roach poisons. The horse's breath may have the odor of garlic. The first signs of intoxication are colic and a hemorrhagic diarrhea. These signs may be quickly followed by coma and death. Alternately, some horses experience a symptom-free interval lasting 2 to 4 days, which is then followed by signs of liver and kidney failure. There is no specific antidote. Treat as described above.

Zinc Phosphide. This substance also is found in rat poisons. Zinc phosphide in the stomach releases phosphine gas, which has the odor of garlic or rotten fish. Intoxication causes rapid labored breathing, colic, weakness, stumbling, ataxic gait, convulsions, and death within 2 days. Treat for poisoning as described above. There is no specific antidote, but the stomach should be lavaged with 5 percent sodium bicarbonate, which raises the gastric pH and delays the formation of gas.

Rodenticide Anticoagulants. Rat and mouse poisons containing dicumarol-related compounds block the synthesis of vitamin K. Vitamin K is essential for blood clotting. A deficiency of vitamin K results in spontaneous bleeding. There are no signs of poisoning until the horse develops spontaneous bleeding with passage of blood in the urine or stool, bleeding from the nose, or hemorrhages beneath the gums and skin. The simultaneous use of nonsteroidal anti-inflammatory drugs such as Butazolidin potentiates the bleeding.

The first-generation anticoagulants (Warfarin, Pindone) require repeated consumption to produce a hemorrhagic effect. However, the newer and more commonly used second-generation anticoagulants (of the bromadiolone and brodifacoum classes) require but a single exposure.

Warfarin is the drug used for treating jugular thrombophlebitis and navicular disease. An overdose can result in the same effect as the accidental ingestion of a rodenticide.

A closely related condition is dicumerol poisoning. Dicumerol is found in sweet clover contaminated by a mold. The elimination of moldy hay will prevent this problem.

Treatment of spontaneous bleeding caused by all anticoagulants involves the administration of fresh whole blood or frozen plasma in amounts determined by the rate and volume of blood loss. Vitamin K_1 is a specific antidote. It is given immediately by subcutaneous injection and repeated at intervals as necessary until the activated clotting time (ACT) returns to normal. Second-generation anticoagulants remain in the horse's system for several weeks and require prolonged observation and treatment.

INSECTICIDE POISONING

Insecticides (discussed in chapter 2, Parasites) constitute a large group of toxic compounds to which the majority of horses are exposed and at potential risk for poisoning.

Organophosphates and Carbamates. These compounds, used extensively in pesticides and dewormers, are the most frequent cause of insecticide poisoning. Organophosphates include dichlorvos, malathion, coumaphos, stirofos, Haloxon, and trichlorfon. The most commonly used carbamates are Sevin, pyrantel pamoate, and pyrantel tartrate. Organophosphates are a particular problem when topical insecticides are applied to a horse shortly after it has been dewormed with either dichlorvos or trichlorfon. This combination of two sources can result in overdose and toxicity.

Signs of toxicity with organophosphates and carbamates are hyperexcitability, colic with tucked-up abdomen, muscle tremors, patchy sweating, profuse salivation, diarrhea, and a stiff-legged gait progressing to staggering. Collapse followed by respiratory failure is terminal. Seizures do not occur with insecticide poisoning.

The organophosphate Haloxon has been shown to produce recurrent laryngeal nerve paralysis in foals. In adults, it produces paralysis of the anus, bladder, and pelvic limbs.

Treatment: Following oral ingestion, remove contents from the stomach by gastric tube and prevent absorption by administering activated charcoal and a sodium or magnesium laxative as described above for the treatment of poisoning. Hyperexcitability and salivation are controlled with intravenous atropine. Repeat subcutaneously as needed. The specific antidote for organophosphate poisoning is 2-PAM (protopam chloride). It should be given as soon as the diagnosis is suspected. Tranquilizers and morphine should be avoided since they may exacerbate symptoms.

Chlorinated Hydrocarbons. Chlorinated hydrocarbons, of which the prototype is DDT, are used in field and seed sprays, and as dusts against plant pests. Their use has been curtailed because of persistent toxicity in the environment. Only lindane, methoxychlor, and toxaphine are approved for use around livestock. Chlorinated hydrocarbons are readily inhaled and easily absorbed through the horse's skin. Toxicity can occur from repeated or excessive exposure. Signs of toxicity occur rapidly. They include hyperexcitability with twitching of the face, followed by muscle tremors that begin at the head and progress backward to involve the neck, shoulder, trunk, and rear legs. Seizures and convulsions are followed by respiratory paralysis and death.

Treatment: There is no specific antidote. Following oral ingestion, flush out the stomach and administer activated charcoal followed by mineral oil and a laxative as described above for the treatment of poisoning. Seizures are controlled with intravenous Valium or pentobarbital. For skin exposure, the coat should be washed thoroughly with soap and water to remove residual insecticide.

Shock

CIRCULATORY SHOCK

Circulatory shock is a state of low blood flow. It is the result of a cardiac output insufficient to meet the body's needs for oxygen. An adequate cardiac output requires a healthy heart, open vessels, and sufficient blood volume to maintain pressure. Any condition that adversely affects one or more of these parameters will produce shock.

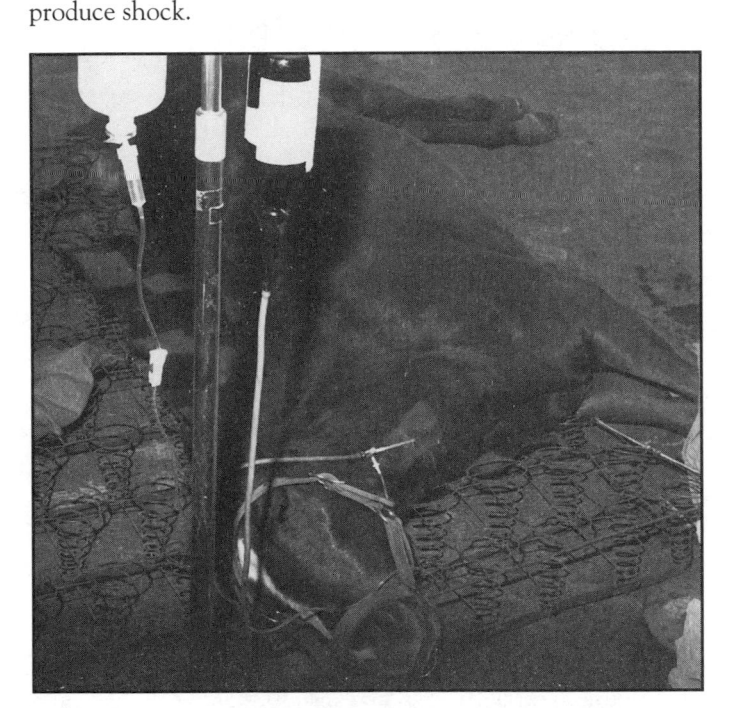

Circulatory shock requires immediate restoration of blood volume and tissue perfusion on the premises.

The body attempts to compensate for inadequate circulation by increasing the heart rate, constricting the skin vessels, and maintaining fluid in the circulation by reducing the output of urine. This becomes increasingly difficult when vital organs are not getting enough oxygen to carry on these activities. After a time, shock becomes self-perpetuating. Prolonged shock causes death.

Common causes of shock are dehydration (profuse diarrhea, excessive sweating), hemorrhage, severe colic, peritonitis, blood-borne infection, heat stroke, snake bite, electrocution, poisoning, and major trauma. Foal septicemia is the most common cause of shock in neonates.

Treatment: First evaluate the horse. Is he breathing? Does he have a heartbeat? What are the extent of his injuries? Is he in shock? If the horse is in shock, summon your veterinarian and proceed as follows:

1. If the horse is unconscious, check to be sure the airway is open. Clear secretions from the mouth with your fingers. Pull out the tongue to prevent it from blocking the airway. If possible, maintain a position in which the head is level with the body.

2. Allow the horse to assume the most comfortable position. An animal will naturally adopt the least painful position that allows it to breathe.

3. Control bleeding as described below for wounds.

4. To slow the progress of shock:

   • Calm the horse and speak soothingly.
   • When possible, splint or support broken bones before moving the horse.
   • Cover the horse with a coat or blanket to provide warmth. Do not wrap tightly.

Veterinary treatment involves rapid rehydration with large volumes of intravenous salt solutions to maintain blood pressure and tissue perfusion. Other steps that may be indicated include the administration of oxygen, blood transfusions, corticosteroids, antibiotics, and various drugs to support the circulation.

The outlook depends upon the cause of the shock and how quickly treatment is initiated.

ANAPHYLACTIC SHOCK

This is an acute hypersensitivity reaction that develops after a horse has been exposed to an allergen to which it is highly sensitive. The allergens most frequently involved in anaphylactic reactions are the penicillin antibiotics, vaccines, and the immune serums.

Anaphylaxis can be localized or generalized (systemic). For example, a local reaction to an insect bite may consist only of itching and a hive-like swelling around the site of the bite. With a systemic reaction, the itching, swelling, and hives become generalized, or appear elsewhere on the body. A severe systemic anaphylactic reaction is accompanied by anxiety, sweating, marked difficulty breathing, diarrhea, a drop in blood pressure, shock, collapse, and death.

Signs of anaphylaxis are produced by histamine and other vasoactive substances released by mast and basophil cells in response to the challenge of the allergen.

Treatment: Early recognition of severe anaphylactic shock is essential. Sudden anxiety with difficulty breathing following either a vaccination or the administration of a drug are indications to treat. The specific antidote is epinephrine. Mild reactions are treated with 1 to 2 ml of a 1:1,000 epinephrine solution given intramuscularly (IM) or subcutaneously (SC). Life-threatening reactions require the immediate administration of 4 to 8 ml of the 1:1,000 epinephrine solution IM or SC, or 3 to 5 ml of the 1:10,000 solution intravenously (IV) via the jugular vein over 3 to 5 minutes. (Note the different solutions for IM and IV administration.) Repeat epinephrine every 15 minutes as necessary. If time permits, a permanent IV line should be established, as further medications and large volumes of fluid may be necessary to support the circulation.

An injectable corticosteroid (dexamethasone 0.1 mg per pound) is frequently administered for its anti-allergic effects. An antihistamine such as pyrilamine maleate at a dose of 0.5 mg per pound by IM or IV injection is often sufficient for a mild local reaction, and is useful in a severe reaction as a complement to the above medications.

Prevention: As a precaution, do not administer a drug or vaccine that has produced any sort of allergic reaction in the past, including hives. Drugs used for treating anaphylactic shock should be available in the medical supplies of all facilities that routinely give injections to horses.

Snake Bites

Poisonous and nonpoisonous snakes are widely distributed throughout the United States. Snake bites tend to occur during the spring and summer when snakes are most active. Horses are usually bitten on the nose. In general, bites of nonpoisonous snakes do not cause swelling and pain. They show teeth marks in the shape of a horseshoe (no fang marks).

In the United States there are four poisonous species: rattlesnakes, cottonmouth moccasins, copperheads, and coral snakes. The diagnosis of poison snake bite is made by the appearance of the bite, the behavior of the animal, and identification of the species of snake. (Kill it first if possible.)

PIT VIPERS (RATTLESNAKES, MOCCASINS, COPPERHEADS)

Identify these species by their large arrow-shaped heads, pits below and between the eyes, elliptical pupils, and the presence of fangs in the upper jaws. The most dangerous snake for horses is the large rattlesnake commonly found in the western and southwestern United States. It is easily identified by its characteristic rattle.

Pit viper venom produces red blood cell hemolysis and destroys tissue by breaking down proteins. It is also a depressant to the heart.

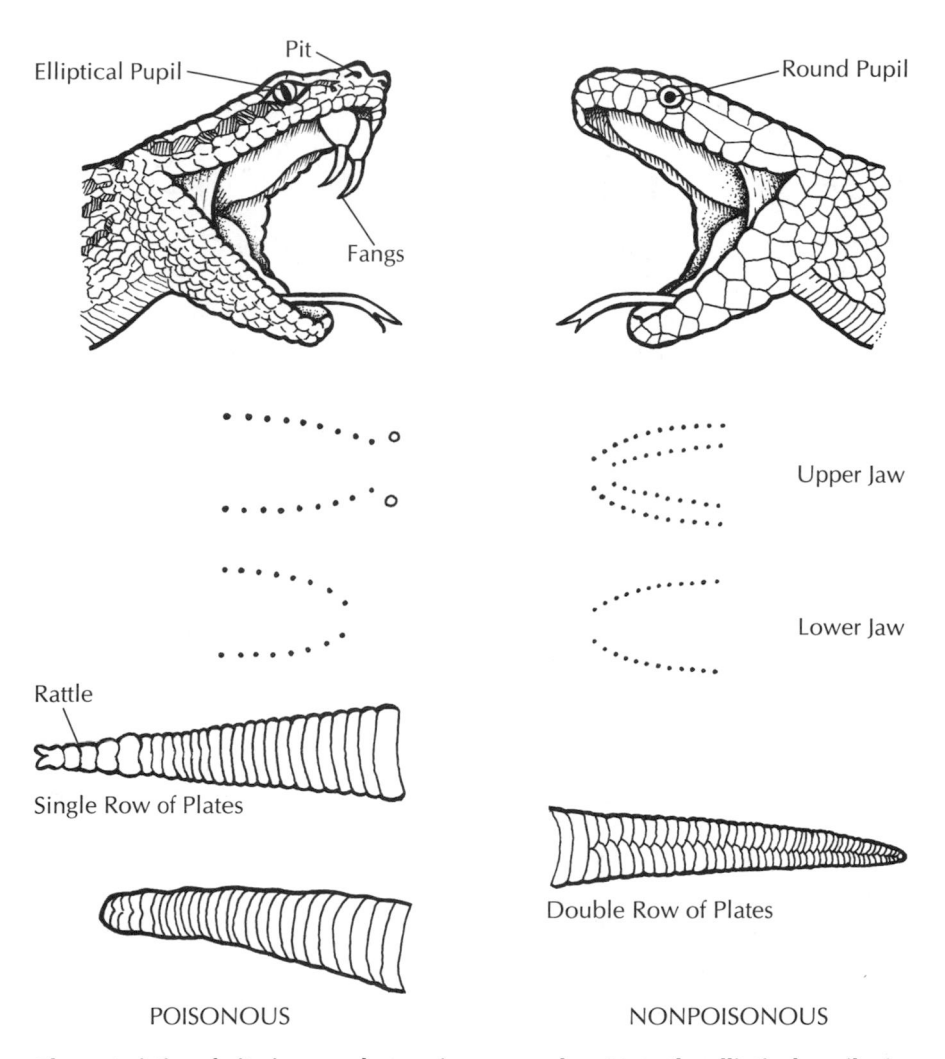

Pit

Elliptical Pupil

Fangs

Round Pupil

Upper Jaw

Lower Jaw

Rattle

Single Row of Plates

Double Row of Plates

POISONOUS

NONPOISONOUS

Characteristics of pit vipers and nonpoisonous snakes. Note the elliptical pupil, pit below the eye, large fangs, characteristic bite, and single row of subcaudal plates on the belly of the pit viper.

The Bite. The strike of the rattlesnake, and to a lesser extent that of other pit vipers, causes tissue swelling around the bite. When the horse is bitten on the nose (most common), the swelling may be mistaken for a bee sting or spider bite. Identification of two puncture wounds in the skin (fang marks) will reveal the true cause.

In a severe case, however, the whole head including the nose, eyelids, and ears may be swollen to an extreme degree, giving rise to nasal obstruction and difficulty breathing. A frothy bloodstained discharge may drain from each nostril.

Behavior of the Animal. Signs and symptoms depend on the size and species of snake, location of the bite, and amount of toxin absorbed by the horse. Most horses experience few signs other than swelling at the site of the bite. With a severe reaction, the horse will become depressed and weak. When death occurs, it is caused by respiratory failure or cardiac arrest.

CORAL SNAKE

The coral snake, found primarily in the southeast, is an infrequent cause of snake bites. This snake has a retiring nature and lives in a habitat different from that of most horses. Identify the coral snake by its rather small size, small head with black nose, and vivid-colored body bands of red, yellow, white, and black, with the red and yellow bands always next to each other. Fangs are present in the upper jaw.

There is a species of nonpoisonous snake that resembles the coral snake. It can be told apart because the black bands are bordered by yellow bands on both sides.

The Bite. The local reaction is less severe but the pain is excruciating. Look for the fang marks.

Behavior of the Animal. Coral snake venom is neurotoxic (destructive to nerve tissue). Signs include paralysis, convulsions, and coma.

TREATMENT OF ALL SNAKE BITES

Fortunately, because of the large size of the adult horse, poison snake bites are rarely fatal. Foals are at somewhat greater risk of systemic reactions and death.

The first step is to identify the snake and look at the bite. If the snake is nonpoisonous, cleanse and dress the wound as described later in this chapter (see WOUNDS). If it appears that the horse has been bitten by a poisonous snake, summon your veterinarian and proceed as follows:

1. Restrain the horse. Snake bites are extremely painful. If the horse is recumbent, see SHOCK.

2. Keep the horse quiet. Venom spreads rapidly if the horse is active. Excitement, exercise, and struggling all increase the rate of absorption of toxin.

3. If the bite is on the leg, apply a constricting bandage (handkerchief or strip of cloth) several inches above the bite. You should be able to get a finger beneath the bandage. Loosen the bandage every hour for 5 minutes.

4. Cold water packs can be applied to the bite at 15-minute intervals to reduce swelling. Ice packs, however, cause additional tissue damage and should not be used.

5. Washing the wound may upset the horse and increase venom absorption. Later, under controlled conditions with the horse sedated, the wound should be thoroughly cleansed, irrigated, and disinfected.

6. Incising the fang marks and applying suction in the field is not a practical undertaking for most equine snake bites and may increase anxiety and struggling. In particular, *do not attempt to suck out the venom, as you could absorb the toxin.*

Antivenins are available through your veterinarian. They are not always necessary for the adult horse but may be indicated for the foal. To be maximally effective, antivenin must be given within 2 hours of the snake bite. Swelling and nasal obstruction respond to corticosteroids. Snake bites frequently become infected. Antibiotics, tetanus prophylaxis, and wound care are important.

Sudden Unexplained Death

A horse may be found dead without obvious explanation. Intentional poisoning comes to mind first. However, most poisonings are accidental and not caused by malicious intent.

All unexplained deaths should be investigated in an effort to establish the cause. Measures may need to be taken to protect other animals on the property.

A postmortem examination in the field may disclose the cause of death and thus eliminate the suspicion of poisoning. If the cause is not readily apparent, samples of blood, urine, stomach contents, and tissue from the kidney, liver, brain, spleen, hair, or hoof should be taken and sent to a laboratory for tissue and chemical analysis. It is also important to send samples of feed, water, weeds in the area, and suspect animal baits. These studies can be expensive. This needs to be taken into account when deciding how thoroughly to pursue the investigation.

The following are some causes of sudden unexplained death, listed in approximate order of frequency:

- Peritonitis caused by acute gastric dilatation and ruptured gastric ulcer, colonic perforation, or intestinal strangulation.
- Poison plant ingestion.
- Forage toxicities including botulism, moldy corn poisoning, sorghum toxicity, blister beetle poisoning, and Rumensin ingestion.
- Cardiac arrhythmias causing cardiac arrest from unsuspected heart disease.
- Poison bait ingestion.
- Lightning strikes.
- Fatal infections including anthrax, equine infectious anemia, bacterial diarrhea, rabies, and equine piroplasmosis.
- Head and neck trauma caused by falls or running into posts and walls.
- Anaphylactic shock caused by insect stings, spider bites, and vaccinations.
- Poison snake bites.

Despite laboratory studies, the exact cause of death may never be determined. The most probable cause of death is then based on circumstantial and laboratory evidence, and the clinical judgment of your veterinarian.

Wounds

In the care of wounds, the most important considerations are to (a) first stop the bleeding, and (b) then prevent infection. Be prepared to restrain the horse before you treat the wound (see HANDLING AND RESTRAINT).

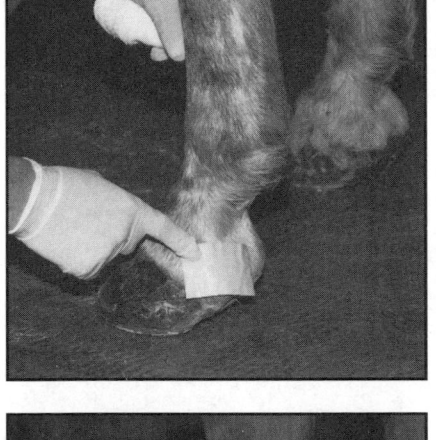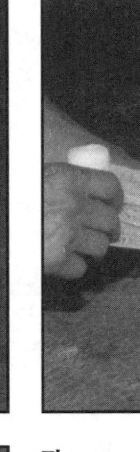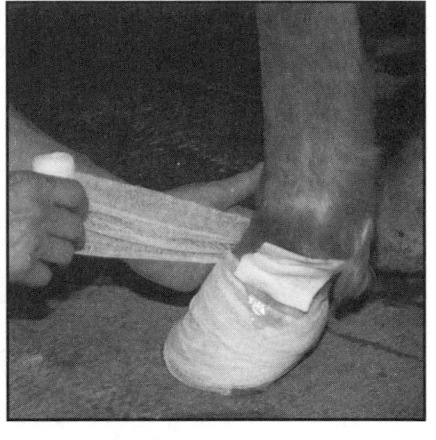

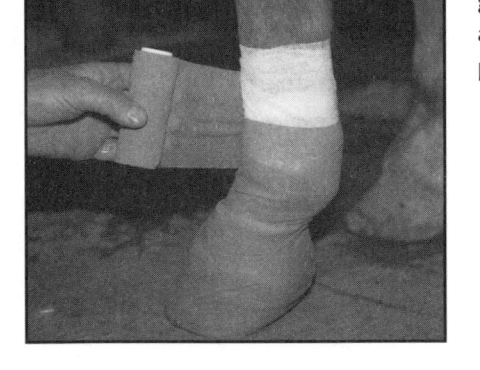

The pressure dressing. Place sterile pads over the wound. Cover with a gauze roll. A stretch bandage helps to apply even pressure. It should not be pulled too tightly.

CONTROL OF BLEEDING

Bleeding may be *arterial* (the spurting of bright red blood) or *venous* (oozing of dark red blood), and sometimes both. Do not wipe a wound that has stopped bleeding. This will dislodge the clot. Do not pour peroxide on a fresh wound. Bleeding then will be difficult to control.

The two methods used to control bleeding are the pressure dressing and the tourniquet.

Pressure Dressing. If the wound is on the leg, take several pieces of clean linen or sterile gauze, place them over the wound, and bandage snugly. Watch for swelling of the limb below the pressure pack. Swelling indicates impaired circulation, in which case the bandage must be loosened or removed.

If material is not available for bandaging, or if the wound is on the body, place a pad on the wound and press firmly. Hold it in place for 15 minutes.

If blood soaks through the bandage, or bleeding persists after the pad is removed, apply further pressure (or a tourniquet) and notify your veterinarian. An arterial bleeder may need to be tied off.

Tourniquet. A tourniquet may be required to control a spurting artery. Tourniquets can be used only on the legs and tail. The tourniquet should be placed above the wound (between the wound and the heart). Take a piece of cloth or a gauze roll and loop it around the limb. Then tighten it by hand or with a stick inserted beneath the loop. Twist the loop until the bleeding stops. A tourniquet should be released for 5 minutes every 30 minutes to allow blood to enter into the limb below the tourniquet.

TREATING THE WOUND

Horses are more susceptible to tetanus than most other domestic animals. Accordingly, all wounds should receive prompt tetanus prophylaxis. If the horse has been immunized against tetanus, it should be given a booster shot now. If the vaccination history is unknown and the wound is either heavily contaminated or a deep puncture wound (tetanus-prone wound), tetanus toxoid and tetanus antitoxin should be given in two different intramuscular locations. Follow with a second tetanus booster in 4 weeks.

All wounds are contaminated with dirt and bacteria. Proper care and handling will reduce the risk of tetanus and prevent some infections.

Extensive wounds and those requiring the application of casts will require chemical restraint, a local or regional anesthetic, and occasionally a general anesthetic. These wounds should be treated by a veterinarian. Cover the wound with a sterile dressing to prevent further contamination while awaiting veterinary instructions (see PRESSURE DRESSING, above).

The five steps in wound care are skin preparation, cleansing, debridement, wound closure, and bandaging.

Skin Preparation. Remove the original protective dressing and cleanse the area with a sterile surgical scrub solution. The two most commonly used solutions are povidone-iodine 10 percent (Betadine) and chlorhexidine diacetate 2 percent (Nolvasan). In the concentrations provided in the stock solutions, these preparations are irritating to unprotected tissue. Scrub the skin around the wound but avoid contact with the open wound. Then start at the edges of the wound and clip the hair back to prevent long hair from entering the wound.

Note that 3 percent hydrogen peroxide, often recommended as a wound cleanser, has little value as an antiseptic and is extremely toxic to tissues. It is not recommended for application to a fresh wound.

Cleansing. The purpose of cleansing is to remove dirt and bacteria. Vigorously scrubbing out a wound with a brush or gauze pad will further traumatize the wound and negate the benefits of cleansing.

Wound lavage is a nontraumatic and highly effective method of cleansing a wound. It involves irrigating the wound with copious amounts of irrigating fluid until the tissues are clean and glistening.

Tap water is a suitable and convenient lavage solution. Tap water has a negligible bacterial count and is known to cause less tissue irritation than sterile or distilled water. To provide antibacterial activity, add chlorhexidine or Betadine to the water. Studies show that chlorhexidine has the greater residual killing effect, but either solution is satisfactory when correctly diluted.

To dilute chlorhexidine, add 25 ml of the 2 percent stock solution to 1,000 ml water (0.05 percent irrigating solution). To dilute povidone-iodine, add 10 ml of the 10 percent stock solution to 1,000 ml water (0.1 percent irrigating solution). (Note that a quart is a little less than 1,000 ml.)

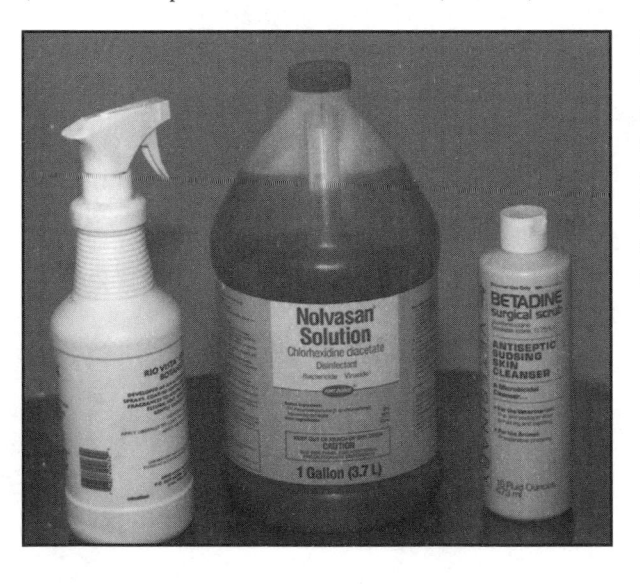

Nolvasan and Betadine solutions should be diluted prior to wound application. For lavage pressure, a plastic spray bottle is equal to a syringe with a 19-gauge needle.

The effectiveness of wound lavage is related to the volume and pressure of the fluid used. A bulb syringe is a low-pressure system and requires correspondingly more fluid to achieve a marginally satisfactory wound cleansing. A large glass or plastic syringe with a 19-gauge needle is sufficient to remove a moderate amount of dirt and bacteria. A home Water-Pik unit (used by people), or a commercial lavage unit, provides a high-pressure stream of fluid and is most effective. A garden hose with a pressure nozzle would also work well as the initial lavage, followed by one of the above to deliver the antiseptic surgical scrub.

Debridement and Closure. Debridement, which follows wound lavage, is the removal of devitalized tissue and any remaining foreign material using tissue forceps (tweezers) and scalpel. Before starting, put on sterile surgical gloves and be sure all instruments are clean. Devitalized tissue and foreign matter are removed by scalpel dissection. Experience helps to determine the difference between normal and devitalized tissue, and to control bleeding that results from the scalpel dissection.

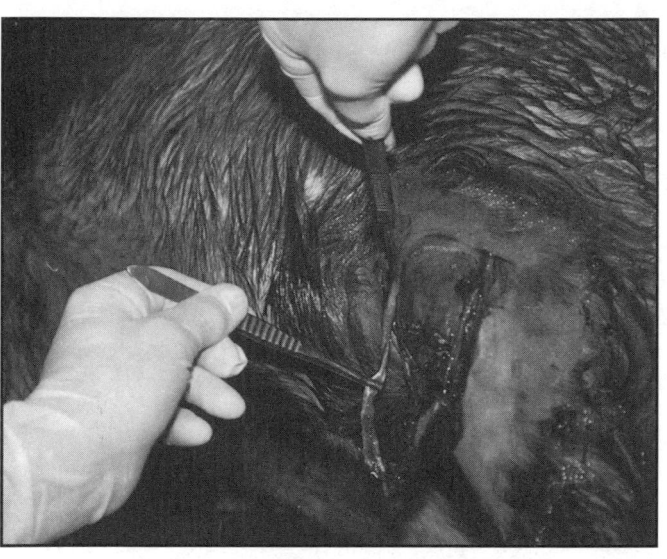

Debridement is the removal of devitalized tissue which predisposes to wound infection.

The next decision is whether to close the wound or allow it to heal by secondary intention. Wounds that are sutured and then become infected pose a serious risk of sepsis. Infections in open wounds, however, are far less troublesome.

Wounds that have been heavily contaminated are likely to become infected. These wounds should not be sutured. Similarly, wounds older than 12 hours should not be sutured. Suturing should not be done if there are signs of inflammation in and around the wound, as this indicates impending infection.

Puncture wounds are quite likely to become infected. The external opening should be enlarged to provide drainage, after which the tract should be irrigated with a dilute antiseptic surgical scrub solution. Bites are heavily contaminated puncture wounds. With all animal bites, keep in mind the possibility of rabies. Puncture wounds should not be sutured. Administer tetanus prophylaxis as described above.

Fresh lacerations on the face are best sutured to prevent infection, minimize scarring, and speed recovery. Small lacerations may not need to be sutured. Lacerations on the leg usually cannot be closed because the skin is too tight and the sutures will pull through.

Occasionally it is possible to close a wound that has been left open for several days and has developed a bed of clean granulation tissue. These wounds have acquired resistance to infection. Suturing such a wound is called *delayed primary closure*.

The length of time that sutures should remain depends on the location and other characteristics of the wound. Most sutures can be removed within 14 to 21 days.

Extensive, complicated wounds that must be left open should be cared for initially at a veterinary hospital. These wounds are likely to become infected and require intensive management including (in many cases) lavage and debridement on a daily basis. Since open wounds heal by secondary intention, it may take weeks or months for the skin to close.

Small open wounds can be treated at home. Medicate twice daily with a topical antibiotic ointment such as Triple Antibiotic Ointment. Recent evidence suggests that a steroid-antibiotic ointment (started after 7 days) may increase the rate of skin closure. The horse should be confined to a clean stall until the surface of the wound has a protective scab. Restrict access to muddy paddocks and pastures until the wound is healed.

Infected wounds with a covering of pus will require the application of moist sterile dressings. A number of topical antiseptics are effective in treating superficial wound infections. They include chlorhexidine and Betadine diluted as described earlier; Furacin Topical Cream or Solution 0.2 percent; Silvadene Cream 1 percent; and topical antibiotics containing bacitracin, neomycin sulfate, and polymyxin B sulfate. Apply directly to the wound, or first place on a gauze pad. Change the dressings once or twice daily to aid in the drainage of pus.

Oral and intramuscular antibiotics will not prevent wound infections but are indicated in the presence of cellulitis or abscess (see PYODERMA).

Most wounds on horses will heal with minimal scarring and a good functional result if the wound does not become infected, and if it is protected from fly attacks. Flies seriously complicate the process of wound healing, promote infection, and cause the formation of excessive fibrous tissue in the wound. To protect the horse from flies and other biting insects, see INSECT CONTROL in the Parasites chapter.

BANDAGING

Wounds can be bandaged or not, depending on their location. Wounds about the head are best left open to facilitate treatment. Many wounds of the upper body are difficult to bandage and do not benefit greatly from being covered.

Bandaging has the advantage of protecting a wound from dirt, manure, and fly attacks. It also restricts movement, compresses skin flaps, eliminates pockets of serum, and keeps the edges from pulling apart. Bandaging is most effective for extremity wounds. In fact, all leg and foot wounds should be bandaged.

Foot and Leg Bandages. Unlike the temporary pressure dressing, the foot and leg bandage will remain for some time. It is important to pad the extremity well to prevent the bandage from becoming too tight and shutting off the circulation. Place several sterile gauze pads over the wound and cover with one or more large pads to completely surround the leg. Wrap with an elastic bandage, starting with

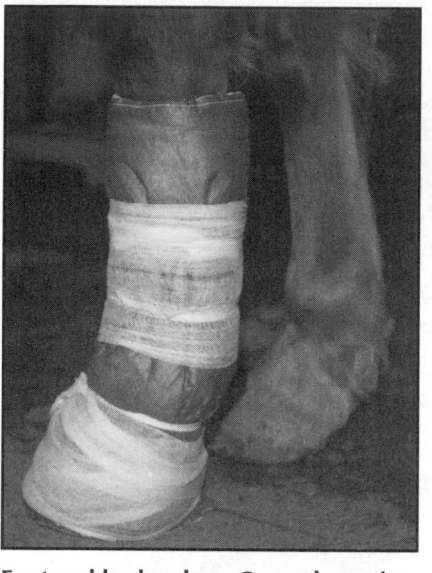

Foot and leg bandage. Cover the entire circumference of the leg with a soft pad and hold in place with a gauze roll.

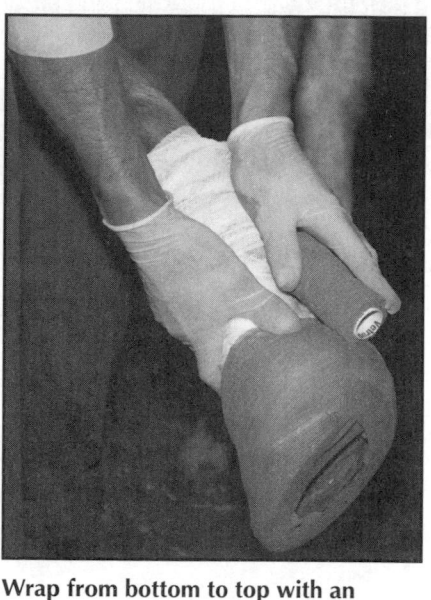

Wrap from bottom to top with an elastic bandage, maintaining even tension without cinching the wrap.

The hoof should be included. This helps to immobilize the joints.

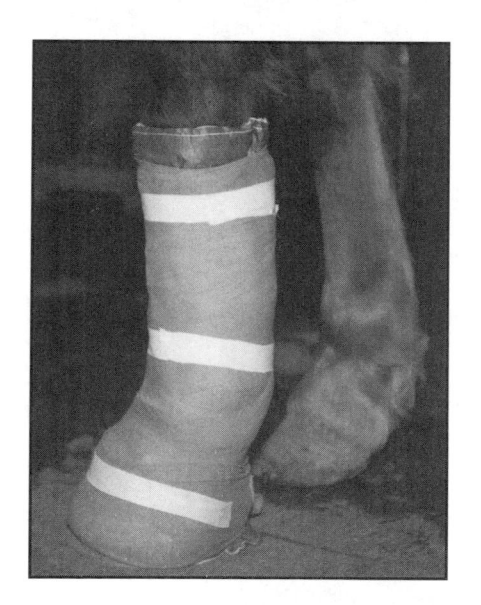

the hoof and working up the leg. Be sure to overlap as you go. This prevents the skin from forming ridges and becoming pinched beneath the bandage. If this happens, the skin can become devitalized. Do not cinch the wrap, but roll it around the leg without stretching the fabric. This will prevent the cumulative effect of an elastic bandage becoming too tight. Flex the joints beneath the bandage several times to ensure the bandage is secure, but not so tight as to interfere with the circulation. If there is doubt about the adequacy of circulation, loosen the bandage.

Bandages over clean, healing wounds can be changed every 2 to 3 days, but should be inspected twice daily for signs of excessive pressure, limb swelling, slippage, drainage, or soiling. If any of these are present, replace the bandage. Polyvinyl duct tape can be used to waterproof the bandage.

A draining or infected wound will need to be redressed at least daily. The bandage should be sufficiently bulky to absorb the drainage without soaking through. Disposable diapers can be used for bandages that incorporate the foot.

For foot wounds that require prolonged treatment, a protective boot or shoe with a removable treatment plate can be used. Wounds of the sole are discussed in chapter 12, Musculoskeletal System.

PARASITES

Intestinal parasites are among the most serious and common health problems affecting the horse. During their passage through the host, worms injure organ systems and create problems that lead to anemia, diarrhea, weight loss, poor condition, and general debility. In young individuals they can permanently damage the lining of the bowel, creating malabsorption and nutritional deficiencies that interfere with growth and development. Worms are a predisposing cause in 90 percent of all cases of intestinal colic.

While all this is inescapable, there is much you can do to keep your horse relatively untroubled by parasites and at the top of its form. In horses, good parasite control goes hand in hand with good health. Control is best accomplished by a routine deworming program as described below, and by utilizing environmental practices aimed at reducing exposure.

Worms (Intestinal Parasites)

Because intestinal parasites are so ubiquitous and easily transmitted, it is not possible to rid horses of all internal parasites or to prevent reinfection. One should assume that all horses are infected with worms.

Deworming programs are primarily aimed at controlling bots and the large and small strongyles. In young foals, the aim is to control the above plus ascarids. Tapeworms and threadworms are not as common, but should be treated when known to be present.

DEWORMING AGENTS (ANTHELMINTICS)

Table I shows the currently recommended deworming agents and their effectiveness against common internal parasites.

Most deworming agents can be divided into five principal classes according to their chemical structure and mode of action. They are the (1) benzimidazoles (BDZs); (2) organophosphates; (3) piperazines; (4) carbamates; and (5) avermectins (ivermectin).

The benzimidazoles include among them mebendazole, thiabendazole, cambendazole, fenbendazole, oxfendazole and oxibendazole. Febantel is a closely related compound that is altered in the horse's body to function as a benzimidazole. The benzimidazoles are highly effective against strongyles and pinworms. All but thiabendazole are excellent against ascarids. The benzimidazoles have a high margin of safety and can be given to foals and pregnant mares after the first trimester. This often makes them the drugs of choice for sick and stressed horses. However, the emergence of small strongyles resistant to BZDs has become a significant problem. Oxibendazole is the only BZD currently effective against small strongyles.

The organophosphates are represented by dichlorvos and trichlorfon. Dichlorvos is moderately effective against strongyles. Both are good to excellent against ascarids, pinworms, and bots. Organophosphates should not be used in combination with tranquilizers because of adverse reactions.

Organophosphates may be present in some insecticide preparations for use on the horse, such as sprays, powders, or dips. Therefore, avoid using topical insecticides containing organophosphates within 1 to 2 weeks of deworming with an organophosphate, as there could be a buildup of chemicals resulting in toxicity (see POISONING in chapter 1, Emergencies).

Organophosphates should not be given to foals under 4 months, or to mares past mid-pregnancy.

Piperazine is excellent for ascarids. However, because it is a fast-acting agent, it should be avoided in heavy infestations because of the danger of causing toxicity and worm impactions (see ASCARIDS).

The carbamates include pyrantel pamoate and pyrantel tartrate. Pyrantel has a wide margin of safety and, like the benzimidazoles, is preferred in foals, late-gestation mares, and sick or stressed horses. It is excellent against all the common worm parasites except bots. In addition, it is effective against tapeworms when given at twice the normal dosage. Many strongyle species that develop resistance to BZDs are responsive to pyrantel.

Ivermectin has a broad spectrum of activity against both intestinal and insect parasites and is effective against drug-resistant strongyles. It also kills migrating larvae. Ivermectin should be included in all deworming programs because of its unique effectiveness against the tissue stages of large stronglyes, ascarids, Onchocerca, and bots.

When choosing a product for its specificity and spectrum of activity, *look for the active drugs listed on the label*. Preparations containing the same drug carry different names when marketed by different companies. In addition, many proprietary deworming agents on the market are made up of more than one class of drug.

DEWORMING YOUR HORSE

In general, deworming agents will never be completely effective in ridding a horse of all parasites. There are several reasons. First is the continuing problem of reinfection. As a horse grazes on pasture, it automatically becomes reinfected by ingesting larvae present in grass and forages. Second, most dewormers (with the exception of ivermectin) attack only the adult worms in the intestinal tract. They do not kill and remove encysted larvae and stages migrating in the horse's tissues. This is especially true for strongyles, ascarids, and strongyloides. These larvae escape the drug and thus serve as a basis for further infection. Third, the development of drug-resistant worms is a continuing problem, especially in the case of the small strongyles that have become resistant to the benzimidazoles. Therefore, to administer an effective deworming program several important points should be considered:

- Deworm all horses on the premises at the same time. Little is accomplished if some horses are left untreated since these will contaminate pastures and paddocks used by all.

- Deworm at regular intervals using one of the programs described below. This has the advantage of achieving and maintaining low levels of infestation. It also avoids the danger of killing too many worms at one time and producing a large mass of deteriorating worms that can cause toxemia or bowel obstruction.

- The dewormer must be highly effective for the species in question, and be used in correct dosage. Dividing a dose between two horses means that neither receives an adequate dose. If the horse spits out some of the dewormer, many worms will survive and the horse will remain infected.

- Treatment of expectant mares is necessary to prevent foals from becoming overburdened with parasites shortly after birth. Deworming during pregnancy is discussed in the section CARE AND FEEDING DURING PREGNANCY.

- Labels should be read and understood completely before using the dewormer. Be sure to follow instructions in regard to preparation and dosage. Above all, *do not overdose*. Anthelmintics are toxic.

Dewormers can be added to the feed, given by drench or stomach tube, or injected by syringe into the back of the horse's mouth (see HOW TO GIVE MEDICATIONS).

DEWORMING PROGRAMS

Three programs (interval, seasonal, and daily) have proven effective in controlling internal parasites. Each has certain advantages when applied to variables such as climate, geographic location, number and concentration of horses, convenience, expense, and history of parasite problems in the past. Because of variables involved, it is important to include your veterinarian in the selection and implementation of the program.

Interval Deworming. Deworming at intervals is commonly employed. The standard interval is 8 weeks or less, but varies according to local conditions and should be determined by fecal examinations performed every 2 weeks after a deworming.

Table 1 DEWORMING AGENTS

Drug	Bots	Habronema	Ascarids	Strongyles	Thread	Pinworm	Tape	Lungworms	Comments
Piperazine	—	+++	+++	+++	—	—	—	—	Used with BZDs against resistant small strongyles.
Organophosphates									All organophosphates:
Dichlorvos	++++	—	+++	++	—	+++	—	—	Do not use past mid-pregnancy. Do not use with insecticides or tranquilizers. Narrow margin of safety.
Trichlorfon	++++	—	++++	—	—	++++	—	—	
Carbamates									
Pyrantel pamoate	—	++++	++++	++++	–+++	++++	++	—	Safe and effective.
Pyrantel tartrate	—	—	++++	++++	—	++++	—	—	
Benzimidazoles (BZDs)									
Thiabendazole		+++	++	++++	++	++	—	—	All BZDs: Do not use during first 3 months of pregnancy. Resistant small strongyles an emerging problem.
Cambendazole		+++	++++	++++	++++	++++	—	—	
Mebendazole		++	++++	++++	++	++++	—	+++	
Febendazole		++	++++	++++	++	++++	—	—	
Oxfendazole		+++	++++	++++	++++	+++	—	—	
Oxibendazole		+++	++++	++++	++++	+++	—	—	
Febantel (Pro-BZD)	—	++++	++++	++++	+++	++++	—	—	
Avermectins									
Ivermectin*	++++	++++	++++	++++	++++	++++	—	++++	Kills migrating larvae of most internal parasites. Broad spectrum. No resistance.

++++ Excellent, +++ Good, ++ Fair, — No effect

*Also effective against the filaria of Onchocerca, larvae of Habronema, and arterial larvae stages of strongyles.

These examinations disclose the length of time that parasite eggs remain suppressed after treatment. In general, this interval is 6 to 8 weeks in the central United States, with marked increases in fecal egg concentrations occurring thereafter. When fecal egg concentrations rise sooner, a shorter deworming interval should be selected.

Interval deworming can be performed on a fast or slow schedule. On a fast schedule, the deworming medication is changed each time it is given. By changing dewormers, the parasites are continually exposed to a new anthelmintic drug, thus preventing the development of resistance to a single drug.

Example of an Adult Fast Schedule

January	Oxibendazole
March	Pyrantel pamoate
May	Oxibendazole
July	Ivermectin
September	Pyrantel pamoate
November	Ivermectin

On a slow schedule, the same dewormer is used every 2 months for 1 to 2 years. In theory, drug-resistant worms should emerge when the dewormer is not rotated. In practice, drug-resistant worms do not develop if ivermectin is used once or twice every 12 months in place of the selected dewormer. In fact, since resistance to ivermectin has never been demonstrated, ivermectin itself can be used as the selected drug in a slow schedule.

Paste dewormers are easy to give. Restrain the head. Insert the syringe through the interdental space and depress the plunger.

Foals should be treated for strongyles, ascarids, bots, and threadworms at 8 weeks of age and every 2 months thereafter.

Foals

It is important that selected dewormers be effective against ascarids, strongyles, bots, and threadworms. It is recommended that the first deworming be given at 2 months of age and subsequent treatments be given at 2-month intervals thereafter. When the foal reaches 1 year of age, it is placed on the same program as adult horses living on the premises.

Example of a Foal Deworming Schedule

2 months	Ivermectin
4 months	Pyrantel pamoate
6 months	Oxibendazole
8 months	Ivermectin
10 months	Pyrantel pamoate
12 months	Oxibendazole

Alternately, ivermectin can be used every 2 months instead of rotating the drugs. Ivermectin has the broadest spectrum, it is safe, and drug resistance has not been a problem.

On farms with threadworm problems, foals should be dewormed at 3 weeks of age with ivermectin or oxibendazole. Mares harboring threadworms should be dewormed within 12 hours of foaling. This reduces milk-borne transmission and environmental contamination by larvae.

Seasonal Deworming Program. The seasonal program is designed for adult horses living in the north central United States and Canada, and similar temperate climate zones. This program controls parasites while reducing cost, labor, and the likelihood of producing drug-resistant worms.

The first dewormer is given in the spring before adult strongyle egg numbers begin to peak. The result is that egg shedding is less, and therefore the transmission of worms during the grazing season is significantly reduced. In addition, a dewormer effective against bots, such as ivermectin or an organophosphate, should be given in the late fall or early winter, about 1 month after a hard freeze kills bot flies. Waiting 1 month insures that all ingested bot larvae will have had time to reach the stomach. An additional bot treatment in midsummer is recommended.

Example of a Seasonal Deworming Program

May	Oxibendazole
July	Ivermectin
December	Ivermectin

The Continuous or Daily Program. In this program the horse is fed pyrantel tartrate (2.64 mg/kg) in alfalfa pellets on a daily basis to control the adult intestinal forms of large and small strongyles, ascarids, and pinworms. Pyrantel tartrate does not kill tissue stages of these worms, but (when used on a daily basis) does kill larvae before they begin their tissue migration. This has a great advantage for elderly and stressed horses, and in circumstances in which other methods have failed to reduce egg counts and numbers of infective larvae.

One other asset of daily deworming is that, as opposed to other programs, pyrantel tartrate does not have to be given to all horses on the premises to control worms in a single individual. This is advantageous for boarding facilities and for farms where horses come and go frequently.

A potential drawback is the risk that feeding low levels of a dewormer will lead to the development of drug-resistant worms. However, this does not appear to be a problem with pyrantel tartrate, a dewormer to which no parasite has yet developed resistance.

Pyrantel tartrate does not kill bots. Accordingly, a boticide should be administered in midsummer and late fall as described above.

Environmental Control of Parasites

Environmental control of parasites is an integral part of an effective worm management program. To decrease exposure to worm larvae and eggs, implement the following steps:

- Remove manure and old bedding from stalls daily, and at regular intervals from corrals and paddocks. Dispose of it properly. Manure should be composted for 1 year before being used as fertilizer on pastures.
- Harrow pastures in hot dry months to break up and spread horse manure.

- Feed hay or grain in cribs or mangers. Avoid feeding horses on the ground. Prevent horse manure from contaminating water troughs.

- Avoid overstocking and overgrazing pastures. Pastures that have been extensively grazed should not be restocked for 4 to 12 months, depending on seasonal influences. Note that larvae are killed rapidly in hot dry climates, less rapidly in cool damp climates, and least rapidly in cold climates.

- New arrivals should be dewormed with ivermectin and quarantined for 3 weeks before being introduced to resident horses. As soon as possible put them on the same deworming program as other horses on the premises.

- Perform fecal examinations 2 or 3 times a year to monitor the effectiveness of the deworming program. Fecal exams should be performed 14 days after deworming. Horses on an effective deworming program should not be passing parasite eggs at 14 days. On large farms, monitoring 10 percent of horses provides a representative sample.

Diseases Caused by Certain Worms

STRONGYLES

Strongyles are species of roundworm that number among them some of the most harmful and damaging of all internal parasites of the horse.

These parasites are arbitrarily divided into two groups, called the *large strongyles* and the *small strongyles*. The harmful effects of the large strongyles are much greater than those of the small ones. The larvae of the large strongyles migrate through the horse's circulation and damage blood vessels. The larvae of the small worms remain in the wall of the gut.

The life cycle of the two species is similar up to a point. Female worms lay eggs that are shed in the feces. Under favorable environmental conditions, the eggs become free-living larvae in 1 to 2 weeks.

Larvae present in grass and forage are ingested by grazing horses. At this juncture the effects of the two species are different.

Large Strongyles (Bloodworms). There are 3 important species but S. *vulgaris* is the most harmful. The infection rate is between 70 and 100 percent. Once ingested, the larvae of S. *vulgaris* penetrate the wall of the intestine and enter the arteries that supply blood to the digestive organs. The larvae of the other two species migrate to the liver, flanks, tissues around the kidney, and pancreas. Damage to arteries caused by S. *vulgaris* leads to thrombosis (clotting), embolism, and the development of aneurysms.

An embolus is a blood clot in a large vessel that breaks off and travels to a small vessel, where it creates a blockage. This destroys part of the blood supply to the organ, in this case a segment of bowel. In humans, the result would be perforation of the bowel and peritonitis. However, perforation is not common in horses because of a remarkable network of cross-connections in the arterial supply to the intestine. These cross-connections compensate for areas of interrupted blood flow. It has been suggested that this collateral circulation is an evolutionary adaptation to millions of years of selective pressure imposed by these parasites.

An aneurysm is a sac-like enlargement of the artery. Aneurysms have the potential to rupture and cause internal bleeding. This is infrequent because aneurysms are filled with clotted blood and fibrous connective tissue. Aneurysms are dangerous primarily because they produce emboli.

Episodes of thrombosis and embolism are the main cause of the colic and abdominal pain which accompanies repeated attacks of strongyles. Arterial thromboembolism is diagnosed by rectal palpation.

Having lived in the arteries for about 5 months, the larvae of S. *vulgaris* return to the intestine and develop into adult worms, where they attach by suckers to the wall of the bowel. Microscopic bleeding occurs where the worms attach and reattach. A heavy infection can cause severe anemia. The entire life cycle takes 11 months.

Small Strongyles. Small strongyles are the most common internal parasite in adult horses and occur frequently in foals.

Larvae penetrate the wall of the intestine, where they encyst. During this stage they produce colic, bleeding and anemia, protein loss, and intestinal malabsorption. In spring (and during times of stress), larvae rapidly emerge from the gut wall and cause severe diarrhea.

Prevention of Strongyles: Control of strongyles is the number one priority in all deworming programs. The eggs of both small and large strongyles do not appear in the feces for 9 to 12 months. However, it is safe to assume that irrespective of fecal exam, the horse is or will soon be infected.

Note that the arterial stage of S. *vulgaris* is not killed by most dewormers (ivermectin being the exception). Therefore it is important to eliminate the nonmigrating stages before they penetrate the tissues. This can only be accomplished by utilizing a proven deworming program as discussed earlier. An occasional treatment does not offer protection and will not prevent the potentially devastating consequences of these parasites.

Small strongyles have developed resistance to BZD dewormers. Using agents in rotation mitigates this problem. The inclusion of ivermectin in all deworming programs is highly recommended.

ASCARIDS

The most harmful species of roundworm is called *Parascaris equorum*. This adult worm lives in the small intestine and may achieve a length of 12 inches. *P. equorum* is the major worm problem in nursing and weanling foals. It occurs rarely, if at all, in horses over 2 years of age.

The female worm produces eggs that are shed in the feces. These eggs are highly resistant to environmental influences and remain infective for months or years.

Eggs are taken up by the foal in contaminated feed and water. The eggs hatch in the small intestine and produce larvae which penetrate the wall of the gut. The larvae then migrate through the liver and reach the lungs. Here they enter the breathing tubes and are coughed up and swallowed. Back in the small intestine, they mature into the adult worm. The entire process takes about 10 to 12 weeks.

The symptoms of ascarid infection depend upon the burden of parasites and whether a large number of eggs are ingested at one time or a small number over a long time. Under natural circumstances, infection tends to be chronic and ongoing rather than sudden and overwhelming. The major adverse effects of ascarid infection are malnutrition and growth retardation. Severely infected foals display an unthrifty appearance, a rough hair coat, and a potbelly. A huge number of worms produces diarrhea.

When larvae are migrating in the lungs, the foal may exhibit a persistent cough or nasal discharge. Adult worms in the intestine may produce colic. Following the administration of a rapid-acting dewormer such as piperazine, a large mass of dead worms can form a blockage that leads to intestinal obstruction. This can be avoided by using a slow-acting dewormer such as oxibendazole and repeating it a second time.

Prevention of ascarids involves interval deworming starting at 8 weeks of age and continuing every 2 months until one year of age. P. equorum does not develop resistance to dewormers. The same dewormer can be used as often as necessary.

THREADWORMS (STRONGYLOIDES)

The threadworm of concern in horses is Strongyloides westeri, the first intestinal parasite to mature in young foals. It does not produce illness in the adult.

The infection is acquired primarily through larvae ingested in dam's milk. Since foals eat manure routinely, they can also ingest larvae shed in the mare's feces. The larvae migrate to the lungs and return to the intestines, where they mature into adult worms. The entire process takes less than 2 weeks. By 16 weeks of age, foals develop resistance to threadworms and maintain minimal infection.

The major illness caused by threadworms is mild to moderate diarrhea that often occurs at 9 to 16 days of age, the same time as foal heat diarrhea. Characteristically, the foal does not appear ill and suckles normally.

A disease in humans called cutaneous larvae migrans (creeping eruption) can be caused by the larvae of threadworms. As the larvae penetrate the skin, they cause lumps, streaks beneath the skin, and itching. The disease is self-limited.

Treatment: Threadworm infection should be considered a likely cause of moderate diarrhea in all suckling foals even though in some cases the diarrhea is due to other causes. A deworming agent effective against threadworms should be administered. Oxibendazole and ivermectin are effective. A prompt clearing up suggests that threadworms were the cause of the diarrhea.

Prevention: Reduce the burden of infestation by removing manure and changing the stall bedding on a daily basis. In areas where threadworms are a problem, deworm foals at 3 weeks of age. Also deworm the mare 12 hours postpartum to prevent milk-borne and fecal transmission.

STOMACH BOTS

This infection is caused by the larval phase of the bot fly. Adult flies are nearly as large as bees. They do not bite, although fly attacks may agitate the horse and cause alarming escape behavior. Since this fly is found in all parts of the United States, virtually all horses are infected.

There are three common species of bot fly. They differ only in where they lay their eggs on the horse and how their larvae reach the stomach.

Gastrophilus intestinalis, the most common bot fly, glues its eggs to the hairs of the chest, shoulders, and forelegs. The eggs hatch quite rapidly in response to an increase in temperature that occurs as the horse licks its legs or brings its warm breath in contact with the eggs. The larvae enter the surface of the tongue and burrow into the muscle where they remain for one month. Later they molt, are swallowed, and attach themselves to the lining of the stomach.

Eggs of the species *Gastrophilus nasalis* are deposited on hairs beneath the jaw or on the throat ("throat bots"). Eggs hatch into larvae in 6 days. The larvae find their way into the mouth and burrow into pockets between the molar teeth. Here they undergo a second molt, are swallowed, and attach themselves to the lining of the stomach.

Gastrophilus hemorrhoidalis eggs are deposited on the short hairs of the lips and follow the same sequence as above. This species is rare.

Bots larvae in the stomach of an untreated horse.

Bot larvae spend about 10 months attached to the wall of the stomach. In spring they release their hold and pass out with the manure. The larvae burrow into the ground and remain in a pupal stage for 3 to 5 weeks. Soon after, adult flies emerge.

Signs of bots vary with the stage of infestation. Larval ulcerations in the mouth can cause pain on eating and lead to weight loss and unthriftiness. A more serious problem is caused by the stomach larvae, which produce colic, ulcers, and rarely perforation with fatal peritonitis (see STOMACH AND DUODENAL ULCERS).

Treatment: Assume that all untreated horses living in temperate zones are infected with bots. Bot treatment should be given in late fall one month after a killing frost. A second treatment is recommended at the beginning or middle of the bot season. Organophosphates and ivermectin are the anthelmintics of choice. They are effective against both the mouth and stomach stages of bots. Horse feed supplements containing stirofos (an organophosphate) can be given to kill bot larvae in the stomach.

Prevention: Sponging the horse's neck, shoulders, chest, lips, and forelegs once or twice a week with warm water can reduce the number of larvae that enter the mouth. Insecticides containing insect growth regulators (IGRs), when used as directed and applied to the above areas, prevent hatching of bot eggs on the horse's hair. This lowers the burden of infection. See also INSECT CONTROL.

PINWORMS (OXYURIS)

Pinworms are common parasites, occurring primarily in stabled horses. Pinworms cause intense anal itching. The horse backs up against a post or wall and rubs its tail and hindquarters back and forth incessantly. In time the skin becomes excoriated and the hair is rubbed off, giving the characteristic "ratty"-looking tail. One other cause of severe tail itching and hair loss is the tail mange mite (see MANGE).

The adult pinworm lives in the colon. The egg-bearing female migrates through the anus and deposits her eggs on the horse's perineum. The eggs are sticky and adhere to fences, bedding, stable walls, and other spots where the horse rubs its bottom. Eggs hatch within one week. Infective larvae drop to the ground, where

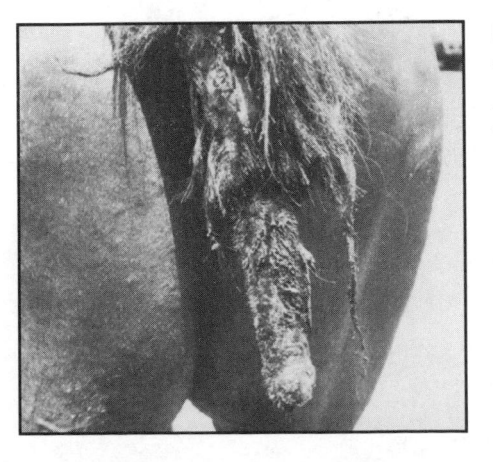

Pinworms are one cause of severe tail pyoderma. Photo: *Equine Medicine and Surgery,* **American Veterinary Publications.**

they contaminate feed. Once ingested, they pass to the colon and develop into adults. The entire life cycle is complete in 8 weeks.

While the above sequence is typical, pinworms sometimes complete all stages of their life cycle in the horse's large intestine. When this happens, a large burden of adult worms can cause inflammation of the colon and episodes of colic.

Treatment: Pinworm eggs can be found by applying a clear tape to the perineum and then examining the tape under a microscope.

Reduce the burden of infestation by cleaning the anal area with warm soapy water daily. Use disposable paper towels to avoid transmitting eggs to other horses. Pinworms are sensitive to many deworming agents (Table I). The anthelmintics used in routine deworming programs will also control pinworms. Horse pinworms cannot be transmitted to people, dogs, or other domestic animals.

TAPEWORMS

There are three species of tapeworm which infect the horse. Yearlings and 2-year-old horses are affected more frequently than older horses.

Tapeworms depend upon mites that live in pasture grass as intermediate hosts for one stage in their life cycle. Eggs are passed in the feces and ingested by the mites. The horse acquires the tapeworm by eating an infected mite while grazing. Adult worms develop in the horse and take up residence in the small and large intestine, where they achieve a length of up to 12 inches. It takes 4 to 8 months to complete the cycle.

Tapeworms ordinarily produce little in the way of symptoms. Worm masses have been implicated in causing intussusception and bowel obstruction.

Treatment: The diagnosis is made by finding tapeworm eggs on stool examination, and occasionally by seeing egg cases in manure. Egg cases resemble kernels of rice and are capable of movement.

Niclosamide, and pyrantel pamoate at twice normal dosage, are effective anthelmintics, although not approved by the FDA for the treatment of tapeworms. Veterinary consultation is recommended. The inclusion of pyrantel pamoate in a deworming program can provide some benefit against tapeworms.

LUNGWORMS

Lungworm infection in horses has been related to contact with burros and donkeys. These animals appear to be the natural hosts but seldom show evidence of infection. In older horses and ponies the disease occurs sporadically. Foals, if infected, do not show symptoms.

Adult worms up to 4 inches in length live in the lungs and lay eggs in the breathing tubes. The eggs are carried by ciliary action toward the larynx where they are swallowed and passed in the feces. Eggs hatch within a matter of hours. The larvae are ingested by the grazing horse, penetrate the wall of the bowel, and are carried to the lungs. Because eggs hatch rapidly, feces should be examined for larvae rather than for eggs. A special technique is required.

The principal signs of lungworm infection are a persistent cough of several months' duration, along with labored breathing on exertion, and loss of weight and appetite. Wheezes can be heard with a stethoscope. These signs are like those of chronic obstructive pulmonary disease (COPD), which is far more common than lungworms. Association with donkeys, however, should raise the suspicion of lungworms.

Treatment: Ivermectin is effective and should be administered every 8 weeks. Separate horses from donkeys, or treat donkeys concurrently.

STOMACH WORMS (HABRONEMA)

There are three species of stomach worm which infect the horse. These small worms live in colonies in the wall of the stomach. Eggs, which pass in the feces, are picked up by adult stable and house flies that serve as intermediate hosts. Habronema larvae escape from the mouthparts of these flies as they feed on wounds or around moist areas of the body, especially the inner corners of the eyes and the male genitalia. To complete the cycle, the horse must swallow larvae or an infected fly.

In most cases, stomach infection is asymptomatic. However, a large burden of worms can produce a severe gastritis. One species produces tumor-like enlargements in the wall of the stomach. If one of these ruptures, a fatal peritonitis ensues. This is rare. The most common problems with habronema are larval attacks directed at the skin (summer sores) and eyes (conjunctivitis).

Treatment: Fly control is important and will reduce the incidence of skin and eye infections. Ivermectin is effective against both the adult worms in the stomach and larvae in the wounds and eyes. A routine deworming program controls stomach worms.

HAIRWORMS (SMALL STOMACH WORMS)

The small stomach worm *Trichostrongylus axei* infects cattle and horses. Horses grazed with cattle are more likely to develop infection. The adult worm is small and slender, measuring less than $1/2$ inch in length. It lives deep in the wall of the stomach. Severe infestation produces gastritis with ulcers, weight loss, and anemia. The diagnosis is difficult to make because the eggs of hairworms are similar to the eggs of strongyles.

Treatment involves the administration of ivermectin. Routine deworming every 8 weeks controls these worms.

Insect Parasites

Flies, mites, ticks, lice, gnats, and mosquitoes are common insect parasites that can irritate and injure the horse. Many of these insects also present a health problem in that they carry equine diseases. Most of them are blood-sucking. A heavy infestation can cause dermatitis, unthriftiness, anemia, and in severe cases even death.

INSECT CONTROL

This is of major importance. To prevent parasites on the horse, it is necessary to reduce their number by attacking them in the stable or on the premises. It is also helpful to provide insect protection by applying or administering appropriate repellents and insecticides.

Insecticides and Repellents

Pesticides recommended for use on the horse and in the barn or stable include pyrethrins (natural and synthetic), organophosphates, organochlorides, insect growth regulators, synergists, and repellents. In addition, the oral deworming agent ivermectin can be used to kill lice, mites, and ticks feeding on the skin of the horse.

Pyrethrin. A natural extract of the African chrysanthemum flower, it kills quickly but has little residual activity because it is rapidly degraded in the environment by ultraviolet light. Pyrethrin has low potential for toxicity and is considered among the safest of insecticides. It is found in many shampoos, sprays, dusts, dips, foggers, and premise sprays.

Pyrethroids. These are synthetic compounds that resemble pyrethrin in structure but are more stable in sunlight and therefore have longer residual activity. Permethrin is a commonly used synergized pyrethrin. Others include resmethrin and tetramethrin.

The insecticidal effects of natural and synthetic pyrethrins are potentiated when combined synergistically with piperonyl butoxide, which works by inhibiting the insect's own enzymes.

Organophosphates. These insecticides are unstable and do not persist long in the environment. They are among the most toxic to mammals. Coumaphos, malathion, stirofos, and dichlorvas (DDVP) are incorporated into products for use on the horse. However, it is important to use them exactly as directed by the manufacturer.

Insect Growth Regulators (IGRs). Methoprene (PreCor) and Fenoxycarb are two hormone-like compounds that prevent larvae from developing into adults. They do not affect the cocoon or adult stages. Both are degraded by sunlight and therefore used mainly for indoor treatment. Methoprene is used in foggers and premise sprays alone or in combination with pyrethrins or organophosphates to provide a spectrum of ovicidal and adulticidal activity.

Synergists. Synergists are compounds such as piperonyl butoxide and MGK 264 that can act alone but are frequently added to commercial insecticide preparations to enhance the total effectiveness of the product.

Repellents. MGK 326 and Stabilene are two repellents commonly used on horses. Repellents do not kill parasites, but in many cases the use of repellents is the easiest and most convenient means of offering protection from fly species and mosquitoes. To be effective, repellents must be applied frequently (at least once a day).

Premise Control

This can be accomplished by mechanical or chemical methods. One mechanical method used in stables, barns, and indoor enclosures is the electronic bug-killer. Since flies roost at night, the bug-killer is only effective against mosquitoes and gnats. The apparatus must be installed carefully and placed out of reach of horses. Flypaper strips attract and capture flies. However, they usually do not significantly affect the fly population.

Manure attracts flies and is an excellent breeding ground for insect parasites. *A well-planned manure disposal system is essential.* If manure must be stockpiled before being taken away, store it well away from horse facilities.

Chemical control methods are effective and should be used on a routine basis. Many different chemical companies provide insecticide products for use in stables and barns. Study the label to determine the product's effectiveness and safety. To assure effective control, prepare and apply the product according to the written instructions. Do not use insecticide products on horses unless they are specifically recommended for that purpose. Many of these products should not be inhaled, ingested, or allowed to make contact with the skin and eyes. Familiarize yourself with the signs of insecticide toxicity and be prepared to treat accordingly (see INSECTICIDE POISONING).

The major insect problem in horse stables and barns is the fly. For fly control, residual insecticide surface sprays provide long-term kill. Permethrin (2570) kills stable flies for 6 to 8 weeks. These products are sprayed to the point of drip run-off on surfaces where flies roost. Remove all horses before spraying.

Space sprays provide a quick knockdown. They can be sprayed directly on resting flies or used as mists or fogs. Try to time the spray or fog with the daily pattern of fly activity. Dichlorvos, Naled, and pyrethrins are used in space sprays. Remove all horses before spraying.

Dichlorvos (0.46 percent granules) is a fly bait that can be sprinkled on the ground or on wet sacking. One pound added to a gallon of water makes a liquid spray. Other fly baits are commercially available, but can be extremely toxic to horses and must be used with caution to prevent accidental ingestion.

Stirofos is an organophosphate insecticide present in certain commercial larvicides, including Endrol and Equitrol. When added to the horse's feed on a daily basis, stirofos kills horsefly and stable fly larvae hatching in the manure. It does not control horn or face fly larvae, which develop only in fresh cow manure. If the horse is a finicky eater, start by feeding small amounts and build up to the amount recommended on the label.

Control on Horses

A number of insecticides are safe and effective for use on horses and aid in the control of external parasites. To be effective, some insecticides must be applied daily during peak insect season. However, too frequent application can lead to toxicity. For this reason the pyrethrins and permethrins, having the widest margin of safety, are often the best choices for frequent application.

Topical insecticides can be applied using one of several methods including hand-washing with a sponge, application by mist or spray, and dusting or powdering. To assure safety and effectiveness, follow the manufacturer's recommendations with regard to preparation, dosage, and route of administration. Some horse dewormers contain chemicals similar to those found in topical insecticides. Use of one of these shortly after deworming could lead to a toxic accumulation. As a precaution, do not use a topical insecticide of the same class as the dewormer within 2 weeks of deworming.

With most topical insecticides, the effects are transient. Daily application will be necessary to maintain protection. An exception is a product called Poridon (piperonyl butoxide), which lasts up to a week with a single application. Poridon is a thick viscous material that hardens to a flexible film. It contains an ingredient that causes the insecticide to migrate out of the film and move down the coat from one hair to the next. Eventually a large area of the coat is covered with the product.

Apply 3 to 4 ounces down the middle of the horse's back from the poll to the base of the tail. The product can be applied on the face as a bead line from the forehead to the nose (avoid contact with the eyes), and as a line down the front or back of the legs. Poridon works especially well during the bot fly season. It is effective against all species of flies, mosquitoes, and Culicoides gnats. It will not discolor the hair or irritate the skin. It is not absorbed and is safe to use on pregnant mares.

Specific insect parasites and how to control them are discussed in the following paragraphs.

FLIES

All flies pass through four stages of development: egg, larva (or maggot), pupa, and adult. This can occur in a few weeks, but some species take a year to complete their life cycle.

The non-biting flies (housefly, face fly) feed on secretions from the eyes, nose, and mouth, and on open wounds often produced by the bites of other insects. Bot flies, which lay their eggs on the hair of the horse, have no functional mouth parts and do not bite as commonly believed. The *biting* flies (stable fly, horsefly, deer fly, horn fly) are blood-suckers, as are most species of the gnat or black fly.

Housefly and Stable Fly. These flies lay eggs in manure piles and decomposed plant debris, including hay and bedding. They feed primarily during the day. At night they roost on nearby vegetation or on the rafters of barns and stables.

These species carry diseases including equine infectious anemia, anthrax, and summer sores. Houseflies feed on secretions from the eyes, nose, and mouth. As such, they are capable of transmitting contagious conjunctivitis and eyeworms. The bites of the stable fly produce skin lumps covered by black scabs, which are called external parasitic nodules. These painful nodules are made worse by rubbing and biting at the skin.

For control on the premises, residual insecticide surface sprays, quick-kills using space sprays or foggers, and fly baits are effective.

Face masks prevent conjunctivitis caused by flies feeding on eye secretions.

Plastic strips impregnated with insecticide provide some protection against house and face flies.

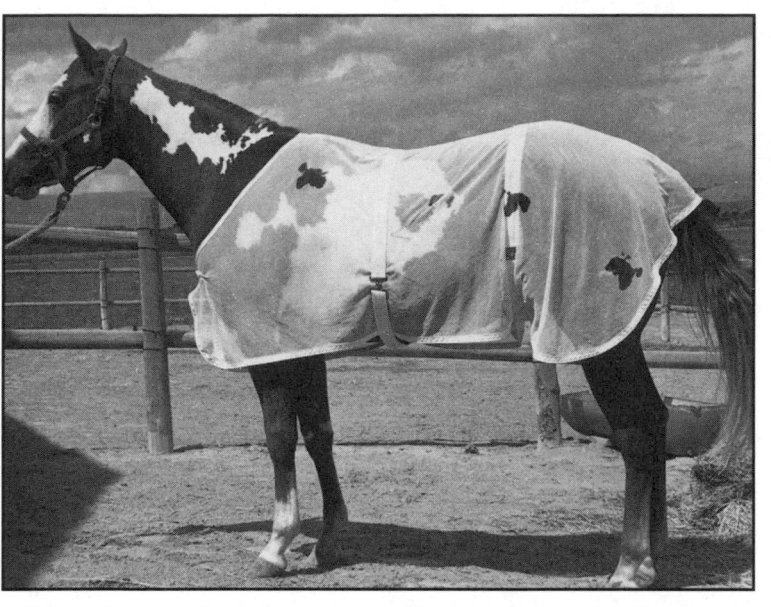

A light nylon covering helps to protect the body from stable flies, houseflies, and other incessant biters.

Face masks are effective exclusion devices. They are especially useful if the flies are causing conjunctivitis.

For control on the horse, use an insecticide hand-wash or direct mist spray. Effective chemicals include coumaphos, dichlorvos, dioxathion, malathion, pyrethrines, and piperonyl butoxide. Apply to the head, neck, chest, withers, and abdomen. To control the stable fly, also apply to the lower body and legs. Applications should be repeated at least every other day. Feed supplements containing stirofos can be given to kill fly larvae that hatch in the manure.

Face Fly and Horn Fly. These flies breed only in cow manure and therefore attack horses pastured near cattle. The face fly produces intense irritation as it feeds on mucus secretions from the mouth, nostrils, and eyes. It is a vector for eyeworms and transmits a contagious form of conjunctivitis. Face flies feed for a limited time and are difficult to control. Face masks are effective exclusion devices. Plastic strips impregnated with an insecticide and fitted to the halter may help to protect the face. Better control can be achieved by using an insecticide wipe-on. Apply to the face, muzzle, and around the eyes on a daily basis.

The biting horn fly is relatively easy to control with residual insecticide sprays applied at intervals stated on the product label. A light spray to the shoulders, neck, and withers usually is sufficient.

Horsefly and Deer Fly. These flies are incessant biters. The bites are painful, result in blood loss, open the way to screwworm attacks, and frequently become infected. In addition, horseflies are the vectors for more than 35 horse diseases, including equine infectious anemia. Vicious attacks can make the horse unmanageable and lead to escape activities such as running and kicking.

These flies lay their eggs in leaves and moist soil around the edges of ponds and ditches and in wooded areas. The breeding source is difficult to control, but stabling is effective because it removes the horse from the fly's locale. Most species of horse and deer fly will not enter stables.

Control on the horse is like that described for the stable fly. The insecticide employed, however, should be labeled as effective against the horsefly. Two such insecticides are resmethrine with cyclopropane carboxylate, and tetramethrin. Frequent application of a repellent is often the most practical solution.

Blowfly and Screwworm Fly. These flies deposit their eggs in open wounds such as those produced by castration, trauma, and the bites of other insects. The navel stump of the newborn is a favored site. The eggs develop into maggots.

Maintain good wound care as described in the section on Wounds. Apply a dust or aerosol spray containing coumaphos or lindane into and around an open healing wound once a week.

Gnats. There are many species of gnat. The most common bloodsucking species are the buffalo gnat (black fly) and the "no-see-ums" (Culicoides). Some species spread vesicular stomatitis. Breeding sources are so variable that source control is impractical.

Gnats are highly irritating to horses and initiate head-tossing, ear-twitching, skin-twitching, and incessant biting or rubbing. The ears are favorite sites for attack. Peak fly activity occurs at twilight, at night, and at dawn.

Black flies secrete a toxin capable of causing cardiac and respiratory depression. Swarm attacks have been known to cause death.

Bites that are caused by gnats ooze serum and form scabs or blisters. The skin may become sensitized by repeated attacks. This leads to dermatitis and hair loss.

To control gnats on the horse, apply on a daily basis insect repellents and insecticides containing pyrethrins with piperonyl butoxide, resmethrin with cyclopropane carboxylate, or tetramethrin. Be sure to get the product well on the inside edges of both ears. Petroleum jelly applied in a like manner is a good skin protectant. Ear nets are especially useful for protection against gnats. Stabling horses before sunset is helpful.

MOSQUITOES

Mosquitoes are of particular importance because they transmit Eastern, Western and Venezuelan equine encephalomyelitis. Some horses are unusually sensitive to mosquito bites and can develop an allergic dermatitis.

Mosquitoes lay their eggs directly on water. Common breeding grounds include ponds, horse troughs, drainage ditches, and water puddles. Control of breeding areas depends largely on eliminating standing water. Spraying for mosquitoes by aircraft can be most effective.

The most active mosquito feeding period is the first two hours after sunset. Stabling before sunset, and the application of repellents and insecticides as described for gnats, are the most effective forms of control.

LICE

There are two species of lice that infect the horse. Biting lice feed only on skin scales. Sucking lice feed on the horse's blood. When present in large numbers, they can cause severe anemia, weight loss, roughened hair coat, and growth retardation in young horses. Horse lice are species-specific. They are rapidly transmitted from horse to horse but do not attack people.

Adult lice are pale-colored insects about 2 to 3 millimeters long and can be seen by parting the hair in sites of skin involvement. They lay eggs (called nits) which look like white grains of sand attached to the hair shafts. Nits are difficult to brush off. Inspection with a magnifying glass makes identification easy.

Adult lice cause intense itching. The most commonly involved sites are the head, face, ears, neck, back (topline), and the area around the base of the tail. As the horse rubs, bites, and scratches at the irritation, there is traumatic loss of hair and the development of scabs and sores on the skin. Infestation is more common in winter than summer.

Treatment: Lice are sensitive to a number of topical insecticides including coumaphos, dichlorvos, and malathion, which can be administered by high-pressure and other sprays, pour-ons, powders, and dips. Retreat in 2 weeks to kill new lice hatching from residual eggs. Blankets, halters, saddles, and other accessories may harbor lice or nits. Wash thoroughly or rub on a pesticide solution. Retreat articles in 2 weeks. The oral dewormer ivermectin kills lice on the horse. The dose is 0.2 mg/kg body weight. Repeat in 14 days.

CHIGGERS

Chiggers, also called red bugs, are the larvae of a mite that uses birds, reptiles, and rodents as the primary host. In the absence of a natural host, they will attack horses. A heavy infestation causes intense itching, rubbing, and biting, with traumatic skin damage especially on the head, neck, chest, and legs. Repellents and residual insecticides afford some protection.

Chiggers can be controlled by a pesticide wash containing coumaphos or malathion. A single application is sufficient. Wait 1 month before putting your horse back into a chigger-infested pasture.

TICKS

Ticks are found in nearly all parts of the country and are especially prevalent in spring and fall. Horses are most likely to acquire ticks when in pasture, after trail rides, and when transported long distances.

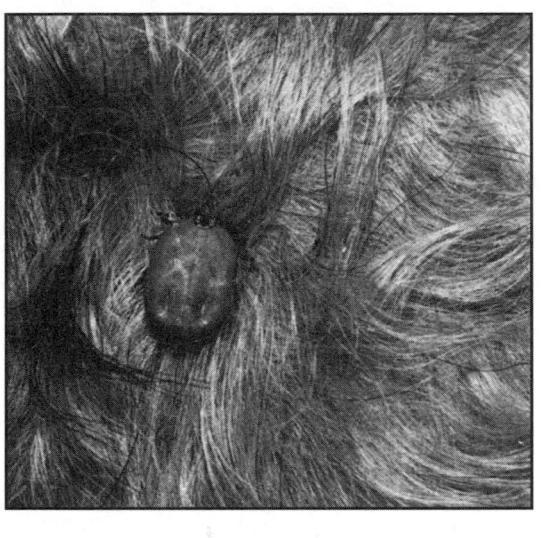

Engorged female tick.

The male tick is a small flat insect about the size of a match-head. A "blood" tick is a female tick, about the size of a pea, feeding on the horse. Ticks can be found anywhere on the horse but many species prefer the ears (see EAR TICKS). Always check the inside and outside of the ear flaps when tick contact is possible.

Horse ticks have a complicated life cycle. Some species employ three hosts, including wild and domestic animals and man. Most ticks remain on the horse throughout their lives, where they feed and mate. It takes about one year to complete the life cycle.

Diseases transmitted by ticks include Lyme disease, equine piroplasmosis, equine ehrlichiosis, and tick-bite paralysis. Tick bites predispose to screwworm attacks. A heavy infestation can cause anemia.

Treatment: If your horse has one or two ticks, the easiest thing to do is to remove them. Grasp the tick with tweezers and gently tease it off the skin. A drop of alcohol or nail polish applied to the tick may cause it to release its hold. If the head remains fixed to the skin, there is no cause for concern. It causes only a local reaction which clears in a few days. Ticks carry diseases dangerous to humans. Accordingly, do not squeeze or crush a tick with your bare fingers. Once removed, ticks can be killed by putting them in rubbing alcohol.

When many ticks are present, apply a topical insecticide (organophosphate or pyrethrin) or administer ivermectin paste as described in the section on Lice. Retreat in 7 days.

Prevention: For outdoor control, cut tall grass, weeds, and brush. Treat the premises with an insecticide preparation. Spraying the horse with a garden hose at high pressure after trail rides will remove many ticks before they attach. Insecticides and repellents labeled as effective against ticks can be applied liberally to the legs and underside to prevent ticks from getting and staying on the horse. Apply before riding in tick-infested areas and again after the post-ride spray.

Chapter 3

INFECTIOUS DISEASES

Infectious diseases are caused by bacteria, viruses, protozoans, fungi, and rickettsia, which invade the body of a susceptible host and cause an illness.

Most infectious diseases are often transmitted from one animal to another by contact with infected urine, feces, and other bodily secretions; or by the inhalation of germ-laden droplets in the air. A few are sexually transmitted. Others are acquired by contact with spores or bacteria in the soil, which get into the body through the respiratory tract or a break in the skin.

Antibodies and Immunity

An animal immune to a specific germ has chemical substances in its system called antibodies, which attack and destroy that germ before it can cause an illness.

Natural immunity exists that is species-related. A horse does not catch a disease which is specific to a dog, and vice versa. Some infectious diseases are not specific. They are capable of causing illness in several species of animal.

When a horse is exposed to an infectious agent to which it is susceptible, it becomes ill and begins to make antibodies against that particular germ. When the horse recovers, the newly formed antibodies will protect against reinfection and continue to do so for a variable length of time. The horse has acquired active immunity to that particular infection.

Active immunity can be induced artificially by vaccination. Through vaccination the animal is exposed to heat-killed or live and attenuated germs capable of stimulating antibody production but incapable of causing illness. Since active immunity tends to wane with the passage of time, booster shots should be given at regular intervals to maintain a high level of antibody response.

Run-down, malnourished, or debilitated horses may not be fully capable of responding to a challenge by developing antibodies and building immunity. Such horses can be vaccinated, but should be vaccinated again when in a better state of health.

61

There is another type of immunity called passive immunity that involves the direct transfer of antibodies from one animal to another. In many species, including man, the infant is born with antibodies and immunoglobulins obtained while in utero. However, in horses antibodies are not passed across the placenta. The foal is born without circulating immunoglobulins and can acquire them only through ingestion of colostrum during the first 18 hours, when antibodies are free to cross the intestinal mucosal barrier. By 24 hours, this barrier closes and antibodies are no longer absorbed.

The length of passive protection is dependent upon the antibody level in the blood of the mare at the time of foaling. A mare vaccinated within 3 months of foaling has the highest levels, and her antibodies will protect her foal for 16 weeks. Of course, if the mare were not vaccinated against a particular disease, her foal would receive no protection.

Passive antibodies can bind up or neutralize vaccine antigens, rendering them less effective. This is one reason why vaccinations do not always produce solid immunity in very young foals. Revaccination at 3 months of age is recommended for all foals vaccinated shortly after birth.

Another method of providing passive immunity is to inject a horse with serum from another horse who has a high level of type-specific antibody. Tetanus antitoxin is an example of such an immune serum.

Vaccinations

Vaccines are highly effective in preventing certain infectious diseases in horses, but failures can occur from improper handling and storage, incorrect administration, or the inability of the horse to respond. Stretching out a vaccine by dividing one ampule between two horses is another reason for failure to take.

The immunity acquired after completing a primary vaccination series will not be maintained if the horse does not get the required annual boosters. If a horse with immunity is exposed to a disease, vaccinating it after exposure will not prevent or alter the course of the disease.

Although allergic reactions following vaccinations are uncommon, the handler who administers his or her own vaccines should be prepared to recognize and treat acute anaphylaxis (see ANAPHYLACTIC SHOCK in chapter 1, Emergencies).

Young foals are highly susceptible to certain infectious diseases and should be vaccinated against them as soon as passive immunity begins to wane (Table I). These diseases are Eastern and Western equine encephalitis, rhinopneumonitis, tetanus, and equine influenza. The risk of infection does not diminish with age. High levels of protection should be maintained in all horses for life.

For other diseases, vaccination is recommended in areas where endemic conditions exist or the risk is high. These diseases are rabies, strangles, anthrax, Venezuelan

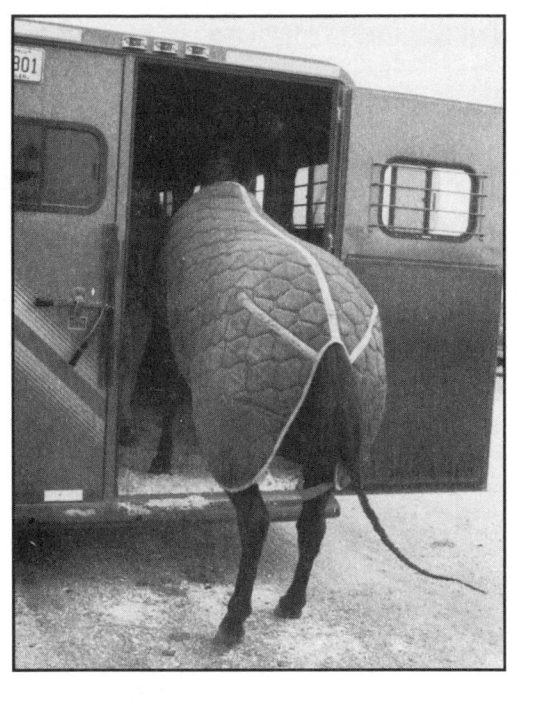

Horses that travel extensively are exposed to endemic diseases and require additional vaccinations (Table II).

equine encephalitis, botulism, Potomac horse fever, and equine viral arteritis. The immunization schedule for these diseases is given in Table II.

Special Circumstances. Tetanus is a major concern for newborn and suckling foals. The vaccination schedule for foals who acquire passive immunity from their mothers is shown in Table I. In the circumstance in which the mare was not vaccinated against tetanus, the foal should receive both tetanus antitoxin and tetanus toxoid within the first 24 hours of life. To complete the initial series, give a tetanus toxoid at 4 weeks and 4 months of age.

Tetanus antitoxin is no longer routinely given to newborn foals because of the potential for serum hepatitis. In fact, tetanus antitoxin is contraindicated in all immunized horses whose vaccination series is current. The two indications for tetanus antitoxin are a tetanus-prone wound occurring in either an unvaccinated horse or one in whom the vaccination status is unknown. In these individuals, administer tetanus antitoxin and tetanus toxoid at two different intramuscular injection sites. Follow in one month with a second tetanus toxoid.

Early immunization for rhinopneumonitis and influenza is recommended for foals whose mothers were never immunized, since these foals do not have passive immunity against these diseases. Foals should be immunized at 1, 2, and 3 months of age, and then given boosters every 3 months until mature.

If a primary vaccination series begins in an older horse, follow the same immunization shown for Foals/Weanlings in Tables I and II.

Table I IMMUNIZATION SCHEDULE

(Minimum Recommended for All Horses)

Disease/vaccine	Foals/ Weanlings	Yearlings	Pleasure	Performance	Broodmares
Tetanus Toxoid*	3 mos, 4 mos	12 mos	Annually	Annually	Annually, 3 to 6 weeks before foaling
EEE, WEE	3 mos, 4 mos	12 mos, in spring	Annually, in spring	Annually, in spring	Annually, 3 to 6 weeks before foaling
Equine Influenza	3 mos, 4 mos, 5 mos, repeat every 3 mos	Every 3 mos	Biannually	Every 3 mos	Biannually, with booster 4 weeks before foaling
Rhinopneumonitis (EHV-1 and EHV-4)	2 mos, 3 mos, 4 mos, repeat every 3 mos	Every 3 mos	Optional, biannually if elected	Every 3 mos	5th, 7th and 9th month of pregnancy (inactivated EHV-1 vaccine only)

* Administer after injury or surgery if the horse has not been vaccinated within the past 6 months.

All vaccines: Follow the recommendations of the manufacturer to avoid improper administration.

Table II IMMUNIZATION SCHEDULE

(Recommended for Horses in Endemic and High Risk Areas)*

Disease/ Vaccine	Foals/ Weanlings	Yearlings	Pleasure	Performance	Broodmares
Rabies	A single vaccination at 12-16 wks	Annually	Annually	Annually	Annually before breeding; not while pregnant
Strangles	3 vaccinations at 3 wk intervals, beginning at 8 weeks	Biannually	Biannually	Biannually	Biannually, 3-6 wks before foaling
Venezuelan (VEE)	3 mos, 4 mos	Annually, in spring	Annually, in spring	Annually, in spring	Annually, 3-6 wks before foaling
Potomac Fever	3 mos, 4 mos	Annually or biannually	Annually or biannually	Annually or biannually	Biannually, 3-6 wks before foaling

continues

Disease/ Vaccine	Foals/ Weanlings	Yearlings	Pleasure	Performance	Broodmares
Equine Viral Arteritis	3 mos	Annually	Annually	Annually	3-6 weeks before breeding; not while pregnant
Botulism	currently not recommended	Annually	Annually	Annually	3 vaccinations at 4 wk intervals, last dose 2-4 weeks before foaling
Anthrax	2 vaccinations, 3 wks apart	Annually, in spring	Annually, in spring	Annually, in spring	Annually, in spring; not while pregnant

*To learn if the disease is endemic in your area, check with your veterinarian or state university extension agent.

All vaccines: Follow the recommendations of the manufacturer to avoid improper administration.

Bacterial Diseases

SALMONELLOSIS

Salmonellosis is the most common cause of infectious diarrhea in the adult horse and an important cause of septicemia in foals. For a discussion of salmonella bacterial enteritis in newborns, see chapter 16, Pediatrics.

Many species of salmonella are infectious to horses, although the majority of cases are caused by S. typhimurium. Salmonella are remarkably resistant to environmental factors and remain alive for months or years in soil and manure. Adult horses become infected by ingesting bacteria present in feed and water. Once the numbers reach a critical threshold, outbreaks of infection occur and may reach epidemic proportions. The seriousness of the illness bears a relation to the size of the bacterial dose. With a small dose, infection may be asymptomatic.

Adult salmonellosis occurs as an acute illness and as a chronic intermittent diarrhea. Recovered horses can become symptomatic or asymptomatic carriers.

Enteric salmonellosis is the name given to the acute diarrhea. This is a severe inflammation of the small and large colon, often complicated by toxicity related to the absorption of bacterial endotoxins. The onset is sudden, with high fever and colic and the appearance of a foul-smelling, watery, green to brown diarrhea. The horse becomes intensely ill and rapidly dehydrates. Death can occur within 12 hours. Atypical cases are found in which the only symptoms are fever, colic, and a mild diarrhea.

Stressed horses are most susceptible to enteric salmonellosis. Common stresses include hard training, deworming, pregnancy, overcrowding, hot weather, coexistent illness, surgery (especially in the abdomen), prolonged transport during which food and water are withheld, and the administration of antibiotics that alter the intestinal flora.

Horses that recover from diarrhea may shed salmonella in their manure for several weeks or longer. These *asymptomatic shedders* generally pass small numbers and do not appear to pose a threat to healthy horses.

Chronic long-term shedders have been identified. Some of them suffer from chronic intermittent diarrhea and pass watery or "cow pie" stools. Episodes of diarrhea are usually triggered by stress. During such episodes, these *symptomatic shedders* pose a threat to other horses.

Salmonella are difficult to recover on stool examination. At least five negative stool cultures are required to exclude the diagnosis. In chronic diarrhea, three times that number are required. Tissue culture obtained by rectal biopsy is more accurate and should be employed along with multiple stool cultures for chronic diarrhea.

Treatment: Salmonella develop resistance rapidly to antibiotics, which renders antibiotic treatment to control diarrhea largely ineffective. One indication for antibiotic therapy is to prevent septicemia in the severely ill horse. A commercially available hyperimmune serum (Endoserum) has been shown to provide some protection against the effects of the endotoxin.

The most important objective in treating infectious diarrhea is to correct the deleterious effects of dehydration and electrolyte and protein losses. This is accomplished with intravenous salt solutions and plasma. Large volumes are often required.

The anti-inflammatory drug Banamine is given to lessen the effects of the endotoxin. DMSO is employed for its antioxidant effects. Both drugs are given intravenously.

Control: Isolate infected horses in an area distant from other horses. All personnel should wear rubber gloves, outer protective clothing, and rubber boots, which should be left in the isolation area. Wash with disinfectant soap. Extreme care must be taken to avoid contaminating food intended for people. S. *typhimurium* is a leading cause of epidemic outbreaks of food poisoning. It is estimated that nearly a thousand people die in the United States of salmonella food poisoning each year.

To control the spread of bacteria, thoroughly clean and disinfect the isolation area. Remove all manure and organic material. Clean barns and stalls with a hot steam spray or use an iodine-based disinfectant. A phenol-containing solution such as Kerol Disinfectant, or a bleach solution (1:32 dilution), can also be effective, provided that all organic material is first removed.

Contaminated pastures should not be used by horses for one year.

STRANGLES

Strangles is a severe acute upper respiratory and throat infection caused by the bacteria *Streptococcus equi*. The disease is named after the noise the horse makes when there is an exceptional amount of purulent discharge in the nose and nasopharynx.

Strangles is transmitted from one horse to another by infective secretions and by contaminated feed, watering troughs, stalls, and horse equipment. In newborns, S. *equi* is a cause of foal septicemia.

Strangles generally occurs in horses 1 to 5 years of age. Symptoms appear 2 to 6 days after exposure. The illness begins with a nasal (and sometimes eye) discharge which is at first watery and mucus-like, and later becomes thick, yellow, and purulent. This is accompanied by a dry, painful cough.

During the next 10 to 14 days, the untreated horse develops large, swollen, tender lymph nodes (a) high in the neck in back of the lower jaw (submandibular adenopathy), and (b) at the back of the throat (retropharyngeal adenopathy). Swallowing is painful. The horse often stands with its head held down and neck stretched out.

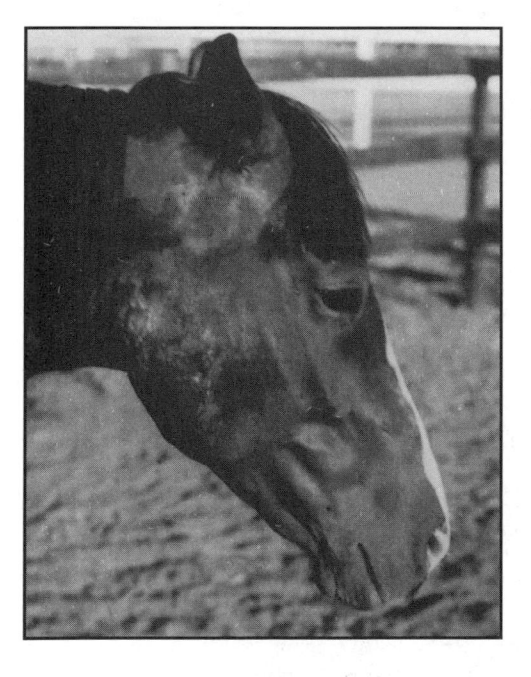

Abscesses in the submandibular area, typical of strangles. Photo: *Equine Medicine and Surgery*, American Veterinary Publications.

After a few days the neck lymph nodes soften, break down, and discharge a thick, creamy pus. The temperature falls and the horse feels better. The draining neck wounds heal slowly with scarring.

Occasionally an abscessed lymph node in the retropharyngeal area drains internally and infects the guttural pouches and sinuses. From these sites the horse may repeatedly aspirate infected secretions, resulting in bronchopneumonia.

Signs that the guttural pouch may be involved include difficult and painful swallowing, shortness of breath, a purulent nasal discharge, and excessive salivation. A *retropharyngeal abscess* may damage the nerves at the back of the pharynx, causing paralysis of the swallowing muscles or paralysis of the muscles of the face and ears. The diagnosis of retropharyngeal abscess is made by soft tissue x-rays of the neck, by endoscopy, and by diagnostic ultrasound.

A well-recognized complication of S. *equi* infection is the bloodstream spread of bacteria to other parts of the body, particularly to the lymph nodes of the intestine. This specific syndrome is called *bastard strangles*. It is characterized by weight loss, episodes of colic, and a general decline in health despite attempts at treatment.

Purpura hemorrhagica, an uncommon sequel to strangles, is characterized by a purplish discoloration of the mucous membranes caused by capillary bleeding. The bleeding appears 1 to 3 weeks after the onset of illness. It is accompanied by labored breathing and swelling of the head, belly, and limbs. The mortality rate is 50 percent.

Treatment: Strangles should be treated by a veterinarian. It is important to confirm the diagnosis. This is done by taking smears and cultures of infected discharges. Abscessed lymph nodes are helped to drain by applying warm Epsom salt poultices. Abscesses that do not drain spontaneously should be drained surgically when fluid-filled and soft.

Horses with strangles should be isolated from other horses and kept in a warm, dry stall. Wrap the legs. Feed a soft diet such as soaked pellets or chopped wet hay. Fresh water should be available at all times and the horse should be encouraged to drink. Good nursing care is important. Clean the nostrils to remove thick secretions.

S. *equi* is sensitive to penicillin, but the timing of antibiotic administration is important. In the early stages before lymph nodes enlarge, high doses of Procaine Penicillin G will arrest the disease. However, when antibiotics are started after the development of lymphadenopathy, they appear to delay drainage and may even cause an abscess to drain internally. However, in the severely ill horse, high doses of Penicillin G should be given irrespective of lymphadenopathy and should be continued throughout the course of the illness, including at least 5 days beyond the last abscess.

Bastard strangles and purpura hemorrhagica require hospitalization and intensive veterinary management.

Prevention and Control: Strict hygiene is important. S. *equi* bacteria can remain infective for up to one year. Scrub and disinfect or steam-sterilize the premises as described in the section on SALMONELLOSIS.

A vaccine against strangles is available but its usefulness is questionable. The immunity that follows vaccination (as well as natural infection) is short-lived. Outbreaks of strangles have occurred on farms where horses have been vaccinated in strict accordance with the manufacturer's directions. Furthermore, vaccines have been associated with abscess at the injection site as well as febrile and other reactions. The M-protein vaccines appear to cause the fewest reactions.

Vaccination is currently recommended on farms where strangles is endemic, and for horses visiting such farms. It is especially important to protect newborn foals. This is accomplished by vaccinating mares in late pregnancy and foals beginning at 8 weeks of age (see Table II).

TETANUS AND OTHER CLOSTRIDIAL INFECTIONS

Several species of clostridia produce disease in horses. The bacteria or their spores are found in soil contaminated by horse and cow manure and are present in the intestinal tract of most animals, where they do not cause illness.

All clostridial species produce powerful exotoxins. These lethal toxins are responsible for the major effects of the illness. Botulism, caused by C. *botulinum*, is discussed in chapter 17, Feeding and Nutrition.

Tetanus (Lockjaw). This noncontagious disease affects almost all animals, including man. It is caused by *Clostridium tetani*. Horses are more susceptible to tetanus than other domestic animals. This is because horses possess less natural immunity and are subject to many tetanus-prone injuries. There is considerable variation in the signs and symptoms of equine tetanus. Death is not inevitable. Some horses experience a mild illness and recover with treatment.

Tetanus infections occur in wounds where the oxygen content is low. The ideal environment is a deep puncture wound which has sealed over. The rusty nail is the classic example, but any cut or injury can serve as a portal of entry. Wounds of castration and docking are quite prone, as are wounds of the sole of the foot. Bacteria in infected wounds produce a potent neurotoxin that is transmitted along nerves and ascends to the spinal cord. Toxin is also absorbed locally and carried by the bloodstream to the brain.

Symptoms of tetanus can appear as early as one week after injury, but may be delayed for several weeks. A wound will be present but often is difficult to locate. Early signs are colic and vague stiffness. They are followed by spasms in the jaw, neck, hind limbs, and the muscles around the wound. A characteristic sign, called protrusion of the third eyelid, is the appearance of a film over the inner third of the eyes. This sign, when present in the above setting, is considered diagnostic of tetanus. The protrusion is best seen when the horse is excited or tapped under the chin.

As the disease worsens the horse develops labored breathing. Stiffness develops in the front and rear legs, causing the horse to adopt a sawhorse stance with its neck stretched out and head extended. The tail is held out stiffly (pump-handle tail), the ears are erect, and the nostrils are flared. There is great difficulty in backing or turning. The jaw muscles contract so that the horse is unable to open its mouth or swallow (lockjaw). Food and water dribble from the mouth. In the final stage the horse goes down, assumes an arched appearance, and dies of respiratory paralysis.

The above sequence is characteristic of fatal tetanus. However, not all horses progress to recumbency.

Treatment: Early surgical treatment of the wound is critical in stopping the progress of the disease. This involves opening the wound widely, removing all devitalized tissue, irrigating thoroughly, injecting penicillin into the wound, and leaving the wound open for effective drainage. High doses of intravenous penicillin are used routinely. Tetanus antitoxin, tranquilizers, muscle relaxants, intravenous fluids, and skilled nursing in a veterinary hospital alter the course for the better. If the horse survives more than 7 days, the outlook for recovery is good.

Prevention: Cleanse and dress all fresh wounds as described in chapter 1, Emergencies (see Wounds). This will prevent most cases of tetanus.

Immunize all foals and adult horses as described in Table I. (See also Special Circumstances, earlier in this chapter, for when to use tetanus antitoxin in prophylaxis.) To heighten immunity and maximize protection for the newborn foal, pregnant mares should be given a tetanus booster 3 to 6 weeks before foaling.

Malignant Edema (Gas Gangrene). Malignant edema is a rare, frequently fatal soft tissue infection caused by *Clostridium septicum*.

Like tetanus, malignant edema occurs in unclean wounds, particularly those caused by sharp objects. Common sites are cuts about the feet and legs. In these areas there is less muscle and more connective tissue, which appears to favor spread of the infection. It also occurs in wounds of castration. It has been known to follow intramuscular injections.

Signs appear within 1 to 2 days. There is pronounced swelling and sometimes gas in the tissues. A blood-tinged gelatinous fluid oozes from the wound.

Other signs of gas gangrene are caused by absorption of exotoxin. They include high fever, depression, progressive swelling of the head or legs, difficulty breathing, and death.

Treatment: Early surgical treatment of the wound, as described for tetanus, is essential. Antibiotics are used routinely. Intravenous fluids, steroids, and blood transfusions may be indicated to limit spread of the infection and treat shock and septicemia.

Prevention of the disease is like that described below for ulcerative lymphangitis.

Intestinal Clostridiosis. Intestinal clostridiosis is a severe, often fatal acute colitis caused by the bacteria *Clostridium perfringens*, normally present in small numbers in the colon of healthy horses. The symptoms are like those of enteric salmonellosis, colitis X, and Potomac horse fever. It is difficult to tell these four diseases apart.

Signs and symptoms of intestinal clostridiosis are due to a exotoxin produced by the bacteria. The onset is sudden with pronounced listlessness and apathy, high fever, rapid pulse, and explosive diarrhea which is watery, dark-colored, and foul-smelling. The horse moves with difficulty and usually lies down. Shock and dehydration are important early features. Tremendous quantities of fluid and electrolytes are lost in the diarrhea.

Treatment: Immediately notify your veterinarian in the presence of any large-volume diarrhea. A stool smear may reveal high numbers of *C. perfringens*. If so, this helps to make an early diagnosis. In any case, cultures should be taken to identify conclusively the cause of the diarrhea. Large volumes of intravenous fluid therapy are essential. Penicillin in high doses is effective when started before shock and collapse.

Banamine is employed for its anti-exotoxic effects. *C. perfringens* antitoxin types C and D are available, although most cases of intestinal clostridiosis are caused by type A. Maintain strict hygienic precautions to prevent human exposure.

Prevention: Long-term use of the antibiotic tetracycline has been associated with some cases of intestinal clostridiosis. Tetracycline should not be used for prolonged periods if some other suitable antibiotic is available.

COLITIS X

Colitis X is a toxic disease of the cecum and large colon that produces severe watery diarrhea and shock. It occurs in adult horses and is usually fatal.

It has been suggested that colitis X is a form of intestinal clostridiosis or salmonellosis in which bacteria, for reasons unknown, cannot be cultured. A stressful episode (surgery, hard training, transportation, deworming), or the administration of the antibiotics Lincocin or tetracycline, often precedes the outbreak of diarrhea. However, colitis X can occur in horses who have not been stressed and who are in all other respects entirely healthy.

Signs are sudden pain in the abdomen accompanied by an explosive, watery, and sometimes bloody diarrhea. Shock and collapse occur rapidly. The horse often dies within a matter of hours.

Colitis X is almost impossible to tell apart from the other causes of acute infectious colitis (salmonellosis, intestinal clostridiosis, and Potomac horse fever).

Treatment: In many cases, the colitis occurs so rapidly that treatment is not possible. With early diagnosis, the horse's life may at times be saved by intensive intravenous fluid therapy, antibiotics, and other supportive measures as discussed above in the treatment of intestinal clostridiosis.

LYME DISEASE (BORRELIOSIS)

Borreliosis is a disease of horses, man, and other animals, caused by a bacteria called *Borrelia burgdorferi*. The bacteria requires an intermediate rodent host, either the white-footed mouse, the California kangaroo rat, or the dusky-footed wood rat. Many species of immature tick feed on these rodents and acquire the bacteria. After the ticks develop into adults, they feed on large mammals. The bacteria are transmitted by the ticks' saliva.

Infection in the horse spreads slowly. Symptoms may not appear for weeks or months. An arthritis affecting one or more joints is the typical finding. It is characterized by intermittent pain and swelling which may involve tendons and ligaments as well as joints. These signs often suggest an injury rather than an infectious disease. Rarely the bacteria infects the brain or eye, causing encephalitis or uveitis.

The diagnosis is made by detecting serum antibodies to B. *burgdorferi*. A rise in the serum antibody level over several weeks is considered indicative of recent exposure.

Treatment: Antibiotics effective in humans appear to be effective in horses. Early treatment gives the best results. Unfortunately, diagnosis is often delayed. The borreliosis bacteria attaches closely to the horse's body cells. Even with effective antibiotics, the horse may require medication for up to 2 years.

Prevention: Keeping ticks from parasitizing the horse is the best prevention. If possible, remove horses from brushy pastures in the spring and fall when ticks are most active. Check your horse regularly by feeling its entire body with your hands for bumps (ticks) attached to the skin. Remove ticks as described elsewhere (see TICKS). Spraying the horse with a garden hose at high pressure after trail rides will remove many ticks before they attach. Insecticides and repellents labeled as effective against ticks can be applied liberally to the legs and underside to prevent ticks from getting and staying on the horse. Apply the product before riding in tick-infested areas and then again after the post-ride spray.

There is no vaccine available to prevent Lyme disease.

ULCERATIVE LYMPHANGITIS

Ulcerative lymphangitis is an infection of the lymphatic system of the legs. Most cases are caused by a bacteria called *Corynebacterium pseudotuberculosis*; a few are caused by *Rhodococcus equi*. Ulcerative lymphangitis is found in dirty stables where horses are crowded under conditions of poor sanitation.

Bacteria gain entrance through cuts or abrasions in the skin. The first sign is swelling involving the lower half of the leg. The hind limbs are affected more often. Abscesses occur beneath the skin along the lymphatic channels. These abscesses open and discharge a thin bloody fluid which later becomes thick and yellow. As the abscesses heal, new ones develop above the old. Lymphatics along the course of the leg become thick and cord-like. Often the limb appears to be healed but later breaks open with new nodules and draining sores. Although lymphangitis is seldom fatal, scarring of the lymphatics can lead to permanent restriction.

A variation called "pigeon chest" is reported in California and some western states. The horse develops an abscess over the sternum or occasionally in the groin. The infection is thought to be spread by ticks, horseflies, and perhaps other insects.

The diagnosis of ulcerative lymphangitis can be confirmed by tissue biopsy or culture of wound discharge.

Ulcerative lymphangitis should be distinguished from sporotrichosis and glanders. Glanders, one of the oldest diseases known among horses, has been largely eradicated. Rare cases do occur. It is caused by a species of *Actinobacillus*. The cutaneous form of glanders produces lymphangitis and abscesses beneath the skin that closely resemble those of ulcerative lymphangitis. Glanders also attacks the lung and membranes of the nose. It is highly infectious, nearly always fatal, and presents a serious hazard to human health.

Treatment: Isolate infected horses. Antibiotics, surgical drainage, and wound irrigation are important. Other measures include poultices, dressings, anti-inflammatory drugs for pain and leg swelling, and physical therapy. Relapse is common, but some cases heal without scarring and restriction.

Prevention and Control: Horse should be kept in clean, dry stalls. Use only clean curry combs and brushes. Remove nails and other sharp objects in stalls and paddocks. Treat skin injuries promptly to prevent infection (see WOUNDS). Observe suitable antiseptic precautions when handling and caring for infected wounds and dressings to prevent both human exposure and transmission of disease to other horses. Disinfect the stable or isolation area as described for salmonellosis.

BRUCELLOSIS

This disease is caused by the bacteria *Brucella abortus*. In the United States it is now quite rare, owing to successful efforts to eradicate the disease in cattle. The horse becomes infected by ingesting contaminated feed or water, or by direct penetration of the bacteria through the mucous membranes.

Equine brucellosis is difficult to recognize because of its nonspecific symptoms. They include intermittent fever, loss of spirit, muscle stiffness, and reluctance to move. Tendons and joints can become infected, although this is not common. Serum agglutination assays (paired samples taken 2 weeks apart) will show a rising antibody level to B. *abortus*, indicating exposure.

Two conditions associated with B. *abortus* are fistulous withers and poll evil. Both occur when bacteria gain entrance through a break in the skin, causing a deep-seated infection characterized by the formation of one or more draining sinus tracts or fistulas which discharge pus. The tracts close spontaneously or with treatment but are prone to recur.

Poll evil affects the poll of the head just behind the ears. The disease first presents as a swelling on one or both sides of the poll. There may be a history of a blow, such as striking the back of the head against the top of a door. Involvement of the neck ligament causes intense pain when the horse moves its head.

Fistulous withers involves the bursal sac overlying the first thoracic vertebral spines. The initiating event may be pressure at the withers from a badly fitting saddle or harness. Extensive involvement can lead to osteomyelitis of the vertebrae.

Not all cases of poll evil and fistulous withers are caused by B. *abortus*. The bacteria *Streptococcus zooepidemicus* and *Actinomyces bovis* may be found alone or combined with B. *abortus* in some cases. In addition, the hair-like worm parasite *Onchocerca cervicalis*, discussed in chapter 4, Skin, has been implicated in the early stages of fistulous withers and poll evil.

Treatment: In cases of proven B. *abortus* infection, the horse should be quarantined to prevent contact with other horses and humans. Brucellosis causes undulant fever in humans. Infected discharges should be handled with extreme caution.

Poll evil and fistulous withers are difficult to treat because of their deep-seated nature. Antibiotics are effective in the early stages but have limited use when the condition becomes chronic with draining sinuses. Ivermectin is given to limit or eliminate potential *Onchocerca* involvement. Vaccination with live strain 19 *Brucella* vaccine (subject to local regulations) may help to resolve the disease when

Brucella is cultured. If the condition becomes chronic, wide surgical removal of devitalized and infected tissue is required for permanent cure.

Prevention: Keep horses away from infected cattle. Horses should not be allowed into pastures used by such cattle for at least 3 months. A vaccination program is not available.

TUBERCULOSIS

The tubercle bacillus infects man and all domestic animals. There has been a steady decline in equine tuberculosis with control and eradication of the disease in livestock. Horses apparently possess some natural resistance.

Tuberculosis is not a respiratory infection in horses as it is in most other animals. Bacteria gain entrance through the digestive tract and infect the lymph nodes of the intestine and spleen. Later they progress to the bloodstream and involve the liver, lungs, bone, and other organs.

Early diagnosis is difficult because of the nonspecific signs, the principal one being chronic progressive weight loss. Fever, cough, and rapid breathing occur late in the disease. Diagnosis is confirmed by biopsy or by culturing the tubercle bacillus from infected discharges. Skin tests for tuberculosis are not reliable in the horse.

Treatment: Generally it is not practical. The obvious hazard to human health makes euthanasia the only acceptable choice.

ANTHRAX

Anthrax is a highly contagious, rapidly fatal disease which affects nearly all animals. Man possesses some natural resistance.

The disease is caused by *Bacillus anthracis*, a spore-forming bacteria which remains dormant in soil for up to 50 years. Horses acquire the disease by grazing on infected pastures. The bacteria enter through abrasions in the mouth or by direct passage through the intestinal tract.

The first indications of acute anthrax are high fever and colic and the appearance of hot swollen areas on the neck, throat, and belly. The horse develops rapid breathing, stupor, staggering gait, coma, and death. Bloody discharges occur from the body orifices, particularly from the rectum. Sudden unexplained death should alert one to the possibility of anthrax.

The diagnosis is suspected because of the characteristic signs and symptoms, especially a bloody discharge with swelling at the throat. It is more likely to be suspected in areas where anthrax is endemic. Microscopic examination of a blood sample may show the characteristic.

Treatment: Quarantine infected horses. Anthrax is a distinct hazard to human health. Great care must be exercised in handling sick horses. Because of rapid progression, death often occurs before treatment can be started. Penicillin, when given early in the illness, may prove effective.

Prevention and Control: A horse exposed to anthrax should be isolated and treated with penicillin at the first sign of fever (temperature 1 degree above normal).

Public health measures require that carcasses be burned or buried in lime. Pastures, paddocks, stalls, and other contaminated areas should be disinfected with a 10 percent formaldehyde solution.

Horses living in anthrax-endemic areas should be protected by a vaccination program. The first dose of anthrax spore vaccine should be given in spring 4 months before the warm, dry summer months. A second dose 3 weeks later is recommended. Maintain immunity with annual boosters. Side effects, including local inflammation at the injection site and febrile reactions, occur commonly. Do not administer antibiotics within 1 week of vaccination as this may interfere with the vaccine's take. In an anthrax outbreak, all horses at risk should be vaccinated, with the exception of breeding mares.

Viral Diseases

RABIES

Rabies is a fatal disease which occurs in nearly all warm-blooded animals, although rarely in rodents. Rabies in dogs and cats has been greatly reduced by mass vaccination. The usual source of infection for horses is a bite from an infected skunk, fox, bat, or raccoon. Other wild animals serve as a reservoir for the disease and account for sporadic cases. Any wild animal that allows you to approach it without running from you is acting abnormally. Rabies should be suspected. *Do not pet, handle, or give first aid to such an animal.*

The rabies virus is present in infected saliva and generally enters at the site of a bite. However, saliva on an open wound or mucous membrane also constitutes exposure to rabies. The average incubation period in horses is 3 weeks to 3 months, but may be as long as 6 months. The virus travels to the brain along nerve networks. The further the bite is from the brain, the longer the incubation period. The virus then travels back along nerves to the mouth, where it enters the saliva.

Signs of rabies in horses are variable and often suggest some other neurological disorder or an infectious disease. Horses seldom exhibit the furious form of rabies and "go mad" and attack people as do dogs. However, unprovoked excitement and frank crashing about may occur and make the horse extremely dangerous.

Horses typically suffer from the paralytic form of rabies. The signs of paralytic rabies are apathy and disinterest in surroundings, weakness, staggering, difficulty swallowing, frothy salivation, inability to drink, and various degrees of lameness and limb paralysis. Thrashing convulsions and coma occur before death.

A distinguishing feature of equine rabies is its rapid course. Death generally occurs within 5 days of symptom onset. Accordingly, *any rapidly fatal illness accompanied by weakness or paralysis suggests the possibility of rabies.*

Treatment: There is no effective treatment for rabies.

A horse who has been exposed to rabies—and particularly if bitten by an animal suspected of having rabies—should be placed in strict isolation. This holds true even if the horse is known to be vaccinated for rabies. Notify your veterinarian, who will report the incident to the state health authorities. If the attacking animal was a domestic dog or cat, a protocol for impounding and observing the animal should be initiated through your veterinarian. If the attacking animal was a wild animal that escaped, there is no way to prove it was not rabid. In that case, post-exposure treatment should be given to the immunized horse as described below.

When the animal is captured and confined, observation of the animal will determine its state of health. If the animal was either killed at the time of the attack or dies subsequently during confinement, its brain should be removed and sent to a laboratory equipped to diagnose rabies from antibody studies. The only definite determination of rabies is through autopsy.

Postexposure treatment depends upon the immune status of the horse. If the horse was previously vaccinated against rabies, give a rabies booster now. For prognostic purposes, prior to giving the booster, a blood sample can be drawn and sent to the Department of Veterinary Diagnosis at Kansas State University, Manhattan, Kansas, to determine the horse's rabies antibody titer at the time of exposure. A titer greater than 1:5 is considered protective.

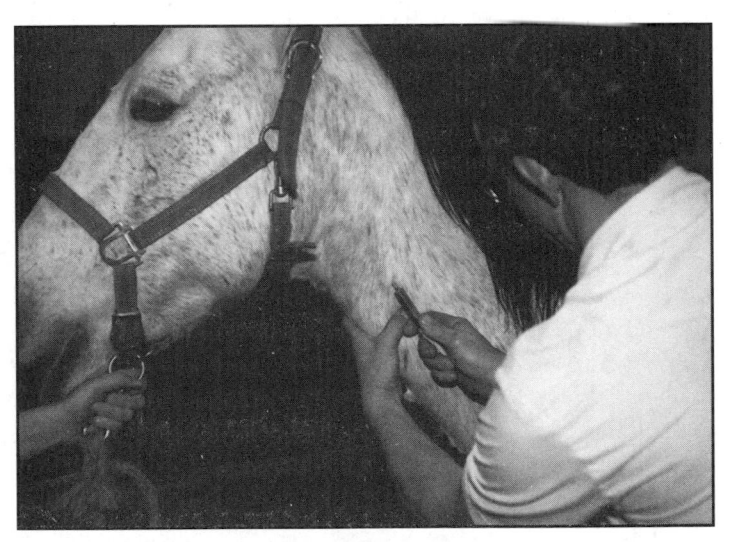

If a vaccinated horse has been exposed to rabies, a serum sample will show whether the horse is protected.

If the horse was never vaccinated against rabies, do not begin a vaccination series now as it is too late to develop rabies antibodies, and vaccination will serve no purpose. If it is proven that the attacking animal had rabies, the horse should be immediately euthanized. If rabies exposure is not conclusively established, the horse should be quarantined and observed for 6 months. If symptoms develop, the horse must be put down.

Pre-Exposure Immunization: Human preventive vaccines are available for high-risk groups including veterinarians, animal handlers, cave explorers, and laboratory workers.

Prevention: Rabies can be prevented by vaccination. There are 3 killed rabies vaccines approved by the U.S. Department of Agriculture. A single annual vaccination is required. Rabies vaccination is not recommended for breeding mares. Because this disease is rare in horses, vaccination is suggested only in areas where rabies is endemic. Consult your veterinarian or local health department for information on local rabies incidence.

EQUINE VIRAL ENCEPHALOMYELITIS (SLEEPING SICKNESS)

The three mosquito-transmitted infectious diseases that attack the central nervous system of horses are *Eastern equine encephalomyelitis* (EEE), *Western equine encephalomyelitis* (WEE), and *Venezuelan equine encephalomyelitis* (VEE). EEE is the most virulent, with fatality rates of 70 to 90 percent. WEE is least virulent, with fatality rates of 20 to 50 percent.

EEE occurs along the Eastern seaboard, the Gulf Coast, and around the Great Lakes. It also occurs in Alberta, Canada, and Central and South America. WEE occurs in the United States commonly from the Mississippi Valley westward. It also occurs in Mexico and in Central and South America. Venezuelan equine encephalomyelitis was first described in Colombia. It subsequently migrated through Mexico into Texas and is now endemic in South and Central America, Mexico, and the West Indies.

All three viruses are transmitted by the bite of a mosquito that must first feed on an infected bird or rodent. The horse is considered a "dead-end" host for the virus of WEE. That is, once a horse becomes infected, the levels of virus in its blood are too low to permit further mosquito transmission. This often happens with EEE as well. However, with VEE the levels of virus in the blood are high enough to infect feeding mosquitoes. Thus VEE horses can serve as a reservoir for infection.

Equine encephalomyelitis presents a hazard to human health. Cases occur each year and a small percentage are fatal. Contact with infected horses is not a problem because people, like horses, acquire the disease from the bite of an infected mosquito. Outbreaks in horses actually serve as a warning, since they usually precede signs of human illness by 2 to 3 weeks.

Equine encephalomyelitis begins 1 to 3 weeks after a mosquito bite and generally lasts 5 to 14 days. Signs and symptoms of all three diseases are similar.

The first indication is a high fever which lasts 1 to 2 days and may go unnoticed. The fever is followed by the onset of acute encephalitis. Signs of brain inflammation include compulsive walking and circling, loss of coordination, and apparent blindness. The horse may crash into walls and fences. Later the horse becomes extremely depressed and oblivious to its surroundings, standing with his head held low, tongue hanging out, and ears and lips drooping. The stage is called "sleeping sickness" because of the characteristic nodding of the head as if going to sleep.

Spinal cord involvement (myelitis) produces a staggering gait, weakness, and muscle twitching. The final stage is paralysis. The horse sinks to the ground, develops seizures, and is unable to breathe.

Some horses who recover may have impaired vision, permanent muscle weakness, and a behavior disorder or learning disability. These horses are called "dummies."

Suspicion of equine encephalomyelitis is based on the appearance and condition of the horse, geographic location, occurrence during the mosquito season, and knowledge of other cases in the area. A serologic blood titer greater than 4 times normal is highly suggestive. Isolation of the virus from the blood or brain is diagnostic.

Treatment: It is directed at supporting the horse through the acute phase of the illness. Intensive nursing care is critical for a successful outcome. Confine the horse to prevent self-injury. Wrap the legs. Provide free access to water. Anti-inflammatory drugs are indicated for fever and muscle pain. Valium or pentobarbital is used for seizure control. Feed a palatable semi-liquid diet such as 1 to 2 pounds alfalfa pellets per 100 pounds weight of the horse per day, soaked in water to form a thick slurry. If necessary, administer feed and water by stomach tube. Antibiotics are used only to treat secondary bacterial infections. Steroids may be of benefit. Intravenous fluid supplements may be required.

Once the horse goes down, the outlook is poor. Good nursing care involves rolling the horse several times a day to prevent both pressure sores and the myopathy of prolonged recumbency. Well-padded bedding is essential. Maintain the sternal position if possible. An indwelling catheter can be used to empty the bladder and keep the horse clean and dry.

Prevention: Encephalomyelitis can be prevented by vaccination. All three vaccines are effective. Frequently EEE and WEE are combined as a single injection. Both are indicated for all horses. Annual boosters should be given in the spring at least one month before the mosquito season. In areas where mosquitoes are present all year long, give a booster every 3 to 6 months. Vaccinate pregnant mares with inactivated vaccine 3 to 6 weeks before foaling.

An outbreak of VEE has not been reported since 1971. Accordingly, VEE vaccine is no longer widely used in the United States but may be indicated in endemic areas including Texas and the southwest.

Control mosquitoes as described in chapter 2, Parasites.

EQUINE VIRAL RESPIRATORY DISEASES

Viral respiratory diseases are highly contagious, often serious illnesses of horses. They spread rapidly and are transmitted by airborne inhalation and contact with the respiratory secretions of infected or recently infected individuals. To contain these illnesses, it is important to isolate infected horses during the contagious period (which lasts 4 to 6 weeks after infection) and to use good hygiene in handling and caring for sick horses.

Signs and symptoms are so similar that it is difficult to tell these diseases apart without tests from a research lab. These special tests are not always available to practitioners in time to be of use in planning treatment, and so usually are not performed.

Respiratory viruses attack the breathing tubes and disrupt the protective blanket of mucus which lines the trachea and bronchi. This leads to a cough which persists for several weeks after the attack. Secondary bacterial infections are common.

Uncomplicated viral respiratory illnesses should not be treated with antibiotics or combinations containing antibiotics and steroids. Antibiotics often reduce the population of protective bacteria in the upper respiratory tract. This allows virulent bacteria to proliferate. Steroids, being immunosuppressive, may actually lower a horse's natural resistance and make the disease worse.

Antibiotics are reserved for treating secondary bacterial infections. As a rule, if fever persists more than 5 days and is accompanied by a mucopurulent nasal discharge (snotty nose), antibiotics are justified. Cultures from tracheal washings, which provide a bacterial diagnosis, are preferred to empirical antibiotic therapy.

Equine Influenza. Also known as the "flu," this contagious illness is caused by two species of myxovirus subdivided into several strains, each capable of causing rapidly developing outbreaks of respiratory disease. These viruses attack the lining of the entire respiratory system, including the lower respiratory tract where complications can lead to pneumonia. Young and old horses are most susceptible.

After a short incubation period, the disease begins with a high fever that lasts about 3 days. A characteristic feature of influenza is the dry hacking cough which later becomes moist and productive. This is accompanied by a clear or mucoid nasal discharge. The cough usually persists for several weeks, even though the actual illness lasts 3 to 7 days. Other signs include runny eyes, loss of appetite, apathy, and muscular stiffness.

Influenza is a relatively mild infection but secondary complications may occur, the most common being bacterial rhinitis. The nasal discharge becomes thick and pus-like, and the breathing is noisy. A persistent fever and labored respirations suggest the onset of pneumonia.

Treatment: Isolate the horse to prevent spread of the disease. Stall rest is important. The stall should be dry and well-ventilated. Closing a stable (to keep it warm) will invariably increase respiratory symptoms. If the stable is cold, apply a horse blanket. Wrap the legs. Provide clean water and a palatable diet free-choice. Butazolidin is used to control fever and muscle stiffness.

Restrict exercise until the cough disappears. The horse should be rested at least 3 weeks and perhaps longer. A rapid return to exercise and training is associated with relapse and chronic bronchitis.

Prevention: Vaccinations will prevent influenza infections or reduce their severity. However, immunity to influenza following vaccination or recovery from natural infection is short-lived, seldom persisting for more than 12 months. In addition, epidemics may be caused by new virus strains. Accordingly, vaccines may have to be modified from time to time to provide the best coverage. Current vaccines contain strains A-1 and A-2.

For these reasons, frequent vaccination is recommended by most veterinarians. Although the manufacturers of the vaccines recommend annual boosters, yearly boosters simply do not provide adequate protection for the majority of horses. The recommended flu immunization schedule for foals and adult horses is shown in Table I. This schedule assumes that a newborn foal is protected during the first 3 months of life by passive antibodies acquired from its mother's colostrum. If the dam was not vaccinated, these antibodies are lacking and influenza vaccine should be administered to the foal at 1, 2, and 3 months of age (3-dose primary), and then every 3 months until maturity. The same recommendation applies to rhinopneumonitis below.

Rhinopneumonitis (Herpesvirus 1 and 4). Equine herpesvirus is the most common cause of respiratory illness in foals, weanlings, and yearlings. It is highly contagious and spreads rapidly throughout a farm, often following the arrival of a new horse carrying the virus.

The principal sign is a copious nasal discharge (snots) which becomes mucoid and pus-like if secondarily infected. Foals may develop a dry cough that persists for 2 to 3 weeks. A severe or fatal foal pneumonia is the major complication of rhinopneumonitis.

In pregnant mares, EHV-1 produces epidemic abortions late in pregnancy. These "abortion storms" can affect the majority of pregnant mares on the premises. The abortion occurs weeks or months after exposure to the virus.

Occasionally instead of aborting, the mare delivers a foal with pneumonia that dies within the first week of life.

A neurological form of EHV-1 occurs in mature horses and in mares who have aborted. Signs include staggering gait, loss of coordination, and various forms of paralysis (see EQUINE HERPES MYELOENCEPHALITIS).

Treatment: It is like that for equine influenza discussed above.

Prevention: Immunity following vaccination and natural infection is short-lived. Frequent vaccinations are required to maintain resistance. It is most important to protect foals, yearlings, stallions, and broodmares. The suggested immunization schedule is shown in Table I. If the dam was not vaccinated, follow the same recommendation for early vaccination of foals as described above for influenza.

Rhinopneumonitis vaccines containing EHV-4 may be the vaccines of choice for foals, weanlings, yearlings, and pleasure horses, since the majority of respiratory infections are caused by EHV-4. Broodmares should continue to be vaccinated with EHV-1, the strain responsible for nearly all recorded abortions.

Vaccines are now available which combine 2 inactivated strains of influenza (A-1 and A-2) with EHV-4. This combination may be especially suitable for foals.

Adenovirus and Rhinovirus Infections. Adenoviruses produce mild respiratory illnesses in young horses. However, this virus group is a common cause of serious illness and death in neonatal foals lacking maternal antibodies (see LACK OF COLOSTRUM). In foals of Arabian or part Arabian ancestry suffering from a combined immunodeficiency syndrome (CID), adenovirus infection is fatal. Thus adenoviruses appear to be opportunistic invaders, causing serious illness only in foals who lack normal immunity.

Rhinoviruses are highly contagious but generally produce few symptoms. The horse may have a fever, runny nose, conjunctivitis, cough, and occasionally a sore throat. There is no specific treatment other than rest and good nursing care.

There are no commercial vaccines available to prevent adenovirus or rhinovirus infections.

Equine Viral Arteritis (EVA): Most horses are exposed to equine viral arteritis but only a few develop symptoms. EVA takes its name from the injury it produces in the walls of small arteries. Small bleeding points called petechial hemorrhages appear on the mucous membranes inside the nostrils and on the conjunctiva that covers the whites of the eyes. The conjunctivitis and red swelling about the eyes can be taken as a visible sign of a generalized arteritis. The disease is spread by respiratory secretions and can be transmitted venereally in the semen of an infected stallion.

The acute respiratory illness produced by EVA is like that of influenza. Typically, fluid accumulates in the abdominal wall (*ventral edema*), scrotum, sheath, and hind limbs. Other signs include apathy, loss of appetite, colic, diarrhea, and dehydration.

A major problem associated with EVA is viral abortion, discussed in the section Infectious Causes of Abortion.

Treatment: Treatment of respiratory illness is like that described for equine influenza. Immunity is lifelong.

Prevention: A vaccine has been developed that protects breeding stock. It should be considered in areas where EVA is endemic. Note that vaccination produces seroconversion. This could complicate the interpretation of tests required for exporting the horse. In some states, vaccination requires prior approval from the state veterinarian. Vaccinate mares and stallions (1 dose) 3 weeks prior to breeding. Do not vaccinate mares during pregnancy. An annual booster is required.

EQUINE INFECTIOUS ANEMIA (SWAMP FEVER)

Equine infectious anemia (EIA) is a retrovirus infection transmitted in blood, saliva, urine, milk, and body secretions. Blood-sucking flies, mosquitoes, and other biting insects are the usual vectors for transmission. However, the virus can also be spread by blood transfusions and unsterile syringes, and can cross the placenta and infect the foal.

The frequency of EIA in the United States has been significantly lowered by control measures introduced in the mid-1970s. The disease is now infrequent.

EIA-positive horses remain infected for life and thus present a continuing hazard to other horses. Risk of transmission is greatest when the horse is acutely ill or in a state of relapse, at which time virus blood levels are high enough to infect feeding insects.

Three distinct types of illness are described, but symptoms overlap.

The *acute* illness is characterized by high fever, severe anemia, weakness, swelling of the lower abdomen and legs, weak pulse, and irregular heartbeat. The anemia is due to the rapid breakdown and destruction of red blood cells. The mortality is high. Sudden death may be the first indication.

The *subacute* illness progresses more slowly and is less severe. It is characterized by recurrent fever; weight loss; anemia; and swelling of the lower chest and abdominal wall, penile sheath, scrotum, and legs. An enlarged spleen is often felt on rectal examination. The horse may be jaundiced.

The *chronic* illness is characterized by recurrent fever and anemia. The horse tires easily and is unsuitable for work. A relapse with reversion to one of the above types is possible weeks, months, or even years after the original attack.

EIA is a rare cause of abortion. Abortion can occur at any time during pregnancy, during a relapse when the virus enters the blood. The majority of sick mares abort. However, a few give birth to healthy, unaffected foals.

EIA should be suspected in any horse with periodic fever and anemia. It can be confirmed by a positive Coggins (AGID) or C-ELISA blood test.

Treatment: It is directed at supporting the horse with blood transfusions and good nursing care. Steroids are contraindicated as they increase the potential for relapse. There is no effective treatment to clear the carrier state.

Prevention and Control: Regulations require that all horses who test positive for EIA must be reported by the testing laboratory to federal authorities. The owner of the horse is given the options of putting the horse to sleep, branding and quarantining it at least 200 yards from other horses for life, or shipping the horse to a recognized research facility.

Horses who do not show signs of EIA are assumed to be healthy. However, even though the disease is infrequent, outbreaks of EIA continue to occur. Accordingly, it is wise to isolate visiting mares and new horses until a negative Coggins test can be obtained.

VESICULAR STOMATITIS

Vesicular stomatitis is a contagious viral disease affecting cattle, horses, and swine. It is transmitted by a blood-sucking black fly and possibly other biting insects, and by contact with contaminated tack and equipment.

There is a short incubation period followed by fever and listlessness. Small blister-like blebs containing clear fluid (*vesicles*) then appear on the mucous membranes of the mouth and tongue, in the nose, and on the coronary bands of the feet. As the disease progresses, the blisters swell and break, leaving raw painful ulcers. Infected horses generally drool copiously, refuse to eat and drink, and may show signs of lameness.

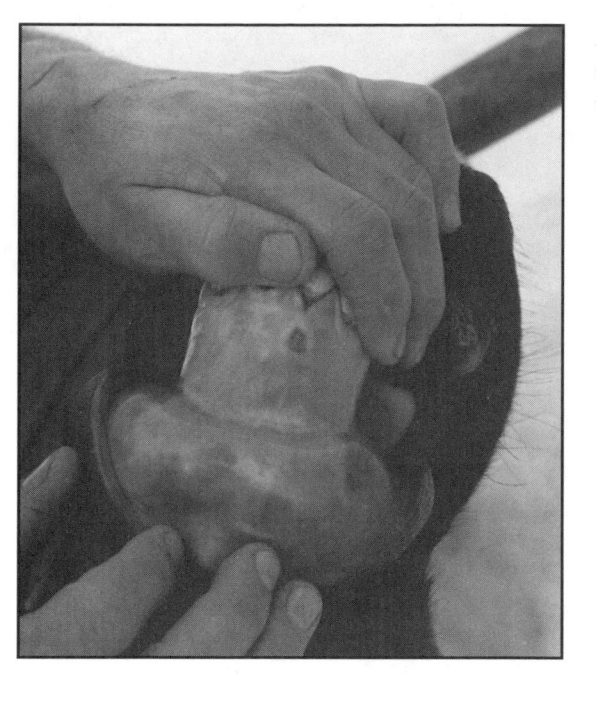

An ulcer on the gum, similar to a late stage of vesicular stomatitis.

Vesicular stomatitis can be transmitted from infected horses to people. In humans, vesicular stomatitis causes blisters in the mouth and influenza-like symptoms including fever, muscle aches, headaches, and malaise.

All vesicles contain live virus. To prevent illness, wear rubber gloves and avoid direct contact when handling sick animals.

Treatment: Notify your veterinarian. Infected horses must be quarantined. Treat stomatitis as described in chapter 7, Oral Cavity. The horse will recover from the virus in 1 to 2 weeks, but occasionally the vesicles become secondarily infected and require antibiotics.

Prevention: Insect control helps to prevent further transmission (see INSECT CONTROL). Avoid close contact with horses from areas where the disease has been recently diagnosed. Do not share feed or water buckets between horses. A commercial vaccine has been developed. Its use in endemic areas is regulated by state and USDA animal health authorities.

Rickettsial Diseases

Rickettsia are microorganisms primarily parasitic in arthropods (ticks, mites, lice, and fleas), but occasionally infecting higher animals, including humans. They are grown with difficulty in the laboratory.

EQUINE EHRLICHIOSIS

Equine ehrlichiosis is a noncontagious disease of horses caused by *Ehrlichia equi*. This rickettsia is transmitted to the horse by the bite of a tick. The disease was first discovered in northern California, where it is still most often found. It also occurs in parts of the Rocky Mountains and Midwest.

In horses younger than 3 years of age the disease is mild. Fever is invariably present. Other signs include listlessness, loss of appetite, slight swelling of the legs, and muscle stiffness.

In horses over 3 years the above symptoms are more pronounced. The horse is reluctant to move and experiences marked swelling of the legs, particularly the hind limbs. A staggering gait with loss of coordination is characteristic.

Equine ehrlichiosis should be suspected when a febrile illness occurs during tick season in an endemic area such as Northern California. Blood smears taken within the first 3 to 4 days of illness show inclusion bodies in white blood cells. These inclusion bodies signify the presence of rickettsia.

Treatment: The antibiotic oxytetracycline is highly effective against rickettsia and should be given for 7 to 14 days. Improvement begins almost at once. Confine the ataxic horse to prevent self-injury. Wrap the legs to reduce swelling. Cortisone may be of benefit. To prevent relapse, complete the full course of therapy and rest the horse for 3 weeks.

Control: Control ticks as described in chapter 2, Parasites (see TICKS). Inspect your horse after riding in tick-infested areas. Rickettsial infections can be prevented if ticks are removed within the first 2 to 3 hours.

POTOMAC HORSE FEVER (EQUINE EHRLICHIAL COLITIS)

Potomac horse fever (PHF) is a diarrheal disease whose exact mode of transmission is unclear, although an insect vector is suspected. The disease was first reported along the Potomac River in Virginia and Maryland where it is still common, and tends to remain endemic on certain farms. It also occurs in river valleys throughout New England and the Midwest. It is infrequently seen in the western United States, occurring seasonally in the months of summer.

The infection is mild and undiagnosed in about half the cases. Horses with symptoms develop high fever and diarrhea after an incubation period of 10 days. The stool is watery and profuse, often described as "pipestream." There is profound listlessness and loss of appetite.

Mild to severe laminitis can occur 3 to 5 days after the onset of diarrhea. While toxicity, shock, and dehydration do occur, horses that die usually do so from complications of acute laminitis.

Potomac horse fever is difficult to tell apart from enteric salmonellosis, intestinal clostridiosis, and colitis X, three other infections which cause severe and often fatal diarrhea in horses. Paired serum samples taken 2 weeks apart are diagnostic if they show a rising PHF antibody titer. However, often the test is not diagnostic.

Treatment: Intravenous oxytetracycline is the antibiotic of choice. It is most effective when given early in the disease. Severe diarrhea is treated with intravenous fluids to prevent dehydration and shock. General supportive care is like that described earlier for salmonellosis.

Prevention: Immunization will prevent the disease or lessen its severity, provided that the vaccination series is completed 3 to 4 weeks before exposure to infection. Immunization is indicated in PHF-endemic locations. Administer 2 doses 3 to 4 weeks apart. An annual or biannual booster is required, depending on the product employed.

Systemic Fungus Diseases

Fungus diseases which invade and spread throughout the body are called *systemic*. Fortunately, systemic fungal diseases are not common in the horse. When present, they tend to occur in chronically ill or immunosuppressed individuals. Prolonged treatment with steroids and/or antibiotics can change a horse's pattern of resistance and allow a fungus infection to become established. Infrequently, a healthy robust horse develops a systemic infection.

Systemic fungus infections do not respond to conventional antibiotics and require intensive veterinary management. The drug of choice for most systemic fungus infections is amphotericin B. This drug requires close monitoring due to its potential for kidney toxicity. Ketoconazole and newer drugs in the same class have been employed, but their effectiveness has yet to be established. When a fungus infection becomes systemic, euthanasia is often recommended.

Fungus infections are not contagious in the usual sense, but can be transmitted to man by accidental puncture wounds or direct contact with open sores.

Fungus infections of the skin and outer surface of the body are discussed in chapter 4, Skin.

The following systemic fungal diseases can occur in the horse:

Histoplasmosis. This disease is caused by a fungus found in the central United States near the Great Lakes; the Appalachian Mountains; and the valleys of the Mississippi, Ohio, and St. Lawrence Rivers. Spores are found in soil contaminated by the dung of chickens, birds, and bats. Most infected horses suffer only a mild respiratory illness. However, on rare occasions the disease can become systemic. The signs are chronic cough, recurrent bouts of pneumonia, difficulty in breathing, and loss of weight and muscle substance.

A skin test shows whether a horse has been exposed to the disease. It is often positive in horses who live in an area where histoplasmosis is endemic. This suggests that inapparent infection is common.

Horses should not be stalled in buildings that also house chickens.

Blastomycosis. This disease is found in the same geographic locations as histoplasmosis. A skin form is characterized by nodules and abscesses which ulcerate and drain. The systemic form is similar to histoplasmosis.

Coccidioidomycosis. This is a mild respiratory infection which on rare occasions can become systemic and spread to all organs of the body. It is found in dry, dusty parts of the southwestern United States and in California. Serologic blood tests are available which may help to make the diagnosis.

Aspergillosis. The disease is acquired by the inhalation of spores found in damp hay. It generally occurs in stabled horses. It can be prevented by stable cleanliness. The signs are those of a rapidly fatal illness accompanied by severe diarrhea. Alternately, the horse may suffer a chronic wasting disease similar to that of histoplasmosis.

Cryptococcosis. This disease is acquired by inhalation. The fungus grows well in bird dung, in particular the droppings of pigeons. Infection begins in the nasal passages and extends to the lower respiratory tract, where it causes pneumonia. Infection of the surface of the brain is responsible for cryptococcal meningitis.

Avoid stabling horses in enclosures that house pigeons, chickens, and other birds.

Protozoan Diseases

Protozoans are one-celled organisms invisible to the naked eye but easily seen under the microscope. Protozoan disease are uncommon in horses.

Equine protozoal myeloencephalitis is an inflammation of the brain and spinal cord caused by a protozoan that migrates randomly through the central nervous system. It is discussed in chapter 11, Nervous System.

Dourine is a fatal sexually transmitted disease present in some less developed countries but eradicated in the United States. There are two protozoan species that cause diarrhea in young horses. They are discussed in chapter 16, Pediatrics.

EQUINE PIROPLASMOSIS (BABESIOSIS)

This is a protozoan infection transmitted by a tropical horse tick. The disease is endemic to Southeast Florida, Texas, Mexico, and Central and South America. The protozoan attacks red cells, causing a rapid hemolysis with severe anemia and hemoglobinuria. Infected horses develop high fever, swollen limbs, weakness, rapid pulse, pale gums, and swelling of the eyelids and face. Death can occur in 1 to 2 days. Horses who recover may serve as carriers for several years.

The protozoan can be seen microscopically in red blood cells. This establishes the diagnosis.

Treatment: Drugs effective against the protozoan are available to treat the illness and eliminate the carrier state. The disease is best prevented by controlling ticks as described in chapter 2, Parasites.

SKIN

The skin of the horse is remarkably strong and sensitive. Despite its apparent toughness, however, it is easily damaged by cinches, girths, and horse tack, and by rough handling with the wrong type of grooming equipment. Once the surface of the skin is broken and disturbed by trauma or a skin disorder, the condition tends to spread rapidly and becomes a major problem to the horse and its owner.

Skin is a barrier that keeps out bacteria and other foreign agents. It is involved in the synthesis of essential vitamins. It provides sensation to the surface of the body. It gives form to the body and insulates the horse against extremes of heat and cold.

The outer skin layer is the epidermis. It is a scaly layer which varies in thickness on different parts of the horse's body. It is thinnest over the muzzle, around the lips, in the skin creases of the groin, and beneath the front legs. In these areas it is most easily traumatized.

The epidermis is modified to form horn-like growths called chestnuts and ergots.

Chestnuts are located on the front legs above the knees and on the back legs below the hocks. Contrary to popular belief, they do not represent the vestiges of missing digits.

Ergots are found at the back of the fetlocks. Their size varies among different breeds. In some horses they are hidden by long hair feathers.

The next layer is the dermis. The dermis gives rise to the skin appendages, which are the sweat glands, sebaceous glands, and hair follicles.

Sweat glands are present everywhere on the body except the legs, and are most numerous behind the ears, on the neck, and on the chest and flanks. Sweat is alkaline, salty, and produces the horse's characteristic odor.

Sebaceous glands open directly on the skin and discharge an oily or waxy substance called *sebum*. Sebum coats the hair, waterproofs the coat, and causes the individual hairs to lie flat. It also gives the coat its luster or shine. Frequent brushing and grooming increase the secretion of sebum and make the coat "bloom."

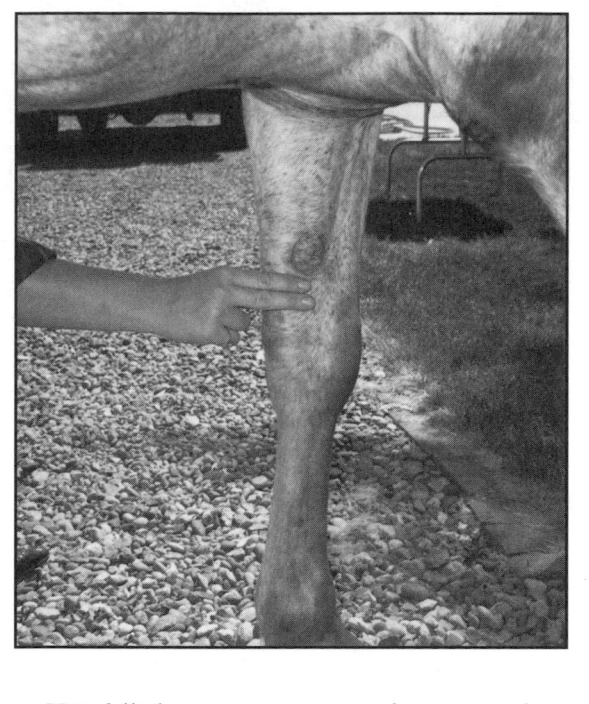

Chestnuts, like human fingerprints, are unique to each horse. They can be used for accurate and permanent identification.

Hair follicles are present everywhere except beneath the tail, around the genitalia, and on the inside of the thighs.

Beneath the skin is a layer of fat which insulates against extremes of temperature. Wasting diseases with loss of subcutaneous fat cause the skin to become dry and hidebound, especially over the ribs.

The horse's outer hair coat is composed of long heavy guard hair. Tiny muscles called *piloerectors* connect to the roots of guard hair. When these muscles contract, they make the hair stand out, thus trapping warm air and providing better insulation in cold weather.

Beneath the outer coat is a dense, thick undercoat. The undercoat is shed in spring and fall. At such times the horse should be groomed vigorously to remove dead hair.

Additionally, the horse possesses hair of a different quality that is not shed. This is the hair of the eyelashes, mane, and tail, and the tactile hair of the muzzle.

A condition called *patchy shedding* may occur in the spring. Some horses shed large patches of hair all at once, producing bare areas 8 to 10 inches in diameter. The skin is perfectly normal. There is no itching, but the condition may be mistaken for a fungus and the horse treated for ringworm. A similar loss of hair can occur several days after a high fever.

Seasonal shedding in horses is not associated with matting and clumping. Mats, clumps, and a disordered appearance suggest a fungus infection.

Hirsutism is the name given to excessive growth of the hair coat. This uncommon condition occurs primarily in aging mares. A growth of the pituitary gland is

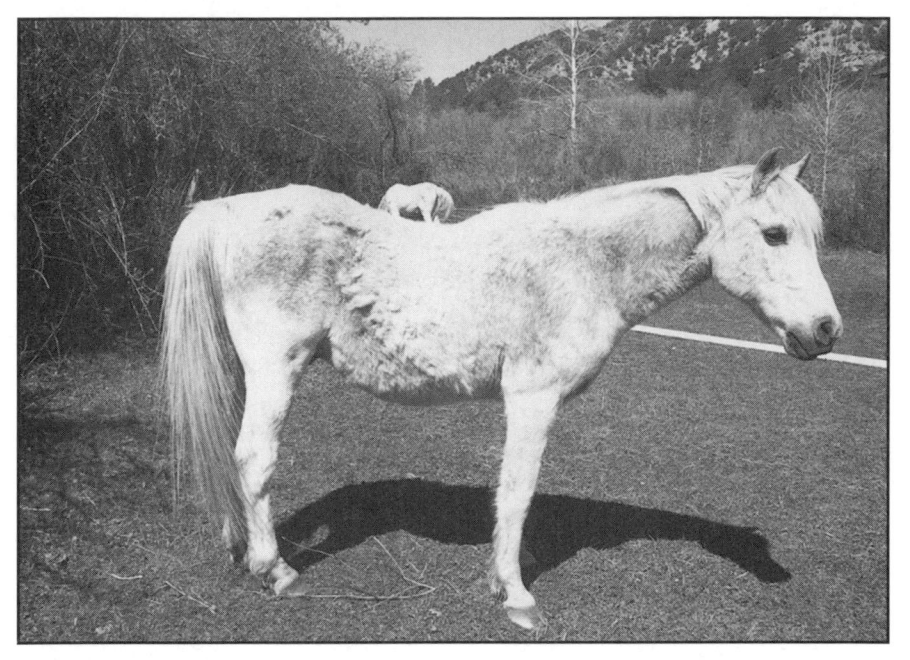

Patchy shedding is normal in spring.

An old, malnourished mare with chronic founder and a hirsute coat.

another cause. Hirsute hair is exceptionally long and coarse and often becomes matted and curly.

The color of a horse's coat is determined by cells at the roots of hair follicles, called *melanin granules*. The specific color is mediated by variations in the density and distribution of these granules, controlled by complex genetic influences not fully elucidated in the horse. A saddle sore or girth gall can damage the melanin layer and result in an area of depigmentation, seen as a spot of white hair.

The appearance of the coat is a good indication of the health of the horse. The coat of a horse in good health is smooth, fine, and glossy. The coat of a horse in ill health is dry, coarse, "staring," and lacks the luster and shine imparted by the skin oils.

How to Avoid Coat and Skin Problems

GROOMING

Brushing for a few minutes each day will help to keep your horse free of skin and hair problems. Brushing removes dirt and debris and also stimulates sebum production.

Horses at pasture usually cannot be groomed daily, but still should have their feet cleaned and coat brushed at regular intervals.

Grooming should be a pleasurable experience for both you and the horse. If the horse grows to dislike the basic routine, a simple procedure becomes most difficult.

Grooming tools that are especially useful are listed below. Your choice will depend on the character and condition of the horse's coat.

- The Body Brush. This is a fine soft brush used over the entire body. It is the principal tool in grooming. Brushes with natural bristles produce less static and broken hair than those of the nylon type.

- Curry Comb. Rubber and metal combs are available. Rubber combs are less likely to injure the skin. Metal combs are best reserved for removing hair from grooming brushes. Combs are useful in grooming horses with long thick coats. They are also good for loosening dirt and removing loose hair during shedding. Apply the curry comb firmly but gently in small circles over the neck and body. Do not use a curry comb about the head or below the knees and hocks.

- Dandy Brush. This coarser brush is used on the lower legs to remove mud. It also can be used to brush out the mane and tail.

- Sweat Scraper. This is a flexible strip or curved solid piece of metal used for scraping off moisture after exercise or bathing. It helps speed up the drying process before grooming.

- Drying Towel. A drying towel can be made from an old blanket cut into sections 2 to 3 feet square. Wool is best for absorbing moisture. Cotton or burlap can be used to dry and polish the coat.

- Grooming Cloth. This is a dry cloth used to wipe off the head, nostrils, and base of the tail, and to apply hair conditioners.
- Hoof Pick. This is a small metal pick used for cleaning the frog and sole.

A horse should be groomed before and after a workout. Before saddling, clean the feet with a hoof pick and go over the horse lightly with a brush. Be sure to remove dirt and surface debris from the withers, back, and girth (saddle area).

A horse coming in hot and sweaty from a workout should be walked and not permitted to drink water until cooled.

Scrape off surface moisture and rub the horse down with a drying towel. When dry, remove mud and loosen surface dirt on the neck and body with the rubber curry comb, and on the legs with the dandy brush.

While standing on one side of the horse, begin brushing using the body brush in a circular pattern. Begin at the neck and work down the front of the chest and side of the shoulder. Brush the foreleg, back, belly, loin, croup, and hind leg. Cross to the other side and repeat the routine. Lean against the horse for better leverage.

Brush the head, mane, and tail. A dandy brush or a wire dog brush are the easiest to use on the mane and tail. Only a soft brush should be used on the face and ears.

Wipe the face, eyes, nostrils, and dock with a moist sponge. Give a final polish to the coat with the grooming cloth.

As a final step, clean the feet with a hoof pick. Start at the frog and work toward the toe. Strokes are taken away from the handler. For more information, see HOOF CARE in chapter 12, Musculoskeletal System.

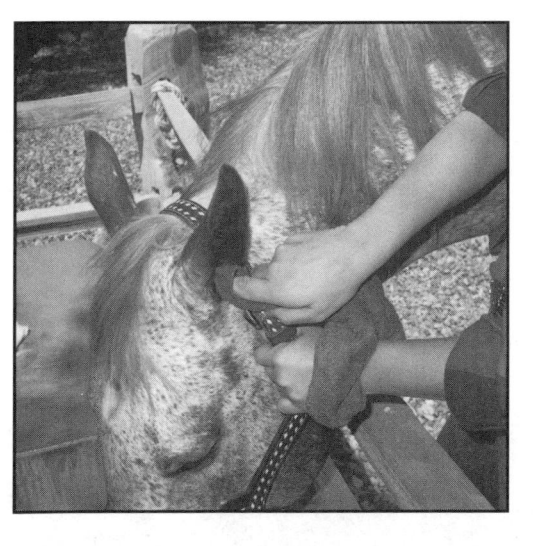

Gently wipe the inside of the ear flap with a damp cloth to remove dirt and loosen skin flakes.

BATHING

How frequently to bathe depends on the use of the horse and the condition of its coat. Over-bathing removes skin oils and leaves the coat dull and dry. Avoid bathing in cold weather. Chilling lowers a horse's resistance to infection and pre-disposes to respiratory diseases.

Horses shed in the spring and fall. A bath helps to remove loose hair, scurf, and dirt. Exhibition horses are bathed in preparation for horse shows. If you plan to show, it is a good idea to get your horse used to the bath routine.

When bathing your horse, use the same systematic approach as described for grooming. Note that shampoos remove dirt, but also remove skin oils that protect the hair and give the coat its sheen. A good horse shampoo should effectively remove dirt but be mild enough to preserve the natural skin oils. Commercial shampoo and hair conditioners are available. The products in current use are protein-based natural moisturizers and are designed to coat the hair shaft in a manner like that of sebum. Follow the directions on the label.

A body sponge is used to apply the wash. Use lukewarm water. After soaping thoroughly, rinse the horse well to remove all residual soap from the coat and skin. Remove excess moisture with the sweat scraper and towel the horse vigorously. Cover the horse with a blanket and walk until dry.

The best results are obtained when shampoos are used infrequently, the coat is rinsed thoroughly to remove all soap residue, and the coat is brushed frequently between baths.

SPECIAL BATH PROBLEMS

Skunk Oil. Skunk oil can be removed from your horse's coat by soaking it in tomato juice and then bathing the area as described above. Commercial skunk deodorizers are available.

Tar and Paint. Trim away excess coat containing tar, oil, or paint when feasible. Soak the tarry spots in vegetable oil and leave overnight. In the morning, remove with soap and water. If the substance is on the hoof, apply nail polish remover and follow it with a good rinsing. Do not use petroleum solvents such as gasoline, kerosene, or turpentine, as they are extremely harmful to the skin and feet.

OTHER GROOMING CONSIDERATIONS

Horse blankets are used to keep the coat clean for exhibition purposes after a bath, to protect the horse from flies and biting insects, and to provide additional warmth for a sick horse. It is a good idea to blanket a horse while traveling in a horse trailer. This prevents chilling and protects the skin from injury.

Some horse owners like to blanket a horse during winter because this seems to prevent excessive growth of the hair, induces earlier spring shedding, and produces a better-looking show coat. However, blanketing decreases a horse's adaptation to cold weather and thus may not be advisable in some circumstances (see COLD WEATHER CARE AND FEEDING, in chapter 17, Feeding and Nutrition).

Be sure the blanket fits properly so that it won't slip and frighten the horse. Blankets should be worn only when a horse is stalled or can be easily observed in a paddock. It is not safe to turn a horse out to pasture wearing a blanket. If the horse will be exposed to rain, the blanket should be waterproof.

Pulling the mane and tail is done to thin and even-out hair for the sake of appearance. Tails generally are shortened to about 4 inches below the hock.

Grasp only a few hairs at a time and slide your hand up close to the roots, then give a quick jerk. The longest hairs on the underside are worked first. Scissors should not be used to shape the tail as this will give a poor cosmetic appearance.

Occasionally the mane is "roached" or clipped, either for cosmetic reasons or to prevent snarling.

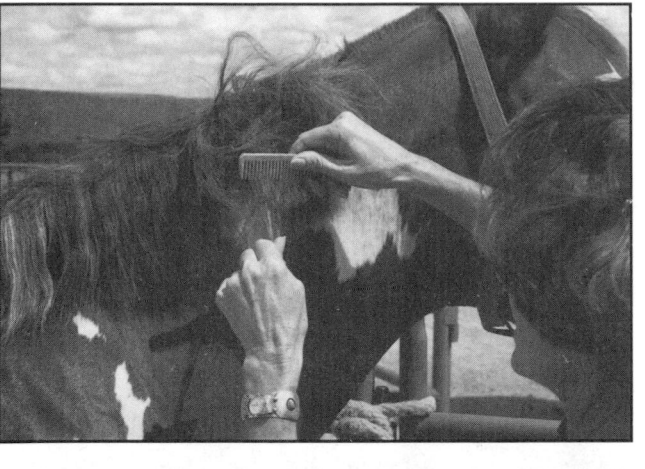

Work the mane by hand to remove snarls and even out the hair. Use electric clippers to roach the mane. Photo: Peggy Gilbert.

Body clipping is done to prepare a horse for show, or to facilitate the cooling-down process after strenuous workouts. A clipped horse chills easily and must be protected from cold. This involves housing the horse in a heated facility; or in less inclement weather, the wearing of a horse blanket.

Cleaning the Sheath. The sheath is a double fold of skin surrounding the penis. There is a pocket within the glans penis above the urethra called the *urethral diverticulum* (see the diagram of the male reproductive system in chapter 14, Sex and Reproduction). Smegma can build up within the sheath, causing irritation and swelling of the sheath and penis. A heavy accumulation of smegma in the urethral diverticulum (called a "bean") can compress the urethra and interfere with the passage of urine. Male horses should have their sheaths cleaned at least once every 6 months. Males with white skin such as Pintos and Appaloosas are especially prone to smegma formation and may have to have their sheaths cleaned more often.

Before cleaning the sheath and penis, the horse should be restrained (see HANDLING AND RESTRAINT). Ivory soap in warm water makes a good wash solution. Do

Clean the sheath and penis with mild soap and water.

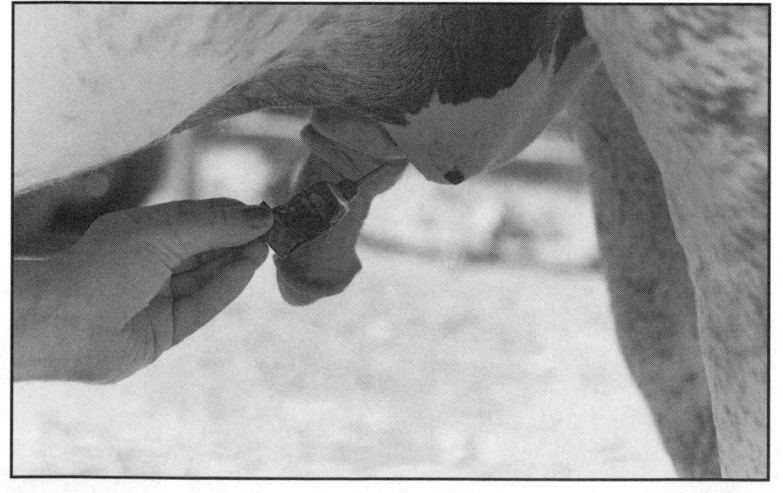

If the sheath is inflamed, instill an antibiotic ointment.

not use iodine-containing preparations such as Betadine or antiseptic soaps such as chlorhexidine. They can be extremely irritating to the prepuce and penis.

Soap your hand well, then use your fingers to loosen and gently remove an accumulation of smegma in the folds of the skin sheath. As the penis extends, it should be washed in the same manner. If there is an accumulation of smegma in the urethral diverticulum, manually evert the diverticulum and clean the recess. Rinse thoroughly with plain water to remove all soapy residue. If the sheath or diverticulum is swollen or irritated-looking, instill an antibiotic preparation such as Triple Antibiotic Ointment.

Grooming equipment and horse tack should be cleaned and disinfected from time to time to prevent the spread of skin diseases. Several commercial tack washes are available. If possible, keep separate tack for each horse.

Leather apparel should be cleaned with saddle soap and protected against cracks and drying with a good leather oil such as neatsfoot oil. Check the reins, cinch straps, and stirrup straps. Repair or replace components that show wear.

What to Do if Your Horse Has a Skin Problem

A horse that repeatedly rubs up against fences, posts, stalls, and other objects, or bites and scratches at its skin, has an itchy skin disorder. To determine the cause, consult Table I.

There is another group of conditions in which hair loss is the principal sign. These diseases do not cause the horse much discomfort—at least not at first—but you will notice patchy hair loss from specific parts of the body. Usually these patches are circular and about 1 to 2 inches in diameter. Scabs and skin flakes are sometimes present. To determine the possible cause, see Table II.

When a horse has a painful skin condition, you will see pus and other signs of infection on or beneath the skin. Often the skin becomes abraded and infected as a result of rubbing and scratching. In that case you must treat both the itchy skin disorder and the secondarily infected skin. The common types of skin infection are listed in Table III.

During the course of grooming your horse, you may discover a lump, bump, or growth on or beneath the skin. To learn what it might be, consult Table IV.

The diagnosis of skin disease can be difficult. The picture is often clouded by the presence of wounds, insect bites, and secondary trauma caused by rubbing and biting at the skin. History becomes important in deciding what caused the initial insult. Considerations such as age, sex, breed, change in activity or diet, contact with other animals, emotional state, exposure to skin irritants, and environmental influences then become important determinants.

The following tables serve as an aid in the diagnosis of skin diseases. To facilitate identification, some skin ailments are listed in more than one table.

Table I ITCHY SKIN DISORDERS

Insect Bites: A common cause of itching in the fly season. Bumps, blisters, scabs, crusty areas, and occasionally hair loss occur where insects bite.

Queensland Itch (Culicoides Dermatitis): The most common insect bite allergy in horses. Caused by gnats. Excoriations, crusts, and scabs. Intense itching with hair broken and rubbed off.

Ventral Midline Dermatitis: Caused by the migrating phase of a hair-like worm transmitted by gnats. Produces moist, crusty, shallow ulcerations, typically centered along the midline on the undersurface of the abdomen but sometimes on the face and eyelids. Hair is lost around ulcerations.

Hives: Round raised wheals scattered over the body with hair sticking out in patches. Swelling of the face or eyelids can occur. Usually caused by inhaled allergens, occasionally by allergens in the feed.

Irritant Contact Dermatitis: Red bumps with crusting and hair loss. Found around the muzzle, feet, legs, saddle girth, and other areas in contact with irritants. Healed skin may turn white (depigmentation).

Allergic Contact Dermatitis: Same as above but requires repeated or continuous contact with allergen (e.g., horse tack, rubber bit). Dermatitis may spread beyond area of contact.

Pemphigus Foliaceus: A rare condition caused by an allergic response to a substance in the horse's own skin. Initially produces blisters, scabs, and scaly skin; later ulcerations appear with oozing of serum and crusting.

Mange: An intensely itchy skin disorder caused by mites. Red lumps followed by scabs, crusts, and patches of hair loss are found all over the body, but especially on the poll, mane, tail, and legs. Mites in ear canals cause head-shaking. Hair is lost due to rubbing.

Chiggers: Intensely itchy skin disorder caused by larvae of mites. Traumatized skin found about head, neck, chest, and legs. Seasonal and regional in chigger-infested pastures. See chapter 2, Parasites.

Lice: Intense itching caused by 2 to 3 mm pale-colored insects found around head and face, ears, topline, and base of tail. Hair rubbed off; skin excoriated. See chapter 2, Parasites.

Photosensitivity Reaction: Requires exposure to sunlight. Redness, swelling, and weeping of serum. The outer skin may peel as in sunburn. Usually confined to white or lightly pigmented and hairless areas of skin.

Summer Sores (Habronema): Caused by the larvae of stomach worms deposited in open wounds and sores. Occurs only in the fly season. Suspect this when a clean wound or sore suddenly enlarges and becomes covered with a reddish-yellow tissue that bleeds easily.

Pinworms: Intense itching and tail rubbing primarily in weanlings and young horses. "Ratty" look to the tail. See chapter 2, Parasites.

Table II DISORDERS IN WHICH HAIR IS LOST

Patchy Shedding: Normal type of shedding. Produces bare patches up to 10 inches in diameter. Skin is healthy and hair grows back in 3 weeks.

Ringworm: Highly contagious skin fungus. Usually occurs in fall and winter. Commonly located in the saddle girth area. Scaly, crusty, or red circular patches with central hair loss are typical. May see matted clumps of hair which fall out easily.

Seborrhea: A flaky, scaly condition that looks like dandruff. Usually symmetrical. Bare circular patches occur where crusts peel off. May resemble ringworm.

Rain Scalds: A fungus infection that occurs in rainy weather. Characterized by tufts of matted hair which look like large drops of water. Tufts come out leaving bare patches about an inch in diameter. May resemble ringworm. Skin often becomes secondarily infected.

Irritant Contact Dermatitis: Red bumps with crusting and hair loss. Found around the muzzle, feet, legs, saddle girth, and other areas in contact with irritants. Healed skin may turn white (depigmentation).

Allergic Contact Dermatitis: Same as above but requires repeated and continuous contact with allergen (e.g., horse tack, rubber bit). Dermatitis may spread beyond area of contact.

Tail Pyoderma: Furunculosis and abscesses that occur on the skin of the tail from self-mutilation. The tail is severely abraded. Look for an underlying itchy skin problem such as tail mites or pinworms.

Selenium Toxicity: Loss of hair from mane and tail ("bob-tail" disease). Cracks in hoof wall may cause severe lameness. See chapter 17, Feeding and Nutrition.

Lymphosarcoma: One or more subcutaneous masses or nodules resembling hives, as seen in the *cutaneous* form.

Table III SKIN INFECTIONS (PYODERMA)

Cellulitis and Abscess: Painful, hot, inflamed skin or pockets of pus beneath the skin. Look for an underlying cause (itchy skin disorder, foreign body, skin wound). One or more abscesses beneath the jaw suggests strangles.

Folliculitis (Summer Rash): Hair-pore infection that occurs in the saddle area in hot weather.

Furunculosis: A deep-seated hair-pore infection with draining sinus tracts to the skin.

Tail Pyoderma: Furunculosis and abscesses that occur on the skin of the tail from self-mutilation. The tail is severely abraded. Look for an underlying itchy skin problem such as tail mites or pinworms.

continues

Table III SKIN INFECTIONS (PYODERMA) (CONTINUED)

Ulcerative Lymphangitis: Begins in extremity wounds with swelling of the leg and the appearance of abscesses along the lymphatic channels. The abscesses open and drain pus. Discussed in chapter 3, Infectious Diseases.

Malignant Edema: Begins in dirty wounds about the legs and face. A soft, hot, painful swelling that progresses rapidly and produces a toxic form of gas gangrene. Discussed in chapter 3, Infectious Diseases.

Poll-Evil: A deep-seated infection at the poll, characterized by swelling on one or both sides of the poll, then the formation of one or more draining sinus tracts to the skin. Discussed in chapter 3, Infectious Diseases, under BRUCELLOSIS.

Fistulous Withers: The same as poll-evil but occurs at the withers.

Rain Scalds: A fungus infection which occurs in rainy weather. Characterized by tufts of matted hair that look like large drops of water. Tufts come out leaving bare patches about an inch in diameter. May resemble ringworm. Skin often becomes secondarily infected.

Sporotrichosis: A draining sore or ulcer at the site of a puncture wound, usually on the leg. Nodules appear along the lymphatic channels, ulcerate, discharge pus, and heal slowly. Caused by a fungus.

Grease Heel (Mud Fever): An infection at the back of the fetlocks and/or the heels, characterized by a greasy exudate that mats the hair. Proceeds to cellulitis and ulceration. Grape-like clusters may appear.

Summer Sores (Habronema): Caused by the larvae of stomach worms deposited in open wounds and sores. Occurs only in the fly season. Suspect this when a clean wound or sore suddenly enlarges and becomes covered with a reddish-yellow tissue that bleeds easily.

Ventral Midline Dermatitis (Onchocerciasis): Caused by the migrating phase of a hair-like worm transmitted by gnats. Produces moist, crusty, shallow ulcerations, typically centered along the midline on the undersurface of the abdomen but sometimes on the face. Hair is lost around ulcerations.

Table IV LUMPS, BUMPS, AND GROWTHS ON OR BENEATH THE SKIN

Warts (Papillomas): Smooth, raised, flesh-colored bumps on the muzzle and lips of young horses. Usually disappear in 3 months.

Sarcoid: The most common tumor in horses. Takes a variety of shapes. May be flat with hair loss, ulcerated, or cauliflower. Found around eyes and anywhere on the body. Affects horses of all ages.

Tender Knots: Frequently found at the site of a shot or vaccination. Resolve spontaneously. Often painful.

continues

Cattle Grubs: Painful nodules beneath the skin; found at the withers, neck, and back. May have a breathing hole to the skin.

Squamous Cell Carcinoma: A hard, flat or ulcerating growth found on older horses of the lightly pigmented breeds, especially in hairless areas exposed to sunlight. Most common on the face and genitalia. Does not heal.

Melanoma: A dark brown to black nodular growth, usually on the underside of the tail; sometimes about the vulva, anus, male genitalia, eye, or mouth. Commonly found on old gray horses.

Phycomycosis (Leeches): A deep-seated fungus infection that often occurs at the site of a cut, usually on the leg but sometimes on the head and abdomen. A fast-growing bulbous mass of grayish-pink tissue which discharges infected material through numerous sinus tracts.

Lymphosarcoma: A mass or nodule beneath the skin. Occasionally the overlying skin becomes ulcerated with loss of hair.

Abnormal Sweating

ANHIDROSIS (ABSENCE OF SWEATING)

Anhidrosis is loss of the ability to sweat in response to exercise or increased body temperature. Sweating is under the influence of the adrenal hormone epinephrine. When released into the bloodstream, epinephrine acts directly on certain receptors in sweat glands, causing them to secrete. The reason why horses with anhidrosis do not sweat when stimulated is not known. One theory is that epinephrine receptors become less sensitive to the effects of the epinephrine. Hair follicles that do not sweat become plugged by dried sebum. This is a contributing factor.

Anhidrosis occurs primarily in horses living in hot, humid climates, particularly in Florida and along the Gulf Coast. It also occurs in horses following relocation from a temperate climate to a subtropical climate such as the above. Performance horses, especially racehorses, are most often affected, but pleasure horses also suffer from this disease.

Anhidrosis may be partial or complete, and the onset can be sudden or gradual.

Sudden signs appear in hot weather after exercise. The affected horse exhibits a fast pulse, high fever, dry skin, and rapid labored breathing with flared nostrils at rest. These horses are called "breathers." Unless failure to sweat is noted by the owner, the horse may be treated for a respiratory infection.

Horses with gradual onset exhibit poor exercise tolerance, loss of weight and condition, a dry, rough hair coat, and patchy hair loss initially over the face. With long-standing disease, the skin becomes dry, scaly, and excoriated over the body.

The diagnosis of anhidrosis can be established by injecting a patch of skin with epinephrine or terbutaline sulfate. A normal horse drips sweat from the patch within

30 minutes. A horse with anhidrosis either does not sweat from the patch, or sweats only when the injected dose is greatly increased.

Treatment: There is no specific drug to restore sweating. Some horses with temporary anhidrosis apparently adapt or revert to a normal sweating pattern when moved to a cooler climate. If this is not an acceptable alternative, provide fan-cooled or air-conditioned facilities during the summer, and exercise the horse judiciously in warm weather to prevent overheating.

Avoid supplementing the ration with grain and concentrates. The addition of 4 ounces of Lite (low-sodium salt) to the evening ration is beneficial. Horses with anhidrosis are at increased risk for heat stroke and should be monitored accordingly. See HEAT STROKE in chapter 1, Emergencies.

HYPERHIDROSIS (EXCESSIVE SWEATING)

Excessive sweating has many causes. It should be thought of as a symptom rather than a specific disease.

Horses can break out in a "cold" or "hot" sweat. Cold, clammy sweating is seen when a horse is emotionally upset or in pain. The temperature drop is due to shunting of blood away from the skin.

In contrast, a hot sweat is due to increased flow of blood through the skin. It has the specific purpose of cooling the horse. Hot sweats are seen after exercise and occur with high fever. Heavy sweating after a light workout suggests lack of condition.

Profuse sweating occurs after the administration of certain drugs such as epinephrine and acepromazine. It is also characteristic of tetanus, encephalomyelitis, and epinephrine-secreting tumors of the adrenal gland.

Patchy sweating over the neck, shoulders, and ribcage is seen with organophosphate insecticide poisoning.

Allergies

An allergic reaction is caused by a foreign protein (allergen) that invades the horse's immune system and triggers the release of histamine and other substances that result in self-injury. This is called a *hypersensitivity reaction*.

Before a horse can become sensitized to an allergen in the environment, it must have been exposed to it at least once before. In the allergic horse, repeat exposure to allergens such as pollens, molds, grasses and weeds, insect bites, certain feeds, and drugs trigger a reaction typified by itching, hives, occasional sneezing, coughing, and tearing. The skin and respiratory tract are the targets for allergic symptoms in horses.

There are two kinds of hypersensitivity reaction. The *immediate* type occurs shortly after exposure, while the *delayed* type occurs hours or days later. Insect bites are examples of both types; there can be an immediate or a delayed response.

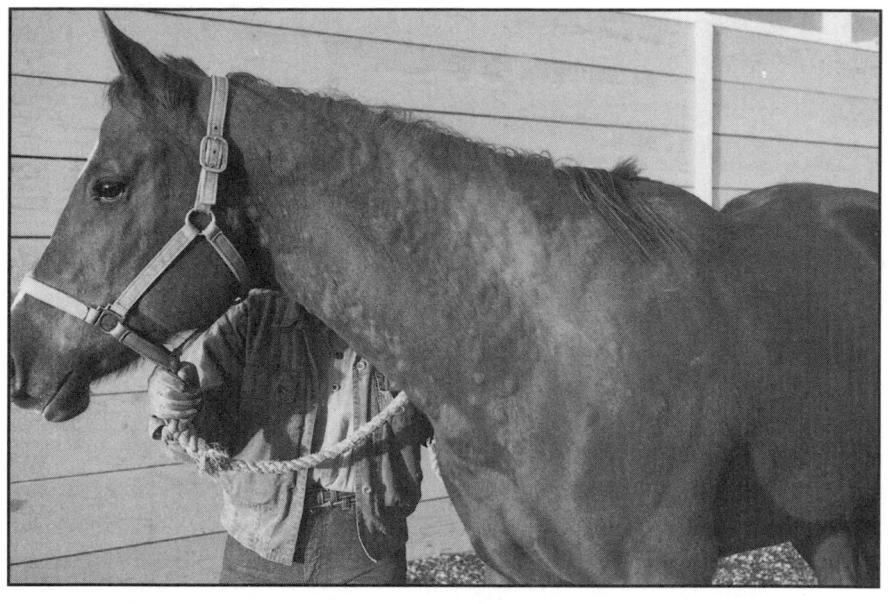

Hives. An allergic reaction to a vaccination. Note the wheals on the neck.

Anaphylactic shock is a life-threatening hypersensitivity reaction of the immediate type discussed in chapter 1, Emergencies.

HIVES (URTICARIA)

Hives is the appearance of round raised wheals on the skin, ranging in size from less than an inch to several inches in diameter. The hair sticks out in patches over parts of the body. There may be swelling of the face or eyelids. These wheals, which are not painful, pit with pressure. The horse may or may not itch.

Episodes of hives that come and go and last only a few hours are usually caused by inhaled allergens and less commonly by allergens in the feed. Inhaled allergens known to cause hives in horses include: the down of bird feathers; cigarette and tobacco smoke; pollens of numerous trees, bushes, plants, and weeds; grass and grass seeds; and dust, rusts, and molds.

Vaccinations and injected drugs are occasional causes of hives. Insect bites can but usually do not produce hives.

Treatment: Horses with hives usually recover spontaneously without treatment. A course of short-acting corticosteroids can be considered. With recurrent hives, attempt to identify the offending allergen. Intradermal skin testing is the best way to identify an inhaled allergen. Successful avoidance in the case of airborne pollens may not be practical. A course of desensitizing injections may be effective in this situation.

When an ingested allergy is suspected, first take the horse off all sweet feeds and supplements. If this does not prevent recurrence, switch to pellets or alfalfa hay.

CONTACT AND ALLERGIC CONTACT DERMATITIS

These two conditions are discussed together because they produce similar skin reactions. Both are caused by contact with a chemical. Whereas all horses coming into contact with an irritating chemical will develop a skin irritation, only horses allergic to a chemical will develop a hypersensitivity response.

A contact dermatitis of either type causes itchy red bumps and fluid-filled blisters that become crusted and sometimes secondarily infected. Hair is lost in the area of inflamed skin. The healed skin becomes thicker, rougher, and darker.

Contact dermatitis occurs around the muzzle, lower legs, feet, and in sites (like the saddle area) having contact with horse tack.

Common irritants are acids and alkalis, insecticides, detergents, solvents, soaps, and petroleum by-products such as creosote and tar.

Common allergens include dyes and preservatives in horse gear; chemicals in topical insecticides and horse liniments; and various plants including poison ivy and poison oak. Rubber bits can cause reactions around the mouth. The site of the reaction frequently indicates the cause of the dermatitis.

Treatment: Identify the skin allergen by removing the horse from all possible exposure for 1 to 2 weeks. If the problem clears, re-expose the horse to the suspected allergen. If the dermatitis returns, the diagnosis is established. Once the allergen is known, prevent further exposure. When an irritating chemical has made contact with the skin, wash gently with warm water to remove all residue. Treat secondary skin infection with a topical antibiotic such as nitrofurazone or Triple Antibiotic Ointment.

VENTRAL MIDLINE DERMATITIS (ONCHOCERCIASIS)

Ventral midline dermatitis is a skin disease caused by the filarial phase of a hair-like worm called *Onchocerca cervicalis*. The adult worm lives in connective tissue of the horse's neck. The majority of horses in the United States are infected, but only a few develop a dermatitis. It is believed that the skin response is due to an allergic reaction to the dying microfilaria.

The filaria migrate under the skin and settle primarily on the midline of the abdomen from the chest to the groin, especially around the umbilicus. Other sites are the withers, face, eyelids, and legs. At these sites the parasites produce an itchy skin disorder with redness, moist shallow ulcerations, crusting and scaling, and patchy hair loss. Spots up to 10 inches in diameter can develop. Scarring and loss of skin pigmentation are late occurrences.

These open sores attract Culicoides gnats and other flying insects. Gnats feeding on the open sores pick up filaria and introduce them to a new host. Biting flies and other insects exacerbate the skin disorder and create pyoderma.

Treatment: Ivermectin paste is completely effective in ridding the horse of filaria within 2 to 3 weeks. Minor reactions can occur with its use. Veterinary supervision is advised.

Adult worms are not affected by deworming agents and therefore serve as a reservoir for recurrent infection. To keep the skin free of disease, ivermectin must be repeated at 4-month intervals. A deworming program incorporating ivermectin, as described in chapter 1, Parasites, will effectively control onchocerciasis.

NOTE: The filaria are capable of penetrating the eye and producing uveitis, a leading cause of blindness in horses (see chapter 5, Eyes).

SUMMER SORES (HABRONEMA)

Summer sores are caused by the larvae of stomach worms. These larvae are deposited by stable and horse flies as they feed around moist areas on the body, especially the sheath of the penis and corners of the eyes. Larvae also are deposited in open wounds.

Summer sores at the corners of the eyes and on the penis often assume a growth-like (granulomatous) appearance, resembling a sacroid or squamous cell carcinoma (both discussed elsewhere). A skin biopsy is the best way to make the diagnosis.

An open wound or sore in the fly season that suddenly enlarges, ulcerates, and becomes covered with reddish-yellow tissue which bleeds easily, should be suspected of being a summer sore. Over the raised round surface of the wound is a gritty, greasy-looking exudate containing rice-sized, yellow, calcified dead larvae.

Summer sores may heal, only to break out again next season. This suggests that a hypersensitivity reaction, related to the presence of adult stomach worms, is a factor in some cases. Horses with summer sores are nearly always heavily parasitized by Habronema. Severe itching is present.

Treatment: Early summer sores respond well to ivermectin paste, which is effective against both the adult worms in the stomach and the larvae in the wound. The inclusion of ivermectin in a deworming program will reduce the frequency of summer sores.

Skin preparations containing organophosphate insecticides, wettable powders, and antibiotics can be applied beneath dressings or massaged into larger open sores with good results. Your veterinarian can provide you with a suitable prescription.

INSECT BITE ALLERGIES

Flies, mites, ticks, lice, gnats, and mosquitoes are insect parasites that can irritate and injure the horse. Most of them are blood-sucking. The mouth parts of the biting flies, in particular, tear the skin and do considerable physical damage. Hypersensitivity reactions will occur if the horse is allergic to a substance in the saliva of the insect. For more information, see INSECT PARASITES.

Culicoides Dermatitis. Also called Queensland itch and summer eczema, this is a seasonal recurring skin disorder caused by the bites of Culicoides gnats, also called midges, "no-see-ums," and sand flies. It is the most common insect-bite allergy in horses.

The saliva of these gnats contains a protein which causes an intense allergic reaction characterized by severe itching. Hair is broken and matted, particularly around the mane, poll, and tail. Hair loss occurs in these areas. The skin shows excoriations, crusts, and scabs. Secondary bacterial infection is common. Thickening of skin and loss of hair pigmentation are late developments.

Although Culicoides hypersensitivity is the most common cause of mane and tail rubbing, the stable fly, horn fly, and black fly also produce an allergic dermatitis difficult to distinguish from Queensland itch. In some cases more than one insect may be involved.

Treatment: Topical corticosteroid preparations help to reduce skin inflammation and allergic reaction. In severe cases a short course of steroids may have to be given by mouth or injection. Consult your veterinarian. Treat secondary pyoderma as described below.

Control: Culicoides gnats feed primarily at dusk, night, and dawn. To prevent exposure, stable the horse before dusk. Gnats are reluctant to enter barns. The Culicoides gnat breeds in stagnant water and can fly only about $1/4$ to $1/2$ mile. Eliminating stagnant water within these flight limits effectively controls the gnat population.

Many topical insecticides do not repel gnats. Poridon, however, is effective against gnats as well as flies and mosquitoes. One application lasts 7 days. Apply as directed by the manufacturer.

Pyoderma

Pyoderma is a bacterial skin infection that drains pus. Many cases are the result of self-mutilation. When a horse rubs or bites at a persistent irritant to its skin, the skin becomes infected. The pyoderma started only because some other itchy skin disorder was there first. Always look for another skin disease before concluding that pyoderma is the only problem the horse has.

CELLULITIS AND ABSCESS

Cellulitis is an infection of the deep layer of the skin. Most cases are caused by puncture wounds, scratches, and lacerations. Horses are particularly prone to such injuries. Many wound infections can be prevented by proper early treatment of wounds as described in chapter 1, Emergencies (see WOUNDS).

Signs of cellulitis are pain (tenderness to pressure), warmth (the skin feels hotter than normal), firmness (not as soft as normal), and change in color (it appears redder than normal).

As infection spreads out from a wound, you may feel tender cords which are swollen lymphatic channels. Regional lymph nodes may enlarge. This is a stage beyond cellulitis and is characterized by two diseases discussed elsewhere (ulcerative lymphangitis and malignant edema).

A *skin abscess* is a localized pocket of pus. Pimples, pustules, furuncles, and boils are examples of small skin abscesses. An abscess is fluctuant and feels like fluid under pressure.

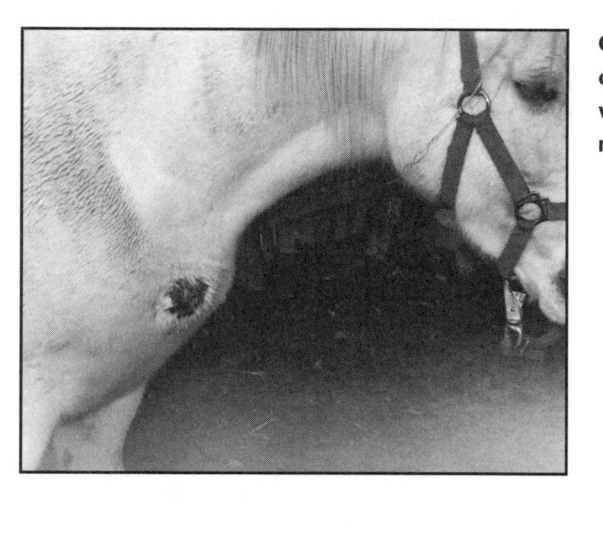

Cellulitis and furunculosis of the skin of the chest wall, the result of a neglected wire cut.

The following skin infections are of particular importance:

Folliculitis ("Summer Rash"). This is a hair-pore infection nearly always caused by a Staphylococcus species. It tends to occur in hot weather as a consequence of excessive sweating and friction to the skin from ill-fitting tack. Small pimples appear, usually at points of contact in the saddle or harness areas. These pimples enlarge and form pustules. The pustules rupture and exude pus. Crusts form and the hair becomes matted.

Folliculitis can be prevented by good hygiene, such as brushing and cleaning the skin and coat after workouts, and using clean dry blankets beneath saddles.

Furunculosis. This is a deep-seated hair-pore infection with draining sinus tracts and patchy hair loss. It is a progressive form of folliculitis and more difficult to treat.

Tail Pyoderma. This condition begins as an itchy skin disorder caused by mange mites or pinworms. As the horse scratches, rubs, and abrades the skin of its tail, secondary staph infection occurs and pustules develop. The ailment is complicated by furunculosis, and by abscesses that rupture and drain in an unending cycle. Hair is lost on the top of the tail. Treatment is most difficult.

Treatment of Pyoderma: Any underlying itchy skin disorder should be treated to eliminate rubbing, biting, and self-mutilation.

Localize the skin infection by clipping away the hair and applying warm soaks for 15 minutes 3 times a day. Saline soaks, made by adding a cup of Epsom salts to a gallon of warm water, make a good poultice. Daily Betadine scrubs help to loosen scabs and promote cleanliness. Topical antibiotics such as nitrofurazone or Triple Antibiotic Ointment are of value and should be applied 2 to 3 times a day.

Pimples, pustules, furuncles, boils, and other small abscesses that do not drain spontaneously should be lanced with a sterile needle or scalpel. If a cavity is present, flush with a dilute antiseptic surgical scrub (see Treating the Wound). Keep the skin open and draining until the cavity heals from below.

Foreign bodies such as splinters beneath the skin must be removed with forceps, as they are a continuing source of infection.

Oral or injectable antibiotics are used in treating wound infections, cellulitis, abscesses, furunculosis, and tail pyoderma. Most skin bacteria respond well to penicillin, oxytetracycline, or trimethoprim-sulfadiazine. Those that do not respond promptly should be cultured and an antibiotic selected on the basis of sensitivity tests.

GREASE HEEL (SCRATCHES; MUD FEVER)

Grease heel is an infection of the skin at the back of the pastern and heel. It occurs most commonly in breeds having long fetlock hair. Two other predisposing factors are trauma to the skin and wet, muddy footing.

Grit on track surfaces, rough stubble in fields, or bites of chigger mites often cause the initial scratches or breaks in the skin, which become infected by a variety of bacteria, especially Staphylococcus. The result is a painful pyoderma in which a greasy exudate of serum accumulates and mats the long hairs. Swelling, hair loss, and ulceration occur as the disease progresses. The horse may become painfully lame and exhibit a stringhalt-like gait. Occasionally heaps of granulation tissue produce grape-like clusters. The skin cracks and exudes a foul odor.

Treatment: Clip the hair and apply saline soaks and Betadine scrubs as described for the treatment of pyoderma.

In mild cases you can apply zinc oxide paste or calamine lotion to dry up the skin. Treat irritated or infected skin by applying an antibiotic-corticosteroid ointment such as Corticosporin. Dress and cover with an ace bandage.

You should see improvement rather quickly. If not, consult your veterinarian. Oral or injectable antibiotics are needed to treat cellulitis. Grape-like growths should be burned off or removed surgically.

Prevention: Stable horses in clean surroundings with dry bedding. Keep the hair at the heels and pasterns short. Always clean the feet after exercise.

PEMPHIGUS FOLIACEUS

This is an uncommon scaling and crusting autoimmune skin disease caused by the development of antibodies to a substance present in the horse's own skin. Half the cases occur in Appaloosas.

The disease begins with the development of small blisters on the lower body. The blisters rupture and form scabs and scaly skin. Fever, listlessness, and swelling of the legs and male genitalia are common. In time, the process becomes generalized.

The diagnosis is made by taking a skin biopsy.

Treatment: Steroids can arrest the disease. Foals and yearlings may stay in remission when the dosage is tapered and discontinued. Older horses tend to relapse and require lifetime treatment. Anticancer drugs which suppress the immune response may be of value.

MANGE

Mange is rare in horses. It is an intensely itchy skin disease caused by tiny spider-like insects called *mites*. Mites live on the surface of the skin or in tunnels a few millimeters beneath the skin. Females deposit eggs in burrows or beneath scabs. Eggs hatch in about 4 days. Mites reach maturity soon thereafter and live only 1 to 2 weeks. The whole cycle takes only 15 to 20 days.

There are 4 species of mite which infect the horse:

The sarcoptic mite, the cause of scabies, burrows beneath the skin of the head, ears, neck, chest, flank, and abdomen. Small red bumps appear around the burrows. As the horse rubs, paws, and bites at the skin to relieve the irritation, the resulting trauma produces further skin injury with crusts, weeping serum, loss of hair, and thickening of the skin. Secondary bacterial infection is common and complicates the picture. Sarcoptic mange is highly contagious and easily transmitted to people.

The psoroptic mite, also called the tail mite, produces lumps and patches of hair loss over the poll, mane, and tail. It is not transferable to man. This mite has been eradicated from horses in the United States.

The chorioptic mite causes leg or foot mange. It is found below the hocks and knees. These mites live on the surface of the skin and produce scabs, crusts, and patches of hair loss. The disease may be difficult to distinguish from grease heel.

The demodectic mite causes demodectic mange, common in dogs but rare in horses. These mites live in hair follicles and sebaceous glands and produce hair loss about the head, neck, and withers, giving a moth-eaten appearance to the hair coat. The mites are transmitted from dam to foal during nursing.

Ringworm and "summer sores" may look like mange, but can be told apart by examining skin scabs and scrapings under a microscope; or in difficult cases, by taking a skin biopsy to look for mites.

Treatment: Horses with mange should be isolated or quarantined to prevent transmission to other horses. Be sure to keep their tack separated also.

Mange should be treated by a veterinarian. The treatment of sarcoptic, chorioptic, and psoroptic mange involves the use of topical insecticides. A thorough dipping or high-pressure spray application is required to saturate the skin. While washing, dislodge scabs with a stiff brush. Several applications at 7- to 10-day intervals are required. There is little information on the use of ivermectin for treating mange mites in horses, but available reports suggest that the drug may be effective in the usual recommended dosage. There is no satisfactory treatment for demodectic mange in horses.

RAIN SCALDS (DERMATOPHILOSIS)

Rain scalds is a skin infection caused by the bacteria *Dermatophilus congolensis*. The organism is activated by moisture. Most horses with rain scalds have been exposed to wet, soggy pastures during a period of heavy rainfall immediately prior to the appearance of skin disease.

The organism is opportunistic and enters through breaks in the skin. Biting fly attacks or grooming with a stiff brush or metal comb often initiate such injuries. In addition, wet skin is more easily abraded than dry skin, and more susceptible to infection.

Rain scalds first appears as pus sticking to tufts of matted hair, giving a characteristic "paintbrush" appearance. The tufts come out, leaving cup-like crusts over the back, rump, saddle area, head, neck, and hind legs. Beneath the adherent crusts is a collection of pus.

In long-haired horses the scalds may spread and join to form large confluent areas of matted hair and crusts. In short-haired horses the scalds usually remain smaller and occur as bumps covered with scabs. Secondary staph infection is common.

Rain scalds can be mistaken for ringworm, and vice versa. Smears taken from the underside of a scab or crust often show the characteristic-appearing bacteria. Cultures confirm the diagnosis.

Treatment: Stable the horse in a dry facility and provide dry footing. Clip away hair and apply antiseptic soak or shampoo (Betadine or chlorhexidine) daily for 7 days, then weekly until healed. It is important to remove scabs with a brush and mild soap. However, if this is too painful or causes bleeding, continue the soaks until the scabs separate easily.

D. *congolensis* is sensitive to most antibiotics. Topical agents work well. A 0.25 percent chloramphenicol solution is quite effective. Apply daily for 5 to 7 days. Oral or injectable antibiotics (oxytetracycline or penicillin) are indicated for severe or widespread involvement. If staph is suspected, obtain a culture and sensitivity, as many staph species are resistant to penicillin.

Fungus Infections of the Skin

RINGWORM

Ringworm is not a worm but a fungus that lives on the surface of the skin. There are five kinds of ringworm in horses. They all cause patchy hair loss.

Ringworm gets its name from its appearance—a rapidly spreading circle with hair loss at the center and a red ring at the margin. Within the circle the skin becomes scabby and sometimes raw. These circular crusty patches usually are 1 to 2 inches in size but may become larger.

Ringworm occurs anywhere on the horse's body but is most common in the saddle area, where it is known as *girth itch*. Other common sites are the face and

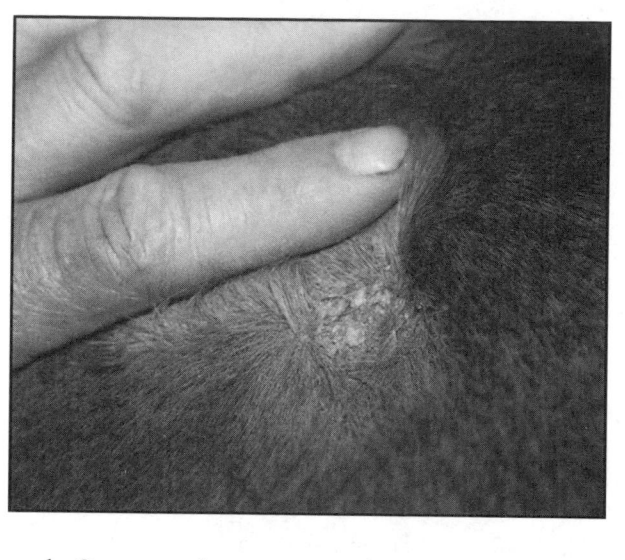

Ringworm, a crusty patch with hair loss, about ¹/₂ inch in diameter.

neck. One type of ringworm produces matted or clumped hair which falls out in large blocks.

The disease is transmitted among horses by contact with contaminated saddles, blankets, and grooming equipment. Humans, especially children, can pick up ringworm from horses.

When the diagnosis is in doubt it can be confirmed by microscopic examination of skin scrapings or by fungus cultures.

Treatment: Most cases disappear spontaneously in 1 to 4 months. To reduce spread and shorten the illness, clip away the infected hair at the margins of the ringworm patch and bathe the skin with Betadine soap to remove dead scales. Small patches can be treated with Tinactin, miconazole, or clotrimazole; all are available at drugstores without prescription. Alternatively, you can apply tincture of iodine 3 times a week.

Phycomycosis. Note the swollen mass of tissue with draining sinus tracts. Photo: *Equine Medicine and Surgery,* American Veterinary Publications.

With extensive involvement, your veterinarian may prescribe a drug called griseofulvin. This drug should not be used on pregnant mares.

To prevent transmission, disinfect grooming equipment, tack, and apparel.

PHYCOMYCOSIS (LEECHES)

Phycomycosis is a deep-seated skin infection caused by a fungus-like micro-organism called *Pythium*. Most cases occur in low prairie land along the Gulf of Mexico. The organism lives in water or moist decaying vegetation, and gains entrance through wounds such as wire cuts. In a very short time the horse develops a swollen mass of devitalized tissue which is gray or yellow in color, and from which numerous sinus tracts discharge plugs of infected material. Bleeding may occur from the surface. These masses, usually found on the lower legs and sometimes actually encircling them, can grow up to 10 inches in diameter. A horse may have two or more of these exuberant growths on various parts of its body. The organism spreads rapidly to regional lymph nodes and occasionally into the abdomen.

It was once thought that elongated masses on the surface of the phycomycosis were parasitic leeches that entered the tissues as the horse stood in water, but this is not the case.

Diagnosis should be made as soon as possible. This requires a biopsy.

Treatment: Only early treatment can cure the horse. The best results are obtained with a combination of immunotherapy and surgery. Immunotherapy involves giving a vaccine prepared from cultures of the Pythium organism. At least three vaccinations are required. While waiting for the mass to get smaller, apply Betadine soaks twice daily. This helps to prevent secondary bacterial infection. Only small phycomycoses respond to vaccination alone. Most masses must be surgically excised after they have ceased to regress. Multiple operations may be necessary.

An infected horse cannot transmit the disease to people or other horses.

SPOROTRICHOSIS

This worldwide disease is caused by *Sporothrix schenckii*, a yeast-like fungus present on vegetation, particularly on the thorns of roses and on plants that carry sharp spicules, or needlelike projections.

A draining sore develops at the site of a puncture wound. This usually occurs on the leg but sometimes on the upper body. Nodules appear beneath the skin along the course of the lymphatics. The nodules ulcerate, discharge pus, crust over, and heal slowly.

The diagnosis is made by taking a sample of wound discharge for fungus culture, or a specimen of infected tissue for fluorescent antibody testing. The disease at times resembles ulcerative Lymphangitis.

Treatment: The frequent application of warm packs is highly beneficial, as the fungus is particularly sensitive to heat. Sporotrichosis often responds to oral iodine therapy when given for several weeks. To prevent relapse, continue treatment 4 weeks beyond healing. In horses that relapse or do not respond to the above, various drugs used to treat human fungus diseases can be tried under close veterinary supervision.

Sporotrichosis can be transmitted to people. Use disposable rubber gloves and hygienic techniques when handling infective material.

Seborrhea

Seborrhea is a flaky, scaly disease of the skin. It is not an itchy skin disorder, and secondary bacterial infection is not always a problem. Seborrhea is classified as either primary or secondary.

Primary seborrhea is rare. It is localized to the mane, tail, and front of the cannon of the hind limbs. Primary seborrhea is sometimes referred to as *stud crud*, even though it is not limited to intact males.

Among disorders known to be associated with *secondary* seborrhea are skin infection, nutritional deficiencies, liver disease, intestinal malabsorption, Vitamin A deficiency, sex hormone imbalances, and autoimmune skin diseases.

In *dry* seborrhea the scaling and flaking looks much like dandruff and the skin is relatively healthy. In *oily* seborrhea scales are held together by sebum, forming thick crusts that are yellowish-brown in color. As the crusts peel off, you may see bare patches of skin up to 8 inches in diameter. With longstanding involvement the skin becomes thickened and inelastic, and the horse generally loses weight and condition.

Seborrhea can resemble ringworm or mange, as all three skin diseases are characterized by patchy hair loss.

Treatment: Secondary seborrhea may clear up with treatment of the underlying cause. Primary seborrhea is incurable but can be managed with topical medications. For dry seborrhea, clip the hair coat at regular intervals and use sulfa or salicylic acid shampoo to keep the skin free of flakes. Benzoyl peroxide and sebum-dissolving shampoos help to loosen scales in oily seborrhea. Thiomar cream or Pragmatar ointment can be applied to individual skin spots. Topical and oral antibiotics are indicated when there is secondary bacterial infection.

Environmental and Traumatic Skin Disorders

PHOTOSENSITIVITY REACTIONS

Photosensitivity is an abnormal reaction of the skin when exposed to sunlight (ultraviolet light). Unlike sunburn, photosensitivity does not require excessive or prolonged exposure. (Sunburn does occur in horses, but only in those with white or light-colored skin.)

A horse becomes photosensitive only after a photodynamic chemical is deposited on or within its skin. A photodynamic chemical absorbs ultraviolet energy and transfers it to the dermis. The process is restricted to the hairless, white, or lightly-pigmented parts of the body, such as the muzzle, ears, lips, vulva, udder, and coronary bands. The result is a skin reaction characterized by redness, swelling, itching, and weeping of serum. The outer layer of skin may peel as in sunburn. Later the skin becomes thickened and fissured. Secondary pyoderma often complicates the picture.

Feedstuffs can contain photodynamic chemicals. The major photosensitizing agent in horses is called *phylloerythrin*, a product formed by the breakdown of chlorophyll in the intestine. Normally phylloerythrin is destroyed by the liver, but in horses with liver disease, toxic levels may reach the skin. This occurs in about 25 percent of horses with liver disease.

Plants that produce photosensitizing chemicals that can be acquired either by direct skin contact or through ingestion include St. John's wort, buckwheat, perennial rye grass, whiteheads, rape ("rape scald"), burr trefoil ("trefoil dermatitis"), alfalfa, and many others.

Drugs may cause photosensitivity, especially the phenothiazines and tetracycline antibiotics.

Involvement of the muzzle and lower legs suggests skin contact with pasture plants. A local skin reaction following application of a topical preparation suggests a photosensitizer in the preparation. Involvement of multiple sites suggests a photosensitizer in the feed.

Treatment: Identify and remove the photodynamic agent, if possible. This may require feed analysis, liver function tests, and investigation of the pasture.

Based on experience, the following steps may be taken:

- Switch to a new ration.
- Bathe the horse and rinse thoroughly to remove any photosensitizers.
- Stop all drugs, especially topicals.
- Keep your horse out of the sun for 2 weeks.

Topical corticosteroids help to relieve itching. Secondarily infected skin is treated as described for pyoderma.

SADDLE SORES, GALLS, AND ROPE BURNS

A poorly fitting or improperly padded saddle can cause a pressure sore, also called a *sitfast*. Skin injuries also occur as a consequence of ill-fitting bridles and harnesses. The rubbed and chafed areas become swollen, bare, and tender to pressure. With continued trauma, these friction sores become infected.

Galls, also caused by ill-fitting equipment (especially saddles), are painful swollen pockets of serum that develop either under the skin or beneath the deeper

A patch of white depigmented skin and hair at the site of an old saddle sore.

connective fascia. Subfascial galls, which are extremely painful, are found most often on the withers.

Rope burns are friction burns, and may involve the full thickness of the skin.

Treatment: Following an acute injury, apply ice packs several times daily for 2 to 3 days. This helps to reduce pain and swelling. Apply zinc oxide salve to raw areas to dry and protect the skin. Deep wounds, such as those produced by rope burns, require clipping of the hair, cleansing with Betadine, and application of topical antibiotics such as nitrofurazone or Triple Antibiotic Ointment. Cover with a sterile dressing. Rest the horse.

Galls beneath the skin usually resolve in 7 to 10 days, but subfascial galls take considerably longer. If the horse must be used at saddle, protect the site with an extra blanket or foam pad. Cut the pad out around the gall or saddle sore to relieve direct pressure.

Rope burns usually occur with ropes made of nylon and hemp. Cotton, which is less likely to produce a burn, is better for tying and picketing.

Tumors and Cancers

A *tumor* is any sort of lump, bump, growth, or swelling such as an abscess. Tumors that are true growths are called *neoplasms*.

Benign neoplasms grow slowly and are surrounded by a capsule. They do not invade and destroy, nor do they spread to other areas. They are cured by surgical removal, provided that all the tumor is removed.

Malignant neoplasms are the same as cancers (also called carcinomas, sarcomas, and lymphomas, depending upon the cell type). Cancers tend to enlarge rapidly. They are not encapsulated. When on the surface they often bleed. They have the potential to spread via the bloodstream and lymphatic system to remote parts of the body. This is called *metastasizing*.

Cancer is graded according to the degree of malignancy. Low-grade cancers continue to grow locally and attain a large size. They metastasize late in the course of the illness. High-grade cancers metastasize early when the primary focus is still quite small or barely detectable.

Tumors are approached in the following manner: Suppose a horse has a solid lump on or beneath the skin. It could be benign or malignant. A decision is made to biopsy the lump. This is surgery during which the lump, or part of the lump, is removed and sent to the pathologist. A veterinary pathologist is a doctor who has been trained to make a diagnosis by visual inspection of tissue under a microscope. An experienced pathologist can tell if the tumor is a cancer. He can often provide additional information as to the degree of malignancy. This serves the purpose of making the diagnosis and, in many cases, gives the rationale for the best treatment.

WHAT CAUSES CANCER?

Cancer is a condition in which rapid cell division and tissue growth occur at the expense of organ-specific function. For example, a cancer arising in a horse's stomach is biopsied via the gastroscope and found to be a mass of tissue which bears only slight resemblance to normal gastric cells under the microscope. The growth in the stomach does not function as stomach tissue nor does it help the horse digest food. If the cancer goes untreated, it eventually interferes with the horse's nutrition and simultaneously metastasizes to other parts of the body. In time, through a number of possible events, it causes the death of the horse.

Cancer is genetically influenced. There are genes which, when present at certain locations on chromosomes, cause cells to become cancers. There are other genes which suppress these genes. There are still other genes which inhibit the suppressors. Thus cancer is a multifactorial and largely unpredictable phenomenon involving the interaction of many genes and chromosomes—all subject to familial and environmental influences.

Carcinogens are environmental influences known to increase the likelihood of cancer in proportion to the length and intensity of exposure to them. Carcinogens are tissue oxidants that gain access to cells, cause alterations in genes and chromosomes, and disrupt the orderly processes that control cellular growth and tissue repair.

Examples of carcinogens known to increase the risk of cancer in people are: ultraviolet rays (skin cancer); x-rays (thyroid cancer); nuclear radiation (leukemia); chemicals (aniline dyes causing bladder cancer); cigarettes and coal tars (causing lung, skin, and other cancers); viruses (causing sarcoma in AIDS patients); and parasites (a cause of bladder cancer).

NEOPLASMS IN THE HORSE

The majority of neoplasms in horses are visible as ulcerations or growths on or beneath the skin. Sarcoid is the most common growth in horses. Next in frequency are squamous cell carcinoma and melanoma. Suspect one of these when there is visible growth of a skin tumor, ulceration of the skin with bleeding, a sore that does not heal, or a nodular brown to black growth in an old gray horse.

Internal cancers are not common in horses. Lymphosarcoma occurs most frequently, followed by stomach cancer.

Neoplasms of the ovary, both benign and malignant, occur in the mare's reproductive tract. Benign fibroid growths of the uterus also occur.

Less frequent sites of cancer in the horse are the oral cavity and nasopharynx, kidney, adrenal gland, pituitary gland, bladder, liver, colon, bone, and udder.

The effectiveness of any form of treatment rests upon early recognition. Early-stage cancers have a higher cure rate than do late-stage cancers. This holds true for all types of cancer. Unfortunately, most internal cancers are asymptomatic and therefore not detected until they are quite large, at which time treatment generally is not possible. Occasionally an ovarian or abdominal neoplasm will be detected unexpectedly during rectal examination performed for some other reason.

The best opportunity for preventing and curing cancer in horses rests upon identifying and treating skin tumors.

BENIGN SURFACE TUMORS

Sarcoids (Blood Warts). Sarcoids are common surface tumors that usually occur in horses younger than 4 years. They are commonly found on the legs, abdomen, head, and around the eyes. Sarcoids range in size from less than an inch up to several inches in diameter. A horse with one sarcoid has 1 chance in 3 of having more.

Sarcoids exhibit a varied appearance. Some are rough and wart-like. Others are red-colored growths that resemble granulation tissue or "proud flesh." Still others are slightly raised nodules. The nodular type is common about the ears and eyelids. An uncommon type is flat, hairless, and resembles a patch of ringworm.

Equine sarcoid has been found by DNA studies to be caused by the cattle wart virus (Bovine Papilloma Virus Types 1 and 2). Possible modes of transmission include direct contact, the airborne route, and an insect vector. Since sarcoids occur at sites of prior trauma, the virus may be introduced through cuts and wounds.

Although sarcoids do not spread to distant parts of the body, these tumors are locally aggressive and have a high recurrence rate after surgical removal (50 percent within 6 months).

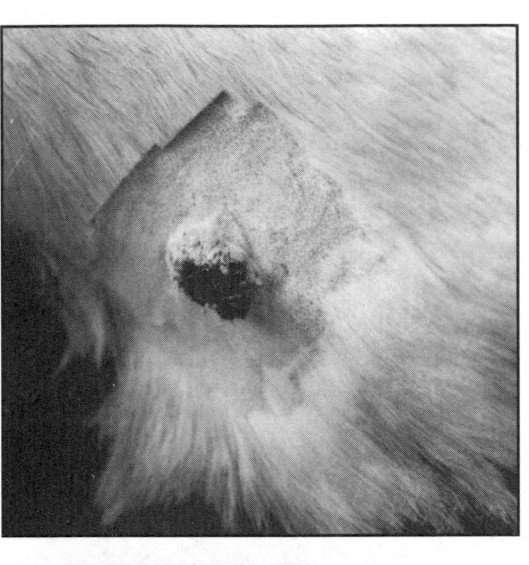

A wart-like sarcoid on the neck.

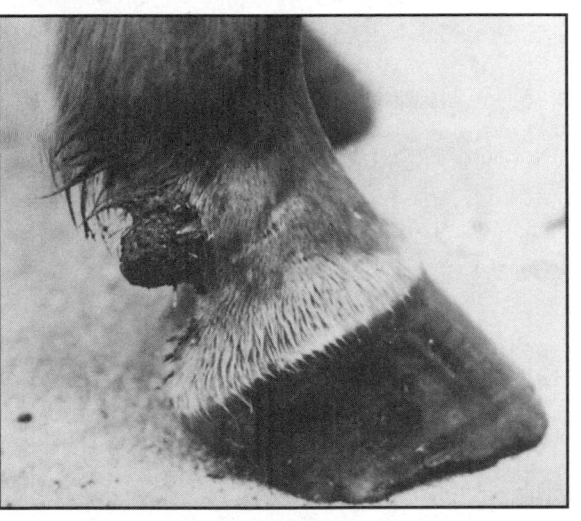

A fleshy sarcoid which developed 4 months after a wire cut to the pastern. Photo: *Equine Medicine and Surgery,* American Veterinary Publications.

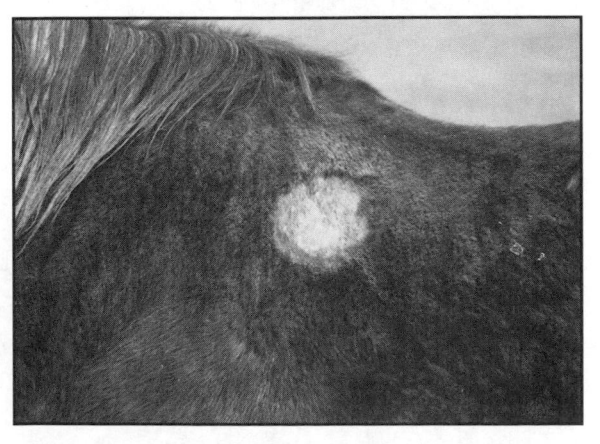

A flat sarcoid resembling a clipped patch of hair with small, grayish, wart-like bumps.

Treatment: Cryotherapy (freezing), often preceded by surgical debulking to reduce the size of the tumor, is the treatment of choice. In this process liquid nitrogen is sprayed onto the surface of the tumor, or nitrogen-cooled probes are inserted directly into the tumor. The tissue is destroyed by rapid freezing and thawing. Immune therapy, in which a commercially prepared vaccine such as EqStim is injected directly into the tumor, also has been used with success.

Surgical excision is an option when the entire tumor, including a surrounding margin of normal tissue, can be removed. This may be difficult or impossible in some locations, especially around the eye. When excision is incomplete, the tumor will recur and be most difficult to treat thereafter.

Radiofrequency hyperthermia is a technique by which radio waves are transmitted through probes inserted into the tumor, causing tissue destruction by heat. This method has been used successfully, especially on wart-like sarcoids on the extremities.

Radiation therapy with radioactive implants is the treatment of choice for recurrent sarcoids.

Warts and Papillomas. Warts in horses are skin papillomas caused by a virus.

Papillomas begin as smooth, raised, flesh-colored lumps that later become gray and horny. They tend to occur in crops on the muzzle and lips of young horses. They also are found scattered on the ears, eyelids, lower legs, and penis.

Treatment: Warts that become irritated and start to bleed can be removed by cryosurgery or chemical cautery (the application of acid). In time, the horse develops immunity to the papilloma virus, resulting in spontaneous regression usually within 3 to 6 months.

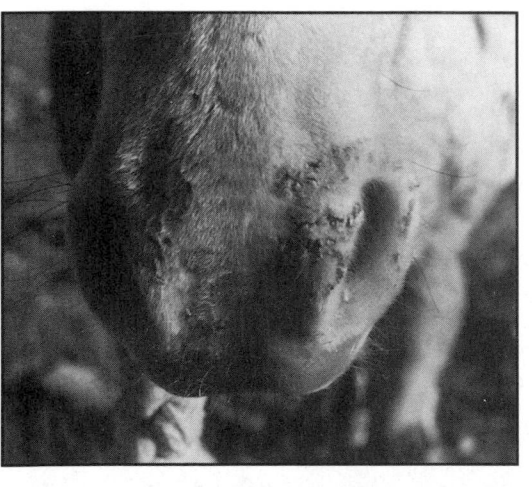

Skin papillomas on the muzzle of a young horse.

Cattle Grubs (Warbles; Hypoderma Nodules). Cattle grubs, about the size of a bumblebee, are the larvae of the warbles or heel fly. This fly, which lays its eggs on the hair of the legs of cattle, may accidentally attack horses pastured with cattle. The eggs hatch into larvae, which then penetrate the skin and make their way beneath it to settle at the withers, neck, and back. While migrating, it is possible for larvae to penetrate the horse's brain and cause parasitic myeloencephalitis. This is rare.

Usually not more than one or two grubs encyst in the horse's tissue. Nodules develop around each grub, and there is a breathing hole to the skin. The resulting lumps are painful and sore and may interfere with the use of a saddle.

Most grubs fail to develop completely and are killed by the host. They become calcified and cause a permanent nodule called a *hypoderma nodule*.

Treatment: Mature grubs that have not calcified are best treated by enlarging the breathing hole with a scalpel and removing the grub with tweezers. Ivermectin in the usual dosage kills migrating larvae. Protection is accomplished through insecticides and fly control as discussed in chapter 2, Parasites. Avoid pasturing horses close to cattle.

Lumps and Bumps. Other benign tumors can occur in the horse.

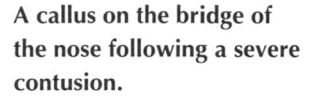

A callus on the bridge of the nose following a severe contusion.

A *lipoma* is smooth round or oblong growth made up of mature fat cells surrounded by a fibrous capsule that sets it apart from the surrounding fat. Lipomas grow slowly and may get to be several inches in diameter. Surgical removal is indicated for cosmetic reasons or to rule out cancer.

A *hematoma* is a collection of blood beneath the skin, caused by a blow or contusion. Small hematomas disappear spontaneously. Large ones may need to be opened and drained.

A tender knot at the site of injection is often present for a few days in horses that have been given their vaccinations. It seldom requires treatment. On rare occasions the injection site becomes infected and an abscess develops.

Sebaceous cysts (wens) are uncommon. A sebaceous cyst is made of a thick capsule that surrounds a lump of cheesy material called keratin. It may grow to an inch or more in size. Eventually it is likely to become infected. Most cysts should be removed.

MALIGNANT TUMORS

Squamous Cell Carcinoma. This common skin cancer tends to occur in older horses with light skin. It can be found anywhere on the body but is most common in the genital and eye regions. Skin in these areas contains less pigment and therefore absorbs more ultraviolet radiation, which damages the skin and predisposes to malignant change.

Squamous cell carcinoma begins as a wart-like growth or flat ulcer with a yellow, infected-looking base. As it grows it becomes firm, nodular, and fleshy, and bleeds easily. It metastasizes only at an advanced stage and then usually to the nearest lymph nodes.

A sore on the penis or sheath that looks like squamous cell carcinoma may be a summer sore. A skin biopsy is the best way to make the diagnosis.

Squamous cell carcinomas arising from the eyelids, the nictitating membranes, and conjunctiva are discussed in chapter 5, Eyes.

Treatment: A growth occurring in an area of light skin pigmentation should be considered a squamous cell carcinoma until proven otherwise. These tumors are best treated by wide local excision if this can be done without damaging vital structures. Radiation therapy, which involves implanting radon probes into the cancer, is useful in reducing the size of the tumor and making it easier to remove. Other successful forms of treatment include cryotherapy and radiofrequency hyperthermia, as described for the treatment of sarcoids.

Melanoma. Melanoma is the most significant tumor in horses. This skin tumor occurs almost exclusively in white and gray horses. In fact, most old gray horses, if they live long enough, will develop one or more of these tumors.

Melanomas are gray or black dome-shaped, hairless, nodular growths about an inch in size when first discovered. They are found frequently at the root of the tail and the perineal region including the anus, vulva, and male genitalia, and less frequently on the head and limbs.

Although melanomas appear benign and may remain inactive for many years, once they begin to grow they spread rapidly. Distant metastases to vital organs are common.

Treatment: All melanomas (except those in the genital and perineal areas) should be removed surgically. Cryotherapy and immune therapy can be considered for larger melanomas, and for those in which surgery is difficult. Perineal melanomas have a low metastatic rate and are removed only if they interfere with urination and defecation. There is no effective treatment for metastatic disease.

Lymphosarcoma. This is the most common internal cancer in horses. It develops in lymph nodes or in organs having lymphoid tissue, such as the liver, spleen, and lung. Lymphosarcoma affects horses of all ages. The cause is unknown.

The disease is divided somewhat arbitrarily into specific types according to the primary site of involvement; however, there is considerable overlap.

In the *intestinal form* there is loss of appetite and weight, mild colic, and the accumulation of subcutaneous fluid in the lower chest and abdomen. A mass may be detected by rectal exam.

In the *thoracic* (mediastinal) form there is lung congestion with fluid accumulation in the chest cavity (pleural effusion). Involvement of the voice box or nasal cavity may cause respiratory obstruction.

In the *cutaneous* (skin) form you may see one or more subcutaneous nodules or multiple bumps resembling hives, usually found on the bridge of the nose, perineum, neck, and elsewhere. These nodules may appear, disappear, and then reappear over an extended period.

A diagnosis of lymphoma is made by removing an enlarged lymph node or biopsying a palpable tumor. If the mass is inaccessible to biopsy, a bone marrow biopsy may be positive. Chest or abdominal fluid, if present, can be withdrawn and sent for cytology. Blood tests usually are not diagnostic.

Treatment: There is no effective treatment for lymphoma, although temporary improvement may follow the administration of corticosteroids. The cutaneous form may be present for years without causing the horse a problem.

Eyes

The eye is an organ with several parts, all of which are uniquely adapted to meet the special needs of the horse.

The large clear part of the front of the eye is the *cornea*. Surrounding it is the *sclera*, or white of the eye, a narrow rim between the eyelids much less conspicuous in the horse than it is in people. The sclera surrounds and supports the entire eyeball.

The thin pinkish membrane that covers the white of the eye is called the *conjunctiva*. It also covers the back of the eyelids. This surface layer contains many nerve endings and is highly sensitive.

The horse's upper and lower eyelids are composed of sheets of cartilage covered on the outside by skin. They don't make contact with the surface of the eye because there is a thin layer of tears between them. The horse has a third eyelid, or *nictitating membrane*, normally not conspicuous but located at the inside corner of the eye. The third eyelid has an important cleansing and lubricating function.

On the upper eyelid are four rows of stiff eyelashes that cross in a trellis fashion. The lower lid generally contains only a few straggly hairs, but there is an inherited tendency for some horses to carry stiff lashes on their lower eyelids. This produces a problem in that these hairs can scratch the surface of the eye.

Tears are secreted by the lacrimal gland, which is rather large in the horse, measuring 2 to 3 inches in diameter. Each lacrimal gland is located in a depression just beneath the supraorbital ridge, a bony arch at the upper part of the eye socket. Tears are carried to the surface of the eye by small ducts which open at the back of the upper eyelids.

Tears serve two functions: They cleanse and lubricate the surface of the eye, and they contain immune substances that help to prevent eye infections.

A normal accumulation of tears is removed by evaporation. Excess tears are pooled near the inner corner of the eyes and carried by the nasolacrimal ducts down to the nose. The openings of these ducts can be seen near the front of each nasal passage by holding open the nostrils.

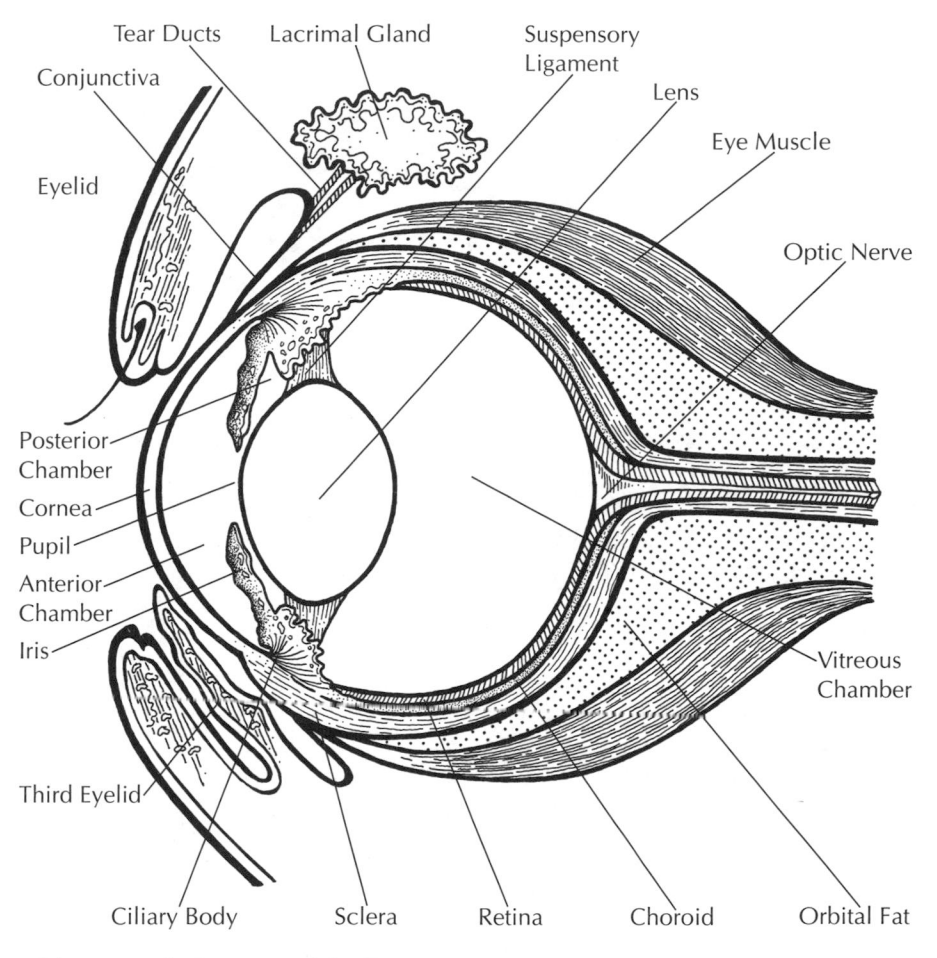

Diagrammatic Structure of the Eye

The opening at the center of the eye is the *pupil*. It is surrounded by a circular or elliptical layer of pigmented muscle called the *iris*, or diaphragm of the eye. In young horses the pupil is round. In horses over five years of age, it gradually assumes an elliptical shape with the long axis horizontal.

The color of the eyes is due to a pigment present in the iris. The usual color is deep hazel or brown with no white around the edges. (A requirement for the Appaloosa is a visible white ring of sclera around the iris.) Occasionally a horse will have blue eyes. This is often associated with white body spots. The Pinto is an example.

The *inner eye* has 3 chambers. The *anterior chamber* is found between the cornea and the iris. It is filled with a clear fluid. The small *posterior chamber* lies behind the iris and in front of the lens. The large *vitreous chamber*, containing a clear jelly, supports the lens from behind and holds the retina in place against the back of the eyeball.

A horse's lens is more spherical than ours and somewhat larger. It is contained within a thin capsule and is attached to the inner surface of the eyeball by a series of fine strands called the *suspensory ligaments*.

The suspensory ligaments attach to the *ciliary body*, a structure composed of muscle, connective tissue, and blood vessels. The ciliary body produces the clear fluid in the front part of the eye.

Light enters the eye by first passing through the cornea and anterior chamber and then through the pupil and the lens. The iris expands and contracts according to the brightness of the light. Light then travels through the vitreous chamber and is received by the retina.

The *retina* is a layer of photoreceptor cells at the back of the eye which converts light into nerve impulses that pass via the *optic nerve* to the brain.

Immediately behind the retina, and within the *choroid* (a layer of blood vessels that nourish the retina), is a special layer of cells called the *tapetum lucidum*. This layer acts like a mirror, reflecting light back onto the retina and producing a double exposure of the photoreceptor cells. It is this layer of cells which makes it seem as though a horse's eyes shine in the dark.

Special Eye Characteristics

Despite the very large size of the horse's globe, eye injuries are not common. This is due in part to a heavy framework of bone that surrounds the orbit. Furthermore, the eyeball is recessed in a cushion of fat capable of being compressed and then moving up into a bony recess called the *supraorbital fossa*. When pressure is applied to the eyeball, it moves backward into the space occupied by the fat cushion and is protected from a blow that might otherwise cause it to rupture.

The third eyelid is attached to the fat cushion at the back of the eyeball. Accordingly, when the eyeball is drawn back into the orbit, the third eyelid moves upward and covers the eye.

The eye is surrounded by a thick layer of muscle, highly developed in the horse, called the *orbicularis oculi*. As the horse shuts its eyes, this muscle closes down tightly. This makes it difficult to lift up or roll out the eyelids when inspecting the eye for an injury or foreign body.

Field of Vision

The shape of a horse's eyeball is quite different from that of most other animals. Whereas in man the eyeball is roughly spherical, a horse's eyeball is somewhat flattened from front to back. As a result the distance from the cornea to the retina is not the same in all parts of the eye. The focal length is a few millimeters longer in the upper part of the eye and a few millimeters shorter in the lower part. This produces a condition called a *ramped retina*. It has important implications, as discussed below.

The human eye focuses on objects at varying distances through the action of the ciliary muscles, which change the shape of the lens. But in horses the ciliary muscles are poorly developed. A horse cannot easily change the curvature of its lens to bring objects into focus. Instead, it accommodates by using the lower part of its retina to see objects at a distance and the upper part (with the longer focal length) to see objects close at hand.

To utilize the lower part of its retina to see objects at a distance, a horse raises its head and brings both eyes together to look straight ahead. The muscles which assist in this process also raise the ears and prick them forward. Accordingly, when a horse is looking afar it stands with its head held high and ears pricked forward.

The opposite occurs when accommodating for near vision. The horse lowers its head and relaxes its eye muscles, which allows the eyes to diverge.

A horse has a wide field of vision (approximately 350 degrees) and can see far out to each side and well behind. However, the binocular visual field is small. Both eyes can be brought together to focus on a single object only in a rather limited field in front (about 65 degrees). At other times the horse sees a different picture with each eye.

There is a blind spot, about 4 to 5 feet in front of the horse, where its vision is blocked by its long muzzle. The horse cannot see this spot unless it lowers its head. When a horse gallops up to a jump, for example, the jump will suddenly enter its blind spot. A rider must be prepared to loosen the reins and let the horse lower its head. Otherwise the horse may fail to see the jump or refuse to take it.

A number of investigators have concluded that perhaps a third of horses are myopic or nearsighted. A small percentage seem to be farsighted. Wild horses appear to be farsighted. From this it has been suggested that domestication and breeding practices may have increased the frequency of myopia in the horse.

What to Do if Your Horse Has an Eye Problem

Your horse has an eye problem if there is matter in the eye; the eye waters; the nictitating membrane is visible; or the horse blinks, squints, or gives evidence that the eye is painful.

A thorough eye examination in the horse requires veterinary assistance and restraint. However, there are certain things you can look for to determine the need to call your veterinarian.

SIGNS OF EYE AILMENT

Diseases of the eye are accompanied by a number of signs and symptoms. Pain is one of the most serious.

Painful Eye. Signs of pain include excessive tearing, squinting (closing down the eye), tenderness to touch, and avoidance of light. The nictitating membrane may protrude in response to pain. The usual causes of painful eye are injuries to the cornea (abrasion or a foreign body) and disorders affecting the inner eye, especially uveitis.

NOTE: *All painful eye conditions should receive prompt veterinary attention.* Eye injuries tend to progress more rapidly in the horse than they do in most other animals, and are more likely to be associated with loss of vision.

Red Eye. Redness of the eye is caused by an increase in the number and size of the vessels in the conjunctiva and nictitating membrane. In addition, the eyelids and conjunctiva may appear puffy and/or swollen. Conjunctivitis is the most common cause of a pink or red eye, but diseases of the cornea (ulcers, keratitis) and uveitis can also produce a red eye.

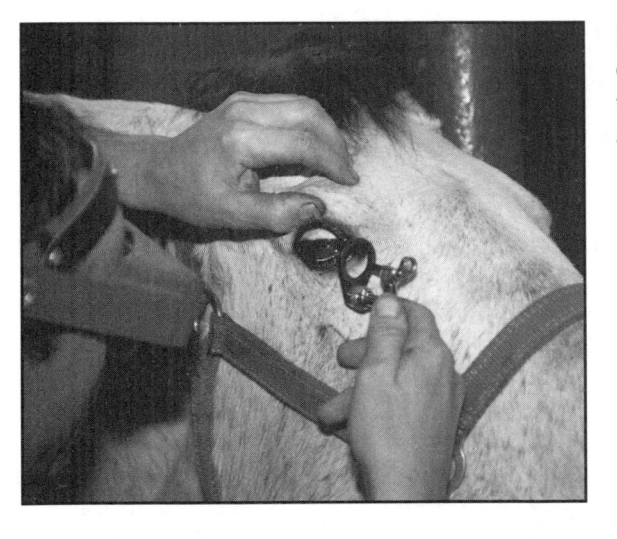

It is easier to perform a detailed eye exam after the horse has been given a regional eye block.

Eye Discharge. The type of discharge helps to define its cause. A watery or mucus-like discharge without redness and pain indicates a problem with the tear drainage system (see TEARING MECHANISM).

Any discharge accompanied by a painful eye should alert you to the possibility of cornea or inner eye involvement.

A discharge from both eyes suggests conjunctivitis or, if the horse exhibits fever and other signs of illness, a viral respiratory disease or strangles.

Cloudy Eye. Loss of clarity or transparency of the surface of the eye indicates an eyeball injury, a disease of the cornea, or an inner eye disorder such as uveitis or cataract. When the cornea is entirely opaque, the owner might think the horse has a "blind eye," but this is not necessarily correct.

Film over the Front of the Eye. This condition is discussed under EYELIDS.

Bulging or Sunken Eye. Abnormal positions of the eye are discussed under THE EYEBALL.

MEDICATING THE EYE

Disorders of the eyelids and conjunctiva can frequently be treated by the use of appropriate ointments or drops. The horse may need to be restrained (see HANDLING AND RESTRAINT). To apply ointment, run a ribbon along the border of the upper eyelid. As the horse blinks, the medication will dissolve and cover the surface of the eyeball. Eye drops, which are applied directly to the eyeball, are more difficult to apply because horses are "eye shy" and will attempt to jerk away. Draw up on the skin above the eye to widen the opening. Ointments and drops must be applied several times a day. Only use preparations specifically labeled *for ophthalmic use*. Check to be sure the preparation is current and not out of date.

Minor eye ailments should not be neglected. If you do not see improvement in 24 hours, consult your veterinarian.

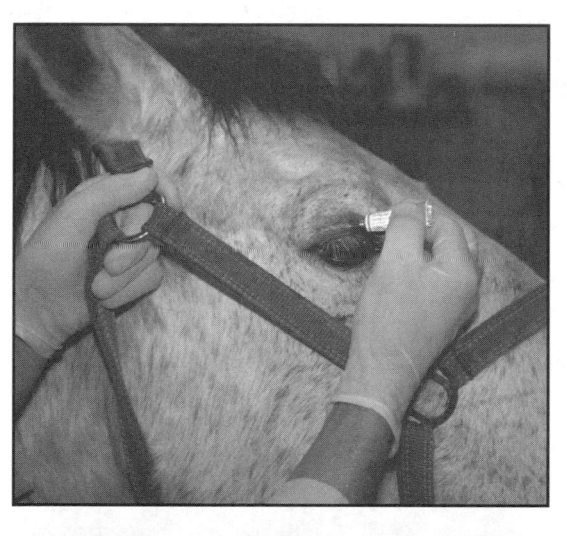

Apply ointment to the upper eyelid. The medication will dissolve and coat the eye.

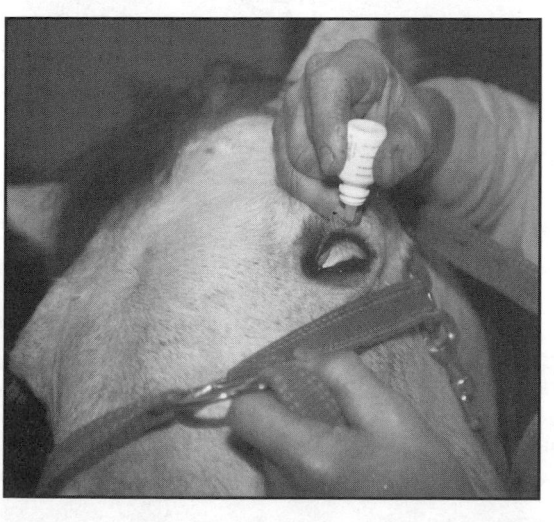

Drops are administered to the surface of the eyeball.

Serious eye disorders require intensive treatment. Your veterinarian may elect to instill the end of a sterile silastic tube into the *subpalpebral space* beneath the upper eyelid. The other end of the tube is taped to the forehead, poll, and withers. This permits eye medication to be given easily and safely and at times specified by your veterinarian. The procedure is particularly useful when the eyelids have to be sutured together to protect an injured eye. The system can be coupled to a small pump for continuous infusion.

An indwelling catheter permits ease of medicating and can be connected to a pump for continuous infusion. Illustration: Mona Frazier.

Long-acting preparations are occasionally injected beneath the conjunctiva. The procedure is often combined with the use of topical ointments or drops.

The intravenous route is the best choice for serious deep inflammations and those that pose a major threat to the eye.

A variety of medications are used in the eye. Some are used to constrict or dilate the pupil; others to treat infections.

Corticosteroid preparations should be used only under veterinary supervision. You should *not* use them to treat injuries that may involve the cornea. Prolonged administration of antibiotics and corticosteroids may lead to fungal infections.

The Eyeball

BULGING EYE (EXOPHTHALMOS)

In this condition, swelling of tissue behind the eye pushes the eyeball forward and causes it to bulge and appear more prominent. Major protrusion prevents closure of the eyelids. The nictitating membrane is often visible.

A bulging eye. Note protrusion of the third eyelid.

Blows which fracture the eye socket cause a sudden buildup of blood or fluid behind the eye. Trailer accidents, horse fights, and running into foreign objects are the most common causes of orbital trauma.

Infections that spread to the eyeball from the sinus or upper teeth also can cause the eye to bulge. This disease is called *orbital cellulitis*. It is an extremely painful condition of sudden onset, accompanied by fever, heat, redness, swelling of the eyelids, and a purulent discharge from the eye. It usually responds to high levels of intravenous antibiotics, although the infection sometimes localizes to form an abscess behind the eyeball (*retrobulbar abscess*).

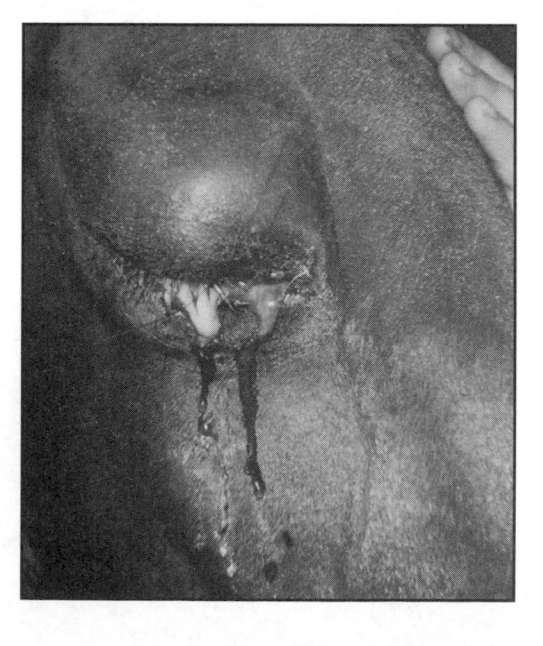

Orbital cellulitis. A bulging eye with a purulent discharge. Photo: *Equine Medicine and Surgery,* American Veterinary Publications.

Glaucoma may result in increased size of the eye and protrusion.

Tumors in the space behind the eyeball are a rare cause of protrusion. Tumors are slow-growing and relatively painless. A variety of benign and malignant growths can occur.

Treatment: All cases of exophthalmos are extremely serious and may cause loss of vision. They require immediate veterinary attention. Ultrasound examination of the eye and orbit may prove helpful in detecting space-occupying masses behind the eyeball. Drugs can be given to reduce the swelling produced by trauma. Surgery may be necessary to replace bone fragments or drain a collection of blood or pus, either behind the eye or within an infected sinus. It may be necessary to suture the eyelids over a bulging eyeball to protect it from injury and keep it from drying out.

SUNKEN EYE (ENOPHTHALMOS)

A sunken eye often develops after a severe eye injury or infection that damages the inner structures of the eye. The eye becomes smaller and sinks into its orbit. When an eye recedes, the nictitating membrane will be visible at the lower inner corner of the eye.

Damage to nerves in the neck can result in a sunken eyeball along with a small pupil, slight drooping of the upper eyelid, and appearance of the nictitating membrane (*Horner's Syndrome*). A guttural pouch infection is one cause of this syndrome.

An abnormally small eyeball is seen in newborn foals as a result of a congenital defect. It is often accompanied by cataracts.

Treatment of the sunken eye is directed as the underlying cause of the problem.

CROSS-EYED GAZE (STRABISMUS)

Strabismus is caused by paralysis of one of the eye muscles. The result is that the eyeball cannot move in a certain direction. This rare condition occurs principally in Appaloosas as a congenital defect. In nearly all cases one or both eyes are rolled in toward the nose. Because of the abnormal visual axis, these horses stumble and exhibit a nervous temperament.

Treatment: The muscles can be operated upon so that the horse will have a more normal field of vision and subsequent improvement in its behavior.

Eyelids

SEVERE SQUINTING (BLEPHAROSPASM)

Severe squinting is a tight shutting of the eye in response to the presence of an eye irritant or foreign body on the surface of the cornea. The reflex spasm of the eye muscles may cause the eyelids to roll in against the cornea. Having once rolled in, the rough margins of the lids rub against the eyeball, causing further pain and spasm.

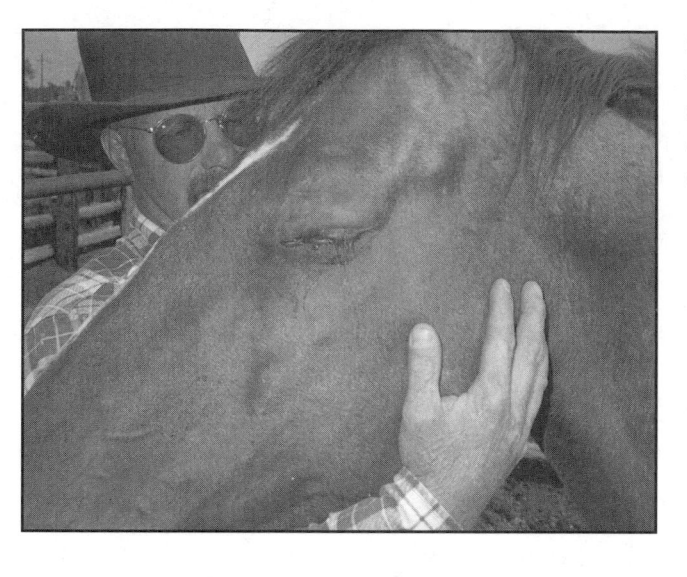

Severe squinting with a tightly shut eye, in this case caused by a painful corneal abrasion.

Painful eye disorders, such as corneal ulcers and uveitis, can also cause reflex spasm of the eye muscles.

A topical anesthetic ointment can be applied to temporarily relieve the pain and break the cycle. This works only for surface irritants. Relief is permanent when the irritant, often a foreign body, can be found and removed. Painful inner eye ailments do not respond to topical anesthetics.

FILM OVER THE EYE (THIRD EYELID)

An opaque third eyelid or nictitating membrane, not normally seen, may become visible in response to illness or injury. When the nictitating membrane is visible over the lower inner corner of the eye, it is said to be *protruding*.

Any painful eye illness causing spasm of the muscles around the eye can cause the eyeball to retract back into its socket and the third eyelid to protrude. Tearing and squinting will occur in this situation.

When both eyes are retracted the condition may be due to tetanus. However, any chronic illness or state of malnutrition that causes the horse to lose weight or become dehydrated (reducing the size of the fat pads at the back of the eyes) can be associated with the appearance of this film across the eyes.

Veterinary examination is warranted to determine the cause of the problem.

PUFFY EYELIDS

Sudden swelling of the eyelids and conjunctiva may be caused by an allergic reaction. Insect bites, inhaled irritants, and allergens in medications are the most common causes. The conjunctiva and eyelids are fluid-filled, puffy, and soft. The puffy eyes may be accompanied by hives in which the hair stands out in an erect manner in little patches over the body.

This problem is of short duration and improves when the allergic agent is removed. Simple cases are treated with Corticosporin or some other eye preparation containing a corticosteroid.

INFLAMED EYELIDS (BLEPHARITIS)

Inflammation of the eyelids tends to occur in younger horses as a result of contact with irritating plants and weeds. It can also be caused by mange mites and ringworm. Horses lacking pigment in the eyelids may suffer from *solar blepharitis*. Blepharitis can be recognized by the thick, reddened, and inflamed appearance of the eyelids. Occasionally crusts and hair loss will occur.

Blepharitis, with crusted inflamed eyelids.

Blepharitis caused by bacterial infection of the eyelids is uncommon. A purulent discharge with crusting and matter on the lids is suggestive. The discharge should be cultured.

A special type of blepharitis and conjunctivitis is caused by the larvae of the Habronema stomach worms. These larvae are deposited by stable flies as they feed around moist areas on the body, including the lid margins and corners of the eyes. Yellow, slightly raised, gritty nodules and open sores develop in the skin of the upper and lower eyelids, and occasionally on the third eyelid and surface of the conjunctiva. Penetration of the eye can lead to keratitis or corneal ulcer. Habrenoma infection is treated with topical corticosteroids and injection of steroids into the nodules. The elimination of larvae is discussed in chapter 4, Skin (see SUMMER SORES).

Treatment: Identify and treat any underlying skin disease or allergic reaction that may be contributing to the blepharitis (see chapter 4, Skin).

An antibiotic-corticosteroid eye ointment such as Neocortef or Corticosporin helps to reduce swelling and inflammation. If the condition does not respond in 24 hours, consult your veterinarian.

Bacterial blepharitis is treated with a topical antibiotic ointment such as Neosporin (no steroid). The application of warm packs may be helpful. Severe cases require the addition of oral antibiotics.

Tattooing the eyelids is the best treatment for solar blepharitis.

EYE IRRITATION FROM HAIR (TRICHIASIS)

Aberrant eyelashes on the upper or lower eyelids can rub on the cornea, producing irritation and injury. Most misdirected eyelashes are the result of an improperly healed laceration of the eyelid. The offending hair should be burned off by electrolysis or removed by surgery.

On occasion, the dock of a long-maned horse will fall in against the eye and cause a similar irritation. These hairs should be removed by clipping, or in some cases by plucking.

EYELID ROLLED INWARD (ENTROPION)

When an eyelid rolls inward, it irritates and damages the surface of the eye. Most cases are due to scarring of the eyelid after an injury or infection. Entropion can also occur as a birth defect in newborn foals.

Treatment: Surgical correction is indicated in adult horses. In newborn foals, it usually is possible to gently evert the eyelids back to their normal position. If this can be accomplished, the procedure should be repeated several times during the first few days. Once a routine of lid manipulation has been established, the condition generally corrects itself in a few weeks. Eye medication is used to prevent infection.

EYELID ROLLED OUTWARD (ECTROPION)

When the lower eyelid rolls out it exposes the eye to irritation. Most cases are due to improperly healed eyelid lacerations. Plastic surgery is necessary to tighten the lid and protect the eye.

EYELID LACERATIONS

The eyelids may be lacerated by barbed wire, nails, and other objects. Lacerations at the margin of an eyelid can affect the cosmetic appearance and function of the eye.

Treatment: Surgical repair is advisable for most eyelid injuries. The earlier the repair, the better the result. A local nerve block and intravenous sedation, or a general anesthetic, is required. Antibiotics are given for 7 days to prevent infection.

TUMORS

Benign and malignant tumors occur on the eyelids and on the nictitating membrane.

Squamous cell carcinoma is the most common malignant tumor. It usually occurs in older horses who lack pigment on their eyelids. Appaloosas appear to be at higher risk. These tumors tend to grow slowly and invade the eye. Finally they spread to lymph nodes in the neck or chest.

The treatment of squamous carcinoma involves surgical excision, radiation therapy, and freezing, often in combination.

Sarcoids are benign tumors of younger horses that occur frequently in the head and eyelid areas. They appear to be caused by a virus. These tumors either grow internally and invade the eye, or externally and break through the skin. They are difficult to treat and tend to recur after removal.

Sarcoids are treated by surgery, cryotherapy, laser destruction, and immunotherapy, often in combination. Immunotherapy involves injecting a commercial extract containing a bacterial cell wall antigen directly into the tumor.

Other tumors occasionally seen are skin papillomas, melanomas, and lymphosarcomas. Melanomas are common in old gray horses.

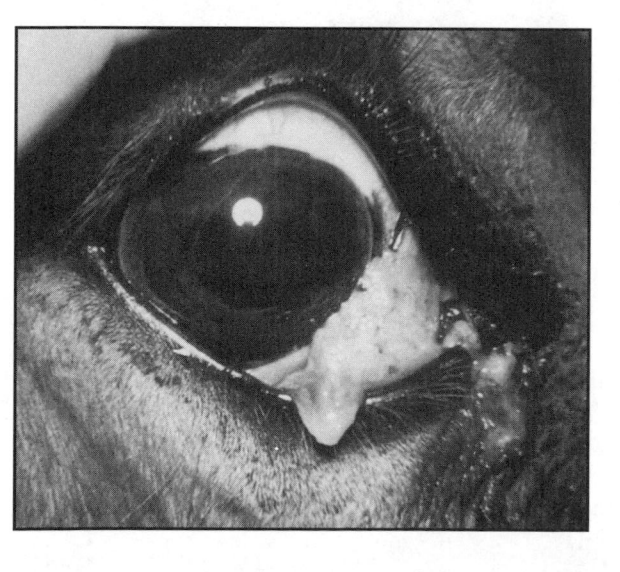

Squamous cell carcinoma of the nictitating membrane. Photo: *Equine Medicine and Surgery,* **American Veterinary Publications.**

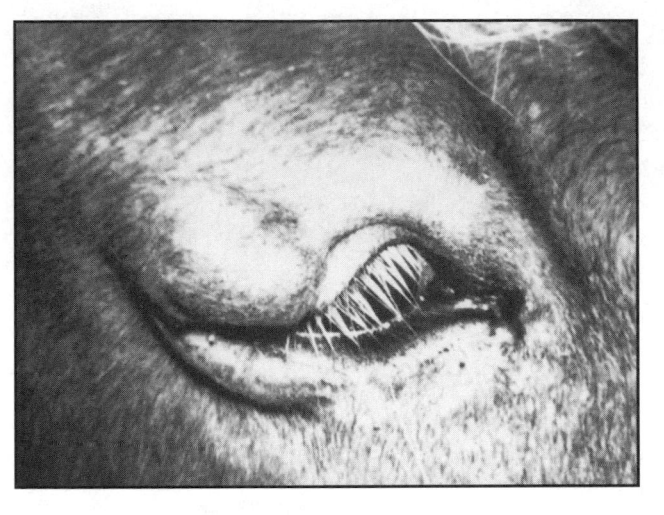

A nodular sarcoid beneath the skin of the upper eyelid. Photo: *Equine Medicine and Surgery,* American Veterinary Publications.

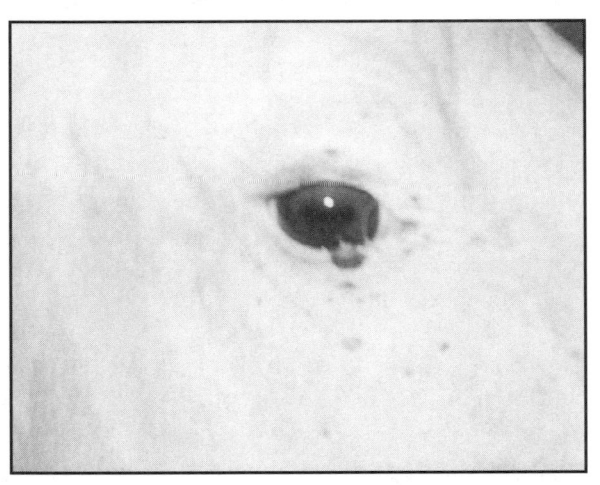

A *melanoma* arising from the lower eyelid.

All growths of the eyelids should be removed at an early stage. For more information, see TUMORS AND CANCERS in chapter 4, Skin.

Outer Eye

CONJUNCTIVITIS (RED EYE)

Conjunctivitis is an inflammation of the membrane covering the back of the eyelids and the surface of the eyeball up to the cornea. It is one of the most common eye problems of horses.

Signs of conjunctivitis are red eyes, swollen eyelids, and a sticky purulent discharge at the corners of the eyes. Conjunctivitis is not painful. When a red eye is accompanied by evidence of pain such as squinting, tenderness to touch, and protrusion of the third eyelid, suspect a serious ailment involving the cornea or inner eye and consult your veterinarian.

Types of conjunctivitis seen in horses are:

Serous Conjunctivitis. This is a mild condition in which the membrane looks reddened and somewhat swollen. The discharge is clear and watery. The usual causes are physical irritants to the eye such as dust, weeds, flies, sprays, and various allergens including those in topical medications.

Serous conjunctivitis often accompanies equine viral respiratory diseases and viral arteritis. Rarely it is caused by the parasite *Thelazia lacrimalis*. This is a small white worm, less than an inch in size, which lives in the space behind the eyelids. These worms must be removed to clear up the eye.

The larvae of Habronema also infect the conjunctiva, as discussed in the section on INFLAMED EYELIDS.

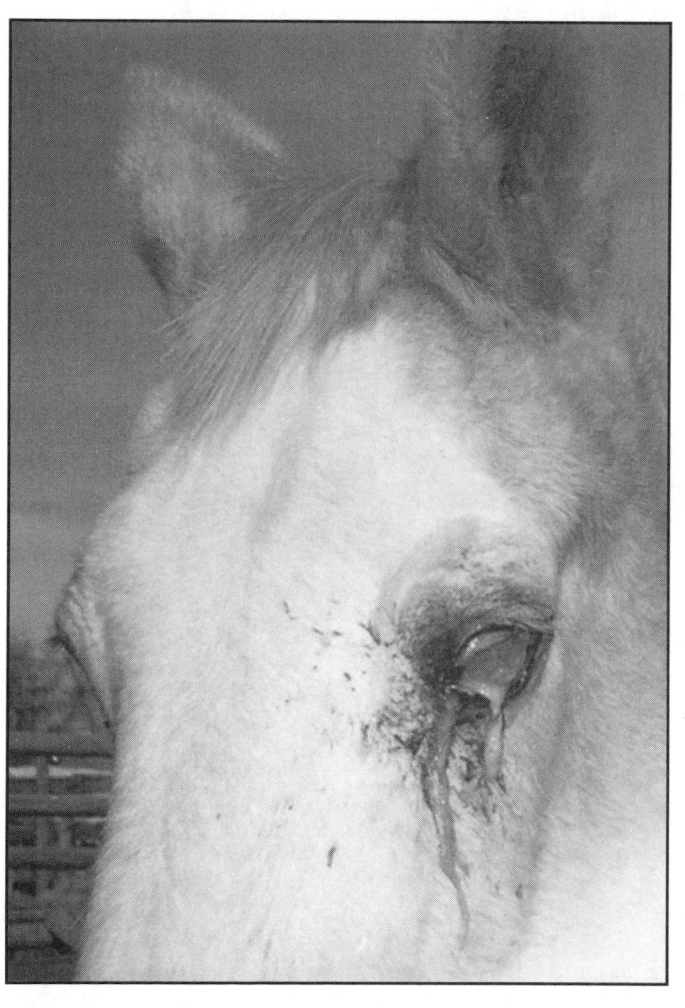

Purulent conjunctivitis. Note the sticky discharge of mucus and pus.

A contagious type of conjunctivitis occurs in foals and occasionally older horses. It appears to be transmitted by house and face flies feeding around the corners of the eyes. A herpesvirus may be the cause. The conjunctivitis generally disappears in about 2 weeks.

The larvae of Onchocerca cervicalis may invade the conjunctiva during aberrant migration. Signs are inflammation of the eye along the upper rim of the cornea. A secondary keratitis may occur. Treatment of Onchocerca is discussed in chapter 4, Skin (see Ventral Midline Dermatitis).

Purulent Conjunctivitis. This often begins as a serous conjunctivitis that later becomes secondarily infected by bacteria. The discharge is then sticky and contains pus and mucus. Strangles and equine viral arteritis may cause purulent conjunctivitis. A bacteria called Moraxella bovis has been implicated in some cases of conjunctivitis in horses. An overlooked foreign body in the conjunctiva or cornea is another cause.

Treatment of Conjunctivitis: Mild irritative forms of conjunctivitis can be treated with an antibiotic ophthalmic ointment such as Gentamicin or Neosporin. The allergic variety responds well to a corticosteroid preparation (Neocortef or Corticosporin). Apply ointments 3 to 4 times a day for 7 to 10 days. You should expect to see improvement within 24 hours. If not, consult your veterinarian. Discontinue a steroid preparation if there are any signs of painful eye, or if the eye worsens under treatment.

Bacterial conjunctivitis that does not respond to topical antibiotics indicates a resistant bacteria, a foreign body, or an injury to the cornea.

HAIR GROWING FROM THE EYE (DERMOID CYST)

A dermoid cyst is a congenital growth which occurs near the corner of the eye. It has a flat, rough surface from which a few short hairs are visible. There is considerable discomfort with tearing and squinting when the horse blinks its eye. Corneal involvement is possible; this interferes with vision.

The dermoid is not a malignant tumor but should be removed because of its irritating effects.

Foreign Bodies and Chemicals in the Eye

Foreign bodies (dust, grass seed, dirt, and specks of vegetable matter) can become trapped behind the eyelids and nictitating membrane. They can also enter and block the nasolacrimal duct system. Signs of a foreign body are tearing and watering of the eye along with blinking and squinting. The third membrane may protrude in response to pain.

Chemicals that may commonly contact the eye include insecticide sprays, detergents, alcohol, antiseptics, and petroleum products.

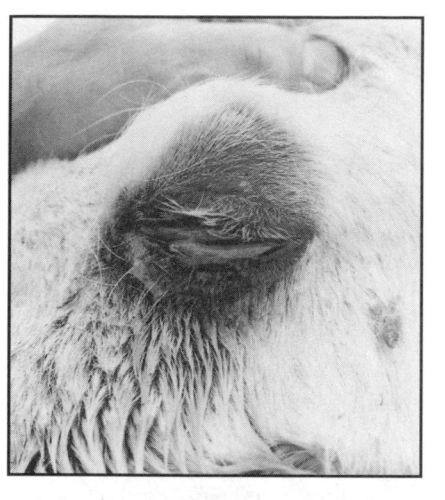

Severe tearing, squinting, and conjunctivitis caused by a foreign body behind the third eyelid.

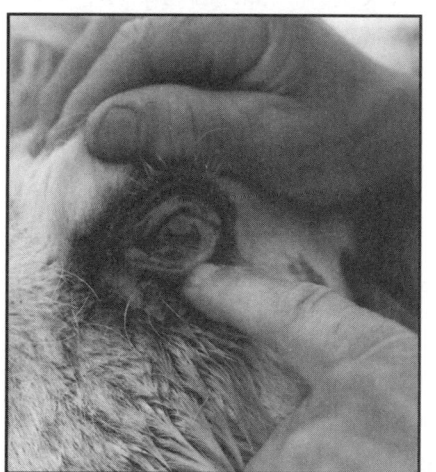

The lids are retracted to examine the eye and the recesses behind the eyelids.

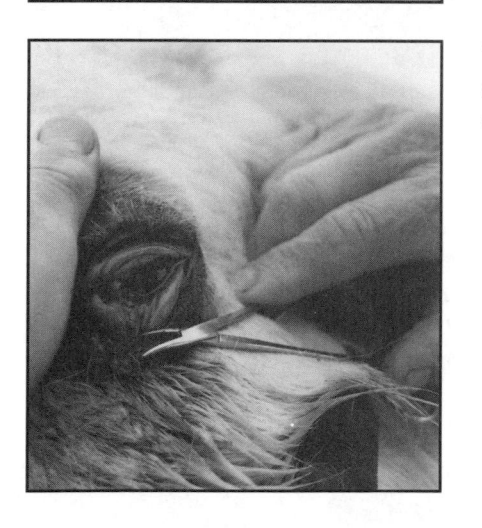

The foreign body may adhere to a cotton swab. If not, it can be removed with a hemostat.

Thorns and splinters can become imbedded in the cornea or penetrate the anterior chamber. Secondary infection by bacteria or fungi is possible.

Treatment: Suspect a foreign irritant when the horse suddenly shows signs of a painful eye. Known exposure to a chemical in the eye requires immediate and repeated flushing of the eye with a syringe and tap water. Due to the associated eye muscle spasm, it may be difficult to adequately flush the eye without a regional eye block and topical anesthetic.

All foreign bodies must be removed as soon as possible. If you are able to see a foreign body on the surface of the eye, you may be able to flush it out by squeezing and gently wiping with a wet ball of cotton. Or you can use a moist cotton-tipped applicator. The foreign body may adhere to it.

In many cases, blepharospasm and swelling of the conjunctiva will make it difficult to examine the eye. The horse will need to be sedated by your veterinarian, after which the orbicularis muscle surrounding the eye can be blocked by an injection and anesthetic drops applied to the eye. The foreign body usually can be identified and removed by blunt-nosed forceps or vigorous flushing.

Thorns and splinters that have penetrated the surface of the cornea require eye surgery and intensive after-care to prevent complications.

The Tearing Mechanism

BLOCKED TEAR DUCT (WATERY EYE)

A blockage in one of the nasolacrimal ducts should be suspected in cases of a unilateral watery or mucus-like discharge which overflows the eyelids and runs down the side of the face. This condition can be distinguished from conjunctivitis and diseases of the cornea and inner eye by absence of pain and redness. The eye discharge of equine viral respiratory disease usually is bilateral and accompanied by nasal discharge and other signs of illness.

Most obstructions in a nasolacrimal duct occur where the duct opens into the floor of the nasal cavity. Stones, foreign bodies such as grass seeds, infections, and tumors are possible causes. A rare cause of obstruction is the eyeworm *Thelazia lacrimalis*, discussed under CONJUNCTIVITIS.

A blockage high in the duct system is usually caused by an eyelid injury or a tumor of the conjunctiva or nictitating membrane.

To see if the drainage system is open, the pool of tears is stained with fluorescein dye. If the dye appears at the nostril, the tear duct is open. If not, the nasolacrimal system can be flushed via the opening in the nasal cavity using a syringe and small catheter. The flushing often removes the blockage and opens the duct.

Dacryocystitis is the name given to an infection of the nasolacrimal duct. It frequently leads to scarring and ductal obstruction. In this situation, your veterinarian may elect to pass a catheter through the duct and leave it in place until healing occurs. Antibiotics and corticosteroids are used to treat the infection and promote healing.

DRY EYE (KERATOCONJUNCTIVITIS SICCA)

Dry eye is rare in horses. It is caused by the absence of tears. Instead of the bright glistening sheen seen in the normal eye, the dry eye presents a dull, lackluster appearance. There is a thick, stringy discharge which is difficult to clear away. Later, as the eye becomes infected, a pus-like discharge may complicate the picture.

Tears are produced by the lacrimal gland and carried to the eye by small ducts that open at the back of the upper eyelids. Infection followed by atrophy of the lacrimal gland can lead to absent tear production. Scarring of the eyelids from severe blepharitis or chronic purulent conjunctivitis can interfere with tear delivery. These are the only known causes of dry eye in the horse.

Treatment: It is directed at re-establishing the flow of tears. It may be possible to do this with drugs. Chronic eye infections should be treated and eliminated.

Cornea

The clear part of the eye is covered by a protective layer of epithelial cells. Most corneal diseases begin with an injury to this protective layer.

The cornea of the horse is more sensitive to injury than that of man and most other animals. Consequently, healing is slower and ulcers on the cornea are more apt to result in complications involving the inner coats of the eye.

CORNEAL ABRASION

Corneal scratches and abrasions are caused by tail-swishing; branch scratches; and foreign bodies such as stones, awns (bristlelike fibers), and feedstuffs which injure the surface of the globe. Scratches on the cornea are extremely painful and are accompanied by excessive tearing, squinting, tenderness to touch, and avoidance of light. The third eyelid may be visible.

With a severe abrasion, the surface of the cornea immediately surrounding the injury becomes swollen, giving it a cloudy or hazy look.

Treatment: Healing of a small corneal abrasion takes place in 24 to 48 hours by a process in which the epithelium thins and slides over a small defect. Larger and deeper abrasions require careful cleansing and removing of loose cells around the edges of the abrasion to promote healing. This is done with a cotton-tip applicator after appropriate sedation and application of anesthetic drops to the eye.

A corneal abrasion will not heal if a foreign body is imbedded in the cornea or beneath one of the eyelids. In all but mild abrasions, veterinary examination is necessary to evaluate and treat the eye injury to prevent the development of corneal ulcer, keratitis, or secondary uveitis.

CORNEAL ULCERS

Corneal ulcers follow injuries to the cornea that progress instead of healing. Ulcers which do not heal promptly often become infected.

Large ulcers may be visible to the naked eye. They appear as dull spots or depressions on the surface of the cornea. Most ulcers, however, are best seen after the eye has been stained with fluorescein.

Treatment: Corneal ulcers are dangerous and must receive prompt veterinary attention. Early treatment is vital to avoid serious complications or even loss of the eye. Corneal scrapings examined under the microscope will show if the ulcer is infected.

Uncomplicated small surface ulcers respond to topical ophthalmic antibiotic ointment applied 4 times a day. Atropine ointment is used to dilate the pupil.

Deep or infected ulcers require intensive antibiotic therapy by subconjunctival injection, subpalpebral infusion, or by the intravenous route. Cultures are taken by corneal scraping and antibiotics selected according to the sensitivities. The eyelids may have to be sutured together to protect the eye and keep it from drying out. Soft contact lenses also have been used for this purpose. Eye surgery to create a flap of conjunctiva to cover the ulcer may be required in difficult cases.

White spots on the cornea may persist after healing. If these scars are large enough to interfere with vision, they can be removed by eye surgery.

Prevention: All painful eye disorders should receive immediate veterinary attention. In particular, foreign bodies should be removed as soon as possible to prevent corneal damage.

Corticosteroids, which are incorporated into many eye preparations used for treating conjunctivitis and inflamed eyelids, should not be put into an eye suspected of having a corneal injury. This may lead to rupture of the cornea.

CLOUDY EYE (KERATITIS)

Keratitis is an inflammation of the cornea. This occurs primarily because of loss of the protective surface epithelium following a corneal injury, and secondarily as a corneal response to an inner eye inflammatory process such as glaucoma or uveitis.

Keratitis is an extremely painful condition accompanied by excessive tearing, squinting, and fear of light. It should not be confused with conjunctivitis, which is characterized by a watery or mucoid discharge with little or no pain.

Superficial (surface) *keratitis* is recognized by loss of transparency of the cornea, which at first appears dull, later hazy, then cloudy and covered by a bluish-white film. A cataract also produces an opaque eye, but this is a disease of the lens and not the cornea. It is not a painful eye disorder.

Ulcerative keratitis occurs when a corneal injury becomes complicated by infection. A purulent discharge runs from the eye. Signs of painful eye are present. There are a number of bacteria which cause this type of keratitis. Cultures and appropriate antibiotics are indicated.

A *fungal keratitis* is not uncommon in the horse, especially if the eye has been treated for some time with antibiotics, corticosteroids, or both. Potentially infective fungal organisms are present in the horse's environment in abundance, particularly in straw bedding and hay.

Treatment of Keratitis: Corneal scrapings and microscopic exam will disclose active inflammatory cells, bacteria, or fungi. Treatment is like that described for corneal ulcer.

The Inner Eye

THE BLIND HORSE

All conditions which prevent light from getting into the eye will impair a horse's vision. Diseases of the cornea (keratitis) and the lens (cataract) fall into this category, as do inflammations of the deep structures of the eye (glaucoma, uveitis). Diseases that destroy the retina invariably produce blindness.

Encephalitis and brain trauma produce blindness when the optic nerve or sight center of the brain has been affected. This is not common.

Most cases of blindness will not be evident on general observation of the eye itself. Ophthalmologic tests are required to make a specific diagnosis.

TESTING FOR VISION

There are signs that a horse is not seeing as well as it should. For example, horses with severely impaired vision often appear uncertain in their movements, step high with great caution, stumble, and tread on objects they usually avoid. Blind horses tend to move their ears constantly and thus may appear unusually alert. Those with partial vision may tilt their heads in an awkward position in order to see better. Occasionally a blind horse will show few if any signs.

Bringing your hand up quickly toward the side of a horse's face to elicit a blink reflex is not a good test for eyesight; there is considerable variation even among sighted horses. In addition, a blind horse may blink if the surface of its eye detects the air current.

A better test for sight is to cover one eye with a blinder and toss cotton balls or gauze pads into the horse's field of vision to see if he follows the object with the tested eye.

An obstacle course made of barrels and hay bales can be used to test for vision. First take your horse through the course without blinders. Then cover each eye separately and repeat the experiment. Keep a loose shank. Visually handicapped horses become frightened and may injure themselves if led through the course on a tight lead.

The loss of one eye is a significant handicap, although many gentle horses with one good eye are able to perform as trail horses and engage in activities not requiring total vision, when guided by an experienced rider. Keep in mind, however, that a visually imperfect horse may "spook" at any time. Therefore, a small child would not be a suitable rider for a horse with restricted vision. In addition, for the safety of both horse and rider, horses with a visual handicap should not be used for barrel racing, track racing, running, or jumping.

After a diagnosis of total blindness has been made, it does not mean the end of the horse's life. The reality is that most horses, even those with normal eyesight, do not really see very well. They rely to a large degree on their senses of hearing and smell. These senses take over and actually become more acute. This makes it possible for them to get around, sometimes almost normally. However, a blind horse should always be confined in a familiar enclosure.

UVEITIS (MOON BLINDNESS)

The uveal tract is composed of the inner pigmented structures of the eye, which are the iris, ciliary body, and choroid. Inflammation of one or all of these structures is called *uveitis*.

Uveitis is one of the most common inner eye disorders of horses and the leading cause of blindness. It has been estimated that 10 percent of horses suffer from this condition.

The signs of *acute uveitis* are a red, painful eye with squinting and occasionally tearing. In addition, the eye often appears "cloudy" or "blind." Other important findings are a small contracted pupil, and a tender soft-feeling eyeball, noted on pressing gently over the closed eye. Signs of *chronic uveitis* are less pronounced.

The condition most likely to be confused with acute uveitis is a corneal injury. In either case, veterinary examination and treatment are essential.

Once a diagnosis of uveitis has been made, there is still the problem of determining its cause. Infected corneal injuries can spread into the anterior chamber and involve the uveal tract, producing a bacterial uveitis. Signs of surface eye infection and corneal damage will be apparent on ophthalmic examination. However, in most cases of acute uveitis, the cornea is clear, indicating a primary inflammation of the deeper structures.

By far the most common causes of primary uveitis are leptospirosis and onchocerciasis. Infrequent causes are strangles, viral arteritis, toxoplasmosis, and brucellosis.

Leptospirosis is an infectious bacterial disease caused by spirochetes. Spirochetes infect cattle, sheep, wild animals, rats, and man. They gain entrance through a break in the skin, or through the digestive tract when the horse ingests food or water contaminated by infected urine, particularly that of rodents. The acute uveitis can occur at the same time as the acute leptospirosis, but typically it appears months or years after the acute infection. Evidence suggests that the uveitis is not the result of active spirochete infection, but instead is caused by an immune hypersensitivity response in which the inner eye structures react to foreign proteins released by the destroyed spirochetes.

Onchocerciasis is caused by a small thread-like worm that lives in the connective tissues of the neck. Adult worms produce microfilariae that migrate beneath the skin to the sternal midline area, where they cause an ulcerative skin condition. During the course of migration beneath the skin, some microfilariae enter the eyelids and progress to the inner chambers of the eye. Like leptospirosis, the intra-ocular inflammation is caused by an immune-mediated response to dying microorganisms within the eye. About half of all horses with skin involvement have eye involvement. Treatment of onchocerciasis is discussed in chapter 4, Skin.

Both leptospirosis and onchocerciasis produce bouts of *equine recurrent uveitis* (ERU), also known as "moon blindness" or *periodic ophthalmia*. Since this "blindness" was observed to come and go periodically, it was thought by cowboys to be controlled by the phases of the moon.

The diagnosis of ERU is based on veterinary examination of the eye; complete blood count; blood chemistry profile; and assays for leptospirosis, brucella, and toxoplasma. Biopsies of the skin, eyelids, or conjunctiva may assist in making the diagnosis.

Treatment: It is directed at preserving vision and reducing inner eye inflammation and recurring episodes. A uveitis complicating a bacterial eye infection must be treated vigorously with topical and intravenous antibiotics and nonsteroidal anti-inflammatory drugs.

Because most cases of uveitis are immune-mediated, corticosteroids are the mainstay of treatment. For acute inflammation, they are given topically on the surface of the cornea as well as intramuscularly. The subconjunctival route may be employed. Butazolidin and other anti-inflammatory drugs are also used. Topical anti-inflammatory drops are available. In addition to the above, atropine drops or ointments are applied at frequent intervals to overcome the contracted pupil and break up adhesions between the iris and the lens. Antibiotics are not given for ERU because this disease is a hypersensitivity reaction.

Treatment is continued until the eye exam reveals a stable condition. Because ERU is often recurrent, the horse should be closely monitored for signs of reactivation, which is an indication to restart treatment.

Deworming preparations that kill larvae of onchocerciasis should not be given in the presence of active inflammation, but may be considered during a quiescent stage. Eye complications are possible. Consult your veterinarian before deworming the horse.

Because of secondary involvement of the cornea, lens, and retina, recurrent uveitis often leads to blindness.

CATARACTS

A cataract is defined as loss of the normal transparency of the lens of the eye. Any spot on the lens that is opaque, regardless of its size, is technically a cataract. To determine if a horse has a cataract, it is necessary to dilate the eyes and perform an ophthalmologic examination.

Cataracts in horses fall into one of three general categories: congenital cataracts, those secondary to eye injuries and uveitis (above), and those related to old age (senile cataracts).

Congenital cataracts may be inherited, although this is often difficult to establish. Some follow eye inflammations that occur in the uterus or shortly after birth. Congenital cataracts generally are noted at about 2 weeks of age, but may not be discovered until much later. These cataracts are not progressive and in some cases do not significantly interfere with vision.

Cataracts are common following eye wounds which perforate the front of the eye and involve the lens. These cataracts are permanent and often progressive.

Equine recurrent uveitis is the most common cause of acquired cataracts in the horse. Because of the intraocular inflammation and subsequent scarring caused by the uveitis, blindness often results even though the cataract itself is not progressive.

As horses grow older there is a normal process of aging of its eyes. New fibers, continually forming on the surface of the lens throughout life, push toward the center. The lens also loses water as it ages. These changes lead to the formation of a bluish haze seen on the lens behind the cornea in horses over 20 years of age. Usually this does not interfere with vision and does not need to be treated. This condition, called *nuclear sclerosis*, is often thought to be a cataract but actually is not. True *senile cataracts* do occur in the aging horse but are not common.

Treatment: A cataract is important only if it impairs vision. Blindness can be corrected by removing the lens (cataract extraction). While this restores vision, there is some loss of visual acuity because the lens is not present to focus light on the retina. The operation is usually reserved for individuals with cataracts in both eyes and who are otherwise good candidates for eye surgery. Horses with cataracts secondary to uveitis are not good candidates. The best candidates are young horses with congenital cataracts and otherwise normal eyes. Foals having cataract surgery should be operated upon as early as possible.

DISPLACEMENT OF THE LENS

When the ligaments holding the lens in place are disrupted, the lens can be displaced forward into the anterior chamber or back into the vitreous chamber. Trauma to the eye, a severe blow to the head, uveitis, glaucoma, and spontaneous displacement owing to poorly developed ligaments are all possible causes of lens displacement.

A displaced lens can cause glaucoma, and likewise glaucoma can cause a displaced lens. It is often difficult to tell which disease came first. Removal of the lens in early cases can maintain vision and reverse glaucoma.

A displaced lens is prone to cataract formation.

GLAUCOMA (HARD EYE)

Glaucoma is due to an increase in fluid pressure within the eyeball. It is rare in horses. When present, it usually is due to equine recurrent uveitis or displacement of the lens.

An eye suffering from glaucoma is extremely tender and has a fixed blank look, which is due to the hazy and steamy appearance of the cornea and the dilated pupil. Tearing, squinting, and protrusion of the third eyelid occur in response to pain. When you press gently on the closed eye with your finger, the affected eye feels harder than the normal one. When glaucoma has been present for some time, the increased intraocular pressure will cause the eye to bulge. Some permanent vision usually is lost before the disease is discovered.

Measurement of intraocular pressure using an instrument placed on the surface of the eye, and inspection of the interior of the eye, are needed to make a diagnosis.

Chronic glaucoma can be managed for a time with drops and medications. Removal of a displaced lens may improve the medical management and restore some vision.

RETINAL DISEASES

The retina is a thin delicate membrane that lines the back of the eye and is an extension of the optic nerve. It is supported and nourished by the choroid, a layer of vascular tissue behind the retina. In retinal disease, the eye loses some or all of its capacity to perceive light.

Common retinal diseases in horses are:

Night Blindness. This disease is due to a defect in certain photoreceptor cells called *rods*. Rods are especially sensitive to light. Their failure to perform results in impaired vision that becomes noticeable at dusk. Daylight vision is unaffected. Night blindness usually occurs in Appaloosas, but not exclusively. It appears to be inherited as a recessive trait. Affected horses often injure themselves repeatedly if left out at night, and should be stalled in a lighted barn. Horses with night blindness should not be used for breeding.

Severe vitamin A deficiency (for more than 1 year) has been reported to cause night blindness. Dietary supplementation may restore night vision.

Chorioretinitis. Inflammation of the retina and its supporting vascular layer is followed by scarring and destruction of retinal tissue. The optic nerve is often involved. The most common cause of chorioretinitis is equine recurrent uveitis (discussed above). Treatment is directed at that condition.

A type of retinal injury can occur after locoweed poisoning.

Optic nerve atrophy has been described as a sequel to severe blood loss, but for reasons unknown this occurs several months after the bleeding episode. Trauma to the eyeball, and conditions causing a bulging eye (described above), are other causes of optic nerve atrophy. Atrophy results in irreversible blindness.

Retinal Detachment. In this condition, the retina becomes partly or totally detached from the back of the eye. Most cases are the result of recurrent uveitis, in which scar tissue pulls the retina loose from its attachments. Others are related to chorioretinitis or severe head trauma. In horses, most detached retinas are of the nearly total type, resulting in sudden and complete blindness.

There is no treatment for complete retinal detachment. With partial detachment, diuretics and anti-inflammatory drugs may help to preserve some vision.

EARS

The ear is divided into three parts. The *outer ear* is composed of the ear flap (*pinna*) and ear canal (*external auditory canal*). The *middle ear* is made up of the eardrum (*tympanic membrane*) and the auditory bones or *ossicles*. The *inner ear* contains the *labyrinth, cochlea,* and *auditory nerve.*

The horse has a well developed sense of hearing. Sound, which is actually air vibrations, is collected by the ear flap and directed down the external auditory canal to the eardrum. Movements of the eardrum are transmitted via a chain of three tiny bones, the ossicles, to the bony canals of the inner ear. Within the bony labyrinth lies the cochlea, a system of fluid-filled tubes in which waves are created by movements of the ossicles. The waves are transformed into nerve impulses, which are then conducted by the auditory nerve to the hearing center of the brain.

The horse has an additional auditory mechanism for sound detection. Vibrations transmitted through the ground can be picked up by the horse's teeth as it grazes, and conveyed to the middle ear through the jawbone.

The ear flap is carried erect and supplied by muscles that allow it to rotate in all directions. A horse will usually rotate its ear toward a sound rather than turn its head. Horses also use their ears to convey such feelings as friendship, acceptance, irritation, dominance, and submission.

The skin on the outside of the pinna is covered with hair and, like the rest of the coat, is susceptible to the same skin diseases. Hair is also present on the inside of the ear flap. Here it is longer, coarser, and directed outward, thereby keeping foreign material out of the ear canal.

Ear Care

The deep recesses of the horse's ears do not need to be cleaned. However, as part of a thorough grooming, it is a good idea to wipe the inside of the pinna gently with a damp cloth to remove dirt and flakes of loose skin.

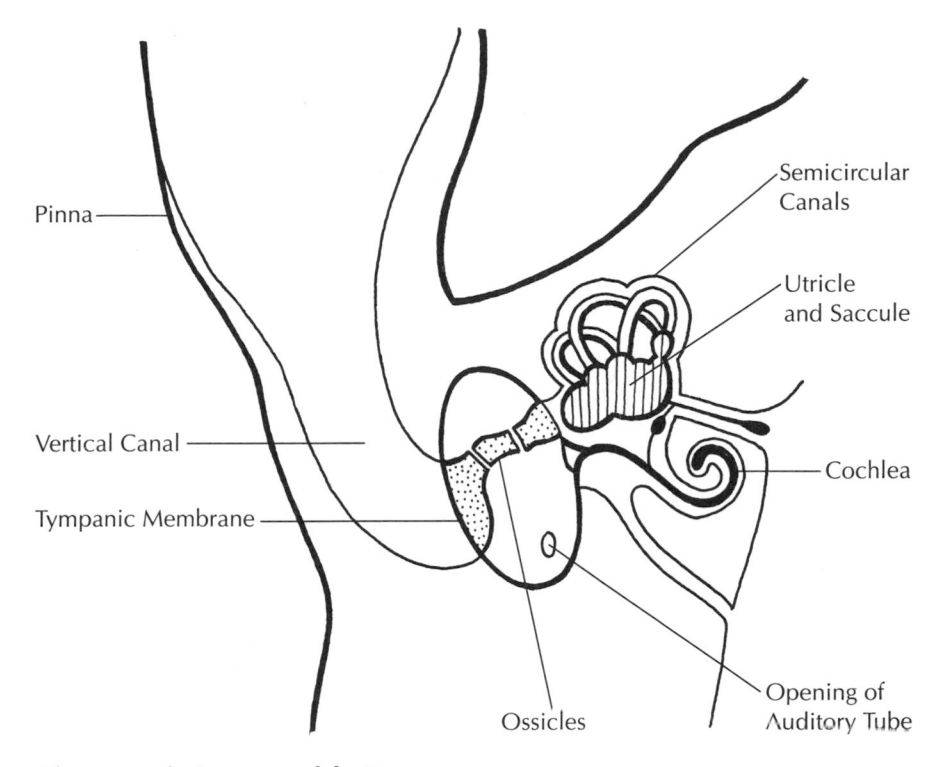

Pinna

Semicircular Canals

Utricle and Saccule

Vertical Canal

Tympanic Membrane

Cochlea

Ossicles

Opening of Auditory Tube

Diagrammatic Structure of the Ear

Do not use soaps, oils, ether, or alcohol on the inside of the ear flaps. These substances are extremely painful and can cause severe skin irritation and possibly infection.

Ear medications are applied by spray or dauber. A dauber is a ball of soft material on a stem. An irrigating syringe can also be used to apply medications.

When applying medication into the deep recesses of the ear, there is a distinct possibility of damaging the auditory canal or tympanic membrane. This procedure, when necessary, should be first demonstrated by your veterinarian.

The Ear Flap

BITES AND LACERATIONS

Bites, lacerations, and puncture wounds of the ear flap are not common. Bites often produce crush injuries with severe swelling. They are prone to infection. Puncture wounds may be complicated by abscesses.

Treatment: Large lacerations, and those involving the cartilages and margins of the ear, should receive veterinary attention. Surgical repair will help to prevent scarring and deformity.

FLY-BITE DERMATITIS

Buffalo gnats, biting midges, and Culicoides flies attack the horse's body, especially the ears. The bites of these blood-sucking insects ooze serum and form blisters and scabs which bleed easily when traumatized. A severe dermatitis with hair loss may ensue.

Treatment: Cleanse the bites and apply a topical antibiotic ointment such as Panolog. Gnats tend to feed in the early morning and evening. If possible, keep the horse inside during these hours to minimize exposure. Ear nets can be used to protect the ears. Insect control is discussed in chapter 2, Parasites.

EAR PLAQUES

Ear plaques are smooth raised areas of depigmentation seen on the inside of the ear flaps. At one time they were thought to be caused by a fungus.

Under the microscope an ear plaque looks like a type of flat wart. There is evidence to suggest that the wart-like skin changes are the result of chronic irritation caused by the bites of black flies. Although they remain for life, they do not become malignant.

TUMORS

The ear flap is conspicuously exposed to ultraviolet radiation, but is also well protected by a dense coat of hair. Accordingly, skin cancer is not as common as one might expect.

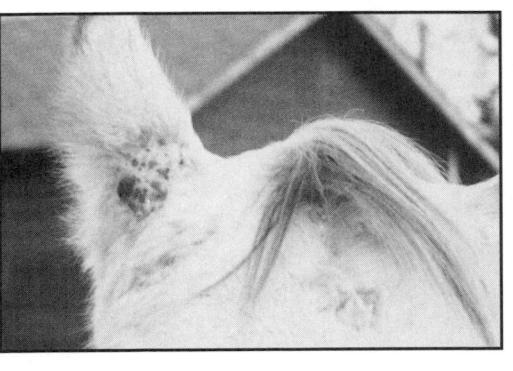

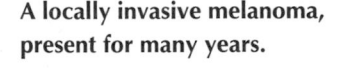
A locally invasive melanoma, present for many years.

Benign and malignant tumors can occur on the ear flap. The most common benign tumor is the sarcoid. Melanoma and squamous cell carcinoma are the most common locally invasive growths. Melanomas tend to occur in gray or white horses. They are rare in colored horses. For more information, see TUMORS AND CANCERS in chapter 4, Skin.

The Ear Canal

FOREIGN BODIES IN THE EAR

Foreign bodies in the ear canal are rare. The coarse hair on the inside of the ear flap forms a barrier and prevents foreign objects from entering the deep recesses. The most common foreign body is the ear tick, discussed below. Splinters of wood and plant material are possible. Signs are head shaking, ear twitching, a head tilt toward the affected side, and rubbing at the ear. A persistent foreign body can lead to an ear canal infection.

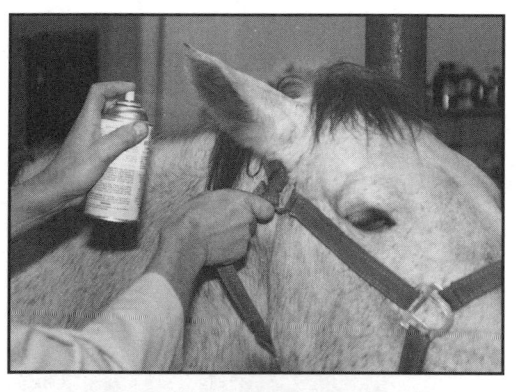

Insecticides can be applied by aerosol spray.

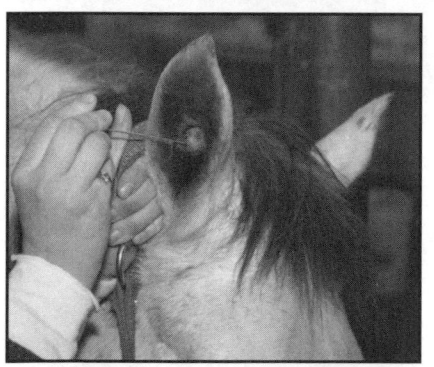

A dauber can be used to medicate the recesses of the external ear. It should not be pushed down into the ear canal.

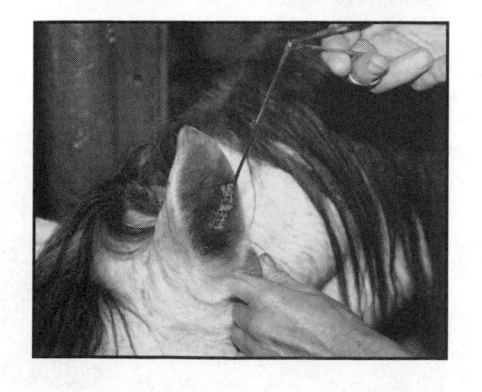

Foreign bodies in the ear canal are removed with alligator forceps.

Treatment: The ear canal is highly sensitive and horses will resist efforts to explore and probe it. Do not attempt to do this yourself. Your veterinarian will usually need to sedate the horse before examining the ear canal. Foreign bodies are removed with a long alligator forceps.

EAR TICKS

Several species of tick live in the ear canals of horses. The major ones are the spinous ear tick, the tropical horse tick, the Gulf Coast tick, and the Lone Star tick. In the case of the spinous ear tick, only the larvae and nymphs are parasitic.

Ear ticks burrow deep in the external auditory canal and are not affected by topical insecticides applied to the body.

Signs are like those of a foreign body in the ear. An infected bite can lead to an ear canal infection, a perforation of the eardrum, or meningitis.

Treatment: Ticks found on the skin of the horse's ear flap should be removed as described in chapter 2, Parasites (see TICKS).

Ear examination and treatment should be performed after the horse has been sedated. Ticks in the canals are killed by instilling an insecticide aerosol, dust, or smear (organophosphate, pyrethrin) into the deep recesses of both ears. The oral deworming agent ivermectin has been used with variable success to kill ticks.

EAR CANAL INFECTION (EXTERNAL OTITIS)

Ear canal infections are not common in horses. Signs are head shaking, tenderness to touch, holding the painful side down, redness and swelling of the ear folds, a purulent ear discharge, and a bad odor.

A tick or foreign body in the ear is the most common cause of external otitis. Ear flap infections can spread to the ear canals. Attempts to examine the ear by poking objects into it can damage the delicate tissues and precipitate an external otitis. A blockage of the ear canal produced by a tumor is a rare cause of external otitis.

Treatment: Cleaning the ear is the most important step in treating external otitis. Cleaning requires sedation and restraint. After the ear has been cleaned, an antibiotic-corticosteroid ear preparation (i.e., Panolog) should be instilled twice daily until the ear is healed. With a severe infection, the ear may need to be cleaned more than once.

Middle and Inner Ear

LABYRINTHITIS (OTITIS MEDIA AND INTERNA)

Infections of the middle and inner ear can be recognized by signs of *labyrinthitis*. The labyrinth is a complex organ composed of three semicircular canals: the utricle, saccule, and cochlea. The labyrinth is like a gyroscope. Its purpose is to synchro-nize eye movements and maintain posture, balance, and coordination.

A horse with labyrinthitis will often assume an abnormal posture with a head tilt toward the affected side. Dizziness, incoordination, and loss of balance are evi-dent in the staggering gait, turning and circling toward the affected side, and ten-dency to lean against walls and fences for support. The horse may exhibit rapid jerking movements of the eyeballs, a condition called *nystagmus*.

The motor nerve to the muscles of facial expression passes through the middle ear and may be involved in middle ear infections. Paralysis of this nerve causes drooping of the ear, lip, and upper eyelid on the affected side. In addition, the horse is unable to close its eye, which can result in the surface of the eye becoming excessively dry.

The usual cause of inflammation of the labyrinth is a bacterial infection of the middle and inner ear. The infection ascends through the auditory tube into the middle ear from an infection in the nasopharynx or guttural pouch. Blood-borne spread from a remote site is possible. Encephalitis, meningitis, and ryegrass staggers can produce signs of labyrinthitis. These signs can also occur with brain tumors, antibiotic-induced damage to the auditory nerves, antifreeze poisoning, and a con-dition called *idiopathic vestibular syndrome*. This syndrome is thought to be caused by a virus. It usually corrects itself spontaneously in 1 to 3 weeks.

The *inner ear/vestibular syndrome* is a characteristic set of signs seen following a blow to the poll with hemorrhage around the brain stem (see HEAD TRAUMA).

Treatment: The treatment of labyrinthitis is directed at the primary disease. Bacterial infections require high-dose antibiotic therapy. The horse should be con-fined to a quiet, well-bedded stall. A dry eye is treated with drops, ointments, and occasionally by temporary suture closure of the eyelids.

Horses that recover from labyrinthitis may exhibit head-bobbing or a coarse tremor of the head, evident during eating or drinking. They are prone to episodes of imbalance and may pose a hazard when used for sport or pleasure.

DEAFNESS

Deafness is seldom a problem because a horse can compensate for a hearing loss by relying on its other senses, particularly its eyesight. Accordingly, signs of deaf-ness are subtle and may go unnoticed for some time.

A horse's ability to hear can be judged by its actions and how it uses its ears. A horse who hears well rotates its ears toward the source of the sound and may turn its head to look. Lack of attentiveness and quiet ears are two indications that the horse is not hearing as well as it should. One way to test this is to approach the horse from outside its field of vision and make a sudden noise. A horse with good hearing will spook or startle. Do not stand directly behind the horse in case it has no trouble hearing and kicks out when spooked.

Loss of hearing can be caused by a middle ear infection (both sides), a head injury, a brain inflammation (encephalitis), and by certain drugs and poisons. In particular, the antibiotics gentamicin, streptomycin, neomycin, and kanamycin can damage the auditory nerves when used for a prolonged period.

ORAL CAVITY

The oral cavity is bounded on the front and sides by the lips and cheeks; above by the hard and soft palate; and below by the tongue and muscles of the floor of the mouth. Four pairs of salivary glands drain into the mouth.

The horse's mouth is remarkably well-adapted to a life of continuous grazing. The prehensile lips are designed to grasp and hold vegetation, while the sharp incisor teeth form an efficient cutting mechanism. The rough surfaces of the cheek teeth grind down plant material and separate the energy portion from the fiber.

Mouth

SIGNS OF MOUTH DISEASE

A horse with a painful mouth will exhibit alterations in eating behavior. Eating slowly is common but not often noticed. Many horses with pain on one side of the mouth will tilt their heads and chew on the other side. A horse with a tender mouth eats selectively, dropping feed that is too coarse. With a very sensitive mouth, the horse may stop eating altogether. Weight loss occurs rapidly once a horse stops eating.

A horse with a painful mouth often won't drink cold water. Some horse avoid chewing by bolting their feed. This not only interferes with feed utilization and nutrition, but also increases the frequency of choke and large colon impactions.

Quidding is the spitting out or dropping of feed after it has been shifted back and forth from one side to the other. This indicates painful chewing.

A young horse with a painful mouth may object to bridle training, throw its head, and bleed from the mouth after being ridden with a snafffle bit. Blood may be found in the feed box.

Common causes of painful mastication include:

- Lacerations of cheeks, gums, and tongue caused by sharp points on cheek teeth, or by dental caps and other teething problems.
- Infected and abscessed teeth.
- Mouth infections such as stomatitis.

Improper mastication results in feed not being properly ground and therefore not adequately digested. Accordingly, horses with chronic mouth pain lose weight and are prone to colic and constipation. This syndrome tends to occur in older horses.

Drooling is an important sign of mouth infection. The saliva is tenacious, brown-stained, and has a fetid odor.

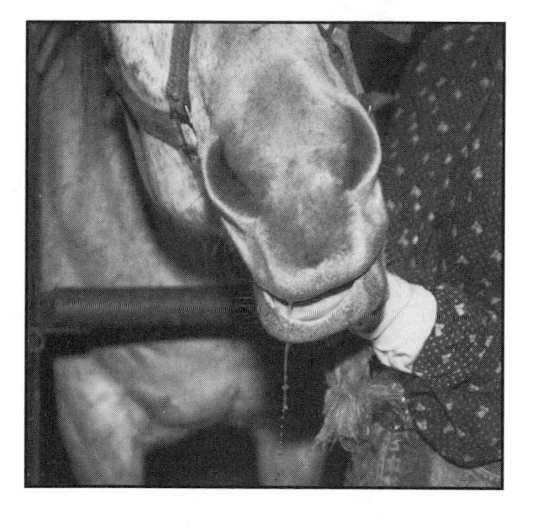

Drooling indicates mouth infection or paralysis of the swallowing mechanism.

A clear salivary discharge indicates the inability to swallow saliva, caused by a blockage or paralysis of the swallowing mechanism. Drooling of saliva also occurs with the use of tranquilizers. A peculiar type of slobbering is caused by the mycotoxin of a fungus present in contaminated legume hay. It disappears when the hay is removed from the ration.

Lolling is a condition in which the paralyzed tongue hangs limply from the mouth between the incisors or protrudes from the side of the mouth through the interdental space. Tongue paralysis occurs with botulism (forage poisoning), encephalitis, meningitis, rabies, and lead poisoning. Yellow star thistle, Russian knapweed, and ergot poisoning also cause tongue paralysis.

Swelling of the face and a discharge from one nostril indicate a maxillary sinusitis caused by the infected root of an upper molar.

HOW TO EXAMINE THE MOUTH

Most mouth disorders will become evident by careful examination of the lips, teeth, palate, throat, and soft tissues of the face and neck. Many horses can be examined with minimal restraint. However, a horse with a painful mouth may resist examination and require forceful restraint or tranquilization.

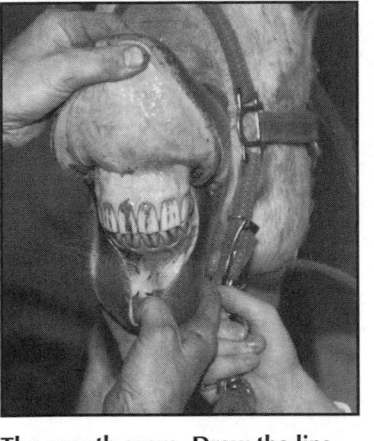

The mouth exam. Draw the lips apart to see the gums and incisors.

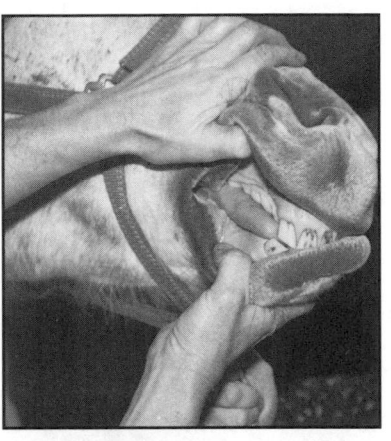

The tongue is visible in the interdental space.

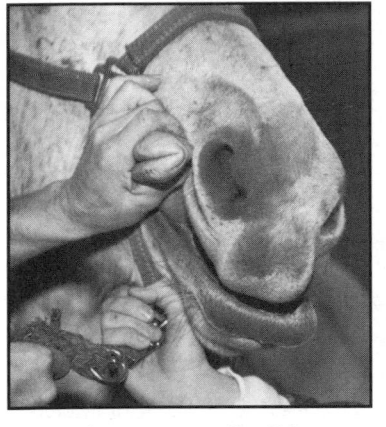

Grasp the tongue and pull it out.

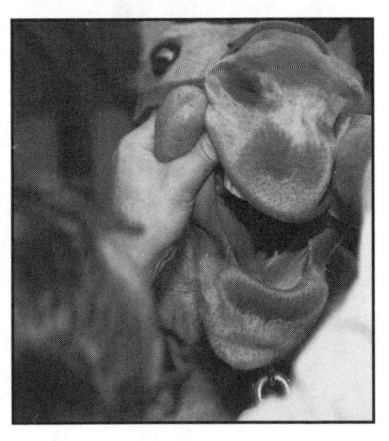

Maintain traction on the tongue. The horse will open its mouth for the examination.

To examine the lips, gums, and incisor teeth, raise the horse's upper lip with one hand while drawing down on the lower lip with the other. The bite is determined by seeing how the upper and lower incisors meet (see INCORRECT BITE).

Healthy gums are firm. In nonpigmented areas the color is pink. Pale gums are a sign of ill health (possibly parasites or anemia). Bluish-gray gums (*cyanosis*) indicate a low-oxygen tension caused by respiratory or circulatory failure. Yellow gums indicate jaundice.

The state of the circulation can be judged by how long it takes the gums to pink up after they have been pressed firmly with a finger. A pink color should return to the blanched area within 2 seconds. A delay in capillary refill of 3 seconds or longer indicates dehydration or shock.

Before opening your horse's mouth, handle him about the head until he relaxes. Then insert the fingers of one hand through the *interdental space* between the incisors and cheek teeth, grasp the tongue, and pull it out. The horse will automatically open its mouth and keep it open as long as you maintain a firm hold on the tongue. With the mouth open, you will be able to see the molars, tongue, and palate. Owing to the dropped position of the soft palate, the nasopharynx cannot be seen through the mouth. This area will need to be examined by nasopharyngeal endoscopy.

LACERATIONS OF THE MOUTH, LIPS, AND TONGUE

The soft tissues of the mouth are common sites for cuts. Most are caused by neglected teeth; others by nails, wire fences, and foreign bodies. Tongue lacerations are usually associated with rough handling and harsh bits. Minor cuts heal rapidly.

Treatment: Bleeding can be controlled by applying pressure to the cut with a clean gauze or a piece of linen. Suturing should be considered when the laceration is large, ragged, or deep; when bleeding resumes after pressure is removed; when the tongue is badly severed; and when lip lacerations involve the borders of the mouth.

A horse with a mouth injury should be switched to a soft diet such as chopped wet hay or soaked pellets. Extensive wounds may require cross-tying and feeding through a nasogastric tube.

FOREIGN BODIES IN THE MOUTH

Foreign bodies in the mouth include foxtail weeds, bearded barley, wire, wood splinters, and wood sticks or corncobs lodged in the dental arch. Small plant awns, burrs, and splinters can become imbedded on the surface of the tongue.

Suspect a foreign body if your horse shakes its head, refuses to eat, and drools. When a foreign body has been present for some time, there will be an offensive mouth odor.

Treatment: Obtain a good light source and, if the horse will cooperate, gently open the mouth. If the foreign body can be seen, it can often be removed. However, many horses with a painful mouth resist handling and require veterinary sedation.

Porcupine Quills. Owing to the natural curiosity of horses, porcupine quills can become imbedded in the face, nose, lips, oral cavity, and skin. Using a surgical hemostat or needlenose pliers, grasp each quill near the skin and draw it straight out in the long axis of the quill. If the quill breaks off, a piece will be left behind. This may result in a deep-seated infection.

Veterinary sedation is usually necessary before quills can be removed from the mouth.

SORE MOUTH (STOMATITIS)

A horse with stomatitis drools, refuses to eat, drinks more than usual, is mouth-shy, and has an offensive mouth odor. The mucous membranes are reddened, swollen, tender, and often contain blisters or a tenacious exudate.

Specific causes of stomatitis include infected teeth, retained foreign bodies, equine viral infectious diseases (e.g., rhinopneumonitis, viral arteritis), photosensitivity reactions, prolonged use of Butazolidin and antibiotics, blister beetle poisoning, and alkaloid plant toxicity.

Vesicular stomatitis is a common contagious viral disease which produces blister-like vesicles on the mucous membranes of the lips and tongue, and on the coronary bands of the feet (see chapter 3, Infectious Diseases).

Treatment: The treatment of stomatitis is directed at correcting the underlying cause of the problem, relieving mouth discomfort, and promoting appetite. Rinse the mouth twice daily with either a 3 percent hydrogen peroxide solution (diluted 1:10), a 10 percent Betadine solution (diluted 1:10), or a 1 percent potassium permanganate solution.

Anti-inflammatory drugs reduce pain and swelling. Antibiotics are indicated for secondary bacterial infection. Eliminate coarse hay. Feed soft mashes and chopped wet hay.

GROWTHS IN THE MOUTH

Solid tumors in the mouth are not common. Growths that ulcerate and exude a bad odor are usually malignant. Squamous cell carcinoma is the most common. It is found most often on the lips, tongue, and gums. Other malignant tumors include fibrosarcoma, melanoma, and lymphoma.

Benign tumors that occur in and around the mouth include sarcoids, papillomas, lampas, cysts, neoplasms of dental origin, and granulomas.

Papillomas (warts) are caused by a virus that is different from the one that causes warts on the skin. Warts in the mouth disappear spontaneously.

Lampas is a swelling of the hard palate just in back of the front teeth. It occurs during eruption of the permanent incisors at 3 to 4 years of age. This hard mass forms a ridge that can project below the level of the upper teeth and cause eating problems. Scraping the palate with a sharp knife and rubbing salt into the wound have traditionally been employed but are not effective. Feed a soft moist ration to encourage eating. The lampas will disappear spontaneously.

A *ranula* (honey cyst) is a smooth, rounded salivary gland swelling in the floor of the mouth on one side of the tongue. When a needle is put into the cyst, a thick, mucus-like, honey-colored material is removed. This often brings about cure without surgery.

Teeth

The horse has 24 deciduous (temporary) teeth and 40 to 42 adult (permanent) teeth. The variation in permanent teeth is due to the presence of 2 canine teeth in the male that are not present in the female.

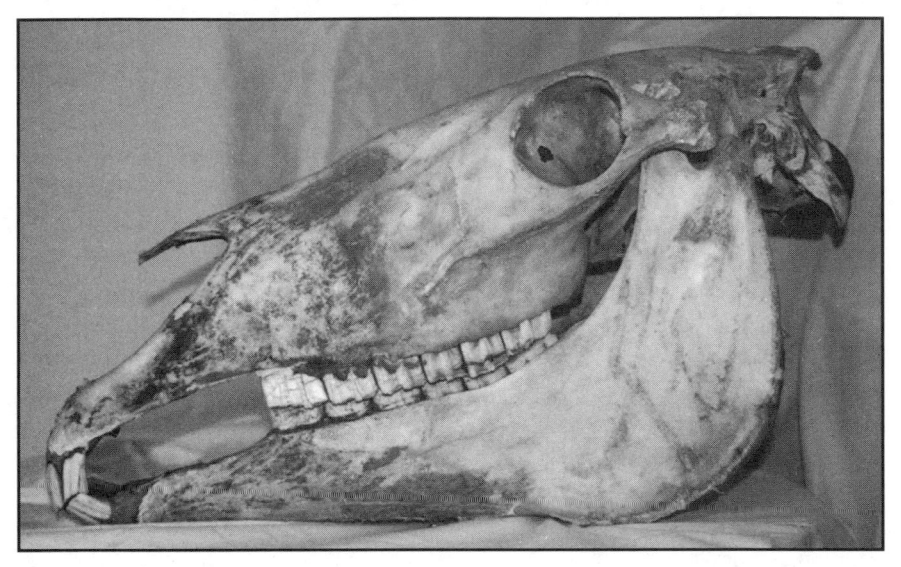

The skull of the horse.

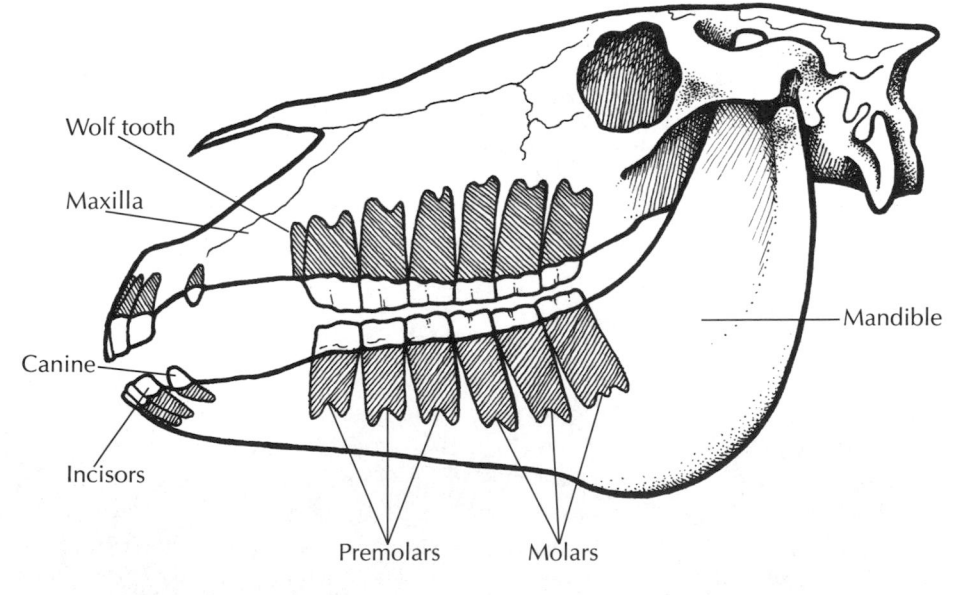

Wolf tooth

Maxilla

Mandible

Canine

Incisors

Premolars   Molars

The position of the teeth.

The top surface or crown of the tooth is covered by a hard substance called *enamel*. Enamel is impervious to bacteria and acids. Beneath the enamel is a softer material called *dentin*, and beneath the dentin is the *pulp* or center of the tooth. The pulp contains blood vessels and nerves. If the tooth cracks, exposing the pulp, the tooth decays rapidly and the root dies.

The root of each tooth is covered by a substance called *cementum* that serves to attach the tooth to the *periodontal membrane* and thus to the bony socket. It is at this very juncture with the periodontal membrane that the tooth is weakest and most susceptible to periodontal diseases and tooth decay.

The teeth of horses are very long, with up to 4 inches imbedded in the bone of the upper and lower jaws. Unlike humans, the teeth of horses erupt continually throughout life at about the same rate as they are worn down by grinding. As each tooth emerges, it is ground and shaped by the opposing tooth.

The nature of the horse's diet and intestinal tract requires that all food must be thoroughly ground between the premolars and molars before being swallowed. If the food is not adequately ground, the horse will not receive the full nutritional benefit of the feed and will lose weight and condition.

In the process of grinding, the horse moves its jaws both up and down and from side to side. In a normal horse, the dental arcades of the upper and lower jaws are

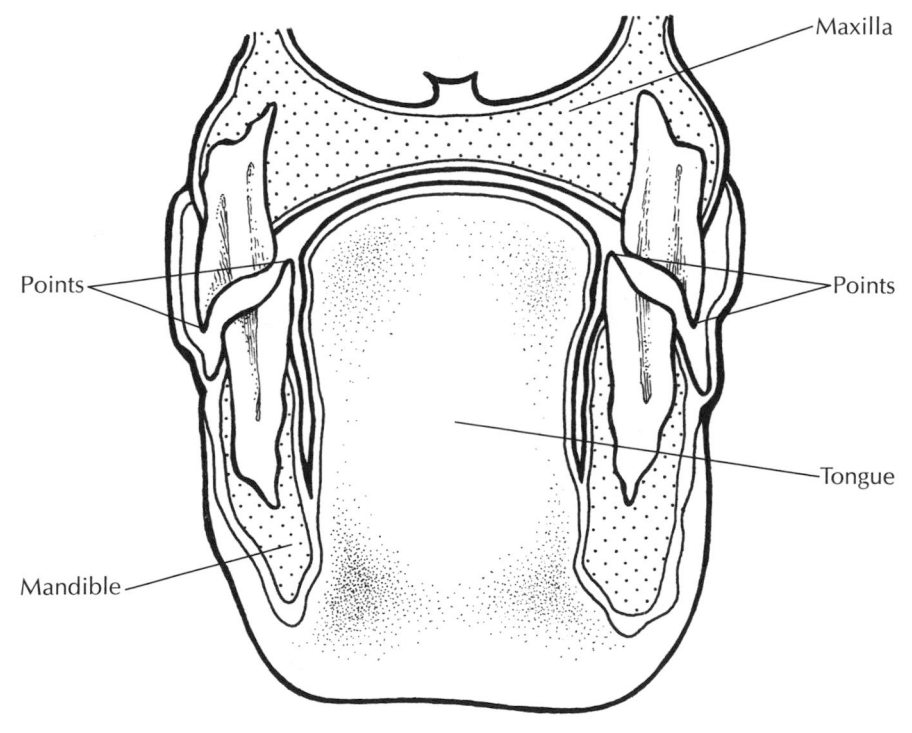

The overlapping upper jaw allows sharp enamel points to develop where the cheek teeth fail to make contact.

not in exact alignment as they are in people. The arcade of the upper jaw overlaps that of the lower jaw by about 30 degrees. The effect of the circular grinding action plus the overlapping arcades creates uneven tooth wear—specifically, the development of points on the tongue side of the lower jaw and the cheek side of the upper jaw. You can test this by sliding your fingers along the spaces between the cheeks and the teeth, feeling for points on the premolars and molars on the upper arcade. When these points are prominent, they interfere with proper mastication and become a source of irritation to the soft tissues of the mouth.

These enamel edges should be removed regularly by filing with a long-handled rasp. This filing, called *floating the teeth*, should be limited to the points of the teeth and should not involve the enamel on the grinding surfaces. For more information, see CARE OF YOUR HORSE'S TEETH.

DECIDUOUS (MILK) TEETH

Foals begin to acquire teeth within the first week of life. The first to appear are the central incisors (I). There are 2 in the upper jaw and 2 in the lower jaw.

All three premolars (P) erupt at 2 weeks. The second incisors appear at 1 month and the third incisors at 6 to 9 months. At about 9 months of age, a foal has a complete set of deciduous (temporary) teeth which total 24 in number.

(Keep in mind when counting teeth that there are 2 jaws and that each jaw has 2 dental arches, therefore a total of 4 dental arches.)

The dental formula for the foal is:

Deciduous (Milk) Teeth: 2 (I 3/3 P 3/3) = 24

PERMANENT TEETH

The first adult molars (M) appear at 9 to 12 months of age. The second molars erupt at 2 years.

At 2¹/₂ years, the central deciduous incisors are expelled and replaced by adult incisors (I). Also at this time, the first and second premolars (PM) make their appearance. The first premolars, commonly called "wolf" teeth, are found only in the upper jaw, or when present in the lower jaw are quite small and needle-like.

At 3 years, the third premolars erupt (although the lower ones may erupt 6 months earlier).

At 3¹/₂ years, the lateral incisors and the third molars are present.

At 4¹/₂ years, the horse attains its corner incisors, fourth premolars, and canine teeth. The canine (C) teeth are usually present in the male but absent or rudimentary in the mare.

By 5 years, the horse has a complete set of permanent teeth, 40 to 42 in number.

The dental formula for the adult horse is:

Permanent (Adult) Teeth: 2 (I 3/3 C I/I PM 3/3 or 4/3 M 3/3) = 40 or 42.

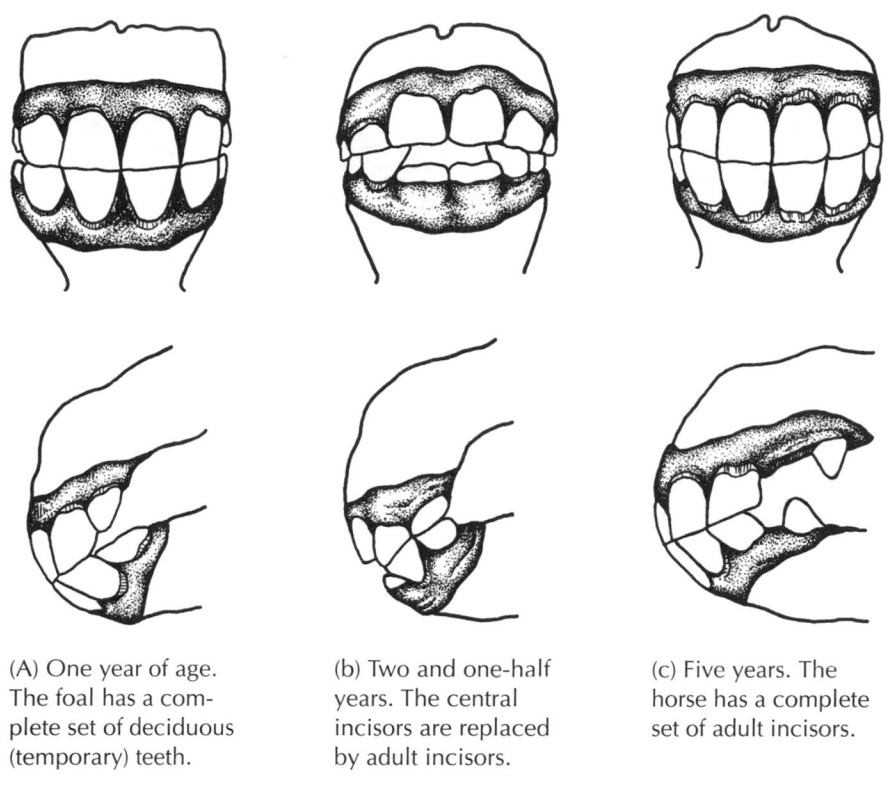

(A) One year of age. The foal has a complete set of deciduous (temporary) teeth.

(b) Two and one-half years. The central incisors are replaced by adult incisors.

(c) Five years. The horse has a complete set of adult incisors.

Aging a young horse, showing the characteristic appearance of the incisors up to 5 years of age.

The age at which the permanent teeth erupt is quite constant. In summary: The central incisors erupt at $2^1/_2$ years, the lateral incisors at $3^1/_2$ years, and the corner incisors at $4^1/_2$ years. This sequence, along with the presence or absence of canine teeth in the male, can be used to accurately determine the age of a horse up to 5 years.

AGING A HORSE BY ITS TEETH

Aging a horse up to 5 years can be easily accomplished as described above.

With experience, it is possible to determine a horse's age up to 30 years with reasonable accuracy by using the order of disappearance of the dental cups, changes in shape of the teeth and jaws, and the appearance of Galvayne's groove.

Dental cups are hollow depressions present in new teeth. As a consequence of bacterial action on retained food particles, these hollows become dark-stained. As the edges of the cups wear down through age and usage, the depressions become more shallow and eventually cease to exist as cups, leaving a white surface with a small dark central pit called a *dental star*.

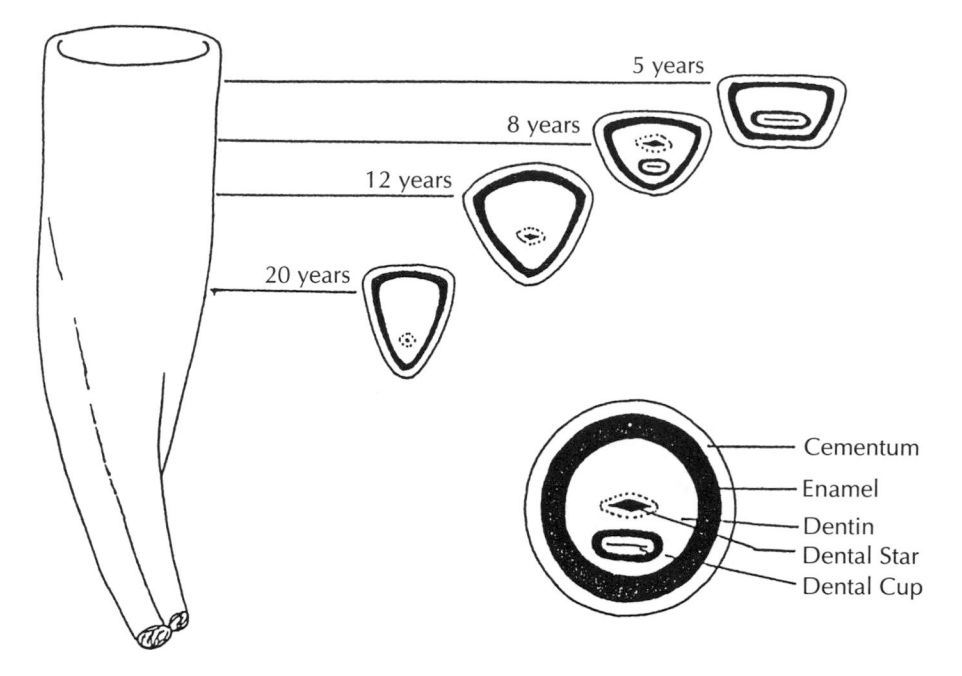

Aging the horse from 6 to 21 years. As the incisor teeth wear with age, the dental cups gradually disappear and the tooth becomes triangular.

The order of disappearance of cups from the incisor teeth can be used to age the horse. Note that the lower incisors wear about 3 years in advance of the upper incisors. Disappearance of the cups and changes in the shape of the teeth follow a generally predictable pattern as follows:

- 6 years: The lower central incisors are worn smooth, with shallow cups in the laterals.
- 7 years: The lower lateral incisors are also worn smooth. The central and lateral incisors begin to assume a more oval appearance.
- 8 years: The lower corner incisors are now worn smooth.
- 9 years: The upper central incisors are smooth, with shallow cups in the laterals.
- 10 years: The upper lateral incisors are now worn smooth. The central and lateral incisors appear somewhat oval.
- 11 years: The cups of all incisors are worn smooth. Thus, at 11 years of age, a horse is referred to as "smooth-mouthed" (referring to the incisors).
- 15 years: The lower incisors appear shorter than the uppers when viewed from the front. All teeth show a distinct dark round dental star in their centers.
- 21 years: The angle of the jaw is distinctly oblique. There is a considerable space between the teeth. The lower incisors may be worn nearly to the gums.

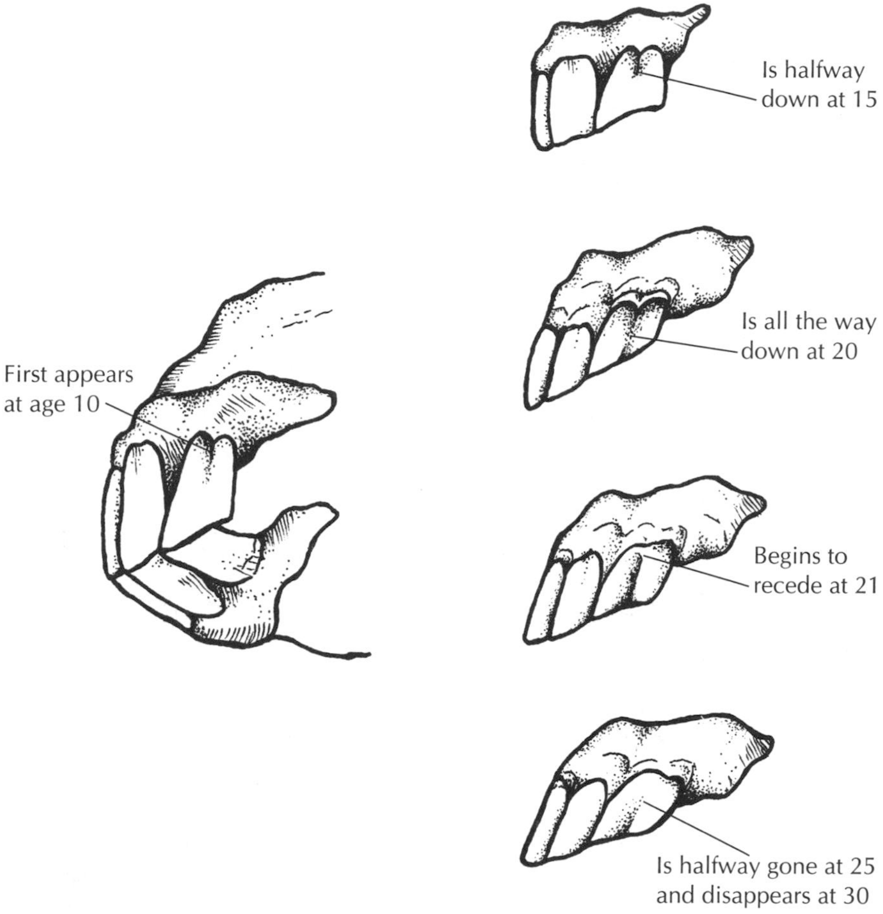

Is halfway
down at 15

Is all the way
down at 20

First appears
at age 10

Begins to
recede at 21

Is halfway gone at 25
and disappears at 30

Galvayne's groove can be used to estimate the age of older horses.

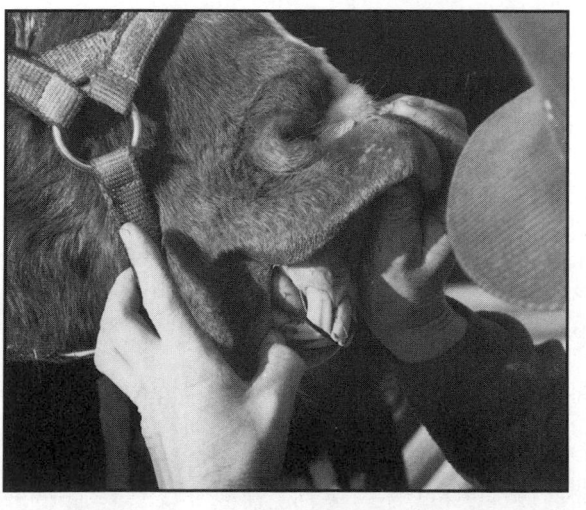

This horse was said to be 12 years old, but judging by Galvayne's groove, the horse is closer to 22.

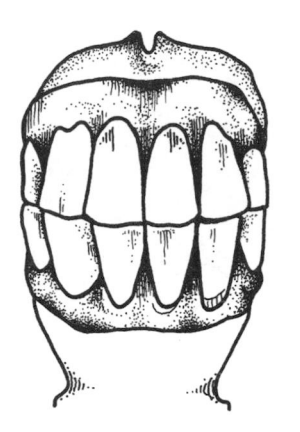

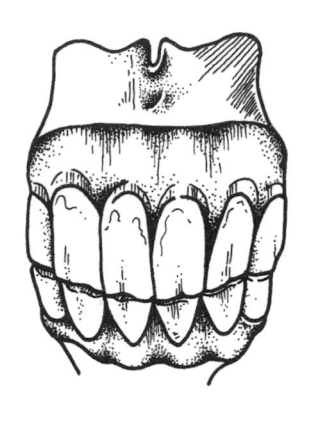

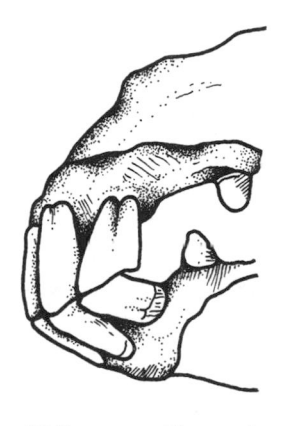

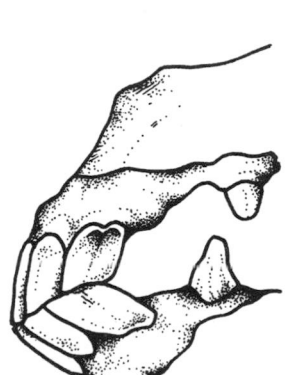

(A) Ten years. The angle of the jaw and teeth is more oblique. The corner incisors are in full contact.

(B) Twenty years. The angulation of the jaw is distinctly oblique. All teeth show wear, especially the lower incisors.

As the horse grows older, age-related changes occur in the shape of the teeth and jaws.

Galvayne's groove can be used to judge the age of horses from 10 to 30 years. This is a groove on the surface of the tooth that appears in the two upper corner incisors only. It first appears at the gum line at 10 years of age. It works its way downward year by year as the tooth continues to wear. At 15 years, the line is halfway down the tooth. At 20 years, the line is present for the full length of the tooth. It then begins to recede from the gum, so that at 25 years it is present in the lower half of the tooth, and is completely gone by age 30.

As the horse advances in age, there is a tendency for the incisors to protrude outward against the lips, creating a jaw and tooth angle that is more oblique. In addition, the gums shrink or recede. The teeth thus appear longer and more exposed when viewed from the side, giving rise to the expression "getting long in the tooth."

TEETHING PROBLEMS

Dental Caps. Dental caps are deciduous cheek teeth that remain attached to adult teeth after the permanent teeth have erupted. These caps are extremely sharp and may cut the cheek or tongue and interfere with eating. Occasionally, a cap becomes partially detached and rotates out to the side, where it damages the cheek and deforms the face.

Dental caps, whether loose or not, should be removed once the adult teeth have emerged from the gum line.

Retained Incisors. Retained deciduous incisors are similar to dental caps except that the retained incisors are in front of the permanent incisors. In most cases, the deciduous teeth are loose and can be removed with dental forceps. If this is not possible, dental extraction should be performed to insure a correct bite.

Supernumerary Teeth. This uncommon problem is due to splitting of the tooth bud. One or two extra teeth (incisors or cheek teeth) may be found in addition to the usual number. Rarely, a horse will have an entire extra row. Dental crowding can result in tooth overgrowth and gaps between teeth that result in gum infection and tooth decay.

Extra teeth that injure the gums or cheeks can be filed or trimmed with dental cutters. Occasionally, extraction will be necessary. A loose supernumerary tooth should be removed.

Absent Teeth. Absent teeth are fairly common. They are caused by failure of normal development of a tooth bud. Unless there is interference with occlusion, no treatment is necessary.

Impacted Teeth. Impacted teeth tend to occur in horses with a foreshortened upper or lower jaw (see INCORRECT BITE). In these conditions, there is insufficient room for the teeth to erupt normally. Some cases are associated with deciduous caps.

If an impacted tooth becomes infected, it should be extracted. Treatment of retained deciduous caps will prevent some cases.

Wolf Teeth. Wolf teeth, present in the upper and rarely in the lower jaw, are vestiges of the first premolars. Delay in eruption and displacement of the wolf teeth by the second premolars can cause abnormal alignment, with sharp points lacerating the lining of the cheeks and tongue. When this occurs the teeth should be extracted.

Wolf teeth may interfere with the bit and be a handicap in training. Prophylactic removal is often requested. Extraction is best done at 18 to 24 months of age.

Canine Teeth. Canine teeth (tusks) are large curved teeth found in the interdental spaces of male horses. In females, they are either missing or very small. Canine teeth are often confused with wolf teeth.

When the canine teeth erupt between 4 to 5 years of age, the gum surrounding the tooth can become sensitive to the bit. A canine tooth that fails to erupt may cause a cyst in the gum. Canine teeth that become long and sharp and interfere with the bridle should be rasped down.

Hooks. Long sharp points may develop on the first upper cheek teeth (second premolars) and the last lower cheek teeth (third molars). There may be a pre-existing malocclusion problem. The long sharp points can lacerate the gums and cause painful mastication. Small hooks can be filed. Large hooks are best cut off. The horse should be adequately restrained or tranquilized.

Split or Broken Teeth. A fractured tooth may be of no consequence, especially when the fracture does not extend below the gum line. However, if the tooth is broken very short or is lost, the opposing tooth will not be ground down and may become long enough to interfere with chewing. The unopposed tooth should be rasped every 4 months to prevent mouth injury. If damage to the broken or split tooth involves the root or surrounding bone, the tooth should be removed.

INCORRECT BITE (MALOCCLUSION)

The bite is determined by seeing how the upper and lower incisors meet. If a horse has a normal bite, the incisor teeth will meet edge to edge. An incorrect bite is one in which the teeth meet in some other alignment. This results in *malocclusion*.

Most congenital malocclusion problems are apparent during the first weeks of life. Severe malocclusion may lead to mouth infections, poor mastication, and impaired digestion of feed. This can compromise growth and development.

Parrot Mouth (Overshot Jaw). This is the most common malocclusion deformity. In this deformity the lower jaw is shorter than the upper jaw. In consequence, the upper incisors overhang the lowers. Because the upper incisors are unopposed, they grow long like rabbit teeth.

When the malocclusion is restricted to the front teeth, it may not cause a problem. However, if the molar teeth are also out of alignment, they will not be ground down and will form hooks and sharp points. These hooks may interfere with the bit and cause considerable pain.

If detected at an early age (less than 6 months), parrot mouth can be treated by applying wire tension bands from the upper incisors to the first maxillary cheek teeth in an attempt to slow the rate of growth of the upper jaw. These braces can be left in place for several months, but should be carefully monitored for adverse effects.

Sow Mouth (Undershot Jaw). This is the reverse of the above. The maxilla is shorter than the mandible, and the lower incisors project beyond the uppers like a bulldog's. It is less common than parrot mouth.

Shear Mouth. In normal horses the upper arcade is always wider than the lower arcade. In the shear mouth this discrepancy is further exaggerated. This produces long, extremely sharp shearing edges on the cheek teeth. A acquired type of shear mouth occurs in old horses who develop age-related changes involving the shape of the mandible.

Treatment of Incorrect Bite: It involves periodically cutting and rasping the teeth to remove points and hooks in an attempt to maintain a normal alignment. Placing the horse on hard feed such as pellets or unprocessed grain may prolong the need for repeated treatments. Because malocclusions have an hereditary basis, horses with such deformities should not be used for breeding.

ABNORMAL WEAR PATTERNS

Abnormal chewing patterns can develop or be present in certain individuals and thus produce abnormalities of tooth wear. It has also been suggested that in susceptible horses some teeth may be innately softer than others, and therefore do not offer equal resistance to wear and usage.

Irrespective of cause, these abnormalities tend to be progressive and get worse with time. In the early stages, they cause subtle performance problems such as interfering with the bit. As the problem worsens, the horse develops painful chewing, quidding, and weight loss. Whole grain may be seen in the feces.

Wave Mouth. This usually occurs in ponies and older horses and results in an abnormal undulating surface of the teeth when viewed from the side. The crests and troughs created by the wave pattern allow some teeth to become too long; others opposing them are ground down to the gum line. Mouth and gum injuries are common.

Mild cases may respond to floating the teeth at frequent intervals. In more severe cases an attempt should be made to even the arcades by rasping, chiseling, and cutting the molars.

Step Mouth. In this disorder there is a sudden change in height of adjacent premolars and molars. In many cases a lost tooth leaves a space that permits an opposing tooth to grow out without meeting resistance. A retained dental cap is another cause of step mouth.

Step mouth is a serious problem, since affected horses have great difficulty chewing and digesting their feed. Treatment involves cutting elongated molars and rasping the teeth at 6-month intervals.

Smooth Mouth. This is caused by equal wear of both the enamel and dentin and produces an absolutely smooth surface on the cheek teeth instead of the rough grinding surface.

In young horses it is caused by a defect in the composition and structure of the teeth. Some cases are related to improper and excessive floating in which the surfaces instead of the edges of the teeth are filed smooth. In very old horses it occurs when the teeth are worn down to the roots.

When the cheek teeth are worn absolutely smooth, the horse cannot grind its feed. These horses experience significant weight loss and suffer from digestive ailments such as colic, constipation, and malabsorption. Whole grain may be observed in the feces.

Young horses who have been improperly floated may, with time, reestablish normal grinding surfaces. In all other cases there is no effective treatment except to feed soft mashes, chopped wet hay, or *processed* grain.

INFECTED TEETH (PERIODONTAL DISEASE)

Horses do not develop cavities in the crowns of their teeth as people do. Instead, dental infection begins near the root of the tooth at the junction of the cementum and periodontal membrane. Periodontal disease predominantly affects the cheek teeth, rarely the incisors.

Periodontal infection is preceded by gum infection (*gingivitis*). In gingivitis the edges of the reddened, swollen gums begin to depart from the sides of the teeth. This creates small pockets and crevices along the edges of the gums. These pockets trap food, become infected, and attack the weak part of the tooth where it joins the periodontal membrane. From here, the infection invades the pulp cavity and leads to root abscesses and bone infection (*alveolar periostitis*). The bone recedes, the roots are exposed, and the stability of the tooth is lost.

Factors which predispose to gingivitis and periodontal disease include malocclusion and abnormal wear patterns, gum lacerations arising from hooks and sharp points on the molars, impacted teeth, split teeth, and fractures of the jaw. In older horses periodontal disease occurs as an age-related phenomenon associated with receding gums, changes in the contour of the jaw, and excessive wear of the teeth.

Abscessed Teeth. A special situation involves the cheek teeth in the upper jaw (maxilla). The roots of these teeth (primarily the first molars) are imbedded in the maxillary sinuses. Consequently, root infections of these teeth commonly cause bacterial sinusitis and a purulent, foul-smelling, persistent discharge through one nostril (see SINUSITIS). A fistula between the oral and nasal cavities may develop. It is necessary to extract the tooth to cure the infection.

The frequency of periodontal disease underscores the importance of regular dental examinations, with early treatment of existing problems to prevent tooth decay and its debilitating consequences.

CARE OF YOUR HORSE'S TEETH

Because your horse's teeth are growing and continually changing, it is important to check the teeth at regular intervals. Veterinary examination is warranted every 6 months until age 2 years, and then annually.

Dental examinations are particularly important in young horses, as their teeth wear faster and form extremely sharp enamel ridges. In addition, young horses may have problems associated with caps or impacted adult teeth. Most dental problems can be treated successfully if they are identified before tooth disease and abnormal wear patterns become fixed and irreversible.

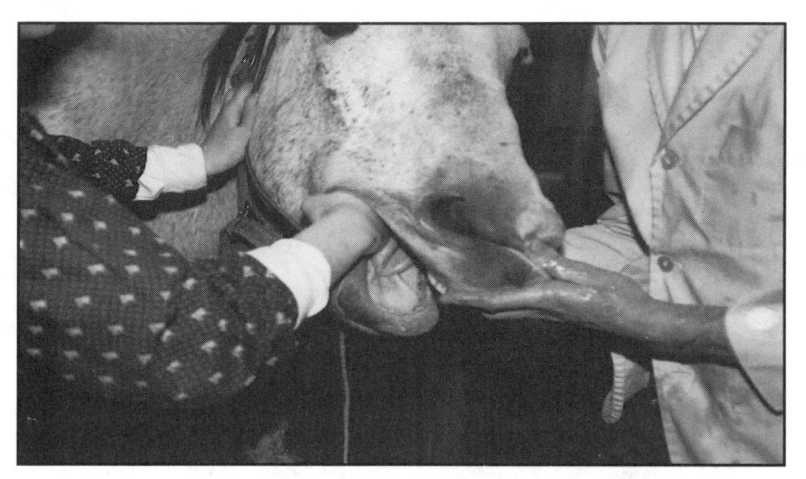

Feeling for points on the molars. The teeth should be checked every
6 months, especially in young horses.

Loose teeth occur in most older horses. However, they do not always fall out by
themselves because the teeth are so tightly packed together. The teeth of older
horses should be examined every 3 months, and any loose teeth should be removed
to relieve discomfort and prevent dental infection.

Floating the Teeth. Floating (rasping) the teeth is performed on a routine basis
once a year after a horse reaches 18 months of age. The purpose of floating is to
control the sharp edges and points present on the cheek side of the upper premolars
and molars, and the tongue side of the lower premolars and molars. The filing is
done with a long-handled rasp. The procedure is not painful to the horse and can
generally be performed with minimal restraint.

These points should be removed with a few strokes of the rasp. Rasping over the
grinding surfaces is harmful and should be avoided.

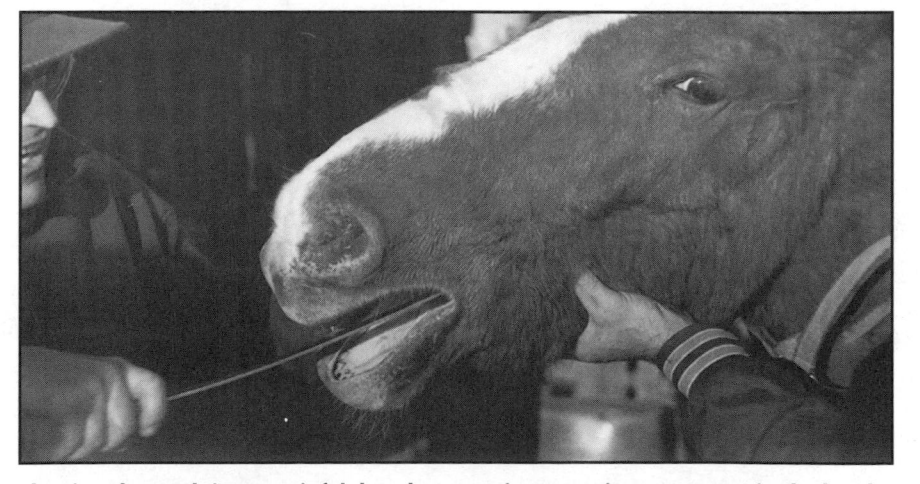

Floating the teeth is not painful, but does require an assistant to restrain the head.

Floating is also used to correct minor abnormalities of wear, such as lowering a tooth that has grown too long.

Other Dental Procedures. Most dental procedures are not painful because the sensitive structures of the teeth are located deep in the tooth. Accordingly, teeth can be filed, chiseled, or cut to a desired length using special dental instruments under physical restraint or IV sedation. Tranquilization is indicated for some cutting procedures that produce a loud report when the tooth is snapped, since this could startle the horse.

Dental caps and wolf teeth can be removed with bone cutters, dental elevators, and forceps. Badly infected teeth or split teeth can at times be removed with long-handled forceps.

When the root is imbedded in bone or the extraction is otherwise complicated, the dental procedure is usually done under a general anesthetic. Some teeth, owing to location, cannot be extracted through the mouth and will need to be repulsed.

Repulsion involves making an incision in the skin overlying the tooth, drilling a hole in the bone to the base of the tooth, and then driving the tooth out from its socket with a dental punch and a mallet. This procedure is not without some danger of damaging an adjacent tooth or fracturing the jaw.

Following dental extraction, withhold hay for several days and provide mash or ground feed. After a tooth has been extracted, the opposite tooth will become too long and a step mouth may develop. The horse will require maintenance dentistry to float the tooth every 6 months.

DIGESTIVE SYSTEM

The digestive tract is a complex system that begins at the mouth and ends at the anus. The lips, teeth, tongue, mouth, and pharynx have been discussed in preceding chapters. The remaining organs are the esophagus, stomach, small intestine, large intestine, pancreas, and liver.

Horses do not have a gallbladder to store bile as people do. Bile from the liver empties continuously into the small intestine.

The *esophagus* is a muscular tube 5 feet long that conveys food down to the stomach. This is accomplished by rhythmic contractions. The lower esophagus enters the stomach at an acute angle, which creates a one-way valve. When the stomach is distended by food or air, pressure closes the valve and prevents reflux into the esophagus. One disadvantage of this mechanism is that the valve also prevents the horse from vomiting to relieve an excessive buildup of gas and fluid. This increases the risk of gastric rupture.

The *stomach* is relatively small when compared to the size of the remaining gastrointestinal tract. While capable of holding 4 gallons, it functions most efficiently when filled to about 2 gallons. Food in the stomach is acted upon by acid and pepsin. Pepsin breaks down proteins into chains of amino acids.

Digestion begins as soon as food enters the stomach. When the stomach is about $^2/_3$ full, the sphincter at the outlet of the stomach relaxes and food passes in a steady stream into the duodenum and small intestine. The rapid ingestion of a large volume of feed causes the stomach to empty rapidly, before the entire meal can be acted upon by the stomach's enzymes. This interferes with total digestion and the proper utilization of feed. This is the main reason why frequent small feedings are preferable to single large feedings.

The *small intestine* is 70 feet long and has a capacity of about 12 gallons. It is located principally in the upper part of the left abdomen and is subdivided into three parts: the duodenum, jejunum, and ileum.

As food enters the upper small intestine, it is acted upon by bile salts from the liver, digestive enzymes from the pancreas, and a mixture of digestive enzymes secreted by the small intestine itself.

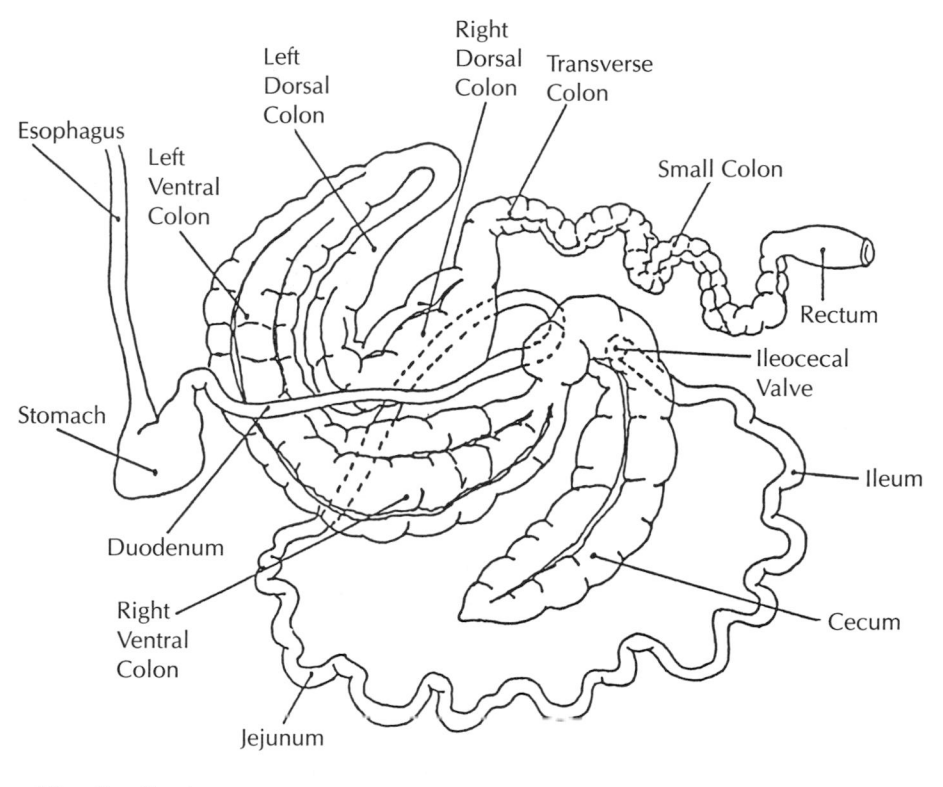

Digestive Tract

The end products of digestion are then absorbed and enter the bloodstream. Blood from the intestines flows to the liver. The liver has numerous functions connected with metabolism. Here the materials of the horse's meal are converted into stored energy.

The remains of the ingested meal, consisting mostly of liquid fiber and roughage, move on into the large intestine.

The *large intestine* is approximately 25 feet long. It is subdivided into the cecum, large colon, small colon, and rectum.

The *cecum* is 4 feet long and holds 7 to 10 gallons. It is a comma-shaped structure located in the right flank, with its tip extending toward the diaphragm. The contents of the cecum are liquid. The cecum contains a large population of bacteria which feed on the digestive chyme and by the process of fermentation break down cellulose. These bacteria also produce essential fat-soluble vitamins that are absorbed by the horse.

The *large colon* is 10 to 12 feet long and holds about 20 gallons of semi-liquid stool. It is subdivided into the right lower (ventral) colon, left lower (ventral) colon, left upper (dorsal) colon, right upper (dorsal) colon, and the transverse colon. All these names refer to the positions of these segments within the peritoneal cavity.

The *small colon* is also 10 to 12 feet in length. In the small colon water is absorbed, and the products of digestion are formed into soft round balls.

The *rectum* is about 1 foot in length. It stores the waste material until it is passed out of the horse's body during the act of defecation.

The *pancreas* is located behind the small intestine. In addition to producing digestive enzymes, the pancreas manufactures insulin. A deficiency of insulin produces *diabetes mellitus*. This disease is extremely rare in horses.

Esophagus

A horse with esophageal disease regurgitates, swallows painfully, and drools.

Regurgitation is the expulsion of swallowed food. It is due to a blockage or malfunction of the swallowing mechanism. When the blockage is *low* in the esophagus, regurgitation occurs about 10 seconds after swallowing.

When the blockage is located at the back of the throat or in the *upper* esophagus, attempts to eat or drink produce coughing, gagging, and the regurgitation of food and saliva through the nose. Food may be inhaled into the lungs, causing an aspiration pneumonia. With a complete blockage, the horse cannot swallow water.

Choke is the most common cause of *sudden* blockage of the esophagus. A slow progressive obstruction is characteristic of tumors and strictures. *Cleft palate* is the diagnosis in a newborn foal who regurgitates milk.

Central nervous system poisons including botulism, moldy corn poisoning, yellow-star thistle, and Russian knapweed. These produce paralysis of the tongue and throat, accompanied by regurgitation and drooling.

Dysphagia is painful swallowing. It occurs under the same circumstances as regurgitation. A horse with dysphagia is noticeably anxious and makes repeated efforts to swallow by lowering its head and stretching its neck. Drooling occurs if the horse cannot swallow. In *strangles*, swollen lymph nodes at the back of the throat are a cause of painful and difficult swallowing.

When an esophageal blockage or paralysis has been present for more than 24 hours, a horse becomes apathetic, stops trying to swallow, and stands quietly beside its water trough.

CHOKE (ESOPHAGEAL IMPACTION AND FOREIGN BODIES)

Choke occurs when the esophagus is blocked by a large bolus of food or foreign material. Choke does not cause respiratory obstruction because the impaction in the esophagus is below the level of the larynx.

Choke tends to occur in horses who eat rapidly and swallow their feed without chewing it thoroughly. It also occurs in horses who have incomplete mastication due to defective teeth, and bolt their food to avoid painful chewing. These are usually older horses. Some horses choke because their esophagus is narrowed by inflammation, ulceration, or stricture.

A horse who chokes displays sudden anxious behavior, backs away from the feed, salivates profusely, coughs, arches its neck and attempts to swallow repeatedly, and regurgitates food and saliva through the nostrils.

Horses can choke on dry grain, which swells when it becomes wet. Sugar beets, a large carrot, pelleted rabbit food, and even hay can cause choke. Pelleted feeds, however, do not seem to cause choke any more frequently than sweet feeds.

Other foreign bodies that can lodge in the esophagus and cause choke include wood and wood shavings, corncobs, milk teeth, fruit pits, and large pills given by bolus.

Treatment: Remove all feed and notify your veterinarian. The impaction will often soften up with saliva and pass into the stomach in a matter of hours. If not, it may do so after the horse has been tranquilized and given an analgesic that helps to relax the esophagus.

With a persistent impaction, your veterinarian may elect to pass a nasogastric tube and gently flush the upper esophagus with warm water to loosen up the wad. This may need to be repeated several times over the next 24 to 48 hours. If this is not successful, the impaction can usually be dislodged under general anesthesia, using a scope to extract the wad or push it down into the stomach. Rarely it will be necessary to open the esophagus and remove the impaction manually. Following such surgery, there is a high incidence of esophageal stricture.

After an episode of choke, the esophagus should be examined with a fiberoptic gastroscope to determine if esophageal ulceration has developed, and also to be sure that the horse does not have a stricture or tumor of the esophagus. As an alternative, the esophagus can be x-rayed using barium paste given orally.

If the esophagus is normal after the impaction has been relieved, it is safe to resume feedings. However, if there is ulceration or an inflammatory stricture, withhold feed (but not water) for 3 to 4 days and then begin feeding a soft diet as described below for stricture. A soft diet can be made by taking pelleted feed and adding warm water to make a mash.

Prevention: Correct any dental problems which may be the cause of improper mastication (see CARE OF YOUR HORSE'S TEETH). Feeding small amounts more often, and moistening the grain, can help prevent recurrent episodes of choke. If the horse persists in gobbling its food, spread the feed over a large surface, mix it with chopped hay, or add several large smooth stones to the feed box and scatter the pellets so the horse will have to sort them out one at a time.

Prevent your horse from chewing wood and plastics. Remove wood shavings from stall floors when necessary.

STRICTURES

A *stricture* is a narrowing of the esophagus caused by inflammatory swelling or scarring. Nearly all strictures are caused by choke.

Following an episode of choke, a temporary stricture caused by swelling of the mucosal layer of the esophagus may lead to repeated episodes for several weeks. These episodes can occur even though you are soaking the horse's feed.

The depth of the mucosal injury determines the depth of the stricture and whether it will respond to treatment. Ulcerating injuries that involve all layers of the esophagus tend to heal with permanent scar tissue.

A squamous cell cancer of the esophagus is a rare cause of stricture.

Treatment: The stricture should be investigated by barium x-rays and/or esophageal endoscopy. A mucosal swelling may subside with the continuation of a soft diet for several weeks. A soft diet consists of a slurry of pelleted feed with added roughage such as chopped alfalfa. Pelleted rations that are nutritionally complete and require no additional roughage are also available. Tight fibrous strictures that remain fixed often respond to the passage of esophageal dilators that stretch out the scar. Multiple (and occasionally periodic) stretchings are required to maintain an adequate passage. In these instances, a soft diet will be necessary for life. Tight, fixed strictures that do not respond to dilatation require esophageal surgery. The surgery is difficult and usually requires referral to a veterinary center.

Many strictures can be prevented by prompt treatment of the initial episode of choke.

Stomach

Diseases of the stomach are associated with indigestion, unthriftiness, and severe colicky pain in the abdomen.

Because of the powerful sphincter mechanism at the gastroesophageal junction, both vomiting and the reflux of stomach fluid into the esophagus are uncommon in horses. In most cases, what is thought to be vomiting is actually choke, with unswallowed food rather than stomach contents coming out through the nostrils.

GASTRIC DILATATION (IMPACTION)

Acute gastric dilatation is a sudden painful distention of the stomach due to a buildup of fluid and gas. The most common cause is grain engorgement. The grain forms a packed mass in the stomach that ferments and draws fluid into itself. Allowing a horse to drink cold water after a heavy workout is another cause of gastric dilatation.

A secondary type of gastric distension occurs when there is an obstruction in the small intestine or colon. The fecal contents of the bowel back up into the stomach. The stomach progressively enlarges because the horse cannot vomit to relieve the pressure.

The pain of acute gastric dilatation is severe and violent. It is accompanied by rolling, sweating, kicking at the abdomen, and turning the head as if to bite at the abdomen. Heart and respiratory rates are increased. The horse may exhibit shock, with cold extremities. Rectal exam will show displacement of the spleen. Peritoneal tap (as described for colic) will show whether the stomach has ruptured. The finding of ingested food in the peritoneal fluid confirms this diagnosis and is an ominous sign.

Chronic gastric dilatation is a milder condition found in horses who crib and swallow large amounts of air. It also occurs in horses who suffer from gastritis, and those who eat and drink immediately after strenuous exercise.

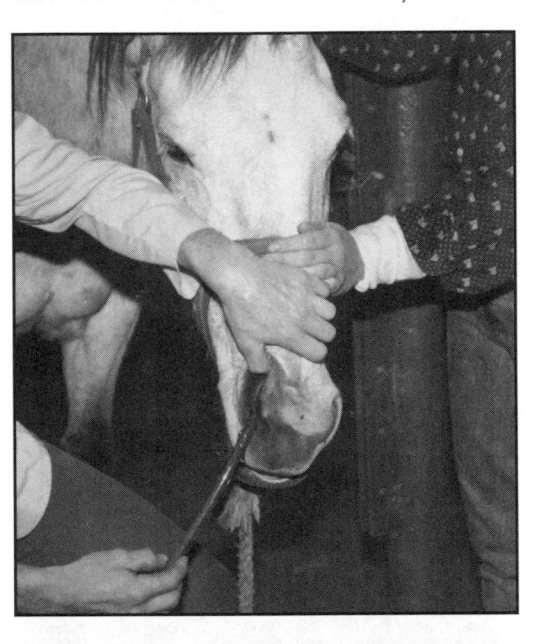

Passing a nasogastric tube is an important initial step in diagnosing acute gastric dilatation, bowel obstruction, and moderate to severe colic.

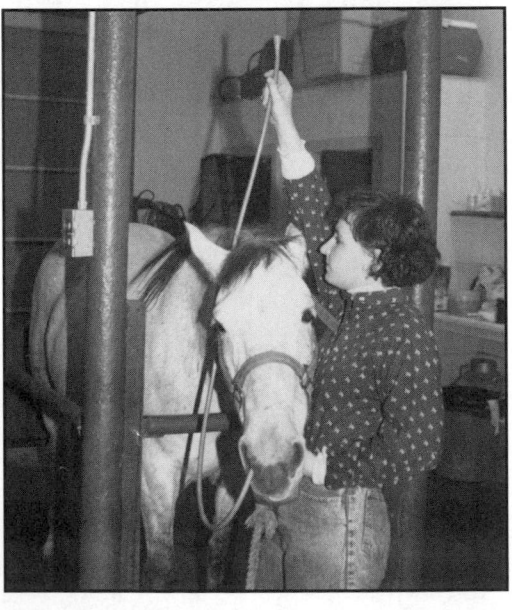

In acute gastric dilatation, air and fluid are expelled as the tube enters the stomach. This brings immediate relief.

Treatment: If the horse shows signs of abdominal distress, notify your veterinarian at once. Gastric rupture is a fatal complication of acute gastric dilatation and is likely to occur if the distended stomach is not decompressed.

The diagnosis of gastric dilatation is confirmed by passing a nasogastric tube. When the tube enters the stomach, air and fluid will rush out the end of the tube. The appearance of the gastric reflux fluid gives some indication as to whether the gastric dilatation is primary or secondary to a bowel obstruction. In the latter instance the gastric reflux is brown and fecal-like. Horses with bowel obstruction require further treatment. See INTESTINAL OBSTRUCTION.

Irrigating and flushing the stomach will relieve a problem caused by overeating or over-drinking. Dioctyl sodium sulfosuccinate (DSS) helps to soften a grain impaction. Mineral oil, which must be given by tube, is also useful for its anti-fermentation effects.

Most horses with gastric dilatation are dehydrated and have electrolyte and acid-base imbalances. These should be corrected by appropriate intravenous therapy.

Note that acute laminitis (founder) may accompany or follow an episode of acute gastric dilatation.

GASTRIC RUPTURE

Rupture of the stomach is a sequel to severe untreated gastric dilatation. Other causes of gastric perforation are ruptured stomach and duodenal ulcers. Rarely a perforated stomach is caused by bots and Habronema worms that invade the wall of the stomach.

As the stomach tears during acute gastric dilatation, there is a brief period during which the pain of distention is relieved and the horse appears to be better. However, within 30 minutes the horse becomes bathed in sweat, develops a rapid heart rate, goes into shock, and dies within a matter of hours.

The diagnosis of gastric perforation can be confirmed by abdominal tap, which shows ingested feed in the peritoneal fluid. Surgical repair cannot be undertaken. The horse should be put to sleep as soon as the diagnosis is confirmed.

STOMACH AND DUODENAL ULCERS

The recent advent of fiberoptic gastroscopy in the work-up of abdominal pain has revealed that gastric and duodenal ulcers are more common than once thought. In foals, ulcers are frequently symptomatic and related to the stresses of weaning and illness. For more information, see ULCERS IN FOALS in chapter 16, Pediatrics.

In adult horses, ulcers are less frequent and often do not produce symptoms when present. An acute rupture may be the first indication, in which case the horse is often found dead from peritonitis.

On gastroscopy, superficial ulcers are patches of inflamed and eroded mucosa covered by white or yellow pus. Deeper ulcers are punched-out areas involving all layers of the stomach wall. Ulcers can be single or multiple and can range in size from less than one inch to several inches in diameter. Ulcers occur in the stomach more frequently than in the duodenum (the first few feet of small intestine).

Stress plays a major role in causing ulcers in horses. Horses are stressed when they are transported over long distances in horse trailers; when they are subjected to overcrowding or a warm humid environment; when they are forced to consume poor-quality feed; when they develop an acute or chronic illness; and when they are forced to undergo sustained hard training.

All the anti-inflammatory drugs—especially aspirin, Butazolidin, and Banamine—can produce ulcers. The risk and occurrence of ulcer disease increases with the duration of NSAID usage. Gastrointestinal bleeding and anemia can occur with these ulcers.

The diagnosis of ulcer usually cannot be made solely on the basis of the symptoms, which include intermittent colic, going off of feed, and a restlessness characterized by repeatedly getting up and down. However, when a horse is under stress or taking anti-inflammatory drugs and exhibits these symptoms, gastroscopic examination is a worthwhile and often rewarding procedure.

Treatment: The first step is to remove all stressful conditions that may be causing the ulcer. Anti-inflammatory medications the horse may be taking should be discontinued if possible.

The ulcer medications used in people are effective in horses. They include the H-2 blockers Tagamet and Zantac; Carefate (a mucosal coating agent); and antacids containing aluminum hydroxide, such as Mylanta. These drugs are best taken in combination and given several times daily. Treatment is continued for at least 3 to 4 weeks. A follow-up gastroscopy may be advisable to ensure that healing is complete.

GASTRIC OUTLET OBSTRUCTION

The scarring associated with ulcers may cause a ring constriction or deformity which prevents the stomach from emptying. The obstruction may be partial or complete. Horses with gastric outlet obstruction experience pain immediately after eating, are reluctant to eat and drink, lose weight, dehydrate, and experience intermittent abdominal bloating and gastric dilatation.

Squamous cell cancer and lymphosarcoma are other causes of gastric outlet obstruction.

Strictures caused by ulcers can be corrected surgically, with a good prognosis.

GASTRITIS

Gastritis is inflammation and irritation of the lining of the stomach. Unlike a stomach ulcer, gastritis involves large areas. The mucosa throughout much of the stomach appears red and swollen, and contains many small ulcerations or areas of erosion. Gastritis occurs in both the acute and chronic form. It is less common than ulcer disease.

Acute gastritis is caused by the ingestion of moldy or spoiled feed, overeating, the consumption of sand, blister beetle poisoning, and the ingestion of chemicals and toxins. The horse with acute gastritis salivates and drools excessively, refuses to eat, and exhibits colic. A severe case of acute gastritis is indistinguishable from acute gastric dilatation. In fact, acute gastric dilatation often develops along with the acute gastritis.

Laminitis (founder) can accompany or follow an episode of acute gastritis.

Chronic gastritis is associated with the long-standing ingestion of poor-quality feeds or foreign materials such as wood shavings, sand, and stones. These indigestible materials irritate the lining of the stomach and often remain for long periods, during which they conglomerate with feed to form impacted food balls called *bezoars*. The bezoars are too large to pass into the small intestine but small enough to intermittently obstruct the outlet of the stomach. The retention of gastric contents favors the overgrowth of bacteria.

Other causes of chronic gastritis include cribbing with the swallowing of large amounts of air; and infection of the lining of the stomach by bots, Habronema, or hairworms.

Signs of chronic gastritis include intermittent colic, lack of appetite, weight loss, unthrifty appearance, a rank odor to the breath, and emaciation. The stool is pasty and soft. The diagnosis is made by gastroscopy performed to evaluate stomach symptoms.

Treatment: The initial treatment of acute gastritis is like that described for acute gastric dilatation. A tube is passed and the stomach thoroughly irrigated to remove the ingested irritant. Intestinal protectants (Pepto-Bismol, Kaopectate) help to soothe an inflamed stomach. Anti-ulcer medications (see above) are often prescribed. It is important to identify and remove the source of the problem.

After an episode of acute gastritis, provide an easily digestible diet, such as one containing bran mashes, green feeds, or fine hay. After 1 to 2 weeks, switch to a high-quality maintenance diet as described in chapter 17, Feeding and Nutrition.

Chronic gastritis is treated by correcting the underlying cause of the condition. This can involve treating a dental problem causing improper mastication. Gastric parasites are eliminated with appropriate anthelmintics. Horses that eat wood and foreign material should be turned out to pasture and provided with exercise and companionship. An obstructing bezoar requires surgical removal.

Small Intestine

Diseases of the small intestine are characterized by colic and intestinal obstruction.

Diarrhea is not a sign of small bowel disease in adult horses. The length and size of the horse's colon compensates almost completely for disorders of the small intestine. Diarrhea of small bowel origin only occurs when there is also disease of the colon. This does not apply to foals, in whom the capacity of the colon is not fully developed.

Diarrhea in foals is discussed in chapter 16, Pediatrics, under FOAL DIARRHEA.

ENTERITIS

Inflammatory disease of the small bowel is called enteritis. Since most cases also involve the colon, and diarrhea is a prominent feature, *enterocolitis* is a more accurate term. Infectious diseases are the most common cause of enterocolitis. They include enteric salmonellosis, actinobacillosis, equine viral arteritis, and rotavirus infection.

Intestinal parasites are another cause of enterocolitis. Adult worms of several species attach to the lining of the small and large intestine and produce inflammation, bleeding, anemia, loss of protein, impaired digestion, and in some cases severe diarrhea.

The migrating larvae of S. *vulgaris* may initiate recurrent episodes of severe colic caused by clotting of the blood supply to a segment of the small intestine. Diarrhea is not a feature.

Treatment: It is directed at the specific infectious disease. Protect your horse by keeping vaccinations current and by maintaining a good parasite control program.

Duodenitis-Proximal Jejunitis (DPJ). This is a severe and often fatal enteritis of unknown cause that begins suddenly with unexplained colic. Dehydration and toxicity develop rapidly. The small intestine ceases to function and passively fills with large amounts of gas and fluid that back up into the stomach, producing *secondary acute gastric dilatation*. The picture closely resembles mechanical small bowel obstruction or intestinal strangulation. The findings on peritoneal tap (as described for colic) help to differentiate these diseases. This is important because, in contrast to the other conditions, horses with DPJ do not require surgery.

Treatment: It involves inserting a nasogastric tube and removing large amounts of fluid and gas. This brings relief from colic, and also obviates the risk of gastric rupture. Large amounts of intravenous fluids are administered along with antibiotics. Prolonged nasogastric tube decompression (up to 7 days) is typical of DPJ.

Granulomatous Enteritis. This disease of the small intestine and colon is occasionally associated with chronic diarrhea. However, most horses experience colic, depression, and weight loss. The cause is unknown. A hypersensitivity reaction to some as yet unknown antigen has been suggested. Rectal examination may disclose enlarged nodes in the mesentery of the small intestine. Some horses respond to corticosteroids, but relapses occur when the medication is stopped.

Colic

Colic is the most common medical emergency encountered by the horse owner. Colic is not a specific disease. It is an indicator of abdominal pain, manifested by signs of anxiety that include tail-switching, pawing, looking back and kicking at the abdomen, sweating, rolling on the ground, and urinating and defecating in small amounts.

Colic is a symptom rather than a disease. It indicates a painful condition in the abdomen.

Colic occurs in indigestion, intestinal spasm, impactions, constipation, intestinal obstructions, feed toxicities, migratory worm infections, peritonitis, and dozens of other conditions, including diseases of the stomach, liver, ovaries, uterus, kidneys, and bladder.

Although the causes are many and varied, it is believed that the majority of colic cases in adult horses are caused by impactions of the cecum and large colon, and spasmodic and flatulent colic (discussed below). Retained meconium and gastric ulcers are the principal causes of colic in foals (see chapter 16, Pediatrics).

The onset of colic usually is sudden. The horse may sit back on its haunches like a dog. Male horses frequently stretch out and relax the penis without urinating. A horse with colic often drops to the ground and thrashes violently while thrusting its feet up in the air. Abrasions and contusions from accidental self-injury are not uncommon.

Colic is an emergency. Call your veterinarian. The first thing he or she will want to do is examine the horse to determine the nature and severity of the colic.

Passing a nasogastric tube and flushing out the stomach is an important diagnostic step and is indicated in all horses with moderate to severe colic. The appearance of the stomach contents may indicate the cause of the colic. In addition, decompression of a distended stomach can lead to dramatic improvement.

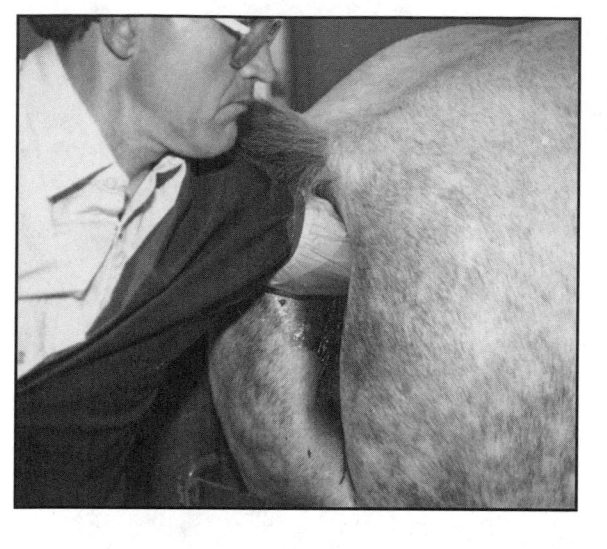

An experienced examiner can frequently determine the cause of the colic by rectal palpation.

Rectal examination is of utmost importance in all cases of colic. It should be performed by a veterinarian, owing to the risk of rectal tears in a colicky horse. Intravenous sedation is often employed to facilitate the procedure. An experienced examiner can often tell the cause of the colic by palpating the small intestine, pelvic colon, bladder, and reproductive organs.

A *peritoneal tap* helps to determine if the horse has a bowel obstruction with impending or actual peritonitis. The tap is performed in the midline of the belly at its lowest or most dependent portion. A long needle is inserted through the skin and into the peritoneal cavity. Fluid is withdrawn and inspected under the microscope for blood, pus, protein, bacteria, and ingested plant material.

As a further step, your veterinarian may elect to administer an analgesic such as xylazine (Rompun). Horses with mild colic frequently respond to pain medication alone and require no further treatment.

Treatment: All forms of moderate to severe colic require intensive medical treatment. In addition to decompressing the stomach and relieving pain, fluids must be given to correct dehydration. This can often be accomplished by giving 1 to 2 gallons of water by nasogastric tube every hour. The IV route is employed if the horse exhibits signs of peritonitis or intestinal obstruction—or if there is a brown, foul-smelling reflux from the stomach tube, which indicates that the stomach is not emptying.

Further medical management is undertaken on the basis of the presumptive cause of the colic, as described below.

Signs of peritonitis, strangulation, or obstruction indicate the need for rapid surgical intervention. These signs include persistent severe pain not relieved by a stomach tube and analgesics; toxemia with a rising temperature; a heart rate greater than 60 beats per minute; a respiratory rate greater than 30 breaths per minute; the finding of blood, bacteria, or plant material on the peritoneal tap; and the finding of a bowel obstruction or displacement of the colon on rectal palpation.

Approximately 50 percent of horses recover from colic surgery. This figure drops to 25 percent if bowel resection is required. Therefore, the best results are obtained when surgery is performed before the need for bowel resection.

For descriptive purposes, colic has been classified as follows:

Impaction Colic. This is a common cause of colic. Most impactions are diet-related—the horse consuming poor-quality or improperly masticated feed. Water deprivation is another cause. Signs depend on the location and duration of the impaction. If the large colon alone is involved, initially the bouts of pain are intermittent and mild. The manure is hard and dry. For more information, see IMPACTIONS.

Bowel sounds are increased in spasmodic and flatulent colic. They are decreased in impaction colic and absent in peritonitis.

Flatulent (Tympanic) Colic. The horse appears bloated and distended and has a great deal of gas throughout the digestive tract. Tapping on the side of the belly produces a hollow drum-like or *tympanitic* sound, indicative of a large volume of air in the colon and cecum. Bowel activity is increased, which is reflected by the loud, high-pitched sounds heard with a stethoscope.

Primary tympany is a form of gaseous indigestion caused by bacterial fermentation of intestinal carbohydrates, often following the overconsumption of lush green grasses, grain, or commercial horse feeds. Occasionally it is due to the ingestion of spoiled feeds. Abdominal pain is intermittent and moderate to severe. Horses with primary flatulence pass a great deal of gas via rectum.

Secondary tympany accompanies bowel obstructions of the cecum or colon. Horses with secondary tympany are acutely ill and soon develop signs of toxicity. They pass little or no gas via rectum.

Treatment: Passing a stomach tube helps to distinguish between primary and secondary tympany. The latter is characterized by a foul-smelling reflux from the nasogastric tube.

Primary tympany responds well to the administration of the antispasmodic dipyrone and the analgesics Banamine and xylazine. Mineral oil (4 quarts) is instilled into the stomach to prevent constipation and treat intestinal irritation. Walking the horse promotes the passage of rectal gas.

Secondary tympany requires surgery to correct the blockage. When the bowel is so distended that rupture is imminent, the distension can be temporarily relieved by inserting a trocar either through the right flank into the cecum or through the rectum into the large colon.

Spasmodic Colic. This colic is caused by powerful contractions of the bowel, which can be recognized by increased bowel sounds and peristaltic rushes. It is believed to be the most common cause of intestinal colic. Nervous, high-strung horses appear most susceptible to spasmodic colic, which may be triggered by fright, anxiety, or drinking cold water after a hot workout.

During spasmodic episodes usually lasting about 10 minutes, the horse rolls, paws, shakes, and kicks. The bowel sounds are loud and rushing, and are often audible without a stethoscope. Between attacks the horse stands quietly. Patchy sweating on the neck is a characteristic finding.

Treatment: Most horses recover spontaneously in less than an hour. For those who do not, treatment is the same as that for primary tympany above.

Peritonitis Colic. The pain is severe, often unrelenting. Signs of shock, dehydration, and toxicity will be evident. Pushing on the abdomen intensifies the pain and will be resisted. When the cause is not obvious, think of a bowel obstruction complicated by strangulation, infarction, or perforation. For more information, see Peritonitis.

Intestinal Obstruction
(Blocked Bowel)

The diagnosis of intestinal obstruction is suspected on the basis of the history and behavior of the horse. The onset is abrupt, and signs are severe. The horse becomes noticeably depressed and exhibits signs of colic and pain in the abdomen. The heart rate increases (often to greater than 60 beats per minute); the pulse becomes weak and thready; the mucous membranes are muddy or cyanotic; capillary refill time becomes greater than 3 seconds; and the extremities become cool and shock-like.

These signs are more pronounced in strangulation and in unrelieved obstruction. They are due to dehydration, loss of fluids into the distended bowel, and in some cases to toxicity and peritonitis.

Insertion of a nasogastric tube may show reflux of partially digested food from a distended stomach. This indicates either a high intestinal obstruction or an obstruction of long standing. When the obstruction is early or low (i.e., in the colon), there is generalized bloating of the belly but little undigested food and gas in the stomach.

Rectal examination is of utmost importance in all cases of abdominal colic and suspected bowel obstruction. An experienced observer can frequently tell the type and location of the obstruction by whether the bowel is in its usual position, and by the feel of the distended loops.

Peritoneal tap (as described for colic) is another important diagnostic test and can be performed in the field. Fluid is withdrawn and inspected for blood, pus, protein, bacteria, and ingested plant material. This helps to determine whether the bowel is becoming gangrenous or if rupture has occurred.

The common causes of intestinal obstruction are discussed below.

IMPACTIONS

Impactions are mechanical blockages that occur when inadequately digested feed or foreign material forms an obstructive mass in the cecum or large colon. Meconium impaction in newborn foals is a special case, discussed in chapter 15, Pregnancy and Foaling (see MECONIUM COLIC).

Impactions tend to occur in horses who consume coarse, poor-quality feed. Horses with dental disease who are unable to chew their feed are also candidates for an impaction, as are horses who simply bolt their meals. In all such cases, the feed is presented to the colon in a poorly masticated, semi-solid state.

Horses recovering from surgery and anesthesia are especially prone to cecal impactions. A decreased water intake, most likely to occur in winter when the water supply freezes, is a common cause of colonic impactions. The ingestion of sand is another cause.

Intestinal parasites are responsible for worm impactions in the small intestine, and may predispose to colon impactions. Abscesses and tumors in the intestinal tract are infrequent causes.

Large Colon Impactions. Impaction of the large colon begins with mild colic, apathy, loss of appetite, increased thirst, and the passage of small amounts of hard manure covered with thick, sticky mucus. The horse's expression is somewhat anxious. The heart rate is less than 50 beats per minute, the pulse is strong and regular, and the breathing rate and temperature are normal. The mucous membranes are pink with a capillary refill time of less than 2 seconds. Listening to the abdomen with a stethoscope reveals the presence of bowel sounds. Pushing on the belly does not intensify the pain.

The signs of an early impaction may go unnoticed. However, with the passage of time, abdominal pain becomes more severe and the horse becomes notably anxious or depressed. The heart rate increases to 55 beats per minute (sometimes over 60). The pulse becomes weak and occasionally irregular, and the respiratory rate is increased. Pale mucous membranes indicate vasoconstriction or internal bleeding. A capillary refill time over 3 seconds indicates impending shock. Dry mucous membranes and loss of skin elasticity are signs of severe dehydration. Bowel sounds are absent if the horse has peritonitis.

Cecal impaction is a serious condition. It begins with mild, intermittent, colicky abdominal pain and depression. These symptoms may persist for days. However, when untreated, severe cecal impaction leads to rupture of the cecum. In fact, some horses may be found dead as a result of sudden overwhelming peritonitis.

Treatment: A horse with a suspected impaction should be examined by a veterinarian. The most important step is to soften the impaction and facilitate passage by liquefying the intestinal contents. With a mild impaction, this may be accomplished by withholding feed and allowing the horse to drink water. As the impaction softens up and begins to pass, the pain subsides. The horse develops an appetite and appears brighter. Temporarily reduce the ration by half.

Severe impactions must be treated aggressively. The horse is sedated with xylazine or Banamine to control pain and relax the bowel. Vigorous hydration is accomplished by administering large volumes of water (6 to 8 quarts per 1,000 pounds horse weight) by nasogastric tube every 2 hours. If the water refluxes from the tube, fluids are given intravenously through large-bore needles placed in both jugular veins.

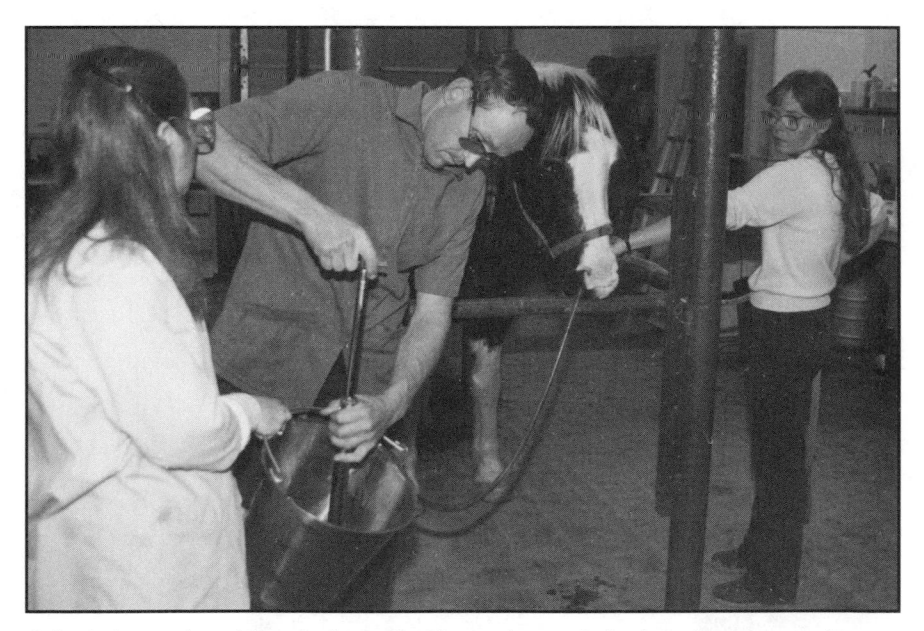

Colonic impaction. After the horse has been vigorously hydrated, 3 quarts of mineral oil are given to facilitate passage.

Dioctyl sodium sulfosuccinate (1 ounce of 5 percent DSS per 1,000 pounds horse weight) or mineral oil (3 to 4 quarts repeated every 12 hours) is given by nasogastric tube to soften the stool. Note that DSS and mineral oil should not be used together. A saline magnesium laxative (Epsom salts) is effective as a cathartic. The magnesium sulfate draws fluid into the intestinal passage, which helps to soften the impaction.

In the seriously ill horse, frequent rectal examinations and peritoneal taps are necessary to monitor progress. Failure to improve, or the advent of signs suggesting impending peritonitis, calls for immediate surgery. To be effective, surgery must be performed before the colon ruptures.

Prevention: If you are able to identify and correct a predisposing cause, there is less likelihood of recurrence. Review feeding practices to be sure the ration is of high quality and digestibility, and that a source of fresh water is available at all times. Perform any necessary dental procedures. Insure that the deworming schedule is up to date.

Sand Impaction. Some horses eat sand for reasons unknown. In sandy soils, unintentional ingestion is possible when grass is short-grazed or pulled out by the roots. Sand is also consumed when hay is fed on sandy ground. States in which this is most likely to occur include Florida and California.

Sand tends to accumulate in the large colon. However, if a significant amount is consumed at one time, a sand impaction can develop in the ileum or ileocecal valve. A continuous low-level intake of sand leads to colic and diarrhea, a condition called *sand enteropathy.* The enteropathy may persist for weeks or months, often terminating in an acute impaction. The weight of the sand in the large colon can produce displacement, torsion, or volvulus.

Rectal palpation will diagnose a sand impaction if the impacted segment is within reach. When not within reach, the volume of sand in the feces can be estimated by filling a rubber glove with balls of fresh manure, adding water, mixing, and observing the amount of sand that settles out in the fingers.

Treatment: It is like that described above for colonic impaction. It is important to administer large volumes of water during the acute attack, either by nasogastric tube or the intravenous route. Failure to replenish fluids lost in diarrhea, dehydration, and sweating makes sand impactions drier and most difficult to pass.

The laxative of choice is psyllium mucilloid (Metamucil). Metamucil forms a jelly in the intestinal tract that collects the sand and lubricates its passage. Administer 1 pound of Metamucil mixed in 2 gallons of water by nasogastric tube. To prevent gel from forming in the nasogastric tube, mix with water just before the mixture is pumped into the stomach. Repeat as necessary, until well after the colic subsides. Usually a considerable amount of sand remains. This leads to recurrence if treatment is stopped too soon.

Surgical removal is necessary for difficult sand impactions and those with unrelieved signs of intestinal obstruction.

Prevent sand impaction by feeding hay in racks or mangers. When horses graze on sandy soils where impactions have occured in the past, dry Metamucil can be added to sweet feeds as a form of prevention.

Worm Impactions. Following the use of a rapid-acting deworming agent such as piperazine in a heavily parasitized weanling foal or yearling, paralyzed ascarids can conglomerate into masses which partially or completely obstruct the small intestine.

Signs are mild to severe colic, which begins shortly after deworming. Gastric distension is an associated factor in some cases. Worms may be present in the feces.

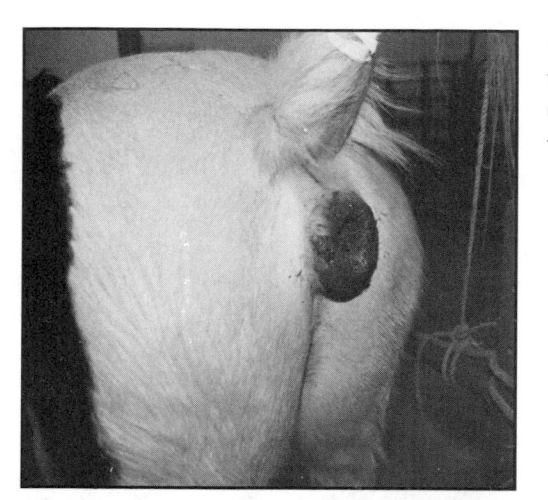

Rectal impaction. Despite forceful straining, the horse was unable to expel the impacted feces.

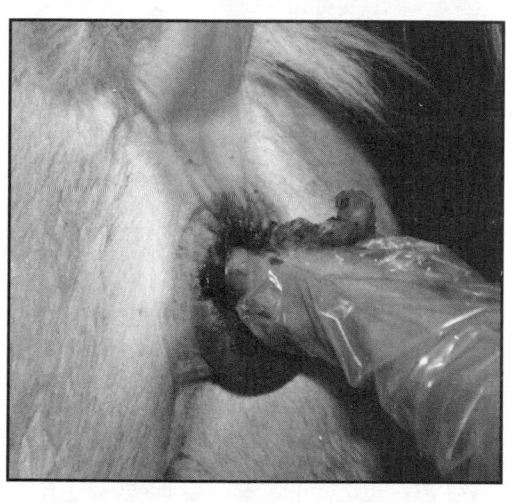

The first step is to remove the dry manure manually.

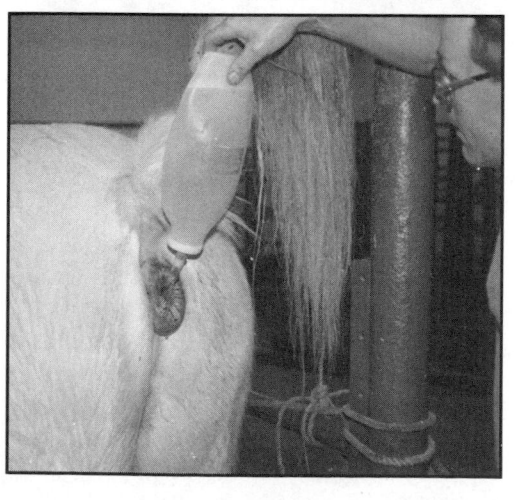

Next a soap water enema is given to flush out remaining balls of hard stool.

In the most severe form, signs are those of an acute intestinal obstruction. Perforation and rupture of the stomach or small intestine is a possibility. Heavy ascarid loads may also be associated with *intussusception*.

Treatment is like that described above for colonic impaction. If not successful, surgery to remove worm masses may be necessary. Worm impactions can be prevented by deworming foals at 8 weeks of age and then every 6 to 8 weeks until they are yearlings.

Rectal Impactions. Fecal material in the small colon and rectum can become so dry and hard that the horse is unable to expel it despite forceful and prolonged straining. The fecal mass appears at the anal opening, which is widely dilated and often everted.

Water deprivation is a common cause of rectal impaction. It is most likely to occur in extremely cold weather when water sources are either frozen over or so cold horses will not consume an adequate amount of water to prevent dehydration. Other causes of rectal impaction are like those described under Constipation.

Treatment: Restrain the horse and manually remove stool from the anus and rectum. Intravenous sedation is often necessary. Administer a soap water enema to stimulate colonic contractions. The enema also helps to lubricate the anal canal and wash out balls of hard stool.

To give a soap water enema, stir a piece of Ivory soap in 2 to 3 quarts of lukewarm water until the water becomes milky. Fill an enema bottle or bag with the solution and connect the tubing of the bag to a flexible rubber catheter. Lubricate the nozzle or catheter with mineral oil and carefully insert it 8 to 12 inches into the anal canal, depending on the size of the horse. Allow the fluid to run in by gravity. Repeat as necessary.

Following removal of the impaction, the horse should be given 3 to 4 quarts of mineral oil by nasogastric tube to break up any impaction in the large colon that may have developed because of the obstruction in the small colon or rectum.

Determine the cause of the impaction and take steps to prevent recurrence.

STRANGULATION

Interference with the blood supply to the wall of the intestine is called *strangulation*. Strangulation is characterized by rapid deterioration in the horse's condition. Signs of strangulation are difficult to distinguish from those of peritonitis. The pain of both is severe and unrelenting. Sweating is pronounced. The horse rolls from side to side and often lies on its back. Dehydration and toxicity occur rapidly.

If blood flow to the strangulated bowel is not restored within 4 to 6 hours, the bowel becomes devitalized and dies. This is called *infarction*. It is followed immediately by rupture and peritonitis. If treatment is to be successful, it must be undertaken before the bowel ruptures. The only effective treatment is to operate and remove the infarcted intestine.

The most common causes of strangulation are:

Volvulus. A segment of intestine can twist on the axis of its blood supply. If the twist is 180 degrees or less, it is called a *torsion*. A twist of 360 degrees is called a *volvulus*. A volvulus results in a sudden shutting-off of the blood supply to the twisted bowel. The bowel itself may be twisted shut at one or both ends.

Volvulus of the small intestine can be caused by adhesions, worm impactions, and motility disorders associated with changes in diet. Migrating strongyle larvae have been known to cause motility disorders. *Lipomas* are a common cause of torsion and volvulus. A lipoma is a fatty tumor on a long stalk attached to the mesentery of the bowel. The lipoma serves as a lead point, causing the bowel to twist.

Groin and navel hernias, internal hernias, and diaphragmatic hernias are other causes of twists and obstructions. An *internal hernia* occurs when a loop of bowel becomes trapped in a pocket between internal organs. A *diaphragmatic hernia* is a hole in the diaphragm allowing the bowel to pass into the chest. Most are apparent at or shortly after birth, causing severe respiratory distress in the neonatal foal. These hernias are rare in older horses.

Volvulus of the colon is not uncommon. The colon in horses is extremely large when compared to that of other animals, and is loosely attached to surrounding structures. For these reasons it is easily displaced, twisted, and kinked. It has been suggested that a horse that rolls from side to side may incur a volvulus, torsion, or displacement of the colon.

The treatment of volvulus is surgical exploration with unwinding of the twisted bowel. If the bowel is devitalized, that segment must be resected.

Intussusception. Intussusception occurs when the small intestine telescopes into an adjacent segment of bowel. It occurs frequently in young horses as a result of enteritis, heavy worm infestation, and dietary changes resulting in disordered peristalsis.

Ileocecal intussusception involves the telescoping of the terminal ileum into the cecum. This is the most common type of intussusception and produces complete obstruction. *Ileal-ileal intussusception* often results in partial obstruction. *Colonic intussusception* does occur, but much less often.

Depending on location, symptoms develop abruptly or gradually. An acute intussusception is indistinguishable from strangulation. When the obstruction is not complete at the onset, signs develop more slowly and may initially suggest spasmodic colic.

The treatment of all types of intussusception is surgical removal of the involved bowel. The sooner this is accomplished, the better the outcome.

Nonstrangulating Infarction. The wall of the bowel can become devitalized as a result of arteritis and arterial occlusions produced by the migrating larvae of S. *vulgaris*. As discussed in chapter 2, Parasites, this does not happen often because the intestinal blood supply of horses contains numerous channels that provide alternate pathways for perfusion. When infarction does occur, the cecum and large colon are the most common sites. Surgical resection is the only effective treatment for infarcted bowel.

Episodes of recurrent thromboembolism *without* infarction occasionally cause colic and abdominal pain in yearlings and young adults. Bowel obstruction is not a factor, although the migrating larvae may also produce an intestinal motility disorder which predisposes to or causes intussusception or volvulus. A conscientious deworming program employing ivermectin every 2 months for life will prevent such episodes.

ENTEROLITHS AND FOREIGN BODIES

Enteroliths are concretions that form in the intestinal tract when mineralized salts are deposited around a central nidus, such as a pebble or other foreign object. A solitary enterolith is usually round. When two or more enteroliths exist together, the grinding effect produces multifaceted concretions.

Horses with enteroliths are found primarily in California and neighboring states, where high concentrations of magnesium ammonium in soil and forage are instrumental in their development. A familial predisposition has been recognized in Arabians.

Enteroliths become symptomatic when they grow large enough to obstruct the bowel. Obstruction usually occurs in the right dorsal colon, transverse colon, or small colon, owing to a narrower caliber of bowel in these locations. The enterolith frequently acts as a ball-valve before it becomes tightly wedged. Accordingly, signs of intestinal obstruction are often preceded by bouts of colicky abdominal pain and the passage of liquid feces. A horse with these symptoms will often be thought to have an impaction. However, when treatment for impaction is not successful, think of an enterolith. The diagnosis can be confirmed by an x-ray showing the calcified mass. Treatment involves surgical exploration and removal of the enterolith.

Foreign bodies in the intestinal tract tend to occur in young horses eating hay nets, rubber, synthetic fibers, nylon, burlap, and other miscellaneous objects. If the foreign body fails to pass spontaneously, it will cause signs of bowel obstruction similar to those of an enterolith and will need to be surgically removed.

DISPLACEMENT OF THE LARGE COLON

The large colon is freely movable within the peritoneal cavity, and when distended by gas can be displaced from its normal position. Large-framed horses are especially prone to displacements. In fact, the larger the horse, the greater the risk.

During displacement, the affected segment of colon becomes partially entrapped, twisted, or pinched off. Torsion, volvulus, or strangulation often complicate the problem.

An uncomplicated displacement usually produces intermittent bloating with mild to moderate colic. While there is loss of appetite, there is little change in the horse's overall condition for a considerable length of time.

The displaced segment can often be felt on rectal palpation. This establishes the diagnosis as well as the type of displacement.

Treatment: There are several types of displacement. Your veterinarian can determine the best method of treatment depending on the specific type.

Fasting for 1 to 2 days, or the insertion of a nasogastric tube into the stomach, often relieves gas in the bowel and permits the colon to return to its normal position. On occasion, rolling the anesthetized horse as well as temporarily laying it on its back may cause the colon to flip back over. Some displacements can be reduced by rectal palpation.

Abdominal surgery is indicated for displacements that fail to resolve and those with signs of obstruction or strangulation.

A horse with a previously displaced colon is prone to recurrence. Treatment of worm parasites and/or a modification in diet may prevent some of these recurrences.

Constipation

Constipation is defined as the infrequent passage of firm, dry manure. Usually it is accompanied by some degree of straining. Constipation should be distinguished from colic, a symptom-complex characterized by sudden severe pain in the abdomen, sometimes—but not always—associated with mechanical blockages and fecal impactions.

A characteristic type of constipation occurs in newborn foals. Treatment is discussed in chapter 15, Pregnancy and Foaling (see MECONIUM COLIC).

Constipation is more common in the older individual, although it may occur at any age. Such horses may pass only small amounts of firm, possibly mucus-covered manure. They may have a rough hair coat and appear unthrifty.

One predisposing cause is dental disease that results in improper grinding of feed and therefore improper digestion. Another cause is worm damage to the lining of the intestinal tract, leading to reduced motility. Feeding too much finely ground grain can cause constipation. In some horses, the intestinal tract simply seems to slow down with age.

Treatment: The horse should have its teeth examined to see if corrective treatment is possible. Put the horse on a good parasite control program. Provide continuous access to clean fresh water. Insure that the horse's water does not freeze and is not too cold to drink.

When the manure is persistently hard and dry, the powdered form of dioctyl sodium sulfosuccinate (DSS) can be added to sweet feeds. To avoid toxicity (severe diarrhea), the daily dose should not exceed 9 mg per pound weight of horse, given every other day. Do not use concurrently with mineral oil.

Milk of magnesia (MOM) is a safe laxative to give for mild to moderate constipation. The single individual dose for an average-sized horse is 8 to 16 ounces. Do not give a laxative to a horse that appears colicky or exhibits any signs of abdominal discomfort, without veterinary approval.

Giving a warm bran mash twice a week is a good preventative measure in older horses.

Diarrhea

Diarrhea is the passage of loose, unformed manure. In most cases, there is a large volume of stool and an increased number of bowel movements. This depends to some extent upon whether the diarrhea is acute or chronic.

Because of the extraordinary size and length of the equine colon, the horse is able to compensate in large part for any inflammatory or irritative process in the small intestine and still maintain a stool of normal consistency. Accordingly, diarrhea is a factor only when there is disease in the colon. This does not apply to foals, in whom the colon is still immature. Foal diarrhea is discussed in chapter 16, Pediatrics.

Diarrhea in the adult horse is discussed below.

ACUTE DIARRHEA

Diarrhea of sudden onset indicates an infectious disease or an acute poisoning. Poor-quality feed, spoiled feed, and ingested irritants do not cause diarrhea in horses as they do in animals with shorter digestive tracts.

When diarrhea is profuse, watery, explosive, foul-smelling, dark green to black, blood-tinged, or bloody, the horse is suffering from infectious colitis. Salmonellosis is the most likely cause because it is the most common.

Certain antibiotics (especially Lincocin and tetracycline) can alter the normal colonic flora and produce an acute diarrhea that is indistinguishable from an infectious colitis.

Nonsteroidal anti-inflammatory drugs, when used over an extended period, can disrupt the blood supply to the mucosa of the cecum and colon and produce a severe diarrhea that is slow to respond to treatment.

Less common causes of acute diarrhea include arsenic and lead poisoning, equine viral arteritis, selenium toxicity, plant poisoning, blister beetle poisoning, and peritonitis.

Treatment is directed at the cause of the diarrhea.

CHRONIC DIARRHEA

Diarrhea that persists for weeks or months is a frustrating problem. Horses with chronic diarrhea gradually lose weight despite a good appetite. Stools are soft and watery and the amount is greater than normal. Large quantities of water are consumed to compensate for losses in the stool.

It is difficult to establish the cause of a chronic diarrhea even with laboratory studies and endoscopic biopsies. Whether the work-up is positive or negative, one of the following may be the cause of the diarrhea:

Chronic Salmonellosis. Horses who recover from enteric salmonellosis can become carriers and shed salmonella in their feces. The stool varies from soft and unformed ("cow pie") to profuse and watery. Treatment with various antibiotics including iodochlorohydroxyquinoline (Rheaform) is possible, but improvement is often temporary. In addition, the carrier horse remains a hazard to other animals and to humans, who are quite susceptible to salmonellosis. Care should be used in handling such horses during a phase of diarrhea.

Intestinal Parasites. Migrating larvae of S. *vulgaris* have been implicated in cases of chronic diarrhea in horses. Although most horses with chronic diarrhea do not have strongyles infection, treatment directed at killing migratory larvae is worth the effort and, if successful, is followed by cure of the diarrhea.

Failure to recognize and treat protozoal diarrhea (discussed in chapter 16, Pediatrics) sometimes leads to diarrhea that continues for weeks or months. The stool is soft and has the consistency of cow manure.

Sand Ingestion. Sand in the intestinal tract can be a cause of chronic diarrhea (see IMPACTIONS).

Chronic Liver Disease. Liver failure may be accompanied by low-volume diarrhea. The stool is the consistency of cow manure.

Tumors. Growths in the digestive tract can produce malabsorption and diarrhea. Lymphosarcoma and squamous cell carcinoma are the most common intestinal tract tumors.

Malabsorption Syndrome. Malabsorption is characterized by failure to absorb nutrients from the small intestine. These horses are unthrifty, malnourished, and, because of protein deficiency, frequently accumulate fluid in the dependent portion of the belly wall (*ventral edema*). Changes in the consistency, color, and amount of stool occur, but the principal sign of malabsorption in the horse is chronic weight loss.

Most malabsorptions are caused by an episode of viral enteritis (in the neonate) or salmonella enteritis (in the neonate or adult). The infectious agent attacks and destroys the nutrient-absorbing villous cells in the lining of the small intestine.

Malabsorption has also been associated with granulomatous enteritis, cryptosporidiosis, liver disease, long-standing worm infections, congestive heart failure, heavy metal poisoning, zinc deficiency, and atrophy of the villous cell of unknown cause. The diagnosis is difficult, and treatment is usually not rewarding.

Rectum and Anus

Diseases of the rectum and anus are associated with prolapse, trauma, and fecal incontinence. Severe itching about the anus can be caused by pinworms, Culicoides dermatitis, and tail mites.

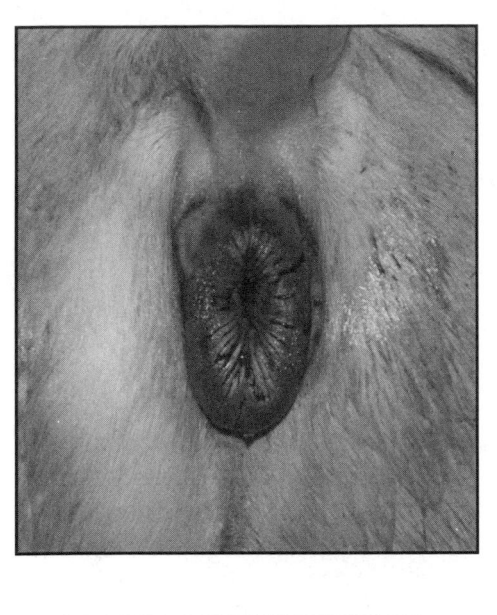

Prolapse of the mucous lining of the rectum, caused by forceful straining.

PROLAPSE OF THE RECTUM

Protrusion of the rectum through the anus is called *prolapse*. Often just the mucous lining prolapses, giving the appearance of a large doughnut. Rarely the entire rectum can turn inside out through the anus and hang over the buttocks.

Heavy straining is the cause. Thus rectal prolapse is associated with constipation, colic, diarrhea, rectal tumors, obstructed bladders, and mares that strain during difficult labor.

Treatment: Notify your veterinarian. The prolapse must be reduced before it becomes excessively swollen and congested. In most cases, an epidural block must be placed to prevent further straining and relax the anal sphincter. Reduction is then accomplished by massaging the swollen tissue and working it back inside the rectum. Following reduction, mineral oil or dioctyl sodium sulfosuccinate (DSS) is given to soften the stool and prevent straining.

When a prolapse has been present for several hours, the swollen and dried-out mucosa becomes devitalized. A surgical procedure to remove the dead layer and repair the mucosa is required. A rectal stricture may follow surgical repair.

To prevent recurrent episodes of prolapse, see CONSTIPATION.

RECTAL LACERATIONS AND TEARS

The anal canal and lower rectum can be torn or lacerated during a difficult delivery as the result of an abnormal foal presentation. Breeding accidents and pelvic fractures are other causes.

The most common cause of a torn rectum is iatrogenic. A rectal injury is a potential hazard whenever a horse is examined by rectal palpation. Some horses have a small rectum, while others have a thin delicate rectum and small-caliber colon.

It is most important that horses be restrained for rectal examinations. Often this involves the use of xylazine (Rompun) to sedate the horse and relax the rectum. In addition, rectal examinations should be done only by experienced personnel.

An injury to the wall of the rectum produces bleeding and the appearance of blood on the glove of the examiner. Shortly thereafter, the horse breaks out in a sweat and strains as if to pass manure. If the tear is deep and extends into the abdominal cavity, signs of peritonitis develop rapidly.

Treatment: Straining is prevented by first giving an epidural block, which also relaxes the rectal canal. The rectum is now carefully examined by finger palpation to determine the extent of the tear. Tears that do not involve the full thickness of the rectal wall have a favorable prognosis and usually heal on their own. Antibiotics are given to prevent infection. Dioctyl sodium sulfosuccinate (DSS) or mineral oil can be given to soften the stool and prevent straining.

A laceration that involves all layers of the rectum but stops just short of entering the abdominal cavity can often be repaired. This is major abdominal surgery and must be done at a center equipped to provide the necessary support. A temporary diverting colostomy (artificial opening in the colon) is required.

A tear that extends into the peritoneal cavity results in fecal contamination and peritonitis. The outlook for recovery is poor even with early treatment. The finding of fecal material on peritoneal tap (as described for colic) confirms the diagnosis. For treatment, see PERITONITIS.

FECAL INCONTINENCE

Loss of control of the rectum occurs when there has been an injury to the spinal cord. Fecal incontinence is accompanied by bladder paralysis and a limp tail. In the male there is prolapse of the penis; in the female, gaping of the vulva. These signs also occur with the cauda equina syndrome.

A perineal laceration during a difficult delivery can create a common passage between the rectum and vagina (*rectovaginal fistula*) through which stool passes via the vagina. This can give the appearance of fecal incontinence.

Treatment is directed at the primary cause. Rectovaginal fistulas can be surgically repaired. With spinal cord paralysis, the stool should be kept soft with DSS and manually removed from the rectum as necessary. See also PARALYZED BLADDER.

Peritonitis

Inflammation of the lining of the abdominal cavity is called *peritonitis*. Peritonitis can be acute or chronic, and localized or generalized.

ACUTE PERITONITIS

Acute peritonitis occurs when there is sudden contamination of the peritoneal cavity by foreign material and bacteria. The common causes are gastric rupture, rectal tears, strangulation of the intestine, bowel obstruction, ruptured bladder, penetrating wounds of the abdominal cavity, and the breakdown of a suture line following bowel surgery.

In mares, peritonitis can be caused by vaginal tears during intercourse, rupture of the large colon during labor and delivery, uterine torsion, and rupture of the pregnant uterus.

In foals, peritonitis can be caused by a ruptured bladder during delivery, navel infections, strangulated hernias, foal septicemia, foal pneumonia, and ruptured gastric ulcers.

Horses with acute spreading peritonitis exhibit intense pain in the abdomen, break out in a sweat, and usually lie down and roll on the ground. Listening with a stethoscope reveals absent bowel sounds. Pressing on the abdomen causes the horse to groan. The belly and flanks feel somewhat rigid or "board-like," owing to reflex spasm of the abdominal wall muscles. Diarrhea may be noted.

When peritonitis is caused by intestinal rupture, signs of shock and dehydration will be evident in the red or muddy mucous membranes, prolonged capillary refill time (3 seconds or longer), and rapid thready pulse (over 60 beats per minute). Death can occur in a matter of hours.

Tapping the abdomen and examining the peritoneal fluid (as described for colic) is the most expeditious way to confirm the diagnosis.

Treatment: It varies with the cause of the peritonitis. In general, horses with acute peritonitis require intensive intravenous fluid therapy, broad-spectrum antibiotics, and correction of acid-base and electrolyte imbalances. Flunixin meglumine (Banamine) is given for pain relief and may help to control endotoxic shock.

Insertion of a nasogastric tube to decompress a distended stomach can lead to dramatic initial improvement. It is advisable to leave the tube in place or to pass it at frequent intervals.

A horse with a continuing source of contamination may be a candidate for surgical exploration. Alternately, in the absence of such a source, your veterinarian may elect to perform *peritoneal lavage*. Catheters are inserted into the peritoneal cavity, and large volumes of salt solution are flushed into and out of the abdomen. This reduces the concentration of bacteria and foreign particles.

With massive contamination or advanced shock and sepsis, the likelihood for success is so remote that it is often advisable to put the horse to sleep.

CHRONIC PERITONITIS

Peritoneal infection can localize to form an abscess, or *chronic peritonitis*. Abdominal abscesses also occur in strangles and foal pneumonia. Migrating larvae of S. *vulgaris* have been implicated in some cases of chronic peritonitis.

Signs of chronic peritonitis are those of gradual weight loss, poor appetite, ill-thrift, and intermittent episodes of colic. If diarrhea develops, the outlook is poor.

Treatment: It is directed at the underlying disease. Antibiotics and deworming agents such as ivermectin may be effective in some cases. Your veterinarian may suggest surgical exploration to drain an abscess or establish a diagnosis.

Liver

The liver has many vital metabolic functions. They include the synthesis of enzymes, proteins and sugars; the removal of ammonia and other wastes from the bloodstream; and the detoxification of drugs and poisons.

The most common signs of liver failure are jaundice, hepatoencephalopathy, and photosensitivity. *Ascites* (fluid in the belly) and *edema* (swelling of the abdominal wall and lower legs) are not as common in liver disease as they are in congestive heart failure. Major blood loss from spontaneous bleeding is rare.

Jaundice. The liver removes bile from the blood. A buildup of bile turns the tissues yellow. This is noted in the yellow appearance of the whites of the eyes and the mucous membranes of the mouth and tongue. Bile excreted in urine changes the color from yellow to the color of tea.

Hepatoencephalopathy. This is a type of encephalitis caused by high levels of ammonia and other toxins in the blood. Ammonia is a product of protein metabolism. It is removed from the circulation and metabolized by the liver. When the liver is sick, ammonia accumulates to toxic levels and exerts a poisonous effect on the brain.

Horses with hepatoencephalopathy develop behavior changes that include loss of appetite, mental depression, aimless wandering, circling, head-pressing, staggering, and frequent yawning. They often appear blind or oblivious to their surroundings and may injure themselves by walking into fences and stepping into ditches. Weight loss and constipation may occur. Coma is a late occurrence.

Photosensitivity. This occurs in about 25 percent of horses with liver disease. The reasons are discussed in chapter 4, Skin (see PHOTOSENSITIVITY REACTIONS).

Chronic liver disease is associated with *cirrhosis*, a condition in which liver cells are destroyed and the liver becomes scarred. Failure does not occur until at least 60 percent of cells are destroyed. When 80 percent are destroyed, recovery becomes impossible.

LIVER DISEASES

A number of diseases, drugs, and toxins can affect the liver and cause death of cells. Involvement of the liver is frequently just one aspect of a generalized disease.

Serum Hepatitis (Theiler's Disease). Most cases of serum hepatitis are caused by a hypersensitivity reaction to a horse antiserum. Tetanus antitoxin is the antiserum implicated in nearly all cases. Because of this association, passive immunization with antisera should be avoided in favor of active immunization whenever it is possible.

In cases of serum hepatitis not associated with the administration of horse serums, there is a seasonal occurrence in summer and fall. Several horses may be affected at the same time. This suggests an infectious cause.

Serum hepatitis begins insidiously with malaise and loss of weight that progresses over several weeks or months and then suddenly culminates in acute liver failure and death in a matter of days. The diagnosis is confirmed by liver biopsy. On occasion, a mildly affected horse responds to treatment and recovers.

Chronic Active Hepatitis. This is an inflammatory liver disease of unknown cause. There is no connection with the virus that produces hepatitis in man. The encephalopathy of chronic active hepatitis is often less severe than it is in other forms of liver disease. The diagnosis is made by liver biopsy. Corticosteroids have been used successfully in some cases. In general, the prognosis for recovery is guarded.

Pyrrolizidine Alkaloid and Aflatoxin Toxicity. The ingestion of plants containing pyrrolizidine alkaloids is a common cause of cirrhosis and liver failure in certain parts of the midwestern and western United States. These plants are not palatable, but accidental ingestion can occur when they are cut and baled with alfalfa or when contaminated grain is threshed and the screenings fed to horses.

Cirrhosis caused by plant alkaloids has an unfavorable outlook. By the time liver failure becomes apparent, the liver is too damaged to recover.

Molds found in stored corn and other feeds produce a series of mycotoxins called *aflatoxins* that are highly toxic to the liver. Fortunately, horses are more resistant to these toxins than are most other domestic animals. Signs are like those of moldy corn poisoning.

Toxicity Caused by Chemicals and Drugs. Chemicals known to cause liver toxicity are carbon tetrachloride and tetrachloroethylene (both present in some dewormers), and toxic amounts of copper, lead, phosphorus, selenium, and iron.

Drugs adversely affecting the liver include inhaled anesthetic gases, antibiotics, diuretics, sulfa preparations, anticonvulsants, arsenicals, and some steroids. Most drugs damage the liver only when the recommended dosage is exceeded or the drug is administered for an extended period.

The horse does not have a gallbladder. However, gallstones can form in the bile ducts and produce obstruction. This is rare, but should be considered in a horse with unexplained jaundice. Other rare causes of bile duct obstruction are roundworms and bots. Cancers and liver abscesses are other causes of unexplained jaundice.

Liver function tests are used to diagnose liver insufficiency and to follow its progress. Liver biopsy is the best way to make a tissue diagnosis when it is important to determine the exact cause of the disease.

Treatment: Treatment of acute liver failure is directed at supporting the horse until there is clear evidence of irreversible damage or the horse shows signs of recovery. Return of appetite is a good sign.

Horses with hepatoencephalopathy should be stalled and sedated with xylazine to protect against self-injury. Intravenous fluids containing 10 percent glucose will maintain an adequate blood sugar. Serum ammonia levels can be reduced by administering Neomycin, mineral oil, or lactulose by stomach tube. Alfalfa hay has a high protein content and should be avoided in favor of mixed-grain rations containing beet pulp, molasses, sweet feeds, and milo or other sorghums. Offer 4 to 6 small feedings a day. Vitamin B, vitamin K, and folic acid supplements are recommended. Good-quality oat hay can be introduced as appetite returns.

Protect the horse from photosensitivity by keeping it indoors from dawn to dusk.

RESPIRATORY SYSTEM

A horse's nasopharynx is made up of the nostrils (nares), nasal cavity, and pharynx. The nasal cavity is divided by a midline septum into two passages, one for each nostril. At the back, these passages open into the throat behind the soft palate.

The two nasolacrimal ducts, which drain tears from the eyes, open onto the floor of the nasal cavity close to each nostril. Because of this arrangement, eye ailments with excessive tearing cause a watery discharge from the nose.

The entire respiratory tree is lined by a delicate membrane. On the surface of this membrane is a layer of mucus which is moved by cilia toward the front of the nose. This *mucociliary blanket* traps bacteria and foreign irritants and thus acts as a first line of defense against infection. However, exposure to cold and dehydration stops the motion of the cilia and thickens the mucus. This reduces the effectiveness of the mucociliary blanket.

The *turbinates* are prominent ridges of bone inside each nasal cavity. They produce air turbulence as the horse breathes in. This helps to warm and humidify the air and also traps foreign particles and irritants at the back of the pharynx, where they can be removed by the action of the cilia.

Because the horse is a nose-breather, the nasal passages must be both large and expandable. During maximal exercise, air flow increases tenfold and the nostrils "flare" to provide a bigger opening. Because of the large size of the horse's nasal passages, foreign bodies in the nose are easily sneezed out and rarely produce problems.

A horse's nose is normally cool and moist. There are no sweat glands in the nose. Moisture is secreted by mucous glands in the nasal cavity.

A warm nose suggests that a horse has a fever and may be somewhat dehydrated. However, this is not always the case. Occasionally a sick horse has a runny nose that is cool because of evaporation. If you suspect your horse has a fever, confirm it with a rectal temperature.

Six pairs of *paranasal sinuses* communicate directly or indirectly with the nasal cavity. The frontal and maxillary sinuses are the most important because they are

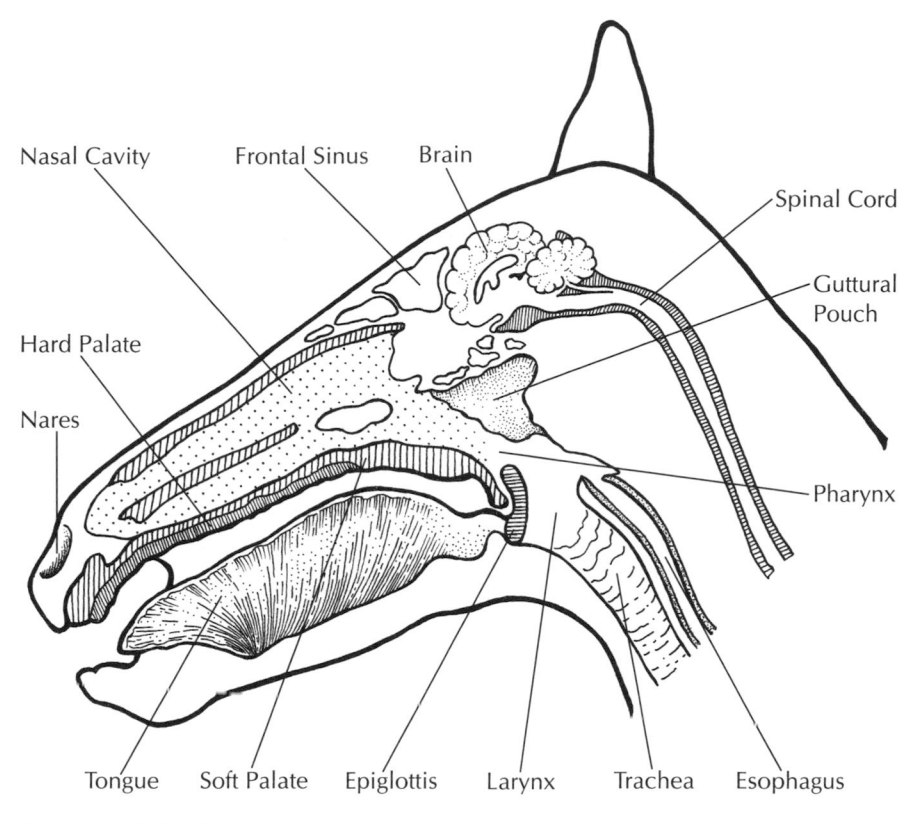

Nasal Cavity Frontal Sinus Brain

Spinal Cord

Guttural Pouch

Hard Palate

Nares

Pharynx

Tongue Soft Palate Epiglottis Larynx Trachea Esophagus

Anatomy of the Head

the most susceptible to sinus infection. In the upper jaw the roots of the cheek teeth are imbedded in the floor of the maxillary sinus. In young horses these roots occupy most of the space in the sinus, but as the horse matures the roots recede and the sinuses become correspondingly larger.

At the back of the pharynx are the paired *Eustachian* or auditory tubes that communicate with the middle ear and equalize air pressure across the eardrum. Each auditory tube has a specialized out-pocket or sac called the *guttural pouch*. These pouches are unique to horses. Ordinarily they are not visible in the neck, but when filled with fluid or air, they can be seen as distinct bulges on each side of the neck just behind the angles of the jaws. The purpose of the guttural pouches is unknown.

A procedure called *nasopharyngeal endoscopy* has greatly simplified the diagnosis of upper respiratory diseases. In this procedure a fiberoptic endoscope is passed into the nasal cavity to view the turbinates, the openings of the sinuses and the guttural pouches, the palate, the back of the throat, and the voice box. Cultures and biopsies can be taken precisely through the instrument. The endoscope can be used to accurately place catheters into a sinus or guttural pouch in order to irrigate and infuse medications.

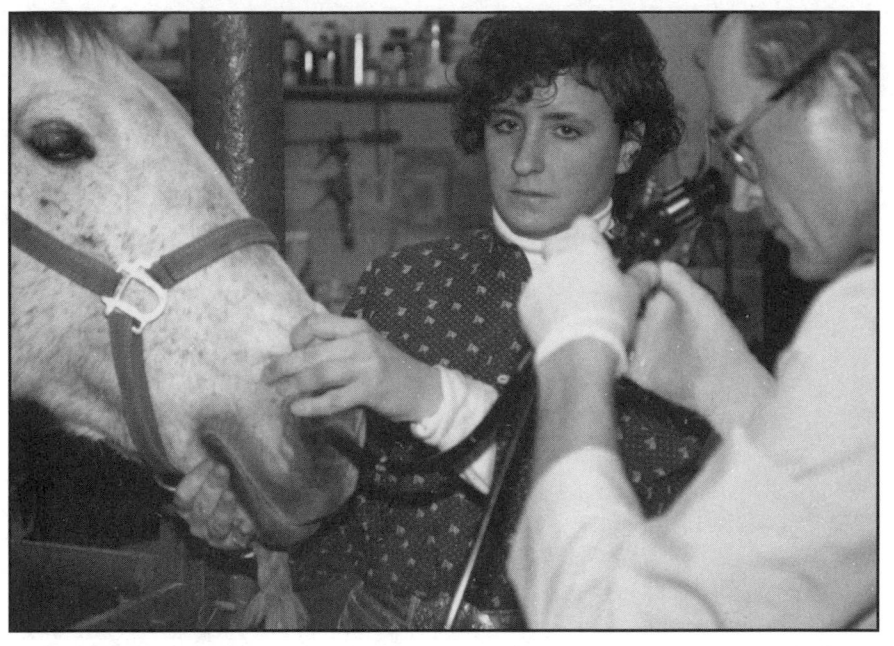

Nasopharyngeal endoscopy has greatly assisted the diagnosis and treatment of upper respiratory diseases.

Bronchoscopy is an endoscopic procedure in which a long scope is passed into the trachea and down into the larger breathing passages. Bleeding may be detected in the trachea of horses with exercise-induced pulmonary hemorrhage (EIPH).

Bronchoalveolar lavage (BAL) is a procedure in which sterile saline is flushed through the scope into the lower respiratory tract, and then the fluid is recovered by suctioning through a channel in the scope.

Trans-tracheal aspiration involves inserting a needle through the skin of the neck into the windpipe. A sterile catheter is passed through the needle into the trachea. Secretions are withdrawn through the catheter.

The secretions obtained by the above methods are cultured and examined under the microscope. This assists in making an exact diagnosis and in guiding treatment.

Signs of Nasal Irritation

RUNNY NOSE (NASAL DISCHARGE)

A discharge which persists for more than a day indicates a disease in the nasal passages, the sinuses, or guttural pouches.

Often you can tell whether a discharge is important by observing its appearance. A watery discharge with sneezing can be due to foreign irritants such as dust or vegetable matter trapped on the mucous membranes. Allergies such as "hay fever" may occasionally produce a clear nasal discharge, but allergic reactions in horses primarily involve the skin and gastrointestinal tract.

A mucoid discharge from both nostrils is characteristic of an equine viral respiratory disease. A thick yellow mucopurulent discharge from both nostrils indicates a bacterial or fungus infection. In the upper airway the most likely sites are the nasal passages, sinuses, guttural pouches, and pharynx. In the lower airway, consider pneumonia and lung abscess.

When you see a puslike discharge from *one* nostril, suspect sinusitis, guttural pouch mycosis, nasal foreign body, polyp, or tumor. Pharyngitis and rhinitis may produce a unilateral nasal discharge. Note that with a guttural pouch infection you can occasionally see a purulent discharge from *both* nostrils even though only one pouch is affected.

The nasal cavity drains best when the head is down. That is why many nasal discharges, particularly those from the sinuses and guttural pouches, are most apparent after a horse has been grazing.

A horse with eye discharge often has nasal discharge. This is because the nasolacrimal ducts drain into the nose.

Colds. Horses don't catch colds as people do. Human cold viruses do not affect the horse. However, young horses are afflicted by a number of viruses of the adenovirus/rhinovirus species which do produce mild symptoms much like the human cold. Usually they are accompanied by a cough, runny eyes, and a sore throat. For more information see EQUINE VIRAL RESPIRATORY DISEASES.

SNEEZING

Sneezing is a reflex resulting from stimulation of the lining of the nose. When a horse sneezes off and on for a few hours but shows no other signs of illness, the sneezing may be due to minor nasal irritation. Sneezing that persists all day long suggests a nasopharyngeal or respiratory tract infection.

Foreign bodies in the nose cause bouts of violent sneezing. The foreign body is almost always expelled, but the irritation caused by it may continue to cause sneezing.

If one nostril appears to be obstructed, a persistent sneezing problem may be due to a foreign body, polyp, or tumor. Check to see if there is less air coming from the nostril by holding a mirror up to the nose and checking for vapor condensation.

NOSEBLEEDS (EPISTAXIS)

Nosebleeds do not occur spontaneously in horses as they do in children. The majority are related to guttural pouch mycosis and ulcerations in the nasopharynx caused by infections, polyps, tumors, and ethmoidal hematomas (see NASOPHARYNGEAL TUMORS). Bleeding tends to occur intermittently, often with the horse at rest. The blood may be mixed with a mucopurulent discharge.

Bleeding from guttural pouch mycosis can be massive and life-threatening. Major bleeds are often preceded by intermittent minor bleeds from one nostril.

Trauma to the face, especially when accompanied by a fracture of the nasal bones, is another cause of nosebleeds.

A nosebleed may be a manifestation of a clotting disorder such as hemophilia, liver disease, warfarin poisoning, or dicumarol (moldy sweet clover) poisoning. These are rare causes of nosebleed.

Exercised-induced pulmonary hemorrhage (EIPH) occurs commonly in race-horses. Infrequently, blood will be seen at the nostrils—suggesting a nosebleed—but the actual site of bleeding is in the lungs.

Nasopharynx

NOSTRILS

Lacerations of the nostrils sometimes result in unsupported flaps of skin that can occlude the airway during inspiration. Failure to repair often results in an obstructing flap of skin, or narrowing of the nostril due to scarring. The laceration is best managed by careful suture repair at the time of injury.

Alar fold stenosis (narrowing of the opening of the nostrils) occurs uncommonly in young horses. Stenosis can result in a fluttering expiratory noise or produce respiratory obstruction. It may be apparent only during exercise. When the narrowing in the nasal openings causes breathing difficulties, the folds can be removed.

Congenitally narrowed nasal passages are another uncommon condition. Horses with this disorder usually have a narrow face and exhibit noisy breathing. These horses have continued exercise intolerance.

Deviation of the nasal septum occasionally occurs as a congenital deformity but most often is caused by facial trauma or a growth in the nasal passage. It can be treated by surgical removal of the deviated part of the septum. The operation is difficult and in most cases must be performed at a center that has the equipment to provide the necessary support.

RHINITIS (NASAL CAVITY INFECTION)

Rhinitis is recognizable by nasal discharge with sneezing, sniffling, and noisy breathing.

Most cases are associated with an equine viral respiratory disease such as equine influenza. The nasal discharge with these conditions is at first watery but soon becomes mucoid, yellow, and thick. Other signs are fever, tearing, blobs of mucus in the eyes, cough, and lethargy.

Another cause of nasal cavity infection is strangles. Strangles is accompanied by high fever, loss of appetite, a dry "throaty" cough, and swelling of lymph nodes at the angle of the jaw and back of the throat. The discharge may be profuse and is always purulent.

A bacterial infection can become established when the nasopharynx has been weakened by a prior viral respiratory disease. Bacterial infections also spread to the nasal cavity from the paranasal sinuses and guttural pouches. A bloody discharge indicates deep involvement with ulceration of the mucosa.

Fungus infections can invade the nasal cavity. The most common is *rhinosporidiosis*. This noncontagious disease produces flat-based or polyplike growths, usually on one side only. These growths bleed easily and occasionally get large enough to obstruct the flow of air. They should be removed.

A foreign body in the nasal cavity produces a malodorous discharge and occasionally bleeding (or blood-tinged mucus) from one nostril. Most foreign bodies can be removed by forceps.

Treatment: The objective of local treatment is to restore normal breathing, prevent or treat infection, and make the horse as comfortable as possible. Gently wipe the nostrils with moist cotton balls to remove dried crusts. Vaporizers help to humidify and restore the integrity of the mucociliary blanket. They are most effective in stalls and closed areas. Nasal sprays, available at drug stores for the treatment of colds in people, can be used to shrink swollen membranes and promote ease of breathing.

A purulent discharge signifies a bacterial infection and indicates the need for antibiotics.

When discharge persists, diagnostic studies are indicated to determine the cause. Fiberoptic endoscopy is the best way to examine the nasal passages, sinuses, and guttural pouches. Cultures taken from the nostrils of horses are unreliable because of the many types of bacteria that normally inhabit this area. Accurate samples can be taken during endoscopy, or your veterinarian can pass a swab or catheter into the nasal cavity to take cultures.

SINUSITIS

The paranasal sinuses communicate with the nasal cavity and are lined by a mucous membrane similar to that of the nose. Therefore nasal cavity infections, particularly those caused by the Streptococcus species, can extend to involve the sinuses. Other causes of sinusitis are abscessed teeth, tumors, and fungus infections of the sinus.

Signs of sinusitis are a purulent discharge from one side of the nose, an eye discharge, and painful swelling or deformity involving the face. Tapping over the sinus produces a dull rather than a hollow sound.

A common cause of *secondary sinusitis* is dental disease, found characteristically in the middle-aged horse. The roots of the upper cheek teeth are embedded in the floor of the maxillary sinuses. When one or more of these teeth become infected, the process erodes into the maxillary sinus. A particularly severe form of purulent sinusitis then ensues. In addition to a copious purulent discharge from the nose, you may notice difficulty breathing, blood in the discharge, a fetid odor, and painful chewing of feed. A communication between the oral cavity and maxillary sinus can develop. This is called a *sinus fistula*. If present, you may see food or plant particles in the nasal discharge.

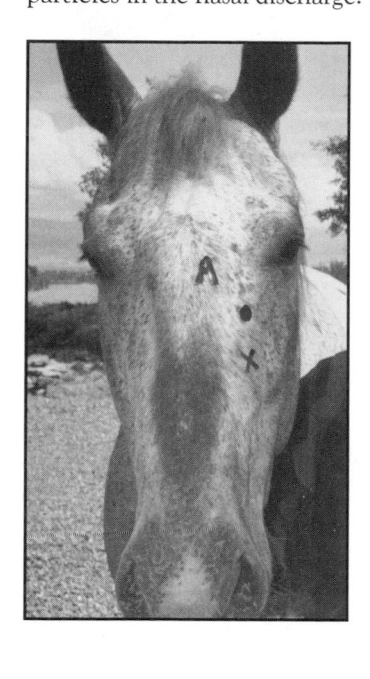

Sites used to bore through the bone to drain the frontal, frontomaxillary, and maxillary sinuses.

Treatment: The diagnosis is made by physical examination and occasionally by the addition of sinus x-rays and fiberoptic endoscopy.

Bacterial sinusitis following a respiratory infection is best treated by instilling a catheter into the sinus through a small hole in the bone. The sinus is flushed and irrigated at regular intervals for several days.

For severe sinusitis, more than one opening may have to be made into the sinus cavity through the face. Large volumes of fluid are flushed into and out of the sinus, which helps to dilute bacteria and debris. Continuous lavage is carried out for 2 to 3 days. Antibiotics can be used along with flushing and drainage, but are not effective when used alone. Abscessed teeth should be removed as described in chapter 7, Oral Cavity, under INFECTED TEETH.

Exercise and grazing help to promote drainage. Turn the horse out to pasture as soon as possible.

Paranasal Sinus Cysts. These are congenital defects resulting from abnormal development of a tooth bud. They occur most often in young growing horses. As the cyst enlarges, it often produces a yellow nasal discharge, swelling of the face, and deviation of the nasal septum. Successful treatment involves removing the entire cyst.

GUTTURAL POUCH DISEASES

The guttural pouches are blind sacs, one on each side of the neck just in back of the angle of the jawbone. They develop as outpockets of the Eustachian or auditory tubes.

Guttural pouch disease produces unilateral nasal discharge and swelling in the neck. The swelling may involve the area of the parotid salivary gland, which overlies the guttural pouch and extends up toward the base of the ear. Pressing on this area produces pain and is often resisted.

Guttural Pouch Empyema. A pouch infection with an accumulation of pus is called *empyema*. There is usually a history of exposure to an infectious respiratory illness such as strangles. Young horses are most often affected. The principal sign is a chronic, intermittent, nonresponsive, unilateral nasal discharge. The discharge is purulent, often bloodstained, and may contain food particles.

A swollen guttural pouch can press on the pharynx, causing difficulty in swallowing, and in very severe cases, respiratory obstruction.

A long-standing empyema is associated with drying and hardening of pus. Over a period of time the pus becomes molded into calcified nodules called *chondroids*. A pouch may contain 30 or more chondroids, some of them quite large and others the size of a small bean.

Nasopharyngeal endoscopy helps to make the diagnosis and obtain pus for culture. X-rays may show an air-fluid level in the distended pouch.

Treatment: Pus in the guttural pouches is best drained by placing a catheter into the pouch through the nose and then irrigating the pouch at regular intervals for several days using a nonirritating saline/antibiotic solution or 1 percent Betadine. The head should be lowered to facilitate drainage and prevent aspiration. For thick pus and chondroids, drainage must be performed through a surgical incision in the neck. A catheter is left in place for flushing and the neck wound is left open for drainage. Horses with respiratory obstruction require urgent tracheotomy.

Guttural Pouch Mycosis (Fungus Infection). *Aspergillus* species are the most common fungi found in guttural pouches. Horses may acquire the fungus from eating damp moldy hay. In addition, the guttural pouches are dark, warm, humid, and poorly ventilated. These factors favor the growth of a fungus.

The most common sign of guttural pouch mycosis is unilateral nosebleed. It usually begins as a mild, intermittent epistaxis, followed in 2 to 3 weeks by a sudden massive hemorrhage. Fungal plaques adhere to the carotid artery and its branches. These arteries pass close to or through the guttural pouches. Weakening of the arterial wall causes bleeding. When the artery finally ruptures, the horse bleeds massively through the nose.

Involvement of a major nerve plexus adjacent to the guttural pouch produces a number of cranial nerve palsies (see chapter 11, Nervous System). The most common is a paralysis of the nerves that initiate swallowing. Horses with this problem often regurgitate food and water through the nose. *Horner's syndrome* (drooping of the upper eyelid), paralysis of the larynx (*roaring*), paralysis of the facial nerve (drooping of the ear, muzzle, and lower lip), and muscle wasting (*atrophy*) of the tongue can occur. Cranial nerve palsies are associated with advanced disease.

Signs of middle ear involvement include head-tilt, staggering, head-shaking, and rapid eye movements.

Treatment: When the diagnosis is made prior to a fatal hemorrhage, tying off the offending artery in the neck can be attempted to prevent bleeding. Nasopharyngeal endoscopy is the only way to effectively examine the guttural pouch and determine which artery is causing the bleeding.

Guttural pouch mycosis is treated much like empyema, except that drugs effective against fungi are used in the irrigating solution. Surgical drainage usually produces better results than medical management, although the outlook for cure is guarded with all forms of treatment. Occasionally a horse with mycosis improves spontaneously.

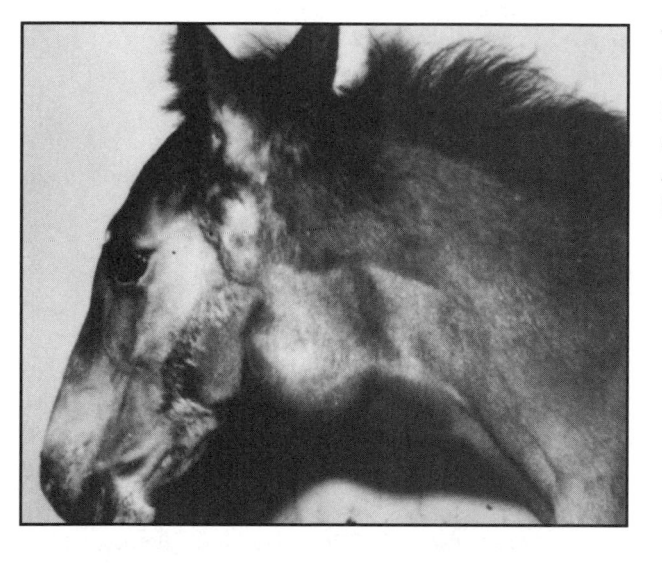

The ballooned-out neck pouch of tympany. Photo: *Equine Medicine and Surgery,* American Veterinary Publications.

Tympany of the Guttural Pouch. Guttural pouch tympany or "bullfrog" disease is a condition in which the pouches become distended with air. It occurs in foals from birth to 18 months of age. Owing to the presence of an abnormal flap of mucosa over the pharyngeal opening of the Eustachian (auditory) tube, a one-way valve traps air in the pouch. The result is a soft, balloonlike swelling in the neck extending from the base of the ear to the angle of the jaw. This does not seem to bother most foals, but the guttural pouch may progressively enlarge to the extent that it narrows the pharynx. This can interfere with swallowing and even cause respiratory distress.

Treatment: The pouch can be deflated by a catheter passed into the auditory tube, or by a needle inserted through the neck. These measures are temporary, as the pouch rapidly refills. They are indicated to relieve an acute pharyngeal obstruction.

Tympany may temporarily correct spontaneously, but surgical removal of the obstructing flap with external drainage of the pouch through the neck is usually necessary.

NASOPHARYNGEAL TUMORS

Tumors of the nasopharynx interfere with airflow in the nasal passage, producing inspiratory noise, nasal discharge, intermittent nosebleeds, and swelling or deformity of the face. The nasal discharge may be mucoid or mucopurulent and blood-tinged.

The most common malignant tumor is squamous cell carcinoma of the nasal turbinates. The most common benign tumor is the nasal polyp. Sarcomas and carcinomas can arise in the paranasal sinuses and guttural pouches. Tumors of dental origin are found in the maxillary sinuses.

A condition called *progressive ethmoidal hematoma* affects the nasal turbinates. This nonmalignant tumor is actually a growth of fibrous connective tissue and blood vessels. The tumor-mass can become quite large, fill the entire nasal cavity, and become visible at the nostrils. The cause is unknown.

Benign tumors such as polyps can be cured by simple removal. Malignant tumors, especially those that deform the face, are extensively invasive and often metastatic. Treatment usually is unrewarding.

Soft Palate and Epiglottis

The soft palate is a flap of tissue at the back of the pharynx. In its normal position the soft palate is down, which seals off the oral airway and opens up the nasal airway. As horses are obligate nose-breathers, the soft palate is always down except when the horse swallows. Note also that as the horse swallows, the epiglottis flips over the trachea like a lid, preventing food from entering the lungs.

The relationship between the positions of the soft palate and epiglottis is important. In the normal relationship the epiglottis is behind (*dorsal* to) the palate, as shown in the illustration *Anatomy of the Head*.

There are certain disorders in which the soft palate and epiglottis produce respiratory symptoms that interfere with athletic performance. Such conditions include swelling of the palate from pharyngeal lymphoid hyperplasia, a condition called dorsal displacement of the soft palate, paralysis of the nerves to the palate, epiglottic entrapment, and pharyngeal cysts.

Dorsal Displacement of the Soft Palate. In this situation the normal relationship between the soft palate and epiglottis is reversed: the epiglottis being in front of, rather than behind or dorsal to, the soft palate. The displacement of the soft palate behind the epiglottis causes a narrowing in the diameter of the nasopharyngeal airway at this level. The displacement is intermittent and usually occurs with forced breathing. There are a number of muscular, developmental, and neurological causes of dorsal displacement. In some horses the cause is unknown.

Symptoms of displacement usually occur during exercise as the horse reaches high speeds. The horse has sudden difficulty breathing, drops its speed, and produces a gurgling noise referred to as "choking down." The diagnosis is confirmed by nasopharyngeal endoscopy and lateral x-rays of the head.

Various surgical procedures are employed. They involve removing a part of the palate and dividing the muscles that raise the larynx during strenuous exercise. The choice depends on what is thought to be the cause of the displacement. With selection of the appropriate operation, the outlook for athletic performance is good.

Epiglottic Entrapment. In this situation mucosal folds surrounding the epiglottis become excessively large, creating a mass that envelops the epiglottis and narrows the air passage. Some cases are associated with a *hypoplastic epiglottis* (an epiglottis that is smaller or less well developed than normal). Epiglottic entrapment occurs in Standardbreds and Thoroughbreds. It is not common.

As a consequence of the narrowed airway, affected horses are exercise-intolerant, breathe noisily during inspiration or expiration, and cough during exercise or after eating. Nasopharyngeal endoscopy reveals redundant folds, often swollen and ulcerated, obscuring the view of the epiglottis.

Treatment involves surgically removing the redundant mucosal folds. Various operations have been employed. Complications include recurrent entrapment (when too little tissue is removed) and dorsal displacement (when too much tissue is removed). A horse with a hypoplastic epiglottis presents a special problem and has a poor prognosis for athletic performance.

Pharyngeal Cysts. These noncancerous growths arise from the back of the pharynx. They are relatively uncommon and seen most often in 2- to 3-year-old racehorses. Signs are similar to those of a soft palate disorder. Diagnosis is by nasopharyngeal endoscopy. Pharyngeal cysts can be removed surgically.

Throat

SORE THROAT (PHARYNGITIS)

Horses do not have tonsils like those of people. However, they do possess aggregates of lymphoid tissues scattered over the back of the pharynx. These lymphoid follicles are well developed and prominent in young horses, but usually regress and disappear at 3 to 4 years of age.

Acute Pharyngitis. Sore throats are associated with respiratory infections such as strangles, rhinopneumonitis, and equine influenza. The throat appears red and inflamed. A purulent discharge coats the back of the pharynx. Other symptoms include fever, noisy respirations, coughing, gagging, pain in the throat on swallowing, and loss of appetite. Enlarged lymph nodes may be felt beneath the angles of the jaws.

Treatment: Anti-inflammatory drugs such as Banamine and Butazolidin relieve pain and encourage appetite and food consumption. Provide a soft diet, or better yet, turn the horse out onto fresh green pasture. Antibiotics alone or in combination with corticosteroids are often sprayed 3 times a day on the back of the throat through a nasopharyngeal catheter. The effectiveness of this is not known.

Frequent vaccination with respiratory virus vaccines (every 4 to 6 months) may prevent some episodes of pharyngitis.

Pharyngeal Lymphoid Hyperplasia (Chronic Sore Throat). In this condition the lymphatic tissue at the back of the pharynx became quite large and diminish the size of the nasopharyngeal airway. This can cause varying degrees of airway obstruction. Signs are decreased exercise tolerance, a "blowing" sound when the horse becomes slightly winded, and a chronic cough—especially at the start or finish of a workout.

One complication of chronic lymphoid hyperplasia is *guttural pouch tympany*. The tympany may be caused by a blockage of the auditory tube from enlarged follicles.

Lymphoid hyperplasia tends to affect racehorses at 2 to 3 years of age. Exposure to one of the equine respiratory viruses often precedes the hyperplasia. Exposure to air pollutants found around racetracks is another predisposing cause. If the diagnosis is uncertain and there is a question of lymphoma, nasopharyngeal endoscopy with biopsy of a follicle will clarify the diagnosis. Chronic lymphoid hyperplasia usually resolves spontaneously by 3 years of age.

Treatment: Ideally the horses should be rested for at least 2 months to allow swollen follicles to get smaller. If rest is not feasible, the horse can be placed on a broad-spectrum antibiotic and treated with nonsteroidal anti-inflammatory medications and topical steroids. If the horse is still unable to return to training and competition, the obstructing lymphoid tissue can be removed by cryosurgery, laser, or electrocautery. General anesthesia is required.

Early recognition of pharyngeal hyperplasia combined with frequent vaccination with influenza and rhinopneumonitis vaccines (every 4 to 6 months) may alter the course of the disease for the better and even prevent recurrences.

Larynx
(Voice Box)

The larynx is an oblong box situated between the nasopharynx and trachea. It is composed of a number of cartilages, including the paired arytenoids. Within the larynx are the two vocal cords that open and close the airway. The vocal cords and muscles of the larynx are supplied by the two recurrent laryngeal nerves.

At the top of the larynx is the epiglottis, a leaflike flap that covers it during swallowing, thus preventing food from going down the windpipe. The larynx is the most sensitive cough area in the respiratory system.

LARYNGITIS

Laryngitis is inflammation of the voice box. It frequently follows respiratory infections complicated by a chronic or persistent cough. Other causes include smoke inhalation and foreign bodies in the larynx.

Signs of laryngitis are a persistent harsh cough that is initially dry but later becomes soft and moist. A nasal discharge may be present. Swallowing can be difficult and painful.

Laryngeal edema is a condition in which the vocal cords and laryngeal cartilages become fluid-filled and swollen. The resultant narrowing of the airway produces a croupy sound, or *stridor*, as the horse breathes in. In its most severe form, laryngeal edema results in complete airway obstruction and death from asphyxiation.

Treatment: The cough is best treated by confining the horse in a warm, dry enclosure and humidifying the atmosphere. Offer a soft or liquid diet. Cough suppressants containing dextromethorphan (DM) can be applied to the horse's tongue.

Laryngeal edema requires urgent treatment, including intravenous corticosteroids. The airway must be kept open. This may require insertion of an endotracheal tube or an emergency tracheotomy.

VOCAL CORD PARALYSIS (ROARING)

Roaring is a common laryngeal problem. It is due to paralysis of one of the recurrent laryngeal nerves (nearly always the left). When one nerve is inoperative, the vocal cord on that side becomes paralyzed and does not retract back to open the larynx as the horse breathes in or out. The resultant narrowing of the air passage is responsible for the characteristic "roaring" or whistling sound that begins as the horse is exercised. In addition, the horse performs poorly and seems unfit. The degree of nerve paralysis may vary, producing a range of disability.

Evidence suggests that some cases of vocal cord paralysis are due to a degenerative process affecting the recurrent laryngeal nerves. The degeneration may be influenced by heredity, and other factors yet to be determined. Acquired nerve injury follows guttural pouch infections, jugular vein thrombophlebitis, lead poisoning, strangles, and tetanus.

Treatment: Fiberoptic endoscopy will reveal a cord that does not open as the horse breathes in. In addition, endoscopy helps to exclude other causes of roaring such as laryngitis, arytenoid chondritis, and dorsal displacement of the soft palate. If the condition interferes with the horse's utility, an operation on the larynx can be considered. There are different procedures. Results do vary and complications can occur.

ARYTENOID CHONDRITIS

Inflammation of one of the paired arytenoid cartilages (*chondritis*) results in progressive enlargement and distortion of the cartilage, eventually leading to partial obstruction of the larynx and symptoms of roaring like those described above.

Arytenoid chondritis usually occurs in young racehorses but has been observed in other breeds. It usually involves only one side. The cause is unknown.

Medical treatment has not been successful. However, many horses with mild disease are able to perform satisfactorily if strenuous exercise is not required. Surgical removal of the affected cartilage can be considered for horses in whom obstruction interferes with athletic fitness. A high postoperative complication rate has been observed. About 50 percent of such horses can return to full athletic performance.

Lower Respiratory System

The lower respiratory system is made up of the *trachea* or windpipe, the *bronchi* or large breathing tubes, the *bronchioles* or small breathing tubes, and the lungs. As the breathing tubes branch, they become progressively smaller until they open into the air sacs. It is here that air exchanges with the blood. The ribs and muscles of the chest, along with the diaphragm, function as a bellows moving air into and out of the lungs.

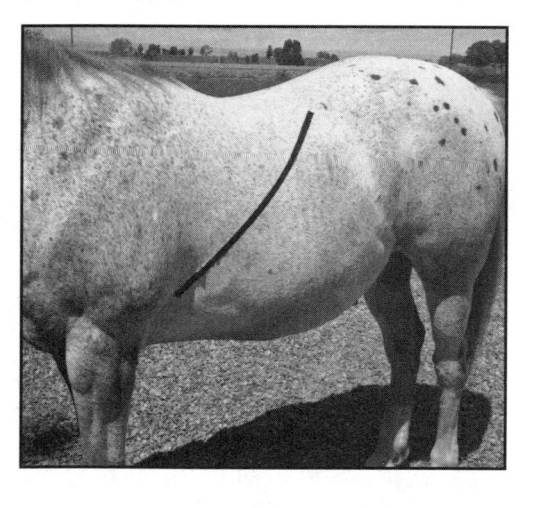

The tape shows the position of the diaphragm, which separates the chest and abdomen.

A horse at rest takes about 10 to 30 breaths per minute. Determine the breathing rate by observing and counting the movements of the nostrils or flanks. The respiratory motion should be smooth, even, and unrestricted.

Abnormal breathing patterns are discussed below.

RAPID LABORED BREATHING (DYSPNEA)

Rapid breathing can be caused by fear, pain, fever, shock, and dehydration. A horse who is winded after exercise may be unfit and out of condition. In the absence of exercise, a rate of 30 breaths per minute or greater indicates a serious condition.

Difficult or labored breathing is known as *dyspnea*. In severe dyspnea the horse stands with its feet spread apart, neck stretched out, and head extended. You may see flaring of the nostrils and an anxious expression, with protruding of the eye-balls. Movement of the chest wall is exaggerated and the flanks heave. Dyspnea is associated with shock and sepsis, heart failure, pneumonia, fluid in the lungs, over-exertion, and chronic obstructive pulmonary disease (COPD).

Cyanosis is the condition in which the blood turns blue because of inadequate oxygen. The bluish discoloration can be seen in the mucous membranes of the mouth, lips, and conjunctiva. This is a grave sign in horses.

Broken wind occurs in horses with COPD and longstanding airway disease affecting the bronchioles. You will observe a prolonged phase of expiration fol-lowed by a second expiratory effort in which the horse contracts its abdominal muscles to squeeze the residual air out of the lungs. This is often accompanied by wheezing.

NOISY BREATHING

Abnormal breathing sounds are most apparent on inspiration but may be heard on expiration.

Whistling and *roaring* are produced by air flowing through a narrow passage in the nasopharynx. Whistling is a high-pitched sound. Roaring is a deep sound and indicates a greater degree of obstruction. The most common causes of both are vocal cord paralysis and displacements of the soft palate.

Blowing occurs on both inspiration and expiration. It can be caused by pulling back too forcefully on the bit, which arches the neck and narrows the cross-sectional diameter of the pharynx. A persistent blowing noise at rest, or at the beginning of exercise, suggests a growth or some other partial blockage in the na-sopharynx, larynx, or windpipe.

Thick-wind is a temporary form of blowing which occurs in out-of-condition horses. It disappears as the horse is brought to fitness.

Trumpeting or *high-blowing* is an expiratory noise which occurs in fresh high-spirited horses at the outset of exercise. It is caused by flapping of the nasal folds and is of no consequence.

Wheezes are whistling, sometimes musical sounds, heard over the trachea and lungs. They indicate narrowing of the breathing tubes from spasm or broncho-constriction. Wheezes are characteristic of acute bronchitis and chronic obstruc-tive pulmonary disease.

SHALLOW BREATHING

Splinting (shallow breathing) is a guarded effort to avoid the pain of a deep breath. To compensate, the horse breathes more rapidly but less deeply. The pain of pleurisy and rib fracture causes splinting.

Fluid in the chest (blood, pus, serum) produces shallow breathing—but without pain.

Wheezes are best heard over the trachea. They indicate acute bronchitis and small airway involvement in COPD.

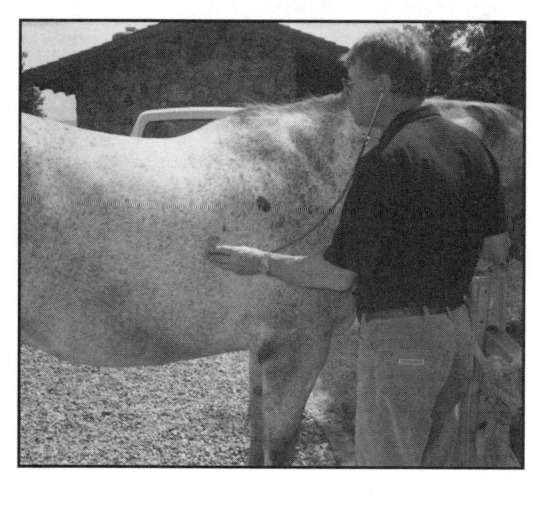

Crackling and bubbling sounds are heard over the lungs. They are present in pneumonia and congestive heart failure.

COUGH

A cough is a reflex produced by an irritation of the air passages. Coughs are caused by infectious diseases, smoke and other inhaled irritants, and by grass seeds and foreign objects in the airway. Upper airway coughs include those caused by acute respiratory infections, pharyngitis, guttural pouch infections, sinusitis, and soft palate disorders. Lower airway coughs are caused by acute bronchitis, COPD, pneumonia, pleuritis, and pleural effusion. Lungworms and the larvae of ascarids also produce bouts of lower airway coughing.

A cough accompanied by fever, sneezing, noisy breathing, and nasal and/or eye discharge, is indicative of a contagious equine respiratory disease.

The circumstances surrounding a cough may suggest its cause. A cough that occurs when the horse is stabled is most likely caused by dust or some other inhaled atmospheric irritant. When it occurs after drinking, it may be due to sinusitis, guttural pouch disease, or leakage of fluid into the windpipe from faulty closure of the epiglottis.

Coughs can be strong and forceful or weak and soft. Loud, harsh, nonproductive coughs are indicative of upper airway disease and are commonly caused by acute respiratory illnesses such as equine influenza, sore throat, guttural pouch disease, and laryngitis. Moist weak coughs are heard in advanced COPD. Soft, painful coughs are heard in pleuritis, rib fractures, and acute pleuropneumonia.

Moist coughs suggest active infection in the lower respiratory system, particularly pneumonia. They occur whenever mucus accumulates in the breathing tubes. The mucus or phlegm coughed up may contain blood. If it appears in streaks, it probably originates somewhere in the upper respiratory tract. The phlegm of pneumonia is homogeneous and red or reddish-brown.

Coughs are self-perpetuating. Coughing by itself irritates the airways, dries out the mucous lining, and lowers resistance to infection. This leads to further coughing.

Treatment: Minor coughs of brief duration are best treated by removing the horse from the source of the irritant. Cigarette smoke, aerosol insecticides, stable dust, and mold should be eliminated from stables and barns, as discussed in the treatment of COPD. Barns and stables should be open and well ventilated. Closing a stable to keep the horse warm is not a good practice, as it invariably increases atmospheric pollutants. Except in unusual circumstances, cough suppressants are contraindicated in horses. The cough is important in eliminating infected secretions from the airway. Mucolytics and expectorants can be of value in situations in which the mucus is thick and difficult to bring up. Your veterinarian can suggest an appropriate preparation.

A cough that persists for more than two days indicates that something is wrong in the respiratory tract. Consult your veterinarian. It is important to diagnose and treat the cause of a persistent cough. Fiberoptic bronchoscopy is the best and most productive test for investigating airway disease. It is indicated in the horse with a persistent cough for whom the cause is not apparent on physical examination or chest x-ray.

ACUTE BRONCHITIS

Inflammation of the *large* breathing tubes is called bronchitis. It is characterized by repeated coughing, often precipitated by cold air and vigorous exercise. The coughing further irritates the lining of the trachea. For this reason the term *tracheobronchitis* may be more accurate.

Acute bronchitis occurs with equine viral respiratory infections and strangles. After the acute infection, the cough may persist for two to three weeks and then should disappear. However, if complicated by secondary bacterial infection, the cough persists much longer. In time the problem may involve the smaller breathing tubes and become one of chronic obstructive pulmonary disease.

Other causes of acute bronchitis are inhalation of smoke, irritant fumes, and industrial pollutants. The use of a breathing tube during general anesthesia may irritate the airway and produce a postoperative tracheobronchitis.

Chronic bronchitis is not a specific diagnosis in equine practice. A chronic cough is considered part of the COPD syndrome.

Treatment: Treat the cough as described above. It is important to restrict exercise in horses with acute bronchitis.

CHRONIC OBSTRUCTIVE PULMONARY DISEASE (HEAVES)

Chronic obstructive pulmonary disease (COPD), sometimes erroneously referred to as *emphysema,* is a common but easily preventable respiratory ailment in horses. COPD in horses is not comparable to COPD in humans.

The cardinal feature of COPD is *small* airway obstruction, leading to chronic cough, shortness of wind, and exercise intolerance. The airway obstruction is reversible until scarring in the breathing passages results in permanent damage. The obstruction can be caused by plugs of mucus and debris in the lower airway, or it may take the form of bronchospasm and wheezing. Inflammation and spasm of these smaller breathing tubes is called *bronchiolitis.*

The common cause of COPD is the chronic inhalation of molds and fungus spores in hay and straw present in barns and stables and particularly in the horse's bedding. Dust, ammonium, cigarette smoke, and other environmental irritants are contributory factors. Exposure to these airborne irritants triggers attacks of coughing, often asthmatic-like and accompanied by wheezing. These attacks are believed to represent an allergic or hypersensitivity reaction to the inhaled allergen. COPD often follows an acute respiratory illness that lowers the horse's resistance to airborne pollutants.

A seasonal allergy has been described. It is known as summer pasture-associated obstructive pulmonary disease (SPAOPD) and appears to be caused by airborne pollens.

Horses mildly affected with COPD breathe normally at rest but become short of breath with exercise. Coughing occurs intermittently, usually when the horse is exposed to dust or cold. The cough is dry and nonproductive.

With continued exposure to the respiratory irritant, the horse coughs more frequently and especially after exercise and feeding. The cough becomes productive and may be accompanied by nasal discharge. Exercise tolerance is more restricted.

In the late stages (*heaves*), there is chronic infection and scarring in the lower airways. The cough is soft and moist and accompanied by wheezing, increased respiratory rate at rest, weight loss, flared nostrils, and a prolonged double phase of expiration. The abdominal wall muscles are used to assist expiration since the lung tissue has lost much of its elasticity. As the abdominal muscles become strongly developed, you will see a "heave line," which is a ridge of muscle running obliquely down the middle of the flank over the ribcage toward the back of the elbow. Horses with heaves are severely restricted in exercise and may become short of breath just walking across a paddock.

Early diagnosis is essential to prevent the disease from reaching an irreversible state. Trans-tracheal aspiration, as discussed at the beginning of this chapter, will

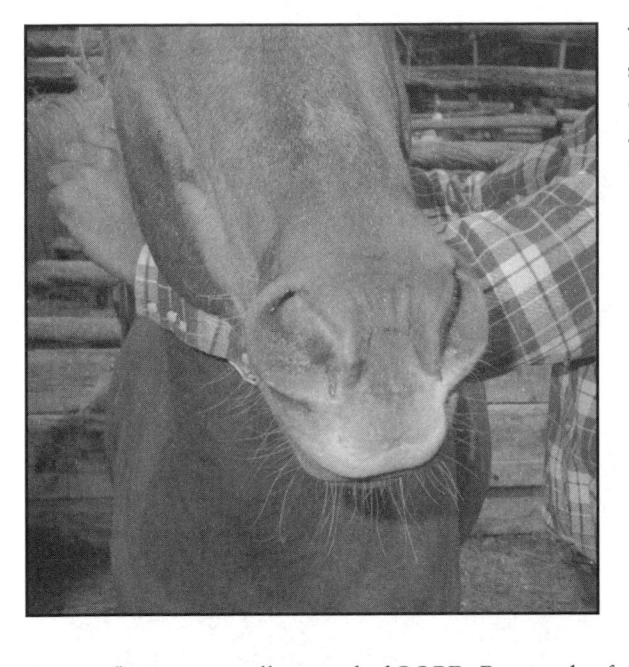

The flared nostrils, shortness of breath, and clear nasal discharge of a horse with heaves (advanced COPD).

show inflammatory cells typical of COPD. Bacterial infection is ordinarily absent. When present, it indicates secondary bacterial involvement or pneumonia. Fiberoptic endoscopy is useful in distinguishing upper airway diseases from COPD.

Lungworm infection may mimic COPD and should be excluded as the cause of a chronic cough.

Treatment: Bronchospasm is a major problem. A bronchodilator can be administered during an acute attack and, if the wheezing clears and breathing is easier, continued use may be indicated. Bronchodilators are usually given for short periods while the adjustments (described below) are made in the horse's environment. A mask inhaler system has been developed for horses which allows metered-dose bronchodilators and other drugs to be delivered quickly and effectively directly to the airways. A drug called sodium chromoglycate, administered by nebulizer, is effective when environmental control is genuinely impossible. Corticosteroids are used to reduce the inflammatory response in a particularly severe attack. These drugs should be administered by your veterinarian.

Mucolytics and expectorants loosen secretions and clear the air passages. A vaporizer also serves this purpose. Antibiotics selected on the basis of culture and sensitivity are indicated for acute infectious relapses. A full course should be given to prevent the emergence of resistant bacteria.

The vast majority of horses with mild to moderate COPD recover with proper treatment and remain asymptomatic. The most important step in the treatment (and prevention) of COPD is to provide fresh air and a dust-free environment. To that effect:

- Keep horses on pasture or in open paddocks and out of barns and stables whenever possible.

An open dust-free barn with good ventilation and a bedding of wood chips will greatly assist in the treatment and prevention of respiratory disease.

- Use peat, shredded paper, or wood shavings for bedding; avoid hay or straw.
- Remove dust, cobwebs, and loose feed from indoor enclosures. Barns and stables should be kept open and well-ventilated. Stalls should be cleaned and the bedding changed on a daily basis. A heated stable that will not be open to cross-ventilation should have a ventilating fan with a capacity of 100 cubic feet per adult horse. In cold weather, only $1/4$ of the capacity of the fan is required. However, closing a barn to keep horses warm is not a good practice.
- Horses should be stalled in well-ventilated boxes with the top door open.
- The concentration of fine particles in the air is highest when a stall is being cleaned and bedded. At such times, move the horse outside.
- Feed hay flakes in hay nets; soak the flakes for a few minutes to reduce dust.
- Fungal spores can be present even in the best-quality hay. Consider switching a horse with COPD to pelleted feeds, hay cubes, or wafers.
- Harvesting hay at higher than usual moisture content, and preserving the hay with organic materials such as a mixture of propionic and acetic acids, will reduce dust in the hay.

PNEUMONIA

Pneumonia is an infection of the lungs. Usually it is classified according to its cause: viral, bacterial, fungal, parasitic, or aspiration in type.

Bacterial pneumonia usually occurs as a sequel to one of the equine viral respiratory infections. The most common causative bacteria is S. *zooepidemicus*, but numerous species can produce adult pneumonia. Individuals most likely to be affected are stressed horses, old horses, horses who are malnourished and debilitated, and very young foals. Foal pneumonia is discussed in chapter 16, Pediatrics.

The general signs of pneumonia are productive cough, high fever, purulent nasal discharge, loss of appetite and weight, and shortness of breath. On listening to the chest with a stethoscope, one can often hear moist crackling breath sounds or rattling and bubbling noises. Trans-tracheal aspiration is used to obtain infected secretions for culture and sensitivity testing. Chest x-ray is indicated to confirm the diagnosis and look for lung abscesses and pleural effusion.

Treatment: Veterinary attention is required. Move the horse to warm dry quarters. Humidify the air. Provide plenty of fresh water. Maintain hydration since this is critical in liquefying secretions and promoting clearance from the respiratory tract. Do not use cough suppressants. Coughing helps to clear the airway. Bronchodilators and plain expectorants may be beneficial if the horse exhibits labored breathing.

Intravenous or intramuscular antibiotics are used in the treatment of bacterial pneumonia, and are often used prophylactically in viral pneumonia to prevent secondary bacterial infection. Most (but not all) of the common bacterial species are sensitive to penicillin. Accordingly, penicillin is started while awaiting the results of antibiotic sensitivity tests. The chosen antibiotic should be continued for at least 1 to 2 months to prevent the secondary complications of lung abscess and pleural effusion.

Immune stimulants such as EqStim are available as adjunctive treatment and may decrease recovery time and protect against relapses.

After recovering from pneumonia, a horse should be rested for at least 3 weeks.

PLEURITIS AND PLEURAL EFFUSION

Pleuritis is a painful inflammation of the membrane which lines the inside of the chest cavity. Infection of this membrane results in fluid accumulation in the space between the lungs and the ribs. This is called *pleural effusion*.

Pleuritis and pleural effusion develop as a complication of pneumonia or lung abscess. The appearance of rapid shallow breathing and splinting in a horse with a cough suggests the development of pleuritis. A characteristic grunting sound may be heard with each breath. As fluid accumulates in the pleural space, breath sounds heard with a stethoscope will become diminished or absent over the lower part of the chest. Ultrasound examination of the chest is of great assistance in determining the amount of fluid accumulation, as well as its composition and exact location.

Acute pleuropneumonia is a particularly severe form of pleuritis and pneumonia. A primary form occurs in racehorses and horses undergoing the stress of shipping. When a horse is carried in a trailer, it cannot lower its head to clear mucus from the nasopharynx. Horses with nasopharyngeal and/or guttural pouch infections are quite likely to aspirate under these circumstances and infect both pleural spaces. Signs are like those of acute pleuritis except that the respiratory distress is usually more severe and you may also see colic, tying up, and swelling of the limbs or lower chest. The pleural fluid may be brown and foul-smelling, which indicates an anaerobic bacterial infection. In this situation the outlook is guarded.

Treatment: It is like that described for pneumonia. Long-term antibiotics are administered in accordance with culture and sensitivity reports. An antibiotic effective against anaerobic bacteria is often required.

A large pleural effusion should be removed by *thoracentesis*. In this procedure a catheter is placed into the pleural space through a large-bore needle inserted between the ribs. The needle is removed, leaving the catheter in place for drainage. A horse will exhibit marked improvement in breathing after the removal of a large pleural effusion. Fluid is submitted to the laboratory for diagnostic tests.

For prolonged drainage, the catheter is exchanged for a large-bore chest tube or a one-way flutter valve. These devices can be left in place for weeks. On occasion, a window must be made in the ribcage to remove thick, tenacious pus.

Maintain nutrition and rest the horse until fully recovered and back to normal weight.

EXERCISE-INDUCED PULMONARY HEMORRHAGE (EIPH)

EIPH is defined as bleeding from the lungs with exercise. It is common among Thoroughbreds, Quarter Horses, Appaloosas, and Arabians. In fact, most racing Thoroughbreds will experience EIPH at some point in their careers. The importance of EIPH is related to its possible etiology as a cause of poor racing performance.

In a typical example of "bleeders," the horse does well in the first three-fourths of the race but falls off markedly toward the end. The horse coughs and repeatedly swallows (blood), cools out slowly, and exhibits respiratory difficulty with rapid labored breathing. Bleeding through the nostrils is observed either immediately after the race or when the horse returns to its stall and lowers its head.

Studies of the airways of racehorses shortly after maximal exercise using fiberoptic bronchoscopy reveal blood in the trachea in the majority of horses, even though blood at the nostrils occurs in less than 10 percent. The amount of bleeding is highly variable. In some horses the amount of blood in the bleeding tubes is extensive and may actually cause the horse to choke up. (There are even reports in which collapse and death have occured from massive bleeding and asphyxiation.) In the majority of horses, however, bleeding is relatively mild.

From these and other studies it appears that not all horses with EIPH experience poor racing performance, and that horses with EIPH who do fail to meet expectations may do so for reasons other than EIPH. However, in the small number of horses with *extensive* bleeding, it seems only logical that an airway full of blood would reduce maximum breathing capacity and oxygen exchange, and that this would be sufficient to account for the poor performance in these individuals.

The exact mechanism by which bleeding occurs in EIPH is a matter of debate. In a maximally exercising horse, the pressure inside the pulmonary capillaries increases greatly at a time when the airway pressure on the other side of the capillary is dropping. In theory, this pressure differential might cause rupture of the blood vessels and bleeding into the air sacs. Alternately, areas of scarring from prior respiratory infections could weaken the capillary bed and allow bleeding to occur. More than one factor may be involved.

The diagnosis of EIPH is made by fiberoptic bronchoscopy. The best time to look for bleeding from the lungs is about one hour after hard exercise. Radioactive scintigraphy has proven to be a useful test in clarifying certain aspects of the disease and in giving a prognosis for return to racing. It is only available at universities and equine centers.

Treatment: The diuretic furosemide (Lasix), given before a race, is the most commonly used drug in the treatment and prevention of bleeding. Surprisingly, although this has been studied, there is no evidence to show that giving Lasix has any influence on racing performance. This is understandable if, in fact, it is true that whether a horse bleeds or not has little if any effect on its performance. However, Lasix does appear to reduce the severity of bleeding in some individuals. Many states regulate its use, both in dosage and when it can be given. In some states the diagnosis of EIPH must be proven before the diuretic is allowed.

Bronchodilators appear to have little therapeutic value. Vitamin C, vitamin K, conjugated estrogen, and various feed additives have all been used empirically but without established benefit.

Management practices (discussed in the section on COPD) that reduce the severity and occurrence of small airway disease offer the greatest potential for improving athletic performance. This is because small airway disease is both a cause of athletic unfitness and a potential precursor of EIPH.

AMMONIA TOXICITY

Ammonia gas, released from urine and manure in bedding, can be a problem in poorly ventilated barns and stalls. Ammonia is an irritant that destroys the natural defense mechanisms that protect the respiratory tract.

Neonatal and young foals are more susceptible to ammonia toxicity than older horses because of their immature respiratory tracts, and because they are closer to the source of gas. However, chronically exposed individuals, whether young or old, run the risk of developing pneumonia.

Treatment: Once you are able to smell ammonia in the stall, the gas is already present in harmful concentrations. Move the horse to a well-ventilated area. If the horse exhibits symptoms, treat for cough or pneumonia as described earlier in this chapter.

Prevention: Bedding should be changed daily, especially in winter months when stables and barns are often closed. Ammonia toxicity will not be a problem in an open, well-ventilated building.

CIRCULATORY SYSTEM

The circulatory system is composed of the heart, the blood, and the blood vessels. The heart is a pump made up of four chambers: the right atrium and right ventricle, and the left atrium and left ventricle. A horse's heart is larger and more rounded than a human's. The right and left chambers are separated by an intramuscular septum or wall. Four valves are present. Their function is to keep blood flowing in one direction.

The amount of blood within the circulatory system of an adult horse weighing 1,000 pounds is 35,000 cc (35 cc per pound). This is about 9 gallons.

The blood is pumped out of the left ventricle into the aorta; passes through arteries of progressively smaller caliber; and reaches the capillary beds of the skin, brain, muscles, kidneys, and other internal organs. Here oxygen and nutrients are exchanged for carbon dioxide and water. The blood then travels back to the heart through veins of progressively larger diameter, finally reaching the right atrium via two large veins called the *anterior* and *posterior vena cavae*.

From the right atrium, blood passes into the right ventricle and out into the pulmonary circulation through the pulmonary artery. The pulmonary artery branches into smaller vessels and finally into capillaries surrounding air sacs (alveoli). Here carbon dioxide is exchanged for oxygen. The blood then passes through veins of progressively larger diameter, finally entering the pulmonary veins. The pulmonary veins conduct blood to the left atrium, after which it enters the left ventricle—thus completing the cycle.

The heart has its own internal electrical system that controls the rate and force of contraction. The heart rate is also influenced by neurohumeral factors. Thus the heart rate increases when the horse exercises, becomes excited, runs a fever, is overheated, or is in shock—circumstances in which more cardiac output is needed. The arteries and veins are also under nervous and hormonal influences. They expand and contract to maintain a stable blood pressure.

There are certain physical signs that help to determine whether a horse's heart and circulation are working properly. Among the most useful are taking

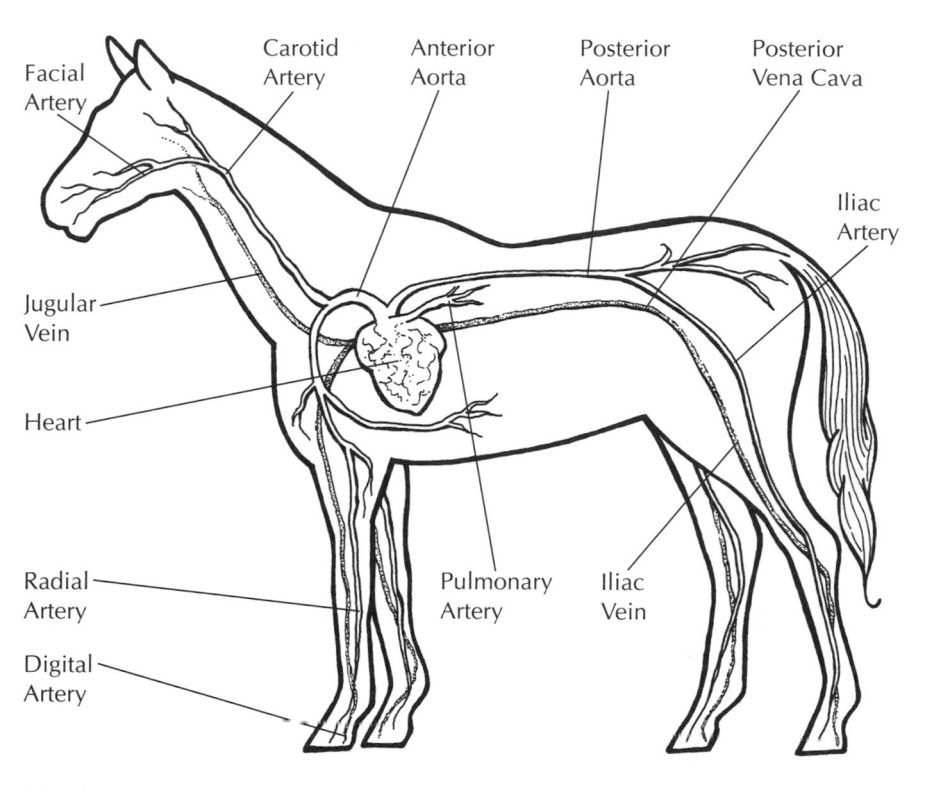

Circulatory System

the pulse, checking the capillary refill time, and looking for dependent edema. Familiarize yourself with normal findings so you can recognize abnormal signs if they appear.

Pulse. The pulse, which is a reflection of the heart rate, can be taken at any point where a large artery is located just beneath the skin. A convenient place to take the pulse is where the external maxillary artery crosses the lower border of the jawbone. To locate the pulse, press lightly with the balls of your fingers as shown in the illustration. The pulse is easiest to locate after the horse has been exercised.

The pulse can also be taken at the inside back of the knee. The knee of the horse corresponds to the wrist in people. Thus taking the pulse here is like taking the wrist pulse in a person.

The *digital* pulse is taken just below the fetlock at the inside of the ankle. Feel for the pulse by firmly pressing with the thumb and fingers in the grooves between the pastern bones and the flexor tendons. Normally the digital pulse is barely detectable; however, it will be strong and pounding in the presence of acute laminitis.

Another way to count the pulse is to feel the beat of the heart itself. Place your hand on the left side of the horse's chest just above the point of the elbow. If the horse is not fat, you should be able to feel the impact of the heart with each contraction.

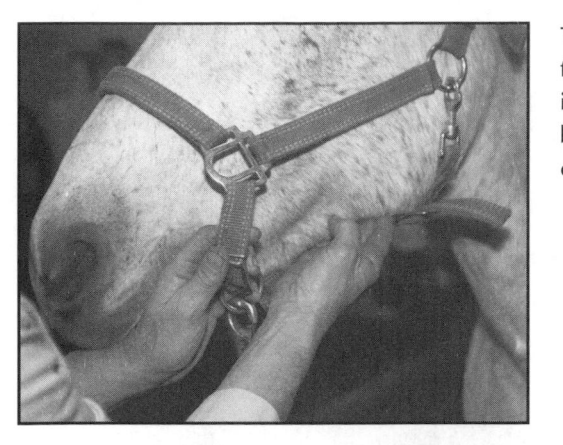

Taking the jaw pulse. With the first two fingers, feel along the inside of the jawbone just below the heavy muscles of the cheek.

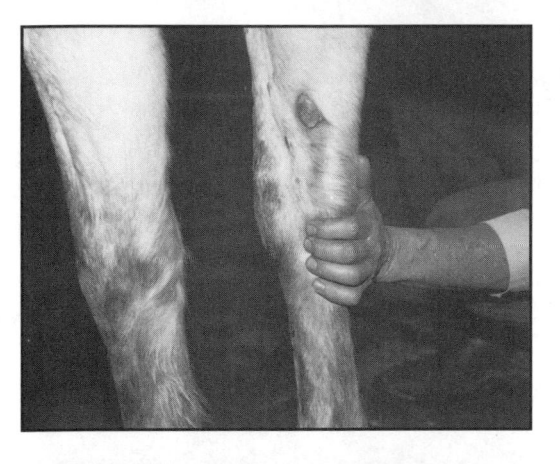

The radial pulse can be taken at the inside back of the knee.

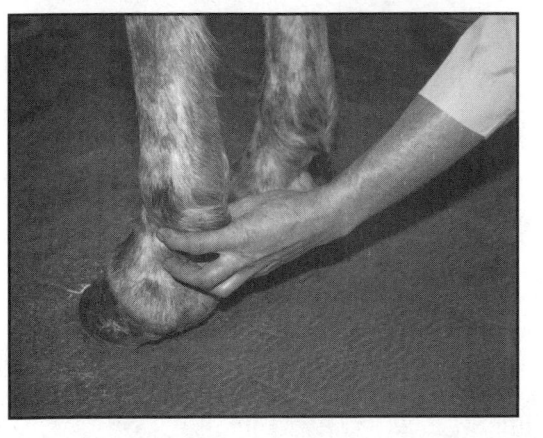

The digital pulse can be felt on the inside, just below the fetlock. The digital pulse is pounding in acute laminitis.

The pulse rate is determined by counting the number of beats per minute. Mature horses run a heart rate of 35 to 45 beats per minute at rest. In 2-year-olds, it is slightly faster. In neonatal foals, 2 to 4 weeks of age, the pulse is 70 to 90 beats per minute.

The pulse should be strong, steady, and regular. A slight alteration in the pulse occurs as the horse breathes in and out. A very fast pulse (over 80 beats per minute in the adult horse at rest) is seen with severe dehydration, blood loss, shock, infection, heat stroke, advanced heart and lung disease, and septicemia. A very slow pulse (under 20 beats per minute) suggests low body temperature, heart disease, pressure on the brain, or a preterminal state with collapse of the circulation.

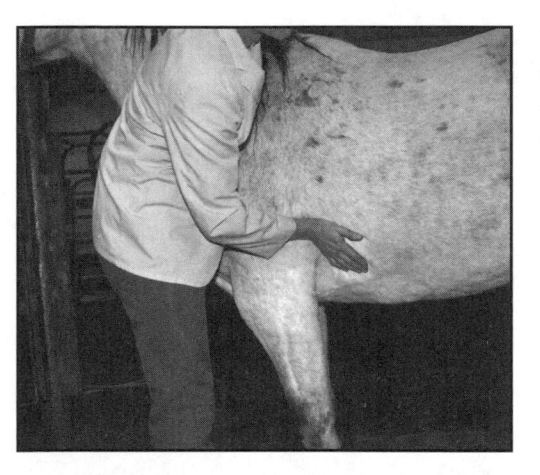

The pulse can also be taken by feeling the heartbeat over the chest just above the point of the elbow.

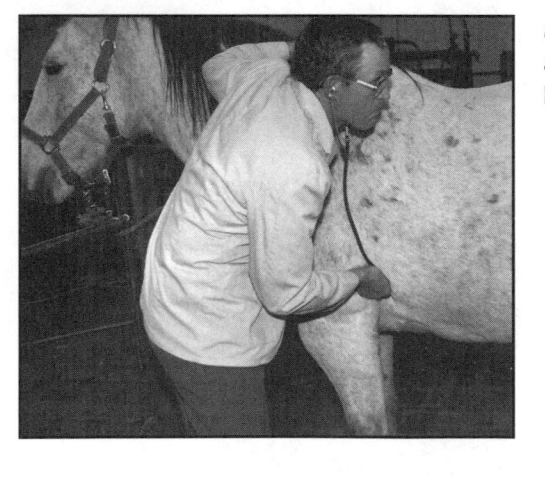

Murmurs, arrhythmias, and abnormal heart sounds are heard with a stethoscope.

Murmurs. Murmurs are caused by turbulent blood flow. Most murmurs are not serious and are called *functional*—that is, there is no disease, just a normal degree of turbulence. It is estimated that as many as 40 percent of foals have a functional heart murmur until up to 3 months of age.

One cause of turbulent blood flow is anemia. The turbulence heard is caused by the low viscosity of the blood.

Murmurs of a more serious nature are caused by valvular heart disease and constrictions in major blood vessels. These murmurs are called *organic*.

The character, sound, location, and amplitude of a heart murmur indicates to the experienced clinician whether the murmur is organic or functional; and it often suggests the diagnosis.

Blood Pressure. A horse's blood pressure is taken with a special cuff placed at the base of the tail over the middle coccygeal artery. It can also be taken around the leg above the digital artery. A horse's blood pressure is difficult to hear with the stethoscope. For this reason, a Doppler ultrasound is often used to take an accurate reading. The normal blood pressure in the standing horse is about 120/70—but there is considerable variation.

Blood pressures are used to monitor the circulation during surgery and to assess the severity of shock, particularly in colic and severe colitis.

Jugular Venous Pulse. Changes in the diameter of the jugular veins in the neck are associated with filling and emptying. During inspiration, the veins empty rapidly and the walls collapse. During expiration, the veins fill rapidly from above. Normally these pulsations are scarcely visible. An exaggerated or very obvious jugular pulse is seen in chronic obstructive lung disease, valvular heart disease, congenital heart disease, and right-sided congestive heart failure—all of which are associated with increased pressure in the venous circulation.

If the jugular veins do not collapse, the veins remain visibly enlarged throughout the entire respiratory cycle. Vein distension, especially when it extends more than halfway up the neck, has the same significance as an exaggerated jugular pulse.

Circulation. By examining the color of the horse's gums, you can obtain important information about the state of the circulation. A pink color is a sign of adequate circulation. A pale color indicates anemia. A gray or bluish tinge indicates a deficiency of oxygen (*cyanosis*). This grave sign can be seen in heart disease, lung failure, and severe colic.

The quality of the circulation can be tested by noting the time it takes for the gums to pink up after being firmly pressed. This interval is called the *capillary refill time*. With normal circulation, a pink color should return to the blanched area within 2 seconds. When the finger impression remains pale for 3 seconds or longer, the horse is severely dehydrated or in shock.

Edema. This is the abnormal accumulation of fluid in the tissues beneath the skin. Edema occurs in dependent locations: the underside of the abdomen (*ventral edema*), the prepuce in males, over the sternum or breastbone, and in all four legs (especially the hind limbs). Edema is characteristic of right-sided congestive heart failure. However, it also occurs in liver disease and in severe diarrhea associated with large protein losses. Malnutrition (a low-protein diet) is another cause. Severe edema can be recognized by the fact that it "pits," or leaves a thumb depression.

Leg swelling not accompanied by edema in other locations may not be an indicator of heart disease or nutritional deficiency. There is a condition called *stocking up* that occurs in unconditioned or inactive horses who are abruptly put to strenuous physical exercise. After exercise, the lower half of the horse's legs may swell. Turning the horse out in a paddock or providing regular exercise each day improves condition and prevents stocking up.

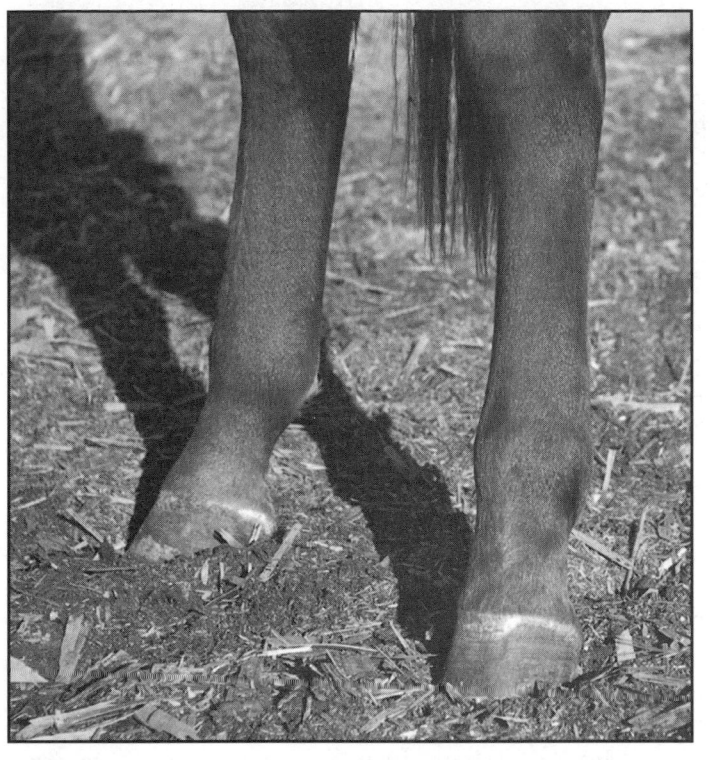

Note the round, symmetrical swelling of the lower legs and fetlocks in stocking up.

Diagnostic Tests. The *electrocardiogram* (EKG) is used principally in diagnosing cardiac arrhythmias and determining if there is evidence of heart disease. Since arrhythmias can appear or disappear with exercise, placing the horse on a treadmill while performing the EKG helps to determine if the arrhythmia is significant and is likely to have an impact on athletic performance.

The *echocardiogram*, which requires ultrasound equipment, is the method of choice for diagnosing the cause of heart disease. A two-dimensional echocardiogram is a cross-section of the heart. This shows the chambers, partitions, valves, and abnormal structures within the heart. M-mode or real-time echocardiography shows the size of the chambers and major vessels, and reveals any abnormal motion of the valves. Color flow Doppler studies map normal and abnormal blood flows. With the above information, the diagnosis, as well as the degree of cardiac impairment, can usually be determined.

Arrhythmias

Heart rhythms follow a fixed pattern that can be seen on an electrocardiogram. Whether the beat is fast or slow, the sequence in which the heart muscle contracts

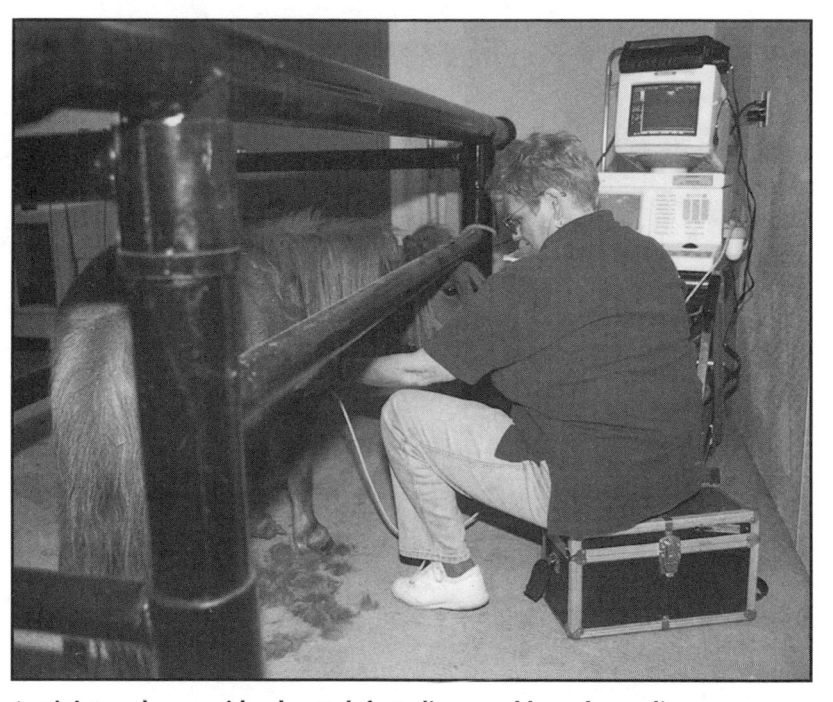

A miniature horse with a heart defect, diagnosed by echocardiogram.

remains the same. This sequence is synchronized to allow efficient filling and emptying of the heart chambers. Various electrical disturbances in the heart's conduction system, called *cardiac arrythmias*, can upset this pattern.

Not all arrhythmias are significant. Physiologic (nonharmful) arrhythmias of various types are common in horses. Such arrythmias occur at slow to normal heart rates and disappear with exercise.

Other arrhythmias, most notably atrial fibrillation, premature atrial and ventricular contractions, ventricular tachycardias, and advanced degrees of A-V block, are likely to appear with sustained or maximal exercise and cause a sudden drop in blood pressure (see CARDIOVASCULAR COLLAPSE). Arrythmias producing collapse can occur in apparently normal hearts; however, in many cases there is underlying (and often unsuspected) heart muscle disease, either myocarditis or cardiomyopathy.

Atrial fibrillation is the most common clinically significant arrhythmia in horses. Episodes of atrial fibrillation can occur in healthy hearts. As the episode begins, the rate converts from normal sinus rhythm to one in which random electrical impulses are sent from the atrium to the ventricles. When the heart rate is fast, the ventricles do not fill and empty in an effective manner. The blood pressure drops during exercise and causes the horse to collapse.

Persistent chronic atrial fibrillation occurs in hearts with congestive failure and atrial enlargement. These horses have heart disease.

A number of cardiac drugs, including magnesium sulfate, digitalis, lidocaine, atropine, and propranolol, used to control arrhythmias and heart failure in humans, are used for the same purpose in horses. These drugs require close monitoring and have effects that are more unpredictable in horses than in people. Usually they are used for short-term effect. There is little experience with long-term cardiac drug treatment in horses. When treating arrythmias, it is equally important to search for and correct any underlying electrolyte or metabolic problem that may have been responsible.

Heart Failure

Heart failure is defined as the inability of the heart to provide adequate circulation to meet the body's needs. It is the end result of a weakened heart muscle. The liver, kidneys, lungs, and other organs are affected by the circulatory insufficiency, causing a multiple organ-system problem.

A diseased heart can compensate for many months or years without signs of failure. Then heart failure can appear quite suddenly and unexpectedly—often immediately after strenuous exercise.

When a diseased heart begins to weaken, signs of right- or left-sided congestive heart failure will occur. Symptoms differ. The treatment of heart disease is directed at preventing and treating the symptoms of heart failure.

RIGHT HEART FAILURE

Signs of right heart failure are more common than those of left heart failure, even though in many cases both sides of the heart fail at the same time.

In right-sided failure, blood pressure increases in the venous circulation, causing dilated neck veins, an exaggerated jugular pulse, edema, and shortness of breath. Dependent edema is visible in the chest area (brisket), abdomen, prepuce, and lower legs. As fluid accumulates inside the abdomen (*ascites*), the horse develops a potbellied appearance.

The slowed circulation causes less oxygen delivery to body tissues. The horse appears lethargic and loses appetite, weight, and condition. Even slight exertion causes muscular weakness and rapid heavy breathing. Murmurs, abnormal heart sounds, and arrhythmias may be present.

Heaves (chronic obstructive pulmonary disease) is the leading cause of right-sided heart failure.

LEFT HEART FAILURE

In left-sided heart failure, fluid backs up into the lungs. Early signs are diminished exercise tolerance, cough, and shortness of breath. They may go unnoticed in the sedentary horse.

As blood pressure increases in the pulmonary circulation, the lungs become congested and fluid accumulates around the air sacs. This is called *pulmonary edema*. An accumulation of fluid in the chest cavity (*pleural effusion*) further reduces breathing room. Respirations become noisy and are often accompanied by wheezing.

In the advanced stages, breathing is labored and the horse assumes a characteristic stance with its feet spread apart and head extended to take in air. The pulse is rapid, weak, and often irregular. Murmurs can be heard over the chest. Any sudden stress or exertion can be followed by collapse.

TREATMENT OF HEART FAILURE

An accurate diagnosis regarding the type of heart disease is essential in planning therapy. This is established through chest x-ray, EKG, and echocardiography.

The two most commonly used drugs are Lasix and digoxin. Lasix is a diuretic used to relieve a fluid buildup. Digoxin increases the force of contraction and slows the heart rate. When using this drug, horses should be monitored carefully for signs of toxicity and evidence of therapeutic response. Little information is available on the long-term use of digoxin since most horses are treated on an acute basis. The treatment of cardiac arrhythmias is discussed above.

Restrict activities to those well within the horse's exercise tolerance. This is of prime importance. Sudden death can occur in horses exercised too vigorously.

Equine Heart Disease

The chief causes of heart disease in horses are valvular disease, myocarditis, cardiomyopathy, pericarditis, bacterial endocarditis, and congenital heart defects. All of these conditions can produce heart failure.

Heart attacks from coronary artery disease do not occur in horses as they do in humans. However, horses with chronic heart disease do suffer collapse in association with arrhythmias and congestive heart failure.

VALVULAR HEART DISEASE AND BACTERIAL ENDOCARDITIS

The exact cause of valvular heart disease in horses is unclear. It has been suggested that degenerative changes in heart valves associated with aging are responsible. Diseased valves are commonly found at postmortem, but in most cases the heart compensates and performance is not affected. When heart failure does occur, it is because the damaged valves don't close securely. This causes reversed blood flow through the leaky valve, creating extra work for the heart, which in time begins to fail.

An acquired form of valve disease (*endocarditis*) is caused by bacteria. *Streptococcus equi*, often associated with strangles, is the most common bloodborne bacteria to infect the heart valves. When bacteria lodge on the valves, they form clumps of infected material. These clumps adhere to the valves and interfere with closure. They also serve as focal points for arterial embolism (discussed below).

The migrating larvae of *Strongyles vulgaris* can adhere to the heart valves—but there is no evidence to suggest they play a role in valvular heart disease.

Endocarditis is the only treatable form of valve disease in the horse. Intensive and prolonged antibiotic therapy is required. This disease can be prevented by prompt treatment of strangles and other bacterial infections.

MYOCARDITIS AND CARDIOMYOPATHY

Myocarditis is inflammation of the muscle of the heart. The damaged muscle loses strength and contracts less forcefully. A variety of infections and toxins can damage the heart. The chief cause of myocarditis is the bacteria S. *equi,* which produces strangles and other streptococcal infections in horses. However, a number of viruses also attack the heart. They include equine influenza, equine viral arteritis, and equine infectious anemia. Cantharidin, the toxic agent in blister beetle poisoning, produces myocardial injury. The long-term use of anabolic steroids has been associated with severe heart damage.

With minimal involvement, the horse may exhibit only mild to moderate exercise intolerance. Most horses experience severe exercise intolerance followed by congestive heart failure. Cardiac arryhthmias are common. Sudden collapse can occur during exercise. Some of these horses die suddenly and unexpectedly, presumably from cardiac arrhythmias.

Cardiomyopathy is a form of myocarditis in which the heart enlarges rapidly. In foals, it is related to a vitamin E and selenium deficiency. In both foals and adults, cardiomyopathy follows the ingestion of Rumensin (monensin), an antibiotic added to beef and poultry feed. The enlarged, flabby heart of dilated cardiomyopathy fails quickly.

Treatment: It is directed at treating congestive heart failure and cardiac arhythmias while giving the horse the opportunity to recover from the underlying illness. With minimal heart muscle damage, the outlook is good. Stall rest is of great importance since physical activity makes the heart more susceptible to injury. The use of corticosteroids to reduce heart muscle inflammation in myocarditis has been recommended. It is controversial in viral myocarditis because steroids are known to lower the body's immune response to the virus.

It is unusual to recover from cardiomyopathy.

PERICARDITIS

The heart is surrounded by a membrane called the *pericardium,* which is continuous with the membrane that lines the chest cavity (*pleura*). Inflammation of the pericardium is called *pericarditis.*

A viral pericarditis can occur as a consequence of an equine viral respiratory infection. However, most cases are of bacterial origin. The infection first involves the lungs and pleura, then extends to involve the pericardium. In some cases, the origin of the pericarditis is unknown.

A characteristic sign of pericarditis is the *friction rub*, a scratchy or leathery sound heard with a stethoscope with each beat of the heart.

Inflammation of the pericardium causes fluid formation within the space between the pericardium and heart wall. This buildup of fluid in the pericardial sac is called a *pericardial effusion*. The pericardial sac is not elastic. Accordingly, fluid in the sac presses directly on the heart and interferes with filling of the chambers. The volume of blood entering the heart is severely restricted. Signs of right-sided congestive heart failure can appear slowly or suddenly, depending on the rate of fluid production.

A second effect of pericarditis is to cause fibrous scarring and contracture of the pericardium, a condition called *constrictive pericarditis*. The effect on cardiac performance is the same as that of pericardial effusion.

Treatment: Congestive heart failure and cardiac arrhythmias are treated as discussed above. Bacterial pericarditis is treated with antibiotics for two months or longer. A pericardial effusion can be relieved by *pericardiocentesis*. In this procedure, a long needle is inserted through the chest wall into the pericardial sac to draw off fluid. This immediately improves cardiac output. If fluid recurs, an operation to remove the pericardium can be considered. However, such surgery is difficult to perform in horses and has been associated with serious complications and death. In general, the long-term outlook for recovery in pericarditis is poor.

CONGENITAL HEART DISEASE (BIRTH DEFECTS)

All forms of congenital heart disease (CHD) are found in the horse. In fact, more than one congenital heart defect may exist at the same time.

A *ventricular septal defect* is a hole in the septum (wall) which separates the two ventricles. Because of the opening, blood can flow from the right to the left side of the heart without going through the pulmonary circulation and receiving oxygen. Septal defects are the most common forms of CHD in horses. Malformations of the heart valves are also common.

A *patent ductus arteriosus* is a persistent fetal artery joining the pulmonary artery to the aorta. This artery is necessary in utero when the lungs are not used for breathing. Normally the ductus closes shortly after birth. A coarse "machinery" murmur as a result of a still-patent ductus is normal up to the third day of life. If the ductus does not close, aortic blood shunting through the pulmonary circulation leads to the development of severe pulmonary hypertension, heart failure, and death.

The extent and severity of symptoms in CHD depends on the type and location of the defect. A small septal defect often does not interfere with the utility and performance of the average pleasure horse, and is compatible with normal life.

Defects that cause exercise intolerance early in life tend to be the most serious and are the least likely to have a good prognosis.

With the exception of patent ductus arteriosus, there is no surgical treatment for congenital heart disease in horses. To be successful, a patent ductus must be closed early in life before the development of pulmonary hypertension.

Most congenital heart defects have a genetic basis. In the interest of breed soundness, horses with all types of CHD should be excluded from breeding programs.

Equine Vascular Diseases

JUGULAR VEIN THROMBOPHLEBITIS

The jugular vein is the usual site for intravenous injections in the horse. Various drugs and irritating solutions injected either into the vein or inadvertently around the vein can lead to inflammation and clotting of the vein (*thrombophlebitis*). Indwelling catheters can introduce bacteria into the vein. When this happens, an infected clot develops, a condition called *septic thrombophlebitis*.

The signs of thrombophlebitis are a tender swollen cord in the neck (the clotted jugular vein), sometimes accompanied by heat, redness, and swelling of the surrounding tissues. With a severe infection, devitalization of surrounding skin can occur. Rarely there can be damage to the nerve plexus in the neck, which results in signs of cranial nerve palsy. An infected clot can give rise to blood poisoning.

Treatment: Apply hot packs and topical DMSO to the neck three times a day until the swelling subsides. Ultrasound examination of the neck is helpful in demonstrating a clotted vein and in documenting its progress or resolution. Anticoagulants (aspirin, low-dose heparin) are considered in special circumstances. An infected indwelling catheter should be promptly removed and, if necessary, replaced in another vein. Culture of the tip of the catheter is indicated, followed by the administration of an appropriate antibiotic.

When extravasation outside the vein is recognized at the time of injection, the irritant can be diluted by injecting large volumes of saline around the vein. This may prevent tissue injury. In the uncomplicated case, the clot dissolves and the vein returns to normal.

ARTERIAL VASCULAR DISEASE

Hardening of the arteries and the deposition of cholesterol in the walls of vessels is not a problem in horses. However, there are two major diseases that cause arterial damage in horses. They are aortoiliac thrombosis and arterial thromboembolism.

Aortoiliac Thrombosis. Thrombosis is clot formation within the artery. There is a characteristic disease involving thrombosis of the abdominal aorta and its major branches that occurs almost exclusively in heavily exercised horses, especially young male racehorses. The mechanism of arterial injury and thrombosis is unknown. One theory holds that these horses are subjected to a routine of training that requires high cardiac output and maximum blood flow to the muscles of locomotion. The pressure of the blood in the aorta and iliac arteries, along with the forceful expansion and rapid contraction of these vessels, causes small tears to develop in the walls of the arteries. These injuries heal with scarring and contracture. Eventually, the passageway narrows and the rate of flow through the channel declines to the point that clotting occurs. In a sense, this is a disease of usage that would not occur in the wild.

The onset of symptoms can be sudden but is more often gradual. The horse is not able to perform as well. Unexplained lameness develops and there is a peculiarity of gait affecting the hindquarters. These gait disturbances become worse with strenuous exercise. The horse may go rigid in the rear, stumble, or collapse. After a lengthy period of rest, the horse does not get better.

On examination, the hind limbs are cool, and sweating may be absent over the hindquarters. The digital pulses are often weak or absent. The horse sometimes inexplicably treads up and down or kicks out with its back feet. Rectal examination may disclose a large pulseless terminal aorta.

The horse must be retired from training and competition. This does not improve the vascular disease, which is irreversible by the time the diagnosis is made.

Arterial Embolism. An embolus is a blood clot that forms in the heart or a large artery, breaks loose, and travels downstream to a smaller artery, where it lodges. The blockage interferes with the blood supply to the organ or tissue affected.

Clots can form in the heart during an episode of atrial fibrillation. They can also develop on valves that have been damaged by endocarditis. These conditions are rare.

The most common cause of embolic disease in horses is that related to the arterial damage caused by the large bloodworm *Strongyles vulgaris*. The subject is discussed in chapter 2, Parasites (see STRONGYLES).

Anemia

Anemia can be defined as a deficiency of red blood cells (*erythrocytes*) in the circulation. The purpose of red cells is to carry oxygen to the tissues.

Red blood cells in horses are quite small when compared to those of man. The number in 1 cubic millimeter of blood is given as 6 to 12 million, with a mean of 7 to 9 million. Thoroughbreds in training tend to have the highest number of erythrocytes. Unconditioned horses are somewhat lower, and "cold-blooded" and draft breeds are the lowest of all. Anemia exists when there are fewer than 6 million erythrocytes per cubic millimeter.

A horse's spleen stores about one-third of the red cells in the body. During any crisis in which additional red cells are needed, these cells are pumped from the spleen into the circulation.

Unlike in most animals, erythrocytes remain in the bone marrow of the horse until they are fully mature—even though the horse may have lost a considerable amount of blood. Thus once the spleen's reserve is used up, there could be a lapse of several days before red cell volume is restored by the release of new blood cells from the bone marrow. Accordingly, the actual number of red cells in circulation after a bleeding episode is quite variable. Serial blood counts are necessary to determine the state of the red cell volume.

Once anemia is identified, its cause can be determined by other blood tests. Bone marrow biopsy helps to show if red cell production is occurring normally.

Causes of anemia include bleeding, hemolysis, infection, and inadequate red cell production.

BLOOD LOSS

Acute blood loss associated with wounds and trauma is discussed in chapter 1, Emergencies.

Spontaneous bleeding beneath the skin and from the nose suggests a clotting deficiency. The most common clotting deficiency in horses is *disseminated intravascular coagulation* (DIC), a condition triggered by overwhelming infection, shock, and acute colitis. DIC is characterized by intravascular clotting throughout the entire capillary circulation, followed by spontaneous bleeding when all clotting factors have been consumed. Horses with DIC are extremely ill and often die.

Other causes of spontaneous bleeding are hemophilia, dicumarol and warfarin poisoning (these follow exposure to moldy sweet clover and rat poisons), and drug-induced immune reactions. Special laboratory studies are required to identify and diagnose these problems. Massive bleeding from the nose occurs in guttural pouch mycosis.

A more insidious loss of blood takes place from the gastrointestinal tract as a result of intestinal parasites (especially strongyle infection), stomach and duodenal ulcers, and cancer of the stomach.

Bloodsucking external parasites (lice, ticks, biting flies) can produce surprising amounts of blood loss in the heavily parasited horse.

HEMOLYSIS AND HEMOLYTIC ANEMIAS

Red cells survive in the circulation for about 150 days, after which they are broken down and destroyed. The iron is recycled by the bone marrow to make new red cells. An acceleration of the break-down process is called *hemolysis*.

Red cells break down into bile and hemoglobin. When hemolysis is sudden and acute, these breakdown products overload the plasma. Accordingly, in an acute hemolytic breakdown, you would expect to see *jaundice* (a yellow cast to the eyes and mucous membranes) and *hemoglobinuria* (the passage of dark-brown urine containing hemobglobin). Common causes of hemolysis include:

Toxins. Oxidizing agents that act on the surface of the red cell and cause hemolysis are found in wild and cultivated onions (*onion poisoning*) and the leaves of the red maple tree (*red maple leaf poisoning*). The venom of rattlesnakes and pit vipers causes red blood cell hemolysis.

Infectious Diseases. Infectious diseases associated with hemolysis include equine infectious anemia, equine ehrlichiosis, and equine piroplasmosis. Bacteria of the Clostridia and Staphylococcus species produce exotoxins that cause hemolysis.

Neonatal isoerythrolysis is a hemolytic disease of newborn foals, discussed in chapter 16, Pediatrics.

INADEQUATE RED CELL PRODUCTION

Most anemias in horses are due to inadequate red cell production. As the erythrocytes become old and outdated, they are replaced by new red cells manufactured by the horse's bone marrow. When for any reason the metabolic activity of the bone marrow is depressed, new red cells are not manufactured as fast as old ones are destroyed.

Chronic illnesses are the most frequent cause of depressed erythrocyte production in the horse. This category includes equine viral arteritis, chronic pneumonia, abdominal abscesses, liver and kidney failure, lymphosarcomas, and cancers.

Iron, trace minerals, vitamins, and fatty acids are all incorporated into red cells. Thus a deficiency in one or more of these nutrients could slow down or stop erythrocyte production. However, this is an uncommon cause of anemia because these nutrients are found in almost all horse rations in more than adequate amounts to meet daily requirements.

Iron deficiency anemia is the one exception. Iron deficiency occurs when iron is lost from the body faster than it is being replaced through the diet. The two situations in which this can happen are chronic gastrointestinal bleeding and a heavy infestation of bloodsucking insects.

Intestinal parasites and stomach ulcers are the usual causes of unsuspected chronic gastrointestinal bleeding. Gastrointestinal bleeding can be diagnosed by checking the manure for occult (microscopic) blood.

Bone marrow depression is rarely caused by an *aplastic anemia*. Aplastic anemias are associated with heavy metal poisoning and exposure to insecticides, organic solvents, and hydrocarbons. Idiopathic aplastic anemia occurs, in which the cause is undetermined.

Bone marrow depression has been found after prolonged Butazolidin administration.

NERVOUS SYSTEM

The central nervous system of the horse is composed of the cerebrum, cerebellum, midbrain (which includes the cranial nerves and brainstem), and spinal cord.

The *cerebrum* is the area of learning, memory, behavior, and voluntary motor control. Diseases affecting the cerebrum are characterized by seizures, mild to marked depression, and alterations in personality and behavior. A well-socialized horse may exhibit signs of aggression or hyperexcitability; wander aimlessly or turn in circles; press its head against objects; exhibit varying degrees of blindness; and yawn continually or make strange noises. Foals may exhibit ineffective nursing behavior, wander away from the mare, appear dumb, and vocalize in a peculiar fashion.

The *cerebellum* is relatively large and well developed in the horse. Its main functions are to integrate motor pathways, coordinate movements, and help maintain balance. Injuries or diseases of the cerebellum result in incoordination, staggering gait (*ataxia*), and muscle tremors. Uncoordinated body movements include awkward jerking of the limbs and bobbing of the head. Gait disturbances can be distinguished from paralysis in that there is no loss of muscle strength in the quarters.

In the *midbrain* and *brainstem* are found centers that control levels of consciousness, respiratory rate, heart rate, blood pressure, and other activities essential to life. At the base of the brain and closely connected to the midbrain and brain-stem are the *hypothalamus* and *pituitary gland*. These structures are vitally important in regulating the horse's body temperature and its hormone systems. They are also the centers for primitive responses such as hunger, thirst, anger, and fright. Diseases affecting this part of the brain cause paralysis of many of the cranial nerves, the effects of which are discussed below.

The *spinal cord* passes down a bony canal formed by the arches of the vertebral bodies. The cord sends out nerve roots that combine with one another to form the peripheral nerves that carry motor impulses to muscles and receive

241

sensory input from the skin. Diseases of the spinal cord produce various degrees of weakness, stiffness, muscle incoordination, and paralysis of the limbs.

The *cauda equina* is the termination of the spinal cord and contains the nerve branches to the sacrum and coccyx. Diseases of the cauda equina produce loss of sensation over the rump, paralysis of the tail, loss of bladder and bowel control, and paralysis of the anal sphincter.

CRANIAL NERVE PARALYSIS

The paired cranial nerves, twelve in number, arise from the midbrain and brainstem and pass directly out into the head and neck through openings in the skull. The most frequently encountered cranial nerve palsies in the horse are:

Optic Nerve (II). Damage to the optic nerve, or the optic center in the brain, produces varying degrees of blindness. The usual causes are trauma, brain abscess, and encephalitis.

Oculomotor Nerve (III). This nerve controls the size of the pupil. Shining a light into the eyes should cause the pupils to constrict and get smaller. With damage to the paired oculomotor nerves close to the brainstem, both pupils become dilated and unresponsive to light. Head trauma and brain abscesses are the most common causes of oculomotor paralysis.

Facial Nerve (VII). This nerve controls the muscles of facial expression. Paralysis causes drooping of the ear, inability to shut the eye or flare the nostril, loss

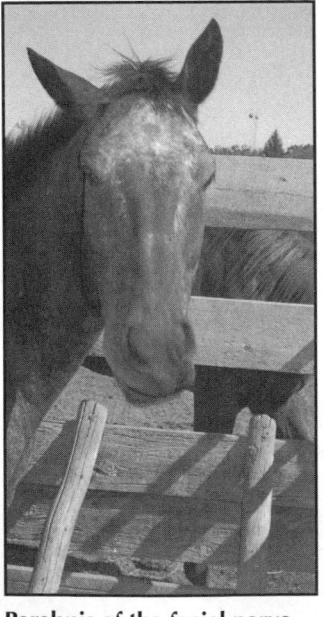 

Paralysis of the facial nerve, causing drooping of the horse's right ear, nostril, and lip.

Paralysis of the tongue, associated with hypoglossal nerve injury.

of skin wrinkles around the nostrils and muzzle, and drooling from the corner of the lip. All these occur on the side of the face that is paralyzed. The most common causes of facial paralysis are guttural pouch infections, jugular vein thrombophlebitis, and trauma to the side of the face. Pressure on the nerve from failure to pad the side of the face during general anesthesia is another cause.

Vestibulocochlear Nerve (VIII). The nerves to the inner ear are important for balance and coordination. Horses with eighth nerve involvement often exhibit a wide-based stance and a staggering gait. There is a tendency to lean, circle, and fall toward the side of involvement. Vestibular disorders are discussed in chapter 6, Ears (see Labyrinthitis).

Glossopharyngeal, Vagus, and Spinal Accessory Nerves (IX, X, XI). The primary function of these nerves is to control swallowing and to produce sounds. Accordingly, signs of involvement include difficulty in swallowing, and a characteristic roaring or whistling sound as the horse is exercised.

The most common causes of paralysis of one or all of these nerves are guttural pouch mycosis and jugular vein thrombophlebitis. Consider also the possibility of lead poisoning.

Hypoglossal Nerve (XII). The twelfth cranial nerve controls the muscles of the tongue. When one side is paralyzed, there is muscle wasting on that side of the tongue, but little difficulty in grazing and swallowing. When both nerves are affected, the tongue is paralyzed, and the horse is unable to eat or drink. Consider rabies, ergot and forage poisoning, lead poisoning, yellow star thistle and Russian knapweed poisoning, and encephalitis.

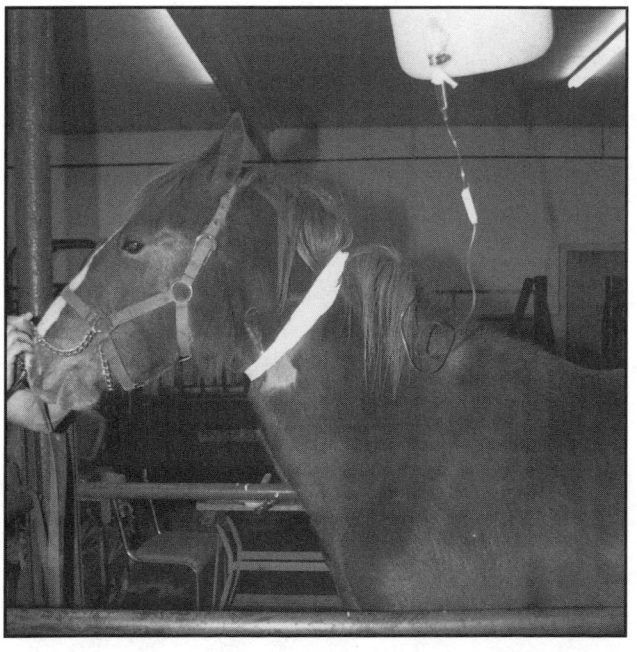

Indwelling IV catheters can cause jugular vein thrombosis, which can result in paralysis of the IX, X, and XI cranial nerves.

NEUROLOGICAL EXAMINATION

History is of paramount importance in diagnosing the cause of a neurological symptom. Consider the following: Is there a recent history of head or neck trauma? Could the horse have been exposed to poisonous vegetation? Is there a history of a recent respiratory infection or abortion? Could a skin laceration or recent surgical incision be the focus of infection? What is the vaccination and deworming history? Has the horse spent time on another farm, or been turned out with a new horse?

Age, sex, breed, and color of the horse are important, as certain neurological disorders are genetically determined.

Next evaluate the horse's general behavior, mental status, head carriage, coordination, and cranial nerve function, looking for abnormal signs like those described above.

Finally, carry out a complete examination of the horse's general body posture and gait, looking for signs of cerebellar, spinal cord, or peripheral nerve involvement as discussed below.

Special tests that may be indicated to make a diagnosis include x-rays of the skull and vertebral column, diagnostic nerve blocks with local anesthetics, muscle and nerve conduction studies, and nerve and muscle biopsies.

A spinal tap is a procedure in which a needle is inserted into the spinal canal to remove cerebrospinal fluid for laboratory analysis. A myelogram is a spinal tap in which dye is introduced into the spinal canal for x-ray studies looking for signs of spinal cord compression. Myelograms are performed under general anesthesia in the horse.

ABNORMALITIES OF POSTURE AND GAIT

Ataxia. The horse should be walked and, if possible, trotted in a straight line. Other maneuvers include walking him on the side of a hill in a circle, walking him over a curb, and making him walk backwards. Signs of ataxia are swaying of the trunk and pelvis, stumbling, dragging the toes, wide-circling, crossing the legs, and awkward foot placement such as stepping on the opposite foot. At rest, the horse will often assume a wide-based stance. When you pick up a foot and cross the legs, the horse may leave them crossed.

Signs of ataxia are caused by disease of the cerebellum, vestibular system, and spinal cord. Cerebellar ataxia is usually accompanied by head-bobbing and fine muscle tremors. Blindfolding the horse makes cerebellar ataxia worse, but has little effect on spinal cord ataxia, in which the stumbling and swaying are caused by lack of limb strength. Vestibular ataxia is discussed in chapter 6, Ears.

Spasticity. This is a stiffness or rigidity of the limbs, seen in spinal cord and cerebellar diseases. A shorter than normal stride occurs in a spastic leg, while a longer than normal stride is seen in a weak leg. Difference in stride length (*dysmetria*) is best detected by walking next to or behind the horse, matching him stride for stride.

Weakness. Weakness is an indication of partial paralysis. It is present in diseases of the spinal cord, musculoskeletal system, and peripheral nerves. A peripheral nerve paralysis is localized to one limb, not accompanied by ataxia, and often associated with localized loss of muscle volume (*atrophy*). Hind leg weakness can be confirmed by walking behind the horse and pulling on its tail. A normal horse can resist this, but a weak horse is easily pulled to the side. Dragging a foot, lacking the ability to extend a joint, and being unable to bear weight on a leg are all signs of a peripheral nerve paralysis.

Head Trauma

Since the brain is encased in bone, surrounded by a layer of fluid, and suspended in the skull by a system of tough ligaments, it takes a major blow to the head to fracture the skull and injure the brain. Such injuries can be caused by kicks from other horses, running into posts, and rearing and falling over backward to land on the poll. Horses are of a generally flighty or nervous disposition; therefore, they are quite prone to head injuries, particularly of the poll.

Skull fractures can be linear, star-shaped, depressed, compound (open to the outside), or closed. Fractures at the base of the skull often extend into the ear, orbit, nasal cavity, or sinuses, creating pathways for brain infection. Open fractures should be suspected if bleeding occurs from the ear canals or nasal passages. Injuries of sufficient magnitude to fracture the skull are often associated with bleeding into and around the brain from ruptured blood vessels. Nevertheless, even head injuries without skull fracture can cause severe brain damage.

Brain injuries are classified according to the severity of damage to the brain.

Contusion (Bruising). This is the most mild sort of injury, in which there is no loss of consciousness. After a blow to the head, the horse remains dazed, wobbly, or disoriented. The condition then clears gradually.

Concussion. By definition, a concussion means a horse was knocked out or experienced a loss of consciousness. A mild concussion is one in which there is only a brief loss of consciousness, while in a severe concussion a horse may be unconscious for minutes or even hours.

After a severe concussion a horse may exhibit a set of characteristic signs and symptoms called the *post-concussion syndrome*. In this syndrome the horse appears depressed, lethargic, or in a stupor; may wander in circles toward the side of the brain injury; and often exhibits blindness or protrusion of the tongue. These signs are due to brain swelling. If treatment is undertaken and the swelling does not extend to the midbrain, the outlook is favorable.

Brain Swelling or Blood Clot. Following severe head injury, there can be swelling of the brain, or the formation of a blood clot from ruptured vessels. Both produce *increased intracranial pressure*.

Brain swelling, technically called *cerebral edema*, is always accompanied by a depressed level of consciousness and often coma. Since the brain is encased in a bony skull, swelling of the brain leads to pressure on the brainstem. As the cerebellum is forced down through an opening near the base of the skull, the vital centers in the midbrain become squeezed and compressed. If this happens suddenly, it leads to death of the horse.

Head trauma is a common cause of cerebral edema. Inflammation of the brain from encephalitis is another cause.

Death also occurs when the brain is deprived of oxygen. Complete interruption of the circulation and oxygen supply for only 5 minutes produces irreversible damage to the cells of the cerebral cortex. This could happen with cardiac arrest and suffocation.

Blood clots can occur between the skull and brain, or within the brain itself. A blood clot produces localized pressure symptoms which do not, at least initially, compress the vital centers. The first indication is a depressed level of consciousness. Often one pupil is dilated and doesn't constrict when a light is shined in the eye. A paralysis or weakness may be present in one or more limbs. Progressive signs indicate the clot is expanding.

Inner Ear/Vestibular Syndrome. This is a characteristic set of signs caused by a blow to the poll with hemorrhage around the brainstem. Typically the horse experiences dizziness, incoordination, and loss of balance. In addition, the horse may exhibit head tilt, rapid jerking eye movements, circling, and evidence of facial nerve paralysis. Horses with vestibular injury often thrash and struggle violently in an effort to stand and therefore are quite likely to injure themselves or their handlers. Horses who recover from labyrinthitis may exhibit head-bobbing, or a coarse tremor of the head, that is most apparent when eating or drinking.

SIGNS OF BRAIN INJURY (INCREASED INTRACRANIAL PRESSURE)

Following a blow to the head, you should watch for signs of brain swelling or the development of a blood clot. These signs can appear anytime during the first 24 hours.

The most important thing to observe is the level of the horse's consciousness. An *alert* horse is in no danger. A *stuporous* horse is sleepy but responds to its handler. A *comatose* horse cannot be aroused. Any change in level of consciousness is an indication to start treatment.

Be sure to check the pupils every hour. They should be equal in size and should constrict when a light is shined in the eyes. A dilated pupil that does not respond to light is a serious sign. Notify your veterinarian. Also notify your veterinarian if the horse becomes recumbent or if its breathing becomes rapid and shallow. Once a horse becomes comatose, it is often too late to begin treatment.

TREATMENT OF BRAIN INJURY

A severely injured horse may have other life-threatening conditions such as a blocked airway, severe external bleeding, fractured ribs, or a punctured lung. Treatment of these takes precedence over the head injury.

Do not attempt to handle a frightened, thrashing, injured horse without professional assistance. The horse should be sedated first to prevent further injury and to facilitate safe examination.

The objective of medical management is to control intracranial pressure and prevent brain swelling. This is accomplished by intravenous medications. The corticosteroid dexamethasone, with or without DMSO (dimethyl sulfoxide), is used for this purpose. Mannitol also is effective but is avoided if there is active bleeding.

Seizures are controlled with an intravenous drug such as Valium, pentobarbital, or xylazine. Antibiotics are indicated for open skull fractures.

Good nursing care is crucially important in the recumbent horse to prevent respiratory complications, muscle damage, and bedsores. Provide a well-padded bed for the horse to lie on, and keep the area clean and dry. Roll the horse from side to side several times a day, or better yet, maintain a sternal position if possible, to prevent pressure sores and the myopathy of prolonged recumbency. Petroleum jelly is a good water repellent and can be applied to the skin to prevent scalds. Maalox (an aluminum hydroxide preparation) helps to heal skin sores and abrasions.

An indwelling bladder catheter may be advisable; alternately, the horse can be catheterized several times a day.

A progression in neurological signs despite treatment indicates increased intracranial pressure from cerebral edema or intracranial bleeding. Exploratory surgery is a consideration. It must be done in a well-equipped equine surgery center.

When coma persists for more than 36 hours, the chances for recovery are slight. However, if the horse shows steady improvement throughout the first week, the outlook for recovery is good. Horses who recover from brain injuries may suffer from seizures, head tilt, head-bobbing, head tremors, and varying degrees of blindness.

Spinal Cord Injuries

VERTEBRAL FRACTURES

Fractures of the spine may or may not be accompanied by injuries of the spinal cord. This depends upon the forces involved and the mechanism of injury.

Vertebral fractures are among the most frequent injuries sustained in athletic training and competition, particularly in racing and jumping. A horse that rears and falls over backward, or stumbles and falls in a somersault, can fracture the spine. Neck fractures are frequently associated with somersaults and head-on collisions. Injuries to the lower spine are most apt to occur when a horse rears and falls over backward, or when it stumbles while backing up and slides into a dog-sitting position.

Following a serious injury to the spinal column, if the horse is recumbent and is able to lift only its head, it is safe to say that the horse has damaged its spinal cord high in the neck. If the horse can raise its head and neck, the injury is in the mid-to-lower cervical spine. If the horse can get up into a dog-sitting position, the injury is at or below the second thoracic vertebra. If the horse can stand yet is ataxic and weak in the hindquarters, the injury is in the lumbar spine. Paralysis of the tail along with urinary or fecal incontinence indicates sacral cord involvement.

The diagnosis and location of a spinal cord injury can be determined by testing for sensation, muscle function, and the presence of abnormal reflexes. X-rays of the neck and back are helpful in showing fractures and dislocations, but do not necessarily reveal the true extent of spinal cord injury. A myelogram is the best way to tell to what extent the spinal cord is compressed or swollen.

Treatment: A horse with a vertebral fracture but no neurological signs of spinal cord injury requires only stall rest and observation. When neurological signs are present, treatment is directed at preventing further spinal cord injury or swelling. Medical treatment is like that described for head trauma.

Surgery to remove bone fragments or decompress the spinal cord is a consideration in all vertebral injuries in which the intact cord is in jeopardy. However, if the cord has been cut, torn, or crushed, the injury is permanent, and surgery is unlikely to benefit the horse.

A paralyzed horse who is recumbent and shows no signs of improvement on medical or surgical treatment during the first 2 to 3 days can be considered to have irreversible damage to the spinal cord, and should be put to sleep to prevent further suffering.

WOBBLER SYNDROME (CERVICAL VERTEBRAL MALFORMATION)

Cervical vertebral malformation (CVM) is the most frequent neurological disease in horses. It is estimated that CVM affects 10 percent of Thoroughbred horses. The wobbly gait and other neurological signs are caused by narrowing of the bone canal and pressure on the spinal cord from malformed vertebral bones. Narrowing of the spinal canal is called *stenosis*.

CVM does not have one specific cause. There are genetic predisposing factors, but CVM does not follow a simple hereditary pattern. Nutritional factors are contributory, especially the feeding of high-energy diets which stimulate rapid bone growth. Foals with CVM have a higher incidence of osteochondrosis, suggesting that CVM may be one of the *developmental orthopedic diseases* (DODs) discussed in chapter 12, Musculoskeletal System. Trauma and biomechanical stresses are also important factors in some cases.

CVM occurs frequently in foals under 1 year of age, but the age group 1 to 4 years is affected predominantly.

CVM is classified according to whether symptoms are made worse by movement of the spine. In *dynamic stenosis*, the most common type, symptoms either appear or are made worse when the horse flexes its neck. In *static stenosis*, symptoms are present but not exacerbated by movements of the neck. This type is relatively uncommon.

Typical signs of CVM are progressive ataxia of the hindquarters (or all four limbs), characterized by clumsiness and wobbling, and a peculiar walk like that of a toy soldier. The neck is usually held stiffly. The horse frequently stumbles and scuffs its toes, or gets its legs crossed and then trips over them and falls. Backing up can be awkward.

Symptoms may be made worse when the horse goes up or down a hill. Owing to weakness in the hindquarters, pulling the tail to one side as the horse walks causes the horse to stumble or sway to that side. This wouldn't happen in the normal horse.

Horses with CVM are subject to frequent falls. Owners and handlers often become aware of the horse's wobbliness and ataxia after a fall. This may give the impression that the fall was the cause of the symptoms, rather than the reverse.

The diagnosis is made by x-rays of the neck. Negative x-rays point to some other cause for the ataxia, such as EDM or EHV-1. When x-rays are consistent with CVM, a myelogram may be requested for more detailed study.

Treatment: Medical therapy is directed at minimizing inflammation at the site of spinal cord compression. This involves the administration of anti-inflammatory drugs including corticosteroids, Butazolidin, and DMSO, either singly or in combination. Stall rest for prolonged periods (6 months or longer) is mandatory for most affected horses. Food and water should be provided at a height of 2 to 3 feet above the floor to minimize neck movement. Foals with mild x-ray changes may stabilize or improve when placed on an energy-neutral diet.

In most cases CVM is a progressive neurological disease, and medical treatment alone is often unsuccessful. Surgery may be considered in selected individuals. The two operations most often used are *dorsal laminectomy*, in which excess bone pressing on the spinal cord is removed, and *intervertebral fusion*, in which two or more adjacent vertebrae are joined together to stabilize the spine. These operations are difficult and may result in complications. The results are best when the surgery is performed on young horses with mild symptoms of short duration. A small number of horses return to athletic performance, and about a third can be used for pleasure riding.

CAUDA EQUINA SYNDROME

The cauda equina is made up of nerves that form the terminal extension of the spinal cord. Injuries to the sacrum that damage the cord can produce paralysis of the tail, anus, perineum, bladder, and rectum. This is called the *cauda equina syndrome*.

Other conditions associated with the cauda equina syndrome include equine protozoal myeloencephalitis (EPM), sorghum grass poisoning, toxicity caused by Haloxon (an organophosphate), and neuritis of the cauda equina.

Neuritis of the cauda equina is a disease of unknown cause which begins gradually or acutely with rubbing and chewing at the tail head, and progresses over several weeks. The tail hangs limply, and the anal and bladder sphincters are paralyzed. Urine drips continually from a gaping vulva or protruded relaxed penis, while feces may appear at the opening of the dilated anus. Hindquarter ataxia and gait disturbances can occur.

This disorder can also affect the cranial nerves, producing a head tilt or facial nerve paralysis. This suggests that an infectious or autoimmune process is at fault.

There is no cure. Manual evacuation of the rectum, catheterization of the bladder, and treatment of urinary tract infections may prolong the life of the horse.

Brain and Spinal Cord Infections

Encephalitis refers to inflammation of the brain, and *myelitis* refers to inflammation of the spinal cord. Most cases of myelitis are subordinate in importance to an associated encephalitis. Specific infections of the brain and spinal cord are discussed below.

ENCEPHALITIS

Encephalitis is a common problem in horses, mainly because of the frequency of equine viral encephalomyelitis. Signs of encephalitis include fever, depression, behavior and personality changes, head tilt, circling, ataxia, incoordination, paralysis, seizures, and coma. How the horse behaves depends upon the parts of the brain most severely affected.

Bacteria also can cause encephalitis. Bacteria gain entrance to the brain via the bloodstream, or by direct extension from an infection in the nasopharynx, sinuses, or guttural pouches. Fungi are rare causes of encephalitis, the principal one being *Cryptococcus*.

Treatment of encephalitis is directed at the primary disease. It is important to prevent brain swelling and to provide good supportive nursing care, as discussed above in the treatment of brain injury. See also Equine Viral Encephalomyelitis.

EQUINE PROTOZOAL MYELOENCEPHALITIS (EPM)

This disease is caused by a protozoan called *Sarcocystis neurona* that invades the brain and spinal cord. This protozoan is a parasite of opossums. The organism is shed in the opossum's feces and contaminates feed and water, or may be picked up and distributed by birds. The horse is not a primary host, which helps to explain the wide variation in clinical signs.

EPM occurs most often in young Thoroughbreds and Standardbreds 1 to 6 years of age. The geographic distribution of the disease follows the natural range of opossums. Most cases are isolated. Outbreaks have not been reported.

The ingested protozoans migrate randomly through the spinal cord and brain, producing a variety of unexplained and highly variable neurological signs. The horse often stumbles or falls repeatedly and may exhibit a head tilt. Over a period of days, weeks, or months, the horse develops weakness, lameness, and muscle wasting in one or more limbs, frequently on different sides of the body. The ataxia and muscle weakness are progressive. Finally the horse goes down and is unable to get back up.

Diagnosis is based on clinical suspicion and neurological findings. A diagnostic blood test using fluid from a spinal tap has recently become available. EPM mimics many neurological diseases. However, it should be the number one consideration for any horse with unexplained neurological signs along with weakness, ataxia, and muscle wasting.

Treatment: It is directed at stopping the progress of the disease. Good results have been obtained using a drug combination (trimethoprim and pyrimethamine) according to a strict protocol. The drugs may need to be given for 2 to 3 months. Complications may require discontinuation. DMSO has been used intravenously to reduce inflammation and swelling of the brain and spinal cord. Corticosteroids ordinarily are not used because they lower the horse's immune response to the parasites. Recovery from neurological signs will depend on the amount of tissue damage caused by the protozoans. Some horses have permanent neurological deficits.

PARASITIC MYELOENCEPHALITIS

This disease is similar to EPM, but instead of a protozoan it is the larval stages of *Strongyles vulgaris*, *Habronema*, *Hypoderma*, and other worms that migrate aimlessly through the brain and spinal cord. Worm encephalopathy is less common than EPM, but the symptoms are nearly indistinguishable.

Treatment: Ivermectin, thiabendazole in high doses, and febendazole are effective against the larval tissue stages of nematodes. Anti-inflammatory drugs reduce inflammation and swelling around the killed parasites. Corticosteroids are contraindicated. Improvement follows treatment, but neurological deficits may persist.

EQUINE DEGENERATIVE MYELOENCEPHALOPATHY

Equine degenerative myeloencephalopathy (EDM) is a progressive disease involving the spinal cord and brainstem. It occurs in young horses 1 to 3 years of age. Most affected horses develop clinical signs by 1 year of age. EDM produces symptoms like those of the wobbler syndrome discussed above. EDM is found in the northeastern United States, but occurs throughout the United States and in parts of Europe. It may affect one or many foals on the same farm.

Evidence suggests that EDM is related to a deficiency of vitamin E. Foals with EDM often have a history of being fed pelleted feeds and cured hay, while not being fed fresh hay or forage that contains ample amounts of vitamin E. There is also an hereditary predisposition to EDM in a number of breeds including

Standardbreds, Thoroughbreds, Arabians, Appaloosas, and Morgans. Thus it appears that both a familial predisposition and a vitamin E deficiency play a role.

EDM begins either gradually or suddenly, usually in foals 4 to 8 months of age. Initial signs are clumsiness and weakness in the legs. The gait is erratic, with the feet sometimes crossing and interfering. The hindquarters frequently are more severely affected than the forequarters, resulting in a wobbly ataxia with pelvic swaying, scuffing of the back feet, and sliding back on the rear into a dog-sitting position.

EDM is difficult to distinguish from CVM and other forms of myeloencephalopathy, but can be suspected when a young horse develops unexplained weakness and ataxia. X-rays of the neck are normal in EDM. In horses with CVM, x-rays of the neck show spinal column abnormalities.

Treatment: When a foal is diagnosed with EDM before 12 months of age, the daily administration of 6000 IU of dl-alpha tocopherol (vitamin E) mixed in grain with 60 ml of corn oil has been shown to at least partially reverse the neurological signs, especially with mild disease. Improvement begins in 3 to 4 weeks. In older horses with spinal cord degeneration, the signs are irreversible and the disease is chronic and progressive.

On farms where EDM occurs as a familial trait, giving foals 2,000 IU of vitamin E per day has been shown to offer protection. Pregnant mares near term may be given a vitamin E/selenium injection to increase vitamin E levels in the milk.

EQUINE HERPES MYELOENCEPHALITIS (EHV-1)

Equine herpes myeloencephalitis (EHV-1) is responsible for major outbreaks of paralytic disease throughout North America and the world. It also causes abortions in pregnant mares and respiratory disease in young horses. Transmission requires direct contact with virus-containing secretions. Since virus shedding occurs in all EHV-1 infections, all have the potential to result in paralytic disease.

Neurological disease usually affects the hindquarters, although occasionally a head tilt of cranial nerve paralysis will occur. Symptoms develop rapidly, reach a maximum within 48 hours, and usually do not progress thereafter. Initial signs are ataxia and alterations in gait affecting the rear. The horse is reluctant to move and often drags its toes. Tail paralysis, bladder paralysis with dribbling of urine, and loss of sensation over the hindquarters are common signs. The horse may sit on its rear and crawl around in the stall.

The diagnosis can be made by recovering virus in blood or cerebral spinal fluid, or by serum antibody determinations. A technique to identify the DNA sequence of EHV viruses from nasopharyngeal secretions using a commercial test kit may soon provide a means of rapid diagnosis.

Treatment: Anti-inflammatory agents and DMSO are recommended. Mildly affected horses continue to eat and drink and often recover completely in 3 to 12 weeks. The prognosis for the recumbent horse is guarded, although many horses will recover if given intensive nursing care as described in the treatment of brain injury. Complications of recumbency are the usual causes of death.

Vaccination does not prevent the neurological form of EHV-1. However, maintaining a high level of immunity in the local horse population through vaccinations may serve as a barrier to the multiplication and spread of the virus. For vaccination information, see Table I in chapter 3, Infectious Diseases.

MENINGITIS

Meningitis is an infection of the vascular membrane covering the surface of the brain. It is not common in adult horses. Most cases are caused by blood-borne bacteria from an infection elsewhere in the body. Occasionally a nasopharyngeal, guttural pouch, or head and neck wound infection will extend into the brain.

Neonatal meningitis occurs in newborn foals who do not suckle during the first 18 hours of life and so fail to acquire protective colostral antibodies (see LACK OF COLOSTRUM in chapter 16, Pediatrics). The infection is blood-borne, originating from a septic site such as an infected umbilical stump.

Horses with meningitis exhibit fever and behavior changes including depression, circling, walking into walls, and falling over. These signs are followed by reluctance to move the head (stiff neck), and by indications of cranial nerve involvement including blindness. Ataxia, weakness, epileptic-like seizures, and coma develop rapidly. The diagnosis is confirmed by finding the bacteria in the cerebrospinal fluid.

Treatment: Antibiotics in high dosage are initiated on suspicion of meningitis. Drugs can be changed later in accordance with culture and sensitivity reports. Intravenous fluids are given to correct dehydration. Alcohol sponge baths reduce fever. Seizures are controlled with Valium.

BRAIN ABSCESS

Brain abscesses are not common. Most occur as complications of strangles. Bacterial infections about the head and neck can extend along the paths of cranial nerves to involve the brain.

Signs are like those of meningitis. They include behavioral changes, head tilt, head pressing, aimlessly wandering, and circling. In advanced stages, the horse begins to convulse. Seizures are followed by coma and death. Treatment is like that for meningitis.

Seizures

A seizure is a sudden and uncontrolled burst of cerebral activity that begins with anxiety, followed by sweating, jaw clamping, rolling up of the eyes, collapse, spastic jerking of the legs, and loss of urine and stool. There is a brief loss of consciousness (lasting up to 60 seconds) followed by a gradual return to normal. Usually the horse is able to stand within a few minutes. A post-seizure phase ranging from mild depression to stupor and blindness can last for several hours.

Some fits involve a small focus in the brain. They are called *partial seizures*. Instead of the classic convulsion described above, the horse exhibits strange and inappropriate behavior such as twitching of the face or limbs, head pressing, compulsive running in a circle, and self-biting.

Seizures commonly are associated with head trauma, brain infections, poisoning, insufficient oxygen to the brain, and liver failure. When due to head trauma, the seizure usually begins several weeks after the injury.

Poisons that typically produce severe and sustained seizures are strychnine, antifreeze (ethylene glycol), insecticides, moldy corn poisoning, locoweed, rye grass, and heavy metals.

Hypocalcemia (low serum calcium) produces seizures as well as ataxia, inability to chew or swallow, profuse sweating, and high fever. Most cases are associated with lactation. Others are due to blister beetle poisoning, excessive sweating, urea poisoning, and heat stroke.

Arrhythmias cause fainting spells which are often mistaken for seizure, as are the cataplexy spells of the fainting foal syndrome.

Epilepsy is a recurrent seizure disorder of cerebral origin. It is far less common in horses than in people. When the cause is unknown, it is said to be *idiopathic*. When it occurs after head trauma or brain inflammation, it is classified as *acquired*.

In some horses with idiopathic epilepsy, seizures appear to be invoked by specific events such as feeding or saddling. There is a syndrome involving recurrent seizures in estrous mares. It appears to be associated with circulating estrogen. It may respond to removing the ovaries or giving progesterone.

A convulsive syndrome occurs in weanling Arabian foals. It is the only known form of inherited epilepsy in horses. Seizures appear abruptly and increase in frequency over days to weeks. Episodes can be mild to severe and are usually generalized. Eventually the foal is convulsing many times a day. The post-seizure state is often quite marked. Most foals appear to outgrow the problem.

Treatment: If a horse begins to convulse, stand well aside to avoid being injured when the horse collapses and kicks out. Do not attempt to gentle or quiet the horse. After the seizure, notify your veterinarian. He or she may want to examine the horse to determine if the horse has been injured or has any findings that may suggest a cause.

Seizures lasting over 60 seconds may be associated with chemical poisoning. Continuous seizures should be stopped to prevent injury to the brain. Valium or pentobarbital can be given intravenously to stop a continuous seizure. Normally this is possible only when a trained professional is in attendance.

Seizure disorders such as those in Arabian foals or in horses with idiopathic epilepsy can be controlled with drugs. Phenobarbital is the most commonly used anticonvulsant. It is given once a day. The dosage can be reduced if the horse remains free of seizures for 3 months. Riding a horse with a seizure disorder is not recommended.

Peripheral Nerve Injuries

Peripheral nerve injuries result from trauma, infection, and toxicity. The effect of an injury to a major nerve is loss of sensation and muscle weakness or paralysis in the area served by that nerve. Most nerve injuries are associated with major limb trauma. Occasionally an isolated nerve injury occurs. Such injuries are caused by bruises, stretches, tears, and lacerations.

One cause of nerve paralysis is the injection of an irritating medication into or around a nerve. This problem is infrequent but can be a source of concern. The correct locations for giving injections are described in chapter 19, Drugs and Medications.

Diagnostic studies helpful in evaluating nerve function include nerve blocks with local anesthetics, muscle and nerve conduction studies, and nerve and muscle biopsies.

Common nerve injuries are discussed below. All cause lameness localized to one limb.

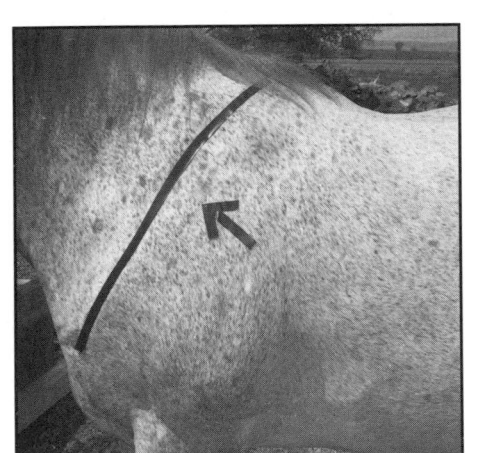

The location of sweeney, a wasting away of the muscles on either side of the scapula (shown by the tape).

Suprascapular Nerve (Sweeny). The term "sweeny" refers to an injury of the supraspinatus and infraspinatus muscles on both sides of the spine of the scapula. Denervation of these muscles produces atrophy. Loss of muscle volume and shrinkage of tissue result in a characteristic prominence of the ridge-like spine.

Nerve damage can occur from continuous pressure on the nerve, from a direct blow to the area, or from a stretch caused by a sudden backward thrust of the foreleg as the horse slips. Sweeny used to be common in draft horses when yokes were used to pull plows.

A horse with sweeny swings its front leg out to the side, a condition known as lateral slippage of the shoulder. Slippage may be accompanied by an audible popping sound. The peculiar shoulder action may further stretch the nerve and aggravate the problem. The lateral slippage occurs before muscle atrophy, which takes several weeks to become evident.

A horse with sweeny can walk without difficulty but has a supporting leg lameness and is not able to participate in athletics. Treatment involves medical management as described below. Surgery to remove a notch of bone to decompress the nerve may be beneficial. It takes 6 months for the full effects of treatment to become evident.

Radial Nerve. The radial nerve in the foreleg is responsible for advancing the leg as the horse steps forward. Injury to the radial nerve can occur with a fracture of the humerus below the shoulder blade, a fracture of the first rib, or pressure on the nerve from prolonged lateral recumbency. If the radial nerve is injured high in the leg, the horse has a dropped elbow and cannot advance or bear weight on the leg. With a low paralysis, the horse stumbles and knuckles over and has a noticeable limp, but is able to bear weight.

Femoral Nerve. This large nerve in the hind limb straightens the stifle joint. It can be injured by a kick or blow to the stifle area. Other causes of injury are exertional myopathy and overstretching of the stifle during vigorous exercise. With femoral nerve paralysis, the horse holds the stifle in a flexed position, has difficulty advancing the leg, and will be unable to extend the stifle to put weight on the leg.

Sciatic Nerve. The main trunk of the sciatic nerve is closely related to the pelvic bone. Most injuries are associated with fractures of the pelvis and sacrum. In foals, deep injections close to the bone in the sciatic area can injure the nerve. The function of the sciatic nerve is to extend the hip and flex the stifle. Paralysis results in major gait disturbances. The limb is dragged, and there are signs affecting both major branches of the sciatic nerve (the tibial and peroneal nerves) as described below.

Tibial Nerve. This branch of the sciatic nerve straightens the hock and flexes the ankle. The nerve is well protected, and isolated injuries are not common. With paralysis, the leg is held with the hock flexed and the ankle straight. This causes the hip to drop on the affected side. The overall stride is strikingly like that of stringhalt.

Peroneal Nerve. The peroneal branch of the sciatic nerve flexes the hock and extends the pastern. The nerve is easily injured in the upper leg near the stifle joint, where it is relatively unprotected by overlying muscle. Trauma from kicks, and prolonged lateral recumbency, are the usual causes.

Paralysis produces a characteristic stance in which the horse holds the leg straight out to the rear with the hoof knuckled over and the front surface of the hoof resting on the ground. As the horse advances and attempts to put weight on the back leg, the foot is dragged along the ground and then jerked to the rear.

Treatment of Nerve Injuries: A nerve that has been bruised or stretched (but remains intact) may recover with time. The immediate need following injury is to suppress swelling and inflammation. This can be accomplished by applying ice packs and dimethyl sulfoxide (DMSO) to the traumatized area. The horse should be rested in a stall for several weeks or months and gradually returned to full activity.

A severed nerve should be repaired as soon as possible. However, the timing of repair depends upon the condition of the wound. Dirty wounds are likely to become infected, which will compromise the repair. In such cases, the repair should be postponed for 3 to 5 weeks.

Healing nerves regenerate slowly—at the rate of about 1 inch a month. Following repair, the joint or limb must be protected while the nerve regenerates. This is accomplished with splints and bandages. Physical therapy involves gentle massage and passive exercises that flex and extend the joints to maintain range of motion. Swimming is a good exercise because the water supports the paralyzed limb.

Occasionally a traumatized nerve becomes entrapped in scar tissue or forms a sensitive mass of nerve fibers at the severed ends. This mass is called a *neuroma*. An operation can be done to free up the nerve or remove the painful neuroma, but the neuroma may reoccur.

MUSCULOSKELETAL SYSTEM

The horse's skeleton is made up of an average of 216 individual bones, connected by ligaments and surrounded by muscles. This is about 12 more than man, but most of this difference is made up of the bones in the tail.

Over the surface of each bone is a layer of dense connective tissue called the *periosteum*. Injuries to the periosteum result in the formation of new bone, which often leads to degenerative arthritis.

The union of two bones is called an *articulation*, or joint. Joint position is maintained by ligaments, tendons, and a tough fibrous capsule, which combine to provide stability and strength to the joint. A layer of connective tissue cells called the *synovial membrane* lines the inside surface of the joint. This membrane secretes a fluid which allows for smooth movement and friction-free gliding.

Elsewhere, interposed between tendons and bony projections, are fluid-filled sacs called *bursae*. These sacs allow the parts to move freely without wear and tear.

Because the horse is such an athletic animal, injuries to all these structures are common.

CONFORMATION AND SOUNDNESS

Breeders and veterinarians use certain terms to describe a horse's overall structure and composition.

Conformation is how various angles and parts of the horse's body agree or harmonize with one another. Standards for registered horses describe the ideal conformation for each breed. These standards are based to a certain extent upon aesthetic considerations, but they also take into account the horse's working purposes.

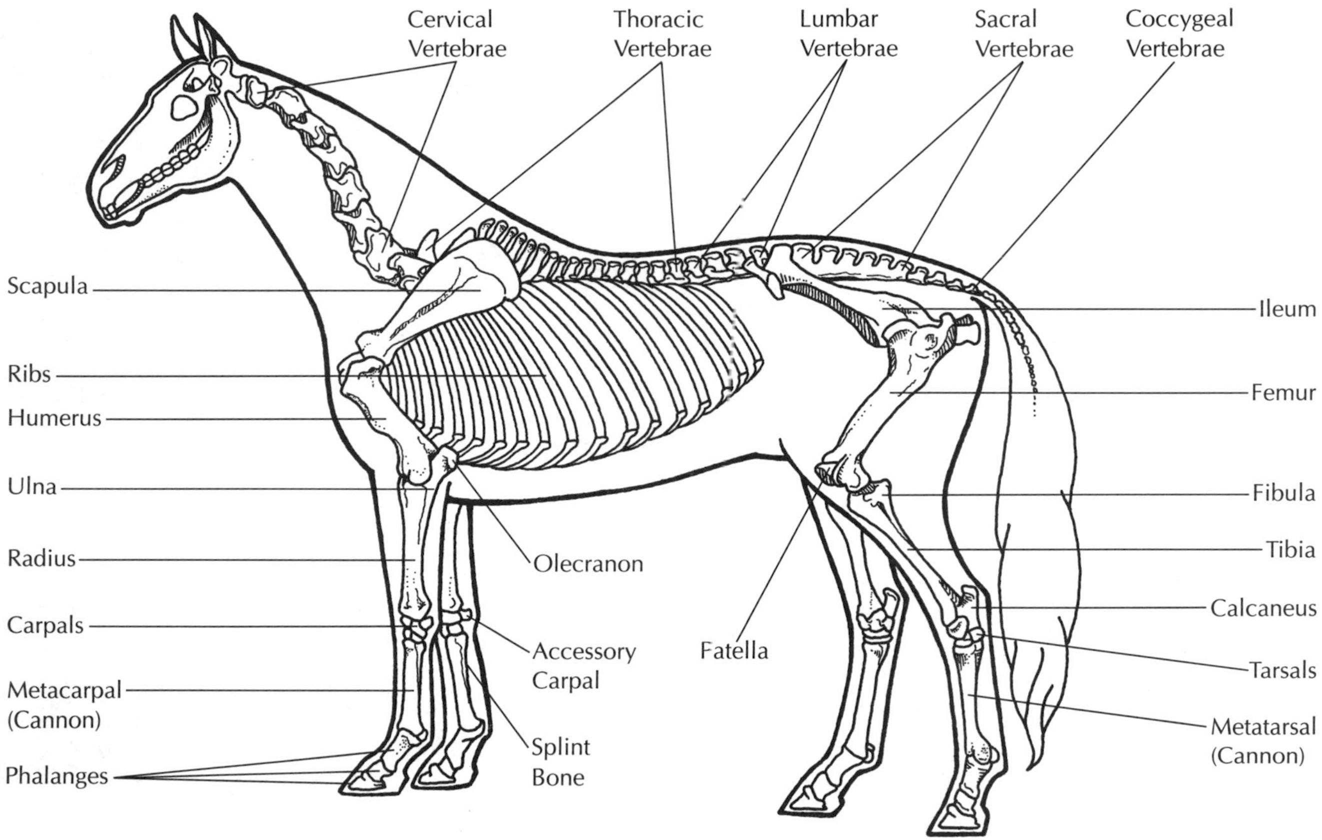

Skeleton of the Horse

Cervical Vertebrae

Thoracic Vertebrae

Lumbar Vertebrae

Sacral Vertebrae

Coccygeal Vertebrae

Scapula

Ribs

Humerus

Ulna

Radius

Carpals

Metacarpal (Cannon)

Phalanges

Splint Bone

Accessory Carpal

Olecranon

Patella

Ileum

Femur

Fibula

Tibia

Calcaneus

Tarsals

Metatarsal (Cannon)

Most breed standards provide some information as to the desired *angle* or slope to the bones of the shoulder, pelvis, and limbs. These angles are determined by comparison with imaginary lines drawn horizontally and vertically through the plane of the standing horse.

Another term used to judge the physical attributes of a horse is *soundness*. When applied to the composition of his musculoskeletal system, it means that in a sound horse, all the bones and joints are in correct alignment to function as intended. In particular, good skeletal conformation is one in which the alignment of the legs is such that there is equal distribution of weight, equal bone pressure, and equal strain on the supporting ligaments when the horse is standing naturally. A horse is considered *unsound* when, by virtue of an old injury or conformation defect, it is unable to perform at the level for which it was intended.

Good conformation is of great importance. Horses who do not possess it are much more susceptible to injuries and bone and joint diseases.

A *blemish* is a defect usually involving the skin, connective tissue, or bone, which more or less diminishes the value of the horse by its unsightly appearance, but does not interfere with or diminish its function.

Judgment must be used in deciding whether a defect is a blemish or unsoundness. For example, thoroughpin and wind puffs could be the result of an old sprain. In that case the consideration would be whether the sprain or injury was produced by poor conformation. If so, the horse would be considered unsound. On the other hand, the horse might have good conformation, in which case the defect is considered a blemish.

Lameness

The forelegs carry 60 percent of the weight of the horse and are subject to a higher incidence of lameness. As a rule of thumb, 95 percent of front leg lameness occurs from the knee down, with the foot being the most frequent site of the problem. This is different in the hindquarters. Only 20 percent of lameness occurs in the foot, with 80 percent occurring in the hock and stifle joints.

Note that gait disturbances can be caused by neuralgic diseases as well as musculoskeletal diseases. If you see bizarre behavior such as head-pressing, staggering, swaying, lack of coordination, head-bobbing, or paralysis, see the section on NEUROLOGICAL EXAMINATION in chapter 11, Nervous System.

The terms "supporting-leg lameness" and "swinging-leg lameness" are used to describe the type of lameness observed.

Supporting-leg lameness is the kind made worse when the horse shifts its weight or support onto the sore limb. The horse will attempt to rest the painful leg by taking weight off it, and will often stand with the sore leg "pointed" well forward of the sound leg. Laminitis and foot wounds are examples of supporting-leg lameness, as are ringbone and navicular disease.

Swinging-leg lameness refers to the fact that the pain is caused by the "swing" or movement of the limb. A horse with a swinging-leg lameness tries to protect the

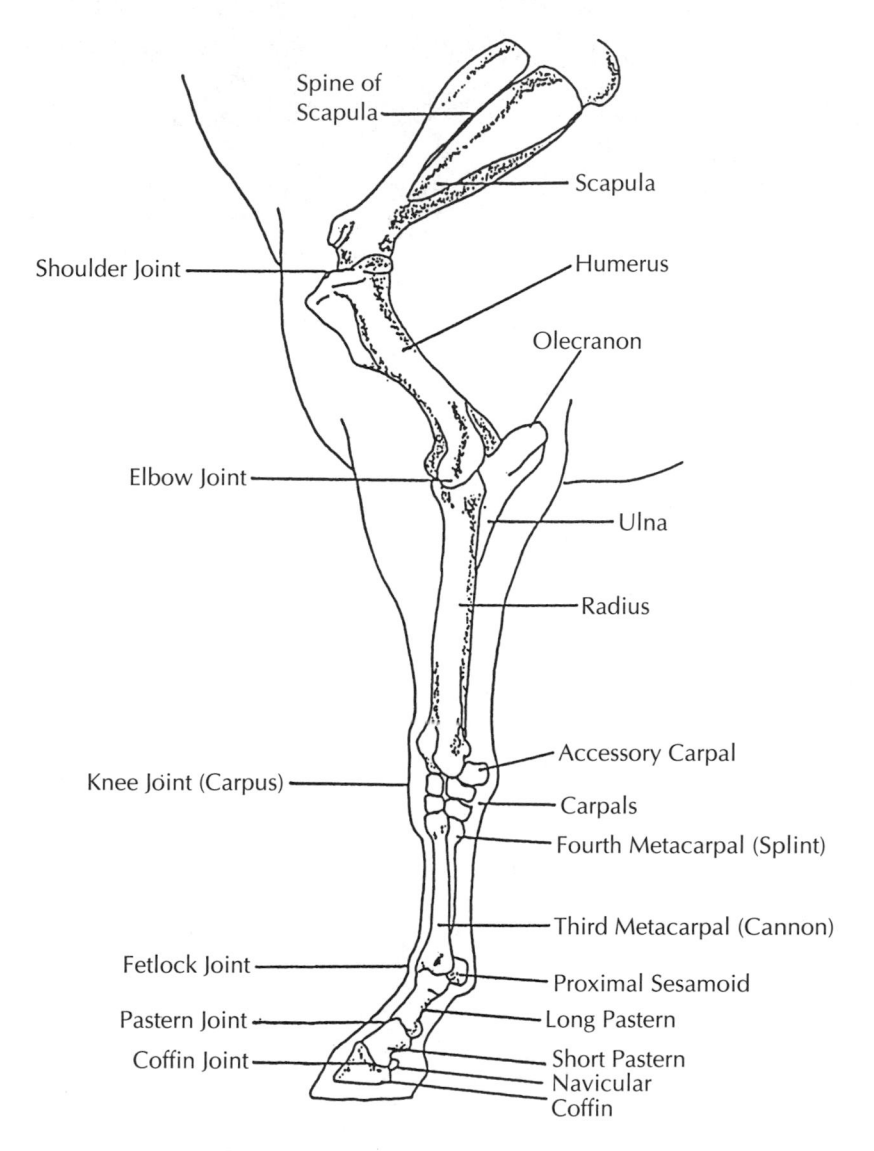

Spine of
Scapula

Scapula

Shoulder Joint

Humerus

Olecranon

Elbow Joint

Ulna

Radius

Accessory Carpal

Knee Joint (Carpus)

Carpals

Fourth Metacarpal (Splint)

Third Metacarpal (Cannon)

Fetlock Joint

Proximal Sesamoid

Pastern Joint

Long Pastern

Coffin Joint

Short Pastern
Navicular
Coffin

Bones and joints of the front leg. Illustration: Rose Floyd.

painful leg by shortening the reach of the leg. This makes for a stilted stride. Muscle strain and joint injuries are examples of swinging-leg lameness.

DETERMINING THE CAUSE

Without a systematic approach to the problem of lameness, it can be most difficult to make a diagnosis. Consideration should be given to the history and circumstances surrounding the onset of the lameness. Which limb is involved, and exactly where is the problem located? Once the site of pain has been identified,

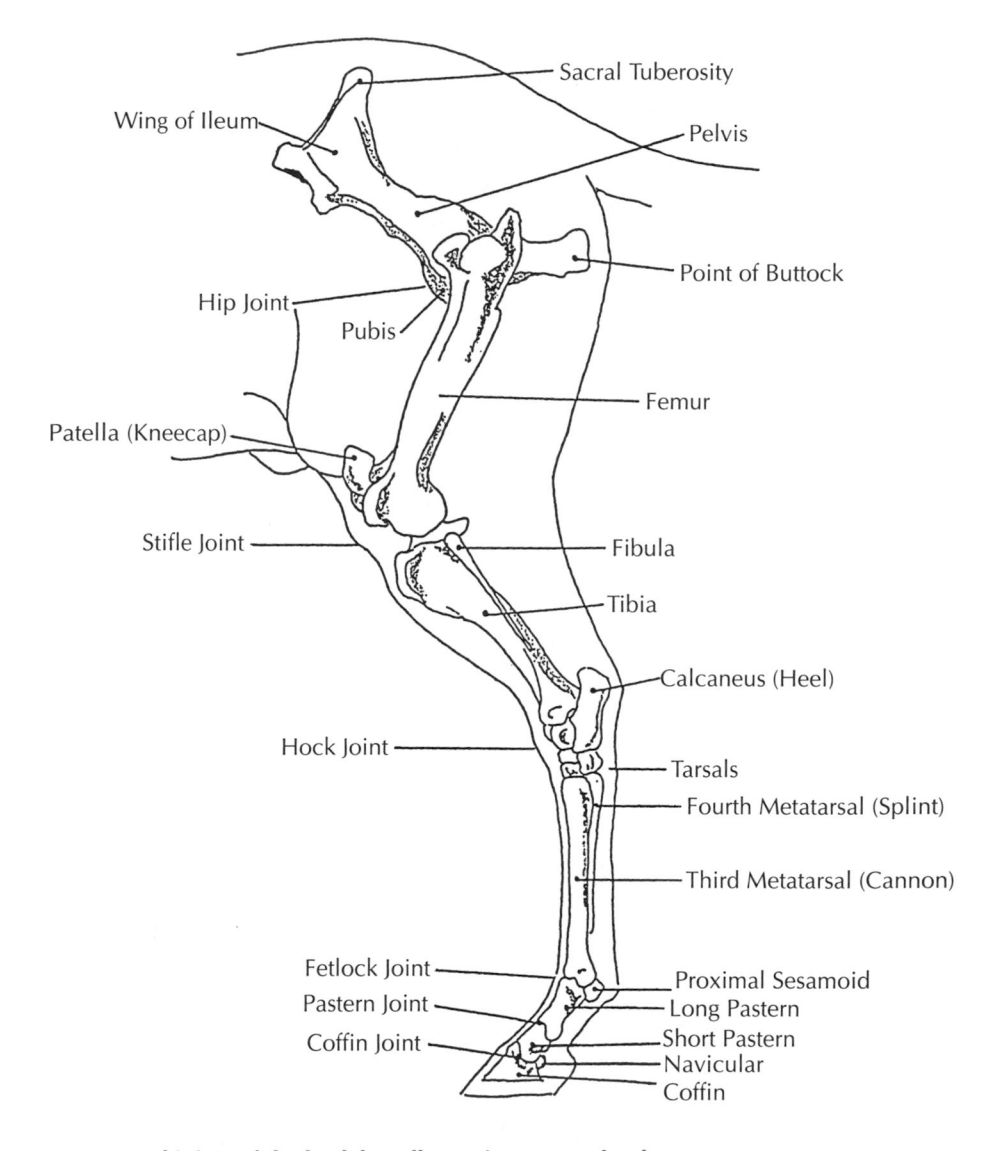

Bone and joints of the back leg. Illustration: Rose Floyd.

you can begin to make a differential diagnosis. If the diagnosis is not apparent after inspection and examination, x-rays and special tests may clarify the problem. Finally, remember this rule: When the site of lameness is difficult to determine, think of the foot when in front and the hock when behind.

History. Lameness of sudden onset suggests laminitis or an acute injury. Ask what happened to the horse just before you noticed the lameness. Were his shoes changed or hooves trimmed? Was he ridden over uneven ground or for a long distance? Could he have been kicked by another horse, or have stepped in a hole? Does he have conformation faults which predispose to injuries?

The condition of the horse is an important factor. When a horse is out of condition, even moderate work or training may sprain a muscle or pull a tendon.

Inspection. Observe the horse while it's standing idle, moving, and then being ridden. Normally a horse stands with its weight evenly distributed on all four legs, and the feet more or less next to each other. If you see a horse standing with one leg flexed, you can be sure there is a reason why he is favoring that leg. A horse with a bruised sole or painful foot usually points that foot or stands with it partly off the ground. A horse with shoulder lameness frequently stands with the heel raised and the toe resting on the ground. If the horse stands with a bend in its knee, suspect an injury to the elbow. If the heel is raised and the knee or stifle is held forward, the horse may have sustained an injury to the heel or fetlock. With a stifle joint injury, the horse often stands and travels with the stifle turned out.

Bone fractures and joint injuries often (but not always) produce some degree of limb deformity. X-rays should be taken. Foot fractures, in particular, are difficult to diagnose without x-rays.

Standing directly in front of the horse, watch his head to see if it bobs up and down with each step. In a horse with a *front* leg lameness, the head bobs down as weight comes down on the *sound* leg. In the *rear* leg the condition is reversed. The head bobs down as weight comes down on the *injured* leg. Note that head-bobbing does not occur with mild lameness.

Next, standing directly behind the horse, see if one side of the rump appears to dip as the horse moves away. This indicates a sore hind limb on the side opposite the dipping.

With a sore stifle, the horse often travels with the stifle pointing out. In addition, he may hesitate before bringing the sore leg forward, which results in dragging of the leg.

Very subtle lameness may not produce visible signs. However, when riding the horse you may notice that he appears unwilling to step out or seems stiff in one leg. Occasionally, one can detect a hind limb lameness by changing diagonals at the trot. The horse's gait feels different on the new diagonal because now you are rising and sitting in time with the sore leg. As you listen at the walk or trot, you should hear equal beats of the hooves. With an irregular beat the horse may be favoring one foot and not putting it down as hard as the others.

A supporting-leg lameness is often made worse by riding the horse in a circle or working him on a lunge line, which forces the horse to put more weight on the inside leg. A left-sided lameness, for example, will show up on a counterclockwise circle to the left. A horse with a supporting-leg lameness is apt to shuffle and stumble, especially on rough surfaces such as gravel. This is particularly characteristic of navicular disease.

A swinging-leg lameness can be brought out by riding the horse down a slope. This requires the legs to move through a greater arc, which increases pain in the sore leg. The horse may compensate by swinging the sore leg out wide or dragging that toe.

Physical Examination. Starting at the feet, perform a systematic examination, working up the legs to the hips and shoulders.

Pick up each foot and examine the sole for a puncture wound, and a bruised sole or corn. It will usually be necessary to clean the hoof thoroughly and possibly remove flaky horn to see the needed detail. A hot or close horseshoe nail is a frequent cause of sole lameness. A hoof tester is indispensable in examining for this and for foot wounds, laminitis, gravel, quittor, and navicular disease. Hot painful front feet should alert you to the possibility of founder.

Run your fingers and thumb along the superficial digital flexor tendons at the back of the fetlocks, looking for swelling, pain, and increased warmth (see TENDONITIS). Swelling of the foot above the coronet is usually caused by ringbone.

Run both hands slowly up the legs. A swollen painful joint indicates inflammation, usually from a recent injury (see JOINT AND LIGAMENT INJURIES). Swelling without pain suggests tenosynovitis and bursitis. In the front legs, a painful swelling along the inside front of the cannon bone indicates bucked shins or splints. On the hind limbs, a bony enlargement on the inside of the leg below the point of the hock is typical of bone spavin. If thickening and swelling is found at the back of the hock, consider curb.

Diagnostic Tests. Veterinarians use certain test to diagnose lameness, and to monitor the course of treatment.

Conventional X-rays. X-rays make it possible to differentiate between soft tissue swellings and bone growths. They are absolutely necessary for diagnosing bone fractures. They do not always provide a definitive diagnosis for lameness, however, because changes seen on an x-ray may not be associated with lameness, and not all causes of lameness produce x-ray findings.

Ultrasonography. This technology employs ultrasound waves in soft tissues to create pictures which can be displayed on a television monitor. Ligaments and tendons that cannot be visualized on x-rays can be seen through ultrasound. This is an excellent way to follow the progress of ligament and tendon healing. It enables the trainer to determine when the horse is ready to return to work.

Bone Scans (Nuclear Scintigraphy). This method of imaging uses intravenous radioactive isotopes and scintigraphy equipment to form a picture of the bone and surrounding tissue. Because of cost and restrictions governing the use of radioactive materials, bone scans are performed primarily at equine medical centers and schools of veterinary medicine.

Nerve Blocks. Local anesthetics are often injected around specific nerves to localize pain and lameness. Anesthesia and pain relief occur in the area supplied by the blocked nerves. Thus if the lameness disappears after the nerve block, the site (if not the cause) of lameness has been identified. Nerve blocks do not always establish a specific diagnosis in that many causes of pain may exist in the same general location.

Neurectomy is the surgical removal of nerves to cause permanent anesthesia and pain relief.

Synovial Fluid Analysis. Synovial fluid is a viscous lubricating liquid containing hyaluronic acid. It is found in joint, bursal, and tendon sheath swellings. The fluid can be removed using a sterile needle and syringe. Normal synovial fluid is clear and pale yellow. The presence of blood indicates that bleeding has occurred into the synovial space. Usually this is because of an acute injury. Pus indicates an infection in the joint or bursa. Laboratory analysis of synovial fluid provides further information.

Arthroscopy. This is a diagnostic procedure which allows direct inspection of the interior of a joint to determine the cause of swelling. A fiberoptic scope is passed through a small incision that can be closed with a single suture. Arthroscopic joint surgery involves the removal of bone fragments, cartilage, and debris. Reconstruction of ligaments is possible.

Tendon Injuries

A tendon is a tough, inelastic band of fibers that connects muscle to bone. Tendons are classified as either *flexors* or *extensors*, depending upon whether they bend the limb or straighten it out. Most tendon injuries in the horse occur in the lower half of the leg.

The large tendon running down the front of the horse's leg is called the *common digital extensor*. This tendon straightens the leg and extends the fetlock, pastern, and coffin joints. In the hind limbs it also flexes the hock joint.

Running down the back of each leg are the two digital flexor tendons. The *superficial digital flexor* tendon forms the rear outline of the leg. The *deep digital flexor* tendon lies beneath the superficial tendon. The combined action of these tendons is to flex the knee and all the joints below. In the hind limbs the flexors also straighten the hock. Each tendon has special "check" ligaments which restrain the tendon and keep it from overstretching (see JOINT AND LIGAMENT INJURIES).

TENDON STRAIN

A strain is an injury to a tendon caused by overuse or excessive use of strength. In a severe strain, the tendon first overstretches and then tears. The area is painful and swollen. Diagnostic ultrasound can be used to visualize the degree of tendon damage and monitor the healing process.

TENDONITIS (FLEXOR TENDONITIS; BOWED TENDONS)

Tendonitis in the horse refers to strains of the superficial digital flexor tendons of the forelegs. These injuries often occur at the end of a long race or a lengthy workout when muscles are fatigued and the horse no longer has the muscle tone to compensate for rapid loading and overstretching of the tendon. Thus the injury occurs most commonly in racing horses, Quarter horses, hunters, and jumpers, but can occur in any horse as a result of a direct blow to the tendon area. Tendonitis of the hind limb is less common, but does occur to some extent in harness racers.

The signs of tendonitis are generalized swelling throughout the area of injury with warmth and pain to the touch. The horse may pull up lame or experience severe lameness shortly after the accident, and stand with its heel off the ground. If the tendon is partially disrupted, you may see "dropping" of the fetlock.

Within the injured tendon there is bleeding and leakage of inflammatory fluids. Released enzymes cause further damage. A pocket of accumulated serum and debris can develop within the tendon itself. The blood supply to the tendon is often disrupted along with its fibers.

In the healing stages, acute inflammatory tissue is replaced by fibrous connective tissue and scar. The tendon becomes thick and bowed out from the leg when viewed from the side. A mild to moderate degree of lameness may be present, which is exacerbated by hard work.

The bow in the tendon is described by its location. A *high* bow covers the upper third of the cannon just below the knee or hock. A *middle* bow (the most common) is found at the mid-cannon bone level. A *low* bow is found at the lower cannon level in the annular ligament area. A *low-low* bow, indicative of *deep* digital flexor tendon injury, is found in back of and below the fetlock joint.

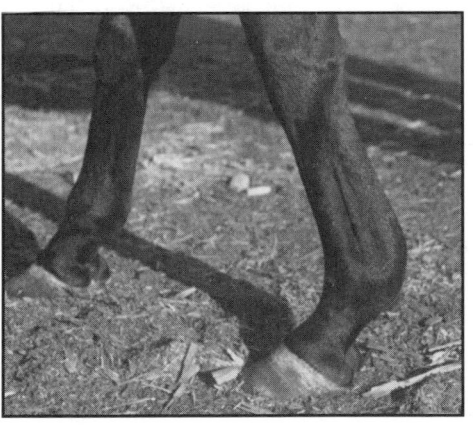

Typical appearance of a bowed tendon.

Treatment: Treatment of acute tendonitis involves reducing the swelling with ice, pressure, and anti-inflammatory medications.

During the first 48 hours it is most important to prevent further damage by resting the horse completely. Begin cold therapy with the application of ice packs for 30 minutes 3 to 4 times a day for 2 days. This slows bleeding, reduces inflammation, and helps to relieve pain. Between applications, immobilize the area and provide counterpressure by wrapping the leg as described in the section BANDAGING in chapter 1, Emergencies. After the first 48 hours, continued benefit can be obtained by alternating the cold packs with warm packs. The warm packs should be applied about 3 times longer than the cold packs (90 minutes to 30 minutes). Continue alternating temperature therapy 3 or 4 times per day for 4 to 6 days. After 6 days, warm therapy alone is recommended to promote circulation and healing.

Banamine is a strong analgesic with a rapid onset of action. Consider initiating treatment with Banamine and switching to Butazolidin as pain and swelling begin to diminish. DMSO gel has anti-inflammatory and antioxidant properties, which are beneficial in resolving harmful inflammatory byproducts at the site of injury. DMSO can be applied topically once per day beneath the bandage, or 2 to 3 times per day on uncovered skin. Corticosteroid injections are no longer recommended for the treatment of tendonitis. Hyaluronic acid injections into the tendon sheath have yielded good results. For more information on analgesics, see ANTI-INFLAMMATORY DRUGS AND PAIN RELIEVERS.

At the beginning of the third week post-injury, remove the supportive bandages and begin passive exercises by moving the joints gently back and forth several times a day. Proceed to light exercise in 4 to 6 weeks.

Early surgical treatment may be indicated in selected individuals, especially those in whom ultrasound shows signs of delayed healing. Various surgical procedures have been used successfully. They include "splitting" of the flexor tendon, cutting of the radial check ligament, and division of the annular ligament.

Firing and blistering are outdated methods of treatment for tendonitits. They are of questionable value and produce further tissue injury.

CONSTRICTION OF THE ANNULAR LIGAMENT

The annular ligament of the fetlock is a tough, unyielding thickening of the sheath that encircles the superficial and deep flexor tendons and forms a canal through which they pass. Contraction of these ligaments squeezes and damages the tendon and prevents it from gliding. The constricting effect is amplified when the tendon swells after an injury. Accordingly, the majority of cases of annular ligament constriction are associated with a pre-existing tendonitis. Direct injury to the ligament accounts for the remainder.

The typical history is that of pain and lameness associated with a tendonitis that fails to improve after several months (as it should with an uncomplicated bow) and gets worse with exercise. In many cases, swelling of the tendon sheath above the annular ligament can be seen and felt. Ultrasound examination is a useful diagnostic test for annular ligament constriction.

All cases of low bow tendonitis should be examined for the possibility of a coexistent annular ligament constriction. An operation to divide the annular ligament and release the constricted flexor tendons is usually successful.

LACERATED AND RUPTURED TENDONS

Tendons can be severed as a result of a deep cut through the leg. They can also be torn or ruptured during athletic competition as a result of sudden overextension or overflexion of a fatigued joint. Struggling to free a trapped leg is another cause of injury.

Damage to a tendon can weaken it to the extent that spontaneous rupture can occur even with normal stress. This can happen with a prior tendon sheath infection, with prior tendon repair, and with advanced navicular disease.

Treatment: Lacerated and ruptured tendons must be surgically repaired. If the wound is clean, this can be done at the time of injury. If the wound is dirty, it is best to treat the wound and repair the tendon at a later date. In either case, antibiotics are indicated.

In the lower leg, a partially ruptured tendon in which most of the fibers remain intact is usually treated by immobilizing the joints above and below the injured tendon. (The same immobilization is used following surgical repair.) The cast can be changed, but should be left for 6 weeks. Afterwards, special shoes may be necessary for several months to protect the tendon from undue strain.

The results of tendon treatment cannot be fully evaluated for 1 year. They are best for extensor tendons and less satisfactory for flexor tendons.

The common sites for tendon injuries are:

Flexor Tendons of the Feet. All degrees of tear and disruption can occur in the feet. If just the superficial flexor tendon is involved, the fetlock will drop but not touch the ground. When both tendons are cut, the fetlock will drop further, bringing the toe up into the air as the horse bears weight. An infected wound increases the amount of scar and decreases the chance for full recovery.

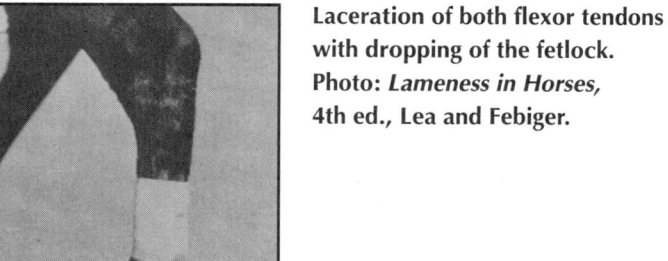

Laceration of both flexor tendons with dropping of the fetlock. Photo: *Lameness in Horses,* 4th ed., Lea and Febiger.

Rupture of the deep flexor tendon usually occurs near its junction with bone at the back of the fetlock joint. Rupture is often preceded by an infection of the sole of the foot, which extends upward to involve the tendon. Navicular disease is another precursor to rupture of the deep flexor.

Extensor Tendon of the Knee (Carpus). This tendon assists in straightening out the knee joint. Rupture occurs just above the knee, usually as a result of being kicked by another horse or by striking the knee against a wall or post.

Signs of rupture are difficult to detect. Careful observation will show that the injured knee flexes more than the normal knee, especially at the trot. Palpation of the tendon will reveal loss of substance when compared to the normal knee.

Peroneus Tertius. This tendon is an integral part of the reciprocal apparatus. It mechanically bends the hock when the stifle joint is flexed. Because rupture occurs above the hock joint, the diagnosis can be made if the hock can be straightened while the stifle is bent.

Rupture of the peroneus tertius requires only stall rest for 6 weeks. Most cases heal and the horse can return to normal activity.

Achilles (Common Calcaneal Tendon). The heel tendon is easily visible as a ridge beneath the skin at the back of the hock and leg. The Achilles is a common tendon, made up of the tendons of the gastrocnemius muscle and the superficial digital flexor of the hind limb.

It is rare for the common tendon to rupture, but when it does, the hock is dropped very nearly to the ground and the limb cannot support weight. More commonly, the gastrocnemius tendon ruptures before the superficial digital flexor. Although the hock is dropped, the horse can still bear some weight.

These injuries are caused by falls with the back legs flexed beneath the body, by being stopped suddenly and pulled back on the hocks, and by making strenuous efforts to keep from slipping while going downhill.

Ruptured gastrocnemius tendons are difficult to treat and usually require casting the limb from the hoof to the stifle for 2 to 3 months and placing the horse in a sling. When the common tendon is ruptured, the prognosis is guarded.

TENOSYNOVITIS

A tendon is surrounded by a sheath of specialized tissue (*synovial membrane*) which secretes fluid that lubricates the tendon and reduces friction when the tendon glides. Inflammation of this sheath is called *tenosynovitis*. The hallmark of tenosynovitis is fluid accumulation in the sheath, which causes obvious swelling. There are several types of tenosynovitis.

Acute Tenosynovitis. This condition is distinguished by a sudden buildup of fluid within the sheath, accompanied by pain, heat, and lameness. There may be a history of trauma. Symptoms are like those of tendonitis and, in fact, both conditions may exist at the same time. Diagnostic ultrasound is useful to distinguish between them.

Acute tenosynovitis can progress to chronic tenosynovitis, with persistent thickening and swelling of the tendon sheath and the development of fibrous bands and adhesions between the tendon and sheath. Chronic tenosynovitis restricts tendon movement and athletic performance.

Treatment of acute tenosynovitis is like that described for tendonitis except that injections of corticosteroid into the tendon sheath are recommended for tenosynovitis.

Septic (Infectious) Tenosynovitis. With bacterial infection, the synovial fluid contains pus and inflammatory enzymes which can digest the tendon. Pain and lameness are severe. Diagnosis is confirmed by ultrasound and by analysis of fluid withdrawn from the infected sheath.

Treatment involves immediate surgical drainage of the abscessed sheath along with the administration of appropriate antibiotics. The outlook is guarded owing to the potential for tendon degeneration and rupture, and the presence of dense fibrous adhesions that encase the tendon.

Idiopathic Tenosynovitis. There are a number of mild conditions that produce tendon sheath swelling but do not produce pain or lameness. In some cases chronic stress appears to be a causative factor; in others there is a history of repeated minor trauma to the tendon sheath. Foals can be born with idiopathic tenosynovitis.

The common types of idiopathic tenosynovitis are:

Thoroughpin. Swelling of the deep digital flexor tendon of the hind limb is referred to as thoroughpin. The distended sheath appears as a soft boggy prominence on the outside of the hock at or below the joint. It rarely causes problems and is considered a blemish.

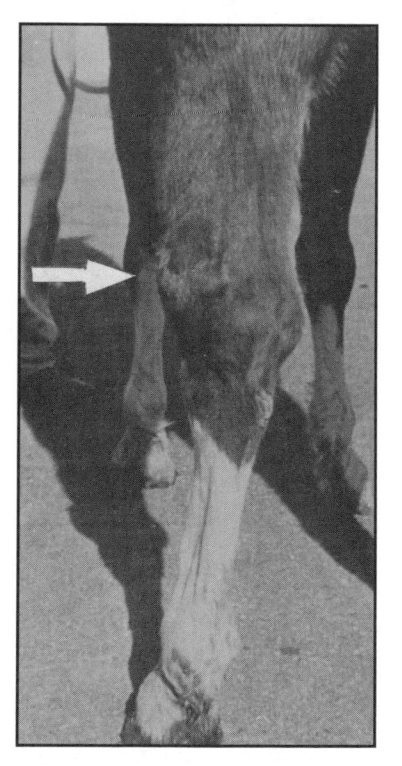

Thoroughpin is a boggy swelling on the outside of the hock at or below the joint. Photo: *Lameness in Horses*, 4th ed., Lea and Febiger.

Bog Spavin. Bog spavin is a swelling of the joint capsule of the hock joint, considered here because of its similarity to thoroughpin. A stress or strain of the hock joint may be the initiating factor, but once the joint capsule becomes distended, the swelling persists. Bog spavin can be distinguished from thoroughpin by the fact that there are not one but three swellings of the hock joint. Two are present on either side of the back of the hock, the third on the inside front of the hock. Bog spavin tends to occur in young horses and disappear as the individual matures.

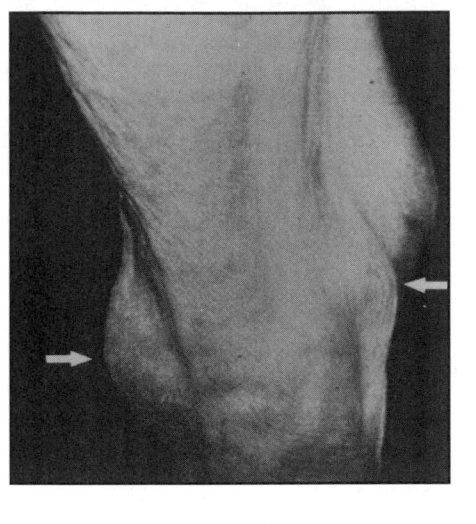

Bog spavin is a tenosynovitis of the hock joint, recognized by swellings on either side and at the back of the hock.
Photo: *Lameness in Horses,* 4th ed., Lea and Febiger.

Wind Puffs (Wind Galls). Generically, the term *wind puffs* refers to synovial swellings of various joints and tendons that do not cause lameness. However, the term is usually used to describe the firm swellings in the area of the fetlock.

A horse in full training who abruptly stops working frequently shows wind puffs on the front and/or back legs. Long straight pasterns, incorrect trimming of the hoof, and heavy training on hard surfaces predisposes to wind puffs, especially in young horses.

Treatment: Swellings caused by idiopathic tenosynovitis can be drained and injected with a corticosteroid for cosmetic reasons; however, they have a strong tendency to recur. Those caused by hard training may respond to a modification in the exercise program.

STRINGHALT

This is a peculiar condition in which there is a sudden upward jerking of the hind leg, accompanied by an involuntary flexion of the hock as the horse steps forward. In severe stringhalt the fetlock may actually shoot forward and strike the undersurface of the abdomen.

While the cause is unknown, the condition appears to involve the tendon of the lateral digital extensor muscle at the hock. Some cases follow trauma to this tendon, and adhesions may form as it crosses the outside surface of the hock joint. Although most cases are isolated occurrences, outbreaks of a stringhalt-like syndrome among horses on pasture have been reported in Australia and New Zealand.

Treatment: Surgery to free adhesions and divide the tendon usually affords immediate improvement, although recovery may be incomplete in some cases. Horses with the stringhalt-like syndrome usually recover spontaneously when removed from pasture.

Bursitis

A bursa is a closed sac lined by a membrane that secretes a lubricating fluid. These sacs are located at strategic points between moving parts and act as cushions to prevent friction and chafing. Trauma to a bursa, either a direct blow or the mechanical stress of racing, produces a painful swelling called *acute bursitis*.

An acute bursitis causes lameness. With rest and anti-inflammatory drugs, the acute bursitis usually resolves. However, with the stresses of repetitive motion at high speeds or heavy loads, the bursa becomes thickened and scarred, and the swelling persists. This is called *chronic bursitis*. It may or may not cause lameness.

Septic bursitis occurs when the bursa becomes infected with bacteria or, rarely, fungi. A good example is *septic navicular bursitis*, which follows a nail penetration injury of the frog of the foot. As the infection works its way up through the laminae of the foot, it rapidly involves the bursa behind the navicular bone. Urgent treatment is indicated to prevent further complications. Treatment of a septic bursitis involves wide surgical drainage of all infected pockets, and the administration of appropriate antibiotics.

Common locations affected by acute bursitis are:

Shoulder Joint (Bicipital) Bursitis. Shoulder joint bursitis follows a kick or blow to the point of the shoulder. Signs are swelling along with a noticeable limp. X-rays are advisable to rule out an associated fracture. With shoulder joint lameness, a horse in motion will often swing its leg out wide in a half-circle.

Treatment: Rest the horse until signs of lameness are gone. Anti-inflammatory drugs such as Banamine or Butazolidin help to relieve pain and swelling. Injections of cortisone into the bursa are often beneficial.

Whorlbone Lameness (Trochanteric Bursitis). This is a painful hip lameness caused by inflammation of a bursa beneath the tendon which crosses the head of the femur. It is the result of tendon overuse that occurs during racing or hard training. It is seen most often in Standardbred racehorses. A horse with trochanteric bursitis carries the foot inward and puts most of its weight on the inside edge of the foot.

Treatment: Injection of the bursa with corticosteroids is often effective. As an alternative, the bursa can be injected with an obliterating agent such as Lugol's iodine solution. Butazolidin is given to relieve pain and swelling. Rest the horse until lameness disappears.

Cunean Tendon Bursitis (Jacks). This is a painful inflammation of the bursa beneath the cunean tendon at the inside of the hock joint. The condition is common among harness racers. In fact, it is said that most Standardbreds will be affected at some point in their racing careers.

Acute bursitis results from a shearing-type stress produced as the foot impacts and pushes off during extended fast pacing or trotting. Improper shoeing and incorrect conformation are believed to contribute. In the majority of cases there is an associated bursitis of the small tarsal bones within the hock joint, causing some experts to refer to the condition as a *cunean tendon bursitis-tarsitis.*

Characteristically, the horse exhibits a "cold" lameness—that is, the lameness diminishes or disappears as the horse warms up. With continued abuse the lameness becomes constant, with the horse putting as little weight as possible on the affected leg, and moving in shorter steps while carrying the leg to the inside. Cunean bursitis is often bilateral, although usually one side is more severely affected than the other. Blocking the cunean bursa with a local anesthetic brings temporary relief and helps to make the diagnosis.

Treatment: Lameness is reversible. Treatment involves corrective shoeing, slower workouts at longer distances, the administration of Butazolidin, and the injection of a corticosteroid and/or hyaluronic acid into the tarsal joints.

Surgery, which involves removal of the cunean tendon, also affords relief. However, this further exposes the horse to shearing stresses and should be reserved for individuals who do not respond to the above management.

Capped Elbow (Olecranon Bursitis). This is a soft boggy swelling of the bursa that overlies the point of the elbow. It occurs in horses who bang the elbow when getting up and down on hard surfaces. It can also be caused by a shoe hitting the elbow when the horse is recumbent. It usually does not cause lameness.

Treatment: The bursa is drained and injected with a corticosteroid or an iodine solution, after which a pressure bandage is applied. This may have to be done several times. Alternately, the bursa can be opened and packed with gauze containing Lugol's iodine solution, or a drain can be left in place until the cavity obliterates. If these procedures are not successful, the bursa can be surgically removed.

Prevent further injury by providing softer bedding.

Capped Hock (Calcaneal Bursitis). This is a boggy swelling over the point of the hock caused by single or repeated trauma, such as kicking a wall or trailer gate. By itself, it is not a cause of lameness.

Treatment: Treatment is like that for capped elbow.

Capped Knee (Hygroma of the Knee). Hygroma is a swelling over the front of the knee caused by pawing and hitting the knee against a wall or getting up and down on hard surfaces. The swelling, which can become quite prominent, takes various shapes.

Treatment: Treatment involves needle aspiration of the fluid sac and injection of a corticosteroid. In chronic cases, permanent swelling is treated by opening and draining the hygroma or removing it by surgery.

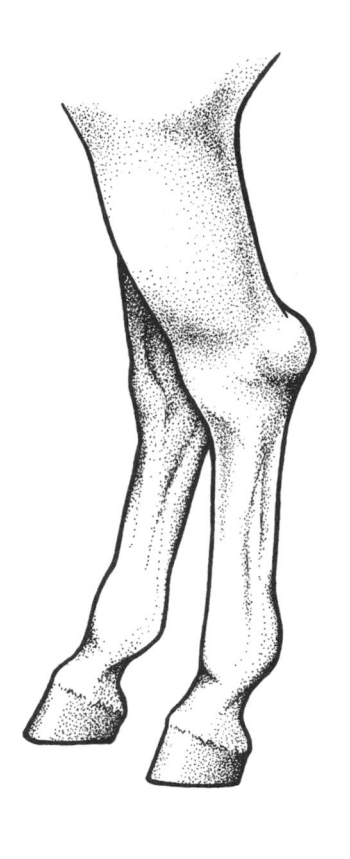

Capped hock is a soft swelling caused by repeated trauma.

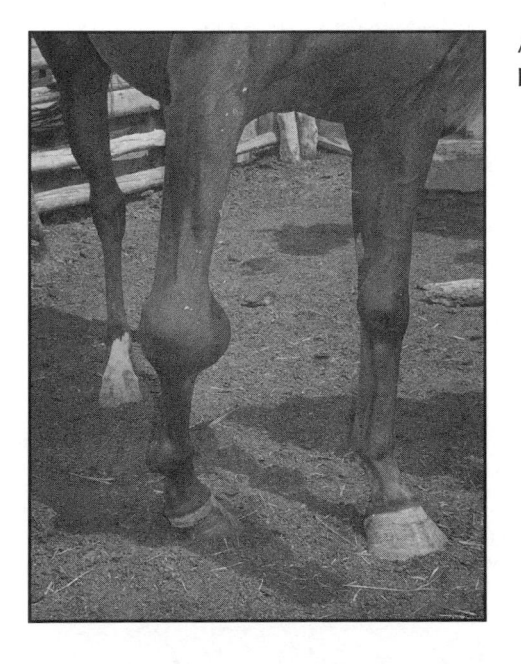

A long-standing hygroma of the knee requiring surgery.

Joint and Ligament Injuries

A joint injury involves a stretching or tearing of the joint capsule and its supporting ligaments by forced movement of the joint beyond its normal range. An injury to a ligament is called a *sprain*.

A *mild* sprain is one in which a few fibers of the ligament are torn, resulting in swelling, stiffness, and often a limp. As the integrity of the ligament is not lost, a mild sprain responds to rest and a support bandage.

A *moderate* sprain is one in which there is a tear of the ligament but the ends do not separate. The signs are pain over the joint, bleeding into the joint or soft tissues, swelling, and restriction of motion (causing lameness). There may be some degree of looseness in the joint. This type of injury requires casting and prolonged rest.

In a *severe* sprain, the ligament and/or joint capsule is completely disrupted. Loss of integrity may result in dislocation *(luxation)* of the joint.

In the horse there is an apparatus composed of muscles, ligaments, tendons, and connective tissue, whose function is to support the horse as it stands; to diminish compression during locomotion; and to protect the horse from injuries that might occur from overextension of the fetlock, pastern, and coffin joints. This apparatus is called the *stay apparatus*.

The stay apparatus is further subdivided as follows:

The check apparatus. This refers to ligaments that restrain the knee and hock joints, and also to the superficial and deep flexor tendons in all four legs. The check apparatus allows a horse to sleep on its feet by locking or "checking" its lower legs in extension with little muscular effort.

The reciprocal apparatus of the hind limb. This insures that there will be reciprocal flexing of the hock joint when the stifle joint is flexed, and conversely that the hock will extend when the stifle extends. The reciprocal apparatus also aids in preventing fatigue when the horse is standing. Structures in the reciprocal apparatus include the peroneus tertius muscle, superficial digital flexor tendon, and gastrocnemius tendon.

The suspensory apparatus of the fetlock. This is of prime importance in absorbing the shock of concussion and in supporting the fetlock. The fetlock is the one joint subject to the greatest stress. The suspensory apparatus includes the suspensory ligament, the paired sesamoid bones and their ligaments, and the superficial and deep flexor tendons.

The *suspensory ligament* is a wide, thick, elastic, tendonlike band which arises from the back of the cannon bone above and attaches to the back of the upper third of the long pastern bone below. In its course from top to bottom, the ligament divides into two branches that surround and partly encase the two proximal sesamoid bones. Where the two branches attach to the long pastern bone, they also join the common digital extensor tendon. All these attachments serve to cushion impact and prevent extreme overextension of the fetlock joint.

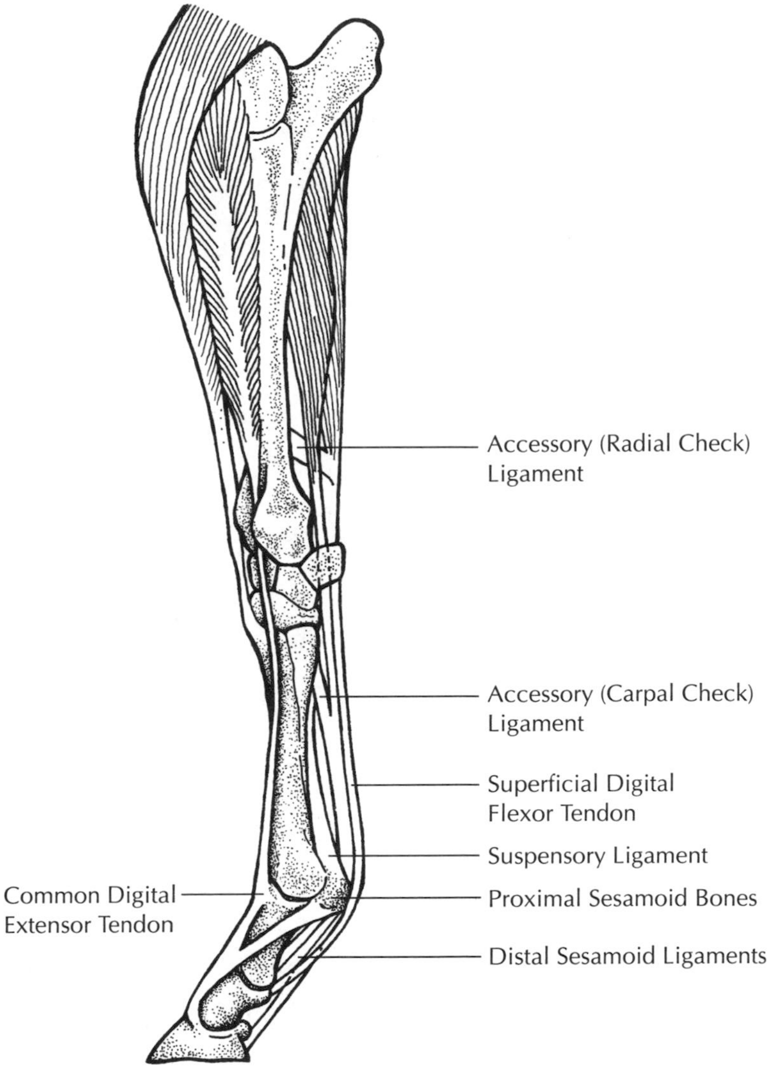

Accessory (Radial Check) Ligament

Accessory (Carpal Check) Ligament

Superficial Digital Flexor Tendon

Suspensory Ligament

Proximal Sesamoid Bones

Distal Sesamoid Ligaments

Common Digital Extensor Tendon

The stay apparatus of the front leg.

Sprains (Ruptures) of the Suspensory Apparatus of the Fetlock

This serious injury is a common cause of fetlock breakdown in the Thoroughbred. It occurs when the horse's weight comes down on the overextended fetlock under the extreme stress of racing. All degrees of tear of the ligament can occur, from mild sprains to complete ruptures of the suspensory ligament and its two branches.

Signs are sudden lameness and extensive swelling at the fetlock joint. The horse often stands with its entire weight on the uninjured leg. When weight is trans-ferred to the injured leg, the fetlock may sink to the ground. Severe fetlock sprains are difficult to tell apart from fractures of the sesamoid bones, which occur because of stress and fatigue during a long race (referred to as "breaking down on the race-track"), from sprains of the distal sesamoid ligaments, and from fractures of the fetlock joint and long pastern bone. In fact, massive injuries can be associated with all of the above as well as injuries to the digital arteries and tendons.

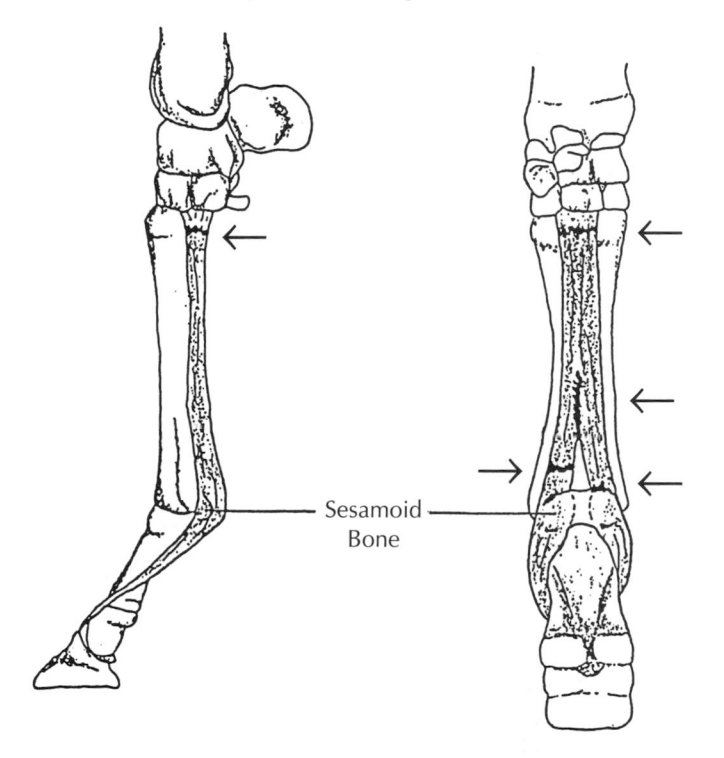

Sesamoid Bone

Sprains of the suspensory ligament of the fetlock, showing where tears are most common. Illustration: Mona Frazier.

Treatment: Veterinary examination and x-rays are indicated in all fetlock inju-ries. A variety of measures are employed in the treatment of fetlock sprains. They include splints, casts, special shoes to raise the heel, and in difficult cases fusion of the joint. With massive injuries, treatment is difficult or impossible.

SPRAINS OF THE DISTAL SESAMOID LIGAMENTS

The three distal sesamoid ligaments run between the proximal sesamoid bones and the back of the short pastern and coffin bones. Injuries occur for the same reasons as those given for sprains of the suspensory ligament, described above. The onset of lameness is sudden. Swelling is present over the course of the ligaments, and pressure over the ligaments causes pain. An exact diagnosis is made with ultrasound, which is also used to monitor the progress of healing.

When trauma is sufficient to disrupt the ligaments, it may also cause fracture of the fetlock. One problem with severe injuries of this ligament is late calcification (see SESAMOIDITIS).

Treatment: Confine the horse for 6 weeks and support the leg with bandages. For severe strains, the leg should be put in a cast. Butazolidin helps to reduce pain and swelling. Return the horse to work slowly, as this area is quite prone to reinjury.

SPRAINED KNEE (CARPITIS)

Carpitis is an exercise-induced sprain of the ligaments that stabilize the interior of the knee joint. These sprains tend to occur in racehorses, hunters, and jumpers. Poor conformation with incorrect alignment of the knees is a major contributing factor.

Carpitis is common in young horses who have just started to train. Signs include varying degrees of heat, swelling, pain, lameness, and reluctance to bend the knee. The swelling is noted over the front of the joint.

Carpal lameness can be confirmed by a joint block. The knee should be x-rayed to exclude a fracture (see KNEE JOINT (CARPAL) FRACTURES).

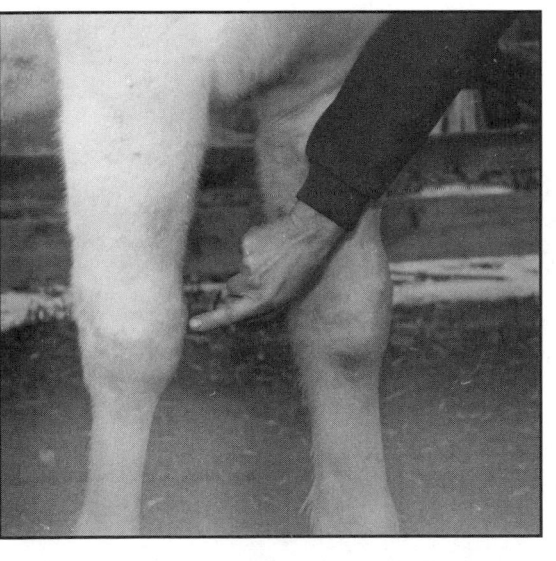

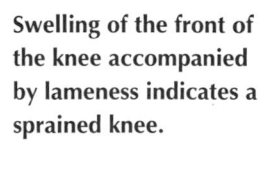

Swelling of the front of the knee accompanied by lameness indicates a sprained knee.

Treatment: Rest the horse for 2 to 3 weeks. Failure to do so may result in fractures of the small bones within the joint. Butazolidin relieves pain and swelling. Joint injections with hyaluronic acid have been recommended. Most horses can return to competition with adequate rest, but poor knee conformation increases the likelihood of recurrence.

SPRAIN OF THE ACCESSORY LIGAMENT OF THE SUPERFICIAL DIGITAL FLEXOR TENDON

The accessory ligament (radial or superior check ligament) of the knee is a strong fibrous band that arises from the back of the radius and joins the superficial digital flexor tendon. The accessory ligament can be sprained during sudden over-extension of the fetlock and knee joints, which forcefully elongates the flexor tendon and rips the attached ligament. This occurs primarily in racehorses.

A horse with a sprained accessory ligament walks gingerly and puts toe and heel on the ground at the same time as if walking downhill. Swelling will be seen at the back of the knee joint.

Treatment: Anti-inflammatory agents relieve pain and swelling. Confine the horse to a stall for 6 weeks. Apply support bandages to the knee. During the next 2 months the horse can be put in a short run. Ultrasound examination at 6 and 12 weeks is used to monitor healing of the ligament.

SACROILIAC STRAIN

The sacroiliac joints are stabilized by strong ligaments that join the iliac bones to the sacrum and thus to the backbone. Ligament injuries occur after slips and falls, which may also fracture the ileum or pelvis. There is a type of chronic sacroiliac strain associated with certain gaits such as trotting and pacing. This is a problem among harness racers.

The signs of sprain are stiffness and pain in the hindquarters, occasionally associated with lameness in one or both hind limbs. A common complaint in hunters and jumpers is that the horse refuses to jump. When there is looseness (subluxation) of the sacroiliac joints, the sacral tuberosity on one or both sides will become prominent over the high point of the rump (*hunter's bump*).

Treatment: Rest the horse in a box stall for 1 to 2 months. Anti-inflammatory drugs reduce pain and swelling. The outlook for returning to prior levels of performance is guarded. In difficult cases, local irritants can be injected about the ligaments to cause scar tissue, which may help to stabilize the pelvis.

DISLOCATION OF THE HIP

Dislocation of the hip is unusual because the round ligament, one of the strongest ligaments in the body, holds the head of the femur tightly in the hip socket. In fact, the ileum usually fractures before a hip will dislocate.

Signs of dislocation are shortening of the affected limb and swelling over the joint. A complete dislocation is a veterinary emergency. Reduction under general anesthesia must be accomplished without delay. If this cannot be accomplished by traction on the limb, the joint can be opened and the hip replaced surgically. The prognosis for utility is guarded.

STIFLE LAMENESS (GONITIS)

The stifle joint, which includes the kneecap and its ligaments, is the largest and most complex joint in the horse. Swelling of the stifle joint, when accompanied by lameness, is called *gonitis*. Gonitis is a descriptive term that does not denote a specific diagnosis. Joint blocks and arthroscopy can assist in determining the cause of stifle joint swelling. A complete set of x-rays is essential in all cases. Severe stifle joint injuries are often complicated by bone fractures (see STIFLE JOINT FRACTURES).

As a sequel to stifle joint injury, many horses develop degenerative arthritis. These horses will not return to sound condition.

Gonitis can include any of the following:

Upward Fixation of the Patella (Locked Kneecap). In this condition, one of the ligaments of the kneecap catches over the inner ridge of the femur and causes the hind limb to be locked in extension. When the horse is required to move forward, it is unable to advance the leg normally and drags the toe. A variation of locked kneecap exists in which the kneecap intermittently catches and suddenly releases, jerking the leg forward in a manner somewhat resembling stringhalt.

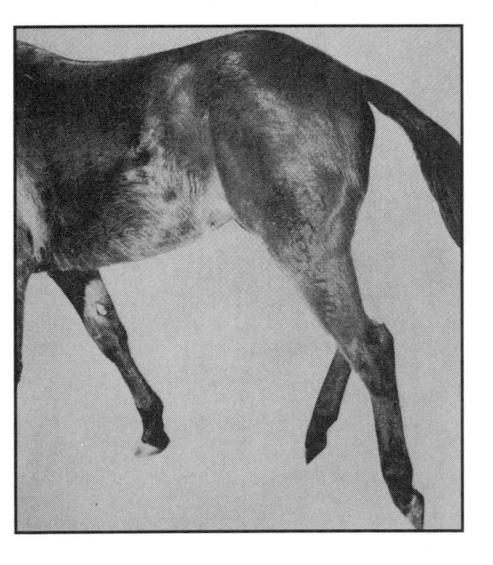

Locked kneecap. The stifle joint is locked in extension as the horse attempts to pull the leg forward. Photo: *Lameness in Horses,* **4th ed., Lea and Febiger.**

A maneuver for releasing a locked kneecap is to back the horse while at the same time pushing inward and downward on the kneecap. This often causes it to release. The horse can then move forward with ease.

Horses and ponies with straight stifle joints are predisposed to upward fixation of the patella. The condition is often bilateral.

Treatment involves stall rest for 1 to 2 weeks. When recurrent, surgery can correct the problem. It involves division of the constricting ligament.

Rupture of the Collateral Ligaments. The inside (medial) collateral is the ligament usually ruptured. The injury is caused by a sudden force applied to the outside of the joint. With rupture of either ligament, the joint becomes unstable and is subject to degenerative joint disease. Treatment is unsuccessful. Chronic lameness results.

Rupture of the Cruciate Ligaments. Two cruciate ligaments are found inside the joint. They join the femur above to the tibia below. A severe wrenching or twisting injury can tear the cruciates. The outlook is like that for rupture of the collaterals.

Sprain of the Joint Capsule. If a joint capsule is stretched but does not rupture, recovery to performance level is possible. Treatment involves absolute stall rest for 2 to 3 months followed by gradual return to full activity. Irritants are sometimes injected to promote scarring in an effort to stabilize the joint. Unfortunately, joint capsule injuries are often accompanied by tears of the cruciates and collaterals.

CURB (SPRAIN OF THE PLANTAR LIGAMENT)

Curb is a thickening and enlargement of the plantar ligament, which often is preceded by an injury to the ligament. The plantar ligament is located at the outside of and just below the point of the hock. Conformation defects such as cow hocks and sickle ("curby") hocks predispose to curb. Occasionally a foal with faulty hock conformation is born with a curblike condition.

Sprains of sufficient magnitude to cause curb occur when a horse is pulled up sharply on its haunches. Kicking walls and going too strongly over a jump are other causes.

Signs of acute sprain are lameness with pain and swelling over the ligament. The horse often stands with its heel off the ground.

In chronic curb the horse may not be lame but the tissues are thickened, and swollen scar tissue is visible at the characteristic site.

Treatment: Rest the horse. Apply ice packs for 30 minutes 3 to 4 times a day for 2 days and wrap between treatments to reduce swelling. Continue with alternating temperature therapy as described for tendonitis. Oral and topical anti-inflammatory drugs, and hyaluronic acid injected around the ligament, reduce pain and swelling. For horses with good conformation the outlook is favorable.

Periostitis

Bones are covered by a thick layer of connective tissue called the periosteum. Inflammation of this layer is called *periostitis*. Injuries that result in stretching or tearing of the periosteum initiate a series of events which begin with bleeding and inflammation beneath the periosteum. The mixture of blood clot, serum, and inflammatory enzymes then converts to fibrous scar tissue that contracts, calcifies, and becomes incorporated into the bone at the site of injury. This is called *new bone formation*. It is the distinguishing feature of periostitis.

Since ligaments attach to the periosteum, forces that stretch ligaments can stretch and tear the periosteum. One example is the chronic stretching of ligaments that occurs with prolonged training on hard surfaces. This stress is amplified when the horse lacks good conformation.

Another cause of periosteal injury is a direct blow to the periosteum and bone. Specific types of periostitis are discussed below.

BUCKED SHINS AND STRESS FRACTURES OF THE CANNON BONE

Bucked shin is a periostitis of the front surface of the cannon bone. It is common in the foreleg but rare in the hind limb.

Bucked shins occur frequently in young Thoroughbreds during the first weeks of training. Horses that run on turf rarely develop this problem, whereas horses that run on hard surfaces are likely to do so. As the foot strikes the ground, the front surface of the cannon experiences greater compression than the back. The causes the periosteum on the front surface of the cannon to buckle and tear. At the same time the bone can develop cracks and fissures called *stress fractures*. The bone then responds to the percussion injury by periosteal remodeling, while new bone is deposited at fracture sites to maintain strength and durability.

Signs of acute periostitis are a warm, painful, firm swelling over the front of the cannon bone. Lameness increases with exercise. The gait is choppy. When only one leg is involved, the horse tends to rest that leg. When both legs are involved, which is the usual situation, the horse shifts weight from side to side.

Treatment: X-rays should be taken to identify the injury and look for stress fractures. Relieve acute inflammation and swelling with ice packs, pressure bandages, and Butazolidin as described for tendonitis. Apply support bandages and rest the horse for at least 1 month to prevent recurrence. Cortisone injections help to reduce periosteal inflammation.

If the injury becomes calcified, a permanent blemish results. However, this does not interfere with performance.

SPLINTS

Splints is a strain or tear of the interosseous ligaments that bind the splint bones to the cannon bone. This is a lameness of young horses. A heavy training schedule, benched knees, improper shoeing, and developmental orthopedic diseases are predisposing causes.

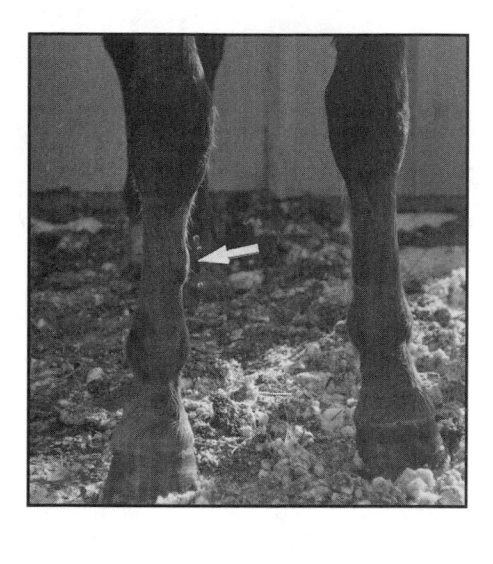

Splints in a young horse.

The periosteal swelling is typically found on the inside of the front leg about 3 inches below the knee. Pain, warmth, and a hard swelling will be noted in this area.

A splint bone can be cracked or fractured by direct trauma. This also produces a type of periostitis, but technically not the same as true splints because the interosseous ligament is not involved.

Treatment of splints is similar to that described for bucked shins. X-rays should be taken to rule out the possibility of a bone fracture. If the interosseous ligament becomes calcified, it may interfere with the suspensory ligament of the knee. This can require surgical correction.

SESAMOIDITIS

Sesamoiditis is a periostitis of the paired distal sesamoid bones. It follows sprains of the distal sesamoid ligaments, described above. The periostitis and new bone formation occur at points where the suspensory ligament attaches to the bone above, and the two distal sesamoid ligaments attach to the bone below.

Sesamoiditis tends to occur among hunters, jumpers, and racing horses 2 to 5 years of age. Long sloping pasterns make the horse more susceptible.

Signs are varying degrees of lameness along with pain and swelling, which is visible over the sesamoid bones at the back of the fetlock. Both front feet may be affected.

Treatment: X-rays and diagnostic ultrasound are needed to confirm the diagnosis. Apply ice packs followed by compression dressings as described for tendonitis. Butazolidin relieves pain and swelling. If the lameness is severe, immobilize the fetlock joint for 2 to 3 weeks with a cast up to the knee. Corrective shoeing can be done to relieve tension on the ligaments.

These bones have a poor blood supply and must be protected from additional trauma during the slow process of healing. This requires a prolonged period of rest (several months) followed by a gradual return to training or activity.

Digital neurectomy may be considered if the horse does not respond to the above.

RINGBONE

Ringbone is the name given to all forms of periostitis and new bone formation that occur below the fetlock joint. Most cases involve the forelegs. *High ringbone* involves the pastern joint area, while *low ringbone* affects the coffin joint area. While new bone develops around these joints, it does not always involve the joint spaces. High and low ringbone can coexist in the same foot. When present, this leads to fusion of the pastern and coffin joints.

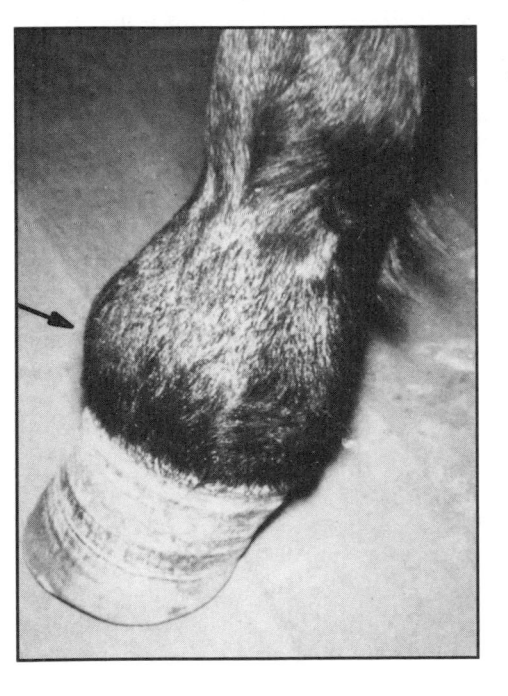

Bone enlargement above the coronet, typical of ringbone. Photo: *Equine Medicine and Surgery,* American Veterinary Publications.

The initiating factor is chronic pulling and tearing of tendons and ligaments related to the stress of concussion on hard surfaces or making quick stops, sharp turns, and twisting movements at high speeds. Straight pasterns and high heels increase stress in the pastern and coffin joints and make the horse more suscep-tible. Occasionally there is a history of a direct blow to the pastern, causing peri-osteal reaction and bone injury.

Heat, swelling, and pain are evident in the characteristic locations. With high ringbone, the swelling is most pronounced over the pastern joint. In low ringbone it is found just above the coronary band. The horse may show pain when the site is squeezed. Lameness is present at all gaits and upon turning. With extensive new bone formation, the hair on the coronary band stands.

Buttress foot, also called *pyramidal disease*, is a specific type of ringbone caused by excessive strain on the common digital extensor tendon as it inserts on the front of the coffin bone. The new bone that forms in this location gives a bulky, pyramid-like look to the foot. The outlook for buttress foot is unfavorable.

Rachitic ringbone is a fibrous tissue enlargement of the pastern in young horses under 2 years of age. As there is no bone involvement, it is not a true ringbone. It is caused by a deficiency of calcium, phosphorus, or vitamins A, D, and C, either singly or in combination. Dietary correction is the appropriate treatment.

Treatment of Ringbone: X-rays are needed to diagnose ringbone and to determine the extent of involvement. Treatment undertaken during the acute phase before new bone develops involves immobilizing the leg in a plaster cast from the hoof to just below the knee. The cast should remain for 4 weeks. Butazolidin helps to relieve pain and swelling. Steroids injected into the soft tissues may be of value before the cast is applied, but injections into the joint can lead to further damage and should be avoided. Rest the horse for several months. Full roller motion shoes are of value because they shorten the horse's stride and reduce stress on the pastern and coffin joints.

Once new bone growth occurs, treatment is less successful. Involvement of joint surfaces almost always leads to osteoarthritis and permanent disability. If the coffin joint is affected, there is little likelihood that the horse can return to riding condition. Digital neurectomy relieves pain. When the pastern joint is affected, surgical fusion of the joint with screws or plates, followed by casting and a rehabilitation program, can produce a good result, especially for the hind limb.

Developmental Orthopedic Diseases

This is a group of related conditions linked by a common pathological process: a breakdown in the mechanism by which cartilage is converted to bone. Among these diseases are osteochondrosis, osteochondritis dissecans, physeal dysplasia, angular limb deformities, flexural limb deformities, and the wobbler syndrome.

The mechanism by which cartilage is converted to bone is called *endochondral ossification*. Ossification occurs at three sites in the bone. The first, in the shaft of the bone, is called the *diaphysis*. The second is the *physis*, or growth plate, located at the junction of the shaft with the head of the bone. The third is the *epiphysis*, which is the surface of the head of the bone that articulates with the joint. The process of ossification is complex. Any mistakes along the way can either delay the ossification process or leave damaged cartilage, which fails to mature into healthy bone. Abnormal cartilage is prone to fracture, fissure, and break into small fragments which enter the joint and become *joint mice*. Cystic spaces can develop within mineralized bone. And delayed ossification or uneven bone growth can result in angular limb deformities.

Until recently it was thought that overfeeding and mineral imbalances were the major causes of what were called *nutritional bone diseases*. Now that other influences are recognized as important contributing factors, the name of this group has been changed to *Developmental Orthopedic Diseases* (DOD).

Some horses appear to have a genetic potential for developing DOD, but whether the horse develops the disease or not depends upon external factors and the degree to which they influence the endochondral ossification process. Some of these external factors are: either too much or too little energy in the ration; a deficiency of calcium, phosphorus, or microminerals in the diet; heavy exercise or hard training during rapid growth; bone and joint injury; hormone diseases; and events that occurred in utero before the foal was born.

High-energy diets have long been recognized as precursors to DOD. A growing foal needs adequate amounts of dietary energy, protein, calcium, phosphorus, and the microminerals copper, zinc, and manganese. Accelerating the rate of growth from 1 pound to 2½ pounds a day increases energy and other nutrient requirements by 65 to 70 percent, and calcium and phosphorus by 95 percent. If energy is supplied but there is insufficient calcium or phosphorus in the diet, growth still proceeds rapidly but without adequate mineralization of bone. This results in an increased risk of diseases associated with defective cartilage and immature bone. A deficiency of the microminerals copper and zinc also results in defective cartilage formation. For more information, see MINERALS in chapter 17, Feeding and Nutrition.

The most common feeding practices responsible for nutritional imbalances in the growing horse are feeding too much grain; feeding alfalfa hay without adding phosphorus to the ration; and feeding a grass hay and grain mix inadequate in calcium, phosphorus, and protein. Adding excessive amounts of vitamins and minerals to the ration is another cause of bone disease. How to feed the growing horse is discussed in chapter 16, Pediatrics.

To treat developmental orthopedic diseases related to overfeeding, remove alfalfa and grain from the horse's diet and provide as much good-quality grass or cereal grain hay as the horse will eat. This feeding regimen decreases the protein and energy portions in the ration and allows a slower rate of growth and recovery.

Specific DODs are discussed below.

OSTEOCHONDROSIS AND OSTEOCHONDRITIS DISSECANS

Osteochondrosis (OC) is an extremely common disease in the growing horse. One study reported OC in more than two-thirds of all racehorses in the northeastern United States. OC results from a primary defect in the process by which cartilage is converted to bone. In one manifestation of OC, thickened cartilage within the joint undergoes fragmentation and breaks into loose pieces of cartilage (joint mice). This form of the disease is referred to as *osteochondritis dissecans*. Another characteristic disturbance in OC is the *subchondral bone cyst*, found beneath the outer shell of the bone. Some of these cysts become quite large and are prominent x-ray findings.

The common joints for OC in order of decreasing frequency are the stifle, hock, shoulder, fetlock, cervical spine, knee, elbow, and hip.

Symptoms commonly appear in young horses 1 to 2 years of age who have just started performance training. A typical history is that of a swollen joint accompanied by mild or no lameness. X-rays usually reveal diagnostic findings.

Treatment: The goal is to restore the horse to athletic fitness and prevent damage to the joint. Conservative treatment involves stall rest for up to 6 months, along with correction of dietary imbalances. Joint surgery is a widely accepted alternative and can often be done in young horses using the fiberoptic arthroscope. Most joints affected by OC are amenable. Devitalized cartilage and loose fragments can be removed through the instrument. Results depend upon the location, type, and severity of the disease. Return to racing is possible.

Prevention: The frequency and/or severity of OC can be reduced by good management practices, beginning with care and feeding of the pregnant mare as described in chapter 15, Pregnancy and Foaling. It is important to maintain steady growth of foals from the neonatal period to 2 years of age, in particular avoiding growth spurts associated with feeding high dietary carbohydrate and energy. The daily ration should provide concentrations of copper and zinc as described in the same chapter. The growing foal needs moderate exercise, but hard, prolonged, and stressful exercise can damage growing cartilage.

PHYSEAL DYSPLASIA

Physeal dysplasia, also called *physitis* and formerly (and inaccurately) called *epiphysitis*, is a generalized bone disease causing lameness in young horses. The disease is characterized by enlargement of the growth plates located at the junction of the shaft with the head of the bone. This creates a flaring at the end of the bone, causing the bone to assume the shape of an hourglass on x-ray. The bones commonly affected are the radius, tibia, and cannon bones.

Physitis occurs in rapidly growing foals up to 2 years of age, with a peak incidence between 6 and 12 months. The disease may appear as an isolated event or affect several horses on a breeding farm. Signs are intermittent lameness and joint stiffness of varying severity. Pain, heat, and swelling are detectable at sites of bone involvement.

A combination of several factors appears to contribute to the development of physitis. They include genetic predisposition, rapid growth, obesity, trace mineral deficiency, calcium/phosphorus imbalances, and excessive and strenuous exercise.

Physitis is most likely to occur in overweight active foals on high grain rations low in calcium and high in phosphorus. The frequency of the disease is increasing, perhaps because more breeders are selectively feeding for rapid growth and maximum mature size.

Physitis is also known to occur in association with other developmental bone diseases, including wobbler syndrome, angular limb deformities, osteochondrosis, and flexural limb deformities.

Treatment: Perform a comprehensive analysis of the feeding program, including ration analysis. It will often be found that dietary energy and/or protein is in excess of recommendations for growing horses (see chapter 16, Pediatrics). A calcium/phosphorus imbalance or deficiency may be identified. Adjust the ration accordingly.

Butazolidin diminishes pain and stiffness. Use it for short periods only. Exercise should be restricted but not eliminated because stall confinement can cause flexural limb deformities. Many horses "grow out" of physeal dysplasia, especially if nutritional problems are corrected and strenuous exercise curtailed until the bone disease becomes inactive. Some horses, however, develop cystlike areas in bones, angular limb deformities, or flexural limb deformities that ultimately impair utility.

ANGULAR LIMB DEFORMITIES

Angular limb deformities refer to knock-knees and bowlegs. Other knee joint deformities are considered here for convenience.

When angular limb deformities are apparent at birth, they are called *congenital*. Congenital limb deformities are caused by abnormal limb positions in the uterus, nutritional imbalances in the mare, neonatal hypothyroidism, and unequal growth between the two sides of a long bone.

Deformities that appear days to months after birth are called *developmental*. Developmental deformities can be secondary to incomplete ossification (or collapse) of the small cuboidal bones in the knee or hock joint. Some cases are caused by joint injury during the first few weeks of life. Premature foals are at greatest risk and should be monitored closely.

Note that many normal foals have some degree of limb crookedness, which may not straighten out until they are yearlings. On visual inspection as seen from the front, if the knock-kneed or bowlegged limb is greater than 15 degrees off vertical, the deformity is significant and a veterinarian should be consulted.

Knock-Knees (Carpus Valgus). These knees are deviated toward one another when viewed from the front. When the cause is congenital, the knees often straighten in a short time. Foals who acquire deformities after birth often need veterinary treatment, as described below.

Bow-legs (Carpus Varus). This is the reverse of knock-knees; the limbs bow out. The outlook is like that for knock-knees.

Bucked or Sprung Knees (Anterior Deviation). In bucked knees, one or both knees are flexed forward so that the joints appear rounded over at the front when viewed from the side. This conformation restricts movement and causes a shortened stride. The fetlock may become knuckled.

The involvement of both knees indicates the cause is congenital. When one knee is involved, a limb injury should be considered.

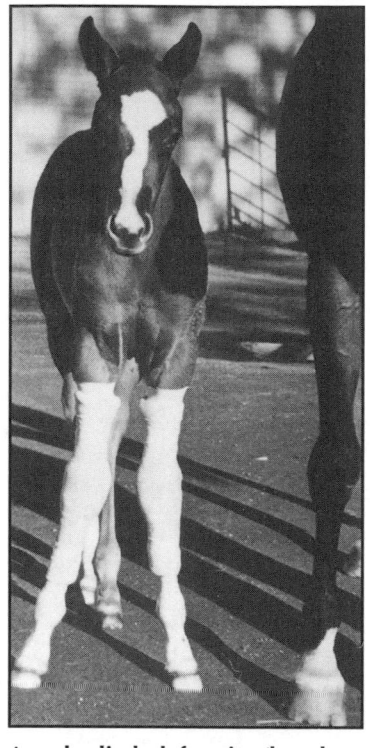 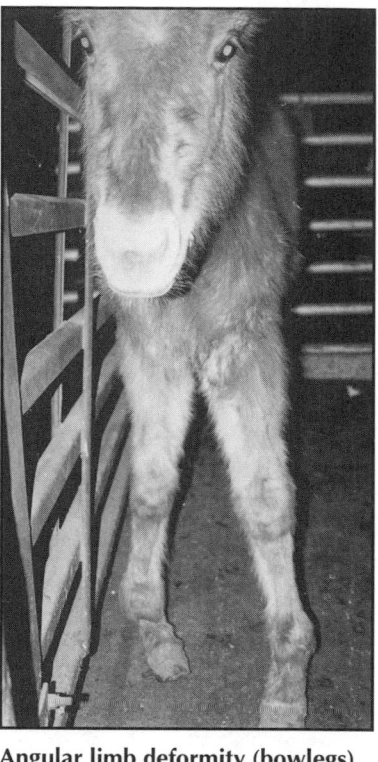

Angular limb deformity (knock-knees) treated with tube casts. Photo: *Equine Medicine and Surgery,* American Veterinary Publications. Courtesy of Dr. J. A. Auer.

Angular limb deformity (bowlegs) caused by severe nutritional deficiencies.

Calf Knees (Backward Deviation). This is the reverse of the above, in which the knees are shallow at the front and rounded at the back. Because of abnormal stresses imposed by this conformation, chip fractures of the carpal bones are frequent.

Benched (Popped) Knees. Also called "offset knees," this is a conformation in which the cannon bones are set too far to the outside, with the result that most of the weight is carried on the inside splint bones. The majority of cases are congenital. Young horses with benched knees are prone to injuries of the knees and lower legs, particularly to splints and sprains of the fetlock joint.

Treatment of Knee Joint Deformities. Early recognition and treatment are vital. The longer a foal walks on deformed legs, the greater the likelihood of permanent damage. Treatment decisions are based on x-ray and physical findings. The simplest therapy is stall rest with 5 minutes of controlled exercise several times a day. A second option is the application of splints, tube casts, or braces. Surgery is recommended when the deformity is severe or has failed to improve with conservative management. Results for surgery are best when it is performed before 3 months of age.

FLEXURAL LIMB DEFORMITIES IN FOALS

Flexural limb deformities, also called *contracted digital flexor tendons*, are seen most commonly in the fetlock joint, coffin joint, and knee joint. Young horses from birth to 18 months of age are affected. The basic condition involves a shortening of either the deep, the superficial, or both digital flexor tendons in the forelegs, and occasionally the hind limbs. Most deformities are bilateral.

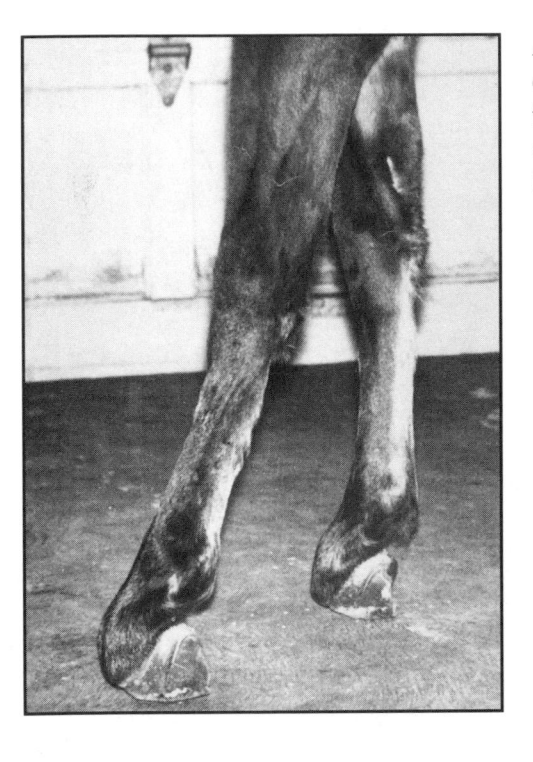

A foal with severely contracted digital flexor tendons in both front feet. Photo: *Equine Medicine and Surgery,* American Veterinary Publications.

The exact mechanism by which these deformities occur is unknown. One theory is that rapid growth of long bones exceeds the ability of the flexor tendons and check ligaments to lengthen accordingly, thus pulling the fetlock joint or coffin joint into flexion. Another theory is that a painful condition causes temporary muscle contracture, which prevents elongation of tendons and ligaments. Trauma, or a developmental orthopedic disease such as osteochondrosis, may be the cause of the limb pain. Most studies have found that nutritional excesses and imbalances are commonly present with flexural deformities.

Flexural deformity of the coffin joint produces a raised heel and *club foot*. With mild deformity, the pastern is straightened and the foal appears to walk on its toe.

In severe contracture, the foot knuckles over and the foal bears weight on the front of the fetlock.

Involvement of the fetlock joint (*fetlock flexor deformity*) causes knuckling at the fetlock, with the foot remaining flat on the ground. A third common contracture involves the knee joint (*carpal deformity*).

Treatment: In the newborn foal with mild deformity involving the coffin, fetlock, or knee joint, the tendon will usually stretch in a few days with corrective treatment. This involves walking the foal for 10 minutes 2 or 3 times a day. Physical therapy includes joint extension exercises and the application of support wraps.

Deformities that appear after the first few weeks of life may also respond to conservative treatment. Reduce energy intake and balance the ration. Trimming the heel helps to stretch and lengthen the tendon.

When the deformity is severe or progressing in spite of conservative treatment, surgery is advised. The most frequently used operation involves dividing the inferior check ligament, which allows the flexor tendon to lengthen. The superior check ligament, and even the suspensory ligament, can be cut in advanced cases. The prognosis for complete recovery depends on the location and severity of the flexural deformity, the age of onset, and response to treatment. For mild congenital flexural deformities, the outlook is excellent.

Arthritis

The term *arthritis* describes a number of joint ailments characterized by inflammation, degeneration, and new bone formation in and around joints.

When there is a history of an injury to a joint, or to the ligaments supporting a joint, the resulting arthritis is called post-traumatic arthritis or *degenerative joint disease*.

An *acute serous arthritis* is characterized by a swollen, tender, fluid-filled joint along with a tendency to favor the limb. It is the result of either a joint stress or injury. This condition is also called *acute synovitis*. It does not necessarily progress to degenerative joint disease.

Infectious (septic) arthritis occurs when bacteria from the bloodstream invade joints. If the infection destroys cartilage, there will be irreversible damage. A form of septic arthritis called *joint ill* occurs in young foals. It is discussed in chapter 16, Pediatrics.

Degenerative joint disease is the most common arthritic problem in adult horses. It is the end result of various injurious processes, many of which are discussed below.

The lameness associated with arthritis is that of stiffness and diminished range of motion. With an arthritic flare, there is joint swelling, pain, and tenderness over the joint.

Bone and joint x-rays are indicated in the diagnosis and treatment of all types of arthritis.

Treatment of Arthritis: Acute serous arthritis is treated like a sprain. Rest the horse. Apply cold and alternating temperature therapy as described for *Tendonitis*. Topical application of DMSO with or without steroids can reduce joint inflammation. Butazolidin helps to relieve pain and swelling. The joint can be aspirated and/or injected with corticosteroids, hyaluronic acid (HA), DMSO, Palosein, or polysulfated glycosaminoglycan (PSGAG). PSGAG occurs naturally in joint fluid and is said to promote healing of cartilage. For more information, see ANTI-INFLAMMATORY DRUGS AND PAIN RELIEVERS in chapter 19, Drugs and Medications. After a flare-up, the horse should be returned to activity slowly. Proper shoeing of a horse with faulty conformation helps to relieve abnormal stresses on joints. In advanced stages, a surgical procedure may be indicated to relieve pain and improve serviceability.

Septic arthritis requires the empirical use of high-dose broad-spectrum antibiotics while awaiting culture and sensitivity reports based on fluid withdrawn from the joint. Antibiotics should be given for several weeks. It may be necessary to open and drain the joint, inject antibiotics into the joint, or aspirate it repeatedly to remove infected fluid. Butazolidin relieves pain and swelling. This facilitates joint movement and prevents adhesions. Early and appropriate care of wounds, as described in chapter 1, Emergencies, will prevent many cases of septic arthritis and bone infection.

Counterirritation describes a number of long-established techniques that involve burning, pin firing, or blistering of the skin and connective tissues over joints, tendons, and ligaments. Most of these techniques are outdated and have been replaced with the use of drugs such as hyaluronic acid, Palosein, and PSGAG.

The following are some specific arthritic problems.

BONE SPAVIN (JACK SPAVIN)

This is the name given to arthritis of the hock joint. The hock is composed of an improbable column of bones subject to compression, rotation, and stretching of the ligaments that unite them. Hard use damages cartilage and also produces periostitis, the end result of which is degenerative arthritis. Sickle and cow hocks predispose to joint injuries.

Bone spavin is seen in horses ridden hard at a gallop. It is an occupational hazard among racehorses, hunters and jumpers, and western horses used for barrel-racing, roping, and cutting.

When bone spavin has been present for some time, you will see a bony enlargement on the inside of the leg below the point of the hock. This protuberance is called a "jack."

In the early stages before bony enlargement, x-rays or bone scans will show signs of bone erosion. This is called a "blind" spavin.

Spavin typically begins as a "cold" lameness. A cold lameness is present before exercise, disappears as the horse warms up, and returns when the horse cools down. Because of pain on the inside of the hock, the horse tries to carry most of the weight on the outside of the foot. The hoof or shoe may show wear on the outer edge.

The spavin test is performed as follows: The hock is flexed by holding the foot up close to the lower abdomen for 2 minutes. The foot is then released and the horse immediately trotted. With a positive test, the horse shows lameness on the first few steps.

Treatment: All stressful activity contributing to the lameness must be discontinued. Intermittent use of low-dose nonsteroidal anti-inflammatory drugs, and hyaluronic acid injections into the joint, are beneficial. Corrective shoeing is helpful. In advanced cases, dividing the cunean tendon and/or fusing the hock joint relieves pain and makes the horse serviceable.

OSSELETS

Osselets is an arthritis of the fetlock joint which begins as a chronic stress injury to the joint capsule from the repeated concussions of hard training and racing. Upright pasterns are predisposing. One or both front feet may be affected.

In the initial stages, there is stretching or tearing of the fetlock joint capsule with signs of acute serous arthritis. This stage is referred to as "green" osselets.

"True" osselets represents a more advanced stage and refers to the visual presence of swelling and new bone growth on the outside front of the fetlock joint.

The stride in osselets is short and choppy, with the horse tending to plant weight on the outside edge of the hoof.

The outlook for "green" osselets is favorable if the horse is rested until all signs of inflammation are gone. When new bone growth involves the joint surfaces, treatment is difficult. This is especially true if the horse has upright pasterns.

SHOULDER JOINT ARTHRITIS (OMARTHRITIS)

Shoulder joint arthritis usually occurs as a complication of a joint fracture. In most cases there is a history of being kicked by another horse or running into a solid post or door. Osteochondrosis of the shoulder joint in growing horses may cause sufficient joint injury to lead to a degenerative arthritis.

A horse with a shoulder joint lameness lifts its head when stepping down on the painful leg, swings the bad leg out wide instead of carrying it straight ahead, and stands with its good leg in advance of the painful leg. Swelling and tenderness about the shoulder joint may be evident. A nerve block can help to locate the site of lameness. X-rays showing arthritic bone changes within the joint are diagnostic. When a chip fracture or joint "mouse" is identified, it should be removed.

Steroid injections into the joint followed by hyaluronic acid (HA) afford temporary relief. With new bone formation, the outlook for recovery is poor.

Broken Bones

Broken bones are caused by accidents such as being kicked by another horse, taking a hard fall, stepping into a hole, running into fences and posts, or being hit by a car. In addition, horses are prone to high-torque and compression injuries of the legs and feet.

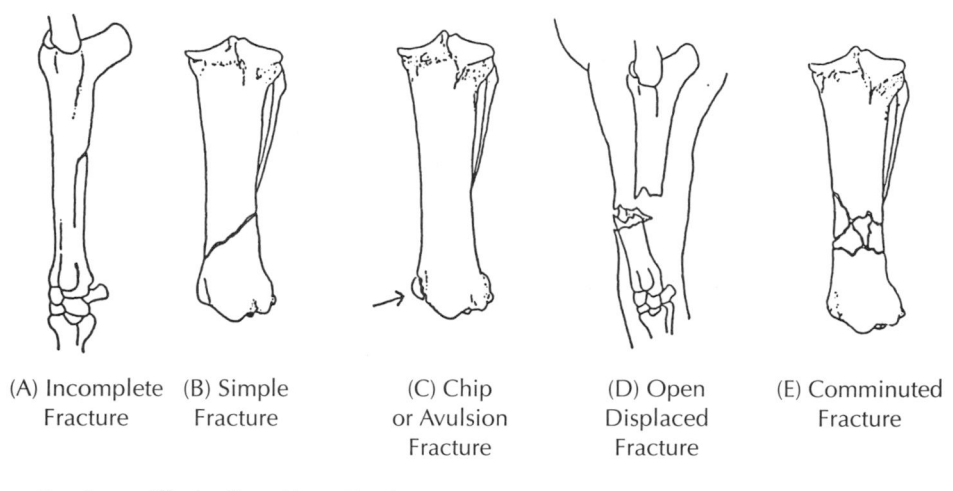

(A) Incomplete   (B) Simple   (C) Chip   (D) Open   (E) Comminuted
  Fracture   Fracture   or Avulsion Displaced   Fracture
                                 Fracture   Fracture

Fractures. Illustration: Mona Frazier.

Bone fractures are classified as open or closed. A closed fracture does not break through the skin. With an open or *compound* fracture, the bone makes contact with the outside, either because of a wound which exposes it, or because the point of the bone punches through the skin from the inside. Open fractures are considered dirty, as they are automatically contaminated with dirt, debris, and bacteria.

Osteomyelitis, or bone infection, is a potential hazard with all open fractures. Long-standing bone infection is called *chronic osteomyelitis*. It is characterized by fever, lameness, pain, and swelling, and a discharge through a sinus tract connecting the infected bone with the skin.

Comminuted fractures are multiple breaks in the bone, like a shattered windshield. A large force is necessary to cause multiple breaks to occur. This results in marked instability and a most difficult problem in treatment.

Bone fractures are recognized by limb deformity, shortening of the leg, swelling at the site of injury, and inability to put weight on the leg. Stress fractures of the cannon bone and chip fractures involving the joints below the elbow and stifle are not obvious on visual inspection. X-rays are needed to make the diagnosis.

How to treat a bone fracture depends upon a number of factors, including the location and type of the break, whether the affected bone is involved in direct weight-bearing, the age and weight of the horse, and the resources available to the veterinarian. In general, treatment falls into one of three categories:

The first is complete rest. The horse must be confined to a box stall for several weeks or months. For weight-bearing fractures, the horse may need to be placed in a sling. However, many horses will not tolerate slinging.

The second is to apply splints, braces, and casts. Lightweight polyvinyl chloride pipe splints are effective. They can be removed easily to inspect the skin for pressure sores and to administer physical therapy to the joints. Ideally, splints and casts should be applied to immobilize the joints above and below the fracture site.

The third approach is repair the fracture with an operation. One of the following procedures may be employed:

Arthroscopy. This is an excellent approach for chip fractures that enter the joint. The small surgical incisions heal with minimal scarring and restriction. However, arthroscopy is not suitable for all joints.

Open Reduction, Internal Fixation. This operation involves making an incision over the joint or fracture, bringing the ends into alignment, and then maintaining the desired position with various metallic devices, including screws, pins, and wires, or rods inserted down the center of the shaft. Compression plating is a procedure in which a metal plate is laid across the fracture site and secured above and below by bone screws.

Arthrodesis (Joint Fusion). Fractures involving joints often lead to painful post-traumatic arthritis. Fusion of the joint will relieve pain and make the horse more serviceable, although some degree of permanent lameness will result. Arthrodesis is a surgical procedure in which bone grafts are placed in and around the joint to accomplish this purpose. Bone grafts can also be used to heal certain types of fractures, such as those of the proximal sesamoid bones.

The prognosis for a successful outcome is guarded if the horse will have a residual lameness or handicap and thus cannot return to the activity for which it was intended. A poor prognosis is for multiple fractures, comminuted fractures, open fractures (often complicated by bone infection), fractures involving the weight-bearing surfaces of joints, unstable fractures, and fractures that cannot unite because of poor blood supply. In some cases treatment is most unlikely to be successful and may even be impossible.

The following fractures can occur in the horse:

Fractures of the Shoulder (Scapula and Humerus). These fractures are uncommon. A large force is necessary to fracture the scapula or humerus. Such a force could occur with a hard fall on the shoulder, being kicked by another horse, or running into a solid object.

Simple fractures of the scapular spine heal with stall rest. Comminuted fractures are more difficult to treat successfully. If the horse recovers, permanent lameness and shoulder joint arthritis are to be expected.

The humerus usually breaks in mid-shaft, causing either a spiral or oblique fracture. The horse is unable to bear weight on the limb. The radial nerve may also be injured, producing a "dropped elbow." Treatment is complicated by rotation of the bone fragments, angular deformities, persistent radial nerve paralysis, and technical problems associated with attempts at surgical reduction and stabilization. The prognosis is guarded.

Fractures of the Forearm (Radius and Olecranon). The radius and ulna are fused to form a single bone in which the olecranon process is the remnant of the ulna. All manner of fractures can occur in the forearm, usually as a result of hard falls, direct blows, and stepping into holes.

A horse with a broken forearm is unable to bear weight and exhibits obvious swelling and deformity. These fractures are difficult to immobilize. The prognosis is guarded to poor. Results, however, are good for young horses with nondisplaced stress fractures treated with stall rest.

Knee Joint (Carpal) Fractures. The knee is composed of 3 movable joints made up of 8 bones arranged like blocks in 2 layers. A combination of one or any of the 8 bones can fracture. Chip and slab fractures are most common. A slab fracture is a vertical fracture through one of the blocks. Knee joint fractures tend to occur in racehorses who fatigue at the end of a hard race and come down heavily on an overextended knee. The direction in which the horse is raced influences which front leg is affected. Horses that race in a counterclockwise direction (United States) have more chip fractures in the right leg, whereas those that race in a clockwise direction (Europe) have more chip fractures in the left leg.

The large accessory bone at the back of the knee joint also can break. This produces a characteristic swelling on the outside of the knee joint.

Chips in the joint can be removed surgically using an arthroscope. Many horses can return to racing. Slab fractures are fixed in place with screws. The prognosis for racing is guarded. Accessory bone fractures tend to pull apart after repair; however, if left alone, they eventually form a fibrous union.

Cannon and Splint Bone Fractures. Breaks can occur anywhere along the lengths of these bones and can enter the joints above and below. Fractures entirely across the long axis, comminuted fractures, and those that enter joints require extended therapy and often cannot be treated successfully.

Small fissure fractures may develop in association with ligament stress and concussion (see BUCKED SHINS AND STRESS FRACTURES OF THE CANNON BONE). These fractures are incomplete. Treatment, which is favorable, is like that for bucked shins.

Fetlock Joint and Long Pastern Bone Fractures. Chip fractures involving the fetlock joint are common in racehorses. These are stress fractures related to overextension of the pastern joint at racing speeds. They are often bilateral. The chip most often comes off the long pastern bone at the joint lip. The diagnosis cannot be made without x-rays. A small chip can be treated with adequate rest for 4 months. Large chip fractures, and those displaced into the joint, require surgery. Arthroscopic removal is preferred. The prognosis is good if treatment has been uncomplicated.

Longitudinal and comminuted fractures of the first phalanx tend to occur in Western performance horses in whose events sudden turns, slides, and twists are combined with axial compression. Surgical treatment offers the best results. The prognosis is guarded.

Fractures of the Sesamoid Bones. Sitting side-by-side at the back of the fetlock are the two proximal sesamoids. Fracture of these bones is almost an occupational disease of racing horses. The forelimbs are most frequently affected in Thoroughbreds and Quarter Horses, whereas the hind limbs are most frequently affected in the Standardbred. When the fractures involve both sesamoid bones, the horse may actually "break down" on the racetrack and need to be removed by ambulance. In this situation the suspensory apparatus is lost. This becomes a most difficult problem in treatment.

Broken sesamoids heal slowly. In young horses, casting the leg for 4 months has been successful. In performance horses, and those with displaced fractures, surgical fixation and bone grafting offer the best results. The prognosis for return to racing is guarded.

Pastern and Coffin Joint Fractures. Fractures of the short pastern bone occur most often in the hind limbs of Western performance horses, especially those wearing heel calks, which prevent foot rotation when the horse changes direction. A "pop" may be heard at the time of injury. Chip fractures can be treated with stall rest or arthroscopic surgery. More extensive fractures require special casts or internal fixation with plates or screws. The prognosis for athletic performance is guarded.

Fractures of the coffin bone are stress-related. They tend to occur in the front feet of racehorses exercised on hard surfaces. The foot should be immobilized in a full bar shoe with quarter clips, and the horse should not be worked for at least 8 months. Prognosis for racing is guarded.

There is a characteristic fracture which occurs at the site where the common digital extensor tendon inserts on the coffin bone. Sudden traction on the tendon can crack the bone and pull the extensor process free of the coffin bone. Unlike most fractures in the lower leg, this fracture usually does not produce acute lameness. With lack of treatment the foot assumes a triangular shape and eventually takes on the typical appearance of *buttress* foot. Treatment involves application of a cast and the administration of anti-inflammatory drugs. Prognosis is guarded.

Navicular Bone Fractures. Navicular fractures are rare. Most are associated with navicular disease, discussed later in this chapter. Hind limb fractures can occur from kicking walls and posts. Navicular fractures are difficult to diagnose. X-rays are required.

The navicular bone heals poorly. These fractures often do not unite. Treatment is similar to that described for navicular disease.

Broken Ribs. Broken ribs are caused by kicks and blows to the chest wall. In the newborn, they occur during the birthing process. Signs are pain and swelling over the ribs, frequent coughing, and reluctance to move. Fracture of the first rib may cause "dropped elbow" if the radial nerve is involved.

The end of a broken rib may enter the chest cavity and puncture the lung. If the lung collapses, the chest cavity fills with air. This is called a *pneumothorax.* In most horses the right and left chest cavities are incompletely separated. This permits air to pass from one side to the other, in which case the pneumothorax occurs on both sides. This causes extreme difficulty in breathing and often death.

Uncomplicated rib fractures heal spontaneously in several weeks. Complete rest is important.

Pelvic Bone Fractures. Horses that slip and fall on their sides, or struggle during casting while their hind limbs are tied, may sustain a fractured pelvis. (*Casting* is a procedure in which ropes and lines are used to throw a horse down on its side.) The ileum can be broken in many places, but the most common sites are the wing, shaft, and sacral tuberosity.

When the tuberosity is fractured, the horse appears to have a flattened or "knocked-down" hip on that side. This type of fracture also occurs when a horse runs through a narrow gate.

Rectal and vaginal examination may reveal pelvic bone asymmetry and bone crepitus (crackling) when the horse shifts its weight. X-rays are difficult to perform, requiring general anesthesia with the horse on its back. However, a bone scan can be done with the horse standing. Hot spots will be seen at fracture sites.

Pelvic fractures cannot be treated surgically. Confine the horse to a box stall for at least 3 months. Slinging the horse is of benefit, but many horses will not tolerate it. Complete healing takes at least a year. The prognosis for return to service is guarded.

Femur Fractures. Young foals occasionally break a femur during casting and halter breaking. These injuries often involve the growth plates. In the adult a considerable force is required to fracture the femur. The broken bone fragments usually override. This makes it difficult to maintain alignment. Surgical treatment is the only available method, but even with compression plates and rods the prognosis among horses over a year of age is poor.

Stifle Joint Fractures. The stifle is a complex joint which incorporates articulations between the femur and tibia and the femur and kneecap. Fractures of the kneecap can occur from kicks to the knee. During a race a horse's leg could strike an upright post at high speed. A force sufficient to break the patella often produces soft tissue injury to the ligaments and capsule of the joint. The damaging blow may fracture the end of the femur as well.

Other fractures at the stifle occur as a result of crushing or twisting injuries of the limb, often associated with joint dislocations. A chip fracture in the stifle joint is rare. Consider osteochondrosis.

Simple patellar fractures heal with stall rest for 3 to 5 months. Surgical repair is indicated for complicated breaks. The outlook is guarded.

Severe stifle joint injuries are difficult to treat successfully and often heal in a bad position. This frequently leads to serious complications such as stifle lameness.

Tibia and Fibula Fractures (Gaskin). The *gaskin* is the area between the stifle and hock joints. The tibia and fibula are the bones of the gaskin. The fibula is seldom broken because it is rather small and well protected by muscle.

All types of fractures can involve the tibia, including those into the joint. The most common cause is a kick from another horse. Incomplete fractures are often preceded by stress fractures. With a complete fracture, the horse is unable to bear weight on the leg. If obvious deformity is not apparent at the time of injury, x-rays are necessary to make the diagnosis.

Stress fractures are best treated by strict stall confinement for up to 3 months. With complete fractures, internal fixation with plates and screws has been successful in selected foals. In adult horses, fractures of the tibia are most difficult to treat. The outlook for recovery is poor.

Hock Joint Fractures. The hock is a complex structure composed of ten individual bones, which make up several movable joints.

Fractures generally occur because of a direct blow, such as a kick from another horse. Twisting injuries also can produce fractures. These tend to occur among barrel-racers, Thoroughbreds, and horses shod with heel calks. X-rays and bone scans are used in diagnosis.

Broken bones in the weight-bearing axis heal poorly. Surgery has been employed successfully in a few cases. It is unlikely that many horses with such fractures can return to full performance. Degenerative joint disease with permanent lameness can be expected.

Other fractures, such as those of the calcaneus, can be treated successfully in selected cases by removing chips or stabilizing the fragments with screws. Badly comminuted fractures of the calcaneus cannot be treated.

In young horses hock injuries frequently involve growth cartilage, in which case healing often produces a false joint and permanent lameness.

Muscle Diseases

MUSCLE STRAIN

A muscle strain is an injury caused by overuse or overstretching of muscle fibers. The signs are a painful swelling accompanied by lameness. In a *mild* strain only a few fibers of the muscle are stretched, swollen, or torn. In a *severe* strain the entire muscle may be torn free from its attachments; or the muscle itself may tear.

The muscles most commonly involved by athletic performance injuries are those of the croup and the back of the thighs.

Injuries sufficient to cause muscle strain may also strain ligaments and tendons. Diagnostic ultrasound helps to distinguish between these conditions and monitor the healing process.

Treatment: Muscle strains respond to massage by hand or ultrasound. Anti-inflammatory medications, both orally and topically, are of considerable value. Naproxen (twice daily) appears to be the best analgesic for muscle pain. The horse should be rested until the injury is healed.

SORE BACK AND LOIN SYNDROME

The longissimus dorsi muscle runs down the back from the neck to the sacrum. This muscle, as well as the two psoas muscles which lie beneath it, are strained in racing or jumping. Ill-fitting tack is a contributing factor.

A horse with a strain of this muscle group will be stiff and drag its hind toes. Pain and spasm cause a shortened stride and gait alterations suggestive of hind-quarter lameness. The horse may twist itself over the jumps instead of going over strong. With pressure over the loins the horse may groan and drop its back. The involved muscles will be firm, warm, and painful. The abdomen is tucked-up and tense.

Treatment: Rest the horse. Anti-inflammatory drugs help to relieve pain and swelling. Hot packs and ultrasound promote blood flow and relieve spasms. Vitamin E and selenium have been used in treating and preventing certain muscle disorders and may be of benefit.

Check to see if the saddle and tack are too tight by placing a string down the back between the saddle and pad. Once in the saddle, you should be able to draw the string out easily if the tack is properly adjusted.

OVERLAPPING OF THE SPINOUS PROCESSES

The ridge down the center of the horse's back is composed of the spines of 18 thoracic and 6 lumbar vertebrae. Normally the vertebral spinous processes are separated by interposed muscle. In this disease, the spines impinge upon each other or overlap. This causes pain and muscle spasm. An overlap involving two or more spines can occur anywhere along the back, but most often affects the saddle area. Friction caused by the spines rubbing together results in a periostitis with new bone formation.

Horses with a swayed back are more susceptible to overlapping spinous processes and back pain.

In some horses with overlapping spinous processes there is a history of falling or going over backward. This would suggest that a back injury produced the condition. However, not all such horses have a history of back injury. Undoubtedly many cases are caused by activities that produce maximum flexion and extension of the spine. The problem is most prevalent in hunters and jumpers. Horses with a weak or swaybacked conformation are most commonly affected.

Signs are like those described for sore back and loin. Downward pressure on the back is painful. The horse often resents being saddled and gives evidence of pain when the cinch is tightened. Diagnosis is based on physical examination and x-rays which show narrowing of the spaces between the spines, and occasionally an overlap.

Treatment: A mildly affected horse should be confined and not ridden until free of symptoms. Treat as described for sore back and loin.

Severely affected horses may require surgery. This involves the removal of the tops of the spinous processes. Two months of stall rest and one month of light exercise are required before the horse can be ridden.

BONE FORMATION IN MUSCLE (OSSIFYING MYOPATHY)

Following a tearing injury to a muscle, healing can be complicated by the development of excessive fibrous connective tissue and, later, bone formation in the muscle. This is called *ossifying myopathy*. Characteristically the injury occurs in the semimembranosus and semitendinosus muscles at the back of the thigh at the level of the stifle joint. In this location these muscles are especially prone to sprains and tears.

The presence of scar and bone severely restricts action of the muscles. There is a characteristic gait in which the back foot, just before touching the ground, is suddenly jerked back several inches. This is opposite to the direction of stringhalt. The back of the thigh at the site of ossification is hard to the touch.

Treatment: The most satisfactory method of treatment is surgical, which involves removing the ossified muscle or dividing the tendon of the semitendinosus. Improvement usually is apparent shortly after the operation. Not all horses remain free of symptoms, however, as new fibrous adhesions can form.

MYOPATHY OF PROLONGED RECUMBENCY

Horses under a general anesthetic for more than 2 to 3 hours, and horses who become recumbent for long periods in the lateral position, are subject to a myopathy caused by the weight of the horse pressing on the dependent muscles. This causes a decrease in the arterial blood flow to the compressed muscles, with local tissue oxygen deficit. For reasons not well understood, in one form of this disease the myopathy becomes generalized.

The typical history is that of a long anesthetic. The horse generally stands after the operation and at first seems normal. In a short time the horse develops signs of muscular weakness, becomes wobbly and unstable, may exhibit a dropped elbow or stifle, or knuckles over at the fetlock. The affected muscles become hard, swollen, and painful.

If the myopathy is severe or generalized, it is unlikely that the horse will be able to regain or keep its feet. Myoglobin produced by dying muscle may appear in the urine and give it a dark brown color. Death can occur from shock or kidney failure.

Treatment: Treatment is like that described for exertional myopathy (see chapter 1, Emergencies). Nonsteroidal anti-inflammatory drugs relieve pain and swelling. Wrap the opposite limb with a support bandage. Attempts to minimize post-anesthetic myopathy include expeditious surgery, positioning the patient on a well-padded surface, and avoiding certain anesthetic agents that may predispose to generalized myopathy.

Prevention: When a horse goes down for any reason and requires good nursing care, it is important to maintain the sternal position if possible. If this is not possible, turn the horse from side to side every 2 hours and provide soft padding. Foam rubber eggshell padding is a good bedding and also helps prevent pressure sores.

Exertional myopathy is discussed in chapter 1, Emergencies, and nutritional myopathy and myotonia are discussed in chapter 16, Pediatrics.

The Foot

The foot refers to the hoof and all its internal structures. Most causes of lameness are found in the foot. An understanding of the anatomy and physiology of the hoof is necessary to identify these causes correctly.

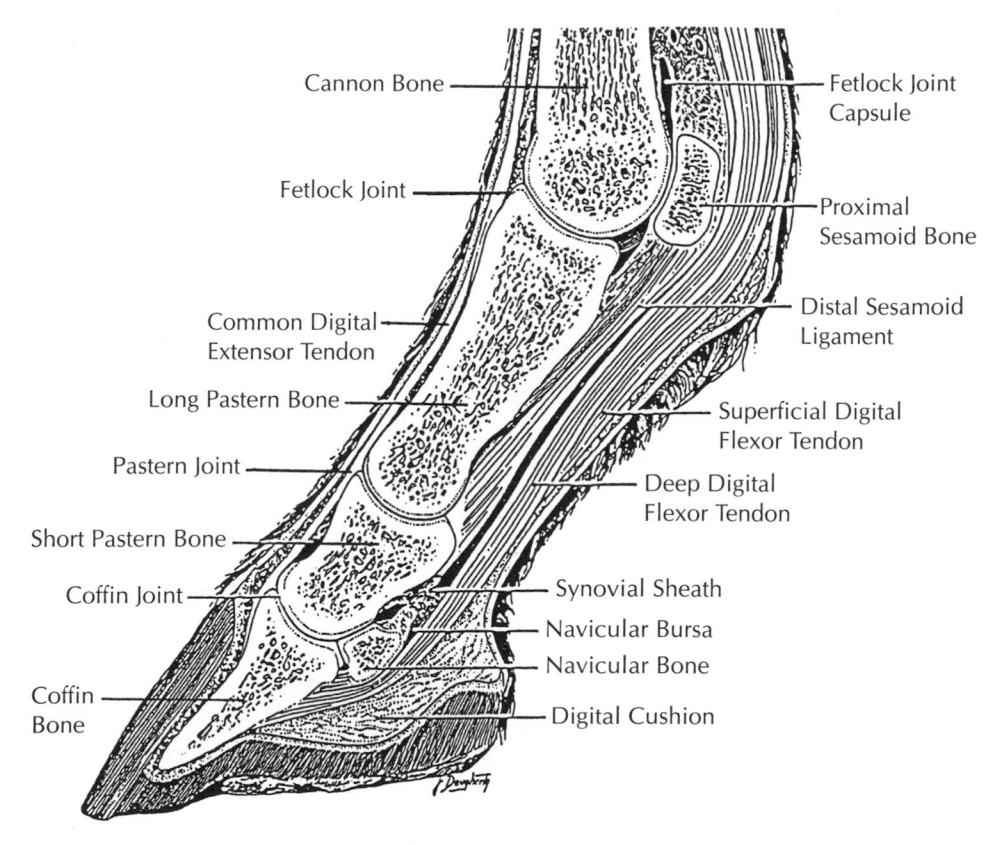

Side View of the Fetlock and Foot. Illustration: *Lameness in Horses,* 4th ed., Lea and Febiger.

A comparison can be made between the bones of the human wrist and hand and the bones of the lower foreleg of the horse.

The knee or *carpal joint* corresponds to the human wrist. Everything below the horse's knee represents bones of the human hand. Whereas the human has five metacarpal bones, only three bones (the second, third, and fourth metacarpals) are present in the horse. These bones are called the *cannon* and *splint* bones. The *fetlock joint* is the same as a knuckle joint. Everything below the fetlock joint corresponds to the human finger. In essence, the horse has adapted a conformation that places all of its weight on a column of bones comparable to the human finger.

The first bone in the human finger is called the *proximal phalanx*. In the horse the proximal phalanx is also called the *long pastern bone*.

The next bone in the human finger, the *middle phalanx*, is the *short pastern bone*. And the last bone, or *distal phalanx*, is called the *coffin bone* (which is buried in the foot).

There are two joints in the human finger. The first, or *proximal interphalangeal joint*, corresponds to the *pastern joint* in the horse. The second, or *distal interphalangeal joint*, corresponds to the *coffin joint*.

To continue the comparison with the human finger, imagine that the fingernail extends all around the finger like a thimble. In this analogy, the outer *insensitive laminae* of the horny hoof is like the fingernail. The bed from which the nail is formed corresponds to the inner *sensitive laminae* of the horse's hoof.

The coffin bone is shaped like the hoof. It is a hard, spongy bone with many perforations for vessels and nerves to pass through the bone and supply the sensitive structures surrounding it.

On each side of the coffin bone are grooves that serve as lines of attachment for the *lateral cartilages*. These are thin plates that slope up and end above the coronary band. They can be felt beneath the skin at the heel, and help to shape the bulbs.

The *navicular* is a wedge-shaped bone positioned at the back of the coffin joint. It is enclosed by the wings of the coffin bone. The navicular bone serves as a pulley or fulcrum for the deep digital flexor tendon.

THE LAMINAE

The inner *sensitive* laminae of the hoof is called the *corium*. The corium is a highly vascular layer of specialized tissue modified from the dermis of the skin. It attaches to the coffin bone and lower edges of the lateral cartilages. The corium manufactures the *insensitive* (or epidermal) laminae, which in turn becomes the horny tissue of the hoof wall and sole.

Each part of the corium is named for one of the five insensitive laminae which it produces. These structures are: the *perioplic corium*, which produces the periople (a wax-like waterproof covering that minimizes moisture evaporation from the hoof); the *coronary corium*, which produces the wall of the hoof and supplies its nutrition; the *laminar corium*, which lines the inside hoof wall from the coronary band to the sole; the *solar corium*, which produces the horn of the sole; and the *frog*

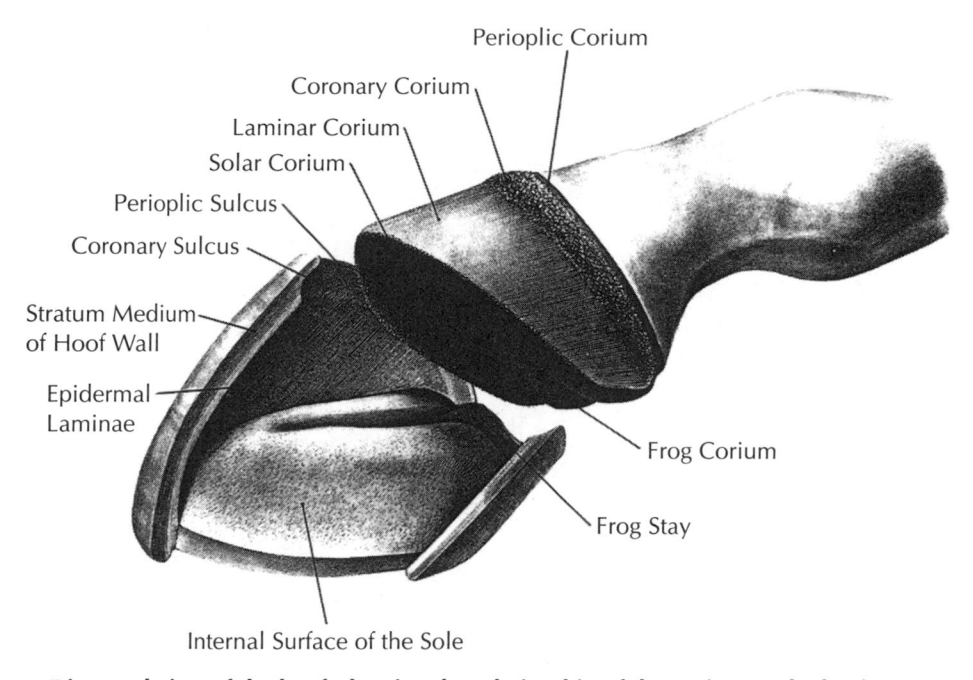

Perioplic Corium

Coronary Corium

Laminar Corium

Solar Corium

Perioplic Sulcus

Coronary Sulcus

Stratum Medium
of Hoof Wall

Epidermal
Laminae

Frog Corium

Frog Stay

Internal Surface of the Sole

Dissected view of the hoof, showing the relationship of the corium to the laminae of the hoof wall. Illustration: *Lameness in Horses,* **4th ed., Lea and Febiger.**

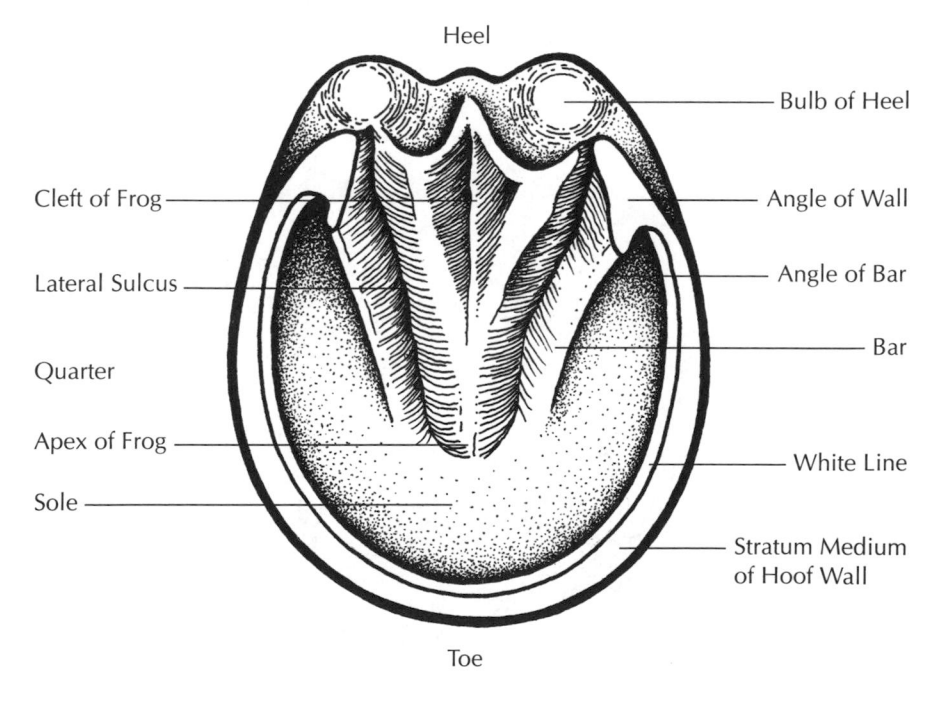

Heel

Bulb of Heel

Cleft of Frog

Angle of Wall

Lateral Sulcus

Angle of Bar

Bar

Quarter

Apex of Frog

White Line

Sole

Stratum Medium
of Hoof Wall

Toe

Ground (Solar) Surface of the Hoof.

corium, which produces the horn of the frog. The dissected view of the hoof shows the relationship of these five inner sensitive laminae to the insensitive laminae they produce.

THE ELASTIC TISSUES

The elastic tissues capable of altering shape in response to foot impact are the digital cushion, hoof wall, sole, frog, and bulbs of the heel.

The *digital cushion* is the main shock absorber of the hoof. It is a wedge-shaped elastic structure bounded by the lateral cartilages at the sides, the deep digital flexor tendon above, and the horny frog below. The back of the cushion forms the bulbs of the heel.

The hoof wall is composed of three layers. The outer layer consists of horn cells that give the hoof its gloss and protect it from excessive drying. Located at the hairline along the top of the hoof wall is the *coronary band* (coronet). This is the primary source of growth and nutrition for the hoof wall. Injuries to the coronary band usually leave a permanent defect which extends the length of the hoof.

The middle layer is called the *stratum medium*. It is thickest at the toe and gradually becomes less thick at the heels, although it is slightly reinforced at the angles where the bars are formed. (The angle of the wall and bar is called the *buttress*.) The middle layer incorporates pigment cells which, when present, give the hoof its color. A nonpigmented hoof will not be any weaker than one with pigment.

The inner layer of the hoof wall fuses with the corium, which attaches in turn to the coffin bone. This relationship is important because it explains how the weight of the horse is transferred to the bearing edge of the hoof wall, and not to the cupped sole of the foot as one might expect.

The *ground surface* of the hoof is composed of the sole, frog, bulbs, and bearing edge of the hoof wall. The ground surface is oriented into four quarters called the toe, the heel, and the two side quarters.

The *sole* is a thick plate of flaky horn that covers most of the ground surface and is rounded in such a way that when viewed from the bottom it is hollowed out or concave. This is important because if the sole were allowed to make contact with the ground, lameness would result from sole bruising.

The *frog* is an elastic wedge-shaped mass of horn that fills a triangular space at the back of the foot. The triangular space is created by two ridges or *bars* that separate the frog from the sole. The bars converge and run forward to end just short of the apex of the frog. At the back, the bars terminate in the *bulbs* of the heels. Just inside the bars are two grooves called the *lateral sulcii*, which spread slightly when weight is placed on the frog.

In the center of the frog is a deep depression known as the *central sulcus* or *cleft*. If you could view it from the inside of the hoof, this cleft would present as a ridge called the *frog-stay*. The frog-stay acts as a wedge pressing into the digital cushion.

Around the perimeter of the ground surface of the hoof is the *white line*, which represents the inside edge of the hoof wall at its junction with the sole. The white line marks the border between the sensitive and insensitive sole. It serves as a guide to show where nails should be driven when shoeing.

In the unshod horse, weight is carried on the bearing surface of the hoof wall, and on the bars and frog. The bearing surface of the hoof wall should be level with the frog to distribute the weight evenly.

The foot receives an excellent blood supply from the two digital arteries. Blood goes back to the heart through a network of veins called the *coronary plexus*. This plexus is located between the lateral cartilages and surrounding hoof wall. In this location the coronary plexus acts like a hydraulic cushion. Since these veins do not contain valves, blood can flow out of the coronary plexus when the foot expands and back into the plexus when the foot contracts.

THE HOOF AS A SHOCK ABSORBER

The shock of concussion is diffused and dissipated laterally against the hoof wall. It is not transferred vertically to the ground, which would greatly increase concussion and musculoskeletal injuries. A number of shock-absorbing mechanisms aid in dissipating this force.

As the foot strikes the ground, downward pressure flattens out the concave surface of the sole. This distributes weight laterally against the hoof wall, which expands about 1/4 of an inch. Now the reason for the bars is shown. If the hoof wall formed a continuous ring uninterrupted by the bars, expansion of the hoof could not take place.

With heel pressure the horny frog, aided by the frog-stay, compresses the digital cushion, which then flattens and pushes the lateral cartilages outward in opposite directions. To make room, venous blood is squeezed out of the coronary plexus.

As weight is removed from the leg, the above structures spring back to their original positions. This is known as *contraction* and aids in propelling the horse forward.

The conformation of the knee and hock joints also helps to reduce the shock of impact. These semi-flexed joints are composed of a number of bones arranged in layers and capable of yielding in three planes.

One other shock-absorbing structure is the navicular bone, supported by the deep digital flexor tendon and its ligaments. During concussion, the navicular shuttles the load from the digital cushion through to the short pastern bone, thereby bypassing the coffin bone and relieving some of its load.

All of these mechanical aids are of singular importance in preventing musculoskeletal and foot injuries and in maintaining the health and fitness of the horse.

Hoof Care

Horses living outdoors on varied terrain wear and grow their hooves in a natural fashion. In contrast, the domestic horse living in paddocks and stables, with infrequent exercise and limited opportunity to toughen his feet, is susceptible to a number of hoof problems. A program of daily inspections and hoof cleaning, routine hoof trimming, and application of horseshoes for those horses that require them, will prevent many of these problems.

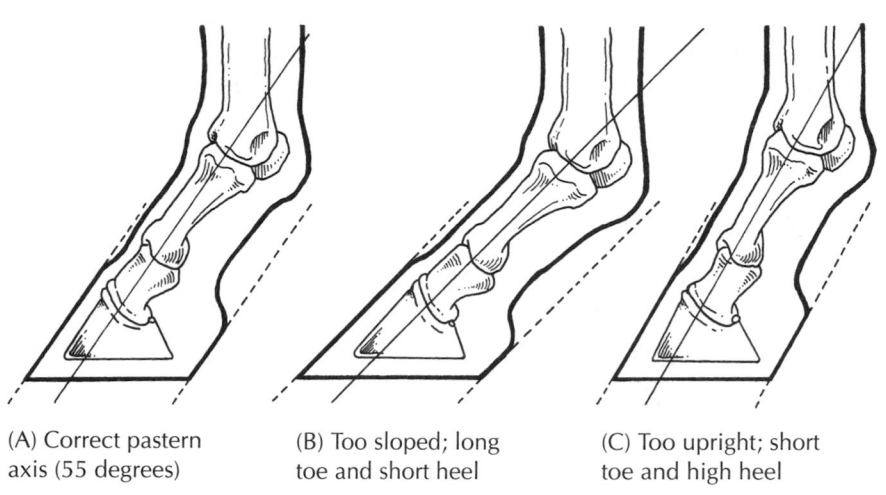

(A) Correct pastern axis (55 degrees)

(B) Too sloped; long toe and short heel

(C) Too upright; short toe and high heel

Hoof pastern axis of front foot.

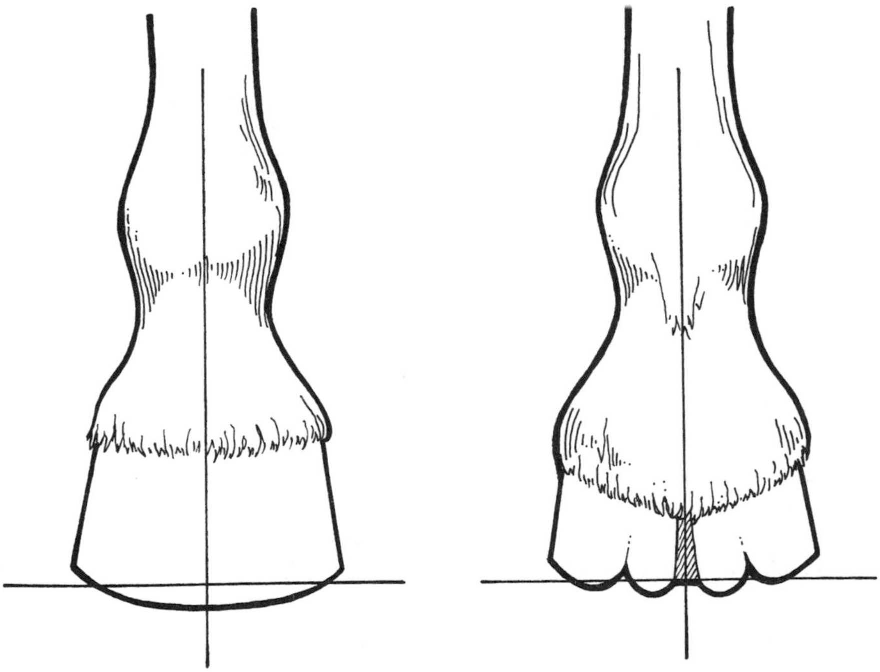

Front view

Rear view

Balanced hoof. The weight of the horse is evenly distributed, and the sole makes level contact with the ground.

Good stall and paddock sanitation is essential to good foot care. Corrals, paddocks, and stalls containing a buildup of urine and wet manure predispose to thrush and canker.

It is important to clean a horse's hooves before and after each workout, daily if the horse is stabled, and at least once a week if on pasture. Remove all debris from the sole and frog, using the hoof pick as shown in the illustration. Give special attention to the central cleft and both lateral sulcii of the frog.

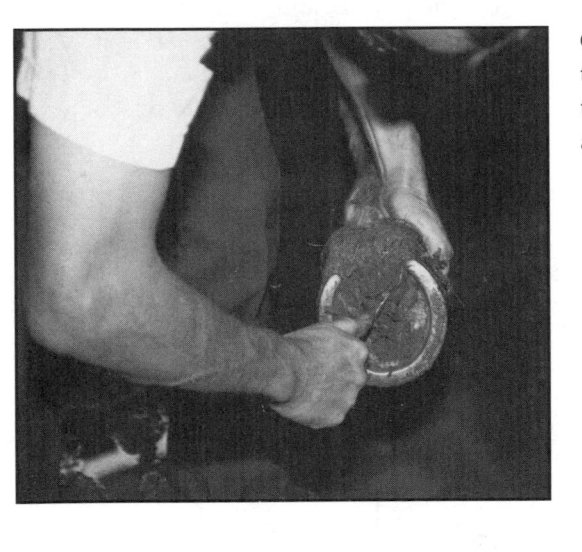

Cleaning the hoof. Start at the frog and work toward the toe. Strokes are made away from the handler.

Lack of environmental moisture has been implicated as a cause of hoof drying and cracking. Thus recommendations for improving hoof moisture content have included applying mud packs or commercial hoof dressings, and allowing the water tank to overflow, creating mud for the horse to stand in several times a day.

Recent observations suggest that excess moisture, especially frequent wet-to-dry episodes which expand and contract the hoof, may do more harm than good. For example, hoof dressings and mud packs can remove the periople, a wax-like moisture barrier which protects the hoof wall from absorbing too much water. A hoof that absorbs too much water, or contains a persistently high moisture content, becomes less elastic. The soft, crumbly horn tends to peel and separate, and does not hold horseshoe nails well.

The health of the outer hoof is related to the health of the inner sensitive structures of the foot. Regular exercise stimulates circulation, maintains health of the corium and elastic tissues, and balances moisture content internally. If the external moisture can be kept at a constant, relatively dry level, and frequent wet-to-dry episodes can be avoided, most hoof problems related to drying and cracking will be eliminated.

Many farriers recommend that hoof dressings be used sparingly. Hoof dressings containing turpentine are particularly deleterious. When hoof dressings are used for a therapeutic purpose such as cracking of the bulbs of the heels, an animal grease product such as lanolin or fish oil is preferable. A commercial hoof sealer, which penetrates the outer hoof better than a dressing, may be of benefit as a moisture barrier when a horse must be kept in unusually wet or dry conditions.

An appropriately balanced diet is essential for normal growth and healthy appearance of the hoof. Overfeeding and underfeeding are the chief causes of poor hoof growth in the foal. A balanced ration should also provide adequate amounts of calcium, biotin (from vitamin B complex), and the essential amino acid DL-methionine. Supplementing a diet with gelatin, amino acids, and other dietary additives will not, however, produce a better hoof if the foal is eating an appropriate creep or weanling ration. Inadvertently adding selenium to a diet already meeting selenium requirements can have serious deleterious consequences, including hoof wall degeneration or even loss of the foot.

HOOF TRIMMING

In the mature horse, the hoof grows about $^1/_3$ inch each month. In the foal, the rate is $^1/_2$ inch each month. Growth is most rapid during spring, and slowest during hot and cold weather.

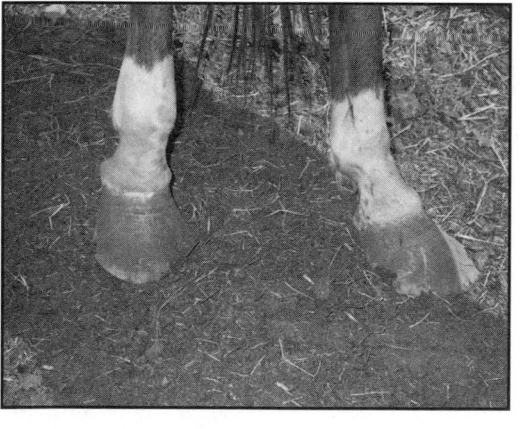

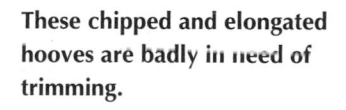
These chipped and elongated hooves are badly in need of trimming.

Few horses are allowed the amount of exercise needed to keep their hooves worn down. Shod horses, in particular, require frequent trimming because the horseshoe, which is interposed between the ground and the hoof, prevents hoof wear. Accordingly, if the horse is shod its hooves should be trimmed about every 5 to 8 weeks. If the horse is not shod, frequency of trimming will depend on wear.

Since a horse's toe grows faster than its heel, if the hoof is not trimmed frequently enough the foot becomes unbalanced. After 7 to 9 weeks the excessively long toe alters the horse's gait, which may result in injury and poor performance. The long toe also contributes to the development of sole bruises, corns, and contracted heels.

Trimming the hoof.
Pare away excess
sole and frog with
the hoof knife.
Photo: Eric Ervin.

Using hoof nippers,
trim the walls until
even with the frog.
Photo: Eric Ervin.

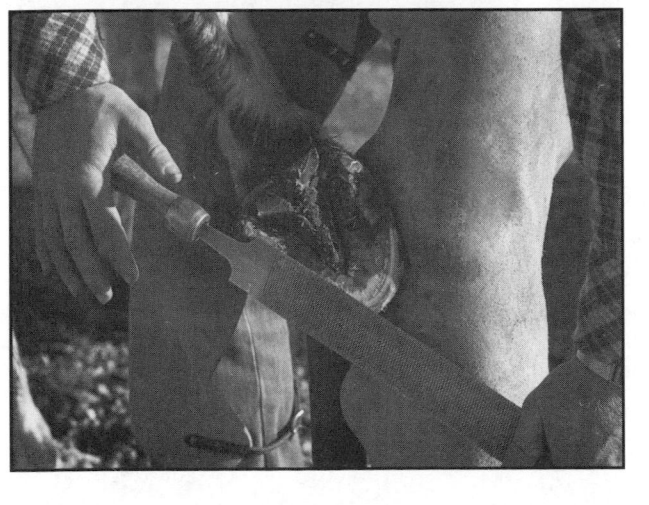

Rasp both sides of
the hoof wall at the
same time until they
are level and smooth.
Photo: Eric Ervin.

Although many horse owners employ the services of a farrier, some may elect to trim the feet themselves. The tools required for trimming are a hoof paring knife, hoof nippers, and a rasp.

First clean out the feet as described above. Using a hoof knife, pare away excess sole and frog. Hoof nippers are used to trim the hoof walls. The object is to trim the walls evenly, and to trim just enough of the wall to make the bearing edges level with the surface of the frog. This distributes weight evenly between the frog and walls. Complete the leveling process by rasping both sides of the hoof wall across the bearing edges from side to side at the same time.

There is a strong temptation to trim the hoof so that it corresponds to an ideal hoof and pastern axis. If the horse does not possess this angle naturally, abnormal stresses will be placed on the supporting ligaments of the pastern and foot. Accordingly the best job of trimming is that which preserves whatever angle is normal for the individual horse.

Some errors to be avoided are:

- Trimming and rasping the bearing surfaces unevenly, so that the foot is not level.
- Overtrimming the heels. Dropping the heels puts strain on the sesamoids and may produce lameness.
- Opening the heels. Removing the wide part of the frog, or more of the frog than is normal for the horse, weakens the heels and may lead to contracted heels. Only loose or torn pieces of frog should be removed.

PUTTING ON HORSESHOES

Horses living outdoors on varied terrain do not require horseshoes. Horseshoes have been described as a necessary evil and a product of domestication, stabling, and circumstances that limit the availability of exercise.

However, there are situations in which horseshoeing is almost a necessity. One is to prevent excessive hoof wear when the horse is being worked or ridden on difficult terrain. Performance horses need shoes for traction and other purposes. For stabled horses, shoes should be put on to prevent sole injuries from lack of foot toughness. Corrective and therapeutic shoes are indicated for orthopedic problems.

Horseshoes should be reset whenever the foot is trimmed, which is usually every 5 to 8 weeks. The shoes of racehorses are usually reset every 2 to 4 weeks.

Most horseshoes are composed of flat plates without raised edges or appendages. However, shoes with calks, studs, ice nails, borium spots, and other traction devices can be fitted when there is need for added traction on ice, snow, or mud. A solid raised bar on the toe of the shoe is called a *grab*. Calks and grabs should be of the same height on all shoes to prevent an uneven step or unnatural gait.

All traction devices have the potential for stopping the shoe suddenly while the horse is moving forward. Severe sprains or fractures are possible, especially at high speeds and during performance activities. To prevent such accidents, it is important to build up the traction devices in stages. This requires the close monitoring of an experienced farrier.

Horseshoes can be applied hot or cold.

Hot-shoeing is the application of a fire-heated shoe to the trimmed level hoof. The shoe can be made by the farrier from scratch or modified from a premade shoe

Putting on horseshoes. A protractor is used to measure the hoof angle and size the shoe for the foot.

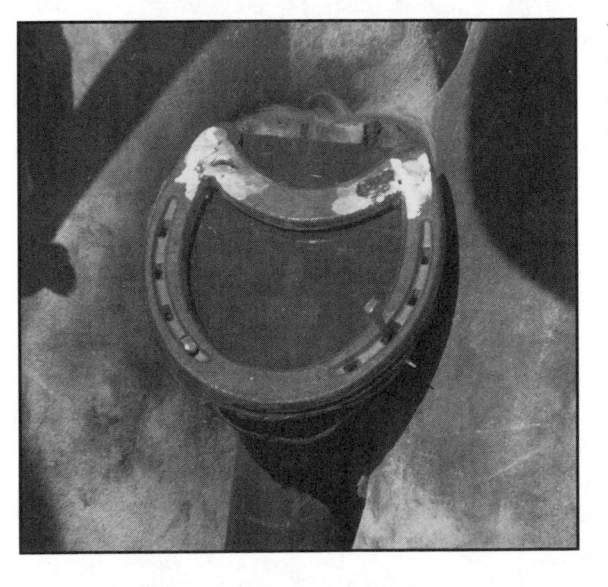

The nail exits about ¹/₂ inch above the bearing edge. Note pad and complete bar shoe, used in corrective shoeing.

using a forge. The hot shoe shows the edges of the hoof that may need further rasping. This ensures an optimal fit between the hoof and the shoe.

Cold-shoeing is the application of a non-heated shoe to the trimmed level hoof. Most farriers can apply cold shoes which are both level and fit the horse well. Many farriers use a combination of hot- and cold-shoeing techniques.

Most horseshoes have holes for 8 nails, but 4 to 6 nails will hold the average shoe. The shoe is sized and fitted to the surface of the hoof. It is then nailed into position. Horseshoe nails are made with a built-in curve. When they are driven into the white line, which marks the border between the sensitive and insensitive laminae, they curve away from the sensitive laminae and exit through the hoof wall about $1/2$ to $3/4$ of an inch above the bearing edge. The end of each nail is twisted off and, when all nails are in, their tips are bent over or clinched. The clinches are then filed smooth, and wax or another substance is used to fill all nail holes. This prevents urine, water, and mud from entering the hoof and causing infection. Finally, any overhang of the hoof wall beyond the shoe should be rasped to bring it into alignment with the edge of the shoe.

"Quickening," also called *hot nailing*, occurs if the nail is accidentally driven into the sensitive laminae. When this happens, the horse immediately jumps or flinches. The offending nail should be taken out. As the nail is removed, blood can frequently be seen on the nail and in the nail hole. The nail hole should be flushed with 7 percent tincture of iodine. Administer a tetanus toxoid booster. If the horse's tetanus immunization history is unknown, see Table 1 in chapter 3, Infectious Diseases.

A *close nail* is one that puts pressure on the sensitive lamina of the foot without actually piercing it. It may cause the horse immediate discomfort, but frequently goes unnoticed for several days or until the horse is exercised and exhibits lameness. The nail causing the problem can be located with a hoof tester or by tapping each nail with a hammer. Removing the offending nail usually cures the problem.

One other cause of immediate lameness is clinching the nails too tightly. If this happens, the nails should be loosened or reset at once.

To remove a horseshoe, open the clinches at the side of the hoof using the chisel end of a clinch cutter. Holding the horse's foot between your knees, use a shoe puller starting at the outside of one heel. Pry the shoe away from the hoof wall while pulling in toward the frog. Switch to the opposite side and repeat the process. Work down the sides toward the toe. Once the shoe is loose, it should come off easily. Avoid prying excessively at any one spot as this might bruise the sole. Check the hoof wall for nail fragments and remove them if present.

LOST SHOES

Eighty percent of lost horseshoes involve the front feet. The loss of a horseshoe is a cause of concern not only because of the potential for hoof wall damage associated with the shoe pulling free, but also because the unprotected hoof is at risk of bruising and cracking.

The majority of horses do not lose shoes. It has been estimated that 20 percent of horses lose 80 percent of shoes. If a horse loses a shoe more than once or twice a year, there will be a specific reason to explain the loss. A bad job of shoeing is seldom the cause, provided the shoes were applied by an experienced individual.

There are a number of possible causes for repeated shoe loss. A wet, muddy environment predisposes to soft hooves that do not hold nails securely, as discussed in the section on HOOF CARE. A conformation problem such as underrun heels may require setting shoes farther back on the hoof, where they project at the heels and can be stepped off by another horse. A horse that toes out can step off a front shoe with either foot. Horses that overreach can clip off a front shoe with a back foot.

Leaving shoes on too long is the most common cause of lost shoes. As the hoof wall overgrows the shoe, the shoe becomes embedded in the sole. The nail clenches are then too long and are pushed away from the hoof wall, resulting in the shoe working free.

Treatment: When a shoe is lost, the hoof must be protected as soon as possible. If this happens on a trail ride, dismount and walk the horse back to the barn or trailer. Clean the hoof and wrap it with a protective bandage or apply a commercially available protective rubber boot. The horse should be kept in a clean dry enclosure until the shoe is replaced.

All shod horses should have their shoes reset on a regular schedule to prevent hoof wall overgrowth, lost shoes, and conformational foot imbalances.

CORRECTIVE TRIMMING AND SHOEING

The purposes of remedial hoof care are to correct (or compensate for) an abnormal hoof/pastern axis, to relieve stresses associated with painful tendon and bone diseases, and to prepare the horse for conventional horseshoes.

Corrective trimming and shoeing should be part of a specific treatment program involving the cooperative efforts of farrier and veterinarian, as each has specific skills and expertise to contribute.

Corrective trimming and shoeing forms an integral part of the treatment of most orthopedic diseases of horses. Laminitis, sand cracks, flat feet, corns and sole bruises, navicular disease, and contracted heels are among the most common conditions for which remedial hoof care is employed. Other conditions include contracted flexor tendons, tendonitis, ligament injuries, ringbone, sidebones, bone spavin, dropped sole, and cunean tendon bursitis.

Foot Injuries and Diseases

FOOT WOUNDS

Wounds of the feet occur commonly in horses. All such wounds are contaminated and frequently complicated by infections and abscesses.

Lacerations of the coronet are caused by barbed wire, sheet metal, and rusty nails. The coronet is quite vascular and bleeds profusely. Since the hoof wall grows from the coronet, an injury involving the coronet can leave a horny ridge or defect in the hoof wall.

Puncture wounds of the sole and frog are a common cause of lameness. In all cases of lameness it is essential to carefully inspect the ground surface of the hoof for a puncture wound. In many cases the object causing the puncture will be visible as a foreign body in the wound, making the diagnosis relatively easy. However, when the object is not visible, the puncture wound can be extremely difficult to detect, especially when it is located in the frog. A hoof tester is of considerable help in locating the site of tenderness.

Puncture wounds of the sole are among the most serious of foot wounds because there is no effective drainage to the outside. An abscess beneath the sole may force drainage at the coronary band, but when this does not happen, serious complications occur. They may include bacterial laminitis, tetanus, septic arthritis of the coffin joint, septic tenosynovitis of the flexor tendon sheath, pedal osteitis, septic bursitis of the navicular, fracture of the navicular, destruction of the digital cushion, and blood poisoning (septicemia).

Treatment of Foot Wounds: All horses should receive a tetanus toxoid booster. If the state of immunity is unknown, see Table 1 in chapter 3, Infectious Diseases.

Lacerations of the skin of the coronet and fetlock are cleansed, dressed, and bandaged as described in the section WOUNDS in chapter 1, Emergencies. Change the dressing daily and confine the horse to a stall. Usually it is not advisable to attempt to close such wounds with sutures because of inadequate connective tissue and problems with contamination.

With puncture wounds of the bottom of the foot, the entire sole and frog should be cleansed and washed. It is important to establish drainage at the point of entrance. This is accomplished by cutting down into the puncture wound with a narrow hoof knife and following the tract to its deepest point, or until the sensitive tissues are encountered. The external opening should be at least 1/4 inch wide. The tract should be irrigated with a dilute Betadine solution (1 to 2 ml added to 1,000 ml sterile saline) and packed with Betadine-saturated gauze. The foot is then bandaged as described in the WOUNDS section. The irrigation is repeated daily until healing is well established. The horse should be closely confined in a clean dry stall. Antibiotics are not necessary for simple, early wounds, but are often prescribed for heavily contaminated wounds of unknown duration.

Sole wounds that drain at the coronary band have already established a tract to the outside. The ground surface of the foot should be treated as described above, and the through-and-through tract thus created flushed once a day for several days. Deep and complicated wounds require veterinary management.

After the infection has been cleared and the wound is clean, apply shoes over full pads to prevent dirt and manure from getting into the cavity and reinfecting the foot.

PUNCTURE WOUNDS OF THE WHITE LINE (GRAVEL)

Gravel is a specific foot infection caused by a puncture wound or crack in the white line that permits infection to invade the deep structures of the foot. Because these infections usually cannot drain through the site of injury, pus will follow the path of least resistance and travel up the white line to drain at the coronary band.

At one time it was thought that a piece of gravel entered the sole of the foot at the white line and worked its way upward. However, this does not occur—except by coincidence.

When you examine the white line in a horse with gravel, you will see black spots. On probing, one of these will be found to penetrate into the sensitive laminae. Pus will often exude from this wound. The sensitive area will be very painful when the foot is examined with a hoof tester.

Treatment: An abscessed pocket under the white line and sole is drained by cutting down and paring out the tract with a hoof knife. If the tract is already draining at the coronet, this opening should be enlarged as well. In long-standing infections an additional drainage hole may need to be made in the hoof wall midway between the wounds of entrance and exit. Treatment is like that described for Foot Wounds.

HOOF WALL CRACKS

A crack is a separation or break in the hoof wall. Cracks are identified according to their location as toe, quarter, or heel. Vertical cracks are classified as grass cracks or sand cracks. Grass cracks start at the ground surface and extend upward; sand cracks begin at the coronet and extend down.

Grass cracks often occur in unshod hooves where the bearing surface of the hoof wall is not trimmed and becomes too long, cracking with percussion. A common cause of hoof cracking and peeling is exposure of the hoof to *too much* moisture (rather than not enough). Especially deleterious are repeated wet-to-dry episodes, which cause expansion and contraction of the hoof wall. A vitamin or essential amino acid deficiency may be a contributing factor in some cases of cracked hooves.

Sand cracks occur as a result of cuts and injuries to the coronet. Gravel can lead to a vertical sand crack.

Horizontal cracks in the hoof wall are called *blow-outs*. They are caused by injuries to the coronary band and hoof wall. A blow-out is an inconsequential finding unless it weakens the hoof wall and set the stage for a vertical crack.

A horse with a crack may or may not be lame. This depends on the location and depth of the crack. If the crack bleeds after exercise, it is deep and extends into the sensitive laminae. Deep cracks are susceptible to infection. If this occurs you will observe a discharge of blood and pus and feel increased heat in the hoof wall.

Hoof cracks do not unite from side to side as do skin wounds. The crack is replaced by new horn that starts at the coronary band and grows down (like a fingernail growing out from its base).

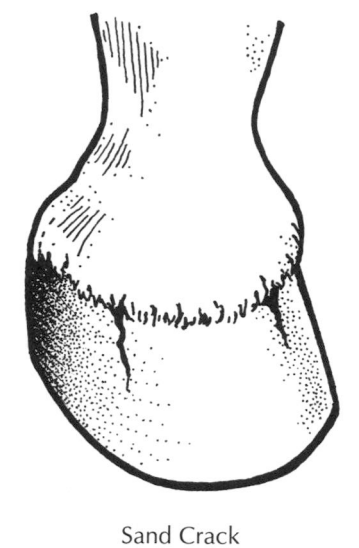 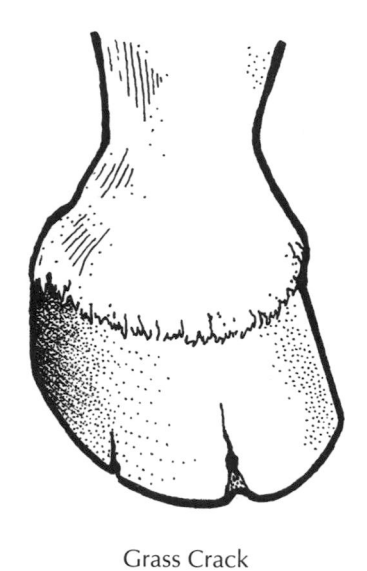

Sand Crack   Grass Crack

Hoof wall cracks can begin at the coronet or bearing edges.

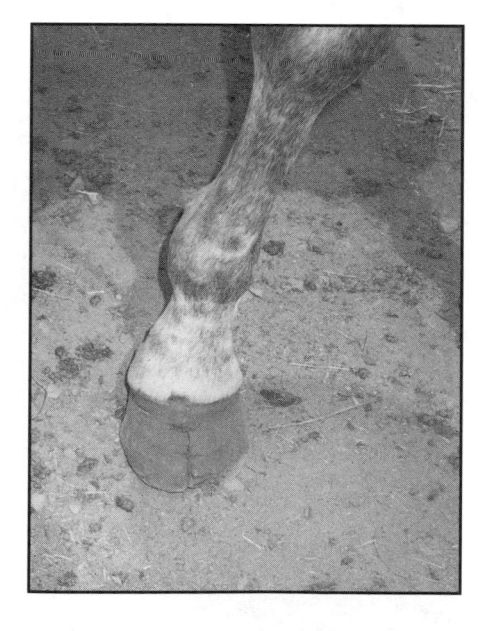

This vertical crack was laced together with wire.

Treatment: This depends upon the location and depth of the crack. The immediate goal is to prevent the crack from lengthening and deepening. For grass cracks, this can often be accomplished by a skillful hoof trimming. Sand cracks usually respond to a combination of professional trimming and application of corrective horseshoes. The shoes must be worn for as long as it takes the crack to grow out. For cracks at the coronet, this can take 9 to 12 months.

Large, deep cracks must be stabilized to prevent the hoof from splitting. Before a crack can be stabilized, however, it must be thoroughly cleansed to remove dirt, debris, and loose horn, which serve as a reservoir for bacterial infection. If the crack is moist or bleeding, it is treated as described for FOOT WOUNDS, and should not be closed until dry.

One technique for closing a vertical crack is to drill holes in the hoof wall on either side of the split and then lace the two sides together with stainless steel wire or heavy nylon. Alternately, the crack can be patched by fastening a metal plate across it. A variety of new prosthetic materials can be used to fill cracks completely or patch across them. These materials resemble the consistency of the hoof wall so closely that once applied they can be nailed into, trimmed, and even rasped along the hoof wall as it grows down.

As a sequel to treatment, protect the hoof from repeated episodes of wetness and dryness, which can make the hoof brittle and less pliable. A hoof sealer is beneficial in stabilizing hoof moisture content if the horse cannot be quartered under ideal conditions. The ration should provide adequate amounts of the amino acid DL-methionine, calcium, and biotin (a component of vitamin B complex). To meet these needs, a nutritional supplement may be indicated.

WHITE LINE DISEASE (SEEDY TOE)

In this disease the white line disintegrates as the result of infection caused by bacteria, yeast, or fungus. The infection starts at ground level and works its way up the white line to the coronary band. The region commonly affected is the toe back to the quarter. The loss of horn creates a hollow space between the hoof wall and the sole that becomes mealy or "seedy." Eventually a deep recess, filled with cheesy material and debris, develops between the sole and hoof wall. The loss of supporting horn coupled with the pull of the deep digital flexor tendon can cause rotation of the coffin bone, like that seen with chronic laminitis.

White line disease seldom occurs in barefoot horses on pasture. Like many other hoof conditions, it is a disease of domestic horse management. The typical horse with white line disease is shod, given limited daily exercise, bedded in damp wood shavings, kept in a wet stall, and exposed to frequent wet-to-dry episodes such as daily wash-downs or walks in wet grass.

Treatment: All diseased horn and unsound tissue must be pared out and removed down to solid healthy horn. In questionable cases, the cavity is packed with Betadine dressings and treated as a hoof infection until healthy horn is observed. The deep recesses are then filled with prosthetic hoof repair material. Egg bar or full support shoes are fitted. With advanced disease, special shoeing techniques are required. All predisposing conditions should be corrected.

CORNS AND BRUISED SOLES

Rocks and other hard objects can bruise the sole and produce lameness. The injury actually involves the underlying sensitive laminae, not the horny sole or frog. Horses with thin soles are most often affected, as are horses with flat feet. Both of these conditions are inherited traits. Another cause of thin soles is removing too much sole or frog when trimming the foot.

Corns are bruises of the sole that occur at the *buttress*, the angle formed by the wall and bar. They occur most frequently on the inside buttresses of the front feet. Improper foot care is the most common cause of corns. When shoes are left on too long, the growing hoof wall can force the heel of the horseshoe to apply pressure to the sole. Applying shoes that are too small, bending the shoe in at the heel, and trimming the heels too low all result in excessive sole pressure over the buttress.

A *dry corn* is characterized by red staining in the horn. This is the result of bruising (bleeding) in the sensitive tissue beneath the horn. In a *moist corn*, serum is present beneath the involved horn. This indicates a more severe injury. In a *suppurating corn*, the corn has become infected, resulting in a draining abscess beneath the horn, which produces death of the adjacent sensitive lamina and digital cushion. Bruised soles are identical to corns, except that they occur at the toe or quarter instead of the heel.

Lameness is the most common sign of corns and bruises. A horse with a corn tends to favor that heel. Cleaning the flaky material from the sole with a hoof knife may reveal characteristic findings. A hoof tester helps to locate the injury.

Treatment: For dry corns caused by improper shoeing, remove the offending shoe, trim the hoof wall, and rest the horse. Do not reapply shoes until the horse is free of symptoms.

Sole bruises are best treated by resting the horse. When limited use is required, the sole can be covered with a suitable hoof packing and a full pad applied beneath the shoe.

Suppurating corns and bruises are treated by removing all diseased horn over the bruise down to the sensitive lamina. Soak the hoof daily in magnesium sulfate (Epsom salt) and bandage the foot to prevent contamination. Initiate tetanus prophylaxis as indicated. Rest the horse until healed. If the horse must be used, the wall and bar in the area of the corn can be removed, and a protective shoe applied to protect the injured area.

If a sole abscess becomes chronic, it can lead to a complication called *pedal osteitis*. This is a thinning and demineralization of the coffin bone. The result is a chronic and persistent lameness which is most difficult to reverse.

The feet of a horse with thin soles can be toughened by taking the shoes off and turning the horse out to pasture on rough ground for 6 months. Alternately, the soles can be toughened using a topical solution containing equal parts of phenol, formalin, and iodine. This requires veterinary supervision. Corrective shoeing helps some horses with flat feet, but there is no cure for the problem.

KERATOMA

Keratoma is a rare tumor or growth arising in the horn-producing cells of the hoof wall, usually in the toe region and less commonly in the sole. There is usually a history of prior injury or hoof disease, but some cases arise spontaneously. Lameness results from pressure on the coffin bone or sensitive laminae.

Keratomas are typically circular and approximately 0.5 to 2.0 cm in size. They may or may not produce an abnormal contour or bulge in the hoof wall. Keratomas of the sole are most commonly recognized during hoof trimming and paring of the sole. A deviation of the white line toward the center of the sole is suspicious.

If the horse is not lame, no therapy is warranted. For keratomas causing symptoms, surgical removal is the only effective treatment. Some keratomas recur after surgery and require further removal. The outlook is good when the keratoma can be removed completely without damaging surrounding structures.

DISEASES OF THE FROG

Thrush. Thrush is a painful bacterial infection involving the central cleft and the collateral sulcii of the frog. It is characterized by a putrid black discharge along with poor growth and degeneration of the horn. When the frog is cleaned with a hoof pick, a soft putty-like material will fall away, revealing sulcii deeper than normal. The infection may extend into the sensitive laminae and infect the digital cushion. A number of bacterial species may be involved, but the anaerobic organism *Fusobacterium necrophorum* appears to be the most common.

Thrush is caused by lack of proper foot care resulting in a buildup of mud and manure that prevents air from getting to the frog. During routine hoof trimming the clefts of the frog should be pared back to make them self-cleaning. When this is not done, flaps of frog tissue can seal in debris and make it impossible to clean out the frog with a hoof pick.

Treatment: Remove the horse from mud and manure and stable it in a clean dry stall. Remove the shoe and thoroughly clean out the frog. Expose the clefts by removing degenerating frog with a hoof knife. Apply a drying agent such as 10 percent formalin or 7 percent tincture of iodine to the cleft and sulcii, and then follow with a topical antibiotic solution such as 10 percent sodium sulfapyridine. Bandage the foot to prevent contamination. Repeat the treatment daily for several days, then once or twice a week until the foot is healed. Your veterinarian may suggest a bar shoe to promote frog regeneration. The prognosis is good when the sensitive structures are not involved.

Canker. Canker is a chronic infection of the horn tissues of the foot. It begins at the frog and progresses slowly to involve the sole and sometimes the wall. The disease is rare and is found almost exclusively in tropical climates.

Canker develops in horses who stand in mud, or in bedding soaked with urine and feces, and who do not receive regular foot care.

The cankerous horn tissue of the frog loosens readily, and when removed discloses a foul-smelling, bleeding corium covered with a curdled-white discharge. The appearance is quite similar to thrush, but can be distinguished by the characteristics of the discharge, severity of infection, and involvement of the sole as well as the frog.

Treatment: Move the horse to a clean, dry stable, or preferably a dry rocky pasture. Treat the foot as described for thrush. Penicillin, both intramuscularly and topically, is an effective antibiotic. Because canker regularly involves the corium, treatment is often prolonged.

Contracted Heels. This is a disorder in which the foot is abnormally narrow or actually contracted, especially at the heels. One or both front feet may be affected. In severe cases the bars may actually touch while the hoof wall, from the coronet down, may slope inward toward the bearing surface instead of outward.

One cause of heel contracture is too little pressure on the frog. This can happen when a horse with a painful foot stands for long periods with its heel off the ground to relieve pressure on the sole. Another cause of heel contracture is an excessively long, unbalanced foot resulting from improper trimming. The racing Thoroughbred is frequently trimmed and shod for a long toe and underrun heel in order to increase the speed of the horse. This is a foot conformation likely to predispose to contracted heels.

Treatment: Therapy is directed at restoring a balanced foot by corrective trimming and shoeing. If the contracted heel is the result of a painful foot, the cause of this must be identified and treated.

SHEARED HEELS AND QUARTERS

The heel of the horse's foot has two bulbs, one on each side. In a balanced foot, both bulbs should contact the ground simultaneously. In a horse with sheared heels, one bulb (and often its associated quarter) strikes the ground first, causing the horse to bear weight on the inside or outside of its heel. This causes an upward displacement of that heel bulb in relation to the other. An important finding on examination is that the heel bulbs can be manipulated back and forth independently and/or displaced in opposite directions.

With selective weight-bearing on one side of the foot for a period of time, the heel and quarter on that side become painful. The resulting lameness is like that seen with navicular disease, which may actually be brought on by sheared heels. Sheared heels also predisposes to hoof wall injuries and thrush.

The most common cause of sheared heels is improper hoof trimming in which one heel bulb and/or quarter is trimmed shorter than the other. In some cases this is intentional, the belief being that changing the balance of the hoof will increase speed at the racetrack, or compensate for some fault in the horse's conformation.

Treatment: It involves bringing the foot back into balance through corrective trimming. In chronic cases, an egg bar or full bar shoe may be required.

LATERAL CARTILAGE DISEASES

Quittor. Quittor is a chronic deep-seated infection of the lateral cartilages of the coffin bone. Destruction of the inflamed part of the cartilage results in the discharge of infected material via a sinus tract that opens at or above the coronet.

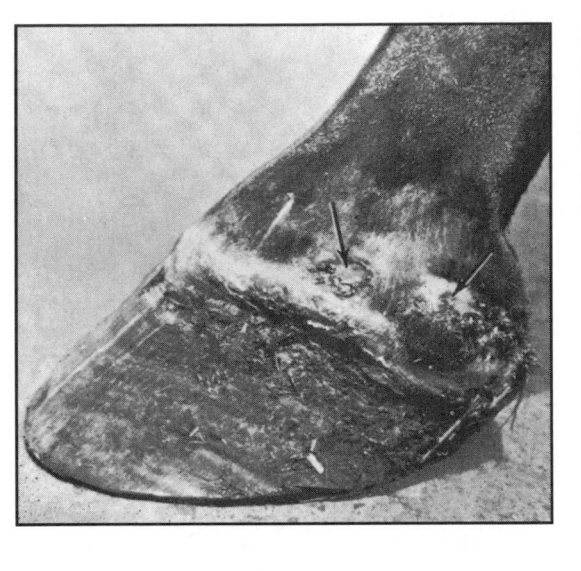

Quittor is an infection of the lateral cartilage of the coffin bone. Note draining sinus tracts. Photo: *Lameness in Horses,* 4th ed., Lea and Febiger.

Injuries near the lateral cartilages, such as being struck by another foot, often precede the appearance of quittor, as do penetrating injuries of the sole.

During an acute attack the horse will be lame. You can see swelling and feel heat over the lateral cartilage near the involved quarter. In the chronic stage one or more sinus tracts are apparent. Periodically these tracts open and drain pus. In long-standing cases some degree of sidebone will be present.

Treatment: The most effective treatment is to remove the destroyed cartilage. Many horses recover completely. In long-standing cases there may be enough damage to surrounding structures to produce permanent lameness.

Sidebones. This name is given to ossification of the lateral cartilages of the coffin bone. It can occur in all four feet but is most common in the front feet. Excessive concussion (often combined with incorrect shoeing) is believed to be the primary factor in converting the cartilage to bone. Faulty conformation is a definite predisposing factor.

Sidebones usually do not produce lameness, except perhaps in the acute ossifying stage when pain, heat, and swelling are found over the quarters. If a horse with sidebones is lame, it is quite likely that some other condition, such as navicular disease, is responsible for the lameness.

Treatment: It is indicated only for relief of lameness. The quarters can be grooved or thinned to permit expansion of the hoof, which helps to eliminate pain. Full roller motion shoes diminish action in the region of the coffin joint. If lameness persists, a digital neurectomy can be performed as described in the section on NAVICULAR DISEASE.

Navicular Disease

Navicular disease is perhaps the most common cause of *intermittent* front leg lameness in horses. Quarter Horses, jumpers, cutters, racers, calf-ropers, and barrel-racers are especially prone to the problem. These horses are subject to unusual foot stresses with hard stops, twists at speed, abrupt changes in direction, and forceful landings on overextended fetlocks. Usually both front feet are affected, but a predominance on one side may lead to the impression that the lameness is unilateral.

The navicular bone is located at the heel of the foot beneath the central one-third of the frog. It is suspended by three ligaments, articulates with the coffin joint, and serves as a support to the coffin and short pastern bones. Behind the navicular is the deep digital flexor tendon, which curves around and attaches to the back of the coffin. Between the navicular and the tendon is a bursa that allows the deep flexor tendon to glide over the bone. All these structures make up the *navicular complex*.

The exact mechanism of injury and pain in navicular disease is not known, but a number of factors are predisposing. They include poor foot conformation (upright pasterns), infrequent or inadequate hoof trimming that results in a long toe and low heel, sheared heels, contracted heels, and improper horseshoeing. All these abnormalities adversely affect the smooth and efficient transfer of weight through the navicular to the ground (see THE HOOF AS A SHOCK ABSORBER).

Among horses with navicular disease, it is believed that tissue stresses are multiplied beyond the capacity of the bone and surrounding supportive structures to adapt. Degenerate changes appear in the bone. They consist of cartilage erosion, bone erosion, and adhesions between the bone and deep digital flexor tendon. These changes may be accompanied by periostitis, bursitis, and tendonitis in the surrounding structures that make up the navicular complex.

Initially the lameness is mild. The horse goes lame for short periods and then appears sound. Later the lameness becomes more frequent. Pain in navicular disease is located in the heel. As a consequence the horse puts its toe down first, sometimes actually stabbing it into the ground, which may cause the horse to stumble on the toe. A stiff, shuffling gait with a shortened, choppy stride is characteristic.

A standard diagnostic test is to apply a hoof tester over the center of the frog. Pain is elicited here because the bone is located beneath the frog. In contrast, a horse with laminitis reacts painfully to hoof testing over the toes. Blocking both posterior digital nerves in the foot helps to determine if the heel is the site of pain. After an effective block, the horse with navicular disease no longer feels pain and moves out freely, unless the condition is bilateral, in which case the lameness shifts to the other leg. Blocking the second leg then eliminates the lameness.

X-rays may reveal suggestive changes in the bone or surrounding tissue but are not always diagnostic. Thus a diagnosis of navicular disease usually must take into consideration all factors, including the history; the horse's characteristic gait; and the results of hoof testing, nerve blocks, and x-rays.

Treatment: Any abnormalities in hoof balance and conformation amenable to treatment should be corrected. This will require the services of a farrier skilled in therapeutic hoof trimming and shoeing. Results may not be apparent for several months.

A hoof tester over the central third of the frog elicits pain in navicular disease.

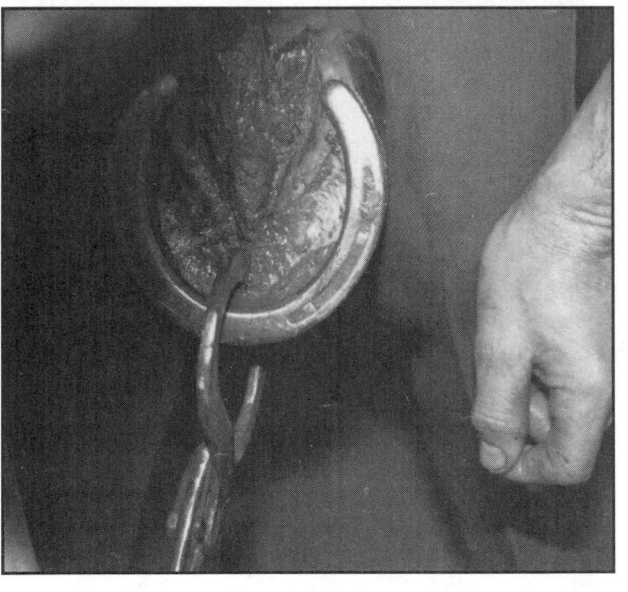

A horse with laminitis reacts painfully to hoof-testing over the toe.

Medical treatment involves the periodic use of Butazolidin and other anti-inflammatory drugs to relieve pain. Analgesics should not be given continuously because of potential side effects, including stomach ulcers.

The drug isoxsuprine hydrochloride appears to offer significant relief for horses with navicular disease. Its mechanism of action is unknown, but horses receiving the drug have shown substantial improvement that can last up to a year after the drug is discontinued. Some veterinarians recommend year-round use of the drug at lower doses. Isoxsuprine hydrochloride is given by mouth. It has few known side effects and can be used concurrently with Butazolidin.

Some horses do not respond to conservative treatment and/or have more advanced disease. For these horses surgery is indicated. The most common operation, *palmar digital neurectomy,* involves removing both digital nerves and all accessory branches that supply the back half of the foot. When successful, the horse will be free of symptoms and can be used safely for all activities, including racing and jumping.

Approximately 20 percent of horses do not respond completely after digital neurectomy. This may be because of tendon disease, adhesions, periostitis, traumatic arthritis of the fetlock joint, or complications resulting from the effects of the operation. Digital neurectomy is not legal in all states on racehorses. In some states the racing commissions regulate the sites of incision.

A second operation is called *navicular suspensory desmotomy.* In this procedure the suspensory ligament of the navicular is divided close to its attachment on the long pastern bone. The operation is difficult and not often used.

Laminitis (Founder)

Laminitis is a metabolic and vascular disease that involves the inner sensitive structures of the feet. The disease begins when bacterial endotoxins and lactic acid

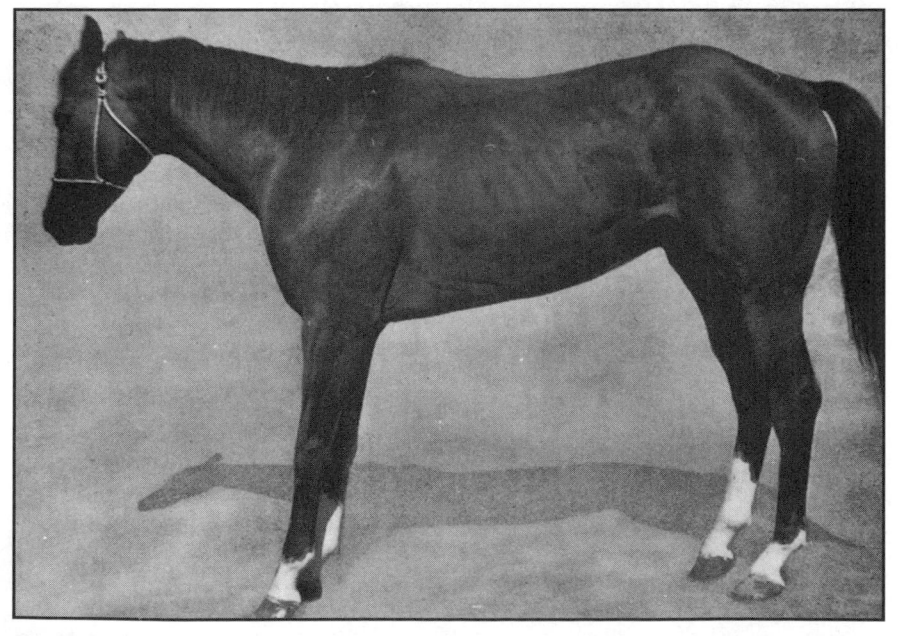

The typical stance of a horse with acute laminitis. Photo: *Lameness in Horses,* 4th ed., Lea and Febiger.

are released into the bloodstream, a condition called *endotoxemia*. Conditions that trigger the release of endotoxins are discussed below.

Endotoxins and lactic acid dilate the large digital arteries to the feet, increasing blood flow while at the same time causing intense constriction of the small capillary vessels that nourish the laminae. The result is a large volume of blood going down to the feet but being shunted around the laminae. Thus deprived of blood and oxygen, the laminae swell. Because the hoof is rigid, the swelling compresses the laminae and causes further tissue compromise. Unless the situation is not relieved, the sensitive inner structures of the feet will die.

Laminitis occurs most often in the two front feet but may occur in all four feet. All horses are at risk, but ponies and stallions are most susceptible.

Founder occurs in both an acute and chronic form.

ACUTE FOUNDER

The most common cause of acute founder is the rapid consumption of excess quantities of carbohydrate—well beyond the daily amounts normally consumed by the horse. The carbohydrate load in the intestinal tract alters the bacterial balance within the cecum, indirectly leading to the release of lactic acid and endotoxins.

Acute founder begins suddenly with high fever and chills, sweating, diarrhea, fast pulse, and rapid heavy breathing. The digital artery at the fetlock exhibits a pounding pulse. The feet are hot and painful. The horse alternately lifts one foot after another and gives evidence of severe pain when the sole of the foot is tapped.

There is a characteristic stance in acute founder in which the two front feet are placed out front to take weight off the toes. When all feet are involved, the horse draws its feet up underneath its belly or lies down. Death in acute founder is uncommon but can occur. With severe laminitis, the hoof may slough.

Acute founder is classified as grass or grain founder, depending on the source of dietary energy.

Grain founder generally does not occur until a horse has consumed at least 25 pounds of grain at one time. However, horses differ greatly in their tolerance to grain consumption. A horse who eats grain on a daily basis has a higher tolerance.

Signs of grain founder do not appear until 12 to 18 hours after the grain has been consumed. When the horse does not exhibit symptoms within the first few hours, it may appear as if the danger is past. However, if the horse consumed a large quantity of grain, it is nearly certain that it will founder. Moreover, once signs do occur, it can be difficult or impossible to prevent permanent foot damage. Accordingly, if you know or even suspect that your horse has consumed an unknown quantity of grain, *consult your veterinarian without delay*.

Grass founder is common among horses grazed on lush, fast-growing summer pasture grasses, particularly clover and alfalfa. This type of founder often affects ponies and fat horses. It can also occur in winter as a result of overfeeding legume hays.

Other causes of acute laminitis include *water founder*, which occurs in hard-working, overheated horses allowed to drink large amounts of cold water before being cooled down. *Postpartum laminitis* is a complication of a severe, often fatal bacterial infection of the mare's uterus which develops during or shortly after foaling. Retained placental tissue contributes to the infection and subsequent endotoxemia. Respiratory and other systemic infections are rare causes of acute laminitis.

The administration of high doses of corticosteroids, used in treating a variety of severe illnesses in horses, has been shown to increase the sensitivity of the laminar capillaries to circulating toxins and other vasoconstrictive substances—thus increasing the risk and occurrence of acute laminitis.

CHRONIC FOUNDER

Laminitis becomes chronic when pain and lameness persist for more than 2 days or when permanent damage occurs to the foot.

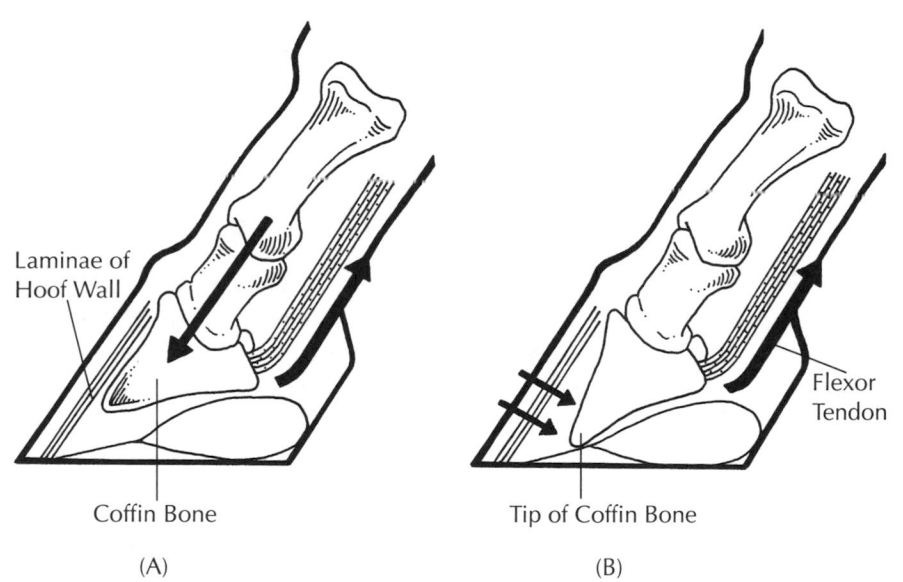

Rotation of the coffin bone. (A) Normal position within hoof. (B) Detached from hoof wall and rotated, with tip pointing down.

An important complication of laminitis is rotation of the coffin bone. This can occur as early as 48 hours after the acute episode, but may not occur until much later. Rotation occurs when the coffin bone becomes detached from the hoof wall and, aided by the pull of the digital flexor tendon, rotates away and drops down. All degrees of rotation from mild to severe are possible. With a severe rotation, the tip of the coffin bone may penetrate the sole of the foot. This is a serious complication and most difficult to treat. Other complications of chronic laminitis include white line disease, thrush, separations of the hoof at the coronary band or sole, and complete loss of the hoof. Damage to the sole corium often produces a long toe that curls up at the end (*slipper foot*).

After an attack of acute laminitis, damage to the inner sensitive laminae causes characteristic changes in the hoof wall. You may see a series of heavy founder rings on the hoof wall. These rings are caused by injury to the coronary band corium. The rings are present for life.

Founder rings on the hoof wall.

Slipper foot is caused by permanent damage to the sole corium in chronic founder.

TREATMENT OF LAMINITIS

Acute founder is a medical emergency. Notify your veterinarian immediately. Do not wait for signs to develop. Remove all feed from the horse's stall; if the horse is on pasture, move it to a paddock or stall.

The object of emergency treatment is to reduce the severity of the attack and prevent rotation of the coffin bone. If this can be prevented or minimized, the horse usually will not suffer permanent disability.

With grain founder, treatment is directed at eliminating the grain from the horse's intestinal tract before it reaches the colon and undergoes fermentation. Pass a stomach tube and coat the intestinal tract with a large volume of mineral oil (3 to 4 quarts per 1,000 pounds body weight). Mineral oil is a laxative and also prevents the absorption of endotoxins. Repeat this dose every 6 hours until all grain has passed through the horse's intestine.

Once symptoms of acute laminitis develop, gently remove the horse's shoes and apply cold packs to the feet. Provide a soft footing (6 inches of sand is ideal) that is comfortable to stand on and reduces tension on the deep digital flexor tendon. A method of reducing the pull of the tendon, and thus minimizing coffin bone rotation, is to apply 18- to 20-degree wedge pads beneath the heels. A similar effect can be obtained by wrapping a roll of elastic gauze beneath the frog. Exercise contributes to coffin bone rotation and should be avoided.

Veterinary management of acute laminitis includes the administration of flunixin meglumine for its beneficial anti-endotoxic properties. Butazolidin is given for its anti-inflammatory properties. When given in combination with Acepromazine, it has been shown to reduce capillary constriction and hypertension. For best results, both agents should be given together by the IV route. After 24 hours, Butazolidin can be given by mouth. During the next 2 weeks, x-rays are taken at intervals to monitor the position of the coffin bone.

Dietary management involves eliminating grain from the diet and replacing it with good-quality grass hay. Begin by offering a few pounds of hay 2 or 3 times a day while watching for signs of relapse. Later grain can be introduced at a rate of 1/2 pound per day. Water should be available at all times. Overweight horses should be put on a reducing diet as described in chapter 17, Feeding and Nutrition (see Obesity). A horse who has foundered once is likely to do so again. Such horses should be watched carefully and not given unrestricted access to lush green pastures. They should never be fed large amounts of grain or fresh hay. Eliminate access to salt during the acute phase.

Foot care is important in the management of chronic laminitis. The goal is to prevent further rotation of the coffin bone and to realign the bone with the hoof wall and sole. This involves corrective hoof trimming and shoeing, and the cooperative efforts of farrier, veterinarian, and horse owner.

Prognosis: Best results occur when symptoms resolve within the first 10 days. Any degree of rotation of the coffin bone is undesirable, but when rotation is greater than 12 degrees, it is most likely that the horse will remain lame regardless of treatment. Cracks and separations of the sole and hoof wall predispose to infection of the inner sensitive laminae. These present major treatment challenges.

URINARY SYSTEM

The urinary system is composed of the kidneys, ureters, bladder, and urethra.

The kidneys are paired organs located on each side of the backbone opposite the 18th ribs. The surface of the left kidney can be felt by rectal palpation.

Each kidney has a pelvis or funnel that siphons the urine into a ureter. The ureters pass on down to the pelvic brim and empty into the bladder. The passageway that connects the bladder to the outside is called the *urethra*.

The urethra in mares is short and wide. It can be catheterized easily by a rigid catheter.

In the male, the urethra is long and narrow. To facilitate handling of the penis and passage of the catheter, the horse should be tranquilized. This also paralyzes the muscle that retracts the penis, allowing the penis to protrude.

The chief function of the kidneys is to maintain water and electrolyte balance and excrete the wastes of metabolism. This is accomplished by *nephrons*, the tiny basic working units of the kidneys.

Equine urine normally is cloudy, strong-smelling, alkaline, and often rather mucoid. After standing for some time it frequently assumes a dark coffee color, the result of oxidation of pigments.

Fresh urine that is dark and coffee-colored suggests the presence of myoglobin seen in *azoturia* (tying-up syndrome), hemoglobin (hemolytic anemia), or bile (seen in jaundice). Certain drugs may cause the urine to turn red when exposed to light.

A urinalysis will distinguish between natural pigments and those present from other causes. Blood in urine cannot be distinguished from pigment unless clots are seen.

The act of voiding is under the control of the central nervous system and spinal cord. A horse can decide when to void, but the actual mechanics of bladder emptying are controlled by a complicated spinal cord reflex.

SIGNS OF URINARY TRACT DISEASE

Dysuria (painful urination) and straining to urinate are the two most important signs of *lower urinary tract* infection. Cystitis, urethritis, and bladder stones are the usual causes. Azoturia should be considered, since the passage of myoglobin can produce pain on urination. Blister beetle poisoning is an unusual cause of dysuria.

A horse with dysuria assumes a stretched-out posture for voiding but does not immediately void. Groaning and contraction of the abdominal wall muscles are signs of straining. In males, the penis is often relaxed and protruded. A horse with dysuria often voids frequently in small amounts. Mares may exhibit urine scalds of the perineum.

Hematuria is the passage of blood in the urine. Microscopic hematuria is blood visible under a microscope. Microscopic hematuria can also be identified by a urine dip stick. When clots visible to the eye are present, the problem is either cystitis or urinary tract stones.

Polyuria is the passage of unusually large amounts of urine. The bladder capacity of the adult horse is about 1 gallon. Horses normally void several times a day. The normal adult horse fed alfalfa hay and having access to water will produce about 4 gallons of urine per day. Much larger volumes are seen in horses who consume large amounts of salt (*psychogenic salt consumption*). Polyuria, if not otherwise explained, indicates chronic kidney failure.

A horse with polyuria exhibits extreme thirst and drinks a lot more than usual to compensate for urine losses. In fact, extreme thirst and continual drinking of water are more likely to call attention to the problem than is the large urine output.

DIAGNOSTIC STUDIES

Owing to the heavy bacterial contamination that occurs in voided specimens from horses, urine is best obtained by inserting a catheter or obtaining a midstream specimen. Sterile technique should be used when inserting a catheter to avoid introducing bacteria into the lower urinary tract and causing infection.

Rectal palpation is a useful examination in urinary tract disease. It often indicates the condition of the bladder and the presence of stones in the lower urinary tract. An enlarged kidney, collecting system, or bladder may be detected by palpation.

Transrectal or abdominal ultrasonography is useful in visualizing the size and appearance of structures in the urinary tract. Small shrunken kidneys, stones, and abnormalities not apparent on palpation are often revealed by the ultrasound. This equipment is also helpful in placing a needle in the correct position for kidney biopsy.

Fiberoptic cystoscopy provides the opportunity to visualize and biopsy the interior of the bladder.

X-rays using injected dye to outline the urinary collecting system are technically difficult to perform in adult horses, and generally are useful only in foals. Plain x-rays of the pelvis may show urinary tract stones.

Blood chemistries provide essential information about kidney function.

Urinary Tract Infections

Infection in the urethra (*urethritis*) is associated with diseases of the male reproductive system. It is discussed in chapter 14, Sex and Reproduction.

BLADDER INFECTION (CYSTITIS)

Inflammation of the lining of the bladder is called *cystitis*. Infections of the urethra in both males and females usually precede the development of cystitis.

The bladder of horses is relatively resistant to infection. Accordingly, cystitis usually does not occur unless there is an additional problem that prevents bladder emptying or lowers natural defenses. Such predisposing conditions include late pregnancy, prolonged labor, bladder stones, and paralyzed bladder.

Signs of bladder infection are frequent painful voiding, hematuria, and straining. A male horse may stand with its penis dropped, and a mare may have a vaginal discharge with scalding of the skin. A catheterized urine specimen reveals pus, blood, and bacteria. Fever and loss of appetite do not occur unless the upper urinary tract is also infected, which is more serious than cystitis.

Treatment: Early diagnosis and treatment will decrease the risk and occurrence of chronic cystitis and/or pyelonephritis. It is important to exclude the presence of bladder stones.

A urine culture and sensitivity should be obtained to screen for the antibiotic most effective against the bacteria in question. A first attack should be treated with antibiotics for 14 days, and a second or recurrent attack for 1 month. Repeat the urine culture 1 week after starting treatment. Change to a new antibiotic if the sensitivity studies show that the first antibiotic was not effective or if bacteria are still present in the urine.

PYELONEPHRITIS

Pyelonephritis is a bacterial infection of the upper urinary tract (kidney, pelvis, ureter). Pyelonephritis may affect one or both kidneys. A bladder infection often precedes pyelonephritis. Most cases occur in postpartum mares, presumably as a result of the stasis of pregnancy.

Signs of pyelonephritis are fever, colic, weight loss, loss of appetite, and depression. These signs are not specific and do not necessarily point to the urinary tract. However, when cystitis is also present, urinary symptoms will be noted.

The urine contains pus, bacteria, blood, protein, and epithelial cells. Rectal palpation and ultrasound studies show enlargement of the kidneys or ureters. When infection has been present for several weeks, laboratory tests and ultrasonography are apt to reveal reduced kidney function and small shrunken kidneys.

Treatment: The treatment of pyelonephritis is like that described for recurrent cystitis. Antibiotics, selected on the basis of bacterial sensitivity tests, should be continued for 4 to 6 weeks. Re-culture in 2 weeks and change the antibiotics as circumstances warrant. Culture again at the end of treatment to be sure the infection has been eliminated. If bacteria are still present, continue treatment.

Pyelonephritis is insidious and chronic in horses. Many cases are not discovered until there is extensive loss of kidney function and localized pockets of pus that are difficult to eradicate with antibiotics. If only one kidney is badly damaged and the other kidney is normal, the damaged kidney should be removed to eradicate a source of infection.

PARALYZED BLADDER

Paralysis of the bladder accompanies spinal cord injuries, the cauda equina syndrome, and equine herpes myeloencephalitis. These diseases are described in chapter 11, Nervous System.

Sorghum cystitis ataxia is a type of bladder paralysis that occurs in horses who graze pastures containing Sudan grass, Johnson grass, Columbus grass, and sorghums. These pastures are found in the southwestern United States. Sorghum poisoning causes degenerative changes in the sacral spinal cord.

Irrespective of cause, a paralyzed bladder empties only by overflow. The characteristic sign is dribbling of urine. When the horse coughs or strains, urine spurts from the urethra. In males, the penis is often relaxed and extended. In mares, the vulva and skin of the buttocks may be scalded. Rectal palpation reveals a large flaccid bladder, often containing stones. There is a pool of static urine and sediment that serves as a culture medium for bacteria of many species.

In addition to the bladder problem, horses with spinal cord disease exhibit varying degrees of hindquarter unsteadiness, with a weaving gait and a tendency for the legs to buckle. There is loss of anal tone.

Treatment: Horses with sorghum cystitis ataxia may improve after the toxic grass has been removed from the diet. Complete recovery is rare.

Management of a paralyzed bladder involves intermittent drainage by urinary catheter as determined by the horse's level of comfort, ability to tolerate the full bladder, and status of infection. Drugs are available that can stimulate bladder emptying and relax the uretheral muscles. Success is uncertain.

Attacks of acute cystitis or pyelonephritis occur and require continuous catheter drainage and antibiotics. The use of prophylactic antibiotics may reduce the frequency of such episodes. Application of petroleum jelly will help to prevent urine scalds. Manual evacuation of stool from the rectum is often necessary to prevent impaction.

Recurrent episodes of pyelonephritis ultimately lead to kidney failure. The longer the horse is impaired, the worse the prognosis.

URINARY TRACT STONES

Stones are not common in horses. The majority occur in the bladder or urethra. Kidney and ureteral stones, although common in people, are rare in horses.

They are usually bilateral and produce chronic renal failure before they are diagnosed.

Bladder and urethral stones affect middle-aged and geriatric male horses. Forages that contain large amounts of calcium, ammonia, and magnesium predispose to stone formation, as do grains containing a high content of phosphorus. Stasis and infection in the lower urinary tract are important associated findings in many horses with bladder stones.

Bladder stones in mares usually pass easily and cause few signs. This is because the urethra of the mare is short and wide.

In stallions and geldings, the long narrow urethra prevents the passage of most bladder and urethral stones. These stones obstruct. Signs of incomplete obstruction are straining, painful urination, and the passage of clots—often noted at the end of urination.

Complete unrelieved urethral obstruction is characterized by severe colic with groaning and rolling. It is likely to progress to rupture of the bladder and subsequent peritonitis.

The diagnosis of bladder and urethral stones can be made by rectal palpation and/or transrectal ultrasound. Passing a catheter to decompress the bladder may dislodge an impacted stone. Fiberoptic cystoscopy is useful in determining the size, number, and location of the stones. This information is useful in planning treatment.

Treatment: Most male horses with lower urinary tract stones require surgery to open the bladder or urethra and remove the stones. The use of prophylactic antibiotics and urinary acidifiers (such as ammonium chloride) after treatment may help prevent the formation of new stones.

Management of a ruptured bladder depends on the size of the tear and whether the horse is voiding after removal of the blockage. The two alternatives are antibiotics alone, or antibiotics plus surgical repair of the bladder.

Rupture of the bladder in newborn foals is discussed in chapter 16, Pediatrics.

Kidney Diseases

Diseases of the kidney attack either the glomerulus (the capillary network that produces the urine) or the renal tubule (the filtering mechanism that concentrates the urine). Signs of disease are those of kidney failure, discussed below.

GLOMERULONEPHRITIS

Glomerulonephritis is an inflammatory disease that targets the glomerulus. It is the most common cause of chronic renal failure in horses.

This disease appears to be related to a malfunction of the horse's immune system. The virus of equine infectious anemia has been identified as a specific cause. Certain strains of streptococcus bacteria have also been shown to cause acute glomerulonephritis in horses. In many cases the cause is unknown.

The diagnosis is established by needle biopsy of the kidney.

Treatment: Corticosteroids may suppress the immune reaction and slow the progress of the disease. However, glomerulonephritis eventually leads to chronic kidney failure.

INTERSTITIAL NEPHRITIS AND NEPHROSIS

These are predominantly diseases of the renal tubules. They are a common cause of acute and chronic renal failure.

A number of nephrotoxic drugs produce interstitial nephritis. Among the most common are the antibiotics gentamicin and neomycin; Butazolidin and other NSAIDs; sulfonamide antibiotics; dewormers containing carbon tetrachloride and tetrachloroethylene; and insecticides containing toxaphene.

Problems with the antibiotics and NSAIDs occur when the recommended dosage is exceeded, or when the drug is administered over a long period. Drug-induced kidney failure is reversible if the drug is withdrawn before permanent damage. Most (but not all) horses recover within a few weeks. Those that do not recover develop chronic renal failure.

Pyelonephritis, and stones that block the ureters, are other causes of interstitial nephritis.

Acute tubular nephrosis is the name given to the kidney damage that occurs with fulminate infections accompanied by endotoxemia, dehydration, and circulatory collapse. Most cases occur with intestinal clostridiosis and other forms of infectious colitis. Early and aggressive treatment of the endotoxemia and circulatory failure offers the best prospect for kidney recovery.

Myoglobin is a pigment released from oxygen-starved muscle. Hemoglobin is released from destroyed red cells. Diseases that cause the sudden release of large amounts of these pigments (*azoturia, hemolytic anemias*) will result in the formation of pigment casts in the nephrons that obstruct the flow of urine and impair circulation to the kidneys. The kidney failure is usually reversible if the horse recovers from the causative illness.

Treatment of nephritis and nephrosis is directed at the primary disease.

Kidney Failure

Kidney failure is defined as the inability of the kidneys to remove nitrogen and other wastes from the blood. The buildup of toxic chemicals produces signs and symptoms of uremic poisoning.

ACUTE KIDNEY FAILURE (AKF)

Acute kidney failure (AKF) comes on suddenly. The predominant signs are severe depression with marked loss of appetite. In early AKF, the urine output is decreased or absent. However, in the recovery phase, the volume is much greater than normal.

Laboratory studies show elevated serum creatinine and blood urea nitrogen (BUN). Urinalysis may show increased protein and numerous white cells. The presence of pathogenic bacteria indicates an infectious origin. Large amounts of hemoglobin or myoglobin pigment in the urine indicate tubular disease secondary to *azoturia* or *hemolytic anemia*. Abdominal or transrectal ultrasound may reveal stones or pyelonephritis.

Causes of acute kidney failure include:

- Shock, when due to sudden blood loss, rapid dehydration, or endotoxemia.
- Complete blockage of the urethra by a stone.
- Blockage of both ureters by stones.
- Rupture of the bladder with urine peritonitis.
- Myoglobinuria, caused by azoturia or the myositis of prolonged reumbency.
- Hemoglobinuria, caused by a hemolytic anemia.
- Exposure to nephrotoxic drugs.
- Exposure to nephrotoxic plants, especially cultivated and wild onions, certain oak species, withered red maple leaves, wild jasmine, locoweed, mycotoxins in cereal grains, and blister beetles in alfalfa.
- Exposure to heavy metal poisons (mercury, arsenic, selenium, and copper).

Treatment of AKF is directed at correcting shock and dehydration, eliminating urinary tract infections and obstructions, stopping exposure to nephrotoxic drugs and poisons, and supporting the horse during the acute phase of the illness.

CHRONIC KIDNEY FAILURE (CKF)

Horses with chronic kidney failure (CKF) do not begin to show signs of failure until 70 percent of the kidney's nephrons are destroyed. At this point the causative illness often is no longer present, making its identification difficult or impossible.

Causes of CRF include:

- Acute kidney failure that has gone on to a chronic stage
- Glomerulonephritis
- Interstitial nephritis
- Chronic pyelonephritis
- Vitamin D intoxication
- Exposure to nephrotoxins
- Kidney tumors

The most important sign of CKF is unexplained weight loss. Unfortunately, this is not specific for kidney disease.

Failing kidneys lose the ability to retain protein, concentrate urine, and conserve water. Accordingly, horses with CKF have an obligatory output of dilute urine, and must drink a large volume of water to compensate. An alert owner may notice that the horse has an extreme thirst, or that its stall is wet a lot more than usual. A urinalysis will reveal that the specific gravity of the urine is low and the protein high.

Because damaged kidneys do not retain protein, the serum protein is low, which favors fluid accumulation in the subcutaneous tissues of the abdomen (*ventral edema*), and marked swelling of the lower extremities. Dependent edema is particularly characteristic of chronic glomerulonephritis.

As kidney function deteriorates further, the horse retains ammonia, nitrogen, potassium, acids, and other wastes in the blood and tissues, a syndrome called *uremic poisoning*. Signs of uremia include depression, refusal to eat, weight loss, anemia, ammonia-like odor to the breath, mouth ulcerations, and an excessive buildup of tartar on the teeth. At the end, the horse falls into a coma.

Treatment: Your veterinarian may wish to make an exact diagnosis by performing a kidney biopsy. This helps to plan treatment and determine prognosis.

It is important to provide unlimited access to fresh water. A salt block should be available as long as the horse does not develop edema or hypertension, in which case salt should be restricted. It is important to restrict calcium in the diet, since uremic horses retain calcium.

Encourage appetite and nutrition by feeding a high-carbohydrate diet, such as good-quality timothy or grass hay with corn grain. Avoid alfalfa and feeds high in protein that increase nitrogen consumption and thus contribute to uremia (see Table II in chapter 17, Feeding and Nutrition). The horse's serum electrolytes (sodium, potassium, bicarbonate), calcium, and kidney function tests should be monitored at frequent intervals. This may anticipate and prevent acidosis, mineral and electrolyte imbalances, and other complications. Some exercise is good for a uremic horse, but stressful activity should be avoided.

SEX AND REPRODUCTION

The Mare

FEMALE ANATOMY

The mare's reproductive system is composed of the ovaries, fallopian tubes (*oviducts*), uterus, vagina, and vulva.

The ovaries are bean-shaped and vary in size from 1.5 inches during the nonbreeding season to 3 inches during heat. In addition to producing the eggs (*ova*), the ovaries produce the sex hormones, which prepare the reproductive tract for mating, fertilization, and support of pregnancy.

The surface of the ovary is composed of a capsule of fibrous connective tissue, which prevents egg follicles from developing on its surface. As a follicle inside the ovary enlarges and prepares to ovulate, the follicle migrates toward a chute-like recess in the ovary called the *ovulation fossa*.

The uterus is composed of a cervix, body, and two horns. The cavity of the uterus is lined by a layer of tissue called the *endometrium*. The body of the uterus is about 10 inches long. Each horn is an additional 8 inches.

The oviducts carry the eggs from the ovulation fossa down into the horns of the uterus. This process takes 5 to 6 days. However, an unfertilized egg can live for only 12 hours. Accordingly, the ovum must encounter a viable sperm in the oviduct within 12 hours of ovulation for fertilization to take place.

The newly fertilized embryo arrives in the uterus at about 6 days post-ovulation. It now begins a state of wandering about in the uterus, passing from one horn to the other, and then back into the uterus, finally implanting in the body of the uterus at the base of one of the horns at 16 days of gestation. This wandering back

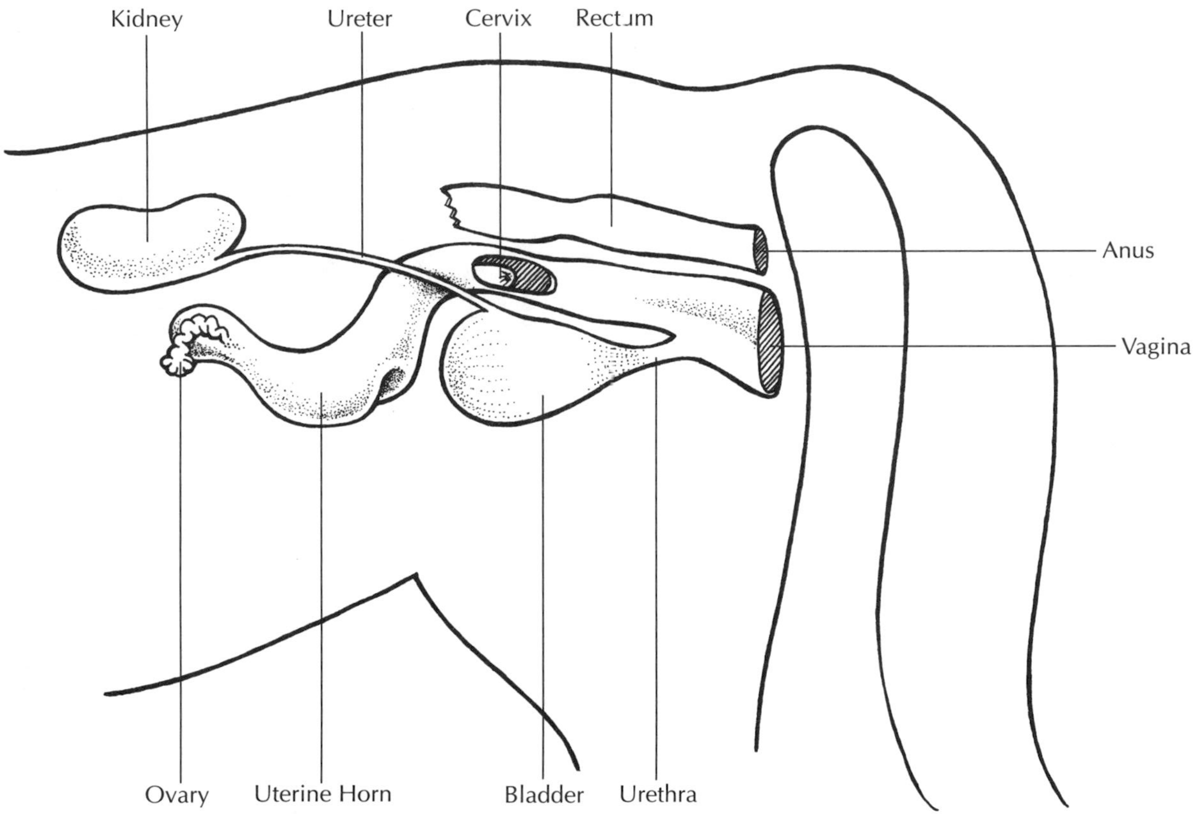

Female Reproductive System

Kidney

Ovary

Uterine Horn

Ureter

Bladder

Cervix

Urethra

Rectum

Vagina

Anus

and forth across the endometrium stimulates the endometrium to stop producing a hormone called PGF2α. This hormone, a prostaglandin, acts on the ovary to cause the corpus luteum (CL) to regress. If the CL should regress, progesterone levels would fall dramatically and the endometrium would shed, causing the embryo to die. Thus by wandering about in the uterus for 16 days, the embryo suppresses the production of prostaglandin and ensures its own survival.

There are three physical barriers that guard the uterus from bacterial infection. The first is the tight cervix, projecting into the back of the vagina, which in the sexually quiescent mare is about the same length and diameter as an index finger. The cervix shortens and widens during the receptive phase of heat, allowing sperm to enter the uterus after breeding. The second barrier is the vulvovaginal sphincter. This is a muscular ring located inside the vaginal opening where the hymen is located in a maiden mare. The third barrier is the arrangement of the vulva, or lips of the vagina, which close the vaginal entroitus. The adult vagina itself is 18 inches long.

NATURAL BREEDING SEASON

The natural or physiologic breeding season should be distinguished from the man-made or operational breeding season discussed below.

Mares are seasonal breeders. The natural mating season is determined by a number of factors including the length of daylight, temperature, nutrition, rainfall, climate, and latitude. After a period of ovarian inactivity lasting through the winter months (called *anestrus*), the natural reproductive season in the northern hemisphere begins in April and continues through September. In high northern latitudes the breeding season is shorter, while in deep southern latitudes mares may cycle all year long.

It has been shown that the length of daylight has a direct affect on ovarian activity. This effect is mediated through the optic nerves and pineal gland. As day lengthens, melatonin secretion from the pineal gland begins to decline. Falling levels of melatonin signal the hypothalamus to release GnRH (*gonadotropin-releasing hormone*).

GnRH is barely detectable during deep winter anestrus, but within 2 to 3 weeks of exposure to increasing day length, plasma levels begin to rise. GnRH triggers the pituitary gland to release first FSH (*follicle-stimulating hormone*), which wakes up the ovaries, and then LH (*luteinizing hormone*), which triggers ovulation.

Both FSH and LH follow a distinct seasonal profile, with plasma LH rising more slowly than FSH in the spring, and dropping more quickly than FSH in the fall. The discrepancy between the timing and presence of these two hormones is the reason why anovulatory heat cycles (heat cycles without ovulation) are seen in early spring and late autumn.

December 22, the winter solstice, is the day with the shortest period of daylight. Seventy percent of mares are in deep anestrus at this time and the number increases to about 85 percent by mid-January. In March, some of these mares begin to develop cyclic ovarian activity. The first cycles may not be accompanied by ovulation; but by the middle of April to the first of May, with the increased number of daylight hours, more sun, warmer temperatures, and green grass, nearly all mares are cycling consistently. Conception rates peak during June.

The advantage of the natural breeding season is that when a mare is bred in summer, she foals in the spring, when conditions are most hospitable for raising a foal.

OPERATIONAL BREEDING SEASON

Thoroughbred racing associations and breed registries have designated January 1 as a universal birth date. In effect, all foals born at any time during the year automatically become yearlings on January 1 of the following year. In the southern hemisphere, the universal (artificial) birth date is August 1. The effect of the artificial birth date is to emphasize early births for larger, stronger weanlings and yearlings. A colt born in January, for example, has an athletic advantage over one born in June. But in order to produce foals early in the year, breeding must begin during the winter months of natural subfertility, creating the man-made or *operational* breeding season, which begins February 15 and ends July 15.

Artificial Light Program. What makes this all possible is an artificial light program. By exposing the mare to increasing photoperiods (natural plus artificial light), winter anestrus can be shortened and the mating season started earlier than would be the case if one depended on length of day alone. Since it takes at least 60 days to induce early ovulation with artificial light, if the breeding season is to start on February 15, lighting should be initiated between November 15 and December 15. The best results are obtained when the mare is exposed to 15 hours of continuous light a day. The full 15 hours can be provided from the first day of the program, or artificial light can be added at the rate of 30 minutes a week until 15 hours of continuous light are achieved.

Artificial light schedules must be consistent. Irregular schedules will not induce heat and may even throw the mare back into anestrus. A 200-watt incandescent bulb or a 400-watt fluorescent light bulb is an effective light for a stall. For pens and paddocks, incandescent, mercury vapor, sodium, or quartz lights are suitable if the intensity of light is such that a newspaper can be read at any point within the enclosure. The lighting system can be equipped with an automatic timer.

THE HEAT CYCLE (ESTROUS CYCLE)

The estrous or heat cycle is the period from one ovulation to the next. The length of the cycle is 21 to 23 days. This may vary by a few days, especially at the beginning and the end of the breeding season.

When a filly reaches puberty, she becomes sexually mature and begins to produce ova. This usually happens between 10 and 24 months of age, with 18 months being the average. At this time she can become pregnant. However, most horse breeders believe that a 2-year-old mare is too immature to be bred. After she is 1 year old, separate the filly from the stallion to prevent accidental pregnancy.

The reproductive cycle of the mare is divided into two phases: *estrus* and *diestrus*. Estrus is the phase in which the mare is actively interested in and receptive to the stallion. This is also when she ovulates. Diestrus is the period of sexual disinterest which begins 24 to 48 hours after ovulation and lasts 14 to 16 days. It is followed by a return to estrus.

Estrus (Heat). The duration of estrus is variable. Early in the year it lasts 6 to 8 days, but by midsummer it decreases to about 4 days.

The hormonal effects which govern estrus and ovulation are complex. In brief, the pituitary gland releases a hormone called FSH (*follicle-stimulating hormone*), which causes egg follicles within the ovary to grow and produce increasing amounts of estrogen. Estrogen prepares the reproductive tract for mating and fertilization, and is also responsible for the behavioral changes of the estrus mare.

When the egg follicle approaches maturity, the pituitary releases a second hormone called LH (*luteinizing hormone*), which causes the follicle to ovulate. Ovulation usually occurs about 24 hours before the end of heat.

Typical stance of a mare in standing heat.

Winking of the labia with presentation of the clitoris.

A mare in standing heat who is receptive to breeding displays typical estrus behavior in the presence of a stallion. She presents her hindquarters to the stallion and, if separated by a partition, leans back against it. The receptive attitude includes a squatting posture, raised tail, flexed pelvis, urination, and spasmodic "winking" of the labia with presentation of the clitoris.

Diestrus (Luteal Phase). Diestrus begins with an abrupt change in behavior in which the mare refuses the stallion and exhibits her rejection by laying back her ears, wheeling, squealing, kicking, and occasionally biting and pawing.

Twenty-four hours after ovulation, the egg follicle in the ovary fills with blood. The blood is replaced in 5 days by the mature *corpus luteum* (CL). The CL is a yellow mass within the ovary that produces the pregnancy hormone *progesterone*. A critical function of progesterone is to prepare the lining of the uterus to receive, support, and maintain the embryo. If the corpus luteum fails in this task, the embryo will be lost.

What happens to the CL depends upon whether the mare becomes pregnant. If pregnancy does not occur, the corpus luteum remains active for only 12 to 14 days. It then undergoes rapid regression. This is followed in 3 days by a new estrous cycle.

If pregnancy does occur, the uterus recognizes the pregnancy (as described earlier) and sends a message to the CL to continue progesterone production until the placenta takes over this task. This transition occurs between day 70 and 90 of gestation.

The laid-back ears of a mare in diestrus.

Abnormal Heat Cycles

Mares are notorious for displaying profound and frustrating inconsistency in their heat cycles. The average interval is 21 to 22 days, but some mares cycle at shorter, longer, or less regular intervals. Maiden mares, and mares over 15 years of age, are most likely to have irregular heat cycles, especially at the beginning and end of the breeding season.

When a mare fails to breed or fails to conceive after breeding, the cause should be investigated. The first step is to determine if the mare is cycling (having estrous periods).

DETERMINING ESTRUS

The standard methods for determining estrus are teasing, rectal palpation, and ultrasonography.

Teasing. The teasing behavior of the stallion and mare indicate to the experienced stallion manager when the mare is receptive and about to ovulate. The most decisive indicator of receptivity is when the mare presents her hindquarters to the stallion, stands in the braced position, and swishes her tail to the side. A positive teasing response normally indicates the mare is cycling. For more information on teasing procedures, see WHEN TO BREED.

Rectal Palpation. The estrous cycle produces changes in the mare's reproductive tract that indicate whether she is experiencing the hormonal effects associated with estrus. These changes can be identified by rectal palpation. Experience is required to interpret the findings. The organs affected by the sex hormones are the uterus, ovaries, vagina, and cervix.

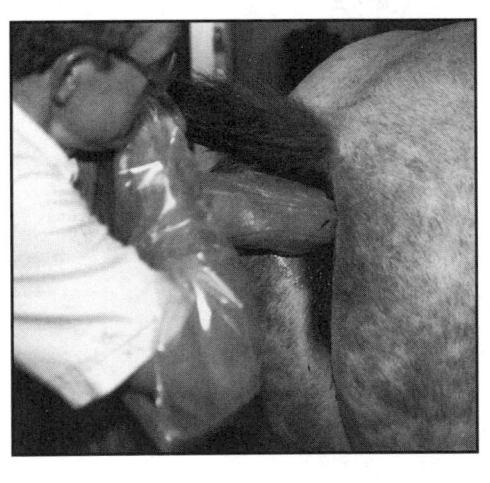

Rectal palpation helps to determine if the mare is cycling.

The horns of the uterus exhibit a degree of firmness (tone) which changes with the heat cycle. During diestrus, the uterus feels quite firm and does not indent on pressure. As estrus and ovulation approach, the wall of the uterus becomes less firm to finger pressure and does not spring back after indentation, a condition similar to pitting edema.

The ovaries are about twice as large during estrus as they are during anestrus. As ovulation approaches, one follicle becomes larger and begins to soften (*dominant follicle*). Ovulation can be expected when the dominant follicle is about 4.0 cm in size. After ovulation, an ovulatory depression can be felt at the site of the follicle (the *corpus hemorrhagica*), which is followed in 5 days by the development of the corpus luteum (CL). The CL lies within the ovary and so cannot be palpated.

During anestrus and diestrus, the cervix is a long firm muscular tube about the size of an index finger, and the canal is tightly closed. Under the influence of estrus, the cervix softens. It becomes shorter by about one-half as the width doubles. The cervix opens to permit the ingress of sperm.

Ultrasonography. Transrectal ultrasound examination helps to confirm the findings of rectal palpation. The uterus during estrus shows characteristic folds caused by estrogen-induced swelling of the endometrium. These folds disappear just prior to ovulation. A follicle about to ovulate changes shape from spherical to teardrop and leaks fluid toward the ovulation fossa.

Anovulatory follicles, a persistent corpus luteum, twin pregnancies, tumors, and other abnormalities also can be seen on ultrasonography.

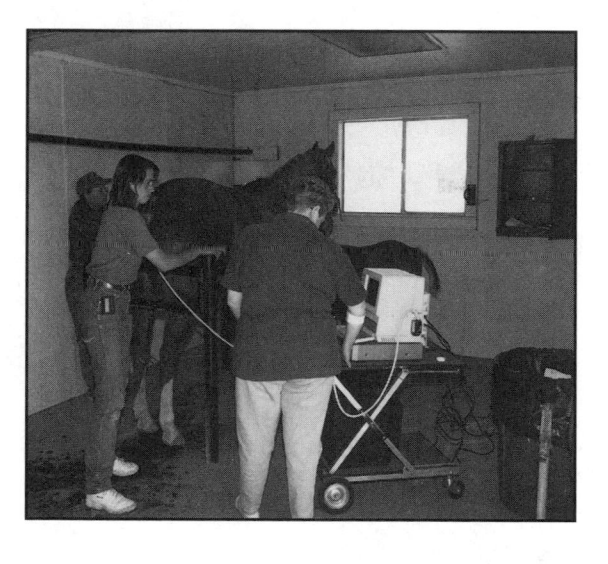

Ovulation, pregnancy, twins, persistent corpus luteum, and other conditions can be diagnosed by ultrasonography.

If it is determined by teasing, rectal palpation, or ultrasonography that the mare is not cycling normally, or is cycling but not reacting normally to the hormonal influences of estrus, the problem may be anestrus, transitional heat period, persistent corpus luteum, silent heat, or (rarely) nymphomania. These problems are discussed below.

ANESTRUS

Anestrus is lack of estrus, or failure to cycle.

Seasonal anestrus is a physiologically normal state of ovarian inactivity that occurs in the winter months. Pregnancy is the most common cause of anestrus during the breeding season.

Absence of cyclical activity and failure to ovulate are closely associated with diseases affecting the uterus. A mare with pyometra or endometritis often will not cycle because the damaged endometrium does not produce prostaglandin. Lacking prostaglandin, the CL persists for long periods during which the mare does not ovulate (see PERSISTENT CORPUS LUTEUM).

A mare who has had an ovariectomy (a fact that may not be known to a new owner) does not have ovaries and will not cycle.

Gonadal dysgenesis, ovarian hypoplasia, and testicular feminization are rare diseases related to chromosomal abnormalities. Mares with gonadal dysgenesis and testicular feminization do not possess functional ovaries. Mares with ovarian hypoplasia may exhibit occasional or very irregular cycles. These abnormalities can be diagnosed by rectal palpation and ultrasonography. Occasionally, chromosome analysis is required. Fertility is not possible in any of these disorders.

The most common tumor of the ovary is a benign granulosa-theca cell tumor. This tumor, which is found most often in mares 5 to 7 years of age, produces large amounts of estrogen. Estrogen exerts a negative feedback on the pituitary, which ceases to produce FSH and LH and thus shuts down the ovaries. On rectal palpation and ultrasonography, the ovary with the tumor is large and the other ovary is small, firm, and inactive. Despite the fact that these mares do not cycle, they may exhibit strong estrus behavior due to high levels of circulating estrogen. Treatment involves removing the diseased ovary.

Tumors of the hypothalamus or anterior pituitary gland can cause cyclic failure by interfering with the production of the sex hormones. These tumors are rare.

Anabolic steroids and testosterone adversely affect the ovaries. Mares receiving these drugs (usually to enhance racing performance) have smaller ovaries and generally do not ovulate. Negative effects can occur for up to 6 months after steroids are stopped. These mares are often aggressive and difficult to cover. Accordingly, performance-enhancing drugs should be avoided when breeding is anticipated.

Debilitation anestrus occurs among run-down, underfed, emaciated mares who are habitually overworked. Chronic diseases, especially a heavy burden of parasites, contribute to a run-down state. Old mares with uncared-for teeth are subject to nutritional deficiencies and weight loss. Rectal palpation reveals small, firm, inactive ovaries. The uterus is flaccid. The mare shows no signs of estrus when teased.

The estrous cycle can often be restored by correcting the cause of debilitation.

TRANSITIONAL HEAT PERIOD

At the beginning (and end) of seasonal estrous, many mares are inconsistent in their heat cycles, exhibiting signs of heat without ovulating. Although actually not an abnormal heat cycle, seasonal anestrus becomes a problem for farm managers who would like to have their mares bred early in the spring so they can foal as close to the universal birth date (January 1) as possible.

Ultrasound findings in transitional estrus include multiple anovulatory ovarian follicles 2 to 3 cm in size. These follicles produce the estrogen that causes the observed signs of heat. The reason these mares do not ovulate is the lag in pituitary production of LH, discussed under NATURAL BREEDING SEASON. Pituitary and plasma levels of LH are not yet high enough during transition to trigger ovulation. Instead of an orderly progression to a dominant follicle which matures and ovulates, seasonally anovulatory follicles all collapse together, after which a new cycle begins. Ultimately, a dominant follicle (3.5 cm or larger) develops at a time when LH pituitary stores are adequate. This results in ovulation, which ends the transitional period.

Treatment: Anovulatory follicles do not require treatment unless breeding for the artificial birth date. The increase in the spring photoperiod will start the breeding season spontaneously in May or June.

The most effective method of hastening the breeding season is to institute an artificial light program as described earlier. Keep the mare in good condition and feed just enough additional energy to permit gradual weight gain. Regular teasing with a stallion is helpful in bringing on early estrus.

A daily progesterone injection for 7 to 14 days may shorten the transition period and advance the first ovulation. Results are inconsistent, but if successful, a normal estrus occurs 3 to 5 days after the injections are stopped. Normal cycles follow, with a 50 percent conception rate on the first service.

Prolonged Estrus. This is a variation of transitional estrus in which the mare shows sustained receptivity to the stallion. A large percentage of mares, especially maiden and barren mares, exhibit this behavior. The cause is failure of the anovulatory follicles to collapse, resulting in a persistently high output of estrogen.

Due to the high estrogen influence, the mare may allow the stallion for 30 days to mount and breed, and may continue to do so for up to 2 to 3 months. This presents problems. If the horse owner is not familiar with the condition, he or she may conclude that since the mare continues to breed without becoming pregnant, she must be infertile. Another problem is that multiple acts of coitus increase the likelihood of developing a bacterial infection of the mare's reproductive tract.

Treatment: Wait 1 month before breeding. During this time most mares will begin to ovulate and can be successfully bred. If immediate breeding is desired and the mare has a mature follicle over 3.5 cm in size, ovulation can often be induced by an injection of human chorionic gonadotropin (HCG). Ovulation should occur within 48 hours. Breed the mare immediately after the injection of HCG in anticipation of ovulation.

In the absence of a preovulatory follicle, a course of progesterone as described above may induce estrus and advance the date of ovulation.

Split Estrus. This uncommon condition is more frequent during the transition period. The hormonal basis is not known. The mare shows to the stallion for a few days, goes out of heat for several days, and then returns to estrus and ovulates. Split estrus appears to be influenced by stress, transportation to the stud, and improper teasing methods. The advent of the natural breeding season should resolve the problem.

PERSISTENT CORPUS LUTEUM (PROLONGED DIESTRUS)

Persistent CL is a common cause of lack of estrus behavior during the breeding season. It lasts 1 to 3 months, with an average of 60 days.

A persistent CL results in prolongation of the diestrus stage of the heat cycle. Some mares with a persistent CL will ovulate during diestrus. However, they will not show estrus behavior or stand for the stud. The reason for this is that high levels of progesterone produced by the CL block the behavioral effects of estrus.

The cause of persistent CL is insufficient prostaglandin (PGF2α) output from the endometrium of the uterus. What causes this to happen in a specific instance is generally not known.

In the nonpregnant uterus, the endometrium synthesizes and releases PGF2α, which travels to the ovary and there causes regression and disappearance of the CL. It follows that conditions which interfere with endometrial PGF2α production or release will be associated with a persistent CL and high levels of progesterone. An endometrium partially destroyed by pyometra or endometritis is an example.

The embryo forces the uterus to recognize pregnancy and inhibit PGF2α release by contacting the entire surface of the endometrium during the initial mobility phase, described earlier in this chapter. Loss of the embryo after this uterine recognition process may prolong diestrus for several days, assuming that remnants of the embryo remain in contact with the endometrium. Thus a prolonged diestrus without other signs may be the only indication of a missed pregnancy.

Another cause of a persistent CL is established pregnancy complicated by early embryonic death (EEG), abortion, or fetal reabsorption *after* day 36 of pregnancy. By day 37, specialized fetal cells called *endometrial cups* interdigitate with the endometrium, forming the earliest attachment of the developing fetus to its mother. The endometrial cups produce measurable amounts of equine chorionic gonadotropin (eCG; formally known as *pregnant mare serum gonadotropin,* or *PMSG*). eCG has the effect of stimulating and prolonging the CL, giving the appearance of a continuing pregnancy. The mare will not return to estrus until the endometrial cups cease to function, which does not occur for several months.

When the embryo is lost *before* day 36, the CL regresses within several days, and the mare returns to estrus.

The diagnosis of persistent CL is made by rectal palpation that reveals a nonpregnant uterus with a long, closed cervix and increased uterine tone. The CL is not palpable because it is buried in the ovary. However, it can usually be seen by ultrasound. A high serum progesterone in the pregnancy range confirms the diagnosis.

Treatment: An injection of prostaglandin causes the CL to regress, provided that the CL has been present for at least 4 to 5 days. The mare will return to estrus in 3 to 5 days. A CL less than 4 to 5 days old will be refractory to prostaglandin. Administer a second dose 7 to 10 days later.

Vaginal douching with sterile saline and antibiotics to stimulate release of PGF2α from the uterus is not as effective as giving PGF2α by injection. Curettage of the uterus is questionable.

Estrogen administration is not effective and will actually prolong the CL.

SILENT HEAT (UNOBSERVED ESTRUS)

Silent heat, also called *behavioral* or *psychological anestrus*, is an emotional disorder in mares characterized by normal estrous cycles but lack of receptivity to the stallion. Veterinary examination discloses the presence of heat and ovulation, but the mare fails to show the normal behavior signs of estrus.

Occasionally what appears to be lack of heat is actually the handler's lack of familiarity with the subtler signs of estrus. Some estrous mares exhibit diminished estrous behavior and require prolonged and intense teasing to demonstrate receptivity to the stallion.

Silent heat is common in nervous mares, shy mares, maiden mares, and mares with foals. *Lactation anestrus* occurs in mares who are extremely possessive of their suckling foals and will not breed when the foal is by their side. Despite the name, these mares are not anestrus, and the condition is not related to lactation. An approach to diminishing the mare's possessiveness is to allow the foal to suckle only four times a day.

A common cause of silent heat is ineffectual teasing practices. Mares should be teased frequently (once a day or every other day) on a regular schedule. Regular teasing helps to bring the mare into heat. Irregular teasing may delay the development of heat behavior, and can lead to missing the moment of receptivity to the stallion.

Intense stimulation and much patience are required when teasing mares with diminished estrus behavior. Techniques such as changing stallions, changing location, and flank and vulvar presentation may be required before mares with prolonged reaction time will exhibit estrus behavior. Most mares, however, when intensively teased at full heat, will show some signs of estrus to the experienced handler and can be successfully bred.

Repeated rectal palpation with or without ultrasounds can be used to time ovulation. An ovulating mare who continues to refuse the stallion can be twitched and hobbled, permitting the stallion to mount and breed at the correct moment. Artificial insemination is another alternative. Reluctant maiden mares often improve after their first successful breeding.

NYMPHOMANIA

Nymphomania is a rare condition characterized by an exaggerated and wanton display of estrus. The cause is unknown. Nymphomaniac mares do not have any genital tract abnormalities and cycle normally. There is a strong association with neurotic behavior, apparently influenced by rising and falling levels of estrogen.

In the *mild* form of nymphomania, the mare's behavior is limited to estrus and abates during diestrus. In the *severe* form, the mare exhibits strong estrus responses (squirts urine, swishes tail, squeals when touched about the hindquarters)—often throughout the estrous cycle—and is extremely aggressive toward horses and people. It is dangerous to perform rectal examinations on nymphomaniac mares, whether mild or severe.

Breeding is difficult or impossible because of the mare's violent aggression when presented to the stallion, or when handled about the hindquarters.

Treatment: Mares with mild nymphomania often respond to removal of the ovaries. Mares with severe nymphomania do not respond to any form of treatment. Euthanasia is recommended in severe cases.

Twins (Double Ovulation)

Although double ovulation occurs commonly, only about 1 percent of conceptions result in twin pregnancies. Twin pregnancies are considered a disaster in horses. The mare's endometrium does not have the surface capacity to support two pregnancies, and one or both fetuses suffer the effects of placental insufficiency.

The majority of twin conceptions result in early embryonic death (EED) with loss of both embryos, an event that may surface only as a prolongation of diestrus. Among fetuses that survive beyond 150 days, 90 percent end in abortions or stillbirths.

Prevention: Monitoring mares with frequent rectal exams during the preovulatory stage of estrus will identify most double follicles. Monitoring is particularly important for twin-prone mares with a history of double ovulation. If ultrasound shows two follicles maturing at the same time, one alternative is to postpone breeding until the next estrus. The other is to tap and evacuate one follicle by needling it through the wall of the vagina. When two follicles mature and ovulate at *different* times, a double pregnancy can be avoided by not breeding until 12 to 18 hours after rupture of the first follicle. Alternatively, the mare can be bred without consideration of number of follicles, and if twin pregnancy occurs, one embryo can be selectively terminated as described below.

Treatment: To preserve treatment options, it is necessary to diagnose twin pregnancy before 30 days' gestation. Rectal palpation and transrectal ultrasound, starting at 3 weeks post-conception, will identify many (but not all) twin pregnancies.

When twin pregnancies are diagnosed, the decision must be made whether to continue the pregnancy, terminate the pregnancy and re-breed the mare on the next estrus, or selectively terminate one embryo. Re-breeding on the next estrus is possible only when the pregnancy is terminated before 37 days' gestation. If it is terminated after 37 days, the endometrial cups, discussed above in PERSISTENT

CORPUS LUTEUM, will prevent the mare from returning to estrus for several months. This nearly always means the mare can't be rebred until the next season. Pregnancy termination is discussed elsewhere in this chapter.

Converting the pregnancy to a singleton by selective termination of one embryo is another alternative. This is commonly done by rectal palpation, then manually grasping and crushing one of the embryonic vesicles through the wall of the rectum. Selective termination does traumatize the uterus and may result in the loss of both pregnancies.

The last alternative is to allow the pregnancy to proceed to term, while supporting the mare with progesterone during the second half of gestation. However, very few twin pregnancies produce live foals.

Preparing for Breeding

Only 60 percent of mares bred annually in the United States produce live foals. The main reasons for this low reproductive efficiency are poor preparation for breeding, uterine infections, and abnormal estrous cycles.

Good preparation begins with the selection of a suitable stallion, the completion of all arrangements for transportation to the breeding farm, and the performance of a prebreeding physical examination during which problems that may prevent breeding or interfere with fertility can be identified and treated. All of this should be done well before the breeding season begins.

Most stallion owners require a health certificate or a statement of gynecological health status with a negative cervical culture, and an up-to-date vaccination certificate. Proof of serological negativity will be required for equine infectious anemia—either a Coggins test (AGID) or C-ELISA. If you plan to cross state lines, an interstate health certificate is mandatory.

Your veterinarian can perform the necessary examinations and cultures (as described below) and provide you with the needed documents.

If the mare has produced foals, a good breeding history should include notes on the health of each foal, past foaling or breeding difficulties, and any prior injuries or infections, as well as a record of the mare's estrous behavior, teasing behavior, and past heat patterns.

To ensure that all vaccinations are current, consult the Immunization Schedule (Table I) in chapter 3, Infectious Diseases. Additional vaccinations (Table II) may be indicated if the mare will be exposed to endemic diseases for which she has not been vaccinated. Discuss this with your veterinarian.

All mares should be on a good parasite control program as described in chapter 2, Parasites. No additional deworming is required in preparation for breeding. Correct any dental problems. Remove the mare's shoes and trim her feet before she is presented to the stallion.

The effect of nutrition on fertility is very pronounced in mares. Both overly fat and excessively thin mares have a difficult time conceiving. The ideal mare should be in good condition or slightly lean coming out of winter anestrus. Her diet should contain all the necessary nutrients and minerals for the adult horse as described in chapter 17, Feeding and Nutrition.

Four to six weeks prior to the breeding season, increase the mare's maintenance ration to produce a gradual gain of weight. This can be accomplished by reducing roughage slightly and adding 2 to 3 pounds of grain to the daily ration. The process is called "flushing." It is thought to improve the mare's chances of conceiving. However, do not add grain to the ration if the mare is already overweight.

Mares taken straight from the racetrack or show circuit just before breeding have a difficult time conceiving. A let-down period of at least 60 days should be allowed for the mare's reproductive system to establish regularity. Mares on testosterone and other anabolic steroids do not display estrus. Anabolic steroids should be withdrawn at least 6 months before the breeding season.

BREEDING SOUNDNESS EXAMINATION OF THE MARE

This is an overall physical examination with special emphasis on the reproductive organs. The soundness exam is routinely performed before each breeding season, at the end of the breeding season in the case of a barren mare, before buying a broodmare or a maiden mare, and whenever a problem is suspected.

Procedures that may be performed (in addition to the standard rectal palpation and speculum vaginal exam) are endometrial culture and cytology exam, endometrial biopsy, transrectal ultrasound, and endocrine assays. Chromosome analysis or cytogenic studies might be indicated for infertile maiden mares. Fiberoptic examination of the uterus is available in some centers. Not all of these procedures are needed for every mare. Indications depend on the reasons for the examination.

The general health and age of the mare are important considerations. Mares over 15 years are more likely to have infertility problems. Bad teeth, nutritional deficiencies, and chronic laminitis (often seen in older mares) are physical handicaps that can interfere with the ability to carry a foal.

Early in the breeding season, some maiden and barren mares exhibit an abnormally long winter coat (*hirsutism*). This winter coat will be lost before the mare begins to cycle. Thus a hirsute coat indicates that estrus will be delayed. Rarely a pituitary problem causes hirsutism.

The reproductive examination begins by inspecting the perineum for the defect called "windsucking" or *pneumovagina*. The windsucking perineal conformation permits air and fecal material to enter and pool in the vagina, resulting in a persistent source of bacterial infection. The top of the vulvar opening should be no higher than 4 cm above the vaginal floor. A long vulva that extends well above the pelvic brim, associated with a sunken anus, creates a sloping perineum that predisposes to pneumovagina. Mares with pneumovagina frequently lose the protective vulvovaginal sphincter. This entire process can occur simply with aging abetted by weight loss, loss of vaginal fat, and the presence of vaginal tears associated with prior deliveries. Thus pneumovagina is most frequently seen in elderly, thin, multiparous broodmares.

The windsucking test involves spreading the lips of the vulva and listening for the characteristic noise of air rushing into the vagina. The test is also performed by applying uniform pressure with the hands on each side of the labia.

The windsucking perineum is the most common cause of genital tract infection, and the primary cause of infertility in the mare. When present, it should be corrected by surgery. The procedure, called a Caslick's operation, consists of removing the mucous membrane from the lips of the vulva and then stitching the lips together, allowing sufficient room for the mare to pass urine. The closure must be opened for each foaling and then resutured.

The next step is to perform rectal palpation. This is accomplished by inserting a well-lubricated, shoulder-length glove into the rectum. Both ovaries, the entire uterus, and the cervix are palpated. Because the rectum is easily ruptured, rectal palpation should be performed only by experienced personnel.

During the breeding season, determining the moment of ovulation is one of the most important indications for rectal palpation. The egg is viable for only a few hours after ovulation. The best time to breed is just before ovulation. Accordingly, many unnecessary breedings can be avoided by knowing that the mare has already ovulated. Collapse of the follicle, indicative of postovulation, can be felt as a crater or pit in the ovary.

The vaginal speculum examination is an important part of the prebreeding exam and should always be performed as a sterile procedure. The mare's tail is wrapped, and the vulva and perineum cleansed with surgical soap. Cultures are taken using a swab inserted through a sterile speculum.

In the maiden mare, a persistent hymen may be found at the vestibulovaginal junction. When the hymen is completely intact, it is said to be *imperforate*. More often, there are transverse bands across the vaginal canal, indicative of a partially intact hymen. When an intact hymen is not opened before breeding, slight bleeding will occur with the first mating. A thin or partially intact hymen can be broken by gentle finger pressure. A thick hymen will need to be cut. The mare can be bred 2 to 3 weeks after opening an imperforate hymen.

The color of the vaginal mucosa indicates the presence or absence of estrus. A glistening pink to red mucosa indicates true estrus. Anestrus is reflected by a pale, dry mucosa. Vaginal cultures are routinely taken from the clitoral sinuses.

The routine examination concludes with manual palpation of the vagina. The speculum is removed. After sterile preparation of the vaginal opening and vault, a gloved hand is inserted into the vagina. The cervix is carefully palpated. In multiparous mares, the cervix is occasionally explored with a finger to palpate and measure the length of the cervical canal.

Extended Examinations. Endometrial culture and cytology, endometrial biopsy, and manual or endoscopic examination of the uterine cavity are indicated

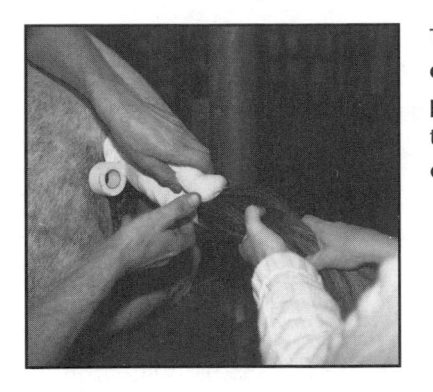

The vaginal speculum examination is a sterile procedure. Wrap the tail to prevent hair from contaminating the field.

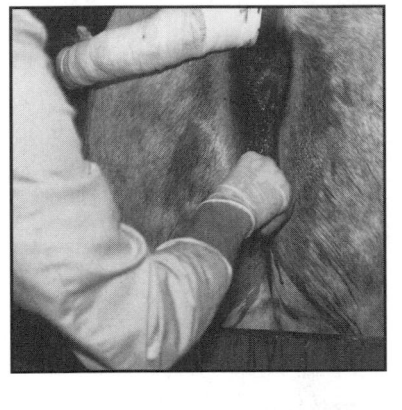

Wash the vulva and perineum with a soap solution and rinse thoroughly.

The vaginal speculum.

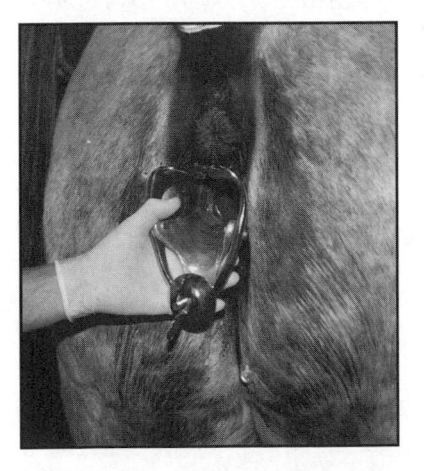

The speculum is inserted. Any discharge indicates infection.

when there is a history of infertility or a finding that requires further medical work-up. All of these procedures are performed using sterile technique.

Any sort of vaginal discharge or yellow fluid on the vaginal floor suggests endometrial infection and the need to assess the uterine cavity by either culture and cytology or endometrial biopsy. A culture from the uterine cavity is a better indicator of endometritis than is a culture from the cervix, since the latter reflects vaginal infection more than it does uterine infection.

Note that when foreign bodies such as instruments and gloved hands are inserted into the cavity of the uterus, there is a risk of introducing infection. Accordingly, such invasive procedures are usually reserved for mares in whom the likelihood of finding and treating a problem outweighs the risks of creating one. On some stud farms, uterine cultures are taken routinely on all maiden mares before breeding. This practice is questionable, since the likelihood of finding endometritis in a maiden mare is remote.

A typical candidate for an intrauterine sampling procedure is a infertile barren mare, a mare with a history of repeated abortions or early embryonic deaths, and a mare with a history of abnormal heat cycles. Other candidates for endometrial culture and/or biopsy include mares presenting for a fertility evaluation as part of a pre-purchase agreement, and mares scheduled for a Caslick's operation (or some other genital procedure) in order to be sure that the rest of the reproductive tract is free of disease.

Endometrial cultures and cytology samples are taken together. A sterile swab inside a plastic case is inserted through the cervix into the uterine cavity. The swab is extended, samples are taken, and the swab is retracted back into its case before being removed from the uterus. The extracted swab is then re-extended and part of the sample is sent for culture while the remainder is looked at under the microscope for cells and bacteria, which if present indicate endometrial inflammation (see ENDOMETRITIS). If the culture grows bacteria, cytology is still needed to show that the bacteria were actually causing the inflammation and were not just contaminants.

In the healthy endometrium, microscopic examination shows a field of uterine cells mixed with fewer than 1 percent white cells, or polymorphonuclear leukocytes (PMNs). The finding of numerous PMNs (more than 1 percent) indicates inflammation. When inflammation is extensive, the gross appearance is like that of pus.

As an alternative to the swab technique, the uterus can be flushed with sterile saline, and the washings cultured and examined microscopically.

Endometrial biopsy provides additional information not fully provided by culture and cytology. It is more precise than culture and cytology and helps to establish the diagnosis of uterine infection when these two studies are equivocal. Most importantly, it quantifies the degree of scarring or *fibrosis* in the wall of the uterus, which correlates with infertility. The biopsy is obtained as described above except the instrument takes a bite of tissue from the wall of the uterus.

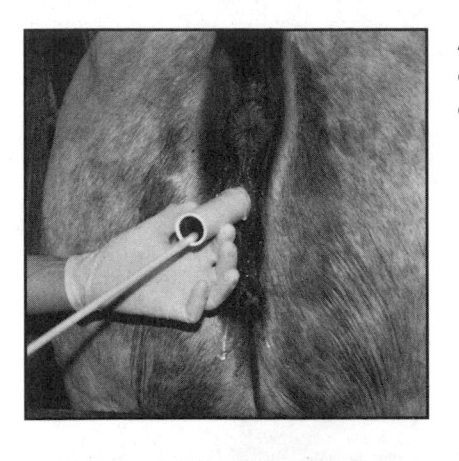

A sterile swab is used to obtain cervical and endometrial cultures.

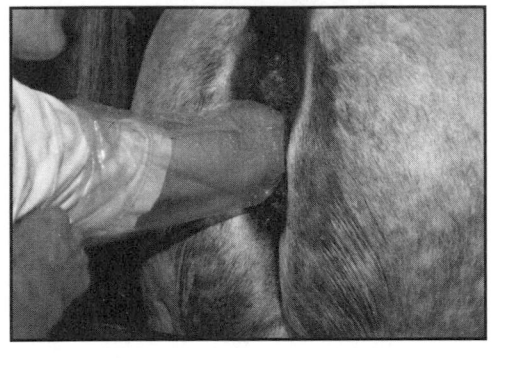

Transvaginal palpation of the uterus completes the prebreeding examination.

Inflammation is determined by counting the number of inflammatory cells. Fibrosis is graded according to the amount of scar tissue surrounding the endometrial glands. Excellent correlation exists between extensive scarring and early embryonic death.

A procedure called *manual palpation* of the uterus is performed by dilating the cervical canal and introducing a gloved hand into the uterine cavity. *Hysteroscopy* is a procedure in which a fiberoptic endoscope is inserted into the uterine cavity to visualize the endometrium, take tissue samples, and perform simple surgery.

The Stallion

The age at which a stallion reaches sexual maturity and begins to produce sperm varies from 1 to 2 years, with an average of 16 months. However, few stallions are used at stud at or before 2 years of age. Even then, the number of services is usually restricted to 2 per week. At 36 months of age the stallion acquires full reproductive capacity. A fertile stallion at 4 years of age can be used 2 or 3 times a day if given occasional periods of sexual rest.

A well-conditioned stallion, turned out for show. Photo: Don Lupton.

MALE ANATOMY

The stallion has two testicles enclosed by the scrotum and located in the pre-pubic region. The testicles produce the sperm, and also the male hormone *testosterone*, which is responsible for the secondary sex characteristics of the stallion. The temperature within the scrotum is 2 to 3 degrees below body temperature. This lower temperature is necessary for sperm production.

The *epididymis* is a coiled tube resting on top of the testicle. It connects the testicle with the spermatic cord. In addition to its transport function, the epididymis serves as a reservoir for sperm during the last 5 to 10 days of maturation. Sperm maturation takes 21 days. If mature sperm are not ejaculated within a few days of maturation, they die and are reabsorbed.

Sperm are transported up the spermatic cord, into the ampulla, and thus to the urethra. Also entering the urethra and mixing with the sperm are the secretions of the three accessory sex glands. They are the *seminal vesicles, prostate,* and *bulbourethral* glands. These glands produce seminal fluid, which provides energy and protective buffers for the sperm. The combination of sperm and seminal fluid is called *semen*.

The sheath surrounding the penis is called the *prepuce*. The prepuce is actually a double layer of sliding skin. The internal layer contains sebaceous glands whose secretions, together with flaking epithelial cells, form a thick waxy material called *smegma*. Smegma tends to collect in the folds of the prepuce and, if not periodically removed, may become a source of infection.

The penis is a cylindrical structure about 20 inches long when relaxed. During erection, cavernous erectile tissue within the penile shaft engorges and the penis becomes twice as long and enlarges in diameter. At the end of the penis is the

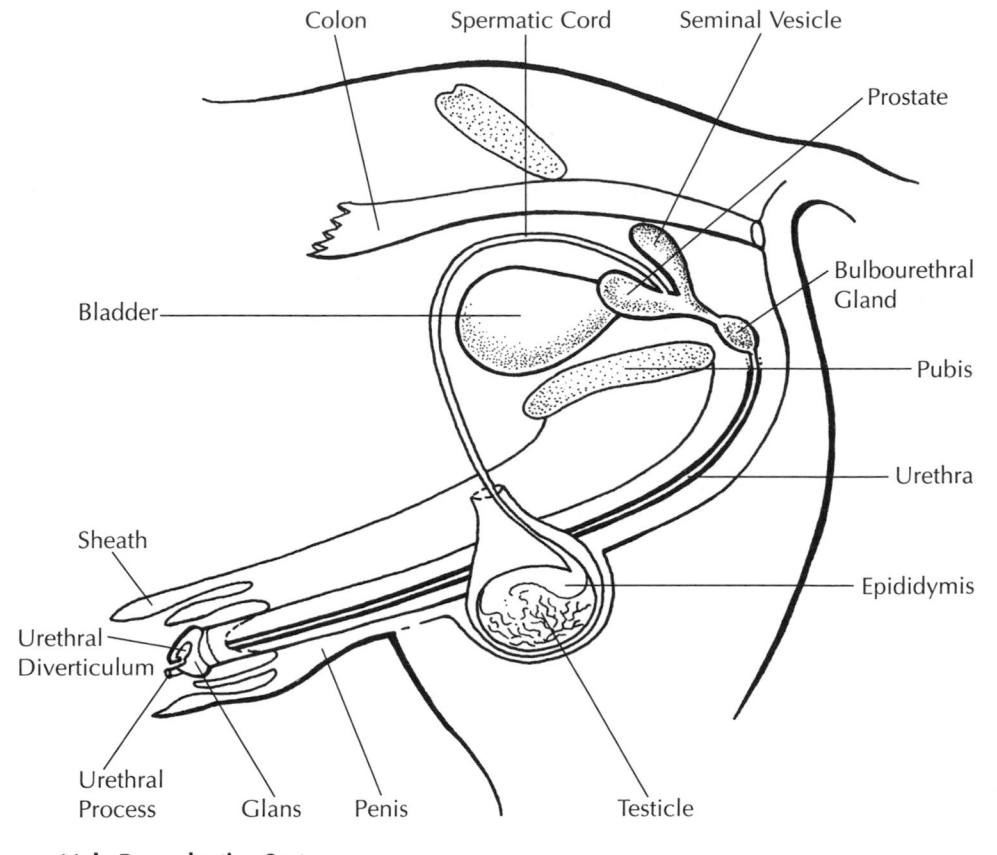

Male Reproductive System

bell-shaped *glans*. In the horse, the urethra projects slightly beyond the tip of the glans. This extension is called the *urethral process*.

There is a pocket within the glans above the urethra called the *urethral diverticulum*. A build-up of putty-like smegma in this pocket, called a *bean*, compresses the urethra, causing spraying and frequent urination. The condition is treated by manually everting the urethral diverticulum and removing the accumulated smegma. The entire sheath and glans should be cleansed as described in Cleaning the Sheath in chapter 4, Skin.

The glans of the penis contains additional erectile tissue which engorges *after* the penis enters the vagina. This marked enlargement of the glans is called "belling" or "flowering." When belled, the penis seats itself against the cervix in such a way that the urethral process is coupled with the opening of the cervical canal (*cervical os*). Thus the semen is ejaculated directly into the uterus. Note that if belling does not take place, ejaculation cannot occur.

A stallion with an exceptionally short penis may be unable to successfully seat the glans during belling. At the opposite extreme, a stallion with an exceptionally long penis may bruise or tear the mare's cervix. This can be prevented by using a breeding role as described in COVERING THE MARE.

Ejaculation is controlled by nerves within the base of the penis which ultimately connect with the sex center in the brain. During coitus, muscles within the penis and urethra contract to expel the semen. An ejaculation consists of about 6 to 8 pulsations. Most of the sperm are present in the first 4 pulsations.

PREPARING FOR THE BREEDING SEASON

Nutritional requirements vary according to the size, condition, activity, and temperament of the stallion. Contrary to popular belief, a stallion's protein requirements do not increase during the breeding season. Furthermore, there are no dietary supplements known to improve sperm concentration or sex drive. Nevertheless, stallions are often overfed and oversupplemented, despite the fact that excess dietary energy is associated with obesity, laminitis, and lack of libido.

The stallion should be fed the maintenance ration for the adult horse as described in chapter 17, Feeding and Nutrition, with adjustments for activity and recent gain or loss of weight. To insure that dietary protein and other nutrients are of the highest quality, only the best feeds should be selected. The diet should provide adequate amounts of vitamin A for healthy sperm production. Water and trace-mineralized salt should be offered free-choice.

A program of good oral hygiene will prevent dental disease and maximize the benefits of the feeding program.

It is not necessary for a breeding stallion to be in top athletic condition. In fact, if the stallion is being intensively trained or in competition, a period of physical let-down is advisable before using the horse at stud.

A stallion should be given daily exercise to maintain cardiovascular fitness and stamina for breeding. Regular exercise enhances fertility by developing muscle tone, improving sex drive, and preventing obesity. Well-exercised stallions are generally less nervous, have fewer stallion vices, and are more confident around mares, and are therefore more consistent in the breeding area.

Since the stallion will be exposed to many outside mares each breeding season, it is most essential that all vaccinations are up to date *before* the season begins (see the Immunization Schedules in chapter 3, Infectious Diseases).

Vaccinations for influenza type A1 and A2 should be performed semiannually or every 2 to 3 months, depending on the prevalence of the influenza. Annual or semiannual boosters afford adequate protection for rhinopneumonitis. Maintain protection against Eastern, Western, and Venezuelan encephalomyelitis. Annual boosters are required, ideally given 1 month before the height of the mosquito season. An annual rabies vaccine is desirable in rabies-endemic areas.

Chronic parasite infections cause weight loss, anemia, diarrhea, and reduced fertility. The stallion should be on a routine deworming program as described in chapter 2, Parasites. Anthelmintic drugs have no deleterious effects on sperm production or reproductive performance.

Hoof and foot care are important. Pain and lameness in the back feet can make it difficult for the stallion to mount. The feet should be trimmed every 4 to 6 weeks. Remove the front shoes to prevent injury to the mare.

Sperm production and libido are depressed during the winter season. An artificial light program, as described for mares, has been shown to improve these somewhat, but the effect is short-lived and may be associated with a rebound depression when high fertility is desired. Accordingly, it is suggested that an artificial light program for stallions not be used.

BREEDING SOUNDNESS EXAMINATION OF THE STALLION

This is a general physical examination undertaken before the breeding season, with special emphasis on the reproductive tract.

The medical history includes notes on past breeding performance and any recent illnesses. A history of an injury to the testicles or penis is important because it could interfere with fertility or reproductive performance. A musculoskeletal injury can prevent the stallion from mounting the mare. A history of being given performance-enhancing drugs is significant since anabolic steroids and testosterone are known to cause testicular degeneration.

Positive and negative experiences during past matings are of great importance in predicting the stallion's present attitude and sexual vigor. It is also important to be aware of the presence of undesirable habits such as biting, kicking, and masturbation, as these require special handling and/or can diminish the stallion's value as a stud.

Veterinary examination of the stallion's reproductive tract is the main focus of the examination. Ultrasound and urethral endoscopy are available when indicated.

Both testicles should be present in the scrotum, and should be of normal size, texture, and consistency. When only one testicle is present, the stallion may still be fertile but should be considered unsuitable for stud. Testicular size is closely related to sperm production and fertility. A stallion with very small testicles is less likely to be potent. Note that the testicles do not begin to develop before 15 months of age and will continue to increase in size until the horse is 4 to 5 years old. Excessive fat in the scrotum is a sign of poor conditioning.

The penis and prepuce are examined for scars, pustules, and growths. Cultures are taken from the urethra, urethral diverticulum, and shaft of the penis. After ejaculation, the urethra is again cultured, as is the semen.

The condition of the prostate, seminal vesicles, and secondary sex glands is determined by rectal palpation. Finally, the inguinal canals are examined for hernias.

The collection and analysis of semen is a most important part of the reproductive examination. This highly technical aspect of stallion management should be carried out by an equine practitioner. The number of sperm per milliliter and the quality of the semen sample help the veterinarian to predict the number of mares a stallion can cover efficiently. Blood in the sample may be associated with infection and infertility. When the semen contains less than 60 percent live sperm cells, there could be a problem with the epididymis or testicles. A pH above normal (alkaline) may be caused by an infection within the urethra or secondary sex glands. The same is true for an increase in the number of white blood cells.

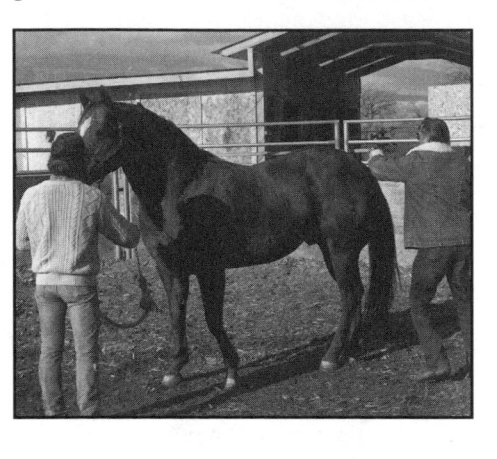

The well-trained stallion who trusts his handlers is apt to be gentle and tractable. Photo: Don Lupton.

HANDLING THE STALLION

Stallion handling requires some special skills that include self-confidence, an understanding of stallion psychology, and the ability to anticipate a stallion's behavior and make quick decisions. It is essential that the stallion handler have the ability to hold the stallion's respect and attention, and the knowledge of how and when to apply physical restraint. These special skills are acquired primarily through practice and experience.

A handler who lacks confidence in his or her ability to control the stallion may overcompensate by becoming overbearing or unnecessarily assertive, actions that make the stallion distrustful and more difficult to handle. This can lead to aggressive behavior and potential injury to the handler, stallion, or mare.

The well-trained stallion who has been gently handled and well socialized early in life has learned that obedience and submission are the normal state between horse and master. When forceful handling is necessary to maintain control, it should be dispatched promptly and without anger, immediately after which the stallion should be required to perform a familiar handling task. This helps to reestablish the authority of the handler. Excessive, inconsistent, and unnecessary punishment will cause many stallions to resent handling, fear or resist restraint, and refuse to display normal mating behavior when presented to a mare in heat.

Avoid a direct confrontation with a stallion (a contest of wills) unless you have the physical restraints in place that guarantee a win. Nothing is more detrimental to the handler/stallion relationship than for the horse to suddenly realize that it is physically stronger and has the upper hand. This stallion will become willful, unpredictable, and potentially dangerous.

There is a natural mating code that experienced pasture-bred mares teach to novice stallions. Mares expect to be courted, teased, and coaxed into a state of readiness. They do not expect to be jumped, assaulted, or mauled, and will force-fully discipline an unruly herd stallion that does not employ good breeding man-ners. However, in the artificial circumstances of hand breeding, these lessons of nature are bypassed. It therefore falls upon the stallion trainer to assume the role of a seasoned mare and not allow the stallion to mount until he has coaxed the mare into a state of readiness.

The essential tool for discipline and control is the combined lead shank, chain, and halter. The lead shank connects to a 2-foot chain with a snap at the end. The snap attaches to the halter. All parts must be stout, in good repair, and should be replaced when worn. The lead can be made of rope, nylon, or leather. Leather is less likely to cause friction burns of the hands.

A chain under the chin is an effective restraint for many stallions.

Even a well-trained stallion is capable of dangerous behavior and must be under firm control at all times.

Control is determined by how the chain is placed. A chain placed over the nose or through the mouth and pulled down hard will exert considerable pain and gain the stallion's immediate attention. However, it may cut the nose or corners of the mouth and leave scars. A chain beneath the upper lip just above the top of the teeth (war bridle) applies pressure to an extremely sensitive area. A chain placed under the chin is less severe, yet remains an effective restraint for many stallions. For more information on halters and leads, see HANDLING AND RESTRAINT. The placement of the chain is one part of the equation. How forcefully the pressure is applied is the other. Each stallion handler has his or her favorite method, developed through usage and experience.

Note that stallion vices are not uncommon, and that even a dependable stallion is capable of doing something totally unexpected and dangerous when in a heightened state of excitement. Accordingly, it is important to have a knowledge of dangerous stallion behavior and a plan of action for dealing with such contingencies.

STALLION VICES

Biting. Biting is perhaps the most common stallion vice. An attempt at biting may be sudden and unexpected, but quite often it is signaled by laid-back ears, raised lips, bared teeth, and a twitching tail.

All biting attempts should be met with a sharp downward jerk on the lead shank. A forceful jab or rap on the muzzle, accompanied by a harsh word, is also effective. Do not slap at the horse's face. Slapping is inaccurate and can make the horse head-shy. Corrective punishment must be administered as the act occurs. All personnel who handle the horse should be aware of this vice and be prepared to administer corrective discipline.

Biting and nipping are much easier to prevent than cure, and must be stopped at an early age. The explorative, nippy behavior of a young colt can turn into a dangerous habit if allowed to go unchecked. Activities that encourage nipping and biting are hand-feeding, allowing the horse to muzzle and lip its handler, and carrying apples or carrots in the pockets. Never assume that a reformed biter has been cured. This vice is hard to correct.

Rearing and Striking. Rearing up on the back legs and striking out with the front feet is a defensive reaction to fear. It is most likely to occur when the stallion is cornered. In a dominant, assertive horse, it is a sign of rebellion or refusal to accept handling. Stallions rear and strike when fighting for herd dominance. Excited stallions frequently rear and paw when preparing to court a receptive mare.

Rearing and striking is dangerous and potentially lethal. It must be anticipated so that precautionary measures can be taken to ensure the safety of people and horses.

Many horses tense up before rearing. A horse is most likely to strike at another horse when in nose-to-nose confrontation. Always stand well to the side, out of striking range, and never in front of two horses who may engage in aggressive behavior. Remain alert to the danger of flailing feet.

A stallion with a history of rearing should be controlled by passing the chain over the nose or between the lips as described above. Do not place the chain under the chin, as in some cases this may actually promote rearing.

To control a rearing horse, jerk down strongly on the lead shank either before or after the stallion rears, but not while the horse is standing up on its hind legs. If the horse throws back his head, he could lose his balance and fall over backwards. After pulling down on the shank, quickly back the stallion several steps. This reestablishes handler control and prevents further attempts at rearing.

Punishment in the form of blows and kicks is difficult to deliver to a rearing stallion and thus is not effective in stopping or preventing the vice. Kicks, in particular, are not delivered with much precision and may leave the kicker off balanced and vulnerable.

Kicking, Crowding, Charging. These aggressive actions may be directed toward people or other horses. Kicking, which can often be anticipated, tends to occur in specific situations. For example, a horse may kick when disturbed during a meal, while being saddled and bridled, as the cinch is tightened, or when handled about the feet or hindquarters. When a kick is anticipated, the handler can be ready to deliver corrective punishment in the form of a jab to the ribs or a jerk on the lead shank, accompanied by a loud reprimand.

A nervous horse may kick when startled outside its lateral field of vision or when approached from the rear. Although this defensive behavior is not vicious, it is nonetheless dangerous and cannot be tolerated. Proper handling and discipline will prevent this.

Crowding is when a horse squeezes a person against the wall of a stall with its body. Punishment in the form of a hard knuckle or sharp pinprick delivered as the horse crowds is often effective. A pointed stick about 2 feet long can be inserted (point outward) between the wall of the stall and the body of the horse. As the horse attempts to crowd, the point of the stick will cause a painful jab.

Lunging or charging is when a horse attacks or attempts to savage an attendant while in a stall or paddock. This type of deliberate aggression has many causes, but improper human socialization and rough treatment appear to be at the root of most cases.

A horse of truly vicious disposition is unpredictable, dangerous, and must be handled at all times with extreme caution. This horse is not suitable as a companion or pleasure horse, and ordinarily is not a good candidate for breeding.

Only the most experienced stallion manager should attempt to break a horse of deeply ingrained aggressive vices. If the horse is a stallion, gelding can be considered. However, there is a good chance that neutering will have no effect on the horse's behavior.

Masturbation. A stallion masturbates by rubbing the erect penis against his belly. For many years it was assumed that masturbation depleted semen reserves and sexual energy. However, recent studies show that masturbation is a normal activity for stallions (and even geldings), and that it does not interfere with stallion fertility or libido. In point of fact, ejaculation rarely takes place. Also contrary to popular belief, masturbation does not appear to be related to, or influenced by, frustration or boredom.

Stallion rings have been used to prevent erection and masturbation and to discourage competition horses from displaying sexual interest in mares. The ring fits snugly around the penis just behind the glans. Problems associated with the stallion ring are irritation, soreness, and blood in the semen. Use of the ring may lead to behavioral mating disorders. For these reasons, stallion rings are not recommended.

Breeding

The three basic methods for breeding horses are: pasture breeding, hand breeding, and artificial insemination.

Pasture breeding is cost-effective and produces relatively high rates of conception.

PASTURE BREEDING

This involves putting a stallion out with a herd of mares in a large natural setting and letting nature take its course. It is most important that all horses be in good health and free of sexually transmitted diseases. Management is limited to preparing the stallion and mares for the breeding season, introducing new members to the herd, and watching for problems.

Pasture breeding is excellent training for young stallions, who learn the code of mating through contact with experienced mares. It may possibly improve conception rates for the marginally fertile stallion. Mares free of reproductive tract disease, but with a history of infertility of undetermined cause, will occasionally become pregnant when turned out into a natural setting with a seasoned pasture-breeding stallion.

Pasture breeding for one mare and a stallion requires no more space than a large paddock. For a herd of 15 to 20 mares, 40 fenced acres is a reasonable acreage.

The stallion's natural proclivity to guard his herd and protect his mares makes it difficult to handle individual horses on a routine basis. Furthermore, the introduction of additional mares into the herd can create jealously among the resident mares. In some cases it is actually the stallion who rejects the new arrival. The new mare must quickly be removed from the pasture to prevent risk of injury. The majority of such problems can be avoided by using proper introduction techniques.

The main disadvantage of pasture breeding is the increased likelihood that a valuable stallion will be injured by a mare's kick. Although the chances of this are small, such an injury could render the stallion unserviceable.

A potential disadvantage of pasture breeding is the limit imposed on the number of mares that a stallion can cover during the breeding season. By skillfully manipulating the size of the herd, removing pregnant mares and replacing them with nonpregnant mares, it is possible to breed 30 to 40 mares in a season. In a hand-breeding operation, it is possible to breed at least twice that number. With artificial insemination, up to 200 mares can be covered in a season. However, when time and expertise are limited and there is ample space, nutritious forage, and a small number of healthy resident mares served by a fertile and sexually confident stallion, pasture breeding is cost-effective and convenient, and produces relatively high rates of conception.

HAND BREEDING

Hand breeding has the advantage of allowing direct management of the breeding process. It also provides the opportunity to select breeding individuals for various complementary characteristics. It is safer from the point of view of sexually transmitted diseases. Injuries to the mare or stallion are less likely to occur. Fertility problems can be identified early in the season when there is still time to achieve pregnancy.

Along with artificial insemination (discussed below), hand breeding is the only practical method of servicing outside mares visiting on the farm for only one or two estrous cycles.

WHEN TO BREED

A mare reaches puberty at about 18 months but does not achieve physical maturity until 36 months old. Since it is desirable for her to be physically mature when she carries her foal to term, most people do not breed a mare until she is at least 3 years of age.

When a mare in heat is receptive to the stallion, she exhibits certain character-istic signs. They include frequent urination, a raised tail, and a "winking" of the vulva as the lips of the vagina contract and relax. Rectal palpation reveals a ma-ture follicle greater than 3.5 cm in size. As the mare ovulates, the follicle ruptures, releasing the egg into the oviduct.

The best time to breed a mare is just before ovulation (see DETERMINING ESTRUS). Ovulation usually occurs 24 hours before the end of estrus, but there is variation. To maximize chances for conception, most breeders recommend cover-ing the mare on the third day of estrus, and every other day thereafter for as long as she remains receptive. On this schedule, motile sperm are present in the mare's reproductive tract at all times when ovulation is likely to occur.

Trying a mare with a stallion across a teasing barrier.

Ovulation can be timed precisely utilizing daily rectal palpation and ultrasound exams. The advantage here is that only one cover will be necessary, timed just prior to, or within 12 hours after, ovulation. When covering occurs 24 hours after ovulation, conception will not occur.

The best way to determine when the mare is in heat is to bring her together with the stallion, or a teaser stallion who assumes that role. The mare's response at the sight and sound of the teaser will determine her level of receptivity.

Teasing. When the breeding farm is large or the stallion is very valuable, it is customary to use another male to do the teasing. The temperament of the stallion teaser is an important consideration. He should be easy to handle but aggressive enough to elicit the signs of heat. The ideal teaser courts his mares consistently and does not lose interest halfway through the procedure. The teaser is allowed to cover one or two mares a season to maintain sexual interest.

A common method of hand teasing involves trying a mare with a stallion across a teasing barrier. This can be a heavy stall door or a tubular steel gate. The barrier should be short enough to allow the stallion to get his head and neck over, and

A mare exhibiting strong signs of estrus, leaning toward the stallion and spreading her legs.

An unreceptive mare swishing her tail and kicking at the fence.

well padded to protect the horses if they kick or strike. The safest teasing wall is one equipped with extensions to protect the handlers.

The stallion is led up to the mare who stands, for example, behind a stall window. The horses are introduced nose-to-nose. If the mare is not receptive, she will lay back her ears and swish her tail violently from side to side. It is most important to maintain control of the mare and anticipate the possibility that she may strike out or swing around and kick at the barrier.

If the mare is receptive, she will lean toward the stallion, spread her back legs, pass water, and show "winking" of the clitoris.

Another method of hand teasing involves leading the stallion past a series of paddocks containing estrous mares. The stallion investigates each one in succession, and the manager makes notes on the readiness of each individual.

In some programs, mares are teased daily while in others they are teased every other day.

COVERING THE MARE

For the safety of the stallion and handlers, the mare should be restrained during the cover. It is impossible to be 100 percent certain that a mare will stand submissively. There is always a distinct possibility that she will panic and kick out at the stallion.

A holding or palpation chute is an effective restraint, but since the stallion cannot mount or dismount at an angle, there is a danger that he will become trapped and injured if he falls off during the mating.

Most breeders prefer to restrain a mare with breeding hobbles. A lip twitch may also be used (see HANDLING AND RESTRAINT). Breeding hobbles consist of a leather strap that buckles around the mare's neck just in front of her shoulders. A rope extends from the lower part of this neck strap down between her front legs and attaches beneath her abdomen to another set of straps which buckle around the hocks. The connection between the front and rear restraints is secured with a quick-release knot. While in hobbles, a mare can walk forward but cannot kick.

Breeding hobbles prevent the mare from kicking the stallion during the dismount.

An especially difficult mare can be fitted with a leather strap that holds up one front leg. The mare will be unable to kick when standing on three legs, but she will lose her balance and fall as the stallion mounts unless the strap is quickly released. This restraint will not prevent the mare from kicking on the dismount, when kicking is most likely.

When the mare is a known kicker, she should be fitted with kicking boots. These boots are made of heavy felt designed to soften the impact. Even when using a kicking boot, the back shoes should always be removed.

If a small or maiden mare is going to be bred to a stallion with a large penis, she could suffer a tear of the vagina or cervix. To prevent this injury, a breeding roll can be used. A breeding roll is a padded cylinder about 5 inches in diameter and 18 inches long. It is covered by a sterile sleeve and placed between the mare and stallion just above the stallion's penis as he mounts. The roll prevents the stallion from penetrating too deeply.

Some stallions have a habit of savagely biting the necks of their mares during mounting and coitus. Painful bites can be prevented by putting a leather neck shield on the mare or by fitting a cage muzzle over the stallion's mouth and nose.

Getting Ready

Before the mare is brought to the stallion, she should be encouraged to empty her bladder. Her tail is then wrapped with a disposable sleeve or bandage. It is important to include all the hair at the base of the tail in the wrap. Loose hair can get caught between the vagina and the penis and lacerate the penis.

The mare's vulva and perineum are then surgically prepped with a mild soap or dilute surgical scrub, using sterile disposable gloves. Rinse thoroughly with lukewarm water to remove residual soap. Dry the hindquarters with clean paper towels. The mare is now ready to be taken to the breeding area.

The stallion is brought into the breeding area and allowed to see the mare if necessary to encourage erection. The extended penis is gently lathered with water or a mild soap solution. Do not use antiseptic solutions such as Betadine or chlorhexidine, which can inflame the skin. Remove smegma from the urethral opening and folds of the prepuce. Rinse with lukewarm water.

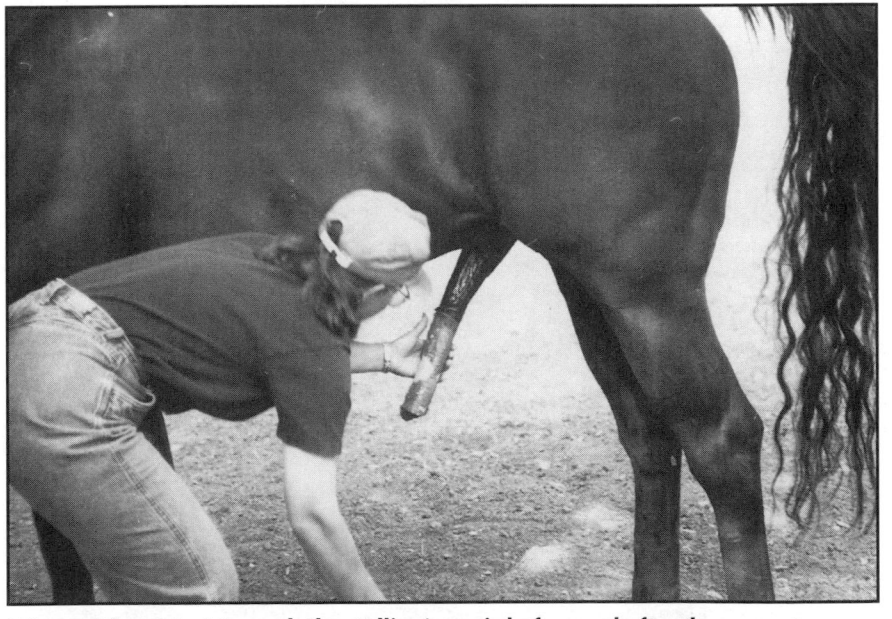

It is most important to wash the stallion's penis before and after the cover, to prevent sexually transmitted diseases.

The Cover

Mating should take place in an area free of distractions. If the mare has a foal at her side, the foal should be kept in a holding pen where it can be seen by its mother.

The procedure for hand breeding requires two or three people. Each person has assigned responsibilities and must know exactly what to expect. The stallion and mare are restrained with a lead shank, chain, and halter, as described in the section HANDLING THE STALLION. The shanks should be of sufficient length so the holders can step back quickly.

The exact positions of the mare and her handler, and the stallion and his handler, are of critical importance for safety and control. *At no time should any handler stand between the two horses, or directly in front of or directly behind either horse.* The mare handler should stand at the mare's shoulder on the same side as the stallion (usually the mare's left side). The duties of the mare handler are to steady the mare, allow her to see the stallion, and prevent her from moving out from under the stallion as he mounts.

The stallion handler stands at the left of the stud's shoulder and leads him calmly and directly to the mare's left shoulder. A 45-degree-angled approach allows the mare to see and prepare for the stallion and is recommended for safety.

As the two horses make contact, either may attempt to bite or strike. Mares can strike with blinding speed. Both handlers must be positioned out of the strike zone and be prepared to move back quickly. Control is obtained by yanking down hard on the lead shank and backing the horses away. When a mare strikes out or kicks at a stud, she is either not in standing heat or is going to be very difficult to cover.

A vigorous stallion, when presented to a quiet mare in standing heat, should greet her vocally, sniff and nuzzle her, display the flehmen response by curling his upper lip, drop his penis, and obtain an erection—all within 3 minutes.

After the initial friendly greeting in which the stallion is allowed to sniff and nuzzle the mare, he is backed away. This greeting and identification procedure is repeated 2 or 3 times as the stallion works down from shoulder to flank. The receptive mare, now suitably coaxed, spreads her legs, flexes her pelvis, and strikes a breeding stance.

The stallion should remain at the left side of the mare until he is fully erect and ready to cover. This takes about 15 seconds for the experienced stud. After receiving a cue to mount, the stallion raises up slightly to the side of the mare and quickly positions himself behind her buttocks for intromission and ejaculation. A third handler (optional), standing beside the mare's left hip, can hold the mare's tail to one side and guide the stallion's penis into the vagina. Guidance is particularly helpful when the mare is tall. This handler should immediately step back after intromission is accomplished.

Breeding averages 20 seconds. The normal ejaculatory pattern consists of 5 to 6 intravaginal thrusts followed by 3 to 5 short thrusts synchronous with ejaculation. As the stallion ejaculates, his tail moves up and down. This is called *flagging.*

The horses make contact. The mare is receptive.

The stallion works down from shoulder to flank.

The stallion must be absolutely ready and fully erect before being given the signal to mount.

It may not be seen in a horse with a high tail carriage, but the pulsations can be felt by placing the hand under the stallion's penis.

The stallion is allowed to dismount at his leisure. As the stallion begins to dismount, the mare handler should turn the mare's head quickly to the left. This causes her hindquarters to move to the right and away from the stallion, which places the stallion out of line should she kick. At the same time, the stallion is backed from the mare.

The stallion is now returned to the wash area to have his penis and sheath cleansed and rinsed as described above. Washing immediately after each service is a most important step in preventing the transmission of sexual diseases.

ARTIFICIAL INSEMINATION

Artificial insemination (AI) is the procedure during which semen is collected from the stallion and introduced into the reproductive tract of the mare. When properly performed, AI increases the number of mares who settle on the first cycle. Other advantages of AI are a low risk of spreading reproductive infections and the elimination of breeding injuries.

Fresh semen is divided into aliquots containing about 500 million sperm in each aliquot, and inseminated into one or more mares shortly after collection.

Cooled transported semen from some fertile stallions will preserve for 3 to 4 days, and can be shipped and used to inseminate mares who would otherwise be unable to breed to that stallion.

Frozen semen can be stored for weeks, months, or even years, and then thawed and inseminated into one or more mares.

AI using freshly collected semen is permitted by almost all U.S. breed registries. However, as of this date, many registries do not permit the use of either cooled transported or frozen-thawed semen. In the hands of skilled personnel, conception rates using fresh semen or cooled transported semen approach per-cycle pregnancy rates similar to those of live cover. Under ideal conditions, pregnancy rates from frozen-thawed semen range from 30 to 40 percent.

The chief disadvantage of AI is that it requires special facilities and equipment as well as personnel experienced in the collection, handling, and storage of semen.

Collection of Semen. Most stallions can be easily trained to use an artificial vagina. Several models are available. All consist of a hollow inflatable rubber bladder surrounded by a cylinder. At the end of the bladder is a funnel that empties into a container for collecting the semen. The bladder is inflated with warm water at a temperature between 110 and 115 degrees F. Sterile disposable liners are available, which protect against chemical and detergent contamination of the semen. An optional filter retains the gel fraction and allows the sperm-rich portion to pass into the sperm receptacle. A sterile nonspermicidal lubricant such as KY Jelly is used to lubricate the interior of the bladder.

The artificial vagina is used in conjunction with a phantom mare or a live "jump" mare. A phantom mare can be made by welding two 55-gallon oil drums together and mounting them on a steel pipe; or one can be purchased. The phantom is padded with several layers of foam and covered with canvas or leather.

A jump mare is a mare in estrus, or more commonly, a mare whose ovaries have been surgically removed, and who is then given estrogen to create artificial heat.

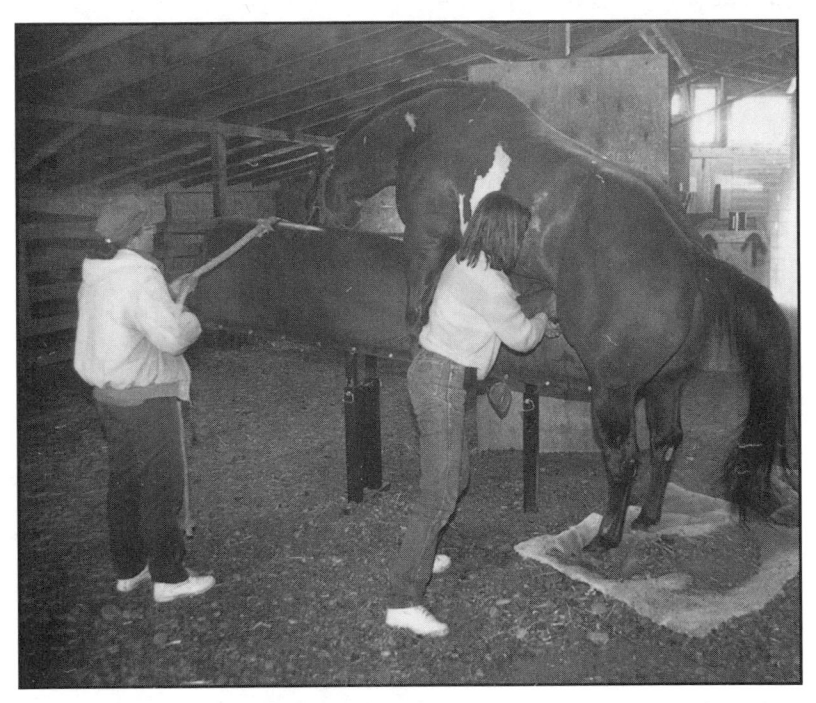

Semen collection for artificial insemination. The stallion mounts the phantom mare.

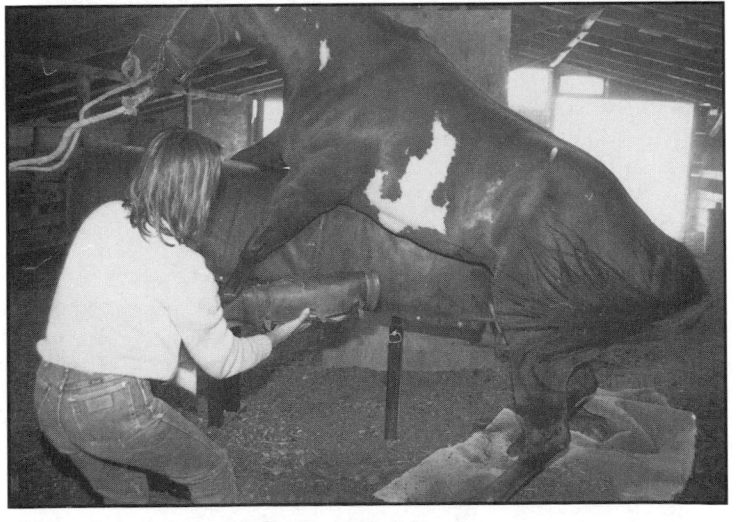

The penis is deflected into the artificial vagina.

The semen is mixed with an extender and can be used fresh, cooled, or frozen.

The stallion is brought into the breeding area and shown the phantom or jump mare until an erection is obtained. The erect penis is washed as described above.

The stallion is then allowed to mount the phantom or jump mare. The stallion handler now directs the erect penis to the side and into the artificial vagina. Ejaculation occurs in the usual manner. After dismount, the penis is washed with warm water to remove lubricant. The filter containing the gel is removed (or the gel fraction aspirated), leaving the sperm fraction in the receptacle. The resulting semen is mixed with an appropriate semen extender containing an antibiotic. Subsequent handling depends on whether the semen will be used freshly, cooled and transported, or frozen.

Inseminating the Mare. The procedure is performed under antiseptic conditions. The mare's tail is wrapped, and the perineum thoroughly washed and dried. An 18- to 20-inch sterile plastic disposable insemination pipette is inserted through the cervical canal and into the body of the uterus. The volume needed to deliver the required number of sperm typically ranges from 5 to 20 ml. Most breeders inseminate at day 2 or 3 of estrus, and continue every other day until ovulation occurs, as determined by rectal palpation or ultrasound exam (see DETERMINING ESTRUS).

BREEDING ON THE FOAL HEAT

The first postpartum heat occurs from day 7 to day 12 after foaling. In some cases, this interval is too short for the uterus to involute and the reproductive tract to return to a normal state of readiness for the next pregnancy. Most breeders simply wait until the second heat cycle at 30 days postpartum, at which time chances for successful pregnancy are greater.

Breeding on the foal heat, however, becomes an important issue when the goal is to maintain a 12-month interval between foals to continue to produce foals close to the universal birth date (see OPERATIONAL BREEDING SEASON).

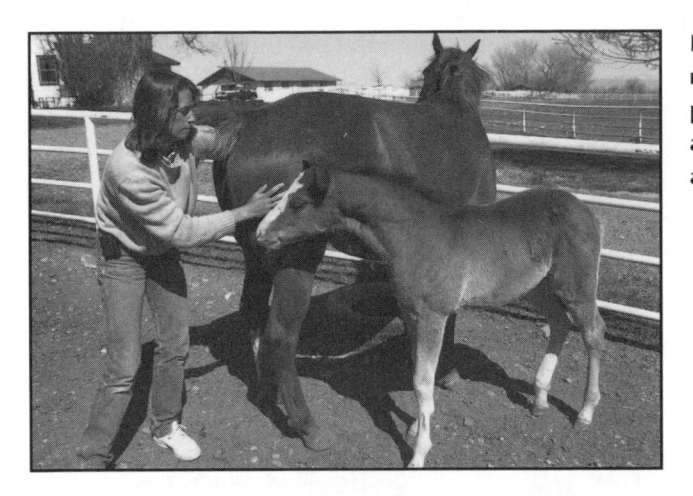

Inseminating the mare. Rectal palpation discloses a dominant follicle about to ovulate.

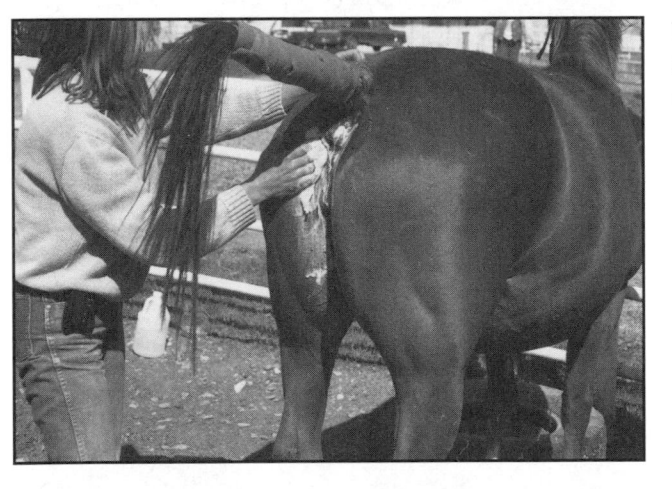

The tail is wrapped, and the perineum washed and dried.

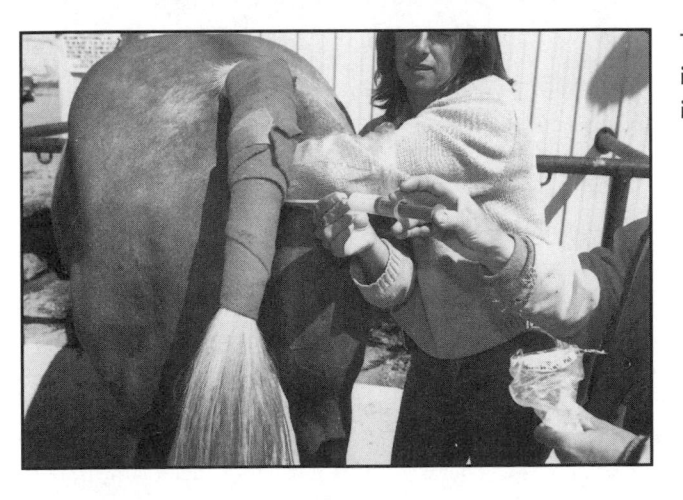

The semen is injected directly into the uterus.

The mare has a relatively long gestation period, averaging 340 days. This leaves only about 25 days between the birth of one foal and the conception of the next, if the mare is to produce foals at yearly intervals. Since the second heat occurs 30 days postpartum, it falls outside this window of opportunity.

Recent ultrasound studies of the uterus reveal that although involution of the uterus is not complete until day 21 postpartum, fertility can actually be achieved earlier. It is the presence or absence of uterine fluid that determines reproductive readiness. Persistent fluid adversely affects embryo implantation and decreases the chances of pregnancy. Ultrasound monitoring of postpartum uterine fluid reveals that after 15 days there is little or no fluid detectable in the uterus in the majority of mares. Thus if the embryo enters the uterus on day 15 or later, the pregnancy should survive.

Note that after conception occurs, there is a 5-day interval before the embryo enters the uterus. Thus if ovulation and conception can be postponed until day 10 or later, there is a good chance that the uterus will be receptive to maintaining the pregnancy. In point of fact, ovulation can be delayed until day 10 or later using a combination of progesterone, estrogen, and prostaglandin. Alternately, the interval between the foal heat and the second postpartum heat can be shortened to less than 30 days by administering prostaglandin alone.

A workable approach that meets all objectives is to monitor the mare by rectal palpation and ultrasound for ovulation and uterine fluid. If it is apparent that the mare will not ovulate until day 10 or later, and there is little or no fluid in the uterus, she can be bred on the foal heat with the expectation of achieving a normal per-cycle pregnancy rate. When ovulation is expected to occur before day 10, or if there is significant fluid accumulation in the uterus, breeding is postponed. Seven days after ovulation, the mare is injected with prostaglandin PGF2A, which shortens diestrus and brings her back into heat ahead of schedule and in time to meet the universal birth date.

Infertility

Low fertility rates are a common problem in horses. Up to 50 percent of mating cycles do not produce live foals. The stallion, the mare, or both may be implicated in the infertility problem.

INFERTILITY IN THE STALLION

Stallion infertility is the inability to fertilize an ovum. The reasons for such failure include impotence (lack of sex drive), physical ailments which prevent coitus, and diseases of the male system which adversely affect semen quality.

Low Libido. Loss of sexual interest and arousal is the most common behavior problem in stallions. A young stallion or a stud who services just a few mares each season often exhibits slow breeding characteristics with long delays in arousal, mounting, and ejaculation. This is considered normal. It improves with usage and experience.

A common psychological cause of loss of libido is a painful or traumatic breeding experience. Rough handling, excessive punishment, or severe discipline can discourage a stallion from expressing normal sexual urges.

Breeding fatigue is a common cause of loss of sexual interest and arousal. While some stallions are able to service two or three mares a day for prolonged periods without becoming sexually fatigued, for many others this schedule is too strenuous. In fact, nearly all stallions show a gradual decline in sexual interest toward the end of the breeding season. On occasion, a vigorous stallion will suddenly stop breeding, exhibiting what is referred to as a stale or sour attitude.

Rarely lack of libido is caused by testosterone deficiency. A stallion recovering from a protracted illness can take several months to regain its normal hormone balance and sex drive. A medically induced cause of testosterone deficiency is the administration of male hormones to enhance racing performance. The administered testosterone suppresses the pituitary, which stops producing gonadotropin. In the absence of gonadotropin, the plasma testosterone level remains low until the pituitary recovers. This can take months.

Treatment: Young stallions typically show remarkable improvement after breeding their first mares. The best way to expedite a successful mating is to try the stallion repeatedly using minimal restraint and lots of patient encouragement. Select an experienced mare who shows strong signs of estrus, who is well-liked by the stallion, and who stands quietly when mounted. A similar approach applies to the experienced stallion who may have been traumatized.

A time-honored method of developing stallion libido is to turn the stud out to pasture with one or more broodmares, as described in PASTURE BREEDING. In the sexually fatigued stallion, a vacation from breeding usually restores low libido. A prolonged period of rest is usually required.

Impotence caused by hormonal rather than psychological factors is difficult to treat with hormone replacement. Unfortunately, the dose of testosterone that stimulates the male libido also depresses sperm formation. One alternative is a subcutaneous injection of gonadotropin-releasing hormone (GnRH) just prior to breeding. GnRH releases stored testosterone. This may temporarily increase sexual arousal without the undesirable side effects associated with injected testosterone.

Male Functional Problems. The stallion may begin courtship with a good libido, become aroused in the presence of an estrous mare, and yet not be able to perform the act of coitus for various reasons, including inability to erect the penis, mount the mare, insert the penis, or achieve normal ejaculation. Some of these problems have a medical basis, others a medical/psychological basis, and the remainder are psychological/management problems.

Penile trauma can produce temporary or permanent loss of the ability to erect the penis. Injury can take the form of a severe laceration, penile rupture, or paraphimosis. The usual cause is a kick to the erect penis during live cover. The use of stallion rings and brushes can result in penile trauma. A poorly constructed phantom mare and misuse of the artificial vagina are other causes of penile lacerations and abrasions.

Premature erection is a condition in which "belling" of the head of the penis occurs prior to intromission, making the penis too large to enter the mare. The situation can be accommodated by lubricating the vagina well and manually directing the penis trough the vulva.

Mounting problems are characterized by repeated attempts to mount, mounting and dismounting, and dismounting prior to ejaculation. The usual causes are joint and back pain. Osteochondritis of the hocks, spine, or pelvis is frequently implicated. Stallions suffering from chronic laminitis or hoof disease experience pain when standing up on their back legs. A common cause of painful mounting is abrasions on the inside of the knees acquired from frequent mounting, particularly of a phantom mare. Nonpainful causes of failure to mount include muscle disease and nerve and spinal cord injuries.

A horse with a painful mounting problem often improves when placed on a course of Butazolidin for 7 to 10 days.

Ejaculatory failure is intromission without ejaculation. The signs of ejaculation (flagging, urethral pulsations, and belling of the glans penis) do not occur. The stallion exhibits poor or irregular thrusts, dismounts as ejaculation appears imminent, or thrusts repeatedly to the point of exhaustion.

Ejaculatory failure is often the final, frustrating expression of other factors including low libido, penile pain, and difficulty mounting.

Treatment: Treatment of the physical problem may not be sufficient to allow the stallion to regain all of his potency. If the horse has learned to associate the act of sexual intercourse with pain, frustration, or danger and punishment, the therapy must also show the horse that sex is painless, safe, pleasurable, and rewarding. This involves a sex therapy rehabilitation program. Some techniques that have proven effective are training the stallion to use an artificial vagina, which can be made more or less stimulatory by adjusting the temperature and pressure; allowing the stallion to socialize with mares more freely; changing broodmares and breeding locations; engaging in longer periods of teasing; waiting patiently for time to heal all wounds; and converting to pasture breeding.

Ejaculation failure has been treated successfully by administering drugs that contract smooth muscles in the genital tract.

Finally, conception can proceed through artificial insemination even if the horse remains functionally impaired. A stallion can be collected while standing using an artificial vagina. Neither mounting nor full erection is necessary for ejaculation. Accordingly, if a valuable stallion is unable to provide live cover for any number of reasons, artificial insemination remains a good alternative.

Semen Quality Problems. Absence of sperm is seen in several conditions that are not difficult to diagnose. They include undescended testicles, testicular hypoplasia, testicular degeneration, acute orchitis, testicular growths, and injuries resulting in testicular atrophy or loss. All are discussed in DISEASES OF THE MALE SYSTEM.

A frequent cause of reduced sperm numbers (and quality) is overuse. Stallions vary widely in their ability to produce sperm in response to breeding demands. Mature breeding stallions can be used more frequently than young stallions. However, excessive use can reduce semen quality in even the most fertile stallion. A good policy is to give all stallions a period of sexual rest during the season.

Semen contaminated by blood (*hemospermia*) or urine (*urospermia*) is abnormal. Blood in semen is believed to interfere with fertility, although this is not proven. However, blood in semen is frequently associated with *Pseudomonas aeruginosa*, a bacteria known to cause infection in the male genital tract. Red blood cells are recognized by the pink to red color of the ejaculate.

Urine in semen is recognizable by the yellow color and large volume of the sample. The effect of urine is to greatly reduce sperm motility.

A large number of bacteria of one species (especially a pathogenic species) is highly suggestive of urethritis or accessory sex gland infection. The presence of numerous white blood cells in the semen confirms this diagnosis.

Horses with any of these semen quality problems should undergo diagnostic studies beginning with bacterial culture of the sheath, the urethra (both before and after ejaculation), and seminal fluid. If further information is needed, other studies such as diagnostic ultrasound of the accessory sex glands and trans-urethral fiberoptic exam of the male genital tract can be performed. The horse should be placed at sexual rest pending diagnosis and treatment.

Nutritional deficiencies can be a cause of infertility. A male who is grossly undernourished and on a very low plane of nutrition will frequently experience loss of libido and may undergo atrophy of the testicles. Any chronic disease associated with weight loss and debilitation reduces sperm production and adversely affects libido. Overweight studs are sluggish and lazy, but this does not affect spermatogenesis and has not been proven to reduce libido.

Anabolic steroids and testosterone can cause testicular degeneration. This effect may be temporary or permanent. Most adult stallions take several months to recover sperm production after male steroids are stopped. A few remain permanently sterile.

Thyroid deficiency is not a cause of reduced fertility. In fact, adult hypothyroidism is a rare condition in horses, although a few cases have been described in Standardbreds and Thoroughbreds. Pituitary and other hormonal causes of reduced spermatogenesis are difficult to identify and treat. In general, hormonal therapies have been disappointing and appear to be of questionable value.

Genetic and chromosomal abnormalities are rare causes of infertility. Due to the complexity of the controlling genes, they are difficult to diagnose. Genetic work-ups must be carried out at schools of veterinary medicine.

Vitamin supplements have no beneficial effect on spermatogenesis or libido. Vitamin A is necessary for sperm formation, but unless a vitamin A deficiency exists (rare if the horse is receiving standard feeds), giving additional vitamin A has no proven value.

INFERTILITY IN THE MARE

Mares who do not conceive after one or two cycles are called *repeat breeders*. Repeat breeders usually cannot conceive because of genital tract infection.

The main cause of mare infertility and fetal loss during pregnancy is infection in the uterus. The windsucking perineal conformation described under Breeding Soundness Examination of the Mare, and the sexually transmitted diseases discussed below, are responsible for the majority of uterine infections.

The second leading cause of mare infertility is abnormal heat cycles, discussed earlier in this chapter.

Behavioral Infertility (Refusal to Mate). Behavioral mating problems are less common in mares than in stallions. The role of the mare in coitus is passive. The main reason the mare refuses the stallion is simply because she is not in standing heat.

Maiden mares, nervous mares, and mares with a foal at the side can be more difficult to breed. The nursing mare can be reassured by placing the foal where she can see it during the breeding process.

A fastidious mare who refuses to respond to a particular stallion may do so when placed with another stallion she knows and likes. A maiden mare who fears stallions in general should be bred to a gentle, experienced, self-confident stud who is not easily put off. She will usually accept this stallion and thus present no further difficulties.

If the mare continues to be recalcitrant, she can be hobbled or restrained by tying up a front leg. Tranquilization can be considered. If these measures fail, artificial insemination remains an option.

SEXUALLY TRANSMITTED DISEASES

Sexually transmitted diseases are a significant cause of sterility and abortion.

Bacterial Infections. There is a normal flora of bacteria on the penis and prepuce of the stallion, and in the vulva and vestibule of the mare, that inhibit the growth of virulent bacteria. When local conditions are disturbed, pathogenic bacteria become established and cause infection. Once a bacterial infection becomes established, it can be passed back and forth during coitus.

Disturbances in the normal flora of the skin of the penis can be caused by the presence of smegma that accumulates beneath the sheath and in the urethral diverticulum. While it is important to keep the penis clean, excessive washing, or the use of detergents and antiseptic solutions such as Betadine or chlorhexidine, removes friendly bacteria and inflames the skin.

Seventy-five percent of uterine infections and a majority of septic abortions in mares are caused by *Streptococcus zooepidemicus*. Other bacteria commonly found around stables and paddocks, and capable of causing infection when sexually transmitted, are species of *Staphylococci, Pseudomonas aeruginosa, Klebsiella, Actinobacter,* and *E. coli.*

When present, the windsucking vagina and the urovagina make it virtually impossible to maintain a normal bacterial flora in the vagina.

Sexually transmitted infections produce vaginitis, endometritis, and pyometra in mares. In stallions, they cause urethritis, orchitis, epididymitis, and infections of the accessory sex glands. A stallion can harbor a pathogenic bacteria and transmit the disease without having a symptomatic infection.

Prevention: Lax breeding practices contribute to the transmission of sexual diseases. While it is common practice to wash the mare's vulva and buttocks before breeding, failure to wash the stallion's penis and sheath *before and after mating* is a critical omission and can lead to a sexually transmitted infection in all the mares he services.

Good hygienic technique involves the wearing of sterile disposable gloves when washing the genitalia. Change gloves between horses. Each horse should have a separate wash bucket with a clean plastic liner filled with warm soapy water. Use only clean linen or paper towels, and discard after use.

A breeding soundness examination (discussed earlier) should be done on all horses before the breeding season. This exam includes endometrial, urethral, and semen cultures. These cultures should identify infected horses.

Treatment: Early diagnosis of bacterial infection may prevent chronic disease and sterility. Treatment is discussed in the sections on DISEASES OF THE MALE AND FEMALE SYSTEMS. A period of sexual rest for at least 2 months is important to prevent relapse. It is essential to re-investigate the mare or stallion with appropriate diagnostic tests to be sure the disease is cured before returning the horse to breeding.

Contagious Equine Metritis. Contagious equine metritis (CEM) is a highly contagious venereal disease caused by the organism *Taylorella equigenitalis*. No cases have been reported in the United States or Canada since 1983, but the disease is important to breeders who import horses from Europe and Japan. Federal regulations impose restrictions on the importation of horses from these countries. CEM is a significant cause of infertility in mares. Early abortions do occur, but this does not happen often because most CEM-positive mares usually are unable to conceive.

In the mare, signs of CEM occur 2 to 6 days after breeding. They include a copious gray to creamy discharge that mats the tail and hindquarters. However, many mares do not show signs of infection. These mares are asymptomatic carriers.

A stallion who harbors T. *equigenitalis* usually does not show signs of infection. The first indication of disease is a high incidence of reproductive failure in the mares he services.

In mares, the diagnosis of CEM is made by taking cultures from the clitoral fossa at any stage of the estrous cycle. CEM survives for long periods in this location. A blood test for CEM is reliable in mares 3 to 6 weeks after exposure, but serological titers decline quickly, and there is no blood test that will detect the carrier state. In stallions, the bacteria survives in the smegma of the prepuce, the urethral fossa, and surface of the penis. Stallions are checked by taking cultures from these areas. There is no blood test available for the diagnosis of CEM in stallions.

Treatment: The CEM bacteria is susceptible to most antibiotics and disinfectants. Treatment in mares with acute infection involves the use of antibiotics orally or by intrauterine infusion. The carrier state in females, however, is difficult to eliminate. Recommendations include washing the genitalia daily with 2 percent chlorhexidine solution and applying 0.2 percent nitrofurazone cream to the clitoral fossa. An operation to remove the clitoris may be advised to eliminate a continued focus of infection.

It is relatively easy to eliminate the carrier state in males. The penis should be cleansed daily with 2 percent chlorhexidine. After drying, nitrofurazone cream is applied to the penis. Prevention involves the use of strict hygiene before and after breeding.

Coital Exanthema. This is a highly contagious viral disease caused by equine herpesvirus type 3. It is spread from mare to stallion by genital contact. It is rare in the United States. It is not a cause of infertility or abortion.

During the acute stage in mares, painful blisters appear quite suddenly on the surface of the vulva and perineum. There is a whitish discharge on the buttocks and tail. The blisters become ulcerated and later scab over.

In the stallion, blisters 1 to 1.5 cm in size form on the glans and body of the penis. These vesicles also develop into pustules and ulcers, leaving depigmented spots after healing. With a severe infection, the penis becomes inflamed and swollen.

Treatment: The disease runs its course in about 2 to 3 weeks. Recovery from infection, however, does not confer immunity; future relapses can occur during serious illnesses and times of stress.

It is important to avoid secondary bacterial infection of the penis. Wash the penis with a mild soap (such as Ivory) and rinse thoroughly. An antibiotic ointment may be useful in preventing infection and helps to soften scabs. Insect control is a major factor because flies can seriously aggravate open sores on the penis. Inflammation of the vulva is treated in a like manner.

The stallion should be rested until the skin of the penis is completely healed (3 to 4 weeks). The mare can usually be bred on the next heat cycle.

Dourine. This disease is caused by a protozoan transmitted during sexual intercourse. Dourine has been eradicated in many countries including the United States, but still occurs in South Africa, Asia, and the former USSR.

In the mare, the initial signs are swelling of the vulva and a vaginal discharge; in the stallion, a urethral discharge accompanied by swelling of the penis, prepuce, and scrotum. As the disease progresses, large round patches of raised skin appear in crops all over the body. Dourine is often fatal. Treatment is impractical as results are poor. Euthanasia is mandatory to prevent epidemic spread.

Diseases of the Female System

Infections in the female reproductive system adversely affect fertility and the ability to carry a foal to term.

VAGINITIS AND VULVITIS

Infections of the vulva and vagina are common and occur after coitus, foaling, vaginal examination, and birthing injuries. The acquired perineal conformation described as "windsucker" or pneumovagina is the major cause of vaginitis and all other genital tract infections in the mare. In this condition, the perineum is sloping, the anus is sunken, and the lips of the vulva and vulvovaginal sphincter do not form a protective seal against fecal contamination of the vagina.

The *urovagina* is an acquired perineal conformation defect similar to the above. Urine refluxes from the urethra and pools in the dependent portion of the vagina near the cervix. This invariably results in vaginal and cervical infections. Urine scalds may be visible around the buttocks and perineum.

Vaginitis and vulvitis are mild infections which by themselves do not cause infertility. The importance of vaginitis is that it can progress to endometritis, particularly when there is a continuing source of contamination.

Uncomplicated vaginitis usually clears spontaneously. Vaginal washes with an antiseptic such as 2 percent chlorhexidine hasten this process. Treatment of urine scalds involves the periodic application of zinc oxide ointment. All predisposing perineal deformities should be surgically corrected.

VAGINAL BLEEDING

A maiden mare with an intact hymen will experience vaginal bleeding after coitus; ordinarily the bleeding is not severe.

A mare that bleeds profusely after a covering may have sustained a tear in the vagina or a laceration of the cervix. A cervical tear is most likely to occur when the mare is bred to a stallion with a large penis. Veterinary repair is indicated.

Coital injuries can be minimized by knowledgeable stallion handling and the use of a breeding roll as described in the section on COVERING THE MARE. An intact hymen should be opened before the breeding season.

Postpartum vaginal bleeding is discussed in Chapter 15, Pregnancy and Foaling.

CERVIX DISEASES

Infection of the cervix (*cervicitis*) is a sequel to infection of the vagina. Occasionally, an infected cervical canal becomes scarred and constricted, interfering with uterine drainage and predisposing the mare to pyometra.

Lacerations of the cervix occur during foaling and less commonly during coitus. A lacerated cervix results in *cervical incompetence*. An incompetent cervix remains partially open. This nearly always leads to infection of the uterus. If the mare is able to become pregnant, the incompetent cervix results in abortion.

Lacerations of the cervix should be repaired. The repair is best done about 1 month after foaling. When a broodmare presents with an incompetent cervix, a purse string suture can be taken around the cervix a few days after service. This may prevent the cervix from opening up prematurely. If the pregnancy goes to term, the suture must be removed before foaling.

UTERINE INFECTIONS

Uterine infection is the most common cause of infertility. The two major predisposing causes of uterine infection are the windsucking vagina and sexually transmitted diseases. In addition, contamination of the uterus occurs whenever the cervical barrier is breached by foaling, vaginal palpation, and all procedures in which instruments are introduced into the uterine cavity.

All mares experience some degree of bacterial contamination after service and foaling. The mare with an intact defense system clears the contamination within a few days. These defenses include all the physical barriers to uterine contamination (a closed vulva, an intact vulvovaginal sphincter, and a tight cervix); a hormonal and immune mechanism that establishes a resistant endometrium; and most importantly, the uterine tone and muscular contractility that causes infected secretions to be expelled rapidly from the uterine cavity.

The older, multiparous, barren mare (who may also have acquired a pneumovagina) is the example of the individual who, because of repeated assaults on her defense mechanisms over the years, is no longer capable of clearing her uterus spontaneously and thus is more likely to harbor infection.

ENDOMETRITIS

Endometritis is an infection of the cavity of the uterus. It is classified as acute or chronic, depending on the severity and duration of the infection. Both are aspects of the same process, and the distinction between them is somewhat blurred.

A mare with endometritis usually appears in good health, yet fails to conceive after several matings. Occasionally, she exhibits a pattern of unexplained fetal loss during pregnancy. A vaginal discharge is sometimes present or can be detected on vaginal exam. Rectal exam is often normal, but may show an enlarged uterus containing fluid. This can be confirmed by diagnostic ultrasound.

A positive uterine culture is not always indicative of endometritis. A mixed bacterial flora in the uterus is common. During collection, the culture specimen can become contaminated by cervical or vaginal bacteria. However, the findings of a pathogenic strain (*Streptococcus zooepidemicus, E. coli, Proteus, Pseudomonas aeruginosa, Staphylococcus species*) on one or more cultures is significant. Cytology and endometrial biopsy will confirm the diagnosis. For more information on these procedures, see the discussion in BREEDING SOUNDNESS EXAMINATION OF THE MARE.

After long-standing endometrial infection, the uterus becomes fibrotic (scarred). Fibrosis interferes with placental attachment. An endometrial biopsy will show the extent of fibrosis, which can then be graded. Mares in category 1 have normal findings (or slight changes), with a 70 percent chance of producing a live foal.

Mares in category 2 have reversible or moderately severe changes, with a 30 to 70 percent chance of producing a live foal. Mares in category 3 have widespread fibrosis and less than a 10 percent chance of producing a live foal.

Treatment: The objective of treatment is to eliminate infection and produce a live foal. The treatment of mares with chronic low-grade inflammation and no symptoms of active infection can be deferred until the time of breeding, as described below. Mares with severe acute endometritis characterized by purulent vaginal discharge should be treated intensely before they are bred.

Antibiotics selected on the basis of sensitivity tests have been the mainstay of treatment in the past. Antibiotics can be given either systemically or by local infusion into the uterus. The advantage of local infusion is that it puts the antibiotic squarely in the spot where it can do the most good. The disadvantage is that infusion runs the risk of introducing new strains of bacteria, which are likely to be resistant to the antibiotic initially selected. Unfortunately, the development of antibiotic-resistant strains of bacteria is a common problem. Even when the drugs are given systemically, superinfection with resistant bacteria as well as yeast and fungi remains a possibility. For these reasons, antibiotics are being used less frequently.

Based on the observation that natural defenses and the ability to clear the uterus of contamination correlate with successful pregnancy, irrigation of the uterus with saline alone (no antibiotic) has become the standard treatment of many veterinarians. Mechanically flushing the uterus appears to successfully eliminate infected fluid, debris, and toxic products.

A balloon catheter is placed through the cervix into the uterine cavity. The cavity is flushed with 1 to 2 liters of sterile saline, and the fluid is recovered by gravity or expelled with the aid of oxytocin. The appearance of the recovered fluid (going from cloudy to clear) indicates the degree of progress and need for further irrigation. An indwelling catheter can be placed to avoid having to enter the mare's reproductive tract each time the uterus is irrigated.

In mares with low-grade infection, flushing is initiated just prior to breeding and then again 6 hours after breeding. The sperm are well up into the oviducts within 2 hours, so there is little likelihood of interfering with conception.

Since natural defenses are most efficient during estrus when the output of estrogen is greatest, shortening the second half of the estrous cycle to increase the frequency of estrus is an adjunctive step that has proven to be advantageous. This is accomplished by giving prostaglandin 5 to 6 days postovulation to regress the corpus luteum and shorten the length of diestrus.

To prevent reinfection after treatment, it is important to correct any anatomical problems such as pneumovagina or incompetent cervix.

Prevention: Before coitus, the mare *and* the stallion should be cleansed and washed as described above. This reduces the frequency of bacterial contamination and the transmission of sexual infections. Invasive diagnostic procedures that breach the cervix should be restricted to medical necessity and should be performed with antiseptic technique. Strict hygiene during foaling also is of utmost importance.

PYOMETRA (ABSCESS OF THE UTERUS)

Pyometra is the accumulation of pus in the uterus. Some cases are related to cervical incompetence, which predisposes to ascending infection; others to cervical scarring that blocks the cervical canal and thus interferes with the protective flushing mechanism by which the uterus rids itself of infection. In many cases, however, there is no explanation for the pyometra.

When scars or adhesions plug off the cervix, several quarts of fluid (up to 60) can accumulate in the distended uterus. Rectal palpation and transrectal ultrasound will easily diagnose this problem. When the cervix is not obstructed, a vaginal speculum exam may reveal pus in the vagina.

Mares with pyometra generally do not appear ill and rarely exhibit signs of toxicity. However, they usually don't come into heat at regular intervals, owing to a persistent corpus luteum (see ABNORMAL HEAT CYCLES), and it is for this reason that medical opinion is usually sought. A persistent CL can be diagnosed by obtaining a serum progesterone level, which is positive when elevated.

Treatment: It involves draining and flushing the uterus with frequent warm saline lavages. Antibiotics are added to treat accompanying endometritis. Despite aggressive treatment, relapse is common. Endometrial biopsy is performed in all cases to determine the amount of salvageable endometrium. In the majority of mares, the extent of endometrial scarring and atrophy make successful breeding unlikely.

Acute metritis is a severe and often fatal disease of the entire uterus caused by a postpartum infection of the mare's reproductive tract during or shortly after foaling. It is discussed in chapter 15, Pregnancy and Foaling.

Diseases of the Male System

THE PENIS

Skin Disorders. A build-up of smegma and bacteria within the prepuce and urethral diverticulum can lead to inflammation of the surrounding skin. This happens in both stallions and geldings.

In addition, bacterial infection can occur when the resident flora of the penile skin is destroyed by excessive washing, particularly with antiseptics such as Betadine or chlorhexidine.

Irrespective of cause, the skin of an inflamed penis and prepuce appears fluid-filled and swollen. The penis may be extended.

Treatment: Cleanse the penis and sheath with warm soapy water to remove smegma. Use a mild soap such as Ivory. If the penis is infected (red, swollen, tender to touch), apply a topical antibiotic ointment. Insect control is a major factor because flies can seriously aggravate an inflamed penis (see INSECT CONTROL). Bacterial infection can be prevented by periodically cleaning the sheath as described in chapter 4, Skin.

The larva of the Habronema stomach worm may be deposited on the sheath or skin of the penis by stable and horseflies. These summer sores (*habronema granulomas*) often cause intense itching and may interfere with urination and ejaculation. Treatment of summer sores is discussed in chapter 4, Skin.

Squamous cell carcinoma is the most common growth affecting the penis. Smegma accumulation is a predisposing cause. The tumor begins as a rough thickened patch of skin, which becomes ulcerated and secondarily infected. Malignant squamous cell carcinomas can metastasize. Sarcoids, papillomas, melanomas, and lipomas are other tumors of the penis. Biopsy is the only way to make an exact diagnosis.

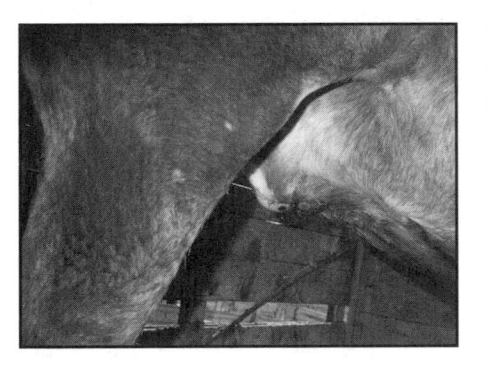

Squamous cell carcinoma is the most common tumor of the penis and sheath.

Penile tumors can be treated by cryotherapy (freezing), by a circumcision-like removal of skin, or by removal of the entire penis. The decision depends upon the size, location, and degree of malignancy of the tumor.

Phimosis. Phimosis is the inability to protrude the penis through a constricted prepuce. Constrictions almost always follow sheath infections, which invariably heal with scarring. Rarely the constriction is congenital, or caused by a growth.

Treatment involves cleaning the sheath cavity with 3 percent hydrogen peroxide solution (dilute 1:10), and then instilling an antibiotic such as Triple Antibiotic Ointment. Antiseptics such as Betadine and chlorhexidine worsen the problem and are contraindicated. Surgical opening of the constricted prepuce may be required.

Paraphimosis. In this condition, the extended penis is unable to return to its former position inside the sheath. There are three types of paraphimosis. In the first, the retractor muscles are "paralyzed." This usually follows the administration of a phenothiazine tranquilizer. In the second, the penis remains engorged because the erectile tissue clots. This follows kicks to the penis during breeding. The third type of paraphimosis is actually *phimosis*, in which the penis manages to extend through a tight prepuce which then forms a constricting band around the shaft of the penis, causing sustained engorgement.

Treatment: Paraphimosis is an emergency. The penis must be returned to its sheath as quickly as possible to prevent further swelling and inflammation that makes reduction increasingly difficult. Ice packs and pressure are used to slowly reduce swelling as the penis is worked back up into the sheath. A purse-string suture through the prepuce prevents the penis from re-extending. The penis is supported with a gauze sling tied around the horse's body. Infection is treated with antibiotics. Sexual rest is essential. An antidote to phenothiazine-induced paralysis is available.

If the penis cannot be manually reduced, two surgical options remain. One is a penis suspension operation; the other is removal of the penis.

URETHRA

Urethritis. Sexually transmitted diseases are the most common cause of infection of the urethra. Sheath infections, *Habronema granulomas*, and growths of the penis are other causes.

A stallion with urethritis often passes blood in his ejaculate (*hemospermia*). Blood in semen is believed to interfere with fertility, although this has not been proven. The signs of urethritis are a urethral discharge and frequent painful urination. These signs may be absent.

Treatment: The presence of infection can be confirmed by cultures and sensitivities. The accessory sex glands may be involved. This is determined by collecting and examining separate phases of the ejaculate. Fiberoptic endoscopy can be used to directly visualize the urethra and the openings of the accessory sex glands, as well as the neck of the bladder. This helps to determine the cause of hemospermia and to rule out stones and tumors.

Urethral Obstruction. Strictures and stones are the most common causes of urethral obstruction. Stones in the urinary tract are discussed in chapter 13, Urinary System.

Strictures of the urethra occur from stallion rings, *Habronema* sores, and sexually transmitted bacterial infections. Note that the tip of the urethra protrudes during erection and can be lacerated by the tail hairs of the mare. A laceration of the urethra frequently goes on to form a stricture. Kicks to the penis can result in post-traumatic urethral scarring.

Smegma may accumulate in the urethral fossa in sufficient amounts to press on the end of the urethra and cause obstruction. This is called a "bean." It is more common in older horses. The chief sign is spraying. Rarely, a tumor of the penis obstructs the urethra.

The signs of urethral obstruction are colic, urine spraying, dribbling, extension of the penis, and frequent difficult urination.

Treatment: A catheter is placed to relieve a blockage. Further treatment is directed at the initiating cause. Clean lacerations of the urethra are repaired at the time of injury. Badly traumatized wounds are left unsutured and allowed to heal around an indwelling catheter.

TESTICLES

Orchitis. Inflammation of the testicle is called *orchitis*. It is sometimes accompanied by *epididymitis,* which is inflammation of the coiled tubules on top of the testicle. Sexually transmitted bacterial infections are the most common cause of both conditions, especially those produced by *Streptococcus zooepidemicus*. The infection starts in the urethra and works its way up to the testicle.

Viruses and parasites are rare causes of orchitis.

Signs of orchitis (and associated epididymitis) are a hard, swollen, painful mass in the scrotum. There is a characteristic hopping gait. The semen contains bacteria, pus, and abnormal sperm. Ultrasound of the testicle is helpful in distinguishing between infection, trauma, and tumor, and to determine if the epididymis is involved. Needle aspiration biopsy of the testicle can be performed in questionable cases.

Treatment: Ice packs are applied to the scrotum to reduce pain and swelling. The testicles are elevated using an external support. Antibiotics selected on the basis of semen culture and sensitivity tests are given intravenously and continued for 1 to 2 weeks after swelling and pain subside. Anti-inflammatory drugs and corticosteroids help to reduce pain and swelling.

Testicular degeneration often follows acute orchitis. Fertility is thus dependent upon the health of the remaining testicle. A testicular abscess or chronic infection may necessitate unilateral castration to clear the reproductive tract of infection and preserve fertility.

Acute epididymitis results in scarring of the tubules. This blocks the passage of sperm. The only effective treatment is to remove the epididymis and testicle.

Testicular Injury. The usual cause of a testicular injury is a kick during mating. A severe blow results in hemorrhage and marked swelling of the testicle. Later the testicle undergoes atrophy and becomes small and hard. Treatment and prognosis are like that for orchitis.

Undescended Testicle. A horse with one or both testicles missing from the scrotum is said to be *cryptorchid*. Testicular descent from the abdomen to the scrotum occurs in utero at about 300 days' gestation. An interruption in the normal sequence of events can leave a testicle in the abdomen (10 percent of the time), or in the inguinal canal (90 percent). Retained testicles are associated with an increased incidence of tumor.

Two to three days after birth, the rings in the abdominal wall close tightly. A testicle that has not passed through the inguinal ring at this time remains intra-abdominal. One that makes it through the ring and remains in the inguinal canal may yet descend. It is reported that descent can occur up to as late as 4 years of age.

Undescended testicles continue to produce testosterone but don't produce sperm. Thus a horse with two cryptorchid testes has all the behavioral characteristics of the stallion but is not fertile. A horse with one normal testicle is fertile, but usually is not used for breeding because the condition is considered to be hereditary.

An undescended testicle can often be felt in the inguinal canal, or can be located by rectal palpation. Ultrasound is useful in locating a testicle that can't be palpated.

Treatment: Castration is indicated for all cryptorchid horses. It is important to find and remove the cryptorchid testicle. This can be technically difficult if the

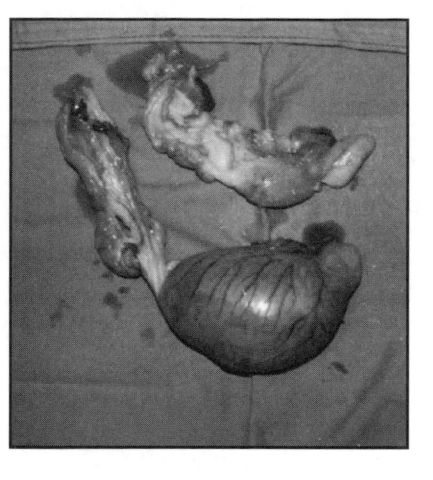

Two testicles. The smaller undescended testicle was found in the inguinal canal.

testicle is intra-abdominal or located out of the usual path of descent (*ectopic*). There is a specific syndrome in which the horse is said to have been gelded but continues to act like a stallion. The cause is a retained testicle missed at castration. A serum testosterone level before and after administering HCG, or a single estrone sulfate measurement, will determine whether functioning testicular tissue is present. If the test is positive, one testicle was not removed, and the horse should undergo an exploratory operation.

Testicular Hypoplasia. This is a developmental disorder in which one or both testicles are small and flabby, failing to reach normal size by maturity. Small testicles are the norm in colts and young stallions. The testicles do not achieve adult size until about age 4. In a normal 3-year-old, the scrotal width should be greater than 3 inches. If it is less than 3 inches, hypoplasia is likely.

Hypoplastic testicles are associated with impaired sperm production. An ejaculate will show either no sperm or a low concentration of sperm with numerous abnormal spermatocytes. The diagnosis can be confirmed by testicular biopsy.

Testicular hypoplasia should be distinguished from testicular degeneration (described below) because the outlook for future fertility is better with testicular degeneration. In testicular degeneration, the testicles were normal before they became small.

Testicular Neoplasms. Benign and malignant testicular tumors are uncommon in the horse. Signs are those of a painless enlargement of one testicle, which may go unnoticed for some time. Bilateral tumors are rare. Malignant tumors tend to grow slowly and can often be cured by orchiectomy. Benign tumors are almost invariably cured by orchiectomy.

The diagnosis is suspected on examination of the testicles. Ultrasound may provide additional information. Fine needle aspiration is the easiest way to obtain tissue for diagnosis.

The effect of the tumor on sperm production is variable, which frequently influences the timing of surgery. If the semen quality is good and the stallion is booked, surgery is often deferred until the end of the breeding season.

There is a higher incidence of tumors in undescended testicles. Early removal of these testicles is the best method of prevention.

Torsion of the Spermatic Cord. A 360-degree twist of the testicle within the scrotum shuts off the blood supply to the testicle. Young stallions are most commonly affected, often during or immediately after strenuous exercise. The testicle will die unless the problem is corrected within a few hours. Signs of torsion are indistinguishable from those of acute orchitis.

The veterinarian should be called at once on suspicion of a swollen, painful testicle. Emergency surgery is indicated when there is a possibility of salvaging the testicle. Unfortunately, in most cases too much time has elapsed and irreversible damage has occurred. Atrophy of the testicle is the usual outcome.

Testicular Degeneration. Testicular degeneration is an acquired condition in which the sperm-producing tissue of the testicles is damaged, resulting in reversible or permanent sterility.

A common cause of reversible testicular degeneration is high fever. In order for testicles to produce sperm, the temperature in the scrotum must be at least 2 to 3 degrees below that of body temperature. Fever raises scrotal temperature. The problem will be further compounded if the horse lies down, bringing the testicles up close to the body. Febrile diseases commonly associated with temporary sterility are equine infectious anemia, pneumonia, laminitis, equine viral arteritis, equine influenza, strangles, and ehrlichiosis.

Prolonged high environmental temperatures with high humidity have been implicated in causing testicular degeneration, as have scrotal hernias in which the heat of the intestine raises the scrotal temperature. In all these conditions, the testicles become small and flabby like those of testicular hypoplasia.

A type of testicular degeneration that can be either reversible or permanent is that caused by the injection of anabolic steroids and testosterone given to enhance racing performance. Early administration (during the first year of life), and continuous administration over the stallion's racing career, appear to increase the likelihood of permanent damage.

Temporary sterility often improves once the cause is removed. It takes 50 to 60 days for regenerating sperm to reach the ejaculate, so any improvement in sperm quality will not be seen for at least 2 months. Frequent semen examinations are required to monitor progress. Sexual rest is necessary. Feed a balanced ration high in protein and vitamin A.

Irreversible sterility follows diseases that destroy the testicles, including testicular trauma and acute bilateral orchitis. These testicles become small as glandular tissue is replaced by fibrous connective tissue.

Heat and Pregnancy Prevention

Progesterone drugs such as altrenogest can be used to suppress signs of heat in cycling mares. Estrous behavior disappears 2 to 3 days after the start of treatment and does not return until treatment is stopped. Progesterone weakens the cellular defense mechanisms of the uterus against infection. This is not likely to be a problem during short-term administration, but extended use is potentially detrimental. Veterinary consultation is advisable before starting a mare on progesterone.

When stallions and cycling mares are kept on the same premises, accidental pregnancies can occur. Stallions are remarkably adept at getting to mares in heat. Confining stallions to box stalls except when under direct supervision is probably the most practical way to prevent accidental matings.

An intact male who will not be used at stud is usually gelded. This controls stallion behavior and makes the horse more serviceable. However, some horsemen prefer to own and ride a stallion.

Due to the magnitude of the operation, removal of the ovaries is seldom done for sterilization purposes in mares.

When accidental or unwanted pregnancy does occur, the two available options are to terminate the pregnancy or allow the mare to carry the foal to term.

PREGNANCY TERMINATION (ELECTIVE ABORTION)

Indications for elective abortion are mismating, accidental or unwanted pregnancy, hydrops amnion, and twin pregnancies. The rationale for avoiding twin pregnancies as well as the methodology for converting a double pregnancy to a singleton is discussed in the section on TWINS.

Elective abortion should be done during the first 4 months of pregnancy. After 4 months, it is safer and better to allow the mare to carry her foal to term.

The two techniques for elective abortion are prostaglandin injection and intra-uterine infusion. The choice of method will depend on the stage of pregnancy.

Prostaglandin (PGF2α). High levels of progesterone are needed to maintain an intrauterine pregnancy. Progesterone is manufactured by the corpus luteum (CL) in the ovary. A single injection of PGF2α given after the formation of a mature CL (5 days after ovulation) and before the formation of endometrial cups (37 days), will cause rapid regression (lysis) of the CL, loss of pregnancy, and return of the mare to heat (see PERSISTENT CORPUS LUTEUM for a discussion of endometrial cups). Before 5 days postovulation, PGF2α will not cause abortion because the CL has not matured.

After 37 days, PGF2α must be administered daily for 4 days. Even though the mare will abort, she will not return to estrus until the endometrial cups cease to function, which takes 120 to 150 days. These mares usually cannot be rebred until the next season.

Intrauterine Infusion. Dilatation of the cervix followed by infusion of a saline/antibiotic solution into the pregnant mare's uterus will cause abortion within 48 hours. The infusion irritates the uterus and causes contractions. In addition, the irritation releases PGF2α. Both mechanisms appear to be involved in causing the abortion.

Just as with PGF2α, intrauterine infusion must be done within 37 days of gestation; otherwise the mare will not cycle for 4 to 5 months.

REMOVING THE OVARIES (OVARIECTOMY)

Removal of both ovaries is a major operation and therefore is not done frequently for sterilization. A complete hysterectomy (removal of the uterus as well as the ovaries) is not done for sterilization in the horse as it is in the dog and cat.

The usual reasons for ovariectomy are to remove an ovarian neoplasm, to eliminate estrous behavior in a mare not valued for breeding, or to modify aggressive or nymphomaniac behavior. Ovariectomy can be done by the vaginal, flank, or midline abdominal approach, depending on the size of the ovaries, temperament of the mare, and preferred technique of the veterinary surgeon. The vaginal approach is the most common because it can be done under local anesthesia with the mare standing, is less expensive, and perhaps has fewer complications.

Two days before surgery the mare should be given mineral oil by gastric tube to remove fecal balls in the colon that might feel like ovaries to the veterinary surgeon. Withhold feed for 24 to 48 hours but allow unlimited access to fresh water.

After the operation, your veterinarian may suggest cross-tying the mare for 1 week to prevent stress in the incision area caused by getting up and down. The mare can return to full activity in 2 weeks. Postoperatively, antibiotics and anti-inflammatory drugs are often prescribed. Postoperative complications, although uncommon, include intra-abdominal bleeding and shock (first 24 hours), wound infection, rupture of abdominal contents through the vaginal or abdominal incision, and peritonitis.

MALE CASTRATION (GELDING)

The primary indication for gelding is to prevent aggressive or stallion behavior in a horse not valued for his breeding potential. A gelding is always more tractable than a stallion and tends to perform better for pleasure and show. A gelding is easier to keep with other horses and shows little or no interest in the estrous mare.

Castration may be indicated for medical reasons including testicular disease, undescended testicles, and inguinal hernia.

Castration can be performed at any age including the first few weeks of life without complications. Most horses are not castrated before 12 to 18 months of age to allow for physical development. When the stallion is castrated after sexual maturity, his libido and sex drive usually persist for 4 to 6 months, but can last for up to a year.

A complete physical examination should precede the surgery. Infectious diseases, anemia, and unthriftiness caused by parasites or malnutrition should be corrected before surgery is undertaken. A tetanus toxoid booster is given to all immunized horses, and tetanus antitoxin is also given if the horse was not previously immunized.

The operation can be performed under local anesthesia and IV sedation with the horse standing or lying on his side.

Post-operative complications are uncommon. They include bleeding, peritonitis, prolapse of abdominal contents through the inguinal ring, spermatic cord infection, and abscess of the scrotum.

After surgery, your veterinarian may ask you to confine the horse in a clean stall or paddock (away from flies if possible) for 2 weeks. Exercise the horse for 15 to 30 minutes twice daily to prevent scrotal swelling.

Consult your veterinarian if the horse exhibits colic, fever, unusual swelling at the site of the operation, or the drainage of purulent material.

PREGNANCY AND FOALING

Pregnancy

GESTATION

Gestation is the period from conception to birth. As reckoned from the first day of successful mating, it averages 340 days with a range of 320 to 370 days. A gestation of 370 days is considered long, but mares have been known to deliver healthy foals after 399 days.

Foals born before 320 days are considered premature. If the foal is born before 300 days it will usually be too young to survive.

DETERMINING PREGNANCY

Failure to show heat 18 to 22 days after service is suggestive but not conclusive of pregnancy. Regular stallion teasing every 1 to 2 days for up to 40 days is required to establish failure to show heat.

Rectal palpation as early as 20 to 30 days is an early reliable indicator of pregnancy, provided the examiner is highly skilled at pregnancy palpation. Transrectal palpation performed between days 40 and 50 is 95 percent accurate. Findings that confirm pregnancy are a uterine horn that is firm and tubular, and a cervix that is firm and contracted. The ovaries should contain follicles no larger than 2.5 cm in size. The uterine wall is thinner at the site of the implanted embryo.

Transrectal ultrasound has added greatly to knowledge of early pregnancy. It is particularly useful in the diagnosis of twins. Between days 15 and 50, ultrasound is 95 percent accurate for the diagnosis of pregnancy. Scanning usually is not done before day 18, but mares with a history of twins or double ovulation should be scanned between days 12 and 15 in order to effectively manage pregnancy reduction to a singleton. The fetal heart is visible on ultrasound by day 30.

The mare immunological pregnancy test (MIP) is the most frequently used serum pregnancy test—because it is accurate, inexpensive, and convenient. The MIP is based on detecting elevated levels of equine chorionic gonadrotropin (eCG) in the mare's serum between days 40 and 120 of gestation. This test is 95 percent accurate. It will not detect pregnancies of less than 40 days' gestation. In addition, should the pregnancy be lost *after* day 37, the test will remain falsely positive due to the activity of the endometrial cups discussed in the section on PERSISTENT CORPUS LUTEUM.

Plasma progesterone levels, and milk progesterone levels in lactating mares, are elevated as early as the 16th day of gestation. These tests are 90 percent accurate.

CARE AND FEEDING DURING PREGNANCY

During the first 8 months of pregnancy, feed the mare her usual ration of high-quality feed. Trace-mineralized salt, which in selenium-deficient areas should contain selenium, should be fed free-choice as the only salt available.

During the last 3 months of pregnancy there is a significant increase in the size of the foal. The mare can be expected to gain about one-half pound of weight per day. This weight represents growth of the foal. Since the mare's weight increases by about 15 percent during the last 3 months, increase the amount of feed accordingly.

The nutrient requirements for an 1,100 lb. mare during the last 3 months of pregnancy are given in Table I in chapter 17, Feeding and Nutrition. In essence, the mare will require an additional 15 percent in dietary protein and energy, and twice as much calcium, phosphorus, and vitamin A.

If you are feeding high-quality alfalfa or legumes, either as hay or pasture forage, most of these additional requirements can be met by the mare's natural tendency to eat more feed. A grain or protein supplement is not required when feeding top-quality hay. However, additional calcium and (especially) phosphorus are needed and should be provided by mineral supplements, as grass and legume hays generally do not contain sufficient amounts of either. To trace-mineralized salt, add a calcium-phosphorus mixture such as monodicalcium phosphate or some other calcium/phosphorus mineral supplement, as shown in Table IV. Alternately, a sample ration as shown in Table V can be used in place of feeding alfalfa.

It is particularly important for the mare to be well nourished at the end of pregnancy in order to maintain milk production and prevent weight loss during lactation. She should be moderately fleshy to heavy with a body condition score (as given in WEIGHT GAIN AND LOSS) of at least 6.

Note that mature grass pastures and hays do not contain enough protein or dietary energy to produce significant weight gain during pregnancy and lactation. Mares on such pastures should be given a supplemental grain mix containing at least 16 percent crude protein at the daily rate of $1/2$ to 1 pound per 100 pounds body weight, to effect weight gain and a body score of 6 to 7. In addition, larger quantities of calcium will be needed than when feeding legume hays.

Water requirements increase greatly during pregnancy. The mare should have free access to clean fresh water at all times.

A moderate exercise program maintains muscle tone and condition. A physically fit mare is more apt to deliver a healthy foal and have fewer postpartum complications. Mares on pasture get adequate exercise. Those confined to a stall or paddock should be taken out and exercised twice a day. A mare can be ridden up to the last month of pregnancy. However, intense physical exercise should be avoided. Overexertion and emotional stress have been linked to pregnancy loss. Transporting a mare over a long distance is a cause of emotional and physical stress, and should be avoided if at all possible, especially during the last 2 months of pregnancy.

Certain vaccinations are suggested during pregnancy (see Table I and Table II in chapter 3, Infectious Diseases). Vaccinations boost the immunity of the broodmare and insure that high levels of antibody will be present in her colostrum.

The risk of abortion following exposure to the rhinopneumonitis virus is significant. Vaccinations provide immunity for only 2 months. It is recommended that vaccinations for rhinopneumonitis be given during the 5th, 7th, and 9th months of gestation. Some practitioners recommend vaccinating mares in the 3rd month as well. A modified live virus vaccine and a killed (inactivated) vaccine have been approved for pregnant mares. Only the killed vaccine is labeled for use in preventing abortions.

Tetanus toxoid, equine encephalitis, and equine influenza boosters should be given 3 to 6 weeks before foaling.

If a pregnant mare develops equine viral arteritis, there is a 50 percent chance she will abort. Preventive vaccination before pregnancy may be indicated in certain high-risk areas.

All horses should be on a regular deworming program as described in chapter 2, Parasites. Internal parasites drain the mare of nutrients, cause tissue damage, decrease her resistance to infection, and have a harmful effect on the fetus. Accordingly, the mare should be on the same deworming schedule as other horses on the premises. Note that because of the risk of abortion, benzimidazole dewormers are not recommended during the first trimester, and organophosphate dewormers are not recommended past mid-trimester. It is routine practice not to administer dewormers during the last 6 weeks of gestation.

On the day of foaling, ivermectin should be given to prevent the passage of threadworms to the foal in the mare's milk. Threadworms cause respiratory and intestinal damage in foals. A foal at risk for threadworms should be dewormed at 3 weeks of age.

Fetal Loss During Pregnancy

The risk of fetal loss may be as high as 30 percent. Pregnancy loss is highest during the period of the embryo. It is more common in mares over 18 years of age and in mares with a history of infertility or prior abortion.

EARLY EMBRYONIC DEATH (EED)

EED is defined as loss of the embryo before day 40 of gestation.

Fetal loss can actually occur even before the embryo implants in the wall of the uterus, owing to unfavorable environmental conditions or a genetic defect in the fertilized egg. Recent ultrasound scanning in early pregnancy reveals that this is common. These early embryos are small and are presumably reabsorbed.

Ultrasound scanning of the cervix after implantation reveals that the cervix is open at the time of early embryonic loss. This suggests that many of these larger embryos are lost by passage through the cervix rather than by true reabsorption.

When pregnancy loss occurs after 37 days, the endometrial cups, discussed in the section on PERSISTENT CORPUS LUTEUM, continue to produce equine chorionic gonadotropin (eCG), which prevents the mare from coming back into heat for 120 to 150 days. This condition used to be called *false pregnancy*.

ABORTION

Abortion is defined as death of a fetus after organ development (45 to 55 days), but before 300 days when the fetus is capable of independent existence outside the womb. A dead foal delivered after 300 days is called a *stillbirth*.

Mares who abort on successive pregnancies should be suspected of having chronic endometritis or a progesterone deficiency. A mare who aborts (or has a history of EED) should have an infertility examination to determine the cause of the problem.

Chromosomal abnormalities and genetic defects incompatible with life usually cause abortion before 90 days of gestation. It is estimated that 1 percent of foals are born with minor abnormalities.

When abortion occurs after the 2nd month of pregnancy, laboratory examination of the fetus and placenta will reveal the cause in about 50 to 60 percent of cases. When postmortem tissue examination is not done, the cause will be known in less than 10 percent of cases. Most diagnostic laboratories prefer to have the complete fetus and placenta submitted in a chilled (not frozen) condition as soon as possible after the abortion. It is particularly important to include the placenta, since abnormalities of the placenta are common causes of sporadic abortion. Until a cause is established, assume that all abortions are infectious and handle the tissues with sterile precautions.

INFECTIOUS CAUSES OF ABORTION

Viral Abortions. The *rhinopneumonitis* virus (EHV-1) is the number one cause of mare abortion in late pregnancy. It is highly contagious and natural or acquired immunity is not well-maintained. Repeated infections keep the virus active in the horse population. Abortion storms, involving nearly all pregnant mares on a single farm, have been reported.

Pregnant mares are likely to be exposed in the fall during the respiratory virus season. The typical signs are a runny nose, conjunctivitis, and dry cough. The virus enters the bloodstream, crosses the placental barrier, and invades the fetus. Death and abortion, however, do not occur until 1 to 3 months after exposure. Therefore the majority of mares tend to abort in late pregnancy. EHV-1 infection does not impair future fertility.

Vaccination will prevent many (but not all) EHV-1 abortions. For more information, see CARE AND FEEDING DURING PREGNANCY.

Another respiratory virus that produces abortion is that of *equine viral arteritis* (EVA). It is shed primarily through respiratory secretions but can be transmitted venereally in the semen of an infected stallion to a mare.

During the acute respiratory illness, the virus crosses the placenta and infects the fetus, resulting in death and abortion shortly thereafter. About half of infected mares will abort.

Stallions, but not mares, can develop a carrier state. Thirty to 50 percent of stallions become carriers. A carrier stallion sheds virus in his semen, either on a temporary or permanent basis. If a mare becomes venereally infected, she can develop a respiratory infection and pass it on to other mares or horses with whom she comes in contact. A serological blood test is available that becomes positive 2 weeks after infection.

Abortions can be controlled to some extent by screening all seropositive stallions to look for the carrier state. This is accomplished by culturing the virus. A seronegative mare (susceptible to EVA) should not be bred to a seropositive stallion unless it has been conclusively established that the stallion is not a carrier; or unless the mare has been given a series of EVA vaccinations. Virus isolation tests on semen or test matings are the only ways to determine if a seropositive stallion is infectious. For more information, see EQUINE VIRAL ARTERITIS.

Equine infectious anemia (EIA) is a rare cause of abortion because the disease is so well contained through testing and isolation of infected horses. A negative Coggins test is a prerequisite for breeding. EIA is transmitted through the bites of bloodsucking flies. Infection can occur during pregnancy. Infected mares do not always abort unless very ill, and may actually give birth to normal healthy foals. EIA is a lifetime infection. There is no vaccination or treatment to prevent or cure the disease. Seropositive horses must be isolated indefinitely as they remain a reservoir for the virus.

Bacterial Abortions. *Streptococcus zooepidemicus* is the most frequent cause of bacterial abortion in mares. This bacteria is found as a part of the normal flora on the genitalia of stallions. When local defense mechanisms break down and bacteria are introduced during coitus in large numbers from an infected penis, a streptococcal infection ascends into the uterus. The bacteria multiply during pregnancy and invade the placenta. This is called *placentitis*. Abortion takes place when the placenta can no longer support the fetus. This usually happens between the 5th and 10th month of pregnancy.

Salmonella, a widespread cause of epidemic contagious abortion in the past, has become less frequent—although occasional outbreaks caused by S. *typhimurium* do occur. The disease is acquired through the ingestion of bacteria from placental and uterine fluids or from contaminated feed, soil, and drinking water. Abortions tend to occur in late gestation. A characteristic feature of salmonella abortion is retention of the placenta. The fetus and products of conception are infective and must be handled with sterile precautions. A preventive vaccine is available but is used infrequently, as the disease is rare.

Leptospirosis is a disease caused by a spiral-shaped bacteria that attacks both man and animals. It is an uncommon cause of abortion during late gestation. The aborted fetus often appears yellow (jaundiced), suggesting the diagnosis.

Leptospirosis is transmitted by contact with the infected urine of rodents, wild animals, sheep, and cattle. Infection in the mare, often mild and inapparent, precedes abortion by about 2 weeks. After recovery from illness, bacteria can be shed in the urine for 2 to 3 months. During this time the mare should be isolated. Antibiotics are not effective in eliminating the carrier state.

Brucellosis is a disease primarily of cattle that occasionally causes abortion in mares. The usual source of infection is contact with soil contaminated by cattle. Pastures used by infected cattle should not be grazed until at least 3 or more months after the cattle have been removed.

Aspergillus fumigatus and other fungi account for a small number of cases of placental infection (15 percent). The mechanism of transmission is like that described for bacterial placentitis. Fungal placentitis tends to produce less initial inflammatory reaction than bacterial placentitis. As a result, abortion (or stillbirth) occurs quite late in gestation (within 1 month of term).

UTERINE CAUSES OF ABORTION

Placental Insufficiency. A poorly developed placenta is the result of preexisting conditions within the uterus (such as chronic endometritis) which interfere with placental attachment and reduce the surface area for placental and uterine interaction. The result of an insufficient placenta is a malnourished fetus that is either aborted or born weak.

Twin Pregnancies. Twins account for 20 to 30 percent of all observed abortions. The mare's uterus simply does not have the surface area to allow two placentas to attach and grow normally. One twin generally develops more rapidly and acquires most of the space. The other twin dies and brings on the abortion of both. Ninety percent of mares who do not abort early in pregnancy do so after 150 days.

It is therefore unusual for a mare to go to term with twin pregnancies. When this does happen, usually one twin is born mummified and the other small and weak. Twin pregnancy is best prevented and treated as described in the section TWINS.

Twisting of the Umbilical Cord. Sudden intrauterine death can occur if the umbilical cord shuts off the blood supply to the fetus. An abnormally long umbilical cord lends itself to this happening. The incidence is given at 1 percent, but the actual incidence may be somewhat lower, because torsion of the cord is often blamed for abortion when there is no other explanation.

Incompetent Cervix. In this condition the cervix, having been weakened by an old laceration, does not seal the uterus. Infection can then gain access to the uterine cavity. If the incompetence is detected before infection develops within the uterus, a suture can be placed around the cervix to tighten the opening. The suture must be removed before foaling.

Hydrops Amnion. This is a swelling of the membranes surrounding the fetus, resulting in an excessive accumulation of fluid in the uterus. It is extremely rare in the horse. Prompt intervention to induce abortion is necessary to save the life of the mare.

Kicks. Kicks and other mare injuries seldom cause abortion. The foal is well protected by a shock-absorbing cushion of fluid.

HORMONAL CAUSES OF ABORTION

Progesterone deficiency caused by inadequate production from the corpus luteum has long been considered a cause of unexplained early pregnancy loss, although the condition has not been well documented in horses. However, some mares with a history of habitual abortion will deliver a live foal when supplemented with progesterone. To be effective, progesterone should be administered in adequate dosage throughout the first 4 months of gestation. After 4 months, the placenta takes over the function of manufacturing this hormone, and exogenous progesterone is no longer required. There are no known adverse effects of giving progesterone.

Estrogen deficiency is not a cause of abortion.

Stress. Physical and emotional stress lowers plasma progesterone levels and releases steroids, which may be the reason why a higher rate of abortion has been noted in mares subjected to stressful events such as prolonged and difficult transportation, intense physical work, episodes of colic, surgery, and a change from a wet cool environment to a hot humid one.

TOXIC CAUSES OF ABORTION

Forage Toxicity. The consumption of certain pasture grasses and poisonous plants has been linked to abortion, difficulty in foaling, and the birth of deformed foals. Among these forages are fescue toxicity, ryegrass poisoning, sorghum toxicity, and locoism. Toxicity of these plants and grasses is not limited to abortion. For more information, see the section FORAGE TOXICITIES.

Chemicals. Drugs and chemicals implicated in causing abortion include phenothiazines, lead, some dewormers (benzimidazoles in the first trimester; organophosphates in the second and third trimesters), and organophosphate insecticides.

Life-Threatening Complications of Pregnancy

Catastrophic events during pregnancy are not common, but when they occur recognition is vital.

RUPTURED PREPUBIC TENDON

The prepubic tendon is attached to the pubic bone and serves as a common tendon for the abdominal muscles. In susceptible mares, the tendon slowly gives way from the weight of the pregnant uterus. Draft mares and fat, idle mares are most often affected. The signs of impending rupture are an excessive accumulation of fluid in the underside of the belly (*ventral edema*) with a sagging pendulous abdomen. Sudden complete rupture is accompanied by shock, collapse, and death.

Treatment: When the tendon gives way gradually, confine the mare, limit exercise, and support the abdomen with a sling until the foal is mature enough to be delivered vaginally or via cesarean section. The damaged tendon cannot be repaired. If the mare survives, she can no longer be used for breeding.

RUPTURED UTERUS

Rupture of the uterus generally occurs when active labor is arrested by a large fetus, twin foals, an abnormal presentation, or some problem that causes difficult and prolonged labor. Rupture can also occur as a sequel to torsion of the uterus.

When the uterus ruptures completely, the foal along with the placenta may be extruded into the abdomen. Sudden vaginal or abdominal bleeding with shock during foaling are signs of rupture of the uterus and indicate the need for rapid delivery or emergency cesarean section. A partial tear of the uterus may go unnoticed during foaling and then cause postpartum peritonitis several hours later.

Treatment: Some partial tears can be sutured through the birth canal after delivery. If this is not possible, then the repair is usually accomplished through a midline incision under general anesthesia.

TORSION OF THE UTERUS

Torsion is a rotation of the uterus about its long axis. It is a rare occurrence. A hard fall, an episode of violent rolling, or an excessively active fetus have been implicated as possible causes. When the uterus rotates 180 degrees, the broad ligaments become stretched. This interferes with the blood supply to the uterus and fetus. A 360-degree rotation, which is even more rare, cuts off the blood supply and results in death of the fetus within hours. The mare goes into shock and collapses.

Torsion nearly always occurs in the last trimester when the uterus increases rapidly in size. An incomplete rotation produces colic, frequent urination, listlessness, and loss of appetite—signs often mistaken for early labor. Accordingly, any mare who exhibits colic in late pregnancy should have immediate veterinary consultation. Rectal palpation will confirm the diagnosis or torsion of the uterus and also indicate the direction of the twist.

Treatment: Rolling the anesthetized mare in the direction of the torsion may correct the rotation. However, in most cases it is necessary to make a flank incision and twist the uterus back to its normal position. If the mare is close to term, the next step is to induce labor. Death of the uterus and fetus requires emergency cesarean section.

Foaling

PREPARATION

When foaling takes place in a pasture-breeding environment, the acreage should be large enough to allow the mare to withdraw from the herd, which she will do instinctively at foaling time. This is especially important because other horses in the herd may harass or even attack a newborn foal at a time when the mother is unable to protect it. When the foal is up and nursing, the mother will return to the herd.

Most breeders prefer to confine the mare where she can be observed and medically attended in the case of an obstetrical emergency. The foaling quarters should be clean, dry, draft-free, and warm—preferably in familiar surroundings away from strange people and other distractions. A box stall is ideal, but a small dry grassy paddock can be equally satisfactory. A good light source is essential. The mare should be introduced to her foaling quarters at least 2 weeks before the expected date of delivery.

The floor of the box stall should be covered with several inches of bedding. Clean straw provides good bedding and firm footing. Sawdust, wood shavings, and sand are poor bedding materials associated with breeding complications after foaling. Change the bedding at least once a day to maintain a clean, sanitary surface.

The equipment you will need includes a bucket of warm soapy water, tail bandages, cotton towels, cloth strips for tying up the placenta, and 2 percent tincture of iodine for the navel stump.

When the mare approaches her foaling time, it is essential to check on her often. A comfortable observation post outside the stall is advantageous. A mare about to foal should be checked on with a flashlight every 15 to 20 minutes during the evening and night, when most mares prefer to foal. Stall-mounted television monitors have been used successfully on large breeding farms.

About a week before the mare is expected to foal, begin to cut back on the amount of feed.

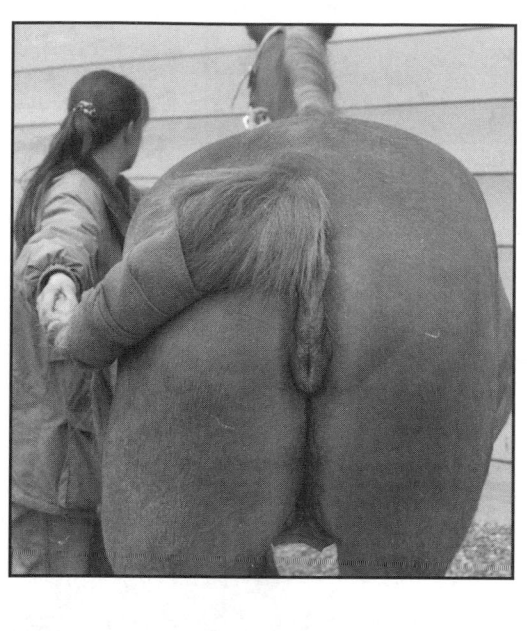

The mare's vulva relaxes, swells, and lengthens within 2 weeks of foaling.

SIGNS OF FOALING

About 3 weeks before delivery, the mare's udder will begin to enlarge, at first swelling at night and shrinking during the day. Within the last 2 weeks before foaling, the mare's vulva swells, relaxes, and lengthens to permit expulsion of the foal.

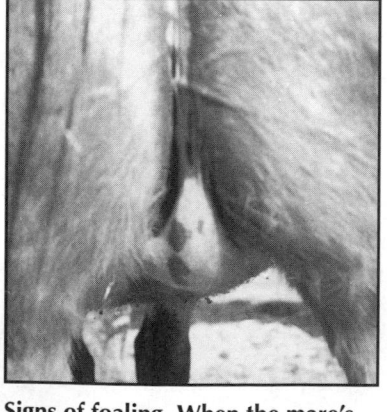

Signs of foaling. When the mare's udder remains full all day long, she is close to delivery.

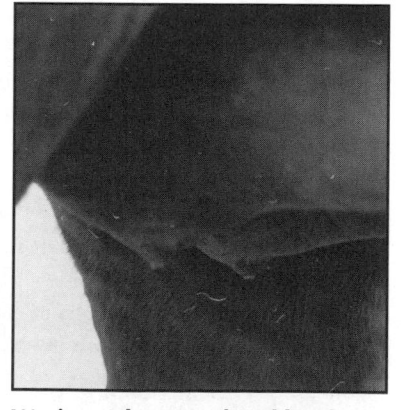

Waxing. A honey-colored bead forms at the end of each teat within 48 hours of foaling.

On the day before foaling, the udder remains full and tense. Clear to serum-like colostrum begins to drip from the udder. This colostrum dries to form a honey-colored bead at the end of each teat. This is called *waxing*. It usually indicates the mare will foal that night. (However, it is not uncommon for udder distension and waxing to occur within a few days before foaling.) When the wax falls from the ends of the teats, the mare may begin to drip a white, opaque milk that is thick and sticky. When the white milk appears, the mare should foal in 8 to 12 hours. If the mare streams milk, she is losing large amounts of colostrum. The colostrum should be collected and frozen. Later it can be thawed and given to the foal.

Mares have some degree of control over the timing of delivery and prefer to foal at night. Eighty percent deliver between the hours of 10 pm and 4 am.

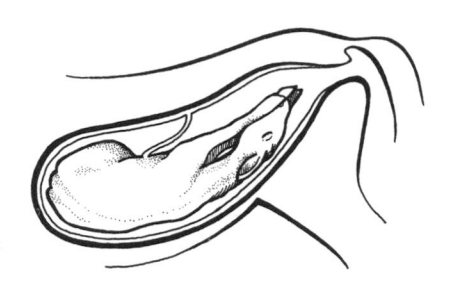

(A) The foal is lying on its back before the mare goes into labor.

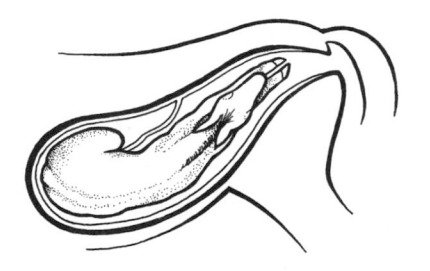

(B) In the first stage of labor the foal rotates with head and legs extended into the birth canal.

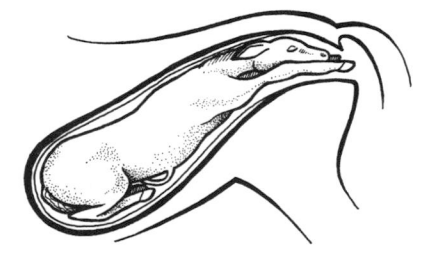

(C) The nose and forelegs pass through the birth canal with the pads of the feet pointing down.

The position of the foal in the uterus during normal delivery.

NORMAL LABOR AND DELIVERY

Although 90 percent of births occur without problems, it is important to be familiar with the normal sequence so you can recognize when something is wrong and either assist the delivery or summon your veterinarian. There are three stages of labor. Normal delivery may be preceded by several bouts of false labor.

A normal delivery. The forelegs and head have passed through the birth canal.

The amnion breaks, allowing the foal to breathe.

FIRST STAGE OF LABOR

During the first stage of true labor (which lasts 2 to 4 hours), uterine contractions gradually dilate the cervix and shift the foal from the resting position into the orientation for delivery. The mare becomes noticeably more active and

The foal rests. The umbilical cord is still intact.

The mare stands, breaking the umbilical cord.

restless, paces in her stall, gets up and down several times, passes small amounts of urine and stool, looks and nips at her abdomen, and sweats and appears to have colic. While these are the customary signs of first-stage labor, keep in mind that some mares pass through the first stage without giving strong indications.

Once you have determined the dam is in the first stage of labor, wrap her tail with a sterile gauze roll and wash her vulva and hindquarters with mild soap and water, as described in COVERING THE MARE.

The end of the first stage is marked by the appearance of the bubble-like amnion protruding from the vulva. Within 5 minutes this membrane ruptures, releasing yellow to chocolate-colored fluid, an event known as "breaking the water." The amnion may rupture within the birth canal, in which case you will not see the bubble.

SECOND STAGE OF LABOR

Second-stage labor is typically brief, lasting 10 to 20 minutes. It begins when the water breaks and ends with the delivery of the foal. After the water breaks, the forelegs should appear at the vaginal opening within 15 minutes.

Forceful contractions of the uterus and abdominal wall muscles during second-stage labor cause the placenta to separate from the wall of the uterus. In the horse, placental separation occurs rapidly, cutting off oxygen supply to the foal. Although most foals are born within 20 minutes, there is a maximum time between rupture of the amnion and delivery of the foal (40 to 60 minutes) after which the foal is at serious risk of death. Accordingly, it is important to record the moment when the water breaks, because from this point forward delivery is on a strict timetable.

After the water breaks, the mare usually lies down on her side with her legs extended. However, some mares get up and down frequently and others stand to deliver.

The normal fetal orientation in the birth canal is the *anterior longitudinal presentation*, in which the foal is aligned lengthwise with its spine parallel to the mother's spine, head tucked between extended forelegs, and pads of the feet pointing down. As the chest enters the birth canal, one leg is placed slightly in front of the other to allow the shoulders to pass through one at a time. During passage through the pelvic opening, the amnion surrounding the foal will in most cases have ruptured. If when the head is delivered the nostrils are still covered with the amniotic sac, remove the membrane to allow the foal to breathe. If the mare stands to deliver, be prepared to catch the foal and lower it gently to the ground.

After the hips have been delivered, the foal usually rests with its hind legs in the mare's vagina for 10 to 20 minutes. *Resist the temptation to break the cord.* Allow this to happen naturally by the movements of the mare.

Once the cord separates, dip the navel stump in 2 percent tincture of iodine. This step is important in preventing navel ill and neonatal sepsis. Tying off the cord is unnecessary and inadvisable in that it may cause cord infection. The stump will dry up naturally.

In the unlikely event that the cord does not break within 30 minutes, you should step in and break it by hand. Grasp the cord firmly 2 to 3 inches from the navel and pull the cord in the direction of the placenta until it tears. Don't cut the cord, as this may produce bleeding.

Once the cord has been severed, tie it in a knot above the mare's hocks to keep her from stepping on the end and tearing the placenta. A strip of cloth is helpful in tying up the cord.

How to revive a depressed foal is discussed below.

THIRD STAGE OF LABOR

In the third stage the placenta is expelled. This occurs in 30 minutes to 3 hours after foaling.

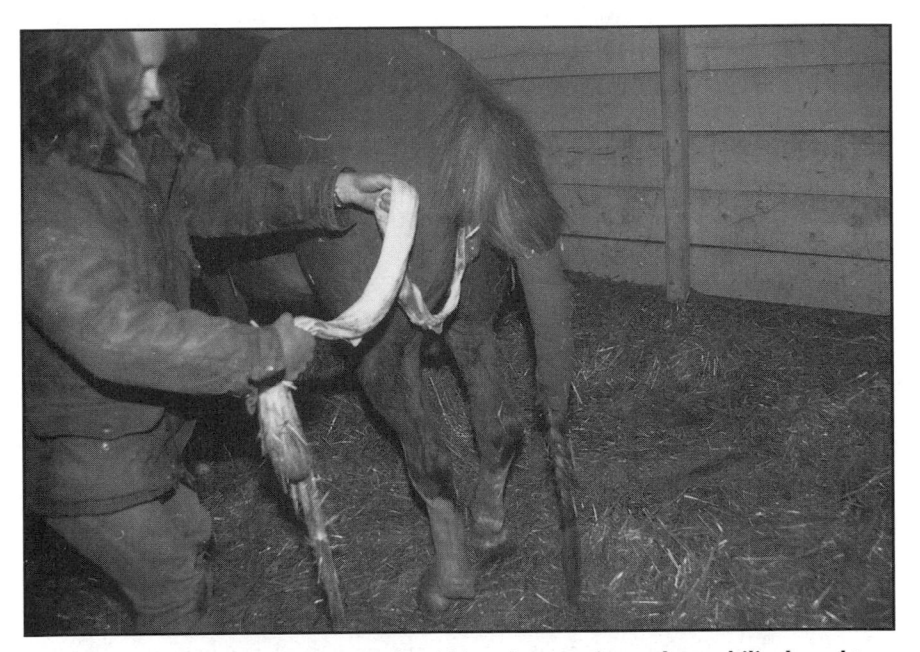

The placenta will pass spontaneously within 3 hours. Tie up the umbilical cord to prevent the mare from stepping on it.

Do not attempt to pull the placenta from the mare's uterus. This will damage the uterus or cause the placenta to tear. If the placenta tears, a piece will be retained. A piece of retained placenta can cause toxic uterine infection.

After the placenta has been expelled, examine both sides to be sure that no missing pieces remain in the uterus. Small tears can be detected by filling the placental sac with water and ballooning it out. An intact placenta resembles a pair of "Dutch britches," a configuration representing the two horns and body of the uterus.

If the placenta does not pass within 3 hours or there is a possibility of a retained fragment, the mare should be examined by a veterinarian at once (see RETAINED PLACENTA).

REVIVING A DEPRESSED FOAL

If a foal does not breathe within 60 seconds, it should be resuscitated at once. Extend the foal's head and remove secretions from its nostrils with a sterile gauze or a clean towel. Rub the foal vigorously all over with a clean towel. If this does not revive the foal, try to stimulate a cough reflex (which activates breathing) by tickling the inside of its nose with a surgical clamp or a piece of straw.

After a prolonged and difficult delivery, some foals are too weak or flaccid to breathe on their own despite the above efforts. You will need to administer mouth-to-nose resuscitation. Close one nostril with the flat of your hand to keep air from exiting. Enclose the other nostril with your mouth. Blow in with enough force to expand the chest. Release both nostrils to allow air to escape. Continue at a rate of 25 breaths per minute while pausing every 30 seconds to see if the foal is starting to breathe.

If you suspect the foal does not have a heartbeat, administer a brisk thump to the side of the chest behind the elbow. This may produce a heartbeat.

AFTER THE DELIVERY

The first few hours are critical in the development of a strong maternal bond between mare and foal. The mare will usually lie quietly, often licking her foal and nickering to it without arising. As she starts to get up, make sure she does not tread on the foal.

Soon after delivery, the foal will roll up onto its chest and attempt to stand. It takes about an hour for a foal to gain enough coordination and strength to stand on its own. If the foal is not able to stand after 2 hours, consult your veterinarian.

As soon as the foal is able to stand, it will begin to search for an udder. This is a trial and error process and does not happen at once. Given time and assistance from its mother, the foal will find the teat and begin to nurse. If the foal is not nursing successfully within 3 hours of standing, something may be wrong and the foal should be checked.

It is good practice to examine the mare in order to be certain that her teats are open, the nipples well-formed and not inverted. It is essential that the foal receive the first milk of the mare, since it contains the all-important maternal antibodies which protect against newborn infections.

Twelve hours after foaling, the mare should be dewormed with ivermectin, which is effective against threadworms, ascarids, and large and small strongyles. In threadworm problem areas, treat the foal at 3 weeks of age. For routine deworming of foals, see chapter 2, Parasites.

Foals at birth are capable of forming antibodies in response to vaccination, although the immune response is much weaker than it will be at 4 months of age. Nevertheless, if circumstances warrant, vaccination against rhinopneumonitis and

After the delivery the mother helps the foal to stand.

The foal has found the teat and is nursing successfully within 3 hours of birth.

influenza can begin at birth and continue at 2-month intervals to provide protection for up to a year.

Tetanus antitoxin is no longer routinely administered since it has been associated with fatal cases of serum hepatitis. It is only indicated if the mother was not vaccinated against tetanus, in which case both tetanus antitoxin and tetanus toxoid should be given. For recommended vaccinations, see IMMUNIZATION SCHEDULE.

The first few hours of the foal's life present an excellent opportunity for handlers to imprint useful resistance-free behaviors on the new foal. These behaviors help to socialize the foal to humans and make the foal easier to handle and train later.

Resistance-free exercises include pressing down on the withers, and lifting and stroking the girth. Repeat until resistance disappears. Other desensitizing exercises include rubbing the ears and head, examining the teeth and mouth, and taking the rectal temperature. Imprinting should be done gradually and gently and with the acceptance of the mother. Do not separate mother and foal for resistance-free exercises. Repeat daily for 3 days.

The postpartum mare is susceptible to constipation and colic. To prevent these problems, cut back her feed by half. Gradually increase it over the next 10 days until she is back on full ration.

During return of the uterus to normal size, the mare will have a dark chocolate-colored vaginal discharge, which disappears by the seventh day. A persistent discharge, a yellow discharge, a heavy bloody discharge, or a foul-smelling pus-like discharge are abnormal. The mare should be checked for delayed uterine involution, retained placenta, and postpartum metritis (see POSTPARTUM PROBLEMS).

Note, however, that a foul discharge is not always present in cases of postpartum infection. Monitor the mare's temperature at frequent intervals throughout this period. A temperature above 101 degrees F indicates fever and infection.

Scaly skin and oily secretions tend to accumulate in the skin fold that divides the udder. Gently wash the mare's udder with warm water and Ivory soap to remove smegma. Repeat as necessary.

Meconium Colic

The foal should begin to pass meconium stools within the first 12 hours. Meconium is a greenish-brown to black material that accumulates in the foal's intestinal tract prior to birth. By the fourth day, meconium is replaced by the yellow feces of the normal neonatal foal.

When meconium is not passed, it becomes painfully impacted, usually in the small colon or rectum. Signs of meconium colic begin within 24 hours of birth. They include straining without passing meconium, restlessness, tail-switching, repeatedly getting up and down, rolling and thrashing, arching the back, and lying in an unusual position. The diagnosis is confirmed by digital rectal examination that reveals firm meconium within the rectum and pelvic colon.

Most foals with meconium colic respond to softening the stool. A prepackaged Fleet phosphate enema will often relieve a simple impaction. The tip of the tube is carefully inserted its full length into the foal's rectum and the enema administered without excessive pressure. Hold the tail down for a few minutes to prevent immediate return of the enema. If no response occurs within one hour, administer a second Fleet enema or a soap water enema.

A soap water enema can be given instead of or along with a Fleet enema. To prepare a soap water enema for a neonatal foal, stir a piece of Ivory soap in 1 pint of lukewarm water until the water becomes milky. Fill an enema bag or bottle with the solution and connect the tubing to a soft flexible rubber catheter. Lubricate the catheter with mineral oil and insert it carefully 10 inches into the rectum. Do not force the catheter as this could lacerate or perforate the rectum. Allow the fluid to run in by gravity.

Your veterinarian may elect to give a dose of mineral oil (250 ml) or a laxative such as milk of magnesia (8 ounces) by stomach tube to complete the flushing-out process. The mineral oil should pass in 24 hours. In unresponsive cases, surgery is required.

Exercise is beneficial for both the mare and her foal. Begin on the first or second day by turning them out into an empty paddock or small field for 15 to 30 minutes twice a day. This amount of exercise will not tire the mare or the foal. Increase exercise gradually as weather permits. By 2 weeks, the mare and foal can be left out most of the day. However, they should be separated from other horses until the foal is 3 to 4 weeks old.

Exercise is good for the foal and the mare. By 2 weeks they can be left outside most of the day. Photo: Don Lupton.

Postpartum Examination. For the safety of the mare and to ensure that she is progressing on schedule, it is a good practice to have your veterinarian examine her by rectal palpation 1 week after delivery. This step is essential if you plan to breed her on the first postpartum heat (see BREEDING ON THE FOAL HEAT).

Prolonged or Difficult Labor (Dystocia)

The prolongation of any stage of labor is called *dystocia*. Most cases of dystocia are fetal in origin. The size or position of the foal creates a blockage in the birth canal that cannot be overcome by intense and forceful straining. In time, the uterus becomes exhausted and is unable to contract, even after the blockage has been removed. This is called *uterine inertia*.

In the horse, the length of the second stage of labor is critical. Once the water bag ruptures and the foal begins to descend, the placenta begins to detach and follow. If the foal is not born within 40 minutes, there is an increasing risk of fetal mortality. Accordingly, urgent veterinary assistance is needed on suspicion of dystocia. A first suspicion would be if the forelegs do not appear at the vaginal opening by 15 minutes after the water breaks.

Beyond risk to the foal, difficult and prolonged labor is associated with frequent mare complications. They include injuries to the birth canal, acute metritis, retained placenta, delayed uterine involution, rupture of the uterus, and prolapse of the uterus.

Common causes of dystocia are discussed below.

ABNORMAL PRESENTATIONS

Abnormal presentations are the most common cause of difficult or arrested labor.

Presentation refers to the alignment of the long axis of the fetus with the long axis of the dam. In a longitudinal presentation, the spine of the fetus is parallel to the spine of the mother. In a transverse presentation, the two spines are at right angles. Presentation also refers to the part of the fetus approaching the pelvic outlet (either head or tail).

Position is the relationship of the back of the foal to the four quadrants of the mare's pelvis: the sacrum, right and left ileum, and pubis. The normal position places the foal's back against the mare's sacrum. Thus the normal orientation is called the *anterior longitudinal presentation*, *dorsosacral position*, with the head, neck, and forelimbs extended.

Malpresentations and malpositions prevent delivery by increasing the size of the presenting parts in relation to the fixed diameter of the pelvic canal.

Suspect a problem delivery if the two front feet do not appear at the vaginal opening within 15 minutes after the water breaks; if the feet appear but you do not see the nose and face following closely; or if you see anything other than the head and nose between the two forelegs with the pads pointing down. The mare should be examined vaginally by your veterinarian as soon as possible to determine the cause of the problem.

The most common *malpresentations* are deviations of the head and neck. In the *lateral deviation*, the neck is bent to the side with the nose pointing toward the hind

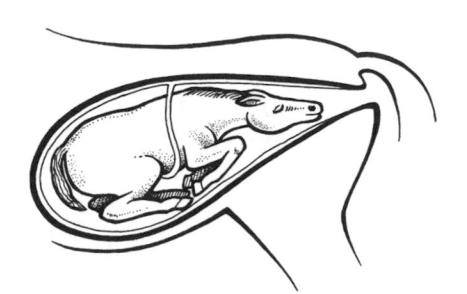

(A) A common malpresentation with the forelegs folded. Push the foal back into the birth canal, then grasp and extend each leg.

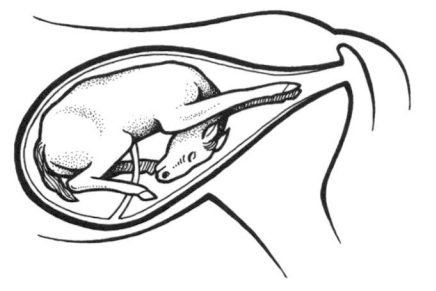

(B) Ventral deviation of the head. Push the foal back into the birth canal, grasp the muzzle, and extend the head.

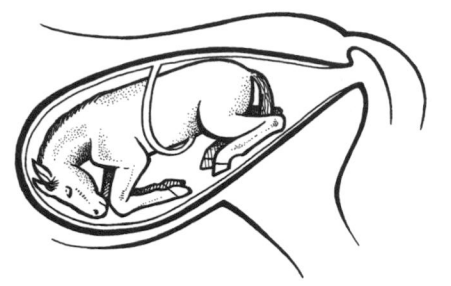

(C) A posterior presentation. Under epidural anesthesia, it may be possible to draw out each back leg. Cesarean section is usually required.

Abnormal presentations.

feet. In the *ventral deviation*, the head is bent down against the chest so the crown (instead of the nose) presents.

A common malpresentation is one in which one or both forelimbs are not extended. A leg can be bent at the elbow and caught in back of the pelvic brim; or folded under the fetus with the feet pointing backward. You might see only one leg at the vaginal opening.

A posterior or backward presentation is when the tail enters the birth canal instead of the head. You might see one or both rear legs protruding from the vulva. In a true breech, the back legs are tucked beneath the body and the rump is the presenting part. The posterior presentation is rare, occurring only in 1 of 500 deliveries.

The most common *malposition* is one in which the foal does not rotate into the normal dorsosacral position. In this situation the foal enters the birth canal on its side—or on its back with the pads of the feet pointing up.

Treatment: Abnormal presentations should be corrected as soon as possible. It is easier to do this before the foal becomes wedged tightly into the birth canal and the uterus is dry and contracted.

Regardless of the malpresentation or position, the legs of a full-term foal must be extended and the neck straightened out before the foal can pass through the birth canal. This is accomplished through the procedure called *repulsion*, in which the foal is pushed back into the uterus far enough to obtain room to grasp and pull out the legs or straighten the neck and extend the head.

The mare should be restrained and kept in a standing position if possible. Epidural anesthesia is of great assistance. Intrauterine manipulation requires the use of sterile technique and a long-arm obstetrical glove. Be advised that if an arm is caught between the foal and the wall of the uterus during a forceful contraction, it can easily be broken. Injuries to the birth canal also can occur during such attempts. Accordingly, intrauterine manipulation by a nonprofessional should be attempted only in a true emergency or when expert help is totally unavailable.

One of the most effective things the handler can do while waiting for the veterinarian is to keep the mare on her feet and walking. This can retard labor for 30 to 60 minutes.

In addition to correcting an abnormal presentation by manipulating the foal's position, *traction* may be necessary. In this situation obstetrical chains and blunt hooks are applied to the fetal parts in order to pull on the foal as the uterus contracts.

Traction becomes less effective with the passage of time. The uterus contracts down around the foal—and the vaginal canal, initially well-lubricated by the ruptured sac, becomes very dry.

Although most cases of mare dystocia can be corrected by obstetric manipulation, cesarean section is occasionally necessary. It is indicated if there has been little or no progress after a reasonable attempt at obstetrical manipulation and the foal is alive with a chance for survival. C-section is discussed below.

If the foal is already dead and cannot be delivered by repulsion and traction, your veterinarian may elect to remove it by *fetotomy*. The fetus is dismembered (using 1 to 2 incisions) and removed in parts. This is not without risk of lacerating the birth canal. If fetotomy cannot be performed with a minimum of dissection, it is safer to proceed to cesarean section.

OTHER CAUSES OF DYSTOCIA

Premature Separation of the Placenta. Separation of the placenta before the foal moves into the birth canal is rare. When it does happen, the placenta precedes the fetus. Signs are those of difficult labor with the appearance of a red basketball-like structure at the vulva. Behind the placenta is the intact water sac, which is prevented from entering the birth canal. The entire process arrests labor and must be immediately corrected to prevent fetal asphyxiation.

Treatment: Rupture the protruding membrane using a pair of sharp scissors. Remove the placental membranes from the foal's nostrils to allow it to breathe. Labor should proceed quickly. Be prepared to revive a depressed foal.

Small Pelvic Opening. A 2-year-old mare may be too immature to have developed an adequate pelvic outlet. A previously fractured pelvis is another cause of a narrow birth canal.

Treatment: Proceed to cesarean section. If the narrow pelvis is diagnosed before labor, C-section can be done electively. The size of the pelvic opening can be determined during the breeding soundness exam.

Twins. The presence of twins frequently prevents normal delivery because neither foal has room to enter the birth canal. The situation is further compounded if one or both of the foals are dead.

Treatment: This situation is difficult to correct if not recognized promptly. When both twins are in a normal anterior presentation, it may be possible to push one back into the uterus to allow the other room to come out. Once the first twin is delivered, the second follows without difficulty. An elective C-section is a consideration when the diagnosis is made during pregnancy.

Uterine Inertia. Mechanical obstruction is the most common cause of uterine muscle fatigue. The uterus is so exhausted that it loses its ability to expel the foal even after a blockage has been corrected. Another cause of inertia is a weak uterine muscle. This can occur with age or chronic scarring.

Treatment: An inert uterus contracts tightly around the foal. This makes it even more difficult to complete the delivery. Cesarean section will be required.

Other less common causes of dystocia are hydrocephalus, contracted foal syndrome, torsion of the uterus, a prolonged pregnancy with a large-sized fetus, hydrops amnion, ruptured prepubic tendon, and vaginal blockages caused by tumors or blood clots.

WHEN TO CALL YOUR VETERINARIAN

Toward the end of the mare's gestation, call your veterinarian and discuss who will be available to cover for an emergency. Do not hesitate to call a veterinarian if you have any concern about the progress of labor. Most equine obstetrical emergencies are associated with impending or actual fetal distress. They will not correct with time. Someone must be prepared to step in quickly and save the life of the foal.

In summary, something is wrong when:

- The mare is in labor for more than 4 hours without rupture of the water bag.
- The water breaks but the front feet are not present at the vulva within 15 minutes.
- The foal is not delivered within 40 minutes.
- The foal presents in any orientation other than the normal anterior longitudinal presentation.
- A thick red membrane (instead of a shiny white one) appears at the vulva, indicating premature separation of the placenta.

- The placenta is not delivered within 3 hours after foaling.
- The placenta appears unhealthy or shows missing pieces.

CESAREAN SECTION

Cesarean section is indicated to retrieve a live foal when arrested labor cannot be easily corrected by obstetrics. It is also indicated to remove a dead fetus that cannot be removed by fetotomy.

Proper operating room facilities must be available to perform cesarean section. Elective and emergency C-sections can be done at equine veterinary hospitals and stud farms with operating facilities. However, emergency C-sections in the field away from anesthesia, padded operating tables, sterile instruments, and support facilities cannot be done successfully.

Survival rates for mare and foal are good for elective C-sections. For emergency C-sections, they diminish rapidly with the length of labor. When used as a last resort, the prognosis for foal and mare survival is poor.

A disadvantage of C-section is that it predisposes a mare to metritis and uterine scarring, which impairs future fertility.

The operation is done through the flank or abdomen with the mare recumbent and under an anesthetic. The foal is removed and the incision in the uterus is closed with interlocking sutures to prevent postoperative bleeding. If a placenta does not separate easily at the time of surgery, it can be freed up and allowed to pass spontaneously in a few hours.

Following cesarean section, a mare may be too weak or exhausted to care for her foal. Due to failure of the recognition process, she may not identify with her foal or be willing to accept it. Accordingly, many C-section foals have to be raised as orphans.

Postpartum Problems

Problems that can affect the mare after delivery are postpartum hemorrhage, injuries to the birth canal, retained placenta, invagination of a uterine horn, acute metritis, and prolapsed uterus. Some mares may have problems with their milk supply, or develop mastitis and edema of the udder. A difficult management problem is the mare who refuses to accept and care for her foal.

HEMORRHAGE

Internal bleeding is a serious, often fatal complication caused by rupture of a large blood vessel in the pelvis or wall of the uterus. Signs are those of severe pain in the abdomen followed by weakness, staggering, pale mucous membranes, shock, and collapse. There is no external sign of bleeding.

Surgical intervention in this situation is not successful. Confine the mare to a quiet stall and keep her as calm as possible. Sedation is of benefit. The bleeding may stop spontaneously.

External bleeding is apparent as bleeding through the birth canal. It is due to a laceration of the cervix, vagina, or perineum, generally caused by the foal's feet or by obstetrical manipulation. Bleeding from the wall of the uterus can occur if the placenta is torn prematurely in third-stage labor.

If you are able to see a bleeding artery, maintain pressure with a sterile dressing and summon your veterinarian. The mare may need to be treated for shock and blood loss. Lacerations that do not stop bleeding should be sutured, if possible. When this is not technically feasible, the uterus and vagina can be packed with strips of petroleum gauze. Lacerations of the cervix should be repaired when uterine involution is complete, 2 to 3 weeks postpartum.

PERINEAL AND VULVAR LACERATIONS

Birth-related injuries to the vagina and vulva are common. A mare delivering her first foal is more likely to sustain such an injury, as are mares who go through difficult or prolonged labor.

Most perineal lacerations are caused by the feet of the foal. The feet can actually tear through the shelf between the vagina and rectum and protrude through the anus. This most often occurs with upside-down presentations.

Vulvar and vaginal bleeding occur from enlarged veins in the hymen area. The bleeding usually is not serious and stops spontaneously.

Treatment: Perineal lacerations should be repaired within a few hours unless the tissue is swollen and hemorrhagic, in which case it is best to cleanse the wound and repair the injury in 3 to 6 weeks.

RETAINED PLACENTA

The placenta is normally expelled 30 minutes to 3 hours after foaling. Bacterial growth in the retained placenta and uterus occurs rapidly. Thus after 3 hours the placenta releases toxic products that initiate postpartum complications, including acute toxic metritis, laminitis, and blood poisoning. The frequency and severity of these problems depends upon the amount of placental tissue retained and the length of time before it is removed.

Retained placenta is nearly always associated with arrested or difficult labor. It is seldom a problem after a normal, uncomplicated delivery.

If the intact placenta does not pass in 3 hours, or if examination reveals a tear or missing piece, notify your veterinarian without delay.

Treatment: It involves the injection or infusion of oxytocin, which stimulates uterine contractions and aids in expulsion of the placenta. If the placenta is not expelled within 2 hours after a course of oxytocin, your veterinarian may infuse the uterus or the retained placenta itself with large volumes of warm sterile water.

In most cases the placenta will be released using one or both of these methods. Antibiotics are indicated when the reproductive tract has been contaminated and when placental passage has been unduly prolonged.

DELAYED UTERINE INVOLUTION

Immediately after foaling the uterus begins to shrink and return to its normal size and shape. This process is called *involution*. It occurs rapidly. By 1 week the uterus is back down to about twice normal size. Some mares are ready to conceive and maintain a pregnancy by the 15th postpartum day. In others, the process takes longer (see BREEDING ON THE FOAL HEAT).

Uterine involution is helped by nursing and exercise. Nursing releases oxytocin, which causes the uterus to contract. Exercise promotes uterine tone and strengthens the abdominal wall muscles.

Delayed involution is important because of the possibility the mare has retained placental tissue as the cause of the delay. In addition, the slow progress of involution in mares with multipariety or advanced maternal age makes it unlikely that these mares can be bred on the foal heat.

Treatment: The size and shape of the uterus can be determined by rectal palpation. If your veterinarian finds that involution is not proceeding according to schedule, he or she may want to administer oxytocin to stimulate uterine contractions. If retained placental tissue is suspected, a uterine biopsy is helpful in confirming this diagnosis.

POSTPARTUM METRITIS

This is an uncommon but serious infection of the entire uterine wall, characterized by the rapid onset of toxemia, blood poisoning, and laminitis. It tends to occur among mares who have had a prolonged or complicated labor, a retained placenta, or massive contamination of the uterus.

Signs of acute toxic metritis begin 12 to 36 hours after foaling. They include fever, increased pulse and respiration, and marked apathy and depression. The vaginal discharge is reddish-brown and foul-smelling. A pounding digital pulse signifies the onset of laminitis.

Treatment: It is directed at evacuating the uterus, which usually contains several gallons of infected blood and pus. This is best accomplished by inserting a large-bore stomach tube into the uterus and flushing it with copious volumes of warm sterile water until the recovered fluid is clear. Antibiotics are instilled when the uterus is empty. This procedure is repeated twice a day as necessary for several days. The mare is also given intravenous oxytocin and antibiotics.

Laminitis may occur at any time with acute metritis and can be severe enough to cause sloughing of the hooves. Intravenous flunixin meglumine is given to prevent the circulatory disturbances associated with the development of laminitis. It is continued until the toxemia is controlled. Shortening the course of toxemia with early vigorous treatment of the infected uterus reduces the likelihood of laminitis.

INVAGINATION OF UTERINE HORN

In this condition one horn of the uterus turns inside-out and projects into the body of the uterus, where it can be felt by intrauterine palpation. Invagination is often associated with a retained placenta in that horn, the invagination occurring as a result of traction during placental expulsion. Signs are colic and restlessness out of the ordinary.

Treatment: The diagnosis is made on postpartum examination performed for colic unresponsive to analgesics. Before replacing the horn back to its normal position, a placenta (if present) must be manually removed. The horn is then kneaded inward until it returns to its former position. Infusion of 1 or 2 gallons of warm sterile water facilitates complete replacement. Aftercare is like that for retained placenta.

PROLAPSED UTERUS

This is an uncommon complication in which the uterus turns inside-out and protrudes through the vulva. Prolonged straining during and after a difficult delivery, and pulling on the umbilical cord in a misguided attempt to deliver a retained placenta, are two common causes.

The uterus must be replaced as soon as possible to prevent shock and further complications. This procedure is quite difficult and requires veterinary management.

Treatment: While waiting for the veterinarian, wrap the prolapse in a clean towel or sheet moistened with warm water to protect the everted uterus from further contamination. Keep the mare on her feet and walking. This slows down contractions and keeps the mare from lacerating the uterus by backing up against sharp objects.

Before attempting to replace the uterus, the mare should be sedated to prevent straining. This is accomplished by drugs, or by giving a caudal or general anesthetic. The uterus is carefully and thoroughly cleansed with disinfectant soap and then worked back through the pelvic opening until it is completely reduced. Antibiotics are placed into the uterine cavity and then the vulva is sutured. Intravenous oxytocin and antibiotics are administered to shrink the uterus and prevent postpartum metritis.

A mare who has sustained a uterine prolapse is apt to do so again on the next foaling.

MARES WHO REJECT OR INJURE THEIR FOALS

A mare learns to recognize and care for her offspring as the foal is born, cleansed, and begins to nurse. Hormonal changes during and after delivery sensitize the mare's central nervous system to the sight, sound, and especially the smell and taste of her newborn foal.

For various reasons, a mare's brain may not respond to the usual sensory stimuli and the imprinting process fails to take place. For example, if a mare has had a prolonged labor or a C-section, exhaustion combined with artificial conditions can derail normal behavior.

Lack of bonding appears to be genetically or environmentally determined. This appears to be true of Arabians, who have a higher incidence of foal rejection than other breeds. Studies suggest that many neglectful mothers were rejected foals themselves, or were raised in isolation away from the companionship of other horses.

There are two main categories of foal rejection. Refusal to allow suckling is the most frequent, whereas aggression toward the foal is the most dangerous.

Refusal to allow suckling generally occurs in first-time mothers. Often it is the pain of a distended udder that seems to generate the fear of suckling. The foal can be injured during the mare's attempts to evade or escape.

Rarely a mare attacks and savages her foal, usually biting it on the withers. Because this behavior is similar to that of the foal-savaging stallion, it has been suggested that it may be caused by masculinization of the mare's central nervous system by mechanisms unknown. Hormone therapy has been attempted, with inconsistent results.

Treatment: The mare who refuses to allow her foal to nurse should be adequately restrained while one or two handlers assist the foal in locating the teat. Once the mare realizes that suckling relieves udder distension and pain, she usually becomes less fearful and readily accepts the foal.

If the mare continues to refuse suckling, she can be restrained in a stall divided by a horizontal bar at shoulder height. The bar is placed so that it holds the mare against a wall but the foal can go beneath the bar to nurse. Tranquilizing the mare is an alternative. However, tranquilizers are passed in the milk and may tranquilize the foal, resulting in ineffective nursing.

The mare who attempts to physically injure her foal is a most difficult problem. Attempts to reunite the foal and dam usually prove futile. The mare and foal must be watched at all times to prevent injury to the foal. Keep in mind that a foal nurses every 15 to 20 minutes during the first week of life. If you do not have the resources to deal with this problem, it is best to remove the foal and raise it as an orphan.

Lactation

The mare's udder is composed of two separate milk sacs, which lie on either side of the midline between her back legs. Each milk sac is composed of two mammary glands. The milk ducts of the two glands come together to form a common duct which opens at the nipple or teat. Thus, although the mare has four mammary glands, she has only two teats.

Milk letdown is controlled by oxytocin released from the pituitary gland during labor and delivery. Tactile stimulation of the teats (suckling, washing the teats) helps to trigger the release.

FEEDING DURING LACTATION

The mare's nutrient requirements during lactation are greater than at any other time in life. A lactating mare produces 3 times her own weight in milk during a 5-month lactation.

Nutrient requirements during the first 3 months of lactation are shown in Table I in chapter 17, Feeding and Nutrition. In essence, the lactating mare requires almost twice as much energy and more than twice as much protein, calcium, phosphorus, and vitamin A.

When good-quality grass hay or grass forage is being fed free-choice, a mare cannot consume enough feed to meet these requirements. However, if you are feeding unrestricted amounts of high-quality alfalfa or lush green legumes, she should be able to consume enough roughage to meet these nutrient needs—with the exception perhaps of phosphorus, which can be supplied free-choice by a salt-mineral mix such as monodicalcium phosphate (see Table IV).

Hay or forage of the above quality is often not available, requiring the feeding of a grain supplement instead. Hay and grain ratios of 50-50 by weight are suitable; or you can use a sample ration as shown in Table V.

The lactating mare needs 30,000 IU of vitamin A per day. Alfalfa and legume hay stored for less than 6 months may meet these requirements. Corn is the only grain that contains significant amounts. In most cases a supplement should be considered. Vitamin A supplements (and supplemented feeds) are of greatest value when used during lactation.

If you have been feeding a commercial ration as the sole source of feed, note that standard horse rations do not contain enough protein for the lactating mare and quite often are deficient in lysine, an amino acid essential for high-quality milk production and growth of the foal. A protein supplement such as soybean meal should be added to the diet. Soybean meal is an excellent source not only of protein but also of lysine.

Some commercial grain supplements are designed to be fed to lactating mares along with hay or equivalent forage. These rations will meet protein and energy requirements when fed according to the directions provided. Foal creep feeds, and mare and foal pellets, are examples.

Keep trace-mineralized salt available for free-choice consumption. A nursing mother requires a great deal of water and should have access to a fresh supply at all times.

NURSING PROBLEMS

One condition that originates with either dam or foal is failure of passive transfer of maternal antibodies, which occurs if the foal does not nurse during the first

18 hours of life. Failure to receive colostrum, the first milk of the dam, is cited as the single most important cause of neonatal infections. For more information, see Lack of Colostrum in chapter 16, Pediatrics.

Insufficient Milk Supply. For the first 2 to 3 months of life, the foal's nutritional requirements are entirely met by its mother's milk.

Absence of milk is called *agalactia*. When the milk does not come in spontaneously after foaling, warm compresses to the udder and an injection of oxytocin may initiate the flow. If not, the problem is most likely due to inherent failure of the mammary glands to produce milk. The foal will have to be raised as an orphan.

Mares on tall fescue pastures in the southeastern United States experience a high incidence of agalactia due to ingestion of a specific fungus that grows on the grass. The fungus produces an alkaloid which blocks pituitary prolactin. Prolactin is the hormone that stimulates milk production.

Insufficient production of milk is suggested by the appearance and behavior of the foal. A foal who is not getting enough milk is thin and nurses vigorously, but never seems to be satisfied.

The volume and composition of milk produced is not related to the mare's consumption of feed, at least not initially. A mare fed less energy than needed will make up the difference at the expense of her own weight and body stores. It is only after she uses up all her reserves and her weight drops to a body condition score of 1 or less (see Weight Gain or Loss) that her milk production begins to decline.

A diet high in energy, protein, and other nutrients, sufficient to produce weight gain back to the ideal condition, will correct this problem. The mare also should be given unrestricted access to water and trace-mineralized salt.

If these measures are not successful, the mare most likely has an inherited defect in milk production. Begin supplementing the foal at an early age as described in the section on The Orphan Foal.

Mastitis. Inflammation of one or more quarters of the mammary gland is called *mastitis*. It usually occurs a few weeks after foaling. It is rare in the mare.

The udder becomes warm, swollen, and painful. The swelling may extend to involve the undersurface of the abdomen. The mare may refuse to nurse or be unable to eject her milk. The milk from the infected gland appears curdled and usually contains blood. Laboratory examination of the milk will show bacteria. Staphylococci and streptococci are the most common.

Treatment: The foal should be temporarily removed and fed by hand as described for the orphan foal. Empty the udders by hand to relieve pressure and continue milk production. Cold packs help to reduce swelling. Antibiotics are started pending the results of culture. The infection responds rapidly to treatment. The foal can usually return to the mare in 1 week. However, if lactation has stopped, nothing can be done to restart the milk flow.

There is a type of noninfectious mastitis caused by eating the leaves, bark, or fruit of the avocado tree. In *avocado poisoning*, milk production stops and does not resume.

Chapter 16

PEDIATRICS

Care of the *newborn* foal is discussed in chapter 15, Pregnancy and Foaling (AFTER THE DELIVERY).

THE NURSING FOAL

Feeding. During the first 2 months the foal receives all of its nutritional needs from the milk of its mother, although it will begin to nibble on the mare's grain and hay when only a few days old. After 2 months of age, the foal's nutritional needs are increasing while the mother's milk supply is stable or decreasing. At or before 2 months of age, begin to feed a creep ration.

A *creep feed ration* is a concentrate mix composed of processed grain specifically formulated to meet the needs of the nursing foal. Studies have shown that after 2 months of age, foals that consume a creep ration free-choice gain weight at a significantly faster rate than foals who nurse exclusively. Furthermore, nursing foals that don't consume a creep ration experience a compensatory growth spurt shortly after weaning when placed on a weanling diet. This compensatory growth spurt greatly increases the risk of incurring a developmental orthopedic disease (DOD). Foals on a creep-feeding program, however, do not experience this growth spurt.

The National Research Council recommends that a creep feed contain 16 percent crude protein, 0.9 percent calcium, and 0.6 percent phosphorus, based on total weight of the ration. Such creep feeds can be purchased from feed stores, or formulated using grains and concentrates (see Table V in chapter 17, Feeding and Nutrition).

Creep feeds are fed free-choice with all the hay or forage the nursing foal will consume. There is no need to restrict the amount of creep feed eaten by the foal until the foal is consuming 4 to 5 pounds a day. When this happens, start feeding $^1/_2$ to $^3/_4$ pounds per day per 100 pounds weight of the foal. If you do not restrict to the above, some foals will consume too much creep feed and thus be at increased

A nursing foal should be dewormed at 2 months of age and given its first routine vaccinations when 3 to 4 months old.

risk for DOD. The creep ration should be divided into equal portions and placed in the creep feeder at least twice daily. Remove moldy or wet feed.

A creep feeding station can be designed by placing a feeder inside a fenced enclosure with an entrance just wide enough for a foal to go in, but too small for a mare to pass through. Alternately, you can place the ration in a feed box with bars across the top spaced so that a foal (but not a mare) can put its nose through. A feeder can be placed in the corner of a stall and screened from the mare by bolting a strong board across the corner at a height that just allows the foal to go under.

Creep feeders in pastures should be placed in areas where the mare grazes. A foal won't use a creep feeder if it means being separated from its mother.

When several foals are using the same creep feeder, some may consume more grain than their daily allotment. It is best to separate and feed them individually. If this is not feasible, reduce the grain ration by half and make up the difference in weight using high-quality roughage such as chopped alfalfa.

Keep trace-mineralized salt available at all times. Studies suggest that increasing the concentrations of copper and zinc in the creep feed to 50 mg/kg dry matter basis for copper and 60 mg/kg for zinc decreases the risk and incidence of DOD. For more information, see Trace Minerals.

Vaccinations. A foal that has received passive immunity through its mother's colostrum is protected from most infectious diseases for about 2 to 3 months. Although newborn foals are immune-competent and capable of forming antibodies in response to vaccination or natural infection, the immune response is weak in comparison to what it will be at 3 to 4 months—when the first vaccination series is usually given. During this transition period between maternal protection and vaccination-produced antibodies, the foal is most susceptible to infectious diseases. It is a good idea at this time to prevent unnecessary exposure to contagious diseases.

When for a specific reason early vaccination at 1 to 3 weeks of age is undertaken, the vaccinations should repeated in 2 months, even though this will increase the number of vaccinations given.

The recommended immunization schedule for foals and weanlings is given in chapter 3, Infectious Diseases (Tables I and II).

Deworming. Most foals are infected very early in life with ascarids, threadworms, and pinworms. Foals also acquire other worm parasites including strongyles and bots. Ascarids, threadworms, and the large and small strongyles in particular, can cause delayed development and maturation, unthrifty appearance, and cough. Even when foals with infection show no signs, enough intestinal damage can occur to adversely affect feed utilization and growth.

At 8 weeks of age, the foal should be started on a deworming schedule as described in chapter 2, Parasites (see INTERVAL DEWORMING). On this schedule the foal is given a dewormer at 2 months of age and every other month until 12 months of age. The mature foal is then put on the same deworming schedule as an adult horse. On farms where threadworms are a problem, foals should be dewormed for threadworms at 3 weeks of age.

THE ORPHAN FOAL

When a newborn foal does not receive adequate colostrum from its true mother, follow the procedure described in the section LACK OF COLOSTRUM.

A foal who is rejected by its mother or orphaned at birth can sometimes be raised by another lactating mare if one is available. Many breeding farms keep a nurse mare with foster mother qualities for this purpose.

Generally most mares will accept an orphan foal within 12 to 72 hours if they are well enough restrained so that the foal can nurse repeatedly without being injured. Tranquilization should be avoided because most tranquilizers are transferred in milk and may sedate the nursing foal. Methods for restraint are discussed in the section MARES WHO REJECT OR INJURE THEIR FOALS.

The first 30 minutes after birth is the best time to substitute a live foal for a stillbirth. Since mares rely primarily upon their sense of smell for close-up identification, it is helpful to make the foal smell like the mare. You can smear the foal with amniotic fluid, or coat the foal with the mare's sweat, milk, or feces. It has been suggested that pouring linseed oil over the foal helps to disguise its odor.

On some farms the use of a milk goat has been successful. Many nannies readily accept foals. The composition of goat's milk is different from mare's milk, but not enough to cause problems. The nanny (or nannies) will have to stand on a raised platform, or the foal will need to nurse on its knees.

If a foster mother is not available, the foal can be raised by hand. This involves the use of a milk substitute and attention to feeding and hygiene. A good-quality commercial milk replacer such as Foal-Lac, Mare's Match, or Mare Replacer is the most suitable substitute for mare's milk. If one of these is not available, you can use a good-quality commercial calf-milk replacer until mare's milk does become available. A good-quality calf milk-replacer is one that contains at least 20 percent crude protein from *milk sources*, at least 15 percent fat, and no more than 0.2 percent crude fiber.

The dietary energy and water requirements of the young foal are extremely high. As a result, a large volume of milk must be consumed. This amounts to 14 quarts per day for a newborn foal. Add to this 1 quart per week until the foal is consuming 18 to 20 quarts per day. Milk replacer is reconstituted with water according to the directions provided. Also follow the manufacturer's instructions in regard to frequency and volume to feed. In general, milk replacer is fed in 4 or more equal feedings beginning with half the daily requirement during the first 24 hours, and increasing to the full daily requirement thereafter. The purpose of starting slowly is to avoid digestive upset and diarrhea.

The milk formula can be given by bottle or bucket. Bucket-feeding is easier and faster than bottle-feeding. Start with a shallow pan, so the foal's nose can touch the bottom. Dip your fingers into the milk and allow the foal to suck on your fingers. If the foal does not suck well, move your fingers against its tongue and palate to stimulate a better suckling reflex. Once the foal begins to suck, encourage it to drink by lowering your fingers along with its head into the pan. It may take only a few minutes or up to 2 hours to teach a foal to drink from a pan, but with time and patience this is easily accomplished.

Once the foal learns to drink from the pan without submerging its nostrils, switch to a plastic bucket with a wide opening. Hang the bucket in a convenient location and keep it full at all times. Foals typically drink small amounts frequently both day and night. Clean all feeding equipment and change buckets every 12 hours. Also provide continuous access to fresh water.

When the foal is several days old, begin feeding milk replacer (milk transition) pellets available from feed stores. Start by putting pellets in the foal's mouth several times a day. Then put as many pellets in a bucket or creep feeder as the foal will eat and keep it refilled. Old pellets should be discarded twice a day.

After the foal is eating 2 to 3 pounds of pellets a day, add a high quality creep feed ration as described in CARE AND FEEDING OF THE FOAL. As soon as the foal is eating 4 to 6 pounds of this creep feed/pelleted mixture a day, the pellets can be stopped. At 4 months of age, the orphan foal can be fed as a normal weanling.

THE WEANLING

Weaning

Wild mares do not wean their foals until they are nearly 2 years old. This lengthy period of bonding and nursing is accompanied by increasing periods of independence, so that when weaning does occur (usually because of a new foal), it occurs quite naturally and without physical or emotional trauma.

Artificially imposed weaning is stressful for both mare and foal. In foals, weaning-induced stress reduces feed intake and growth rate, depresses the immune system, and may cause disease. In its anxiety to return to its mother, the foal may incur injuries.

Most horse owners prefer to wean foals at 5 to 7 months of age, but foals can be weaned at 4 months of age without adverse effects on growth or development. However, foals younger than 4 months of age have yet to attain adult immune status as indicated by levels of serum immunoglobulin (IgG). Accordingly, if there is no medical reason to wean early, it is probably best not to wean until a foal is at least 4 months old.

Prior to weaning, the foal should be in good health, on a vaccination and de-worming program, and eating one pound of creep ration for each month of age daily as well as consuming some hay or pasture. Unless all of these conditions are met at least 2 weeks before weaning, do not wean.

Five days before weaning, eliminate grain from the mare's ration.

There are a number of weaning methods. The abrupt, complete separation of foal and mare works well for a herd of mares and foals. The selected mare is quietly led from the pasture while her foal is distracted. She is stabled or pastured completely out of sight and hearing of the herd. The foal is left in its former surroundings in the company of other mares and foals with whom it is familiar.

An interval, partial separation method seems to produce less anxiety due to the reassuring presence of the mother. On the day of weaning, the mare is led into an adjacent pasture or paddock within sight and touch of her foal but separated by a secure fence that won't injure the foal but will prevent it from nursing. The fence can be made of chain link, small-weave mesh wire, or board with an electric wire.

These 6-month weanling foals have been put together out of sight and sound of their mothers.

If possible, leave the foal in its customary pasture, and in the company of other horses or foals with whom it is familiar. Weaning is complete in 1 week, at which time the dam is removed. To prevent the mare from coming back into milk, the mare and foal should remain separated for 6 weeks.

Feeding

The nutrient requirements of the weanling foal at 6 months of age are shown in Table I in chapter 17, Feeding and Nutrition. Most weanlings will consume 2 to 2.3 percent of their body weight in feed per day. A 6-month-old weanling weighing 462 pounds will thus consume between 9.25 and 10.6 pounds of feed per day.

The daily ration of the average weanling (1,100 pounds mature weight) should consist of a hay-to-grain ratio of 40 to 60 percent by weight. As a rule of thumb, feed 1 pound of grain for each month of age. At the same time, the weanling should consume at least 1 pound of good-quality roughage for every 100 pounds weight. If this amount is not being consumed, cut back on the amount of grain until it is consumed. Heavier breeds and larger horses should be fed slightly less, since they tend to grow more slowly than lighter horses.

A deficiency of calcium, phosphorus, or both will result in a mineral deficiency and the occurrence of lameness and bone disease. These deficiencies can be prevented by insuring that adequate amounts of both minerals are present in the weanling's diet (see Tables I and II). Of equal importance, the diet should contain more calcium than phosphorus to maintain a positive calcium: phosphorus ratio (ideally, 1.25:1). A properly formulated grain mix (Table VII) will contain adequate calcium and phosphorus to meet these mineral requirements. When feed sources are marginal, provide a supplemental mineral mix as described under CALCIUM AND PHOSPHORUS. Also insure that the diet consumed by the weanling (and yearling) contains adequate concentrations of copper and zinc. For more information, see MINERALS.

Table V contains a sample ration, based on a corn/soybean concentrate mix, for weanlings at 6 months of age. Table VI shows the amount of a commercial horse feed to provide along with good-quality hay or forage. Feeding instructions vary with the product. Feed commercial rations according to the guidelines provided.

Overfeeding is a major problem in growing horses. Excessive weight gain, and spurts of growth associated with overfeeding, may cause or exacerbate developmental orthopedic diseases (DODs). Feeding more than 8 or 9 pounds of grain is not necessary or recommended unless hay quality is poor. When feeding a 60 percent grain concentrate mixture, the daily allotment of high-quality legume hay should be restricted to $^1/_2$ pound per 100 pounds weight of the mature horse. After 12 months of age, the amount of high-quality roughage consumed is no longer a concern.

Drying up the Mare

Immediately after removing her foal, stop feeding grain to the mare and reduce her daily hay or forage consumption to 1.5 to 2.0 pounds per 100 pounds body weight. The purpose of temporarily reducing feed and energy is to help stop milk production and excessive udder pressure and discomfort. Apply lanolin or hand lotion to the mare's udder if necessary to keep the skin from drying and cracking. However, do not milk out the mare. Milking stimulates and prolongs lactation. In addition, it is the buildup of pressure that stops the milk from forming. Encourage exercise. Within 1 week the udder should be soft and flabby. When this happens, dietary restrictions are no longer needed.

If the newly weaned mare is in good condition, feed for maintenance. If she is thin, feed additional forage and grain to increase her body weight and condition to moderately fleshy. If the mare is pregnant, see Care and Feeding During Pregnancy.

THE YEARLING

The average yearling achieves 65 to 70 percent of its mature weight by 12 months of age. Growth now slows and nutritional requirements do also.

Diets for most yearlings should consist of 50 percent hay and 50 percent grain by weight. This is a lower grain ratio than for weanlings. Feed 1 pound of grain mix concentrate per 100 pounds weight of the horse per day (up to a maximum of 9 pounds of grain per day) until the horse reaches 90 percent of its anticipated adult weight. This occurs at about 2 years of age. Grain should be fed along with all the good-quality roughage the horse will eat.

A sample ration for feeding a yearling at 12 months of age is shown in Table V in chapter 17, Feeding and Nutrition.

Administer annual booster vaccinations as shown in Tables I and II in chapter 3, Infectious Diseases. The horse should now be switched to an adult deworming schedule as described in chapter 2, Parasites (Deworming Your Horse).

Foal Diseases

A number of diseases affect the neonatal and growing foal. While many of these can and do occur in older horses, they do not pose the same threat to health and life as they do in the foal.

Foals are especially susceptible to certain infections during the first few weeks of life, most notably *foal septicemia, tetanus, rhinopneumonitis, equine influenza*, and *rotavirus infection*. Signs of illness include listlessness, weakness, lack of vigorous suckling, nasal or eye discharge, coughing, lameness, swollen joints, and diarrhea.

Fever is a serious sign in a young foal and always merits professional examination. The normal temperature of the foal is 99 to 102 degrees F. If you suspect illness, take the foal's temperature and notify your veterinarian if the temperature does not fall within this range.

LACK OF COLOSTRUM (FAILURE OF PASSIVE TRANSFER)

Late in pregnancy the mare produces a special milk high in fat, vitamins, minerals, and protein. This is the *colostrum* or first milk of the dam. Of greatest importance, colostrum contains the immunoglobulin antibodies and other immune substances (primarily IgG) which protect the foal from neonatal diseases. Failure of passive transfer (FPT) of immunoglobulins from dam to foal is cited as the single most important cause of neonatal infection and death during the first week of life.

In many species, including man, the fetus receives protection through the passage of antibodies and immunoglobulins across the placenta. This does not happen in the horse. The foal is born without circulating immunoglobulins and can acquire them only through ingestion of colostrum during the first 18 to 24 hours after birth. Immediately after birth, through a special adaptation in the cells of the intestinal lining, antibodies are allowed to cross the mucosal barrier and enter the bloodstream. By 24 hours, this barrier closes and antibodies are no longer absorbed.

FPT can occur for any number of reasons including death of the dam, premature lactation prior to delivery, insufficient production due to maternal illness or advanced age, delay in suckling due to foal weakness or illness, and maternal rejection. Any mare who drips milk prior to foaling is losing colostrum. This should alert her attendants to the possibility of partial or complete FPT. If possible, the milk should be collected and frozen. It can be thawed immediately after delivery and given to the foal by nursing bottle.

Several pints of mare's colostrum must be ingested to provide adequate blood levels of IgG. When there is doubt as to the quantity ingested by the foal, a rapid

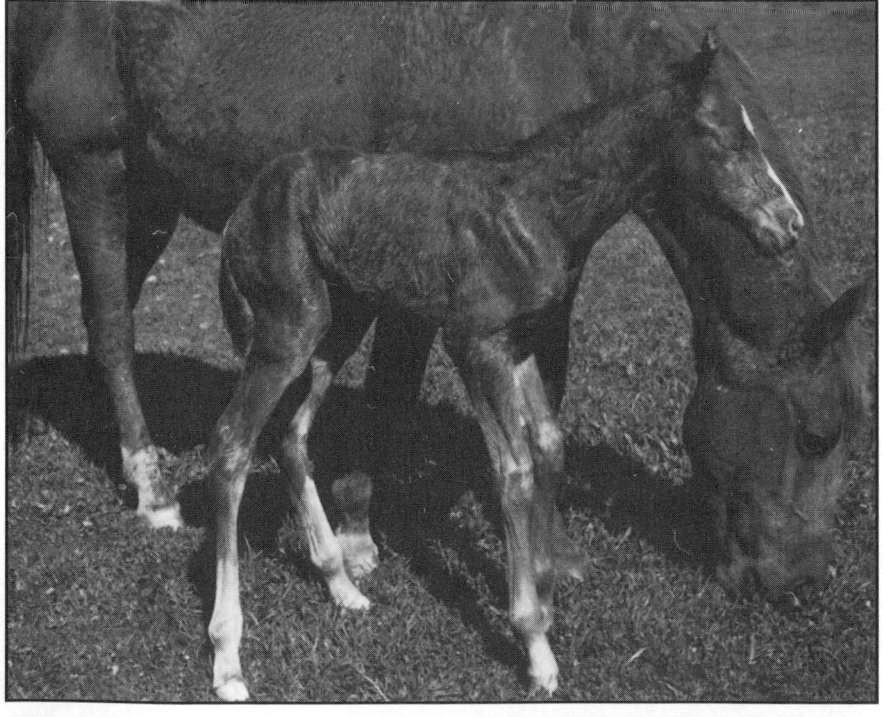

To prevent foal septicemia, it is most important that the foal be up and nursing and receiving colostrum within the first few hours of birth.

bedside IgG blood test (Cite test) can be run on the foal's serum at 12 hours of age to determine if adequate colostrum has been ingested. This test is unnecessary if it is obvious that FPT exists (i.e., by maternal death or failure to suckle). As soon as a colostrum deficiency is diagnosed, colostrum replacement is initiated without delay. Oral colostrum should be administered within the first 18 hours of life to assure success.

Most breeding farms maintain a colostrum bank, obtained by milking 6 to 8 ounces of colostrum from postpartum mares and then pooling it and freezing it for use later. This volume is safe to collect without depriving the foal.

If mare's colostrum is unavailable, the foal can be given bovine (cow) colostrum, equine blood plasma, or freeze-dried equine IgG. The best way to insure that the foal receives the substitute colostrum is to give it by nursing bottle. IgG is better absorbed by bottle than stomach tube.

Treatment of FPT after 24 hours is accomplished by giving 1 to 2 liters of pooled equine plasma by vein. The decision to treat, as well as the amount of plasma to give, depends upon the level of circulating IgG as determined by blood testing, potential for exposure to foal septicemia, and other factors.

Newborn foals are dependent upon colostrum to provide vitamin A. In the colostrum-deficient foal, vitamin A deficiency is prevented by giving an intramuscular injection.

FOAL SEPTICEMIA

Foal septicemia is a rapidly progressive, often fatal systemic infection that affects foals less than 7 days of age. It is the most common cause of severe illness and death in newborn foals. Rather than a specific bacterial infection, foal septicemia is a symptom complex which includes a number of different bacterial pathogens. Some, like actinobacillosis and salmonellosis, are recognized as specific diseases.

The most significant predisposing factor in the development of foal septicemia is FPT, discussed above. Other factors that predispose to neonatal sepsis include prematurity, a complicated birthing, overcrowding, and the stress of cold or wet surroundings. Any foal that does not stand within 2 hours, does not suckle within 2 to 3 hours, or exhibits behavioral or physical abnormalities, is at risk.

The actual source of the infection may be difficult to identify. Some bacteria are transmitted across the placenta and infect the foal before birth. Others are acquired during passage through the birth canal. Ingestion of infected mother's milk or contaminated fodder is another possibility. The respiratory route accounts for some cases. Umbilical stump infection is a serious predisposing cause.

Signs of foal septicemia generally appear at about 2 to 4 days of age and are followed by rapid deterioration. Early signs include weakness, lethargy, and reluctance to nurse (often indicated by engorgement of the mare's udder). An indication of lethargy is an unusual amount of time sleeping or lying on the side. Cough or diarrhea can be the first sign in some infections. By the time the foal appears toxic and has difficulty breathing, swollen joints, shock, collapse, convulsions, or coma, the outlook for recovery is poor.

Because foal septicemia progresses so rapidly, treatment must be started immediately, often without cultures to pinpoint the specific bacteria. There are few clues to distinguish septicemia caused by actinobacillus, for example, from that caused by salmonella or another organism. However, cultures should be obtained because they may modify treatment at a later stage.

Treatment: Since many cases of foal septicemia are associated with partial or complete FPT, serum immunoglobulin levels should be obtained routinely. If the IgG level is low, the foal can be transfused with 2 to 4 liters of plasma. Broad-spectrum intramuscular or intravenous antibiotics are given to treat septicemia and prevent complications. Vigorous fluid replacement is essential to prevent or treat dehydration and shock. X-rays and ultrasound studies may assist in localizing the site of infection.

Supportive therapy is absolutely necessary and often makes the difference between survival and death. Recumbent foals should be kept on a soft mattress, a waterbed, or a suitable protective surface, and kept in the sternal position. If this is not possible, turn the foal from side to side every 2 hours. Prevent chilling and hypothermia with blankets, heating pads, or radiant heat lamps. Intranasal oxygen is of benefit for foals with respiratory distress. Sterile eye lubricants should be applied several times daily to prevent surface drying and corneal ulceration. The perineum of foals with diarrhea must be kept clean and dry. Apply zinc oxide ointment to prevent skin scalds. The umbilical stump should be cleaned twice daily with tamed iodine solution.

Nutrition is vital. If the foal is not strong enough to stand with assistance and suckle, the mare should be milked out and the milk given to the foal by nursing bottle. Mare milk replacer can be used if mother's milk is not available. If the foal is too weak to nurse, the feeding can be given by nasogastric tube.

If the foal survives the initial septicemia episode, localized infections may develop in various body cavities. Joint ill is a common sequel, as is panophthalmitis, an inflammation of all the inner structures of the eyes. Inflammation of the covering of the brain (meningitis) causes seizures and coma.

The prevention of foal septicemia involves the prompt recognition and treatment of FPT; providing clean, dry, sanitary foaling quarters; and using good hygienic techniques when handling the mother and foal during and after delivery.

Following are specific bacterial infections causing foal septicemia.

ACTINOBACILLOSIS (SLEEPY FOAL SYNDROME)

The bacteria *Actinobacillus equuli* is a common cause of foal septicemia. Signs usually appear during the first 48 hours of life. However, sudden death can occur as early as 6 hours after birth. This bacteria may be present in the reproductive system of seemingly healthy mares without producing any illness. This may explain why some foals are infected at birth. Others apparently acquire the bacteria through ingestion.

Infected foals are extremely weak and have difficulty standing and nursing. They appear to sleep all the time and may even be found in a coma. Diarrhea is common. Foals that survive the acute illness often develop septic joints and osteomyelitis (*joint ill*).

Treatment: Treatment is like that for foal septicemia, described above.

NAVEL ILL (UMBILICAL INFECTION)

Navel ill is a serious and frequently fatal disease in newborn foals arising from a bacterial infection of the umbilical structures, which include the artery, vein, and urachus. It is acquired either during foaling or from subsequent contamination of the healing stump. A number of bacteria can be involved, but streptococcus is the most common.

A puslike infected discharge is present. The navel stump is often hot, tender, and swollen. The foal appears apathetic and stops nursing. In the septicemic form, the bacteria enter the bloodstream through the umbilical vessels and spread to the liver, the joints, and elsewhere. The foal may become markedly depressed, go into shock, and die within 12 to 24 hours. Alternately, the foal may not develop an overwhelming septicemia but develop instead the signs of joint ill, as described below.

Treatment: Ultrasound exam of the umbilical structures helps to determine the extent of infection and whether there is an umbilical stump abscess. Intravenous antibiotics should be started at the first signs of navel infection to prevent death or the effects of joint ill. All navel abscesses should be opened and drained, and the infected umbilical structures surgically removed. Supportive care is important. Keep the umbilical area clean and dry and apply a topical antiseptic such as Betadine solution twice daily. Change bedding frequently and keep the stall as clean as possible.

Prevention: Navel infection can be prevented by good management practices such as providing a sanitary environment for foaling; applying tincture of iodine to the umbilical stump after the foal is born; and insuring that the foal receives a sufficient amount of colostrum.

JOINT ILL (SEPTIC ARTHRITIS AND OSTEOMYELITIS)

The infection begins when bacteria enter the bloodstream and invade the bone or synovial membranes of the joint. Note that any type of neonatal infection causing septicemia can cause joint ill. In 25 percent of cases, navel infection is the predisposing cause.

Joint and bone infection can occur in older nursing and weanling foals as a condition separate from foal septicemia. Bacteria gain entrance through the digestive or respiratory tracts, but produce few (if any) symptoms until the foal exhibits a sudden lameness along with one or more hot, swollen joints accompanied by fever (102 to 104 degrees F), listlessness, and loss of appetite. Any foal who exhibits unexplained lameness should be examined by a veterinarian.

The diagnosis is confirmed by aspiration and analysis of joint fluid. Fluid should be submitted for bacterial culture and sensitivity testing. Arthroscopy may be helpful in some cases. Ultrasonography is useful in distinguishing between an abscess around a joint and infected fluid within a joint. Serial x-rays are necessary to identify developing osteomyelitis.

Treatment: It is most likely to be effective when started early in the course of the infection. Massive doses of antibiotic should be given for at least 3 weeks. Septic joints are irrigated every other day for several days, using large-bore needles to infuse and remove large volumes of fluid under pressure. If the infection has been present for more than 1 week, it is usually necessary to open the joint to remove pus and debris. A suction drain is inserted and the leg is immobilized by an occlusive dressing. Stall rest and physical therapy are important to a successful outcome. The prognosis depends on the number of joints involved, their location, and the duration and extent of infection. Foals with bone infection usually develop permanent arthritis.

FOAL PNEUMONIA

Pneumonia is a serious and often fatal infection that attacks newborn foals and older foals up to 8 months of age. In foals older than 1 month, the most common causative bacteria is *Streptococcus zooepidemicus*. *Rhodococcus equi*, found commonly in soil and the intestinal tract of horses, causes a particularly severe illness and may be associated with contagious outbreaks involving up to 50 percent of foals on a farm. Viral pneumonia generally is caused by either rhinopneumonitis (EHV-1) or an equine influenza virus.

Factors that predispose to pneumonia are failure to receive colostrum, overcrowding, cold damp quarters, soiled feed and bedding, an inadequate vaccination and/or deworming program, recent viral respiratory illness, transporting the foal (especially in hot weather), or any physical condition which weakens the foal's resistance. Most of these can be avoided by good management.

Bacterial infection in newborn foals follows the same course as described for foal septicemia. It may be difficult to determine whether the pneumonia preceded the septicemia or occured as a result of it. *Streptococcus zooepidemicus* is the bacteria most frequently isolated in neonatal respiratory infection.

Newborn viral pneumonias are acquired in utero. Shortly after birth, these foals become progressively weak and lethargic and soon develop respiratory distress. Secondary bacterial infection occurs. The majority succumb during the first 7 days. A vaccination program (as described in CARE AND FEEDING DURING PREGNANCY) will prevent most cases.

Pneumonia in foals 1 to 8 months of age usually starts insidiously with lack of appetite, inactivity, and depression. Respiratory signs appear shortly thereafter. They include high fever, diarrhea, rapid pulse, difficult breathing, watery eyes, cough, and a nasal discharge. A thick nasal discharge containing pus is a sign of bacterial pneumonia.

Treatment: A penicillin antibiotic should be started as soon as possible, and can be changed if necessary, subject to culture and sensitivity tests. *Rhodococcus equi* responds dramatically to the combined use of oral erythromycin and rifampin. Antibiotics should be continued throughout the course of the illness and then 1 week longer. Failure to complete a full course of antibiotics is the chief cause of relapse and lung abscess. Good nursing care, as described for foal septicemia, is essential. The foal should be kept in warm dry quarters, treated for dehydration, and given anti-inflammatory drugs to reduce fever. The maintenance of hydration is critical in liquifying secretions and promoting elimination.

Foals with lung abscess require prolonged treatment.

TYZZER'S DISEASE

This rare and rapidly fatal disease occurs in foals under 6 weeks of age. It is caused by an infection of the liver. The causative bacteria is *Bacillus piliformis*. It is not known how this disease is spread, but mares may be carriers.

The onset is sudden with high fever, diarrhea, collapse, and seizures—all occurring within a matter of hours. In most cases the foal is found dead or in coma.

Treatment: Treatment is directed at supporting the foal with intravenous fluids, antibiotics, and anticonvulsants. Unfortunately, the rapidity of the disease makes it difficult to initiate treatment in time to save the life of the foal. The diagnosis is often made at autopsy.

FOAL DIARRHEA

Diarrhea is the most common problem affecting foals. While foal heat diarrhea is mild and inconsequential, infectious enteritis is serious and often fatal. Familiarity with diarrhea illnesses helps to determine when to seek professional assistance.

Foal Heat Diarrhea

Foal heat, or "ninth day diarrhea" (which actually occurs from days 6 to 14), affects nearly all newborn foals. The stool is soft, pasty-yellow, and not profuse. The foal appears unaffected, remains bright and alert, and nurses at regular intervals. The diarrhea is characteristically self-limited, lasting fewer than 7 days.

Since the diarrhea happens to occur when the mare enters her first heat after foaling, it was believed that hormones in the mare's milk caused the diarrhea. In fact, the same diarrhea also occurs in orphan foals. Note that newborn foals normally eat manure and feedstuffs such as grain and hay. It appears that the ingestion of these substances may upset the flora of the foal's immature intestinal tract and cause the temporary diarrhea.

Treatment: Diarrhea of short duration associated with the foal heat requires little treatment. Keep the foal dry and clean around its tail and perineum. Apply zinc oxide ointment to prevent scalding. If the diarrhea persists longer than expected, you can give Pepto-Bismol (20 ml per 100 pounds weight) by syringe (or tablespoon) 2 to 3 times a day for 1 to 2 days. Restrain the foal and insert the medicine into the corner of the mouth. Do not use a laxative or intestinal purgative as this will make the diarrhea worse.

Nutritional Diarrhea

A common type of mild diarrhea is associated with the ingestion of too much milk. It occurs when the mother is a heavy milk producer. Additionally, a temporary lactase deficiency resulting in carbohydrate intolerance may occur in some neonates who are either hand-fed or recovering from a viral enteritis.

Treatment: Diarrhea caused by overingestion of milk can be helped by milking out the mare 2 or 3 times a day. The foal should not be restricted from nursing because the milk is its source of water. As the foal grows, its nutritional needs will increase and it will absorb more milk. This corrects the problem. A temporary lactase deficiency can be treated by giving an oral lactase preparation, such as LactAid, available at health stores.

Parasitic Diarrhea

Threadworms are the first intestinal parasites to mature in the foal, but large numbers are required to cause symptoms. They are transmitted to the foal in the mother's milk. Diarrhea caused by threadworms can appear during the first 2 weeks of life; thus threadworm diarrhea overlaps foal heat diarrhea.

The diarrhea caused by large strongyle infection is associated with severe colic and often constipation. It usually affects foals 1 to 4 months of age.

A heavy roundworm infestation causes diarrhea, colic, poor growth and body condition, nasal discharge, and cough. It usually affects foals 3 to 6 months of age.

Parasitic infestations can be prevented by deworming schedules as described in chapter 2, Parasites.

Protozoal Diarrhea

Protozoans are single-celled organisms occasionally responsible for disease in foals and horses.

Trichomonas. Rarely, sudden severe diarrhea in young horses can be caused by *Trichomonas equi*. This protozoan is a normal intestinal inhabitant. During periods of stress the flora of the intestine changes, allowing Trichomonas to become invaders.

Signs of infection are fever, colic, weakness, and the passage of large volumes of watery greenish stool. The stool does not contain blood. The diagnosis is made by recovering the organism in stool cultures. Without treatment, the diarrhea may continue for weeks or months. With chronic diarrhea the stool is soft and has the consistency of cow manure.

Treatment: Treatment involves correcting dehydration by restoring fluids and electrolytes. An antibiotic effective against protozoans should be started early and continued for at least 1 week.

Cryptosporidiosis. Cryptosporidiosis causes a protozoal diarrhea only in foals. Usually the disease is mild and self-limited, consisting of a watery diarrhea that persists for 2 weeks. However in Arabian foals with combined immunodeficiency disease, and in neonatal foals with FPT, the disease is serious. The diagnosis is made by identifying the organism in the stool.

Treatment involves oral and intravenous fluid replacement. There are no effective antibiotics. Disinfect contaminated areas using ammonia (5 percent), sodium hypochlorite (bleach), or 10 percent formalin.

Bacterial Enteritis

A number of bacterial species produce severe and often fatal infection of the large and small intestine of newborn foals. Failure of passive transfer of colostral antibodies is involved in a high percentage of cases.

Salmonellosis. Salmonella infection is a leading cause of newborn septicemia. This bacteria often settles in other body systems including the lungs, joints, eyes, kidneys, and brain.

Several species of salmonella cause infectious enteritis in foals 1 to 4 months of age. Signs are fever, weakness, and a profuse, watery diarrhea that contains blood. The foal becomes depressed, stops suckling, and quickly dehydrates.

Clostridial Infection. Both C. *perfringens* and C. *difficile* produce highly lethal infectious diarrhea in newborn foals. The diarrhea is bloody, foul-smelling, profuse, and associated with severe colic. It is unusual for a neonatal foal with clostridial diarrhea to live more than 48 hours. In fact, the foal may be found dead before the diarrhea develops. Clostridia are normal inhabitants of the horse's colon; therefore recovery of the bacteria does not necessarily prove a causal relationship. Finding the exotoxin in the foal's stool or serum is more accurate.

Vaccination of pregnant mares with C. *perfringens* toxoid has been advocated on farms with a history of clostridial foal infections. However, the safety and effectiveness of this vaccine is not yet established.

E. coli Infection. E. *coli* is the most common bacteria isolated from blood cultures in septicemic foals. This bacteria tends to seed multiple organ systems. Diarrhea is a late and often terminal event. E. *coli* is an infrequent cause of diarrhea in older foals.

Treatment: Irrespective of bacterial cause, rapid correction of dehydration using large volumes of intravenous fluid is the top priority. Plasma is given to replace protein losses. Salmonella species rapidly develop resistance to antibiotics, which renders antibiotics less effective for salmonellosis than for other types of bacterial enteritis. However, antibiotics are given in all septicemic diarrheas to contain symptoms and prevent seeding of organs. Supportive treatment as described under Foal Septicemia is of great importance.

Rotavirus Infection (Viral Enteritis)

Rotavirus is a highly contagious enteritis that attacks foals up to 6 months of age. Most cases occur in 2-month-olds. This correlates with the interval during which the foal's maternal antibody levels are in natural decline. Older horses usually do not develop the disease but may serve as a reservoir.

Once thought to be confined to Kentucky and the southeastern United States, rotavirus is now worldwide. Annual spring epidemics can involve up to 70 percent of foals on a single farm. Virus is shed in the stool by infected and convalescent foals, and by exposed asymptomatic adults. The virus is rapidly transmitted through contact with contaminated feed, water, bedding, human hands, grooming utensils, and other sources.

Following an incubation period of 18 to 24 hours, the illness begins with pronounced apathy and high fever. The severity of the diarrhea is variable. Some foals experience a few stools of cowpie consistency, nurse lethargically for 1 or 2 days, and then recover. In others the diarrhea is explosive, with the stool appearing watery green to gray in color. A profuse diarrhea, which in the acute form can last 5 to 7 days, results in significant fluid and electrolyte losses. The illness is most severe in foals under a week of age. These neonates dehydrate rapidly.

During the acute infection, the rotavirus destroys the intestinal brush border cells lining the upper intestinal tract. These cells produce lactase and also are responsible for nutrient absorption. The degree of injury is variable. Regeneration may occur within a few days, but some foals sustain a prolonged lactase deficiency and an impaired ability to absorb nutrients. The malabsorption and lactase deficiency can be the cause of another diarrhea, which persists long after the first is eliminated.

Treatment: Administer Pepto-Bismol (20 ml per 100 pounds body weight) 3 to 4 times daily to control diarrhea and protect the lining of the intestine. Zinc oxide ointment is recommended for skin scalds involving the perineum and hind legs. A severely dehydrated foal requires IV fluids and hospitalization. Diarrhea associated with a lactase deficiency is managed by switching to solid feeds and weaning the foal as soon as possible (see WEANING).

Prevention: Sick foals are isolated to prevent spread of disease. Thoroughly disinfect premises and equipment to prevent spread of the virus. Formaldehyde (not bleach) is the disinfectant of choice.

A vaccine for pregnant mares is under investigation. Preliminary studies suggest that after vaccination, antibodies are present in colostrum, and they are at least partially protective for the foal during the first 3 months. Currently the vaccine is not licensed for general use. Horse owners considering the use of equine rotavirus vaccine should contact their state veterinarian.

ULCERS IN FOALS

Ulcer disease is common in foals. In fact, it has been estimated that up to 50 percent of foals will develop an ulcer during the first 4 months of life. These ulcers occur in the stomach, or just beyond the outlet of the stomach in the duodenum, which is the first few feet of the small intestine. The majority of ulcers do not produce symptoms, and disappear with age.

Among horses, stress appears to play a major role in causing ulcers. Stress affects foals in the neonatal period in association with septic diarrhea and other infections.

It also occurs at 2 months when maternally acquired immunity begins to wane; and again at 4 to 5 months in association with weaning.

Symptoms develop in a minority of foals. They include abdominal pain, grinding of the teeth (called *bruxism*), frothy salivation, poor appetite, diarrhea of varying frequency, poor growth, rough hair coat, a potbellied appearance, and a tendency to frequently lie on the back.

Severe complications can occur. The most common is scarring. When this occurs near the outlet of the stomach or in the duodenum, a stricture can develop that partially or completely prevents the stomach from emptying. Affected foals are reluctant to eat and may experience regurgitation and aspiration pneumonia. Ulcers can perforate the stomach or duodenum, spilling intestinal contents into the abdomen and causing fatal peritonitis. The diagnosis can be confirmed by tapping the abdomen and recovering ingested feedstuff.

Examination of the interior of the stomach by gastroscopy is easily performed in foals. It is the best way to make the diagnosis and determine the number, location, and size of the ulcers.

Treatment: The most important step is to treat precipitating illnesses and remove all causes of stress. Medical management employing anti-ulcer drugs is the same as that described for adult horses in chapter 8, Digestive System.

Foals with strictures that prevent gastric emptying can be treated successfully with surgery. Gastric rupture cannot be treated.

NEONATAL MALADJUSTMENT SYNDROME

The neonatal maladjustment syndrome (NMS, also called the convulsive foal syndrome, barker, wanderer, or dummy foal syndrome) is believed to be caused by central nervous system hypoxia (oxygen lack) during or after delivery. The reason for the oxygen deprivation is usually not apparent. All laboratory studies are normal.

Typically, after a rapid uncomplicated delivery, the foal appears normal, but then minutes or hours later loses its suckling reflex and begins to exhibit abnormal behavior. This behavior either gets progressively worse or fluctuates. Indications of brain involvement include seizures with jerking movements of the head and body, followed by spasms of the neck, limbs, and tail, and thrashing of the legs. These convulsions are accompanied by pronounced respiratory distress. The foal often emits a high-pitched whinnying or "barking" sound.

Another characteristic feature of NMS is loss of the righting reflex. This is a sign of spinal cord involvement. The foal is incapable of making the coordinated movements necessary to turn itself onto its sternum or stand alone.

After the barker stage, the foal passes into the dummy stage. During this stage the foal is inert and recumbent, does not respond to stimuli, appears blind, and loses affinity for its mother. Later it becomes extremely active and wanders about aimlessly, bumping into objects.

As a consequence of repeated convulsions, the foal may develop brain swelling as well as thermoregulatory, respiratory, and circulatory failure. This leads to death, which occurs in about half the cases.

Foals suffering from actinobacillosis, foal septicemia, and neonatal meningitis often exhibit symptoms like those of NMS. Accordingly, blood cultures and laboratory studies should be run on all foals exhibiting dummy or wanderer-like behavior, since some of these foals will have an infectious process.

Treatment: The first priority is to control convulsions. This frequently can be accomplished by simply turning the foal onto its sternum. Helping the foal to stand is also helpful. If convulsions persist, Valium or an anti-epileptic drug can be given by intravenous injection. Nasal oxygen is of value. DMSO may reduce brain swelling.

Prevent hypothermia by covering the foal with a woolen or electric blanket and raising the temperature of the stall. Provide a clean well-padded surface for the foal to lie on. Remove all hay and straw.

Foals that were not able to suckle should be given 2 quarts of mare's colostrum by nasopharyngeal catheter within 18 hours of birth. If this cannot be accomplished, see LACK OF COLOSTRUM. Maintain nutrition and water balance by feeding mother's milk and/or warm milk replacer via nasopharyngeal catheter every hour at a rate of 20 percent of body weight per day. Milk the mare, both to obtain milk and to prevent her from drying up. Gastric ulcers are common in convulsive foals. Preventive anti-ulcer treatment is recommended (see ULCERS IN FOALS).

Once coherent, the foal must be trained to walk, nurse, and follow its mother.

Foals surviving the convulsive phase have a favorable outlook. Reflexes return gradually over 2 to 3 days. The suckling reflex is the last to return. Complete recovery with no residual neurological deficit is possible if the foal has adequate IgG levels, does not develop foal septicemia, and is able to stand and suckle within 4 days of birth.

SHAKER FOAL SYNDROME

The shaker foal syndrome is a paralytic disease caused by the ingestion of spores of the bacteria *Clostridium botulinum* present in hay and feeds. The spores grow in the intestinal tract of the foal, releasing a powerful neurotoxin that causes the paralytic signs. The syndrome occurs exclusively in the mid-Atlantic states and is most common in Kentucky, where soils contain a high concentration of spores.

Foals 2 weeks to 8 months of age are most often affected. Symptoms appear 1 to 4 days after the ingestion of spores. The first sign is a generalized weakness. The foal walks with a stiff, stilted gait or may be found lying down. When forced to stand, it trembles and shakes, then drops to the ground and rolls on its side. Paralysis of the swallowing mechanism causes drooling and protrusion of the tongue. Liquids may dribble from the foal's nose and mouth. Death by respiratory paralysis or aspiration pneumonia occurs in 1 to 3 days. The mortality rate is 90 percent.

Treatment is like that described for botulism in chapter 17, Feeding and Nutrition.

Prevention: Vaccination of pregnant mares with C. *botulinum* type B toxoid affords some protection against the shaker foal syndrome. Note that there are 3 types of neurotoxin. Vaccination protects against only type B (the most common), but does not protect against types A and C. Vaccination should be considered in endemic and high-risk areas, especially on farms where the shaker foal syndrome has occurred before. The primary immunization series consists of 3 vaccinations at 4-week intervals, with the last dose given 2 to 4 weeks before foaling. Boosters for adult horses are indicated annually. In immunized broodmares, administer the annual booster 2 to 4 weeks before foaling. The product is not labeled for vaccination of foals.

FAINTING FOAL SYNDROME (NARCOLEPSY-CATAPLEXY)

The fainting foal syndrome is a rare sleep disorder first reported in foals under 6 months of age and subsequently seen in older horses. A biochemical abnormality in the sleep-wake centers of the brainstem is thought to be the cause. Although many breeds are affected, a familial incidence may exist among Suffolk and Shetland ponies.

Signs are those of excessive daytime sleepiness accompanied by rapid eye movements as if the horse were dreaming. The head is held close to the ground, the eyes are closed, and occasionally you will hear snoring.

As the horse begins to fall asleep, its muscles relax. If the horse wakes before it falls, the condition is called *narcolepsy.* But if the horse actually collapses or "faints," then it is called *cataplexy.* Recovery occurs in minutes to hours. Between attacks, the horse is normal.

These attacks are provoked by certain stimuli specific for each individual, such as eating food, being led from a stall, or being stroked or groomed.

The diagnosis can be confirmed by giving a drug which brings on the attack, or giving a drug that eliminates attacks for several hours.

Treatment: An antidepressant drug is available. It acts on the sleep center to suppress the type of disorder associated with this syndrome. It must be given 3 times a day. Oral administration is less consistent than IV administration. The prognosis is variable. In some foals and adult horses, several attacks may occur and then the condition disappears completely. In Shetland and Suffolk ponies, however, the disease is more likely to persist indefinitely.

NEONATAL ISOERYTHROLYSIS

This disorder, also called *hemolytic disease of the newborn,* is of major concern because it affects 1 percent of Thoroughbred foals (although not all show clinical symptoms), and may result in a fatal anemia. It begins shortly after a foal ingests colostrum containing antibodies that destroy its own red blood cells.

These antibodies are manufactured by the mare when fetal red cells of a type incompatible with her red cells cross the placenta and stimulate the mare to develop antibodies to the foreign protein. This generally occurs during a prior pregnancy but can happen during the current pregnancy. A blood transfusion containing incompatible red cells produces the same result.

The antibodies in the colostrum will not attack the foal's red cells if it inherits the same blood type as its mother. However, if the foal inherits its sire's blood type, and if this is the same type to which the mare was sensitized, then incompatibility exists and a hemolytic anemia may develop.

An affected foal is normal at birth, but 24 to 36 hours after suckling experiences weakness and lethargy which may progress to collapse. Heart rate and respiratory rate are increased. The foal often lies with its chin resting on the ground while gasping for air. The breakdown of red cells releases free hemoglobin, which turns the urine a dark tea-color. The liver converts the hemoglobin to bile, which turns the white of the eye yellow (jaundice). In a severe crisis, a foal may die before developing jaundice.

Laboratory studies are used to make the diagnosis and monitor the disease.

Treatment: The degree of hemolysis and attendant anemia depends on several factors, including the amount of colostrum ingested. If the disease is not suspected during the first 24 to 36 hours before the foal develops symptoms, there is no reason to stop nursing, as the mare's milk no longer contains colostrum, and in any case maternal antibodies will no longer be absorbed from the foal's intestine. If the hemolysis is severe, IV fluids may be indicated to wash out hemoglobin before it damages the kidneys. Prophylactic antibiotics are a consideration. Blood transfusions are required only if the anemia is life-threatening. The mare's own blood can be used, provided the serum is first siphoned off and the cells are washed. Otherwise, a different horse of acceptable blood type should be used as the donor. The prognosis is good if the anemia stabilizes and the foal does not develop an infectious complication.

Prevention: When a pregnant mare is carrying a foal with the potential for neonatal isoerythrolysis, you can send a serum sample obtained in late pregnancy to a laboratory equipped to tell whether the mare's serum contains antibodies to foreign red cells. If antibodies are detected, the foal *might* develop hemolytic anemia—depending upon its inherited blood type. Since this cannot be determined until later, as a precaution do not allow the foal to suckle for the first 24 hours and provide an alternate source of colostrum (see LACK OF COLOSTRUM). Leave the foal with its mother but prevent it from nursing by applying a muzzle; or erect a barrier between mother and foal.

Congenital Disorders

Any disorder present at birth is referred to as *congenital*. Some are genetically determined while others are caused by accidents during labor and delivery. Among the more common congenital disorders are the following:

RUPTURED BLADDER

This occurs in somewhat less than 1 percent of newborns, primarily in colts. It is caused by developmental weakness in the wall of the bladder along with bladder compression during delivery. One cause of bladder weakness is urachal infection.

Signs appear within 36 hours. The foal appears depressed, stops suckling, and makes frequent unsuccessful attempts to urinate or passes urine in small amounts. Shortly thereafter the abdomen fills up with urine and the foal has difficulty breathing, suffers seizures, or goes into coma, and develops a number of metabolic derangements including heart arrhythmias.

Treatment: Surgical repair of the bladder can be undertaken successfully if the rupture is recognized within 3 to 4 days. Before surgery the foal requires medical treatment to drain the urine from its abdomen and correct the metabolic derangements.

PATENT URACHUS

This is a common congenital anomaly. The urachus is a tube in the umbilical cord which connects the foal's bladder to its mother's placenta. This channel normally closes at birth when the cord is severed.

When the urachus fails to close spontaneously, urine dribbles from the umbilicus and scalds the skin around the navel. The inflamed macerated skin is an excellent medium for bacterial growth. Infection may ascend into the abdomen via the urachus and produce peritonitis or foal septicemia (see NAVEL ILL).

Treatment: Keep the area as clean as possible and apply a topical antiseptic such as Betadine. Treat urine scalds with zinc oxide ointment. Infected skin requires topical antibiotics or occasionally oral antibiotics. The urachus can often be made to close by chemically cauterizing the opening and channel for about 2 inches twice daily with silver nitrate sticks. If this is not successful within several days, surgical closure is indicated.

BROKEN RIBS

Ribs can be broken during passage through the birth canal. The signs are those of respiratory difficulty, with a characteristic grunt heard as the foal breathes in.

Pneumothorax (collapse of the lung) will occur if the sharp edges of a broken rib puncture the lung. Pneumothorax usually is fatal.

Should a newborn foal exhibit respiratory difficulty, notify your veterinarian. Do not attempt to pick up or restrain the foal by grasping the chest.

HERNIAS

A hernia is a protrusion of an organ, or part of an organ, through an opening in the abdominal wall which would normally close in the course of fetal development. Hernias present at birth or shortly thereafter have a hereditary basis. There is a genetic predisposition for delayed closure of the abdominal ring in most cases. Horses with congenital hernias should not be used for breeding.

If a hernia can be pushed back into the abdomen, it is said to be *reducible*. If it cannot, it is said to be *incarcerated*. Incarcerated hernias are associated with colic and signs of intestinal obstruction. Strangulation and death of a segment of bowel occurs if its blood supply becomes pinched off by the abdominal ring or adhesions. Incarceration and strangulation are surgical emergencies.

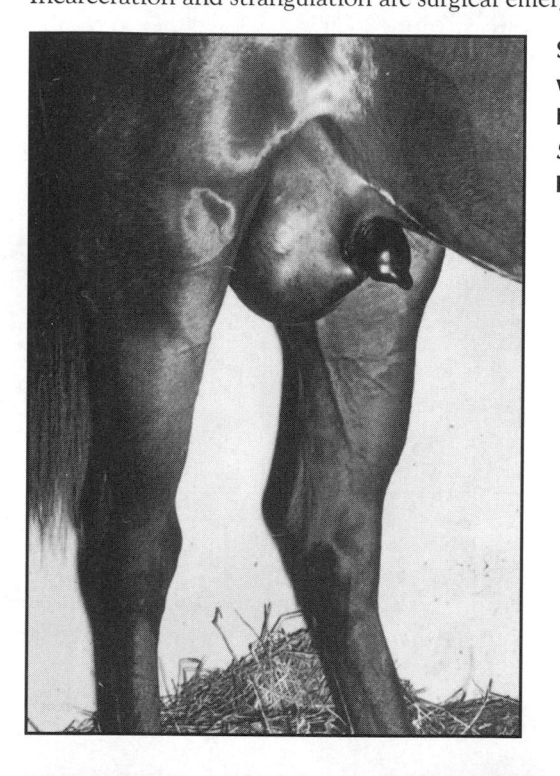

Scrotal swelling associated with a large inguinal hernia. Photo: *Equine Medicine and Surgery,* **American Veterinary Publications.**

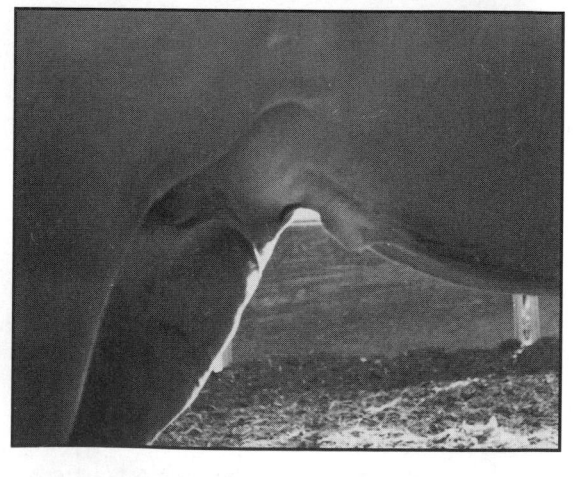

An umbilical (navel) hernia usually closes spontaneously.

Inguinal Hernia. In this situation the hernia sac (containing fat or a loop of intestine) comes through the abdominal ring and into the inguinal canal. If it descends further, it enters the scrotum. Inguinal hernias usually occur in foals, but can occur in stallions as a consequence of trauma, breeding, or physical exertion. Adult-onset hernias are not considered congenital.

Inguinal hernias are detected by palpating over the inguinal canal and feeling for a bulge or swelling. In some stallions, the hernia is detected by rectal palpation. Usually the hernia can be reduced by pushing the bulge back up through the abdominal ring into the belly.

Small inguinal hernias tend to correct spontaneously as the foal grows older. It may be necessary to reduce the hernia several times before this occurs.

Scrotal hernias are large inguinal hernias that descend into the scrotum and produce an obvious swelling around the testicle. In stallions, they can occur quite suddenly after strenuous breeding activity. Scrotal hernias usually produce signs of intestinal obstruction. Rapid surgical correction is necessary. This involves closure of the ring and removal of the testicle on the side of the hernia.

Umbilical Hernia. These hernias occur in both sexes. Ligation of the umbilical cord, manual breaking of the cord, and cord infection with abscess are predisposing causes. Most umbilical hernias close spontaneously by the time the colt or filly is a year of age.

A strangulated umbilical hernia can be recognized by a hard painful swelling at the navel that does not reduce with applied pressure. Rapid surgical correction is imperative.

NUTRITIONAL MYOPATHY (WHITE MUSCLE DISEASE)

Nutritional myopathy is a disease of foals from birth to 7 months of age. It is caused by selenium deficiency. Foals are selenium-deficient because of inadequate intake of selenium by the mare during pregnancy and lactation. One function of selenium is to enhance vitamin E uptake from the gut. Therefore vitamin E deficiency may also exist.

Signs of acute selenium deficiency include diarrhea, muscle pain, and stiffness. In a severe case the foal may develop respiratory insufficiency, heart failure, and death. Post-mortem examination of muscle discloses abnormal fibers that appear white on close inspection. Thus the disorder has been called *white muscle disease*.

Prevention: In areas where selenium deficiency has previously occured, add a selenium supplement to the mare's diet as described in chapter 17, Feeding and Nutrition (see SELENIUM). A selenium injection during the last trimester of pregnancy is recommended, although it may not prevent the deficiency in all foals. It is also important to treat the foal with a selenium injection shortly after birth. It may not be necessary to repeat the injection provided that the foal's creep and weanling diets contain adequate amounts of selenium and vitamin E.

MYOTONIA

Myotonia is a rare muscle disorder of congenital origin affecting foals 3 weeks and older. These foals appear overmuscled. In fact, under the microscope individual muscle fibers appear twice normal in size.

The muscles of the limbs contract rigidly and relax slowly. The first few steps are taken rigidly, but as the foal warms up it moves more freely.

Treatment: An effective treatment has not been established. A similar condition in humans has been treated using quinine-like medications.

CONTRACTED FOAL SYNDROME

The contracted foal syndrome encompasses a group of angular limb and/or spinal deformities in which the foal's bones and joints are permanently twisted into abnormal positions. These deformities occur during gestation and often result in fetal death and abortion.

If the mare carries the contracted foal to term, normal delivery is generally impossible, owing to the flexed position of the forelimbs and increased diameter of the shoulders and chest. Either fetotomy or cesarean section will be required to relieve the blockage. When the foal is able to be delivered alive, it is seldom able to stand and nurse. Surgical correction is rarely successful. The most humane course is to put the foal to sleep.

LIMB DEFORMITIES

Angular limb deformities (knock-knees, bowlegs, bucked knees) and *flexural limb deformities* (contracted digital flexor tendons and clubfoot) are frequently of congenital origin. Some are acquired after birth as a result of improper exercise and nutrition. Acquired deformities are discussed in the section on DEVELOPMENTAL ORTHOPEDIC DISEASES.

When a foal is born with weak or crooked legs, this is not of immediate concern so long as the foal can stand and nurse. Many deviations correct themselves with time. If they do not, casting or bracing can be employed.

EYE DISEASES

Entropion is a birth defect in which the foal's eyelids roll inward, causing the eyelashes to rub against the surface of the eye. *Ectropion* is the opposite condition, in which the eyelids are everted, exposing the eye to excessive drying. These two conditions should be treated to prevent permanent eye damage.

Congenital cataracts are present at birth and are the most common cause of blindness in foals.

Congenital night blindness is a hereditary condition found primarily in Appaloosas.

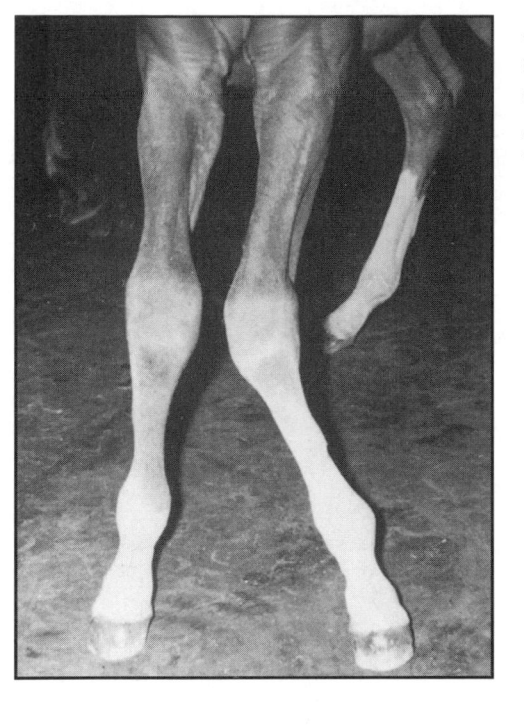

Angular limb deformities (such as knock-knees) may correct spontaneously. Photo: *Equine Medicine and Surgery,* American Veterinary Publications.

A foal can be born with one or both eyes smaller than normal. In some cases there is an almost complete absence of an eye. A small eye is often associated with a congenital cataract.

For more information on these disorders, see chapter 5, Eyes.

CLEFT PALATE

The hard and soft palates separate the nasal and oral cavities. When these structures do not form completely, there is a cleft in the roof of the mouth and an opening between the two cavities at the back of the palate.

Affected foals find it impossible to suckle. They cough, choke, gag, and are unable to swallow milk. The milk comes out the nose when the head is down. Surgical correction can be attempted. The results are best when the defect is small and involves the soft palate only.

COLON ABNORMALITIES

Absence of the anus (*anal atresia*) is a relatively common congenital defect, and may occur in association with anomalies of the urinary and reproductive systems. The entire anus may fail to develop or the rectum may extend down to a well-developed sphincter with a dimple at the site of the anal opening. These latter cases are amenable to surgical correction.

Absence of part or all of the large colon occurs rarely. Surgical repair is difficult. *Aganglionosis* is also called *lethal white foal syndrome* because it occurs in white, blue-eyed, pink-skinned foals born to matings of overo-Paint horses. In this condition the ganglion nerve plexus in the wall of the bowel fails to develop. Lacking this plexus, the colon remains somewhat paralyzed and contracts poorly. This leads to bowel obstruction. Surgical correction is not possible.

HEART DEFECTS

Heart defects are not common in foals. Mild defects may be asymptomatic and compatible with a normal life span. Signs of moderate to severe heart disease include poor growth, lethargy, exercise intolerance, rapid heavy breathing, cyanosis (blue color to mucous membranes of nose, lips, and gums), and collapse. For more information, see CONGENITAL HEART DISEASE.

NEONATAL HYPOTHYROIDISM

Hypothyroidism in newborn foals is characterized by enlargement of the thyroid gland (goiter) along with signs described below. The disease, which begins in utero, generally is caused by the feeding of kelp to pregnant mares. Less frequently it is caused by grazing or consuming plants containing chemicals that block the activity of the thyroid. In either case, the foal does not manufacture or release enough thyroid hormone. The thyroid enlargement is a compensatory effort to boost thyroid production by increasing the size of the gland. The enlarged thyroid in the neck may or may not be visible, depending on its size.

Newborn hypothyroid foals are weak and lethargic; exhibit incoordination and poor righting, and suckling reflexes; and are often hypothermic. Some foals are asymptomatic when born but develop skeletal problems at 2 weeks of age, including angular limb deformities and contracted tendons.

The diagnosis is made by thyroid function tests. Thyroid hormone replacement corrects most of the symptoms. However, any skeletal defects that may have occurred are permanent.

COMBINED IMMUNODEFICIENCY DISEASE

Combined immunodeficiency disease (CID) is a fatal inherited disease of Arabian foals characterized by a deficiency of B and T cell lymphocytes. These specialized cells are essential to the immune system. Affected foals are highly susceptible to infections such as adenovirus pneumonia and, once infected, succumb rapidly.

The diagnosis is made by a blood sample revealing a lymphocyte count of less than 1,000 per ml. Currently there is no treatment for CID.

CEREBELLAR ABIOTROPHY

Incomplete neurological development of the cerebellum is an uncommon disease that occurs almost exclusively in horses of Arabian ancestry, although a similar disorder has been described in Gotland ponies and Oldenburg horses. It tends to occur in individuals from inbred lines. The disease is characterized by a decrease in the number and distribution of specialized neurotransmitter (Purkinje) cells in the cerebellum.

Signs are occasionally present at birth, but usually appear suddenly beyond 6 months of age. Head tremors, incoordination, and staggering gait are characteristic. Often there is a peculiar type of gait called "goose-stepping," most pronounced in the front legs. The foal may buckle in the rear or fall over backwards.

There is no effective treatment. Many mild to moderately affected foals appear to function normally as adults, presumably by learning to compensate.

OCCIPITO-ATLANTOAXIAL MALFORMATION

Occipito-atlantoaxial malformation (OAAM) is a developmental malformation involving the bone socket at the base of the skull and the first and second cervical vertebrae. The effect of the malformation is to narrow the spinal canal and compress the cord. The disease occurs most often in Arabians and less frequently in Morgans and Standardbreds. It is inherited as an autosomal recessive trait.

Some affected foals are born dead. In others, symptoms develop within the first few months of life. Signs include weakness, spasticity, uncoordinated gait, and limb paralysis. The neck is held in a stiff, characteristically erect position, like a "weather vane horse." Bending the neck to nurse can increase cord compression and cause the foal to collapse.

Treatment: Medical treatment is not effective. Surgical decompression (dorsal laminectomy) as described in the section on wobbler syndrome stabilizes or improves symptoms in some foals. The surgery should be performed before cord damage occurs.

HYDROCEPHALUS

Hydrocephalus begins in utero. It is caused by a blockage in the circulation of cerebrospinal fluid in the brain. The fluid is formed more rapidly than it can be removed. The increased pressure around the brain causes the development of a large dome-shaped skull. This skull is often too large to pass through the birth canal, resulting in the necessity for cesarean section or fetotomy to deliver the foal.

Surgery to shunt the fluid off the brain has met with limited success in horses.

17

Feeding and Nutrition

A nutritionally complete food ration for the horse must supply these necessary ingredients: water, energy, protein, carbohydrates, fatty acids, minerals, and vitamins. A certain amount of fiber is important for proper digestion. A number of feedstuffs meet these requirements. The choice depends upon the circumstances under which the horse is kept, the convenience of feeding, availability of hay and pasture, and relative expense. These and other considerations will be discussed in this chapter.

Nutritional Requirements

WATER

The amount of water a horse will require depends upon its body temperature, the environmental temperature, level of activity, and the amount of water present in grass or hay. In general, a mature horse will drink about 10 to 12 gallons of water a day. Hard-working performance horses require up to twice that amount. A lactating mare needs 75 percent more water to replace that lost in milk.

When deprived of water for 2 days, a horse generally refuses to eat and may show signs of colic. With ideal weather and good health, a horse might be able to live for 5 or 6 days without water.

The best policy is to provide plenty of clean fresh water and allow the horse unlimited access to that supply. It is safe to let a horse drink as much as it wants, except immediately after exercise, when it is important to restrict water until the horse cools down.

Not all water sources are safe for the horse. In some parts of the country, such as western noncoastal parts of the United States, the salt content of water is too high, or the water may contain unacceptable levels of fluoride, selenium, arsenic, lead, and other minerals. Water with a heavy blue-green algae growth may contain a toxin that is released after death of the algae bloom. The toxin is poisonous to horses. Stagnant water in ponds or troughs can cause diarrhea and intestinal upsets and should be avoided. The accepted criterion for sanitary water is the absence of coliform bacteria. Presence of E. *coli* correlates with other infectious organisms including salmonella and giardia. In summary, if you are not sure of the purity of your water source, have it analyzed.

Water troughs should be emptied and cleaned at frequent intervals, especially in hot weather. An automatic water delivery system is convenient. Galvanized pipes, however, should never be connected to copper tubing as this results in the release of toxic amounts of zinc.

ENERGY

Energy for metabolism is supplied by dietary carbohydrates, fats, and proteins.

The minimum daily digestible energy (DE) requirements for various classes of horse are shown in Table I, but these are only guidelines. Many factors influence the amount of energy needed by each individual. They include: the mature weight of the horse; his general health and whether he is in optimal condition or recovering from an illness; the effect of cold and inclement weather; and the horse's basic metabolism.

Horses engaged in athletic activity require additional calories. According to the National Research Council (1989), DE requirements increase by 25, 50, and 100 percent for horses engaged in light, medium, and intense work, respectively. Examples of light work are Western and English pleasure, and bridle path hack and equitation. Examples of medium work are range riding, roping, cutting, barrel racing, and jumping. Intense work includes race training, polo, and endurance events.

Energy requirements are highest for pregnant horses, lactating mares, and growing horses.

In humans, the daily caloric requirement for an average adult 70-Kg man is approximately 2,500 kilocalories, which can be expressed as 2.5 Megacalories (Mcal). Foods consumed by humans are highly digestible. If you know the caloric composition of the ration in question, it is not difficult to compute the number of grams that would have to be eaten to provide the necessary 2,500 kilocalories per day.

However, the feeds consumed by horses are not highly digestible. Therefore differences in digestibility must be taken into account when comparing one food ration with another. One method of doing so is to compare the total energy in the feed with the residual energy in the feces. The difference between these two represents the *Digestible Energy* (DE), which is the amount of energy the horse is able to extract from the ration. Thus if the horse required 16.50 Mcal per day, he would

Table I   **MINIMUM DAILY NUTRIENT REQUIREMENTS**

500 Kg (1,100 lb) Mature Weight*

Class of Horse	Weight Kg	Lb	Digestible Energy Mcal	Crude Protein gm	Lysine gm	Calcium gm	Phosphorus gm	Vitamin A (1,000 IU)	Potassium gm
Mature Horse, Maintenance	500	1,100	16.4	660	23	20	14	15	25
Mare, Late Pregnancy	500	1,100	18.8	866	30	37	28	30	31
Lactating, First 3 Months	500	1,100	28.3	1,400	50	56	36	30	46
Nursing Foal, 3 Months Age	155	341	14	650	28	33	20	7	12
Weanling, 6 Months Age	215	462	16	800	34	34	18	10	13
Yearling, 12 Months Age	325	715	20	900	38	32	22	15	18
Two-Year-Old	450	990	18.8	800	32	24	13	20	23

*Source: *Nutrient Requirements of Horses*, 5th ed., National Research Council (1989).

For every 45 Kg (100 lb) above and below 500 Kg (1,100 lb), add or subtract 8 percent from the values given.

DE, mineral, and vitamin requirements for light, medium, and intense work can be estimated by increasing the maintenance requirements by 25, 50, and 100 percent, respectively.

need to consume that amount of feed which would produce 16,500 kcal of DE. The DE in several common sources of feed is shown in Table II.

A horse's ability to digest a ration can be influenced by its overall condition and state of health. Dental disease and loss of teeth are common causes of impaired digestion, as are mouth ailments that interfere with the ability to chew. A heavy parasite infestation is another cause of inadequate energy. A diet deficient in calories or protein will result in a steady loss of weight. Most serious health problems are accompanied by weight loss, which may be the only early indication of a treatable condition.

A chronic deficiency of energy causes loss of weight, lethargy, impaired performance, rough hair coat, and an unthrifty appearance. Mares may experience delayed estrus and fail to breed. Young horses have a reduced rate of growth and a delay in onset of sexual maturity. Despite these outward clues, many owners who see the horse every day fail to recognize weight loss until the situation is advanced. It is a good policy to weigh your horse at regular intervals and keep monthly records. A weight graph is a much better indicator of body condition than is visual inspection.

Table II NUTRIENT CONTENT IN SELECTED HORSE FEEDS, DRY BASIS*				
Feed	Digestive Energy (Mcal per pound)	Crude Protein % in feed	Calcium gm/lb of feed	Phosphorus gm/lb of feed
Hay				
Alfalfa	1.0-1.3	17-22	5.5	1.0
Grasses	0.8-1.0	8-12	2.0	1.0
Grains	0.9	9	1.0	1.5
Grass—forage	0.9-1.1	10-18	2.27	2.0
Canola Meal	1.4	40	3.6	1.8
Corn Grain	1.7	8-10	0.25	1.3
Cottonseed Meal	1.4	45	0.8	5.5
Cow's Milk (whole)	2.55	26	4.3	3.5
Fish Meal	1.4	70	18	12
Molasses	1.6	2-6	5.5	1.3
Oats grain	1.5	14	0.25	1.6
Soybean Meal, 44%	1.6	50	2.0	3.1
Wheat grain	1.75	14-17	0.25	2.0

*These values should be taken as guidelines only. The nutrient content of cereal grains and protein supplements varies little from the values given. Those for hay and forage can vary widely in accordance with types of forage and conditions under which they are grown and harvested. Actual values should be determined by analysis of the feed being used.

Determining Your Horse's Weight

When weighing by scale is not practical, the weight of the horse can be estimated rather accurately using a horse's weight tape (available from feed stores and tack shops). How to use the tape is illustrated in the accompanying photograph. The tape is marked in pounds (or Kgs) of body weight as measured circumferentially at the heart girth. In near-term pregnant mares, the tape underestimates weight by 150 to 200 pounds. This should be added to the result given by the tape.

If a commercial tape is not available, use an ordinary measuring tape and consult the information given in Table III.

Height-weight tapes are available at tack and feed stores.

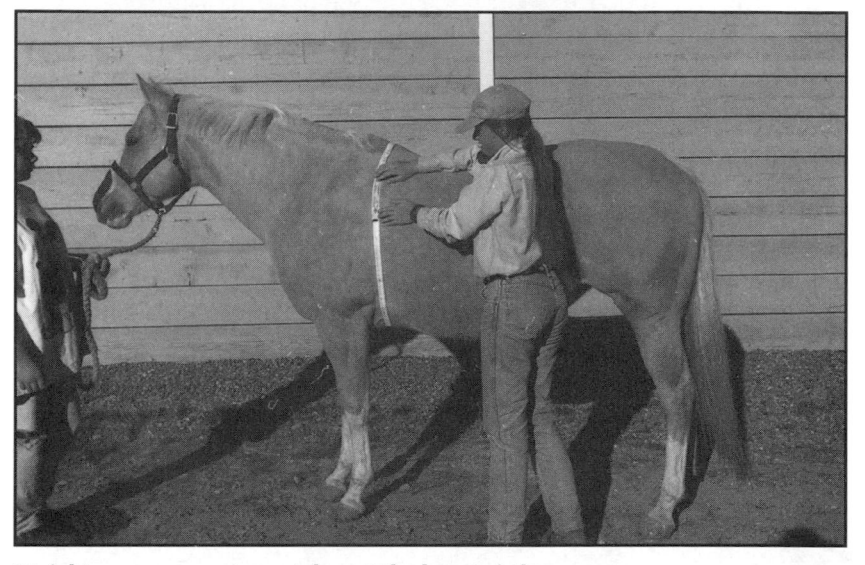

Weight measurements are taken at the heart girth.

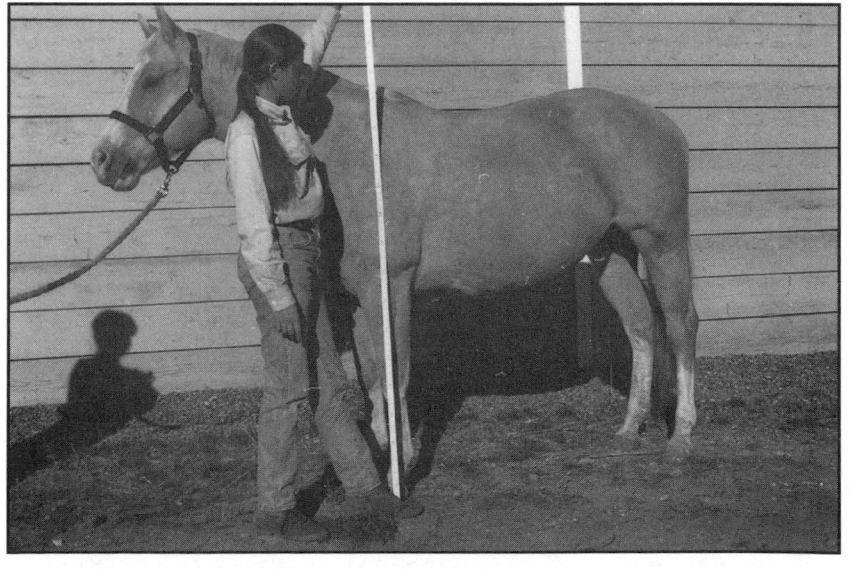

The height is taken at the high point of the withers.

| Table III | **DETERMINING YOUR HORSE'S WEIGHT** | | |
| Heart Girth Length | | Weight | |
Inches	Centimeters	Pounds	Kilograms
30	76	100	45.5
40	102	200	91
45.5	116	300	136.5
50.5	128	400	182
55	140	500	227
58.5	148	600	273
61.5	156	700	318
64.5	164	800	364
67.5	171	900	409
70.5	178	1000	455
73	185	1100	500
75.5	192	1200	545
77.5	197	1300	591

PROTEIN

Proteins are chains of amino acids. Protein is needed to build muscle and body tissue. It is also metabolized to provide energy.

Both the crude protein and digestible protein content of a feed can be determined by laboratory analysis. Crude protein indicates the total amount of protein in a feed. Digestible protein indicates the amount of protein in the ration that can actually be utilized by the horse. When protein alone is stated or given on the label of a food product, crude protein is generally what is meant.

Most protein in natural feeds for the horse is about 75 percent digestible. Thus, if the horse is receiving 16 percent crude protein in his ration, this can be translated into 12 percent digestible protein.

Estimates of the minimum daily crude protein requirements for various classes of horses are shown in Table I. Protein requirements for working horses do not increase greatly over maintenance. In general, the increased feed intake to supply the additional energy for the performance horse will also provide adequate additional protein.

Most feedstuffs serve as sources of protein, but the quality and amount vary considerably. Hays, both legume and grasses, can provide good protein sources. Good-quality pasture also provides protein. The percentage of crude protein in several common sources of feed is shown in Table II.

When the feed intake is inadequate to meet the metabolic needs, protein deficiency and energy deficiency will occur. Underfeeding relative to need is thus one cause of protein and amino acid deficiency. Horses with higher protein needs include those undergoing intense training, those at hard physical labor, growing horses, and pregnant and lactating mares.

Protein deficiency may result from prolonged grazing on pastures containing mature grasses deficient in protein, or from feeding poorly digestible dietary protein that has been heat-damaged.

In mature horses, protein deficiency depresses metabolic activities. The horse becomes lethargic and mentally dull, refuses to eat, loses endurance, becomes anemic, and assumes an unthrifty appearance. Protein deficiency in the pregnant mare can cause intrauterine growth retardation. In the foal it causes suboptimal growth and delayed sexual maturity.

There are at least three amino acids considered essential for growth, but only a lysine deficiency appears to important as a growth-limiting factor. Dietary requirements for lysine are shown in Table I. Soybean meal, rapeseed and canola meal, fish meal, and dried milk and milk products are the protein supplements highest in lysine content.

Protein Supplements

Many feeds do not contain enough protein to meet the nutritional requirements for the lactating mare and growing foal. In these cases a protein supplement, such as soybean meal or a milk product, can be added to the grain or concentrate mix to make up the deficit.

Most protein supplements are of plant origin. They are the byproducts of the extraction of oil from soybeans, cottonseeds, flaxseeds (linseed meal), and other oil seeds. These supplements contain 32 to 50 percent crude protein by weight.

Protein supplements are rated according to quality. *High* quality sources contain all the amino acids needed by the horse in correct amounts. *Low* quality sources are deficient either in protein or in amino acid composition.

Soybean Meal. This is the most commonly used and therefore the most important protein supplement. It is preferred for the young horse because it is high in lysine, an amino acid essential for the growing foal. Soybean meal is rated highest in quality among all plant-source protein supplements.

Soybean meal is sometimes given for 30 days at the end of winter. This aids in the process of shedding and gives a gloss or bloom to the new spring coat.

Cottonseed Meal. Second in popularity, cottonseed meal is more palatable than soybean meal but lower in protein quality and in the amino acid lysine. This may not be a disadvantage in the mature horse.

The major concern in feeding cottonseed meal is that of inducing a *glossypol toxicosis* due the presence of this poisonous pigment found in all parts of the plant (see FORAGE TOXICITIES).

Linseed Meal. This supplement has long been credited with giving a bloom to the coat. However, current methods of extraction remove more oil and fat so that linseed meal no longer has this advantage over other supplements. Linseed meal is palatable and quite digestible. The protein quality is somewhat less than that of soybean meal. The lysine content is low. Linseed meal contains a substance that softens stools. Thus it may have a laxative effect.

Milk Products. Dried milk and milk products are somewhat more costly, but do serve as an excellent protein source for the growing horse because they are high in lysine. Since horses older than 3 years of age lack the enzyme lactase, milk products, if fed in sufficient quantity, will cause diarrhea. This is not a problem in young horses.

Rapeseed Meal and *Canola Meal* (an extract of rapeseed) are important oil seed crops in Canada, Europe, and Asia. These high-quality protein supplements are palatable and contain adequate amounts of lysine. Like soybean meal, rapeseed and canola can be used as the sole source for protein supplementation.

Peanut meal, safflower meal, sunflower meal, gluten meal, fish meals, and various brewer's pellets and grains are examples of other protein sources that can be fed to horses.

CARBOHYDRATES AND FIBER

Carbohydrates are composed of simple sugars. They are classified as either fiber or nonfiber carbohydrates.

Nonfiber carbohydrates, composed of monosaccharide and disaccharide sugars, are the major source of calories for the horse. They are highly digestible and rapidly utilized by the body. When energy needs are low, nonfiber carbohydrates are converted to glycogen and stored in the liver and muscles.

Fiber carbohydrates are that part of the feed high in cellulose and lignin, both of which are poorly digestible and therefore low in energy. Fiber is important for lower intestinal motility and aids in the production of a bulky, well-formed stool.

Feed consisting of plants or plant parts containing over 18 percent crude fiber is termed *roughage*. A mature horse needs 12 to 16 ounces of roughage for every 100 pounds of body weight per day.

When comparing feedstuffs on a per weight basis, feeds containing a low fiber content such as grain will be found to produce 50 to 60 percent more DE per pound than hay, which has a higher fiber content.

Following is the average percentage of crude fiber in several common sources of feed: alfalfa hay (24 to 30 percent); grass hay (30 to 32 percent); soybean meal (7 percent); oats (11 percent); corn grain (2.5 percent); and wheat grain (2 to 3 percent).

FATTY ACIDS

Although most feeds contain less than 6 percent fat, this appears to be adequate to meet the nutritional needs of horses. Fatty acid deficiency has not been described in the horse. Thus a dry, lusterless hair coat is unlikely to be due to fatty acid deficiency. However, experience indicates that coat conditioners and vegetable oil supplements containing fat or fatty acids may give a horse a glossier hair coat, or help the horse shed its coat earlier in the spring. The effect can be obtained by adding 1 to 2 ounces of any polyunsaturated plant or vegetable oil to the horse's ration twice a day. Indications for giving fatty acid supplements are discussed in the section FEEDING THE ADULT HORSE.

MINERALS

Plants, and ultimately the soil in which plants are grown, are the mineral sources for horses. Mineral imbalances can result from too little or too much mineral in the soil; or ultimately factors in the soil may diminish the ability of the plants to obtain the essential elements. For example, there are large areas in which the soil is deficient in iodine, and areas in which the soil contains either an excess or deficiency of selenium. Such areas are well known and have been mapped. Information about the mineral composition of the soil where you live can be obtained from your local extension service, or regional United States Department of Agriculture office.

At least 21 minerals are required in the horse's diet, but the major items of concern in feeding horses are calcium, phosphorus, salt (sodium chloride), and in some geographical areas selenium. Copper and zinc are essential for growth. While a number of mineral deficiencies and toxicities can occur in the horse, with the exception of selenium, calcium, and phosphorus, they are uncommon or rare—provided that average or better quality feeds are used, trace-mineralized salt is available, and excess mineral supplements are not added to the ration.

Salt (Sodium Chloride). Horses have a natural craving for salt. In fact, this is the only mineral for which a natural appetite exists. An adult horse at pasture will consume about one-half pound of salt per week, although this is variable. Horses in training and lactating mares will consume more.

Lack of salt causes decreased appetite and weight loss. It may be responsible for a tendency to lick at urine or eat wood, dirt, manure, and stones.

Salt toxicity can occur if water is restricted and salt is not. The symptoms are colic, diarrhea, paralysis, and death. This could occur if a horse were to drink salt brine, or a salt-starved horse were to obtain access to salt but not to water.

Salt blocks, left to right: plain salt, iodized salt, calcium/phosphorus and trace minerals, and trace-mineralized salt. Keep salt available for free-choice consumption.

To insure that salt needs are met, 0.5 to 1 percent salt can be added to the daily ration or, more conveniently, a salt block or loose salt mix can be made available for free-choice consumption. If salt is available, the horse will consume enough to meet its needs. There is no danger of salt intoxication provided the horse has continuous access to fresh water.

Salt can be provided in loose or block form. More salt may be consumed in the loose form, but adequate amounts will be consumed in either form. A variety of salt blocks and free salt mixes are commercially available. The least expensive is plain salt containing only sodium and chloride. For feeding horses, trace-mineralized salt containing iodine, zinc, copper, and other minerals is preferred, as it provides microminerals that may be absent or deficient in some forages, hays, and grains (see TRACE MINERALS).

Trace-mineralized salt containing higher levels of copper, zinc, and/or selenium is also available, as is salt containing high levels of iodine. Note that none of these salts contain calcium or phosphorus. When additional calcium and/or phosphorus is required, you can purchase a block or loose salt mix containing equal parts of trace minerals, calcium, and phosphorus.

Potassium. Dietary potassium deficiency ordinarily is not a problem because nearly all feeds provide adequate amounts. However, diets high in grain and low in forage—most often fed to horses in training and hard work—may be deficient in potassium. These horses also incur increased potassium losses through sweat, and therefore have a greater need.

A potassium deficit can occur acutely in horses undergoing strenuous training or endurance racing in hot humid weather. Severe diarrhea is another cause of acute potassium loss.

Signs of potassium deficiency include muscle weakness, lethargy, and diminished intake of water and feed. Treatment of loss involves correcting the cause; rehydrating the horse; and replacing electrolytes either orally, by stomach tube, or, in severe cases, by intravenous fluids.

Potassium deficiency is most likely to occur in the high-performance or endurance horse in intense physical activity. A potassium salt supplement is a consideration. The most effective salt is "lite," also called low sodium salt, which is readily available at grocery stores. Lite is half sodium chloride and half potassium chloride, and contains 26 percent potassium. Add 2 to 3 ounces to the horse's daily grain ration.

Calcium and Phosphorus. Calcium and phosphorus are two microminerals of great importance in the horse's diet. Horses are more likely to suffer from calcium or phosphorus deficiency than from any other mineral deficiency.

The mineral content of equine bone is 34 percent calcium and 17 percent phosphorus. Horses require calcium and phosphorus in relatively large amounts for bone growth and maintenance. Growing horses especially need adequate amounts of calcium and phosphorus to support active skeletal growth and development.

Also important is the ratio of calcium to phosphorus in the horse's diet. This ratio should be about 1.2:1 (range 1:1 to 3:1). That is, there should be at least as much calcium as phosphorus in the diet. Phosphorus intakes above calcium intakes can result in *nutritional secondary hyperparathyroidism* and bone demineralization. So long as the intakes remain within an acceptable range and sufficient quantities of both minerals are provided, the horse will adjust its excretion of calcium and phosphorus to maintain the necessary ratio.

A dietary deficiency of calcium, phosphorus, or both will result in mineral deficiency, delayed bone mineralization, and delayed growth. Weanlings and yearlings fail to attain mature stature and may experience pain and lameness from joint and bone injuries, including fractures. Calcium deficiency in the young mature horse produces a condition called Big Head, also known as bran disease. The disease is characterized by a bulging of the face between the eyes and the nostrils, giving a deformed appearance to the head. It used to be more common when bran was fed as a principal ration. Bran is low in calcium, although high in phosphorus.

Many grass hays are low in calcium and/or phosphorus. Horses receiving marginal hay or forage, with or without a grain supplement, are at risk of developing a deficiency of calcium, phosphorus, or both.

Plants containing harmful amounts of oxalate may be found in pasture grasses during summer months. Oxalate binds calcium, decreasing its absorption from the small intestine. A calcium deficiency can occur if the forage does not provide enough calcium to compensate for the losses caused by oxalate. Lactating mares and weanlings, whose calcium requirements are highest, are most likely to be affected by oxalate plants.

Cereal grains do not contain sufficient calcium to support rapid growth. Thus if a young horse receives a high-energy diet containing cereal grains and protein supplements, but does not receive supplemental calcium, growth problems are likely.

Calcium and phosphorus requirements increase dramatically during the last 3 months of pregnancy and during lactation. Unless forage is excellent, mares on pasture should be supplemented (see CARE AND FEEDING DURING PREGNANCY).

Calcium/phosphorus deficiencies or imbalances can be prevented by insuring that adequate amounts of both minerals are present in the horse's diet (see Tables I and II), and that the diet contains at least as much calcium as phosphorus. When feed sources are marginal, provide supplemental minerals by offering a free-choice loose salt mix or salt block containing equal parts of calcium, phosphorus, and trace-mineralized salt (e.g., Pro-phos 12 from Farmland Industries). Remove other mineral sources to encourage consumption.

To treat a calcium or phosphorus deficiency, it is best to give the minerals directly rather than free-choice. One method of administering calcium and phosphorus is to add these minerals directly to 1 pound of sweet feed or moistened grain. Feed half in the morning and half in the evening. When calcium deficiency alone is the problem, you can give limestone (calcium carbonate) at a rate of 1 ounce (28 grams) for every 11 grams of calcium the horse requires in its diet. When both minerals or only phosphorus are deficient, you can give Dical (dicalcium phosphate). One ounce of Dical contains about 6 grams of calcium and 6 grams of phosphorus.

Calcium excess is rarely a problem. Horses can tolerate a dietary calcium intake 5 times greater than that needed for maintenance for long periods without suffering adverse effects. Excess phosphorus, in contrast, is more serious since it can lead to a calcium deficiency. However, an excess of either mineral is unlikely to occur unless the horse is consuming mineral supplements in amounts well beyond daily requirements, or in the case of phosphorus, when bran constitutes a large part of the diet.

Table IV **APPROXIMATE CALCIUM AND PHOSPHORUS CONTENT OF SOME COMMON MINERAL SUPPLEMENTS***

	Gm of Element in 1 ounce (28 gm) of Supplement			
	Calcium (%)	Phosphorus (%)	Calcium	Phosphorus
Limestone (Calcium Carbonate)	38	0	11.0	0
Dical (Dicalcium Phosphate)	22	19	6.5	5.7
Bone Meal	30	14	9	4.0
Monodicalcium Phosphate	16	22	4.8	6.6
Oyster Shells	38	0	11.0	0
Pro-Phos 12 Copper Mineral	12	12	3.4	3.4

*These are approximate or average values. If using some other mineral supplement, to find the number of grams of element in 1 ounce of supplement (2 tablespoons), multiply the percentage shown for the element by 0.28.

Trace Minerals

A number of minerals are required by the horse in very small amounts. Generally they are present in sufficient quantity in the horse's diet or ration. But in some parts of the United States the soil is deficient in one or more of these minerals and therefore the feedstuffs grown in these soils are also deficient.

Selenium. Selenium and vitamin E work together to protect cells from damage caused by oxygen-free radicals. A deficiency of selenium has been recognized in the Great Lakes area, along the eastern seaboard and in the northwest. The dietary selenium requirement for the mature horse is estimated to be 0.1 mg/kg (0.1 ppm) by dry weight of the diet. 0.2 mg/kg is recommended in the last 3 months of pregnancy, during lactation, for the growing foal, and for the working and athletic horse.

Signs of selenium deficiency occur at dietary levels of .05 or less. In very young foals selenium deficiency produces an illness called nutritional myopathy, discussed in chapter 16, Pediatrics. In older horses, selenium deficiency may possibly be associated with a decreased immune response, impaired growth weight, lowered fertility, and reduced milk production. Selenium deficiency is treated by giving an intramuscular injection of selenium and vitamin E. In areas where selenium deficiency in foals has been a problem in the past, the pregnant mare in the last trimester, and the foal shortly after birth, should be given a prophylactic injection.

Trace-mineralized salt containing higher levels of selenium is commercially available and should be offered free-choice in areas where selenium deficiency is a problem. Remove other sources of salt to insure consumption.

Selenium toxicity, a much more common problem than deficiency, is discussed later in this chapter.

Iodine. An iodine deficiency has been noted in high mountain areas and throughout sections of the midwest and western United States. Feeds grown in these areas may contain iodine levels below those needed to supply the horse's requirements.

Iodine excess is caused by oversupplementing with iodine, usually by giving products such as seaweed known to contain high levels of this mineral, but occasionally by giving other iodine-containing horse products.

Iodine is required in the synthesis of thyroid hormone. Thyroid hormone deficiency produces *hypothyroidism*. This is a rare condition in the adult horse, but has been described in Standardbreds and Thoroughbreds. An excess of thyroid hormone produces *hyperthyroidism*, which has not yet been documented in adult horses.

Pregnant mares with iodine deficiency (or excess) can give birth to foals with *neonatal hypothyroidism*, discussed in chapter 16, Pediatrics. This is the major concern with iodine imbalances in the horse.

Iodine deficiency can be prevented by allowing access to a trace-mineralized salt block. However, because there is a wide variation in salt consumption among mares during pregnancy and lactation, a mare at risk of iodine deficiency is best supplemented by adding 1 ounce of trace-mineralized salt to her daily grain mix.

Copper and Zinc. Copper and zinc are the two microminerals of recognized importance for the growing horse. The dietary concentrations of copper and zinc adequate for horses as recommended by the National Research Council (1989) are 10 mg/kg for copper and 40 mg/kg for zinc, as determined by dry-matter basis of diet.

However, recent studies indicate that increasing the concentrations of copper and zinc in the diets of nursing and weanling foals decreases the risk and occurrence of developmental orthopedic diseases (DODs). The exact reason for this is unknown, but it appears that higher concentrations than those previously held necessary to meet nutritional requirements may afford some protection against endochondral ossification defects. It is now recommended that concentrations in creep feeds be increased to 50 mg/kg dry matter for copper and 60 mg/kg for zinc, while concentrations in rations for rapidly growing horses 3 to 12 months of age should be somewhat lower at 25 mg/kg dry matter for copper and 40 mg/kg for zinc. These recommended concentrations have not been associated with any adverse effects.

Iron. The minimum daily dietary requirement for iron is 50 mg/kg in dry-matter basis of feeds. Levels of consumption above 2 gm per day are toxic to the mature horse. Much lower concentrations are toxic to neonatal foals.

Iron deficiency is extremely uncommon in the horse. It occurs only with chronic or severe blood loss, usually related to stomach ulcers or a heavy infestation of worms. A number of vitamin-iron-mineral supplements are available at feed stores. Their value as appetite improvers and energizers is questionable. Those that contain high concentrations of iron pose the possibility of toxicity.

Other minerals required by the horse include *manganese, cobalt, molybdenum, magnesium, sulfur,* and *fluoride.* Fluoride toxicity is discussed elsewhere in this chapter.

In general, average or better forage and most feedstuffs provide adequate levels of these minerals. Deficiencies are rare. Problems are more likely to occur when these minerals are consumed or supplemented in excessive amounts.

VITAMINS

Vitamins are organic substances required in minute amounts for normal body metabolism.

Not all vitamins are dietary essentials. Most vitamins are synthesized by bacteria in the horse's large intestine. In fact, only vitamins A and E must be supplied entirely by the diet.

Vitamin A. Vitamin A is the only vitamin that may be inadequate in rations routinely fed to horses. The daily requirements for vitamin A for various classes of horse are given in Table I.

A deficiency of vitamin A makes a horse more susceptible to respiratory and reproductive tract infections, may cause fertility problems, and can lead to eye difficulties such as night blindness and excessive tearing. It may also cause the horse to develop a dry rough coat.

An excess of vitamin A causes brittle bones, shedding of skin, and symptoms much like those of a deficiency.

Forage plants and grasses contain the vitamin A precursor carotene, converted to vitamin A in the horse's body. This process is not especially efficient. Therefore carotene levels are not good indicators of vitamin A levels.

The best sources of carotene are rapidly growing spring and early summer grasses. Horses that consume such forage for 4 to 6 weeks store enough vitamin A in their livers to maintain adequate serum levels for 3 to 6 months. However, when a horse uses up that supply and does not have access to feeds or supplements containing adequate amounts of vitamin A, a deficiency will ensue.

Properly harvested early-cut legume hay such as alfalfa has adequate amounts of carotene even though much is lost during handling. However, after hay has been stored for 6 months it loses about half its carotene content and may well become deficient.

Accordingly, to prevent vitamin A deficiency when poor-quality hay must be fed for long periods, or when pasture without a significant amount of green color is being consumed for more than 3 months, add 15,000 IU vitamin A to the daily diet. Feed twice this amount to broodmares during the last 90 days of pregnancy and throughout lactation.

Supplements containing vitamin A are available at all feed stores. As an alternative, an intramuscular injection can be given by your veterinarian, which is good for at least 3 months.

Vitamin E. Vitamin E (along with selenium) enhances the body's immune system. Vitamin E deficiency has been implicated as a cause of equine degenerative myeloencephalopathy (EDM). Vitamin E is present in ample amounts in green forages and natural feeds to more than meet daily nutritional requirements. A deficiency could occur if a horse were fed pelleted feeds and/or cured hay for an extended period, as both feeds may contain low levels of vitamin E.

Supplements containing vitamin E have been advocated to improve fertility in mares and stallions. However, there is no evidence to suggest that vitamin E has any benefit in this capacity.

Wheat germ oil and alfalfa meal are excellent sources of vitamin E.

Vitamin D. Deficiency of this vitamin is rare because horses synthesize vitamin D in their skin in response to ultraviolet light. Remaining outdoors for 2 hours a day is sufficient exposure. Good quality sun-cured feeds also produce ample quantities of vitamin D.

Vitamin D intoxication is the most common vitamin toxicity in horses. Vitamin D is incorporated into most vitamin supplements but has little if any therapeutic value. However, such supplements are frequently given in the misguided belief that adding vitamin D will increase rate of growth or improve maximum adult size. The unfortunate result is a decline in health and organ function resulting from calcium deposits in bones, soft tissue, heart, kidneys, and blood vessels. The effects of excessive vitamin D consumption are cumulative. It can take several weeks or months for signs to become evident.

One other cause of toxicity is the ingestion of plants containing vitamin D glycosides. These plants are found primarily in Florida, Texas, southern California, and subtropical areas throughout the world.

Vitamin K. Vitamin K is necessary for blood coagulation. A dietary deficiency does not occur because a horse synthesizes vitamin K in its intestinal tract. However, if a horse ingests a vitamin K antagonist, a deficiency characterized by spontaneous bleeding will occur. For more information, see Rodenticide Anticoagulants.

Vitamin K deficiency also can occur with diseases or conditions that decrease the population of colonic bacteria that manufacture vitamin K. Some of these are prolonged antibiotic therapy, a heavy infestation of worms, diarrhea disease, and colitis.

Nosebleeds are not caused by vitamin K deficiency. Therefore giving vitamin K has no benefit in preventing or treating this symptom. Vitamin K has also been used empirically to prevent exercise-induced pulmonary hemorrhage (EIPH). However, it is not effective in treating this condition, which is due to rupture of blood vessels and not a deficiency in blood coagulation.

Vitamin C. Vitamin C is not needed in the horse's diet since adequate amounts are manufactured by the liver. In man, vitamin C is a dietary essential.

It has been claimed that giving large doses of vitamin C will help to prevent respiratory infections, improve sperm quality and reproductive performance, and prevent nosebleeds, but there are no veterinary studies to support these claims.

B-Complex Vitamins. All B-complex vitamins are produced by bacteria in the horse's intestinal tract and are present in natural feedstuffs in more than ample amounts to meet the horse's needs. A deficiency could occur if the horse were sick and not eating, or, if for the same reasons described above for vitamin K, there were a decreased number of bacteria in the colon.

B-complex supplements are frequently given to hard-working and performance horses. Although benefits are difficult to quantify, many horsemen attest to their value.

When B-complex deficiency is suspected or when additional vitamins are desired, you can safely give up to 30 gm/day of a broad-spectrum commercial vitamin preparation. A similar result can be obtained by giving 12 to 16 ounces of brewer's yeast. Brewer's yeast is high in all of the B vitamins except B-12, which is not needed in the horse's diet.

Feedstuffs

Feedstuffs for horses are arbitrarily divided into *roughages* and *concentrates*.

ROUGHAGES

Roughages are feeds consisting primarily of bulky coarse plants or plant parts with high fiber content and low total digestible nutrients. By definition, a roughage contains over 18 percent crude fiber. Hays and forage pastures provide roughage. These are the most natural and frequently the least expensive feed for horses; therefore they should provide the basis for all horse feeding programs.

Hays. The three types of hay are legumes, grasses, and cereal grains.

Legumes are higher in protein than grasses. Legumes absorb nitrogen from bacteria that live in their roots. These plants then "fix" or convert the nitrogen to protein. The major legumes are alfalfa, clover, birdsfoot trefoil, and lespedeza.

The leaves of legumes contain much more protein than the stems. Accordingly, the amount of leafiness is a good indication of the hay's nutritional value. If the harvest is damaged by weather or excessive handling, the leaves will not be firmly attached to the stems and can be lost during feeding. Legume hay past its bloom when cut is too mature and will not make a good feed.

Grasses commonly fed to horses include timothy, bromes, orchard grass, bermuda, bluegrass, fescue, wheatgrass, and others. Grass hay should be harvested at early maturity because nutrient value and digestibility are best at that time. Grass hay with heads over a half inch long is too mature.

Cereal grain hay, in which the grain is left on the stem and not removed during harvesting, can be cut and used for hay. However, if the heads of the grain are lost only straw remains.

Pastures. Good quality pasture is a nutritious and frequently inexpensive source of feed for horses. Grasses that provide good forage will vary in different geographic areas according to soil content, temperature, and rainfall. A county agent or local extension specialist can provide information on conditions in your area or perform a chemical analysis.

Pastures that contain a mixture of legumes and grasses, a clean water supply, and access to trace-mineralized salt will meet all the nutritional requirements for most horses. However, foals, hard-working horses, and pregnant and lactating mares may require more dietary energy than some pastures can provide.

CONCENTRATES (GRAINS)

Concentrates include a broad class of feedstuffs high in energy and low in crude fiber (under 18 percent). Concentrates are everything in the ration that is not roughage; or that part of the ration composed of grain. Concentrates, because they are low in crude fiber, provide a high concentration of dietary energy in a small volume.

High-energy foods have the potential for overfeeding and can be associated with laminitis, acute gastric dilatation, azoturia, and developmental orthopedic disease. For these reasons, concentrations greater than $1/4$ of the total weight of the daily ration should not be fed except as part of a carefully balanced feeding program, as discussed in the section How to Feed.

Cereal Grains

Cereal grains are the principal high energy source for horses. Pound for pound, they contain about twice as much digestible energy as does hay. As a rule of thumb, a mature horse may be given up to $1/2$ pound cereal grain per 100 pounds weight per day. Hard-working horses and lactating mares can be given up to 1 pound, depending upon the energy content and nutrient quality of the roughage.

Oats. Oats have a higher fiber content than most other grains and therefore are considered by many horse owners to be among the safest of grains. However, oats are expensive, particularly when cost is compared to energy content. One advantage of oats is that they are much less likely to be overfed since the horse would have to eat a larger volume to extract the same amount of energy as in corn, for example. However, a horse will founder on oats if a sufficient quantity is ingested.

Corn (Maize). Corn is a popular feed due to its ready availability. Many horse owners prefer not to feed corn because they feel it is too "hot" a food (i.e., too high in energy). Although corn does contain twice as much energy as an equal volume of oats, when both corn and oats are fed by weight to provide equal amounts of energy, corn does not have a greater tendency to make a horse more high-spirited than do oats. Corn is palatable, consistent in quality, and is the only common grain that possesses significant vitamin A activity. Corn can be fed whole, cracked, or by the ear. It should not be ground finely, as it becomes dusty.

Bran (Wheat Bran). Bran is a poorly digested cereal grain with a low energy content. It does increase the volume of feces excreted and is useful under certain circumstances for this purpose. Contrary to popular belief, it is not a good laxative. In fact, if adequate water is not consumed, it may actually lead to an impaction. This is why bran is generally mixed with water to make a mash.

Wheat, Barley, Milo, and Rye. These grains should not make up more than $1/3$ to $1/2$ of the total grain ration. The reason is they contain a hard kernel or shell which makes them difficult to digest unless they are processed (crimped, rolled, cracked, coarsely ground, or steam-flaked). Wheat has a high gluten content and can produce a doughy ball in the stomach if fed in large amounts. Rye is more susceptible than other grains to a toxin called ergot.

Molasses. Molasses improves taste and decreases dust. For these reasons, commercial manufacturers often combine it with processed cereal grains to make sweet feeds. Wet molasses may be added to a concentrate mix (5 percent of weight of mix) to increase its free-choice consumption and prevent sifting out of minerals.

Molasses is a good vehicle for giving medications. It can also be used as an added source of energy.

Grain Quality and Storage

Government grading standards are one of the best indicators of grain quality. The best quality is grade No. 1, followed in order by 2 through 5. *Sample* grain is the poorest quality. The grade is based on factors such as weight per bushel, moisture content (13 percent or below), broken and damaged kernels (less than 10 percent), presence of foreign material including insects, and degree of discoloration. Grade 2 is adequate for feeding most horses. However, grain generally sold for feed often is not graded. You should inspect it yourself, and the seller should guarantee that it is of good quality or that it may be returned.

Cereal grains containing only a few broken kernels and less than 13 percent moisture can be stored for long periods without loss of nutritional value provided that they are kept in metal containers or dry rodent-proof bins. Plastic containers are not suitable; rodents can eat through plastic rapidly. Grain stored in sacks can become moist and moldy. If so, do not feed it. Note that mold or bacterial growth and insect proliferation generally do not occur at moisture levels below 13 percent.

Galvanized garbage cans with tight-fitting lids are good storage receptacles. Large galvanized metal bins are advantageous for bulk storage.

Always store grain in a room with a horse-proof latch, or in some other secure location where horses cannot get to it. This will prevent accidental engorgement and its attendant dangers of gastric dilatation and founder. Despite such precautions, if the horse should get to the grain supply and consume an unknown quantity of grain, notify your veterinarian at once.

COMMERCIAL HORSE FEEDS

Commercial horse feed manufacturers have developed a variety of feeds nutritionally formulated to meet specific feeding requirements. For example, complete horse feeds containing alfalfa meal, soybean meal, and other cereal grains can be fed as the sole source of daily nutrients. Forage is not necessary. Other products contain cereal grains and/or protein supplements intended to provide extra energy for recreational activities and hard work. Grain supplements are available for late pregnancy and lactation, and for the nursing and growing foal.

Commercial horse feeds are a good choice when good-quality hay or pasture is either unavailable or more expensive than the feed. Other advantages of commercial horse feeds are that less space is required for storage; the horse cannot sort through its food (and therefore wastage is less); and as processed feeds, they are more digestible for the older horse with poor teeth.

National manufacturers produce high-quality grain mixes which meet or exceed nutrient content requirements (Table VII) for the class of horse for which the feed is intended. The majority of these feeds also contain vitamins A and E, and microminerals including selenium, copper, and zinc, in amounts which, when fed according to recommendations, supply all the vitamin and mineral needs of the horse's diet.

State and federal laws regulate the production, labeling, distribution, and sale of animal feeds. The feed tag provides useful information—such as the minimum percentage of crude protein and fat, and the maximum percentage of crude fiber. Although guarantees for minerals and vitamins are not required unless the feed is advertised as either a complete feed or a specific supplement, most national name brand manufacturers supply feed tags showing the complete guaranteed analysis. Feed tags on products from local feed suppliers may not show a complete analysis, but the dealer or the company should be able to provide this information. If not, consider having the feed analyzed or use a different product.

In choosing among competing products, consider the relative cost, nutrient content, quality control, and services provided by the dealer. The feed should be appropriate for the use intended. For example, one formulated for mature horses would not be appropriate for growing horses. Feeds for growing horses should contain protein supplements high in lysine, derived from soybeans or milk products. Because feeds are designed to be fed with forage, failure to provide the needed roughage can lead to digestive disturbances.

Commercial feeds formulated for cattle and other animals should not be fed to horses because they do not meet specific nutrient requirements and may contain toxic ingredients. Rumensin, frequently added to cattle feed to prevent coccidiosis, is highly toxic to horses and will cause severe heart failure and death. Lincomycin, an antibiotic added to swine feeds to increase growth rate, can cause diarrhea and a fatal colitis.

Commercial horse feeds are made up in the form of pellets, cubes, and loose mixes of grain.

Loose grain mixes generally contain molasses, which increases palatability. These feeds are called *textured* or *sweet feeds*. In hot humid weather they are susceptible to spoilage unless properly stored.

Hay is often pressed into wafers or cubes about 1 × 3 inches in size.

Complete feeds are frequently fed as pelleted rations. Pellets are made by grinding seeds and roughage and mixing with molasses, then forcing the mixture through a sieve. *Dehy* pellets are made from fresh-cut alfalfa hay that has been processed to remove water. Pelleting decreases waste, permits longer storage of feed without spoilage, and provides uniform delivery of nutrients. Pellets are easier for horses to chew than grains and may result in better digestibility, especially for the older horse.

Pellets vary in size, the average being about ¼ to ¾ inches in length. While smaller pellets tend to be eaten more slowly, there is no evidence that pellet size, or pelleted feeds in general, cause choke any more often than sweet feeds. Regardless of the feed, the more rapidly it is eaten the greater the likelihood of choke. For the rapid-eating horse who bolts its feed, the rate of consumption can be decreased by feeding smaller amounts more frequently, spreading the feed over a large surface, mixing it with chopped hay, or adding several large smooth stones to the feed box so the horse will have to sort through the rocks to get to the pellets or grain.

How to Feed

Horses choose feeds according to appetite and taste appeal. A true appetite exists only for that which provides energy, and for salt and water. If given a free choice, a horse with a mineral or vitamin deficiency will not necessarily select a feed high in the missing ingredient. The only way to be certain that each horse receives its proper intake of energy and essential nutrients is to ensure that the correct concentrations are present in the daily ration, and that each horse receives its proper share.

Feeding according to weight (not volume) of ration.

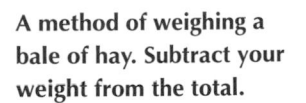

A method of weighing a bale of hay. Subtract your weight from the total.

It is most important to feed rations by weight and not by volume. Tables of nutrition always give the horse's needs by weight of horse and percent of weight in feedstuffs. This allows for a direct comparison of energy and nutrients. This comparison is not possible when comparing volumes.

For example, a 3-pound coffee can holds 2 to 3 pounds of oats. The same can holds 4 to 5 pounds of corn. Furthermore, since corn is more energy-rich than oats, a can of corn may contain 2 to 3 times more energy than a can of oats.

Hay is frequently fed in "flakes," which are sections of the compressed bale. A flake varies in weight depending upon how thick it is and how tightly the hay was compressed when baled. It is a good practice to weigh several samples to get an idea of the average weight of a bale and a flake.

FREQUENCY OF FEEDING

Horses have a relatively small stomach when compared to cattle and other large animals. This limits the amount a horse can safely consume in a single meal.

Under natural conditions while grazing on pasture, a horse grazes 50 to 70 percent of the time, both day and night. Under such conditions, the stomach is never overdistended.

Overloading occurs when too much feed is given in a single meal. This causes over-distention of the horse's stomach, increases intestinal motility, produces a sudden loss of fluid from the plasma into the gut, and increases the risk of colic.

These events can be avoided, and the efficiency of digestion maximized, by feeding stabled and paddocked horses according to the following guidelines:

- Provide enough hay so that the horse will always have something to eat.
- Feed in equally divided amounts at least twice a day, but more often if possible. Horses fed on a consistent schedule are less likely to bolt their food or develop boredom-related vices.
- Feed as little grain as necessary. With small amounts, there is no advantage to feeding more than once a day.
- When horses are fed as a group, ensure that a dominant or aggressive horse does not drive away a subordinate horse. Put out extra feeders at widely spaced intervals to prevent this from happening.

FEEDING THE ADULT HORSE

Care and feeding during pregnancy and feeding during lactation are discussed in chapter 15, Pregnancy and Foaling. Feeding the nursing foal and growing horse are discussed in chapter 16, Pediatrics.

Pasturing. A horse usually can be pastured for 5 to 6 months a year. During the winter season, another feed such as hay or a commercial grain mix will be required.

Most pastures contain more than one type of forage. A mixture containing bluegrass, tall fescue, and orchard grass, or one containing legume hay and grass, provides excellent nutrition. Horses at pasture should have access to clean, fresh water and trace-mineralized salt. To preserve pasture integrity and prevent plant injury and soil compaction, remove horses from pasture after a heavy rain and before irrigating.

A horse should be put out to pasture in a graduated manner to prevent problems of gastric dilatation and founder. This is especially important for fresh green pastures and pastures high in legumes. Begin by turning the horse out for 2 hours the first day. Increase this gradually over the next week. After 2 weeks it should be safe for the horse to remain at pasture full-time.

Feeding Hay. A horse weighing 1,000 pounds needs about 15 to 18 pounds of good-quality hay per day. In selecting hay, the major consideration is not necessarily the kind of hay or even the cutting, but the quality of the hay and its nutritional value in relation to cost—assuming that it is readily consumed and does not contain toxic weeds and plants. To determine the exact composition and nutritional value, you would need to have the hay analyzed. Local extension services can provide information on where this can be done and the cost of the service.

Hay bales should be taken apart and examined for dust and mold, conditions quite likely to be present if the hay was baled while damp. The inside of a properly cured bale of hay should be green and it should have a pleasant odor. Musty or offensive smells suggest mold, a condition which makes the hay totally unsuitable for horse feed.

Ideally, hay should be fed in a hay rack or a wooden feeder. Feeding in a hay net above shoulder level is not a good practice because the horse is more likely to inhale dust and fine plant material, predisposing to bronchitis and heaves. When hay is fed on the ground there is considerable loss due to trampling and scattering, and also contamination of the hay by parasite eggs.

Feeding from a hay rack is more economical and is better for the horse's health.

Feeding Concentrates. Cereal grains are always used in combination with a roughage. Because cereal grains are so high in energy, it is recommended that *a grain or concentrate mix never make up more than half of the total amount of feed consumed each day*, except for horses less than 1 year of age, and for athletic horses undergoing intense physical training. In addition, grain concentrates greater than 50 percent decrease forage intake and create problems caused by lack of fiber.

Rations containing 75 percent hay and 25 percent grain by weight are appropriate for mares in late pregnancy, yearlings at 18 months, and adult horses doing light work.

Table V shows a sample concentrate ration for various classes of horse.

Table V **SAMPLE RATIONS USING CONCENTRATES***

Class Of Horse	Alfalfa	Corn Grain	Soybean Meal	Daily Mineral Supplement
Mature Horse Maintenance	6.8 kg 15 lb	0.5 kg 1.1 lb	0.1 kg .25 lb	Trace-mineralized salt
Mare, Late Pregnancy	5 kg 11 lb	1.5 kg 3.3 lb	0.7 kg 1.5 lb	Equal parts TMS and Dical. Feed 3-4 ounces
Lactating, First 3 Months	5.4 kg 12 lb	3.1 kg 6.8 lb	1 kg 2.2 lb	Equal parts TMS and Monodicalcium phosphate. Feed 6-7 ounces
Nursing Foal, 0-4 Months Age	Free-choice	1.25 kg 2.75 lb	0.34 kg 0.75 lb	Equal parts TMS and Dical. Feed 3 ounces
Weanling, 6 Months Age	2.3 kg 5.1 lb	2.6 kg 5.6 lb	0.55 kg 1.2 lb	Equal parts TMS and Dical. Feed 3-4 ounces
Yearling 12 Months Age	3.0 kg 6.6 lb	2.5 kg 5.5 lb	0.5 kg 1.1 lb	Equal parts TMS and Dical. Feed 3-4 ounces
Two Year Old	4.75 kg 10.5 lb	1.75 kg 3.8 lb	0.1 kg 0.25 lb	Trace-mineralized salt.

*Daily nutrients per horse based upon 500 kg (1,100 lb) mature weight *maintenance*. See also footnotes, *Table I*, for variations attendant upon mature weight and level of activity.

Alfalfa is full bloom, hay, or grazed (18 percent crude protein). *Free-choice* is all the forage the horse will consume.

TMS is trace-mineralized salt containing sodium chloride, zinc, iron, manganese, copper, iodine, and cobalt.

Dical is dicalcium phosphate. When mixed in equal parts with TMS, each ounce of mineral supplement contains 3 gm each calcium and phosphorus.

Wet molasses may be added (5 percent by weight of grain mix) to encourage consumption and prevent sifting out of minerals.

Grain can be fed in wooden feeders, feeding buckets, or nonmetallic feed pans. Horses should be fed individually to prevent overconsumption by a dominant horse. Feeds bags are a good way to insure that each horse receives its correct ration. Remove the feed bag as soon as the horse finishes the grain.

Feeding Commercial Horse Feeds. A commercial ration should meet the requirements for protein and minerals listed in Table VII. Consult the feed tag to be sure the product meets these specific requirements. Guarantees for minerals and vitamins are often provided but are not required unless the feed is advertised as a complete feed or a specific supplement. Feed according to directions on the tag. If the ration is a complete feed, the horse will not need additional fiber, but boredom activities such as wood chewing may occur. If this happens, feed some additional roughage such as long-stemmed hay.

Table VI shows a series of sample rations for various classes of horse using a commercial grain mix.

Table VI SAMPLE RATIONS USING COMMERCIAL HORSE FEED*

(Daily amounts to feed in pounds per 100 pounds body weight)

Class of Horse	Good Quality Hay or Pasture	Grain Mix
Mature		
Idle	1.5 to 2.0	.25 to 0.5
Light Work	1.0 to 2.0	0.5 to 1.0
Mare, Late Pregnancy	Free-choice alfalfa	0.5 to 1.0
Mare, Lactating	Free-choice alfalfa	1.0 to 1.25
Nursing Foal, 0-4 Months	Free-choice alfalfa (creep feed)	1.25 to 1.5
Weanling, 4-12 Months**	1.0 to 1.5 alfalfa	1.5 to 3.0
Yearling, 12-24 Months	Free-choice	1.0 to 1.25
Two-year-old, 24 Months	Free-choice	0.75 to 1.0

*The minimum nutrient requirements in the grain mix are shown in Table VII.

**Weanlings should not be given more than 0.5 lb *alfalfa* per 100 lb anticipated mature weight until after 10 months of age.

Customized Rations. Customized rations are made up from concentrate sources by the individual horse owner or a local feed mill. Commercial rations generally are purchased in volume and so are more economical when feeding a large number of horses. When buying in large amounts, it is advisable to have the ration analyzed to ensure that it is uniform and meets the projected needs of the horse farm.

The procedure for customizing a hay and grain ration is as follows:

(a) Decide how many pounds of hay or equivalent pasture are wanted.

(b) Determine the digestive energy (DE) content per pound of the hay or grass forage from Table II. Multiply by (a). This gives (b), the daily DE supplied by the roughage.

(c) Determine the daily DE requirements of the horse (Table I).

(d) Subtract (b) from (c). This gives (d), the DE which must be supplied by grain.

(e) Determine which grain or grain mix is wanted. If adding molasses, be sure to figure this into the calculations. Adjust the proportions of the mix so the mix conforms to the crude protein (CP) requirements given in Table VII.

(f) Compute the DE/lb of mix from data in Table II.

(g) Divide (d) by (f). This gives (g), the number of pounds of mix to feed.

(h) Obtain daily calcium and phosphorus requirements from Table I.

(i) To get (i), the total grams of calcium and phosphorus wanted in the ration, use Table II and sum the components (hay, grains, molasses).

(j) Subtract (i) from (h). This gives (j), the number of grams of calcium and phosphorus needed to balance the ration.

(k) Using Table IV, convert (j) to the number of ounces of supplement wanted. Add to ration.

Table VII **MINIMUM NUTRIENT REQUIREMENTS IN GRAIN MIX WHEN FEEDING AVERAGE- TO BETTER-QUALITY HAY OR EQUIVALENT PASTURE***

Class of Horse	Crude Protein	Calcium	Phosphorus
Mature	10	0.6	0.3
Mare, Late Pregnancy	16	0.7	0.5
Lactating, First 3 Months	16	0.7	0.5
Nursing Foal	16	0.9	0.6
Weanlings	18	0.9	0.6
Yearlings	16	0.7	0.5
Two-Year-Olds	14	0.3	0.5

*Amounts given are percent of each nutrient in the grain mix. Grain mixes that contain these nutrient levels are available commercially.

Amounts of grain mix to feed are given in Table VI.

Vitamin and Mineral Supplements. The majority of commercial horse feeds contain vitamin and mineral concentrations that meet or exceed the horse's daily needs. Green forages (pasture or hay) are good sources of vitamins A and E. These are the only vitamins not synthesized by the horse and therefore the only vitamins that must be provided in the diet. With the possible exception of equine degenerative myelopathy, vitamin E deficiency has not been described in the horse.

Vitamin A deficiency can occur if a horse does not consume green forage or some other dietary source of vitamin A for several months. Hay older than one year has lost nearly all of its vitamin A activity and is unlikely to be suitable as a dietary source of vitamin A. Horses consuming such hay should be supplemented (see VITAMIN A).

Additional vitamins above daily requirements may possibly benefit the following individuals:

- Draft horses, endurance horses, and racehorses, who may have marginal intake of B vitamins (especially thiamin) relative to needs.

- Nervous, hyperactive, stressed horses, particularly when traveling or showing.

- Broodmares, if there is any doubt about the adequacy of the diet to meet the vitamin needs of pregnancy and lactation.

To prevent vitamin overdose, choose a supplement (preferably in solid form) that provides additional quantities of all vitamins without excessive amounts of any specific vitamin. Administer according to the directions of the manufacturer.

There are specific indications for giving calcium and phosphorus, and the microminerals copper and zinc, as discussed earlier in this chapter.

Allowing the horse free access to trace-mineralized salt will insure that the horse receives adequate amounts of microminerals, and will correct any deficiencies which may be present in feeds. In selenium-deficient areas, utilize trace-mineralized salt containing higher levels of selenium. Remove other sources of salt to insure consumption.

Fat and Oil Supplements. Most horse feeds contain 2 to 4 percent fat, but horses will adapt to the consumption of diets containing 10 to 20 percent fat if sufficient time is allowed for adjustment.

The purpose of adding fat to the diet is to increase energy density without incurring problems associated with high concentrations of grain. These problems include founder, colic, diarrhea, and exertional myopathy. Fat supplements can supply the added energy needs without increasing grain intake or decreasing roughage intake.

Plant or vegetable oils and animal fats are utilized for energy more efficiently than all other sources of feed. Vegetable oils provide about 3 times more DE than an equal weight of cereal grain. Animal fats provide slightly less.

Studies showed that adding 10 percent fat to the ration of lactating mares increased the fat percentage of milk and caused the fat content to remain higher as lactation advanced. Adding 12 percent fat to the diets of racing or cutting horses improved muscle glycogen storage and athletic performance. Beyond 12 percent, performance did not improve and glycogen storage began to decrease.

Among several fat supplements studied, all appeared to be equally effective. Corn, soy, and other vegetable oils were the most palatable.

Because fat supplements are rich in energy, ration adjustment is necessary when feeding these supplements. If the workload does not increase, too much energy will be supplied unless the daily feed intake is reduced. Vegetable oils provide about 4 Mcal DE per pound, or about 8 Mcal DE per quart.

Adding 1 quart (2 pounds) of vegetable oil to 8 pounds of grain results in a 20 percent fat supplement. If the grain and vegetable oil combination makes up half the ration by weight, the concentration of fat in the total ration is 10 percent. Using these figures, one can formulate a 10 or 12 percent fat supplement.

Horses should be started slowly on a fat supplement to prevent digestive upsets and diarrhea. Begin with a small amount and increase it up to the desired 10 to 12 percent over at least 3 weeks. The oil can be added to the grain mix at each feeding or up to a week before. Monitor the horse's weight, eating behavior, and general well-being.

ADDING TO OR CHANGING THE RATION

Most horses prefer the feed they are accustomed to. Accordingly, when the feed is changed, the horse will usually eat less of it—unless the new feed is much more palatable than the old.

Any change in a horse's feeding program, either in type or amount of feed, should be undertaken gradually over a period of several days.

When adding a new concentrate to an established ration, begin on the first day by giving half a pound; then add half a pound a day until the desired level is reached. Be sure to cut back on the amount or hay or forage to avoid giving too much dietary energy. This should prevent colic and founder.

When going off an exercise or training program, the procedure for reducing the amount of grain in the horse's diet is to decrease the grain at the same rate as you decrease the amount of exercise.

When changing the type of hay or grain, replace only 25 percent every other day. It should take about 1 week for the new feed to completely replace the old.

Most manufacturers provide guidelines for adding their products to a current feeding program. Follow these recommendations.

Finally, watch your horse closely as he eats. A sudden change in appetite indicates something is wrong with the feed or the horse.

COLD WEATHER CARE AND FEEDING

Horses adapt well to cold weather and can live outdoors in winter in most parts of the country provided that shelter is available from wind, rain, and snow. A shed open on one side is an ideal shelter for all seasons. Horses grow a long winter hair coat and store a layer of fat beneath the skin, both of which provide excellent insulation. However, when a horse is kept in a heated stable it loses the ability to adapt and is more apt to suffer from chilling and pneumonia when taken outside.

A three-sided shed is an ideal shelter for horses who live outdoors in all seasons.

Horse blankets can be used to prevent chilling. For a horse in winter with a dry coat, the blanket becomes beneficial when the wind-chill temperature drops below 20 degrees F. For a horse in summer with a wet coat, wind-chill discomfort becomes a factor at temperatures below 60 degrees F. For wind-chill temperatures above these levels, blanketing becomes uncomfortable and also decreases hair coat adaptation to cold weather.

Dietary energy is the principal dietary concern in cold weather. Protein, vitamin, and mineral needs are increased slightly. In winter, it is important to feed a ration that gives off a lot of heat. High-quality hay is best for this purpose and is preferred over grain. This is because roughages are digested by bacterial fermentation in the cecum and colon, which produces a great deal of heat. If high-quality roughage is available and the horse has unlimited access to it, it is unlikely that you will need to feed concentrates. However, if high-quality roughage is not available, or the horse loses body weight and condition, then feed some grain.

All grains are satisfactory, but corn has certain advantages. Corn generates twice as much energy as an equal volume of oats. Accordingly, less volume needs to be fed in order to produce the same amount of energy. This leaves more room in the digestive tract for hay. This is the main reason why corn is preferred by many horsemen as a winter feed.

If the proportion of grain in the ration exceeds 40 percent, consider feeding a fat supplement as described earlier (see FAT AND OIL SUPPLEMENTS).

Water requirements for horses in cold weather are often overlooked. Water sources can freeze over. Occasionally the water is too cold for the horse to drink, especially if the horse has bad teeth. A drop in water consumption results in a drop in food consumption and therefore in energy. It will then be difficult for the horse to keep up its weight and body temperature. Inadequate water consumption may

Outdoor tanks should be equipped with water heaters to prevent freezing in cold weather.

cause the stool to become hard and difficult to pass. This is why constipation and rectal impactions are much more common in freezing weather.

Water heaters should be placed in outdoor tanks to keep the temperature in the trough above 45 degrees F. It is important to insure that the water heater is functioning properly by checking the trough daily. If the water heater shorts out, the shock may not be severe enough to injure the horse, but it will keep him from drinking. In extremely cold weather, remove ice several times a day.

Horses have been known to live on snow for limited periods. This is not ideal and should not be relied upon to supply water needs.

Common Feeding Problems

WEIGHT GAIN AND LOSS

It can be difficult to determine if a horse is too fat or too thin. In order to detect weight changes before the horse develops a significant change in body condition, it is important to weigh the horse at least monthly and maintain a record (see Table III, Determining Your Horse's Weight).

Visual inspection is an effective way to estimate body condition. The following scoring system has been developed:

- **Poor** (Score 1): An extremely emaciated horse with prominent bony processes projecting beneath the skin in areas previously covered by muscle. No fatty tissue can be felt. If the condition is slightly better than extremely emaciated, give the horse a score of 2.

- **Thin** to moderately thin (Score 3 to 4): The horse has visible ribs, a slight ridge or prominence down its back over the spinous processes, and a prominent tail head. The withers, shoulders, and neck are accentuated.

- **Well-conditioned** (Score 5): The back is level. The ribs can be felt easily, but are not visibly apparent. There is a layer of fat around the tail head and the withers are rounded over the spinous processes. The shoulders and neck blend smoothly into the body.

- **Moderately fleshy** to fleshy (Score 6 to 7): There is a discernible crease down the back. The ribs can still be felt, but there is a noticeable layer of spongy fat filling the spaces between them. The fat around the tail head is soft. Fat is apparent around the neck, over the withers, behind the shoulders, and along the inner buttocks.

- **Obese** to extremely obese (Score 8 to 9): The above findings are more pronounced. The neck, in particular, is noticeably thickened. The ribs cannot be felt. Fat between the buttocks may rub together. The tail head bulges, the flanks are filled in flush, and the abdomen is potbellied.

An extremely obese horse with a thick, heavy neck: score 8 to 9.

A thin, poorly nourished horse with no subcutaneous fat: score 1 to 2.

Obesity. Overfeeding is the most common cause of obesity. Horses will not adjust their appetites to balance energy expenditure. When given more calories than they need, they will readily consume them.

Keep in mind that energy needs of idle horses are 50 percent less than those of hard-working horses. Be sure to adjust your horse's dietary energy in accordance with its level of activity.

Weight Reduction. Weight reduction is recommended for all horses with body condition scores above 5, with the exception of late-term pregnant and lactating mares, in whom a score of 6 is often desirable.

The 2 methods for getting off weight are calorie reduction and exercise. When both are done simultaneously, the results are better because the loss of body weight is mostly fat. The exercise helps to retain muscle and lean body condition.

Obese horses are to some extent exercise-intolerant. Start an exercise program slowly and advance it as the horse's condition improves. An average adult horse walking for one hour expends 200 extra calories. At a slow trot with some cantering, the horse burns 2,000 extra calories an hour (2 Mcal). With intense work, a horse can expend several Mcal an hour. (Compare this to the 16 Mcal required for daily maintenance.)

Dieting is accomplished not by changing the composition of the diet, as it is in people, but by reducing the quantity of feed. If you are feeding hay and grain, start slowly by cutting back on the quantity of grain until the correct concentration of DE for the new level of exercise activity is obtained (Table I). Since weight loss is wanted, slowly cut back another 10 to 15 percent while maintaining the same level of exercise. When feeding hay alone, follow the same formula.

In severe winter weather, weight loss should be postponed and enough DE supplied to maintain current weight.

A drastic reduction in feed intake should be avoided. In horses, even mild degrees of starvation increase the risk of high blood lipid levels with attendant neuralgic symptoms. Death can occur.

Emaciation. Horses with low body condition scores (1 to 3) are severely undernourished. These horses are in negative nitrogen balance. Refueling must be initiated slowly. The gastrointestinal tract and metabolic condition of the horse will be unprepared for a large protein load. Within 2 to 3 weeks the malnourished horse will begin to gain weight and add lean body mass, much like a growing horse. At this time feed a comparable nutrient-enriched diet.

The Hard-Keeper. A horse who is perpetually thin or seems to require more food than others in a comparable situation is referred to as a hard-keeper.

One or more of the following may be contributing factors:

- The quality or amount of ration fails to meet the horse's energy and/or nutrient requirements. Energy requirements increase as work increases. These requirements must be met by increasing the amount or energy density of the feed.

- The ration is complete but the horse is unable to extract all the dietary nutrients because of dental disease or a heavy burden of worms. Less commonly the horse may have an intestinal disease or a deficiency of digestive enzymes, resulting in a malabsorption syndrome.

- The horse may not be taking in enough feed because a dominant individual is driving it away from the feeder. The horses should be fed from separate feeders spaced widely apart.

Occasionally there is no apparent cause. Some horses seem to be thin by nature. However, the horse who steadily loses weight and condition is a different matter. Something is wrong with the feed or the horse.

Treatment: Nutrient deficiencies should be corrected as described elsewhere in this chapter. A good parasite control program will greatly assist in keeping the horse healthy (see chapter 2, Parasites).

All hard-keepers should be examined for abnormal tooth wear and other correctable causes of dental disease as described in chapter 7, Oral Cavity.

Finally, if the horse's health checks out and the horse is moderately thin to thin, switch to a commercial horse feed or put the horse on pasture containing an abundance of high-quality forage. If pasture is unavailable and you are feeding hay, add cereal grain to the daily ration ($^1/_2$ pound per 100 pounds weight of the horse).

WOOD CHEWING AND CRIBBING

Wood chewing and cribbing are common vices that occur predominantly in stabled horses.

Wood chewing usually does not cause digestive problems as most of the wood is dropped and not swallowed. Occasionally splinters penetrate the soft tissues of the mouth and cause infections and abscesses. Wood chewing, however, can be tremendously destructive to fences, stalls, and wooden siding.

Cribbing, while superficially resembling wood chewing, is a vice in which the horse sets its front teeth on a horizontal solid object such as the edge of a stall window, arches its neck, pulls back, and swallows large gulps of air.

Wood chewing is a destructive vice that is readily copied by other horses.

The major problems with cribbing and wood chewing are wear of the incisor teeth, rarely to such an extent that the horse can no longer graze. In a few cases the horse spends so much time chewing or cribbing that it fails to consume enough feed.

The causes of wood chewing and cribbing are not known. Observation suggests that one or more of the following may be causative or contributing factors: social isolation and lack of companionship; boredom; frustration; lack of opportunity to release tension and nervous energies; need for more fiber; imitative behavior; and vestigial browsing behavior. An hereditary predisposition for cribbing has been identified in some Thoroughbred families.

Treatment: These habits are difficult to stop, but can be minimized by turning the horse out to pasture, preferably with other horses. For stalled horses, you can try hanging a plastic jug from the ceiling to give the horse something to play with; or put up metal mirrors so the horse thinks it has a companion.

If the horse is eating pelleted feed, switch to hay or continue the pelleted feed and add $1/2$ pound of long-stemmed hay per 100 pounds weight of the horse. Make sure the diet contains all the necessary nutrients.

As a deterrent to wood chewing, string electric wires along the top of fences. Wood can be painted with a nontoxic chemical substance to make it unpalatable. Avoid the use of creosote, one of the agents responsible for wood preservative poisoning (discussed below).

The usual method of preventing cribbing is to apply a 2- to 3-inch leather strap around the horse's throat at the narrowest part of the neck. When the horse tries to arch its neck to crib or swallow air, the strap becomes painful. Some straps are equipped with a metal piece at the gullet to increase the discomfort. The crib strap

A well-fitting crib strap will prevent most horses from cribbing.

should be applied snugly, but not tight enough to interfere with breathing. Crib straps usually are effective, but some horses continue to crib in spite of the strap. Another cribbing device which may be effective is a hollow bit in the form of a cylinder with perforated holes. The bit prevents the horse from creating an air-tight seal with its lips. Various surgeries have been developed. They are not always successful and are not recommended.

Horses who crib or chew wood should be separated from other horses who may imitate the habit and acquire the vice.

Forage Toxicities

Forage toxicities are the most common causes of poisoning in the horse. Other causes of poisoning, and the treatment of acute poisoning, are discussed in chapter 1, Emergencies (see POISONING).

FESCUE TOXICITY

Fescue poisoning is caused by an alkaloid-producing fungus that proliferates in fescue grass during the lush stages of growth. This tends to occur on fall pasture, particularly when autumn rains follow a dry summer. Fescue is less palatable than most other pasture grasses. Horses generally will not eat it if something else is available.

Toxicity produces reproductive problems among mares during the last 3 months of pregnancy. There is an increased frequency of prolonged pregnancy, retained placentas, stillbirths, and absent milk production (*agalactia*).

It is easier to prevent fescue toxicity than to treat it. Avoid feeding fescue hay to pregnant mares (or putting them on fescue pastures) during the last 2 to 3 months of gestation. If this is not feasible, supplement the fescue forage with alfalfa or legume hay.

SELENIUM TOXICITY

The daily selenium requirement for the horse is 0.1 mg per kilogram (0.1 ppm) by dry weight of diet. Amounts greater than 5 mg per kilogram are toxic.

Selenium toxicity occurs in areas where soil selenium levels are high. These arid or semi-arid areas are marked by certain indicator plants that accumulate high levels of selenium. These "accumulator" plants are not palatable and are not eaten by the horse except as a last resort. Other selenium "converter" plants, however, including grains and native grasses, absorb lower concentrations and are commonly grazed.

Selenium is taken up by plants more readily in alkaline soils, found principally in the Great Plains and western Rocky Mountains. This is why the disease was known as "alkali disease" to early settlers, who incorrectly surmised that the high salt content in the soil and water were the cause of the symptoms.

Selenium toxicity falls into two categories.

The *acute* form is caused by the rapid ingestion of large amounts of selenium over a short period of time. This usually happens when too much selenium (in the form of selenium supplements) is added to the diet; rarely it is caused by the consumption of accumulator forages.

Horses with acute intoxication may die suddenly from cardiac and respiratory failure. A condition of aimless wandering and stumbling called "blind staggers," seen in cattle and sheep as a result of selenium toxicity, is thought to occur in horses as result of the consumption of locoweed plants containing high concentrations of selenium.

The *chronic* form of selenium poisoning (also called *alkali disease*), which is by far the most common manifestation of selenium intoxication in horses, occurs when a horse grazes forages containing converter plants for weeks or months. The horse becomes run-down and emaciated. Hair is lost, particularly over the mane and tail, giving the name "bob-tail" disease. Breaks and cracks develop in the hoof wall, resulting in foot tenderness and pronounced lameness. The hoof wall may partially or completely slough.

Selenium levels in the horse's daily feed should be less than 2 ppm (2 mg selenium per kg feed). The diagnosis is commonly made by ration analysis, which shows selenium concentrations in feed above these levels. Analysis of hoof and hair samples is also useful in confirming the diagnosis. Elevated serum selenium levels will be found in both acute and chronic poisoning.

Treatment: Remove the horse from pasture. When the roughage or grain is high in selenium, switch to a feed lower in selenium. The new ration should contain 25 percent protein. Specifically, this is a *high* protein ration. The horse also should be given 2 to 3 grams per day of the sulfur-containing amino acids DL-methionine and cysteine.

To prevent selenium toxicity, limit the hours of grazing on problem pastures and use feedstuffs low in selenium. If in doubt, have the ration analyzed. Several additives have been reported to be effective against high levels of selenium in the feed.

LOCOWEED POISONING

There are many toxic species of locoweed or milk vetch, all of which are members of the legume or pea family. They are distributed worldwide. Many horses develop an addiction to these plants and will seek them out even when better forage is available. A horse must consume large amounts of the plant (30 percent of body weight) over a period of several weeks or months to develop the disease.

The substances that cause locoweed poisoning include a neurotoxic indolizidine alkaloid called swainsonine, various nitroglycosides, and selenium (see above). These substances cause different locoweed syndromes.

Locoism is seen most often on high desert ranges in the western United States during spring, when locoweed is most abundant. Affected horses become crazy or "loco" and exhibit such signs as roaring, trembling, salivation, aimless wandering, staggering, respiratory difficulty, and paralysis. These are signs of brain involvement.

Horses who recover from locoism may have permanent neuralgic deficit and are unsafe to ride. The only effective treatment is to remove the horse from pasture or prevent further consumption of rations containing poisonous plants. This must be done early in the course of the disease to be effective.

SORGHUM TOXICITY (MILO, SUDAN GRASS, JOHNSON GRASS)

Sorghum grasses are found in the Southwest and in much of the eastern United States where they are sometimes used as forages. Not all varieties are poisonous. Johnson grass is the most toxic of the sorghums, while sudan grass is the most frequent cause of poisoning.

Poisonous sorghums contain cyanogenic glycosides that are metabolized to cyanide. Levels of cyanide are highest in new-growth grasses. Since toxicity declines in the mature plant, pastures rather than hay are more likely to be associated with poisoning.

Acute cyanide poisoning (rare) is characterized by sudden death preceded by respiratory distress, flaring of the nostrils, staggering gait, involuntary urination and defecation, collapse, convulsions, and respiratory arrest.

The most common condition associated with sorghum toxicity is equine sorghum-cystitis ataxia, seen with the chronic consumption of low levels of cyanide. The signs are incoordination of the hind limbs, urinary incontinence, and paralysis of the bladder. Pregnant mares on sorghum pastures have been known to abort or give birth to deformed foals.

Treatment: Treatment of acute cyanide poisoning involves giving antidotes containing sodium nitrite and sodium thiosulfate. The management of sorghum cystitis is discussed elsewhere (see PARALYZED BLADDER).

Prevent exposure to toxicity by removing horses from sorghum pastures during periods of new growth. These tend to occur when a heavy rainfall follows a frost, after a warm spell, and when the grass has been heavily trampled.

RYEGRASS AND DALLIS GRASS STAGGERS

Ryegrass and dallis grass staggers are caused by mycotoxins produced by molds that invade these grasses. Dallis grass is a common pasture grass in the southern half of the United States. Ryegrass has a somewhat wider distribution. Ryegrass toxicity tends to occur in late summer or fall when pastures are short-grazed and the grass is dry and stubble-like.

Initially a horse with grass staggers exhibits mild excitability and muscle tremors, which progress to dizziness, swaying, staggering, stumbling, and rigidity of limbs. These signs are attributable to neurotoxic biochemical effects that disappear when the horse is removed from the source of toxicity.

Most horses recover within a few weeks, but symptoms may persist for several months.

ERGOT POISONING

Ergot is a fungus that grows on grasses and cereal grains, especially rye. It appears as a black banana-shaped mass about $^1/_2$ inch long replacing part of the grass or grain seed. Improperly stored grain can become contaminated with this fungus. Horses are less frequently and severely affected than other livestock.

Signs of acute ergot poisoning include muscle tremors, excitability, abnormal behavior, staggering, salivation, diarrhea, and paralysis. The ingestion of small amounts over a long time has been reported to cause sloughing of the ears, tail, and hooves. Chronic ingestion in pregnant mares can cause reproductive problems similar to those described for fescue toxicity.

Ergot poisoning can be avoided by keeping the seed heads mowed off in the late summer. Grain should be properly stored, as described elsewhere in this chapter, to prevent growth of mold and fungus.

MOLDY CORN POISONING (BLIND STAGGERS)

Epidemics of an encephalitis-like illness have occurred after the ingestion of moldy corn contaminated by a fungus which produces a nervous system mycotoxin called *fumonisin*.

Moldy corn poisoning is one of the most common toxicities of horses. Outbreaks generally occur in the eastern and midwestern United States from late fall to early spring. Corn put into storage with greater than 13 percent moisture, and corn that is stored in damp areas, is most susceptible to mold. Infected kernels will appear pink to reddish-brown in color.

Symptoms appear after one week or more of continuous consumption of infected feed. Signs of brain involvement include profound depression and little response to stimuli, disorientation, circling, head-pressing, blindness (hence the name *blind staggers*), and occasionally unprovoked frenzy. These signs appear suddenly and end in death, usually within 1 to 4 days.

Treatment: Discontinue feeding corn on suspicion of poisoning. The diagnosis is made by identifying the mold or mycotoxin in the feed. Early cases are treated by eliminating the toxin in the gastrointestinal tract using activated charcoal and laxatives as described in the section on Poisoning.

Another mold found in stored corn and also other feeds produces a series of mycotoxins called *aflatoxins*. Horses are more resistant to these toxins than are other domestic animals. Accordingly, aflatoxin poisoning is rare in horses. Signs are like those of moldy corn poisoning. Liver damage is the major toxic effect.

BOTULISM

Horses are highly susceptible to botulism. Poisoning in foals is called the *shaker foal syndrome* (see chapter 16, Pediatrics). In adults, it is referred to as *forage poisoning*.

Botulism is a paralytic disease caused by 3 potent neurotoxins (A, B, and C), produced by the bacteria *Clostridium botulinum*. Spores of this bacteria are found in soil and water contaminated by decaying plant and animal matter, and also in improperly processed hay and feeds containing animal matter or high moisture content. Paralysis develops after the ingestion of spores or the neurotoxin itself. *C. botulinum* also grows in infected wounds.

Forage Poisoning. Weakness and paralysis appear several days after ingestion of feed or water contaminated by neurotoxin or spores. Often the first indication of paralysis is difficulty in swallowing. The signs are drooling, spilling of feed and water from the corner of the mouth, and regurgitation of food through the nose. Weakness and paralysis, which are progressive over several days, are apparent in the shuffling gait, the tendency to lie down often, and muscle tremors that occur with exercise. Collapse and recumbency are signs of advanced poisoning.

The outlook for recovery is dependent on the amount of toxin ingested. Some horses succumb rapidly to respiratory paralysis in 1 to 2 days. In others, the disease progresses slowly and treatment is possible. Suspect botulism when there is progressive paralysis not attributable to other causes. The diagnosis is confirmed by identifying spores in the feed, feces, or wound.

Treatment: Confine the horse to restrict activity (which exacerbates the disease). Horses with tremors and muscular weakness should be sedated or tranquilized to conserve strength. Eliminate residual poison in the GI tract as described in Poisoning.

A polyvalent antitoxin is available from the University of Pennsylvania (Philadelphia). It greatly improves survival when given in time. It does not reverse established paralysis. Thus if the horse is recumbent and having difficulty breathing, the antitoxin has little effect. Intravenous penicillin is of benefit in the prevention of secondary complications such as aspiration pneumonia. Oral penicillin can exacerbate the release of endotoxin and should be avoided.

The nursing care of the recumbent horse, of the utmost importance, is discussed in chapter 11, Nervous System (see TREATMENT OF BRAIN INJURY). Horses that cannot swallow should receive prompt nutritional support via a stomach tube. Mineral oil should be given periodically to prevent fecal impaction. Wounds infected with *C. botulinum* should be treated aggressively with wound debridement and antibiotics as described in WOUNDS.

Prevention: Horse feeds should be of the highest quality and free of excess moisture, insects, and dead animal parts. Hay should be baled at a moisture content below 15 percent to prevent decay and mold. These precautions will prevent the ingestion of spores in the hay. For vaccination, see SHAKER FOAL SYNDROME.

YELLOW-STAR THISTLE AND RUSSIAN KNAPWEED (CHEWING DISEASE)

Yellow-star thistle and Russian knapweed are members of the sunflower family. The yellow-star thistle became extensively established in northern California and along the Pacific Coast, and has now spread through the southern states to the Atlantic coast. Russian knapweed is a noxious weed in the Rocky Mountain states. Most poisonings occur late in summer or fall when pastures are dry and the plants may be the only available forage. In addition, as these plants are palatable, some horses may acquire a taste for them and actually seek them out. Large quantities of the green or dried plant must be consumed for several weeks before toxicity occurs.

Both plants produce a toxic chemical which permanently damages that part of the brain concerned with picking up and chewing feed. The resulting peculiar attempts at chewing account for the name "chewing disease," by which it is known among ranchers.

An affected horse generally holds its mouth open with the tongue hanging out and thus may appear to have a foreign body lodged in the throat. On closer inspection, it will be seen that the muscles of the lips and jaw are somewhat rigid, giving a wooden look. There is difficulty in grasping feed with the lips, chewing it, and passing it to the back of the throat. Swallowing itself is not impaired.

Treatment: Brain damage is irreversible. The horse will die of dehydration or starvation if not put to sleep to circumvent a painful death.

Prevent poisoning by eliminating pasture weeds with effective herbicides. These annuals should be killed or plowed under before they go to seed. Remove horses from pastures containing these weeds.

POISON PLANTS

Pastures contain a variety of plants, often unrecognized but potentially toxic. Even in well-cared-for pastures, plants can grow along fence lines and remain accessible to horses. Fortunately, most poisonous plants are not very palatable. However, under circumstances such as scarce forage, overcrowding, or the introduction of a new horse into the herd, horses may seek out and eat any green plant—including those that are poisonous.

While numerous plants have been identified as poisonous to horses, the commonly encountered ones, in addition to those described earlier in this chapter, fall into one of these classes (the list is by no means complete):

Those containing *toxic alkaloids, glycosides, resins* and *other substances that can produce sudden death*—usually in a matter of minutes but occasionally in 1 to 2 days. They include *larkspur, monkshood, chokecherry, sorghum grasses, foxglove, poison hemlock, water hemlock, milkweed, oleander, laurels, rhododendrons, death camas, yews,* and *black nightshade*. Many of these plants are ornamentals and unpalatable, and would not be consumed by the horse except under unusual conditions.

Those containing *alkaloids and other substances toxic to the liver*. Among these are the *Senecio*, one of the largest genera in the plant kingdom, containing the *ragworts, stinking willie, rattlebox,* and various *groundsels*. These plants are found over most of the eastern and midwestern United States. They grow in winter and early spring, and are therefore found in first-cutting hay. Cumulative ingestion over

Overcrowded pastures with scarce forage such as the above cause horses to seek out and consume unpalatable plants, some of which may be poisonous.

several weeks is necessary before the liver is affected badly enough to cause signs of failure. When this happens, however, the outlook is guarded.

Those containing *neurotoxins and other substances which affect the nervous system*, producing salivation, head-bobbing, staggering, circling, weakness in forelegs and/ or hind legs, muscle tremors, reluctance to move, falling, and collapse. Some of these are *sagebrushes* of the western United States, *milkvetches, horsetail, white snakeroot, bracken fern* and *Johnson grass*.

The genus *Amsinckia intermedia*, which includes *fiddleneck, fireweed, tarweed, buckthorn,* and *yellow bur weed*, also produces liver failure. These are common weeds of wheat and other grain crops, found throughout the western United States. Troubles develop when contaminated grain is threshed and the screenings are fed to horses.

A third hepatotoxic genera, the *Crotalaria*, are commonly found in the southeastern United States. These plants, which belong to the pea family, include *rattleweed* and *wild pea*.

Treatment: Suspect plant poisoning in any unexplained illness of abrupt onset, especially when accompanied by nervous system signs, colic, diarrhea, sudden collapse, or death. Immediately prevent further access to contaminated feed or pasture. With acute poisoning, begin treatment by eliminating plant toxin from the GI tract as described under Poisoning.

Prevention: Eliminate potentially dangerous pasture plants by digging them out or applying weed killer. Check along fence rows, ditches, and around watering spots, where poisonous plants are most often found. Mow annual weeds before they go to seed. Carefully inspect the hay you feed, and don't feed hay baled with weeds.

Avoid turning hungry horses into strange pastures, as they are likely to eat the first plants they see. Young horses, in particular, are quite inquisitive and likely to ingest dangerous plants. Lawn clippings containing plant cuttings should not be thrown into areas where horses are accustomed to eating hay.

BLISTER BEETLE POISONING

There are over 200 species of blister beetle. Most of them are found in the southern and southwestern United States from Florida through Texas to Arizona, and as far north as Illinois. All contain a poisonous substance called *cantharidin*, which is toxic to the kidneys and digestive tract. Cantharidin on the skin and mucous membranes produces a severe burning sensation followed by redness and blistering. Rubbing the eyes after handling the beetles can cause blindness. A burning sensation on urination occurs after the ingestion of ground beetle extract. This is the basis (unfounded) for its use as an aphrodisiac called "Spanish Fly."

Blister beetles vary in size from $1/4$ to 1 inch in length. They are either black, black with orange stripes on the wings, gray, or yellow-tan with black spots. A characteristic feature is that the head and neck make up about $1/4$ of the length of the insect and about half the width of the body

Blister beetles live in flowering grasses such as alfalfa and clover. When alfalfa is cut and baled in two stages, the beetles escape from the winnows and are not incorporated in the hay bale. But when alfalfa is cut and crimped in one operation, the beetles are crushed and their dead bodies are baled with the hay. Because they tend to congregate in large groups, hundreds of beetles may be trapped in a single flake.

The severity of the toxic reaction depends upon the number of beetles eaten by the horse. When the horse eats more than a few beetles, the signs are those of acute shock, followed in a matter of hours by death. When small numbers are consumed, the horse may exhibit abdominal pain and colic accompanied by fever, profuse sweating, listlessness, rapid heartbeat, and the passage of watery or bloody stool. Bloody urine may be passed in the late stages. Often the horse dips its muzzle in and out of the watering trough to wash the burning from its mouth.

Treatment: Discontinue feeding contaminated alfalfa. Eliminate the toxin in the gastrointestinal tract using activated charcoal and laxatives as described in Poisoning. Mineral oil (4 quarts) should be given repeatedly by stomach tube. Give large volumes of IV fluid to combat dehydration and protect the kidneys. If the horse survives the first few days, complete recovery is likely.

Treat all potentially exposed horses, whether symptomatic or not, with mineral oil.

Prevention: Inspect alfalfa hay for the presence of blister beetles. However, due to the erratic distribution of beetles within baled hay, beetles can be easily missed by random inspection. Since it is generally not possible to examine all hay, it is important to harvest hay in such a manner that blister beetles will not be crushed and incorporated in the harvest. Blister beetles usually are not present in alfalfa cut before the last part of July. Cutting the hay before it flowers lessens the chance of beetles and also increases the nutritional value of the alfalfa.

Eliminate insects by spraying alfalfa with an insecticide preparation such as Sevin. Sevin also kills grasshoppers and other insects. This provides an additional benefit since the larvae of blister beetles feed extensively on grasshopper eggs. Forage containing beetles may be safely grazed.

CATTLE FEED POISONING

Commercial feeds manufactured specifically for cattle may contain substances harmful to the horse.

Rumensin (monensin sodium) is a liposaccharide antibiotic widely used to increase feed efficiency and control coccidiosis in cattle. It is often added to grain mixes intended for poultry and cattle, and it may be incorporated into pasture feed blocks intended for cattle only.

Rumensin is highly toxic to the horse and will produce acute heart failure and death. The signs of acute poisoning are like those of acute selenium intoxication. Death can occur in 12 hours.

Some cattle feeds contain high levels of urea. Urea is an inexpensive source of nitrogen. Although it can be toxic to horses when fed at high levels, the amount in cattle feed generally is not dangerous for the horse. However, urea provides no benefit over other sources of nitrogen.

As a precaution, do not allow your horse access to commercial cattle feeds.

LEAD POISONING

Lead poisoning is uncommon but can occur with prolonged low-level ingestion. Access to lead-based paints can result from improper use or storage. Pastures close to ore-producing or industrial smelting operations may become contaminated with pollutants such as lead. Horses next to busy highways have ingested grasses heavily contaminated with lead from automobile exhaust fumes. This is less of a problem with the elimination of lead from gasoline.

An early sign of lead poisoning is an abnormal inspiratory sound heard during exercise. It is due to paralysis of recurrent laryngeal nerves. Difficulty in swallowing and regurgitation of food through the nose indicates further cranial nerve involvement. Lameness, weakness, and knuckling at the fetlock are signs of peripheral nerve involvement.

A horse with chronic lead poisoning exhibits emaciation, colic, and anemia. There may be a blue "lead line" along the gums at the base of the teeth. The diagnosis is confirmed by a whole blood lead concentration showing a level of 0.30 ppm or greater. Levels over 1.0 ppm indicate a poor prognosis.

Treatment: In mild cases, removing the horse from the pasture or source of contamination may allow for recovery. In more severely affected horses, a lead-binding chelating agent can be used to quickly wash out excess lead from the body. The chelating agent is given intravenously daily in divided doses for several days.

FLUORIDE TOXICITY (FLUOROSIS)

Exposure to inorganic and organic fluoride occurs through contamination of forage, soil, and water. Common toxic sources of fluoride are rock phosphates, phosphatic limestone, or fertilizer-grade phosphates that have not been defluoridated. Wells located near phosphatic rock may contain toxic fluoride concentrations.

A total daily dietary concentration (dry matter) of greater than 40 ppm is considered potentially toxic when consumed by horses for long periods. Water containing more than 4 ppm is marginally safe, and water containing greater than 8 ppm should be avoided.

Signs of fluorosis are primarily related to the musculoskeletal system. There is increased bone thickness, first noted as bumps on the inside of the legs below the knees, then found on the jaw and elsewhere. Intermittent lameness and stiffness appear as the disease progresses. There is a generalized debilitation and unthrifty appearance, with the horse losing weight despite adequate amounts of good-quality feed.

In young horses flourosis affects enamel and dentine, with the result that the teeth develop a characteristic mottled or stained appearance. Dental deterioration and abscesses occur as the disease worsens.

There is no specific treatment for fluorosis. The disease will not progress once the horse is removed from the source of contamination. However, lameness, teeth damage, and bone changes do not regress.

WOOD PRESERVATIVE POISONING

Lumber treated with a phenolic preservative to prevent soil fungus and insect degradation is often used in the construction of farm and stable facilities. The usual chemicals involved are pentachlorphenol (PCP) and creosote.

Exposure to phenolic chemicals occurs by skin contact with treated lumber, and more commonly by direct consumption of the chemical through licking or chewing on treated wood.

PCP speeds up metabolism and produces high body temperature. Signs of acute poisoning include rapid gasping respirations, intense sweating, rapid heart rate, weakness, and coma. Chronic low-level consumption produces anemia and weight loss. The diagnosis can be suspected by the history of licking or chewing at treated wood. It can be confirmed by a PCP blood level.

Treatment: Remove the horse from the source of contamination. There is no specific antidote. The horse with acute intoxication should be treated for overheating as described in the section on HEAT STROKE. Poisoning can be prevented by not using oily, freshly treated wood in areas inhabited by horses.

GERIATRICS

All horses do not age at the same rate. A horse's biological age depends on its genetic inheritance, nutrition, state of health, and lifetime sum of environmental stresses. Of greatest importance is the care the horse has received throughout its life. Well-cared-for horses suffer fewer infirmities as they grow older. But when nutrition, immunizations, parasite control, hoof care, and attention to dental problems are neglected, the aging process is accelerated.

There is no fixed point in life at which the horse becomes a geriatric. As a rule, a horse approaching 20 years of age can be considered elderly, although many horses live well beyond 20—some even into their 30s.

Physical Changes

The horse's physical appearance changes only slowly as it approaches this unique period in its life.

One of the most visible alterations is a sagging in the back, giving a swaybacked curvature to the spine. The slight indentation above the eyes, the *supraorbital fossa*, becomes deeper and more pronounced. The lower lip sinks and becomes droopy.

Musculoskeletal System. Degenerative changes in the muscles may lead to stiffness and intermittent lameness that improves with activity. Most elderly horses have some degree of osteoarthritis, related to the accumulated stresses of activity and usage.

The geriatric horse may still enjoy performing the various skills it was called upon to perform in its youth. Pleasure riding, showing, trail rides, and other moderate physical activities are well within the older horse's capability, but it will not be as quick or as fast as it was when it was young. Since there is a gradual decline in condition, the horse will fatigue sooner and require longer rest periods between events.

Moderate exercise helps to keep joints supple and should be encouraged. However, an old horse should not be asked to exert beyond its level of comfort. A specific condition (such as heart disease) may require that exercise be restricted.

Skin. The older horse is more likely to develop tumors, and this is certainly true for the skin. During periodic grooming, which promotes good skin health and circulation, look for any unusual lumps or bumps on or beneath the skin. On old gray horses, be sure to check beneath the tail, as this is a common site for melanoma.

Heart. Coronary artery disease does not occur in horses. However, valvular heart disease exists in many older horses and may limit cardiovascular fitness in some. While congestive heart failure does occur in older horses, it is related to acquired heart disease and not simply to aging.

Lungs. Chronic obstructive pulmonary disease (COPD) becomes more symptomatic with time. However, COPD, like heart disease, is an acquired condition. Horses who have spent most of their lives outdoors or lived in well-ventilated barns and stables usually do not develop COPD as they age.

Kidneys. Because of scarring and loss of kidney function, many old horses must put out large amounts of urine to eliminate nitrogen and the wastes of metabolism. If these horses do not drink frequently, they are likely to become chronically dehydrated. One of the important side effects of dehydration is increased dryness of the manure. The stool becomes hard and difficult to pass, which contributes to bouts of colic and constipation—painful for the horse and difficult to treat.

As always, it is important to insure that the horse has good access to a supply of fresh clear water. This may mean relocating a water tank from a steep hillside or a far corner of the property to a site closer to the horse's hayrack and shelter. Otherwise the geriatric horse may simply find it too inconvenient to make several trips a day just to get a drink of water.

Teeth. The shape of the jaw changes and the incisors and molars wear down as the horse ages. These changes cause chewing problems and particularly the loss of the ability to grind coarse feeds. In turn, this results in inadequate digestion of feed, loss of weight and body condition, and increased risk of colic and constipation.

Wearing down of the horse's incisors may reach the point that it can no longer graze on pasture or eat long-stemmed hay. Points on the cheek teeth, more likely to form at this age, become a major concern. If chewing becomes too painful, the horse will simply stop eating. Accordingly, routine dental care for old horses is absolutely essential.

Weight. Old horses are much more likely to experience rapid weight changes. Visual inspection for body condition is not as accurate in geriatric horses as it is in younger individuals. A good way to judge body condition is to feel the horse's ribs. Each rib should be distinctly felt, with a slight indentation on either side. If the indentation is deep, the horse is too thin. If the indentation is absent (especially if the ribs can't be felt) the horse is too fat.

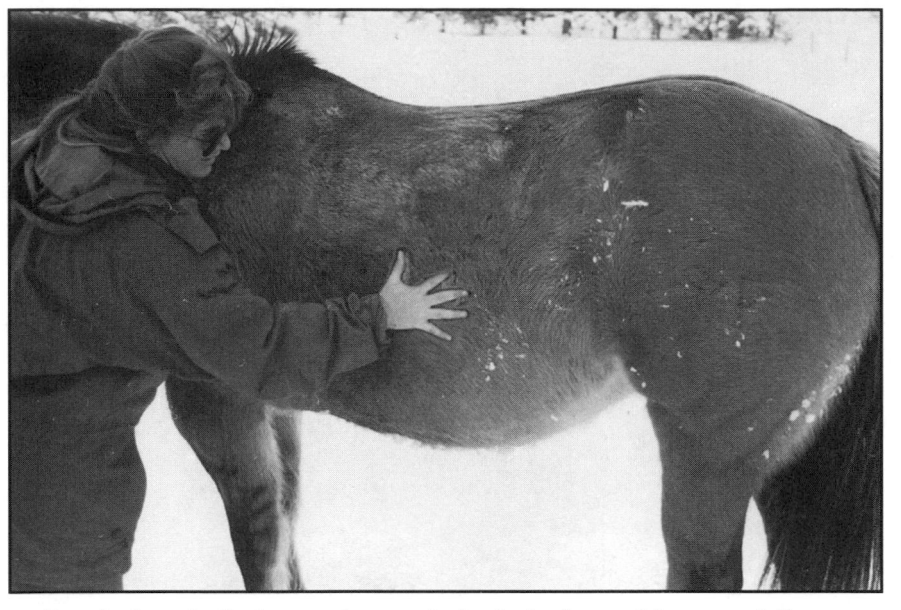

Feeling the horse's ribs is a good way to judge its body condition, especially in winter.

Weight gain occurs if the horse is fed for activity but does not exercise on a regular basis. Obesity is highly undesirable in the geriatric horse. It increases cardiovascular workload and imposes additional stresses on the bones and joints.

Weight loss occurs when there is inadequate feed intake to meet energy needs. In old horses this is usually caused by dental disease, or a lowered pecking order at the feeding station. However, kidney failure should always be considered since it is the most common cause of *unexplained* weight loss in old horses. Liver disease, heart disease, and infectious diseases are uncommon causes. Cancer is an unusual cause of weight loss. If your horse is losing weight, consider asking your veterinarian to run some blood tests to screen for these diseases.

To reverse weight gain or loss, follow the instructions in chapter 17, Feeding and Nutrition (see Common Feeding Problems). Weight adjustments in geriatric horses should proceed slowly. Any sudden change in weight may impose a severe stress. When weight loss is accompanied by protein deficiency (as determined by serum proteins), a protein supplement such as soybean or linseed meal can be added to the daily ration.

Special Senses. The vision and hearing of older horses does not decline with age as is the case with people. Blindness and deafness result from diseases that are acquired at all stages of life. Even when there is loss of eyesight or hearing, however, the horse compensates well by relying on its other senses.

However, loss of taste is a function of aging. This is one more reason why it is important to feed a palatable, high-quality diet as described below.

BEHAVIORAL CHANGES

Older horses are more sedentary, less energetic, and more restricted in their scope of activity. They adjust more slowly to changes in diet, activity, and routine. They are less eager to please and more inconvenienced by work. However, the training and discipline a horse has received during its younger years is not lost. With just a little more patience and effort, the geriatric horse will continue to perform up to expectations.

An older horse may no longer dominate in a social hierarchy at the level it enjoyed during its prime. Younger, more aggressive horses often displace the geriatric individual, who is driven from the feed trough. This leaves the coarser, less nutritious feed for the older horse. Clearly, in this situation the geriatric horse should be fed separately.

Boarding and hospitalization are poorly tolerated in old age. If possible, keep the horse at home. Arrange for a friend or a paid attendant to drop by daily and tend to the horse's needs.

Caring for the Geriatric Horse

Care of the teeth is the single most important consideration in the physical well-being of the older horse.

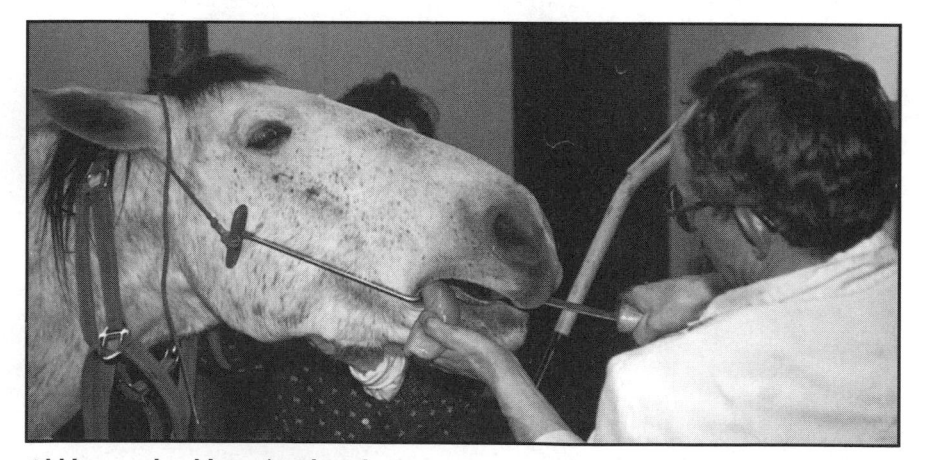

Old horses should receive dental care every 3 months. The points should be filed and any loose teeth removed.

The teeth of old horses should be examined by a veterinarian every 3 months. It is most important to file the cheek teeth to prevent sharp points from lacerating the cheeks and gums, causing a painful stomatitis and reluctance to eat and chew.

Old teeth that become cracked or loose often do not fall out because they are tightly held in place by adjacent teeth. These loose teeth should be removed to promote better chewing and prevent root infections.

The geriatric horse should continue to receive good foot and hoof care. Even though the horse will not be ridden as often, it is still of paramount importance to trim the feet at least every 6 to 8 weeks to maintain good hoof condition and pastern axis. Geriatric horses are less tolerant of musculoskeletal stresses imposed by a long toe, splayed-out foot, or overgrown frog, and are more likely to develop injuries and lameness when the hooves are neglected.

The horse should be kept in a paddock or pasture appropriate to its age and physical condition. Remove environmental hazards and provide a three-sided shelter for inclement weather. Additional bedding in the horse's shelter or stall will add significantly to its comfort.

During cold weather when impactions are most common, it is important to check the temperature of the water supply to be sure that the water is not unduly cold or frozen solid. Horses do not like to drink water at temperatures near freezing. Old horses in particular may not drink enough water to maintain an optimal state of hydration. To insure that the temperature in the tank is at least 45 degrees F, install a water heater. Check the tank daily to be sure the heater is functioning correctly. A heater that is shorted out will deliver a slight shock. It will not hurt the horse, but it will prevent the horse from drinking.

Horses can survive on snow as a source of water. However, this is a drain on calories because energy must be supplied to heat the swallowed snow. This leads to weight loss, inadequate water intake, and risk of colic.

DIET AND NUTRITION

Most geriatric horses require fewer calories than younger horses. Their caloric requirements are close to those of the mature horse at maintenance, shown in Table I in chapter 17, Feeding and Nutrition. Note that overfeeding will result in weight gain. Controlling obesity is one of the most important considerations in keeping an old horse healthy.

The geriatric horse may have difficulty consuming a diet containing adequate amounts of roughage, owing to the condition of the teeth. Compensate by feeding a high-quality hay. Hay for old horses should be fine-stemmed and leafy. Large-stemmed hay is coarse, less palatable, more difficult to chew, and may lead to colic. Poor-quality hay is tasteless, dirty, and contributes to loss of appetite and condition.

Alfalfa is an excellent choice if the horse does not have chronic kidney failure. In kidney failure, the protein and calcium contents of alfalfa are too high, adding to the problems of uremia discussed in chapter 13, Urinary System. A ration containing grass hay and corn is more appropriate for a uremic horse, since it is also low in phosphorus (shown to accelerate the progress of kidney failure).

When alfalfa is not available or should not be used, you can switch to pelleted or cubed feeds. These feeds are easier to chew and digest. Note that feeding small dry pellets to older horses may lead to choke. This is because old horses do not produce as much saliva and therefore the feed is swallowed in a drier state. To prevent choke, moisten the pellets to a gruel-like consistency.

Commercial rations are now available that meet all the nutrient and roughage requirements of the old horse. These products are labeled specifically for senior horses. Commercial products are convenient to feed. They provide a correct balance of calories, fiber, vitamins, and minerals. A semi-moist pelleted form is available, which aids in the prevention of choke.

Old horses need more vitamins and minerals. The absorption of vitamins through the intestinal tract diminishes as the individual ages. In addition, B vitamins are lost in the urine of horses with reduced kidney function. If you are feeding a *complete* commercial ration, you should not need to add vitamin supplements. However, if there is a question about the quality of the horse's diet, or if the horse suffers from kidney or liver disease, it is a good idea to provide supplemental vitamin A and B-complex vitamins. Mineral supplements should not be given unless prescribed by a veterinarian. The horse's kidney function should always be investigated before giving supplemental calcium or phosphorus.

Geriatric horses are more sensitive to extremes of temperature and weather. In hot humid weather, it is important to feed slightly less energy and provide shade or a cool shelter.

In cold rainy weather, energy requirements are greater than normal. Because the older horse may have difficulty meeting these needs through the consumption of greater amounts of feed, these energy requirements can be met by giving vegetable oil (see FAT AND OIL SUPPLEMENTS in chapter 17, Feeding and Nutrition). Vegetable oils provide a high density of energy in a small volume. Moreover, they are palatable and readily consumed. Depending on the horse's weight and need for additional energy, add 1 to 3 cups of corn oil or another vegetable oil to the daily ration. One cup provides approximately 2 Mcal of digestible energy.

Putting Your Horse to Sleep
(Euthanasia)

The time may come when you are faced with the prospect of having to put your horse to sleep. This is a difficult decision to make—both for you and for your veterinarian. Many an old and even infirm horse can be made quite comfortable with just a little more attention to its physical needs and can still enjoy months or years of contented living. But when life ceases to be a joy and a pleasure, when the horse suffers from a painful and progressive condition for which there is no hope of betterment, then perhaps at this time we owe it the final kindness of dying easily and painlessly. This is accomplished by an intravenous injection of an anesthetic agent in sufficient amount to cause immediate loss of consciousness and cardiac arrest.

DRUGS AND MEDICATIONS

Anesthetics and Tranquilizers

Anesthetics are drugs used to block the sensation of pain. Anesthetics can be given as locals, by intravenous sedation, and as general anesthetics.

Local anesthetics are used for operations on the surface of the body, where they are infiltrated locally into the tissue or into a regional nerve. They also may be applied topically to mucous membranes. While local anesthetics (such as lidocaine) have the fewest risks and side effects, they are not suitable for most major operations.

Intravenous sedation involves the use of tranquilizers. Tranquilizers are drugs used to relieve anxiety, to prepare a horse for surgery, and to calm a horse for handling and treatment. The exact mode of action of tranquilizers is variable. Some act on the brain to reduce anxiety; others achieve their effect primarily by increasing the threshold for pain (sedation). The dose that produces sedation in the standing horse is often close to the dosage that causes stumbling and collapse. Accordingly, IV sedation drugs are usually started at low dose and incrementally increased to effect.

Acepromazine, Valium, and other tranquilizers are generally safe and effective when used as directed and in the correct situation. Note that horses can still strike or kick without warning even when properly tranquilized. Use the same precautions as you would around a nonsedated horse.

Xylazine (Rompun) and Detomidine combine both tranquilization and pain control. They are useful for short procedures such as floating the teeth. They are also effective in relieving the pain of colic. Both drugs can be reversed with yohimbine, a valuable consideration if overdose occurs.

To further enhance analgesia while minimizing side effects, drug combinations employing a tranquilizer and a narcotic analgesic are employed. The combination of acepromazine with butorphanol is used most often. Drug combinations allow some painful procedures to be done under IV sedation that would otherwise have to be done under general anesthesia.

General anesthetics render the horse unconscious. Inhaled gases are administered through a tube placed in the windpipe. Halothane is used for longer procedures such as those on the bones, joints, or within the abdomen.

The dose of all anesthetics is computed by the weight of the horse. Nonetheless, susceptibility varies greatly, even among horses of the same weight. Therefore, anesthetics require the services of a trained professional to monitor and control the degree of sedation they produce.

The removal of an anesthetic agent is by the lungs, liver, or kidneys, depending on the specific agent. Impaired function of these organs can cause anesthetic complications. To assure good health before surgery, a complete check-up to include appropriate laboratory tests is advisable. This becomes even more important for the older horse.

If the horse is going to be given a general anesthetic, hay and grain should be withheld for 24 to 36 hours prior to surgery. Access to water should be allowed. Horses on a high-concentrate diet should be weaned to a low-concentrate diet during the preceding week.

The most common post-anesthetic complication is the myopathy of prolonged recumbency, discussed in the section on MUSCLE DISEASES.

Anti-Inflammatory Drugs and Pain Relievers

Analgesics are drugs used to relieve pain. Morphine, pentazocine (Talwin), and butorphanol are *narcotic analgesics* subject to Federal regulation, and must be purchased by prescription. The effect of narcotics on horses is unpredictable. Narcotics can produce excitation, apprehension, and increased muscular activity rather than analgesia and sedation. They are not suitable preparations for home veterinary use.

CORTISONE (CORTICOSTEROIDS)

Corticosteroids are among the most powerful anti-inflammatory agents. The anti-inflammatory properties of cortisone derive from the ability of the drug to enter the cell and alter functions associated with the inflammatory response. However, the suppressive effects are not selective. This means that cell functions associated with cellular immunity and wound healing are likewise suppressed by cortisone. This can delay wound healing for up to a year. The likelihood of wound infection is also increased. All these risks are proportional to the length of steroid usage. They are unlikely to occur when ultra-short-acting steroids are used for only a few days.

Injectable corticosteroids have a limited but real potential for producing acute laminitis. This makes nonsteroidal drugs less risky and a better choice for treating the pain and swelling associated with the majority of musculoskeletal injuries.

A further risk of long-term cortisone usage is adrenal insufficiency. The adrenal gland stops making cortisone because the hormone is being supplied by the medication. Once the medicine is stopped, the horse has no readily available source of cortisone and suffers from a shock-like condition called an *Addisonian crisis*.

Cortisone injections into and around joints are commonly used to reduce swelling and inflammation. These injections can be beneficial when administered under veterinary supervision and *when accompanied by adequate rest*. Too often, however, cortisone masks the pain and lameness associated with the injury, and the horse is returned to exercise or training too soon, with the result that the injury is further aggravated.

Multiple injections into the same joint may produce a condition called *steroid arthropathy*, an accelerated form of degenerative arthritis. One other risk of any intra-articular injection is the potential for producing a septic arthritis (joint infection).

Corticosteroids are often combined with antibiotics, particularly in topical preparations for use in the eye. In some eye conditions, particularly those associated with a virus, secondary effects on the cornea can lead to perforation and blindness. Accordingly, it is important that eye preparations containing steroids be used only with veterinary approval.

NONSTEROIDAL ANTI-INFLAMMATORY DRUGS

Nonsteroidal anti-inflammatory drugs (NSAIDs) are the most commonly used and the safest pain relievers for the horse. These drugs interfere with prostaglandin synthesis and the production of undesirable inflammatory products and enzymes.

All NSAIDs including Butazolidin have the potential for toxic abuse. Toxicity usually occurs when an NSAID is given at twice the recommended dose, or when two or more NSAIDs are given at the same time (the effects being cumulative). The gastrointestinal tract and kidneys are the target organs. All NSAIDs have about the same risk for causing complications.

Ulcers in the mouth, stomach, and large colon occur with long-term use. The effects are loss of appetite, weight loss, GI bleeding, and diarrhea. Kidney damage leads to protein losses in the urine, followed by edema of the limbs, chest, and abdominal wall. Death can occur from colon ulceration or kidney failure. Treatment involves stopping the drug, replenishing protein and electrolyte losses with intravenous fluids and plasma, and administering anti-ulcer medications.

The following NSAIDs are currently used in equine practice:

Salicylates (Aspirin). The short duration of action of aspirin, plus the high dosage required in horses, make aspirin generally impractical for pain relief. However, aspirin in small doses (10 to 20 mg/kg) is employed to inhibit platelet aggregation in acute laminitis and other illnesses associated with intravascular clotting. Thiosalicylate is an injectable salicylate with a longer half-life that has been used for its analgesic effect.

Phenylbutazone (Butazolidin). "Bute" is the most widely used anti-inflammatory painkiller in horses. It is especially effective for injuries involving bone, joint, tendon, and muscle. It can be administered by tablet, paste, powder, or injection, which gives it great versatility. Butazolidin is preferred for long-term maintenance owing to its longer half-life. However, note that long-term use of Butazolidin has been associated with aplastic anemia, although this is rare.

Flunixin meglumine (Banamine). This NSAID has a rapid onset of action, making it the agent of choice in the initial treatment of tendonitis and many musculoskeletal injuries.

Banamine is also a cyclooxygenase inhibitor. It prevents the unwanted circulatory and vascular effects of bacterial endotoxins. Accordingly, it is used for this purpose in the treatment of the endotoxemia associated with acute laminitis, acute colitis, and acute septic metritis.

Naproxen (Equiproxen). This drug is perhaps the most effective nonsteroidal for the treatment of muscle pain and soft tissue injury. It is not as effective in treating joint injuries.

Ketoprofen. This NSAID has a wide spectrum of activity with a relatively low risk of toxicity.

OTHER ANTI-INFLAMMATORY DRUGS

Dimethyl sulfoxide (DMSO). Dimethyl sulfoxide is a powerful free radical scavenger that acts to remove many of the harmful byproducts of inflammation. It has great membrane permeability and passes readily through the skin. It also has the ability to carry other topical drugs along with it, and is frequently used for this purpose along with topical corticosteroids. It should not be used on open wounds.

DMSO is extremely hydroscopic. It rapidly absorbs moisture and becomes diluted with water if left open to the air. When applied to the skin, it draws moisture from the deeper tissue, which explains why it is effective in treating swelling caused by contusions and hematomas. It is not an antibacterial and should not be used for cellulitis.

There are a number of ways of applying topical DMSO. The choice depends on the location of the injury and the reasons for using it. It is best to obtain directions from your veterinarian.

Because DMSO carries other agents along with it, it should be used with caution on skin containing antiseptics, antibacterials, and other chemicals. In addition, wear rubber gloves when handling DMSO to prevent skin contact. Signs of toxicity caused by absorbed DMSO absorption include headache, dizziness, dermatitis, and an oyster-like taste in the mouth.

DMSO as a 10 percent solution is used intravenously in a number of acute disorders including tendonitis, colic, and endotoxemic states, and in the treatment of brain and spinal cord injuries. Solutions of higher concentration, particularly when given rapidly, have been associated with rapid destruction of red cells (*hemolysis*).

Orgotein (Palosein). This drug is a superoxide dismutase (SOD). SOD occurs naturally in the body and acts to suppress harmful superoxide radicals released from inflamed tissue. Within joints, these radicals destroy the enzymes responsible for protecting and nourishing cartilage. Thus Palosein decreases the potential for further damage to joints. Systemic and intra-articular Palosein has proven to be an effective adjunct in the treatment of arthritis.

Hyaluronic Acid (HA). HA is a naturally occurring constituent of the synovial fluid in joints and tendon sheaths. HA prevents destructive enzymes from breaking down cartilage and causing inflammatory adhesions and scars. The intravenous and intra-articular routes of administration have proven to be beneficial in horses with joint and tendon ailments not accompanied by bony destruction on x-rays. Injection into the tendon sheath for the treatment of tendonitis has given good results.

Polysulfated Glycosaminoglycan (Adequan). PSGAG, like hyaluronic acid, occurs naturally in synovial fluid and protects cartilage from stress-induced damage. There is evidence that PSGAG can partially restore cartilage that has suffered some degree of structural damage. Although usually given by intra-articular injections, PSGAG is also available orally and intramuscularly, which has the advantage of treating more than one joint.

Antibiotics

Antibiotics are extracts of rudimentary plants such as molds and fungi. They are capable of destroying some microorganisms that cause disease. Today, many antibiotics are made synthetically from basic chemical structures.

Antibiotics fall into two general categories. Those that are *bacteriostatic* (or *fungistatic*) inhibit the growth of microorganisms but do not kill them. *Bactericidal* and *fungicidal* drugs destroy the microorganisms outright.

Bacteria also are classified according to their ability to cause disease. *Pathogenic* bacteria are capable of producing a particular illness or infection. *Nonpathogenic* bacteria live on (or within) the horse, but don't cause illness under normal conditions. These bacteria are referred to as normal flora. Some actually produce substances necessary to the well-being of the host. For example, bacteria in the bowel synthesize vitamin K, which most animals cannot do for themselves.

WHY ANTIBIOTICS MAY NOT BE EFFECTIVE

Misdiagnosis of Infection. Signs of inflammation (such as heat, redness, and swelling) can exist without infection. A severe bruise is a good example. To be certain of infection, one should see inflammation *and* purulent discharge (pus). The discharge may have an offensive odor. Other indications of infection are fever and elevated white cell count.

Inappropriate Selection. An antibiotic must be effective against the microorganism causing the infection. The best way to confirm that effectiveness is to recover the organism, culture it, and then identify it by colony appearance and microscopic characteristics. Antibiotic discs are then applied to the culture plate to see which discs inhibit growth of colonies. The results are graded according to whether the microorganism is *sensitive, insensitive, or indifferent* to the effects of the antibiotic. Although laboratory findings do not invariably correlate with the results of treatment, antibiotic culture and sensitivity testing is still the surest way of selecting the most effective agent.

Antibiotics sensitivity tests. Discs containing antibiotics on an agar plate show which antibiotics inhibit growth of the bacteria cultured.

Inadequate Wound Care. Antibiotics enter the bloodstream and are carried to the source of the infection. Abscesses, wounds containing devitalized tissue, and foreign bodies such as dirt and splinters are resistant areas. Under such circumstances, antibiotics are unable to get to the source of infection. Accordingly, it is important to drain abscesses, irrigate and cleanse dirty wounds, and remove foreign bodies.

Route of Administration. An important medical decision rests in selecting the best route for administration. The effectiveness of an antibiotic diminishes if it is given by the wrong route. In equine practice, most antibiotics are given intramuscularly. Some are given intravenously and a few by mouth. The choice depends upon the type of antibiotic, the type of infection, the severity of the illness, and whether the GI tract is functioning normally. A horse with colic or diarrhea will not absorb antibiotics well and will maintain inadequate blood levels.

Dosage and Frequency of Administration. The total daily dose is computed by estimating the weight of the horse, then dividing the dose into equal parts and giving each one at a specified time. When the total dose is too low or a dose is skipped, the horse does not maintain a drug level high enough to kill all bacteria.

Factors that have to be taken into account when computing the daily dose are the severity of the infection, the condition of the horse's kidneys and liver, and whether the horse is taking another antibiotic.

COMPLICATIONS OF ANTIBIOTICS

All drugs should be viewed as poisons. The toxic effects of a drug can be more dangerous than the disease. Antibiotics should *never* be given without justifiable indications. Common complications of antibiotics are discussed below and listed in Table I, Antibiotics Your Veterinarian May Prescribe. The list is by no means complete.

Allergy. Antibiotics, more so than other classes of drugs, cause allergic reactions, including hives.

An immediate life-threatening allergic reaction can occur when a horse is exposed to an antibiotic to which it has developed a hypersensitivity through prior exposure. See ANAPHYLACTIC SHOCK in chapter 1, Emergencies.

Toxicity. There is a margin of safety between a therapeutic dose and a toxic dose. Toxicity is related to overdose, prolonged usage, and impaired elimination from the body. Drugs are removed by the liver and kidneys. In failure of these organs, the antibiotic is not broken down and excreted rapidly enough to prevent toxic buildup.

Toxicity can affect one or more systems:

Ears Damage to the otic nerves leads to ringing in the ears, hearing loss, and deafness. The loss can be permanent.

Liver Toxicity can lead to jaundice and liver failure.

Kidneys Toxicity causes nitrogen retention, uremia, and kidney failure.

Bone marrow Toxicity depresses the production of red cells, white cells, and platelets. These effects may be irreversible.

Signs of toxicity are difficult to recognize in the horse. Thus, they can be far advanced before they come to the owner's attention.

Secondary Infection. Antibiotics alter the normal flora that serves as a protective barrier. Pathogenic bacteria are thus freed to multiply and cause disease. The best example of this is the severe enterocolitis that follows the use of antibiotics that change the normal flora of the bowel.

Emergence of Resistant Strains. Strains of bacteria that exhibit resistance to antibiotics evolve when antibiotics are used: (a) for a long time; (b) in too low a dose; and (c) when the antibiotic is bacteriostatic. Microorganisms that develop resistance to one antibiotic often are resistant to others of the same class.

Use in Pregnancy. Certain antibiotics can affect the growth and development of unborn or newborn foals. Tetracycline and griseofulvin are two such antibiotics. They should not be used in pregnancy.

Antibiotics your veterinarian may prescribe are shown in Table I.

Table I ANTIBIOTICS YOUR VETERINARIAN MAY PRESCRIBE

Antibiotic	Dose (By Weight of Horse)	Route and Frequency
Amoxicillin trihydrate	5 to 10 mg per lb	q 8 hr, IM
Ampicillin sodium	10 to 45 mg per lb	q 6 to 8 hr, IM or IV
Ampicillin trihydrate	5 to 10 mg per lb	q 8 to 12 hr, IM
Captan (antifungal)	3 percent solution	Apply topically daily
Ceftiofur	0.5 to 1.0 mg per lb	q 12 to 24 hr, IM
Chloramphenicol palmitate	12 to 25 mg per lb 2 to 5 mg per lb	q 6 to 8 hr, orally (adult horse) q 6 to 8 hr, orally (foal)
Dihydrostreptomycin	5 mg per lb	q 12 hr, IM or SC
Erythromycin	1 to 2 mg per lb 1.0 to 1.5 mg per lb	q 6 to 8 hr, IV Gentamicin q 6 to 12 hr, IM, IV or SC
Griseofulvin (antifungal)	10 mg per lb for 2 weeks 5 mg per lb for 7 weeks	Once a day, orally Once a day, orally
Isoniazid	2 to 10 mg per lb	Once a day, orally
Kanamycin	3.5 mg per lb	q 8 hr, IM or IV
Ketoconazole (antifungal)	13.5 mg per lb	q 12 to 24 hr, orally
Metronidazole	7.0 mg per lb	q 6 hr, orally or IV
Miconazole (antifungal)	2% solution	Apply topically, q 12 hours
Neomycin	1 to 2 grams 0.5 to 1.5 grams	q 6 to 12 hours, orally (adult) q 6 to 12 hours, orally (foal)
Oxytetracycline	3 to 5 mg per lb	q 12 to 24 hr, IV
Penicillin, Benzathine	5,000 to 20,000 units per lb	q 2 days, IM
Penicillin, Procaine G	10,000 to 22,000 units per lb	q 8 to 12 hr, IM
Pyrimethamine	10 mg per lb	q 12 hr for 3 days, then once daily for 27 days, orally
Sodium iodide (antifungal)	10 to 20 mg per lb	Once a day, orally, for 4 to 6 weeks
Spectinomycin	10 mg per lb	q 8 hr, IM
Streptomycin	5 mg per lb	q 8 to 12 hr, IM
Sulfonamides	50 to 100 mg per lb 25 to 50 mg per lb	On day one, orally or IV On subsequent days
Sulfonamide/ trimethoprim	15 mg per lb	q 8 to 12 hr, orally
Tetracycline	3 to 5 mg per lb	q 12 hr, IV
Tylosin	5 mg per lb	q 12 hr, IM

Frequency is how often to give the required dose. Thus if the dose is 10 mg and the frequency is q (every) 8 hours, the total dose in 24 hours would be 30 mg.

Abbreviations: See Table II.

How to Give Medications

PILLS (CAPSULES AND TABLETS)

Pills can be given directly by means of a balling gun *(bolus)*, broken up and added to feed and molasses, or mixed with molasses and given by syringe as described for pastes.

To use the balling gun, load the pill into the cup at the end of the apparatus. Restrain the head. Open the horse's mouth as described in chapter 7, Oral Cavity, under How to Examine the Mouth. Gently insert the tube well into the mouth at the back of the tongue. Depress the plunger to deliver the pill.

NOTE: Pills and tablets should not be given by bolus to foals and small ponies. The esophagus in these individuals is small, and the pill could become lodged in

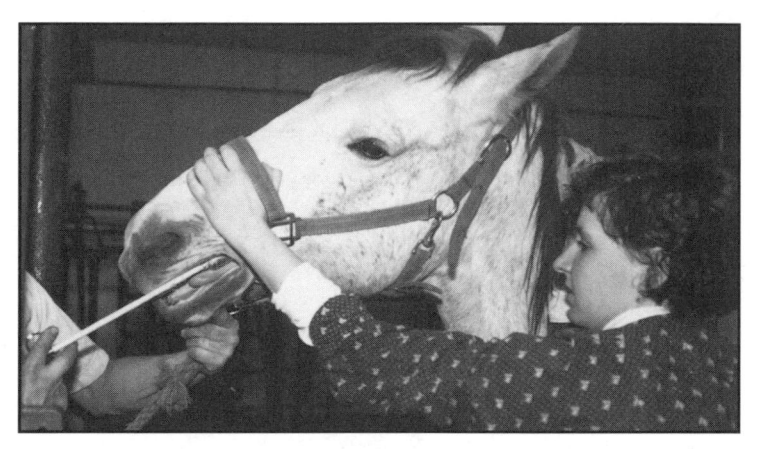

Pills can be given by balling gun. Restrain the head and insert the tube into the mouth at the back of the tongue.

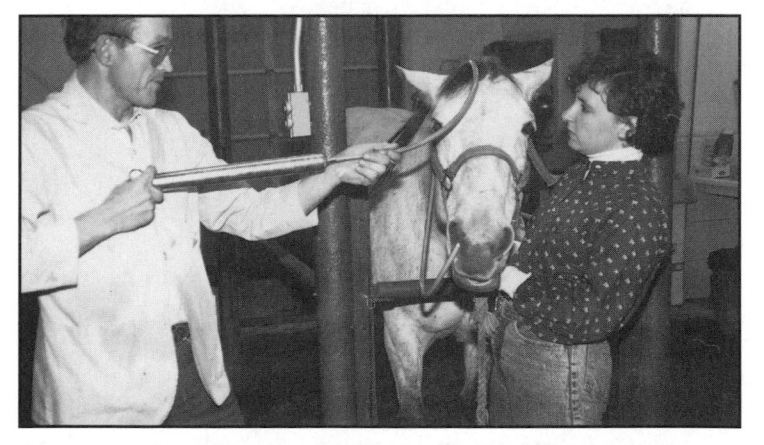

Giving a liquid medication by large-dose syringe and stomach tube.

the swallowing tube. In addition, horses with a history of choke should not be given large pills by bolus (see Choke).

Pills such as Butazolidin and trimethoprim-sulfonamide combinations can be dissolved in water and given by syringe as described for pastes, or broken up and mixed with feed or molasses.

If mixed with feed, a good choice is rolled corn or oats. Add 2 tablespoons of water to a quart of grain. This should be sufficient to get the powder to stick to the grain but not to cause a mush.

If mixed with molasses, the powder can be put into a 60 ml syringe along with 2 ounces of sorghum molasses and delivered like a paste. Molasses is sweet and horses will readily swallow it.

PASTES

Many horse dewormers and some medications come conveniently packaged in disposable syringes, with markings on the syringe to show the number of milliliters of paste to deliver per pound weight of the horse.

Remove all feed before giving the paste. It is easier for the horse to spit out the medication if there is a bolus of food to go along with it.

Insert the end of the syringe into the horse's mouth through the space between the teeth. Depress the plunger. The horse's head should be restrained to prevent it from pulling back and injuring its mouth.

LIQUIDS

Liquid preparations and electrolyte solutions can be given by large-dose syringe, drenching bottle, or stomach tube.

The syringe is used as described for pastes, but with a drenching bottle it is important to raise the horse's chin so that its nose is parallel to the ground. This will prevent the liquid from running back out its mouth.

Mineral oil (and other oils) should never be given by syringe or drenching bottle. Mineral oil, in particular, has no taste and therefore is difficult to swallow. As a result, the horse could inhale the oil, resulting in a fatal aspiration pneumonia. Accordingly, all oils must be given by stomach tube.

STOMACH TUBE

A stomach tube is a plastic or rubber tube about 10 feet long. The tube is introduced through the nose and gently advanced into the esophagus. As the tube passes down toward the stomach, you can often follow its progress as a ripple down the side of the neck next to the jugular vein.

Once the end of the tube is just above the stomach, the medication is flushed down the tube with a large-dose syringe or hand pump. The tube should be flushed with water to deliver any residual medication in the tube.

Improper placement of the stomach tube (into the windpipe) is a potential hazard. The horse may cough as the tube enters the larynx, but this does not always happen. If the medicine is delivered into the lungs, the horse will aspirate and possibly drown. For this reason, a stomach tube should be passed by a veterinarian or an individual trained in its use.

INJECTIONS

It is desirable to have your veterinarian demonstrate the correct procedures for giving injections.

Some injections are given under the skin and others into the muscle. The directions with the product will indicate the correct route.

The injection itself usually is not painful to the horse, but placement of the needle may be accompanied by a brief episode of pain. If this occurs unexpectedly, the horse may shy or possibly kick. For this reason, horses should be restrained for injections. An assistant in control of the halter and lead is adequate restraint for most well-trained horses that are used to being handled and treated. If the horse is high-spirited or not used to being handled, a more secure restraint may be necessary. To learn about restraints, see chapter 1, Emergencies, under HANDLING AND RESTRAINT.

Draw the medicine into the syringe and point the needle up while pressing the plunger to expel air. Remove the needle from the syringe and select the site for injection.

The three best sites for intramuscular injection are the side of the neck, the buttocks, and the back of the thigh (see illustrations).

The skin along the side of the neck is a good place for subcutaneous injections. Here the skin is loose and readily forms a fold when pinched.

Intravenous injections are given into the jugular vein. Experience is necessary to locate this vein and enter it with a hypodermic needle.

To give an *intramuscular* injection, swab the skin with an alcohol sponge. Angle the needle so that it is vertical to the surface of the body. Insert the needle up to the hub with a quick jab. If the horse jerks back, wait a few seconds until it settles down. Then attach the needle to the syringe. Draw back on the plunger and look for blood. The presence of blood indicates that the point of the needle has entered a vein. In that case, the injection should not be given. Withdraw the syringe and start again. Once you see that the injection can be given safely, depress the plunger. Withdraw the needle and rub the skin for a few seconds to disperse the medication. Injections into bones, nerves, and joints can be avoided by giving the shot in the illustrated locations.

For a *subcutaneous* (SC) injection, grasp a fold of skin to form a ridge. Swab the skin with alcohol. Remove the needle from the syringe. Firmly push the needle through the skin fold into the subcutaneous fat. The angle of insertion should be somewhat parallel to the surface of the body to prevent the needle from either going into the muscle or coming out the other side of the skin fold. Repeat the same steps as described for intramuscular injections.

Giving an injection. First alert the horse by tapping the injection site with the back of your hand.

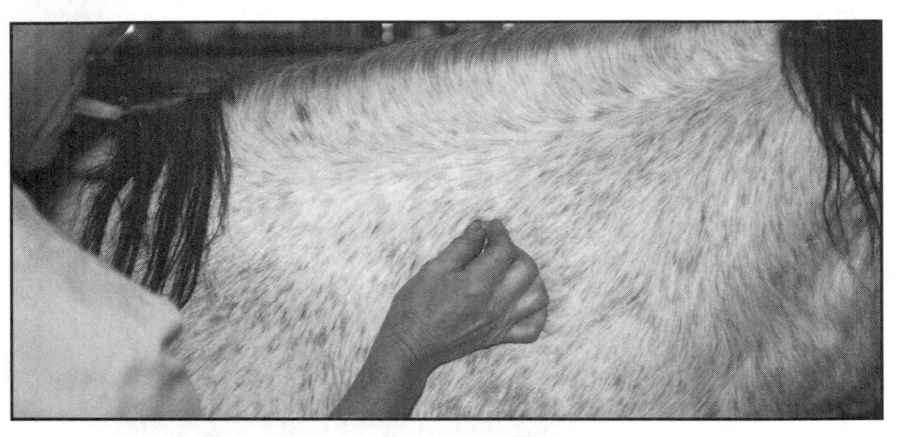

For intramuscular injection, insert the needle vertically before connecting the syringe. If the horse startles, the needle will not break off.

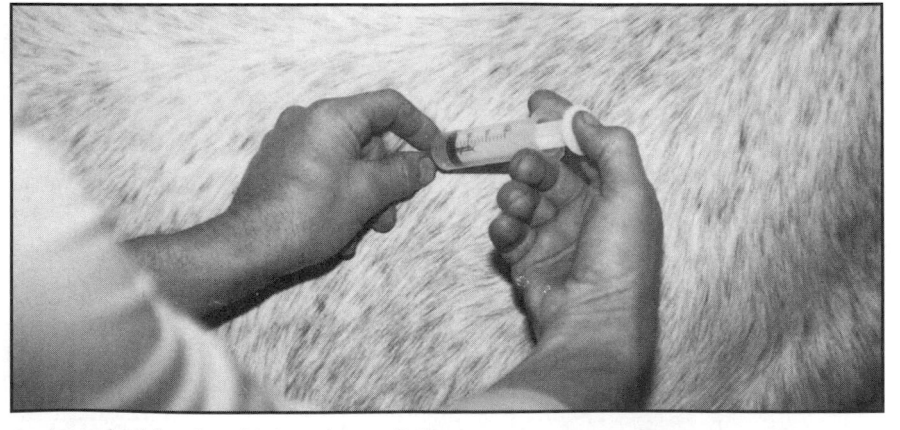

Aspirate for blood and inject the medicine.

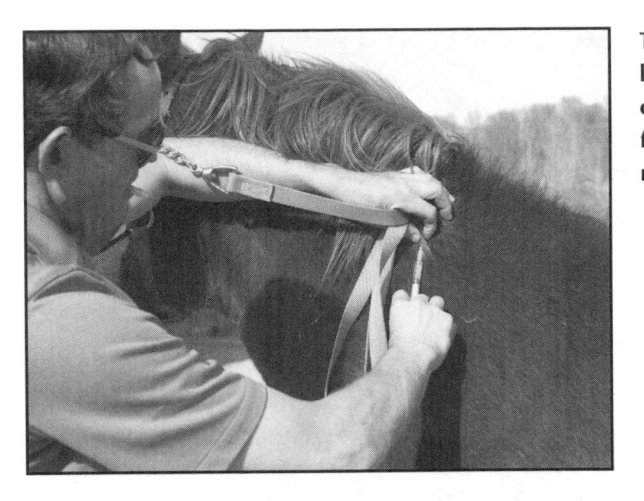

The neck is a good location for subcutaneous injections. Grasp a fold of skin to form a ridge.

The correct site for giving injections into the buttocks. Feel for bone and inject well away from it into the bulging muscle.

An injection can be given into the muscle at the back of the thigh.

ENEMAS

Enemas are used to treat rectal impactions. They are not prescribed on a routine basis. There are better ways to treat chronic constipation, as discussed in chapter 8, Digestive System. In the presence of colic, enemas are contraindicated.

As described in chapter 15, Pregnancy and Foaling, Fleet enemas and soap water enemas are often given to newborn foals with impacted meconium. How to give these enemas is discussed in the section AFTER THE DELIVERY.

The procedure for giving a soap water enema to an adult horse is described under RECTAL IMPACTIONS in Chapter 8, Digestive System.

Eye Medication   How to medicate the eyes is discussed in chapter 5, Eyes.
Ear Medication   How to medicate the ears is discussed in chapter 6, Ears.
Common drugs for veterinary use are shown in Table II.

Table II   COMMON DRUGS FOR VETERINARY USE*

Drug	Description	Daily Dosage (by pound weight of horse)
Acepromazine	Tranquilizer	0.01 to 0.02 mg per lb, IM or IV
Altrenogest	Estrous control	2 mg per 100 lb, orally for 8 to 12 days
Aluminum hydroxide (Amphogel)	Antacid	250 ml q 8 hr, orally
Aspirin	Anticoagulant; NSAID	7 to 50 mg per lb, orally, q 12 hr
Bacitracin	Topical antibiotic ointment	Once or twice daily, as directed
Banamine (Flunixin meglumine)	Anti-inflammatory; analgesic	0.1 to 0.5 mg per lb, q 8 hr, orally, IM or IV
Betadine solution 10 percent	Antiseptic wound cleanser	Dilute to 0.2 percent (2 ml/1000 ml)
Butazolidin (Phenylbutazone)	Anti-inflammatory; analgesic	1 to 2 gm per 1,000 lb., q 12 to 24 hr, orally or IV
Butorphanol tartrate	Sedative	0.02 to 1 mg per lb, IM or IV
Charcoal, activated	Poison antidote	24 ounces (adult); 8 ounces (foal). Mix with water and give by stomach tube.
Chlorhexidine solutions	Antiseptic wound cleanser	Dilute to 0.05 percent (1:40 dilution of 2 percent concentrate)
Corticosporin	Topical antibiotic/ cortisone	Once daily or as directed
Dexamethasone	Corticosteroid (Anaphylaxis)	0.01 to 0.1 mg per lb, orally, IM or IV, single dose
Digoxin	Congestive Heart Failure	0.005 mg per lb, once daily, orally

continues

Drug	Description	Daily Dosage (by pound weight of horse)
Dioctyl sodium sulfosuccinate (DSS)	Stool softener; impaction	7.5 to 30 ml of 5 percent DSS per 1,000 lb, orally (impaction). 4.5 to 9.0 mg per lb, q 48 hr, orally
Dipyrone	Analgesic; fever reducer	10 mg per lb, IM or IV. Repeat as directed.
DL-Methionine	Hoof repair; laminitis	10 to 25 mg per lb, once daily, orally
DMSO (Dimethyl sulfoxide)	Anti-inflammatory	0.2 to 0.5 mg per lb, q 6 to 12 hr, IV; topically (50 percent solution), once daily
Epinephrine 1:1000	Anaphylactic shock	4 to 8 ml per 1,000 lb, IM or SC
Epsom salt (Magnesium sulfate)	Laxative	Adult: 1 pound dissolved in 1 gallon of water (can also use as wound soak). Foal: 5 ounces dissolved in 1 quart water. Orally or by stomach tube.
Glycosaminoglycan (PSGAG)	Joint anti-inflammatory	500 mg IM every 4th day
Hyaluronic acid	Anti-inflammatory	20 to 120 mg IM locally around inflamed tendon
Human chorionic gonadotropin	Synchronize ovulation	2,000 IU, IV, IM or SC single dose
Hydrogen peroxide (3 percent)	Topical skin cleanser	Dilute 1:10 with warm water
Hydrocortisone sodium succinate	Anti-inflammatory	0.5 to 2.0 mg lb, IV drip
Ivermectin	Dewormer; anthelmintic	0.02 mg lb, once, orally
Kaopectate	Anti-diarrhea; GI protectant	2 to 4 quarts per 1,000 lb, q 12 hr, orally
Ketoprofen	Anti-inflammatory	1 mg per lb, q 24 hr, IV
Lasix (Furosemide)	Diuretic	0.5 to 1.5 mg per lb, q 12 hr, IM or IV
Meclofenamic acid (Arquel)	Anti-inflammatory	1 mg per lb, q 12 hr, orally
Metamucil (Psyllium mucilloid)	Laxative (sand impaction)	1 pound per 1,000 lb, dissolve in 2 gallons of water, orally by stomach tube
Milk of Magnesia (Magnesium hydroxide)	Laxative	16 ounces per 1,000 lb, orally (adult); 4 ounces, orally (foal)
Mineral oil	Laxative; GI protectant	3 to 4 quarts (adult); 1 pint (foal). May repeat in 12 to 24 hr. Must give by stomach tube.
Morphine sulfate	Narcotic analgesic	1 to 2 mg per 100 lb, IV, once only
Mylanta	Antacid	200 to 250 ml, 3 times daily
Naproxen	Anti-inflammatory; analgesic	5 mg per lb, q 12 to 24 hr, orally or IV
Neosporin Ophthalmic	Antibiotic eye preparations	Drops: 2 in eye 4 times daily. Ointment: 4 times daily.

Table II   COMMON DRUGS FOR VETERINARY USE* (CONTINUED)

Drug	Description	Daily Dosage (by pound weight of horse)
Nitrofurazone (Furacin)	Antibiotic ointment or powder	Topically daily or as directed
Oxytocin	Milk let-down, Expel placenta	20 to 40 units IM or IV 1 to 3 units IV, once only
Panolog	Antibiotic/steroid ear ointment	Once daily or as directed
Pepto-Bismol (Bismuth subsalicylate)	Anti-diarrhea; GI protectant	1 to 2 quarts, twice daily, orally (adult); 0.2 to 0.5 ml per lb, 3 to 4 times daily, orally (foal)
Prednisone	Corticosteroid	0.1 to 0.5 mg per lb, q 12 hr, IM
Primidone	Foal anticonvulsant	1 to 2 gm, q 6 to 12 hr, orally
Progesterone	Supress estrus Maintain pregnancy	150 mg daily, IM 300 mg daily, IM
Promazine	Tranquilizer	0.5 to 1.0 mg per lb, orally
Prostaglandin PGF2α	Short cycle mare	10 mg, IM, single dose
Pyrilamine maleate	Antihistamine	0.5 mg per lb, IM or IV
Ranitidine	Anti-ulcer	3 mg per lb, q 8 hr, orally or IV
Selenium	Selenium deficiency	5.5 mg per 1,000 lb, IM
Sodium bicarbonate	Treat acidosis	30 gm q 12 hr, orally
Sucralfate (Carafate)	Anti-ulcer; GI protectant	2 to 4 gm per 1,000 lb, q 6 hr, orally
Tagamet (Cimetidine)	Anti-ulcer	3 mg per lb, q 4 to 6 hr, orally or IV
Talwin (Pentazocine)	Narcotic analgesic	0.4 mg per lb, IV
Triamcinolone	Corticosteroid	0.01 to 0.02 mg per lb., IM
Valium (Diazepam)	Seizure control	.02 to 0.2 mg per lb, IV slowly. May repeat in 30 minutes.
Vitamin E	White muscle disease	2,000 IU, orally, once daily (foals)
Vitamin K$_1$	Warfarin; sweet clover	0.2 to 1.0 mg per lb, SC or IM, 1 to 4 times daily
Xylazine (Rompun)	Sedative; Tranquilizer	0.09 to 0.5 mg per lb, IV. Typical dose for sedation is 500 mg per 1,000 lb.
Zinc oxide	Antiseptic salve	Use once or twice daily.

*The dosages given are intended to serve as guidelines only. The exact dose and frequency of administration should be determined by your veterinarian for the individual horse. Always notify your veterinarian for adverse reactions including failure to improve. Preparations used in the Eye must be labeled specifically for *ophthalmologic use*.

Abbreviations: lb (pounds); *mg* (milligram); *gm* (gram); *q* (every); *IV* (intravenous); *IM* (intramuscular); *SC* (subcutaneous).

APPENDIX

Normal Physiologic Data

NORMAL RECTAL TEMPERATURE

ADULT HORSE (mares and stallions): 99.5 to 100 degrees F (37.5 to 37.8 degrees C)

FOAL: 99 to 102 degrees F (37.2 to 38.9 degrees C)

HOW TO TAKE YOUR HORSE'S TEMPERATURE

The only effective way to take your horse's temperature is by rectal thermometer. Bulb and digital thermometers are equally suitable. If using a bulb thermometer, shake it down until the bulb registers 96 degrees F (35.5 degrees C). Lubricate the bulb with petroleum jelly. Raise the horse's tail and hold it firmly; then gently insert the bulb into the anal canal with a twisting motion. Insert the thermometer 2 to 3 inches.

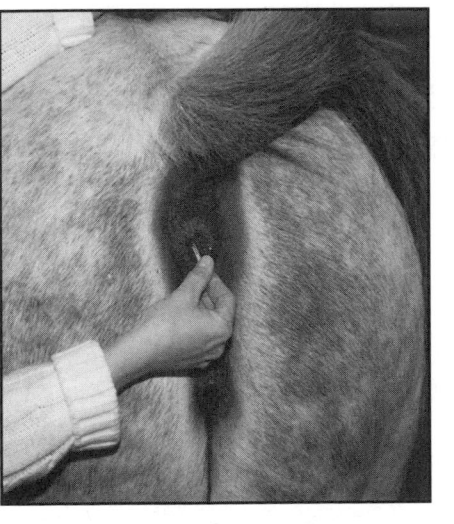

Lubricate the thermometer and insert it 2 to 3 inches into the anal canal. Wait 3 minutes and read.

Hold the thermometer in place for 3 minutes. Remove the thermometer, wipe it clean, and read the temperature by the height of the silver column of mercury on the thermometer scale. If using a digital thermometer, follow the directions of the manufacturer.

Clean the thermometer with alcohol to prevent the transfer of disease.

PULSE

ADULT: 35 to 45 beats per minute at rest

NURSING FOAL (1 month of age): 70 to 90 beats per minute

(Note: To learn how to take the pulse, see PULSE in chapter 10, Circulatory System.)

RESPIRATORY RATE

NORMAL: 12 (10 to 30) breaths per minute

(Note: Determine the breathing rate by observing and counting the movements of the nostrils or flanks.)

REPRODUCTIVE DATA

REPRODUCTIVE MATURITY (MARES AND STALLIONS): 36 months

NATURAL BREEDING SEASON (Northern hemisphere): April to September

LENGTH OF ESTROUS CYCLE: 21–23 days during natural breeding season

LENGTH OF ESTRUS (heat): 4 to 8 days

LENGTH OF GESTATION (pregnancy): 320 to 370 days (average 340 days)

General Index

NOTE: *Pages shown in boldface contain detailed coverage of the item.*